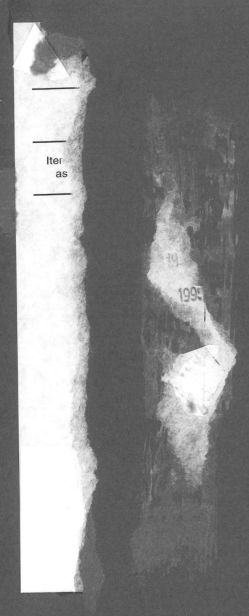

The Irish Derby
1866–1979

LIMITED EDITION

The
Irish Derby

1866–1979

Guy St. John Williams
and
Francis P. M. Hyland

J. A. ALLEN & CO LTD
London and New York

First published in 1980 by
J. A. Allen & Co Ltd
1 Lower Grosvenor Place
London SW1W 0EL

British Library Cataloguing in Publication Data
Williams, Guy St John
  History of the Irish Derby.
  I. Title   II. Hyland, Francis P M
  798'.43'094185   SF357.I/

  ISBN 0-85131-358-2

Set in 10/12 Times Roman by Rowland Phototypesetting
Printed in Great Britain by St Edmundsbury Press, Bury St Edmunds
and bound by Dents of Letchworth

FOREWORD

by Denis McCarthy,

Senior Steward of The Turf Club

Since ancient times Ireland has been the land where the horse is King. It is surprising, therefore, that Irishmen, so eloquent on racing matters, should have written almost nothing on the history of the sport in Ireland. At last here is the book which goes a long way to rectify this omission. Years of painstaking research have resulted in this definitive history of the Irish Derby, which is also by way of being a chronicle of Irish racing for more than a century.

As Senior Steward of the Turf Club, I am delighted to have the opportunity to endorse this long overdue volume and should like to wish its authors every success.

Acknowledgements

The authors gratefully acknowledge the help
given by the following:

The Irish National Library
Kildare Street, Dublin

The Royal Dublin Society Library
Ballsbridge, Dublin

The Turf Club
The Curragh, Kildare

INTRODUCTION

The origins and development of the Irish Derby exemplify the legend of Bruce and the spider, for it was indeed a case of 'If at first you don't succeed . . .' Inspired by the success of the Epsom Derby as the supreme test of the English thoroughbred, the Irish Turf Club instituted the O'Darby Stakes, first run at the Curragh in June 1817 and won by Souvenir. However, this initial attempt did not endure and the race was discontinued after 1824. In 1848 a second attempt was made with the staging of the Curragh Derby, won by Justice to Ireland. This proved as short-lived as the numerous attempts to achieve that cherished ideal which the winner's name so ironically propounded. Finally, in 1864 the Irish Derby Sweepstakes was advertised to be run at the traditional June meeting in 1866. Thus, at the third attempt, was born Ireland's premier race, which has survived, despite many vicissitudes, to achieve international recognition as one of the most important middle-distance tests of successive Classic generations.

Long before it became a race of international renown the Irish Derby had achieved an unique standing in the domestic racing scene. Originally intended to inject glamour into the traditionally mundane Wednesday of the June meeting at the Curragh, the Irish Derby quickly became established as a social occasion. In fact it was its public appeal – particularly to the fairer sex, otherwise seen only at Punchestown on Ladies' Day – that ensured the survival of the Irish Derby in its early years. Shunned by owners and trainers, decried by the sporting press, the race was persistently disappointing as a spectacle, despite added stakes (1869), amended distance (1872) and radically altered conditions (1874). Thus it was popular appeal that made the Irish Derby into the foremost event of the Irish racing calendar, which position it has held unchallenged through the decades to the present day.

The roll of honour of the Irish Derby contains the names of almost all the breeders, owners, trainers and jockeys, whose contributions have collectively achieved recognition for Ireland as one of the most influential centres of the world of the thoroughbred. Though preceded by such distinguished winners as Selim (1866), Ben Battle (1874), Madame du Barry (1878) and St Brendan (1902), the horse that did most to confirm the status of the Irish Derby was Orby (1907). Owned by that enigmatic god-father of Irish racing, 'Boss' Croker, Orby made history when becoming the first Irish-trained winner of the Epsom Derby. By running his national hero in the Curragh Classic Croker conferred an additional glamour on the Irish Derby, which it was to retain throughout the struggle for Independence, the Civil War, crippling economic strictures and two World Wars.

Dominated by English raiders from 1913 to the outbreak of the Second World War, the Irish Derby suffered from the overall stagnation and decline of Irish racing during that period, awaiting another saviour. Fittingly, as with Croker and Orby, the next major influence on the race combined a dynamic man and his outstanding horse. Having made his fortune through an Irish Sweepstakes on English races, Joe McGrath took over Croker's mantle as the colossus of Irish racing. In 1942 his unbeaten champion Windsor Slipper annexed the Irish Derby as the highlight of his Irish Triple Crown. Like Croker before him, McGrath lifted the Blue Riband of the English Turf before making his outstanding contribution to racing in Ireland when persuading the Turf Club to permit the Irish Derby to be transformed into the Irish Sweeps Derby.

Staged for the first time in 1962 and worth over £50,000 to the winner, the Irish Sweeps Derby, through extensive and imaginative promotion, soon became one of the most prestigious races run in Europe. The validity of its claim to be regarded as such is reinforced by the list of Epsom Derby winners that have failed to emulate the double achieved by Orby all those years ago. Moreover, it is surely significant that the roll of honour of dual Derby winners comprises only those true champions of their generations: Santa Claus, Nijinsky, Grundy, The Minstrel, Shirley Heights and Troy. While die-hards still claim that Epsom, with its turns and gradients, tests all facets of the Classic contender, few will deny that the Curragh, with its broad expanses, sweeping bends and demanding straight, is not a truer and fairer test of horse rather than rider.

Irish racing has come a long way since the Iceni raced their horses across the Curragh in the mists of time. Much if not most of that progress has occurred since James Cockin sent Selim from Staffordshire to carry off the inaugural Irish Derby in 1866. The following pages tell the story of the Irish Derby, the horses, the men and the events that made it what it is today; and if at times you feel that we have written a history of Irish racing, we make no apology. For the Irish Derby is the epitome of Irish racing, as it ought to be and may it always remain.

THE CURRAGH

On the Curragh of Kildare
The boys will all be there
With their pikes in good repair
At the Rising of the Moon

The Rising of the Moon, by John Keegan Casey

The Curragh of Kildare is a broad limestone plain some thirty miles south west of Dublin. Bounded by the towns of Newbridge and Kildare, it is bisected by the Dublin–Cork road. The northern portion is dominated by the Curragh racecourse and the other side by the Curragh Camp, the headquarters of the Irish Army. The world 'curragh' in Gaelic means 'horses' course' and The Curragh, as the home of the Irish Derby has long been known, has seen horses pitted against each other since time immemorial. Throughout the annals of Irish history there occur repeated references to horse and chariot racing on the Curragh. The traditional sport and proving-ground of young nobles, racing was governed by a strict and complex set of rules under the old Brehon Law. An integral part of life in Ireland, horse racing survived the eventual conquest of Ireland by the English in the seventeenth century and even prospered under the alien regime. Cheney's Racing Calendar, first published in 1727, records details of Plates and Prizes run on the Curragh, which had already become recognised as the centre of racing in Ireland. In September 1751 the famous match between Black and All Black and Bajazet took place over four miles on the Curragh for 1000gns and a further 10,000gns in side bets.

Just a year earlier Black and All Black had won a £100 Plate at the Curragh put up by the Society of Sportsmen, in time to become the Turf Club, with its headquarters in the Coffee Room in Kildare. When Volume I of the Irish Racing Calendar appeared in 1790 it incorporated the Rules and Orders of the Turf Club. These governed the conduct of racing at the Curragh and, in due course, the application of Turf Club rules became the basis of recognition for race meetings throughout Ireland. In view of the Curragh's pre-eminence in Irish racing and its splendid natural facilities, it was logical that it should become the training centre of Ireland. In the second half of the eighteenth century the prime movers of the sport, such as Lords Waterford, Mountjoy, Conyngham and Rossmore had lodges built on the borders of the Curragh, where their horses were trained and where they themselves stayed during racemeetings. These lodges were permanently staffed by the training grooms and their housekeeper wives. As racing increased in popular appeal, bringing more numerous, if less munificent men to the ranks of ownership, these training grooms gradually made the transition to public trainers, the first to do so being Pat Connolly, who took over Waterford Lodge in 1812.

3

In the ring

The Curragh as it appeared in 1895

Source:
Racing Illustrated.

Grand Stand and enclosure

The Paddock

Across the course

The Paddock

A finish

The advent of the railway made the Curragh more readily accessible to the denizens of Dublin, at that time one of the most glamorous and depraved capitals of Europe. The earlier Royal visits of George IV and William IV, on which they presented Royal Whips to the Curragh, increased the interest of the Society in the Sport of Kings. As cock-fighting ceased to be an integral part of racemeetings, so highwaymen disappeared from the lonely, windswept Curragh, long their favourite haunt. Under the enlightened dictatorship of Lord Drogheda the Turf Club stamped its authority firmly on the conduct of racing. The Irish Derby came into being, heralding a new era, in which racing attracted public, rather than purely participant interest. The progressive dominance of the Irish-bred steeplechaser, supreme at Liverpool, was supplemented by a succession of remarkable flatracers and sires, such as Birdcatcher, Harkaway and The Baron. The long-established four-mile heats across the Curragh gradually gave way to what became the finest natural collection of modern courses in the world, rivalled only by Newmarket. This then is the Curragh, the home of the Irish Derby.

1866

The intensive publicity campaign which preceded the inaugural running of the Irish Derby succeeded beyond the wildest dreams of its promoters. A Race Special from Kingsbridge comprised no less than thirty carriages, thronged with excited race-goers, whose arrival swelled the attendance on the Curragh to record proportions. With the Band of the Third Buffs playing martial airs in the background, all seemed set for a spectacular climax to a delightful afternoon's sports. However, excitement turned quickly to disappointment when only three runners appeared for the feature race. The trio was dominated by Tom King, immediately supported from even money to odds-on, despite a move for Selim. The latter had received a walk-over the previous day, his rivals having failed to reach the post in time! Fire Eater, claiming a 3lb allowance as the produce of an untried mare, was ignored in the betting.

Under the expert supervision of starter M. J. Clancy the small field got away promptly from the Red Post. Charlie Maidment dashed Selim into an immediate lead from Tom King, with Fire Eater already out of contention. Passing the Chains at the entrance to the straight, Lynch attempted to drive the favourite up to the leader, but to no avail. Selim streaked away to win by what the judge, R. J. Hunter, conservatively estimated as three lengths. Despite the size of the field and the bloodless nature of Selim's victory, the occasion was voted a popular success, as evidenced by one journalist, who reported that: 'All returned home much delighted, for, although the fields were small, the quality of the horses was first class.'

Bred by Mr D. Kinsella, a Dublin sporting journalist, Selim was by Ivan, a narrow-backed son of the St Leger winner Van Tromp. A good stayer, Ivan failed by only a head to emulate his sire's success in the St Leger. He got few chances at stud; a pity in view of the excellent record of his progeny, notably Union Jack (Railway Stakes), the brilliant but totally blind Blue Peter and Mainstay. Ivan died in 1865, just as his merits began to receive belated recognition. Selim's dam, Light of the Harem, was out of a full-sister to Birdcatcher and had run second to The Deformed in the Anglesey Stakes when both were owned by R. H. Copperthwaite, a somewhat unsavoury gambler, who subsequently turned his attentions to the English Turf.

In common with all James Cockin's horses, Selim experienced an arduous career. Twice successful in England as a two-year-old, Selim won two races at Chester before crossing to the Curragh in April to beat Fire Eater. Brought back to England, he won at Manchester, before making his triumphant return to the Curragh, where he won on each of the four days. A walk-over on the opening day preceded his success in the Irish Derby and the following day he again defeated Tom King in a three-mile Queen's Plate. On the final day, in Tom King's absence, Selim collected a four-mile Queen's Plate – an impressive week's work, even by the standards of the time. As a four-year-old Selim won at the Curragh, Bellewstown and Londonderry. This good racehorse then retired to stud at Clonmulsk, near Carlow, where he sired nothing better than Bedouin, winner of the Royal Whip.

Tom King, un-named when he ran in the Irish Derby, did once manage to beat Selim on the racecourse. But it was at stud that he was to prove his ultimate superiority, among his progeny being Umpire. That he should have proved the better sire was not entirely surprising, for he was by King Tom out of the dam of Solon. King Tom, second in the Epsom Derby, sired a winner of that race in Kingcraft. Fire Eater, later re-named Rob Roy, won eleven races in five seasons. Retired to stud at Eyrefield Lodge, he became an excellent sire of steeplechasers.

James Cockin, Selim's owner, was an Englishman, whose extensive racing operations were based at Hednesford in Staffordshire, in the competent care of the Toon brothers. Firmly of the opinion prevalent among Yorkshiremen that if the 'orses gallops for owt, let 'em gallop for brass, Cockin had begun his Irish campaign in spectacular fashion in 1865, bringing over Lord Conyngham, with whom he proceeded to win no fewer than seven Queen's Plates. Galled by the invader's success, the Stewards of the Turf Club paid James Cockin the not inconsiderable compliment of amending the articles of Queen's Plates, confining them to horses trained in Ireland for six months previously. The new ruling came into effect in 1868, but proved no deterrent to Cockin, who simply purchased Aneroid from Curragh trainer Pat Doucie and proceeded to collect Queen's Plates with her. For good measure Aneroid subsequently bred Inishowen, Cockin's third and final Irish Derby winner. The best horse bred by James Cockin was undoubtedly Uncas, whose performance in winning eleven races as a two-year-old, eight in Ireland and three in England, left him of little use as a racehorse afterwards. However, it did not impair his stud capabilities and Uncas went on to sire four Irish Derby winners and to establish himself as one of the best stallions seen in Ireland up to that time. With Uncas and Melody Cockin accomplished the coveted Railway, Anglesey and Beresford Stakes treble in successive years, heading the list of winning owners in Ireland no less than seven times between 1860 and 1870. While maintaining his establishment at Hednesford, James Cockin spent the last years of his life in Halifax. On his death in 1876 his stud and stable were disbanded and his bloodstock sold, an event which can scarcely have brought much regret to the Irish racing fraternity.

Charles Maidment, the rider of Selim was then beginning to achieve the recognition which was to result in his winning the jockeys' title in England in successive years, 1870 and 1871, though, curiously, on each occasion he shared that honour, first with W. Gray and afterwards with the redoubtable George Fordham. Charlie Maidment was initially apprenticed at Weever's Bourton stable, where he schooled the full-sisters Emblem and Emblematic prior to their successive Grand National victories. Throughout his long life 'Lucky' Maidment, as he became known, never tired of recounting how, when asked by George Stevens whether he could possibly win the Grand National on two sisters, he had replied, 'Of course you can. I could myself and I'm no steeplechase jockey!' This popular and likeable lightweight achieved his most memorable success when winning the Epsom Derby on Cremorne in 1872. When asked after the race how he had come so close to being pipped on the post by Pell Mell, he replied, with disarming candour, that he had been unaware that such a horse was even in the race! However, he made no such mistake when winning the Grand Prix de Paris on the same horse.

'Lucky' Maidment won the first two runnings of the Irish Derby and headed the list of professional jockeys in Ireland on each occasion. In addition he won the English 'Fillies' Triple Crown on Hannah and the St Leger on Warlock. Successful in the Lincolnshire four times in six years, he won nineteen races at Royal Ascot between 1863 and 1881 and added a second Epsom Derby to his remarkable record when he won on Kisber in 1876. Though he went on riding winners until 1891, 'Lucky' Maidment's good fortune eventually deserted him. In common with many of his cavalier calling he found money easier to come by than to keep, with the result that this once carefree cock of the walk found it necessary to continue riding work at Newmarket until shortly before his death in 1926 at the age of eighty-two.

Wednesday, 27th June, 1866   **3 Ran**   **1m 6f 3yds (Red Post)**

The Irish Derby Sweepstakes of 25sovs each, 10sovs forfeit, for three years old. Colts 8st 10lb, fillies 8st 5lb. Produce of untried sires and mares allowed 3lb. Only one allowance.

(38 subs)

1 Mr J. Cockin's	SELIM (C. Maidment)	8.10
	B. colt Ivan – Light of the Harem by Magpie.	
2 Mr St. George's	TOM KING* (Lynch)	8.10
	B. colt King Tom – Darling's dam.	
3 Mr P. Plunkett's	FIRE EATER† (Jas. Doyle)	8. 7
	B. colt Artillery – Dunsany's dam.	

SP Evens Tom King; 5/4 SELIM; 4/1 Fire Eater.
    Won by 3 lengths.

*Tom King ran un-named.
†Fire Eater was later renamed Rob Roy.

1867

The Derby Day card comprised only four races and had to compete as a popular attraction with a rifle competition at Dollymount and a Field Day in the Phoenix Park. In consequence it was a smaller crowd that witnessed five runners parade for the Irish Derby. The late withdrawal of Knightsbridge, who suddenly fell lame, reduced the field to four, dominated by Red Wine and Golden Plover, from the all-conquering Cockin stable.

At the start Aster whipped around, losing ground, which the fast early gallop never allowed him to make up. The remaining trio raced together to the Chains, where Golden Plover and Red Wine drew away from Columbus. After a short, sharp tussle Golden Plover mastered his opponent, passing the post four lengths to the good. Despite the apparent ease of his victory, both Golden Plover and his immediate victim finished desperately tired, reflecting the severity of the early gallop. Then, as now, fourteen furlongs at the Curragh put a premium on stamina. Golden Plover's success crowned a wonderful afternoon for James Cockin, who won three of the four races on the card.

Golden Plover, a bay colt, was bred by George Oliver and was by Grey Plover, a moderate own-brother to Chanticleer. The best of his get besides Golden Plover were Sir Robert Peel, winner of the inaugural Irish Grand National in 1870 and The Plover, winner of the Railway and Beresford Stakes. Golden Plover failed to follow in Selim's footsteps on the following day when he was defeated. His overall racing record indicates that he was not in the same class as Selim. Red Wine retired to stud at Brownstown Lodge, becoming the sire of the useful 'chaser M'Mahon. Aster,

Wednesday, 26th June, 1867   **7 Ran**   **1m 6f 3yds (Red Post)**

The Irish Derby Sweepstakes of 25sovs each, 10sovs forfeit, for three years old. Colts 8st 10lb; fillies 8st 5lb. Produce of untried sires or mares allowed 3lb. Only one allowance.

(18 subs)

1 Mr J. Cockin's   GOLDEN PLOVER (C. Maidment)8.10
                           B. colt Grey Plover – Alice Gray By Scandal.
2 Capt. Williams's   RED WINE (P. Gavin)   8.10
                           Br. colt Claret – Colleen Dhas Dhu by Arthur.
3 Mr Roberts's   COLUMBUS (late Jug of Punch)   8. 7 (Car 8.9)
                              (T. Kelly)
                           B. colt Colonist – dam Stella by Lanercost.
4 Mr E. Croker's   ASTER (P. Conolly)   8. 7
                           Br. colt Planet – Tidy by Birdcatcher.

SP 7/4 GOLDEN PLOVER; 2/1 Red Wine; 3/1 Aster.
                 Won in a canter, bad third.

9

having disgraced himself in the Irish Derby, went on to win a total of twenty-three races, including the Galway Plate, before also retiring to stud.

In winning the Irish Derby for the second successive year 'Lucky' Maidment preserved a one hundred per cent record in the race, for he never rode in it again. James Cockin could also feel pleased, for Golden Plover's Irish Derby contributed to Cockin's best year in Ireland. Thanks largely to the eight victories of his high-class two-year-old Uncas, James Cockin won more stake money than any other owner since Colonel J. C. Westerna 30 years earlier.

1868

Though reduced from four days to three, the Curragh June meeting still suffered from lack of public patronage on the middle day, Wednesday. This the introduction of the Irish Derby had been specifically designed to overcome, but now lack of owners' support seemed like to defeat this objective. The third running of the Irish Derby – billed as the highlight of the racing year – reached an all-time low. Only two runners paraded for a paltry prize of £115. One of these, Madeira, had only run twice in his life, unplaced in two attempts at this meeting a year previously. Even though he had been brought all the way up from Roscrea, where he was trained privately, his connections did not expect him to prove a match for Michael Dunne's Bee Quick. Bred by his owner out of his famous foundation mare, Queen Bee, Bee Quick had won one of his three races the previous season, besides running that prolific winner, Uncas, to half a length in the Paget Stakes, albeit receiving 14lbs from Mr Cockin's high-class colt. As a three-year-old Bee Quick had won the Madrid Stakes, before being beaten by Columbus in a three-mile match. In what seemed to all intents and purposes to be a walk-over, Bee Quick appeared generously priced at 3-to-1 ON, with many prepared to trade at those odds.

Jumping off at the Red Post, the two colts raced in close company until the straight was reached, at which point Wynne drove Madeira into a clear lead. To the consternation of those who had taken the odds about him, Bee Quick immediately came under pressure. Finding absolutely nothing, the favourite fell further and further behind, as Madeira drew steadily away inside the final two furlongs, passing the judge's box six lengths to the good. In an atmosphere of general dismay, only the layers expressed any pleasure in the startling result.

Bred by Mr Thomas Wright, Madeira was a bay/brown colt by Claret out of Try Back, a daughter of Tom Ferguson's famous horse, Harkaway. Fourth in the Two Thousand Guineas and a winner of eight races in the course of four seasons, Claret was clearly owned by a statistician, for he was advertised in the following terms: 'Claret during his racing career was beaten by seven horses, and he defeated one hundred and fifteen! He is a dark brown, without white, stands sixteen hands high, up to fifteen stone with hounds, beautiful action, without any natural blemish, perfectly sound, a most docile temper, a good grubber, a sure foal getter, and only requires to be seen to be appreciated.' Besides Madeira, Claret sired Blarney, winner of the Anglesey Stakes and a successful sire, and Scots Grey, twice successful in the Irish Grand National. Through his daughter, Claret Cup, herself a good stayer, Claret's name was perpetuated by the deeds of such as La Francaise, winner of the French St Leger, Portmarnock and Carrigavalla, both successful in the Irish Derby at the turn of the century.

Madeira only ran twice more after his surprise success in the Irish Derby, when beaten on successive days at Bellewstown. A bad third to Nelaton on the first day, he ran the same horse to a neck over ten furlongs the next day and then retired to stud, where he got few thoroughbred mares. Bee Quick, whose dismal performance at the Curragh resulted simply from lack of stamina, won subsequently over distances up to a mile, before dropping dead the following year.

'W. Holland' was the 'nom de course' of the Bourke family of Roscrea, who had employed the profits of their successful business concerns in that midland town to create a lavish stud and training stables at nearby Kilmartin House. Whereas the premises remain as a reminder of glories long gone by, the Bourkes found the Turf to be their ruin, and the last of their line died a pauper in England many years later.

The D. Wynne who rode Madeira to victory in the Irish Derby was a nephew of Denny Wynne, the Rossmore Lodge trainer, who had gained fame twenty years earlier as the rider of Mathew, the first Irish horse to win the Aintree Grand National. Known as 'Red Denny', both from the colour of his hair and the necessity to distinguish him from his uncle, the rider of Madeira later became renowned in his own right for his skill in curing horses' ailments, a highly-prized gift in the days when 'vets' were unknown and the horse was the swiftest form of transport.

Wednesday, 24th June, 1868	**£115**	**2 Ran**	**1m 6f 3yds (Red Post)**

1 Mr Holland's   MADEIRA (D. Wynne)   8. 7
                           B/Br. colt Claret – Try Back by Harkaway.
2 Mr Dunne's   BEE QUICK (T. Miller)   8.10
                           B. colt Artillery – Queen Bee.

SP 1/3 Bee Quick.

Won in a canter.

1869

The altered conditions of this year's Irish Derby, whereby the subscription had been reduced and 100sovs added by the Turf Club, had drawn a much healthier response. For the first time the conditions of the race provided an allowance for geldings, of which Mr J. W. Denison's Inishowen took partial advantage. However, he remained a rank outsider in a market dominated by James Cockin's slashing great bay filly Melody, ridden by her Hednesford trainer, Job Toon. Melody merited favouritism not only on her impressive appearance, but also on her outstanding form, for the previous season she had made a clean sweep of the prestige Irish two-year-old events, annexing the Anglesey, Railway, Beresford and Marble Hill Stakes. On form neither The Scout nor Rosette could possibly be expected to give weight to Melody, and her only serious rival appeared to be the unraced filly, Finesse. In a recent, highly secret trial Finesse had reputedly given 21lbs and a beating to The Scout. By now common knowledge, the result of this trial was not enhanced by The Scout's failure to finish no closer than third over three miles on the opening day of the meeting. Nevertheless, The Scout had beaten Howitzer over a mile and a half at the Curragh earlier in the season, and Howitzer had since been successful at Baldoyle. Rosette, the only other runner in the field of six, had last run in a selling race, where she had been entered to be sold for £50. Even though she had finished second, she had failed to attract a bid, even at that price. Both on looks and on form, Melody seemed a 'racing certainty', and the money went down accordingly.

Howitzer took them along at a steady gallop, with The Scout already some lengths in arrears of the other five, and it was not until they reached the half way mark, where Finesse took up the running, that the pace improved. Finesse still led into the straight, where her lack of a previous race found her out, and Melody and Rosette swept past her into the lead. Neck and neck the two fillies thundered up the straight, with Toon and Murphy riding as though the race concerned only them. Almost unnoticed in the growing general excitement, The Scout had steadily been making ground behind the leading pair. Only inside the last hundred yards did Miller launch his challenge on The Scout, forcing his way between the embattled fillies to get his head in front virtually on the line, scoring by a head from the favourite, with Rosette a neck further back in third place. The crowd, already wild with excitement, went wilder still when the judge announced his verdict, for The Scout's success meant that the prize had been kept at home. Once again, the bookmakers were loud in their rejoicing, theirs being a peculiarly profitable form of patriotism.

A fine, strapping bay colt, The Scout had been bred by Mr D. Hewetson and came from the first crop of The Ranger, an excellent racehorse, whose misfortune it was to have scored his most notable victory in France, which any right-minded Englishman regarded as poor form indeed. Although he also won the Yorkshire Cup, The Ranger was overshadowed by his own-brother, Skirmisher, whose success as a three-year-old in the Ascot Gold Cup was rated a far, far greater feat than The Ranger's triumph in the inaugural running of something called the Grand Prix de Paris. Consequently, The Ranger had embarked on his stud career at Conyngham Lodge, the Curragh, where he had sired The Scout. Subsequently repatriated to England, he sired Uhlan, winner of the Doncaster Cup, whose stud career took him to France and later to America.

Pulled out again the following day, The Scout finished second in a three-mile Queen's Plate, with Finesse in third place. He went on to win a further four races that season and then lost his form completely, failing to win anything as a four-year-old, despite three changes of ownership. His final appearance was as a five-year-old, when he failed to reach a place in the Conyngham Cup, over four miles of Punchestown's formidable banks, an unlikely diversion for a modern-day Derby winner, no matter how jaded his palate for racing! Finesse subsequently went on to show that that widely-publicised 'secret' trial might not have been that wide of the mark, for she twice beat The Scout in later races, besides defeating such notables as Billy Pitt and Aneroid over the next two seasons.

The 'J. Johnstone' whose name appears in the Calendar as the owner of The Scout was, in all probability, John Johnston of Hackettstown, Skerries, Co. Dublin, a land agent for the Holmpatrick family, and a prominent owner of the period. No such uncertainty exists about the winning rider, W. 'Billy' Miller, subsequently successful in the Irish Derby on Trickstress, and one of the leading jockeys in Ireland at the time, though he never actually headed the list of winning jockeys.

Wednesday, 23rd June, 1869 £280 **6 Ran** **1m 6f 12yds (Peel Course)**

1 Mr J. Johnstone's THE SCOUT (W. Miller) 8. 7
    B. colt The Ranger – Woodranger's dam.
2 Mr J. Cockin's MELODY (J. Toon) 8. 2
    B. filly Macaroni – Nightingale.
3 Mr P. Keary's ROSETTE (M. Murphy) 8. 5
    B. filly The Ranger or Windhound – Nora.
4 Mr M. M'Cormack's FINESSE (T. Kelly) 8. 2
    B. filly Caractacus – Pardalotte.
5 Lord Strathnairn's HOWITZER (Gray) 8.10
    B. colt Artillery – Cannon Ball's dam.
6 Mr J. W. Denison's INISHOWEN (M. Lynch) 8. 7
    Ch. gelding St Albans – Touchstone mare Lady Sarah.

SP 4/5 Melody; 5/1 Finesse; 7/1 THE SCOUT.
Head, Neck.

1870

Although once again the Irish Derby drew a disappointingly small field, on this occasion quality proved a more than adequate substitute for quantity, for there seemed little to choose between the three thoroughly exposed runners. Dubois had been beaten a head by Billy Pitt in the Madrid Stakes and was widely thought certain to avenge that narrow defeat at a difference of 8lbs. However, Billy Pitt's owner, ebullient bookmaker Paddy Keary, was equally adamant that his colt had made abnormal improvement in the meantime and backed his judgement accordingly. Torn between the two home-trained runners, the large crowd opted for Mr Holland's un-named colt by Rapid Rhone, subsequently named Lord Glasgow, whose English form made him favourite in a lively betting market. Dubois, marginally preferred to Billy Pitt in the Ring, discouraged his supporters by moving scratchily down to the start, in contrast to his free-striding rivals.

Confusion between the almost identical colours of Dubois and Billy Pitt made it difficult to identify the early order. However, it eventually became clear that Billy Pitt held a narrow lead from Dubois and the Rapid Rhone colt. This order was maintained until the three runners passed the Chains, at which point Billy Pitt and the un-named favourite began to draw away from Dubois. In an exciting battle to the line Billy Pitt gradually went a length clear and held on grimly to achieve a hard-fought victory. Although the outsider of the field, Billy Pitt was nonetheless given a warm reception, reflecting the popularity of his jovial owner.

Billy Pitt was bred by the Palmerstown Association, the first commercial breeding venture in Ireland. Unfortunately it did not long survive the death of its founder Lord Mayo, assassinated in 1872, in fulfilling his duties as Governor-General of India. Plum Pudding, the resident stallion at Palmerstown and the sire of Billy Pitt, was an own-brother to the Oaks winner Mincepie. Other good winners by Plum Pudding included Shelmartin, winner of the Anglesey and Beresford Stakes and Grand National, who achieved an unusual double in winning the National Stakes and the Irish Grand National. Another of his progeny, Sugar Plum, won the Galway Plate as a four-year-old. When the Palmerstown Association was disbanded in 1873 Sir Charles Coote paid 425gns for Plum Pudding and installed him at his newly-created 'model stud' at Ballyfin in Queen's County, now called Co. Laois. Billy Pitt, regarded as one of the best horses in Ireland in his day, won ten races in three seasons, before breaking down badly at Cork Park in 1872. At stud he sired a very good 'chaser in Lord Chatham.

Paddy Keary, the owner of Billy Pitt, was one of Ireland's first bookmakers. Known as 'Bank of Ireland Keary' through his insistence upon settling only in Bank of Ireland notes, Paddy Keary lived at Herbertstown House, Co. Kildare, where he kept open house for his many racing friends. Big and burly in stature, forthright and generous in character, Paddy Keary maintained one of the largest strings in training, though he rarely had a runner under National Hunt rules. A long-standing patron of the Connollys' Curragh View stable, Paddy Keary on his side-car was a familiar sight on the Curragh gallops before important races. Of the many good horses to carry his 'White, cerise cap', he regarded Bellman, bought for £40 at a fair in Kildare, as the finest. Bellman defeated the famous North of England Mare, Caller Ou, in an epic duel at the Curragh in 1862. Paddy Keary's side-car overturned as he left the Curragh October meeting in 1872, causing him severe injuries, which led to his death at the age of seventy.

Bucolic Tom Connolly of Curragh View, the trainer of Billy Pitt, succeeded his father, Pat Connolly, the first independent trainer in Ireland. His addiction to alcohol was directly responsible for his death, as the result of a tragic accident, in 1883, having survived his famous father by only three years. During the last years of his life he was assisted at Curragh View by Pat Connolly, no relation of his, but a brother of the celebrated jockey, John Connolly. The best horse with whom Tom Connolly and Pat Connolly were involved was Barcaldine, outstandingly the finest racehorse to come out of Ireland in the latter part of the nineteenth century.

William Canavan, the rider of Billy Pitt, and his equally prominent brother David were sons of 'old' Davy Canavan, the trainer of Valentine, after whom the famous brook at Aintree was named. A hard-riding horseman of the old school, Davy Canavan had little time for the timorous. Asked on one occasion by a prospective English client whether his charge could jump water, Canavan astounded his enquirer by replying, 'Sure why wouldn't he, wasn't he born within sight of the sea!' Like his father and brother, William Canavan made his reputation over fences. On his retirement from steeplechasing in 1898 he emigrated to America.

Wednesday, 29th June, 1870   £220   **3 Ran**   **1m 6f 12yds (Peel Course)**

The Irish Derby Sweepstakes of 15sovs each, 5sovs forfeit, 100sovs added by the Turf Club, for three years old. Colts 8st 10lb; fillies and geldings 8st 5lb. Produce of untried sires or mares allowed 3lb. Only one allowance.

(21 subs)

1 Mr P. Keary's	BILLY PITT (W. Canavan)	8. 7	Connolly
	Br. colt Plum Pudding – Frailty by Knight of the Whistle.		
2 Mr Holland's	LORD GLASGOW* (Walker)	8.10	
	B. colt Rapid Rhone – Hetty.		
3 Lord Charlemont's	DUBOIS (D. Wynne)	8. 7	
	Ch. colt Blarney – It's Curious.		

SP 5/4 Lord Glasgow; 7/4 Dubois; 2/1 BILLY PITT.
                    1 length, 2 lengths.
Winner trained by Mr Thomas Connolly at Curragh View, Curragh.

*Lord Glasgow ran un-named.

1871

Though it continued to grow in popular appeal, the Irish Derby still failed to attract good fields and the sporting press had begun to campaign for altered conditions. Once again only three paraded for the feature event, which appeared to be a formality for the hot favourite, Maid of Athens. Pat Doucie's charge had beaten the Railway Stakes winner Richard the First when winning the National Produce Stakes the previous season. Rattleaway, on whom William Canavan was bidding for a second successive success in the race, did not seem capable of conceding weight to the other pair.

From flagfall Maid of Athens set a strong pace ahead of Rattleaway and Richard the First. Knowing that the favourite was a true stayer, Canavan drove Rattleaway up to join issue fully a mile from home. But his efforts proved in vain, for Maid of Athens immediately went away from him and, maintaining her relentless gallop, crossed the line four lengths clear, having led from pillar to post. Richard the First plugged on bravely to finish only five lengths further back. After three years of upsets, favourite backers were delighted to welcome the gallant winner, as a smiling Tommy Broderick brought her back to scale.

Bred by her owner, 'W. Williams', otherwise Mr Joseph Lyons of Moyanna, Queen's County, Maid of Athens was by Solon out of Colleen Rhue, winner of the Waterford Testimonial Stakes. A wonderful servant to Mr Lyons, Colleen Rhue also produced Kyrle Daly, winner of the Irish Derby two years later, as well as Maid of Erin and Draco, both placed in the race. Solon, one of the last horses to carry the famous livery of Christopher St George of Tyrone House, Oranmore, Co. Galway, won the Madrid Stakes, Kildare Handicap and the Great Surrey Foal Stakes at Epsom. Reputedly a savage at stud, Solon transmitted this trait to many of his progeny, of whom the best was the incestuously-bred Barcaldine, an outstanding racehorse and sire of the Epsom Derby and St Leger winner Sir Visto. In the period between his two Irish Derby winners, Maid of Athens and Sylph (1883), Solon reigned supreme among stallions in Ireland. His progeny scored hat-tricks in the Madrid and Beresford Stakes, yet, for all his success, Solon realised only 55gns at public auction . . . two months before the sensational debut of Barcaldine. In addition to Barcaldine, grandsire of Hurry On and thus ancestor of Santa Claus, Solon left another prepotent son in Arbitrator, an outstanding sire in Ireland, whose best offspring was the St Leger winner Kilwarlin.

Maid of Athens' dam, Colleen Rhue, was by that ill-omened animal Gemma di Vergy. Once dubbed 'the Hope Diamond of horses', Gemma di Vergy brought disaster to all who owned him. He was bred in England by one Mr Cook, who sold him to a certain Mr Palmer. In 1856 Palmer was convicted of poisoning Cook and was hanged. At the sale of Palmer's bloodstock Gemma di Vergy was purchased by Henry, Lord Waterford, better known as 'the Mad Marquis' and the leading owner in Ireland at the time. In 1859 Lord Waterford was killed out hunting, whereupon Gemma di Vergy was sold to a Mr Hamilton, who was certified insane . . . On Lord Waterford's death his Curraghmore Stud was bought by Joseph Lyons, a Queen's County magistrate, who bred horses primarily to carry his own colours. Maid of Athens and Kyrle Daly were the only two runners that Joseph Lyons ever had in the Irish Derby, thereby giving him the unusual distinction of being one hundred per cent successful in the race with more than one runner in it.

After her success in the Irish Derby Maid of Athens was purchased by Mr J. A. Cassidy, the Monasterevan distiller, who rested her until the Curragh meeting in September. Runner-up to Lord Howth's Fluke on the opening day, Maid of Athens was heavily backed for a Queen's Plate on the second day, only to be beaten by her neglected stablemate, Pearlseeker. The scene was colourfully described in The Irish Sportsman and Farmer: 'We shall not soon forget the ecstacy which the metallicians evinced when they saw the pot boil over, and Pearlseeker landing by a length.' Later the same day Fluke achieved a notable giant-killing double when beating Billy Pitt in a thrilling contest. Reappearing on her local track in October, Maid of Athens made her seasonal farewell when successful in a Scurry. Opening her four-year-old campaign in a similar fashion, 'The Maid', as she was affectionately known on the Curragh, did not win again until September when, 'roused by Broderick in his own peculiar and brilliant style', she won a Queen's Plate. Unfortunately for the connections of Maid of Athens, Tommy Broderick, for whom the mare ran much better than anybody else, was suspended for the remainder of the season for disobedience to the starter. Deprived of his services Maid of Athens failed to add to her tally until the final day of the following season. However, her success did not end with her retirement from racing, for she bred numerous winners, including Piraeus, winner of a Liverpool Cup and Grecian Bend, placed in an Irish Derby. The best winner of the Irish Derby since Selim, Maid of Athens, in the parlance of the day, was 'a rattling good mare'.

Maid of Athens had not too far to travel to gain Derby honours, for she was trained within sight of the racecourse by Pat Doucie at Mountjoy Lodge. Doucie was one of the first to follow Pat Connolly's lead in becoming a public trainer, listing among his patrons such as Christopher St George, James Cockin, James Cassidy and

E. J. Irwin, the owner of Faugh-a-Ballagh. Doucie later moved to Melitta Lodge, whence he sent out his third and fourth Irish Derby winners. In 1888 he became private trainer to Richard Newcomen at Turf Lodge, followed by a year as successor to James Dunne at Heath House. Having outlived his jockey son, James, by five years, Pat Doucie died at Mooretown, Kildare and was buried on the morning of the Irish Derby, for which he held the record as a trainer until his death.

Tommy Broderick, the rider of Maid of Athens, was for many years stable jockey to Pat Doucie, sharing the riding with the trainer's son, James. His third and final Irish Derby was gained on Master Ned, owned by James Cassidy and some years later he succeeded Doucie as Cassidy's private trainer at Rathbride Cottage. When ill-health obliged his employer to retire from the Turf Broderick became a public trainer, leasing stables attached to the Grandstand hotel, near the racecourse. However, he soon forsook the rigours and uncertainty of racing for the comparative security of the licenced trade in Kildare. Though overshadowed throughout his riding career, first by Frank Wynne and later by John Connolly, Tommy Broderick was an extremely competent and successful jockey, winning all the major events of the day, in addition to his three successes in the Irish Derby.

Wednesday, 28th June, 1871   **£260**   **3 Ran**   **1m 6f 12yds (Peel Course)**

The Irish Derby Sweepstakes of 15sovs each, 5sovs forfeit, 100sovs added by the Turf Club, for three years old. Colts 8st 10lb; fillies and geldings 8st 5lb. Produce of untried sires or mares allowed 3lb. Only one allowance.

(29 subs)

1 Mr Williams's	MAID OF ATHENS (T. Broderick) 8. 2	P. Doucie
	Br. filly Solon – Colleen Rhue by Gemma di Vergy.	
2 Mr T. Dodd's	RATTLEAWAY (W. Canavan) 8.10	
	B. colt Rattle – Frailty.	
3 Mr G. Gough's	RICHARD THE FIRST (T. Kelly) 8. 7	
	Ch. colt Master Richard – Weatherwise.	

SP 4/6 MAID OF ATHENS; 2/1 Rattleaway; 3/1 Richard the First.
4 lengths, 5 lengths.
Winner trained by Mr P. Doucie at Mountjoy Lodge, Curragh.

1872

The sixth renewal of the Irish Derby saw the distance reduced from fourteen furlongs to twelve, the same as its illustrious Epsom inspiration. This was not in itself sufficient to attract the desired number of runners and The Irish Sportsman was moved to reflect that: 'As time makes its way, and meetings in every part of Ireland are rapidly assuming vast proportions, one cannot help regretting that affairs at the

Curragh have remained so long in statu quo.' In the course of the same broadside the writer appealed to Lord Drogheda, in his capacity as Curragh Ranger, to intervene in order to deter the cavalry units stationed on the Curragh from wheeling, manoeuvring and conducting charges right across the gallops! Nor were his comments without justification, for once again only three runners paraded. In fact, had the English raider, Shelmartin, not been scratched on the eve of the race, he would very likely have received a walk-over. In his absence a smaller crowd than usual faced the prospect of yet another three-runner contest; and a moderate lot they were. In keeping with the generally uninspiring production, staged in unseasonably cold and wet weather, the preceding event degenerated into pure farce. The race in question was a Queen's Plate, with the inevitable three runners. Hiawatha, the early leader, was in the process of being pulled up when his rider realised that the remaining pair had run off the course, their respective riders being busily engaged in '. . . snapping at each other, nor did their dispute end until they had passed the scales.' Hiawatha was then restarted to collect the prize.

Of the three hopefuls for the Irish Derby, two were owned by Paddy Keary and trained by Tom Connolly. Only one of these, the un-named Pleasure colt, had managed to win a race of any description. However, Connolly let it be known that he considered Speculation the better of his pair and this was sufficient to see him start almost favourite with Trickstress, recently third to Maid of Athens over two miles. At least the punters chose correctly, for Trickstress shot off in front and was never headed. Speculation finished a respectful second, with the Pleasure colt tailed off.

Clearly the Turf Club deserved criticism and it was quickly forthcoming in the columns of the sporting press: 'It cannot be denied that the governors of flat racing – the Irish Turf Club – have, for long enough, lain dormant, and have advanced much less the interests of the Turf than they ought to have done . . . The same stupid and illiberal articles are yet in force even in the case of our Irish Derby, although year after year since it was established events proved that its conditions prevented it from becoming what it was designed to be, and its last anniversary possessed about as much interest as a selling race, despite its euphonious title and fairly large value.' Besides demanding improvements to the grandstand amenities, '. . . at present it is rather bleak and ladies do not very much care for it', The Irish Sportsman advocated changing the conditions of the Irish Derby to 'penalise winners and give new beginners some allowances.' In fairness to the Turf Club, the desired amendments were drafted almost immediately, to take effect in 1874.

However, to revert to Trickstress, winner of that much-maligned Irish Derby: she was bred in England by London publican Mr C. Snewing and was by that gentleman's Epsom Derby winner Caractacus, who was exported to Russia within months of Trickstress' triumph. Trickstress had been brought to Ireland by the renowned former steeplechase rider, Mr Allen McDonagh of Athgarvan Lodge, who sold her to Mr A. R. Bourne a short time before the race. Trickstress was pulled out again the following day and, after a great struggle, was beaten a head by Paddy Keary's Commodore at the end of three miles. Speculation won the same day, thus providing compensation for Keary's disappointment in the big race. Thereafter Trickstress completely lost her form, even proving a bigger disappointment at stud. Speculation did manage to win subsequently, but the Pleasure colt, later named

Pleasure Seeker, became a roarer and was sold for 160gns following Keary's death in October.

In a Turf career as brief as it was spectacular, A. R. Bourne gained a reputation as an intrepid gambler, who ran his horses for profit before pleasure. His placing of Trickstress illustrates this point, for on the opening day of the Irish Derby meeting she was announced a certain starter for the Kirwan Stakes, for which she was strongly supported . . . it was reported afterwards that, 'The scratching of Trickstress for the Kirwans made some of the early backers of Mr Bourne's mare feel anything but pleasant.' Later the same season one reads that: 'Egyptian is a great horse when wanted; he may not be on this occasion; but should Mr Bourne entrust him with his confidence and 'coins', be on him, or whatever he puts his pieces on.' For whatever reason, A. R. Bourne, having taken Rossmore Lodge for the 1872 season, installed Thomas Moran as his private trainer and having won his fair share of races, sold off his string at the close of the season and forsook the Sport of Kings.

Wednesday, 26th June, 1872	**£230**	**3 Ran**	**1½m (Peel Course)**

The Irish Derby Sweepstakes of 15sovs each, 5sovs forfeit, 100sovs added by the Turf Club, for three years old. Colts 8st 10lb; fillies and geldings 8st 5lb. Produce of untried sires or mares allowed 3lb. Only one allowance.

(23 subs)

1 Mr A. R. Bourne's TRICKSTRESS (W. Miller) 8. 2 T. Moran
  B. filly Caractacus – Lightfinger by Fazzoletto.
2 Mr P. Keary's SPECULATION (M. Murphy) 8.10 T. Connolly
  Ch. colt Adventurer – Verbena.
3 Mr P. Keary's PLEASURE SEEKER* (M. Lynch) 8. 7 T. Connolly
  B. colt Plum Pudding – Pleasure.

SP Evens TRICKSTRESS; 5/4 Speculation; 5/1 Pleasure Seeker.
  Won in a canter.
Winner trained by T. Moran, private trainer to Mr Bourne.

*Pleasure Seeker ran un-named.

1873

Though the conditions of the Irish Derby had been altered drastically following the fiasco of the previous year, the changes did not apply to this year's renewal. Nonetheless, despite its currently low standing with owners, trainers and the sporting press, the occasion retained its appeal for the public, notably the fairer sex, who were otherwise only seen racing in numbers at Punchestown on Ladies' Day. However, women were not unreservedly welcome on the Curragh, for it was, after all, primarily an Army camp and not all the 'ladies' attended purely for love of racing . . . This long-standing problem was acknowledged in the following tribute to

Sub-Inspector Hume for his 'arrangements', 'whereby the demi-monde, those questionable adjuncts to the Curragh reunions, were confined to an obscure quarter and not, as usual, allowed to block up the roads, or be an eyesore and a nuisance to the occupants of the stand-house.' The coughing epidemic which had ravaged Curragh stables in 1872 meant that few of the Classic generation possessed any meaningful two-year-old form. Of the locally-trained runners only Evora and Kyrle Daly had shown anything in public and Evora now met Kyrle Daly on better terms than she had when beating him on their last encounter. These were the only two even mildly fancied to repel the English raider, Angela. Second in the One Thousand Guineas and third to Marie Stuart in the Epsom Oaks, Angela had been covered by King o' Scots prior to being sent over from Newmarket. Only her persistent tail-switching in the paddock and scratchy action in the preliminaries prevented her being backed as a certainty. By contrast, Kyrle Daly looked a picture of well-being, striding out freely to the post.

The early running was made by the handsome but ungenerous Hooton, who showed the way to Kyrle Daly and Evora, with Angela last. With a mile still to go Kyrle Daly joined Hooton in the lead, going clear four furlongs from home. In the straight Angela and Evora challenged the leader simultaneously, without, however, posing any serious threat to Kyrle Daly, who strode majestically away to win by six lengths and two lengths. Although Angela had clearly not run up to her Epsom form, there could be no gainsaying Kyrle Daly's superiority on the day and the winner returned to a rousing reception.

A handsome bay colt, named after the hero in Griffith's 'The Collegians', Kyrle Daly was bred by his owner, Joseph Lyons. By the recently-deceased Artillery out of Colleen Rhue, Kyrle Daly was thus a half-brother to Mr Lyons previous Irish Derby winner, Maid of Athens, with whom Pat Doucie and Tommy Broderick had also been successfully associated. By Touchstone, winner of the St Leger and an outstanding sire, out of a Birdcatcher mare, Artillery won the Prince of Wales' Stakes at York, the Criterion Stakes at Newmarket and the Ebor St Leger, besides finishing second in the St Leger at Doncaster. In the course of a lengthy career at stud in various parts of Ireland Artillery sired successive winners of the Anglesey, Beresford and Madrid Stakes in the 'sixties, as well as Absentee, winner of the inaugural Galway Plate. Having stood in Ballyshannon, Co. Donegal for the 1872 season, Artillery died at the Mahers' Ballinkeele Stud in Co. Wexford in October of the same year.

Prevented by the cough from running more than once as a two-year-old, and then when palpably unfit, Kyrle Daly had only reached his best shortly before the Irish Derby. Saddled for the Kirwan Stakes the next day, he failed to carry his 7lb penalty successfully. He was then beaten twice over shorter distances by Angela, a very good filly at distances up to a mile, who, because of rheumatism in her knees, required a cut in the ground to show her best form. Having acquired the reputation of being difficult to train, Kyrle Daly changed both owners and stables at the end of the season. Unsuccessful for Mr A. Pringle, he immediately recovered his form when re-sold to Mr T. Coffey, for whom he won twice at the Irish Derby meeting in 1874. Mr Coffey, a newcomer to racing, astonished everybody by entering Kyrle Daly in one of those races to be sold for £25. It cost him 155gns to retain his winner. Later that year Kyrle Daly deadheated for a Queen's Plate at Bellewstown, won the run-off and was then disqualified because his rider, Billy Miller, weighed in with his whip. Though given a chance at stud, Kyrle Daly failed to leave his mark upon the breed.

Wednesday, 25th June, 1873   **£285 10 0**   **5 Ran**   **1½m (Howth Post)**

The Irish Derby Sweepstakes of 20sovs each, 10sovs forfeit and 3sovs only if declared on the 1st May, 1872, 100sovs added by the Turf Club. The second horse to receive 30 guineas and the third to save his stake. For three years old. Colts 8st 10lb; fillies and geldings 8st 5lb. Produce of untried sires or mares allowed 3lb. Only one allowance.

(22 subs)

1 Mr W. Williams's   KYRLE DALY (T. Broderick)   8.10   P. Doucie
                           B. colt Artillery – Colleen Rhue by Gemma di Vergy.
2 Mr R. H. Long's   ANGELA (Loates)   8. 2   (UK)
                           B. filly Adventurer – Stella.
3 Lord Howth's   EVORA (M. Lynch)   8. 5
                           B. filly The Knight of St Patrick – Bessie by Orlando.
4 Mr A. Sedlier's   HOOTON (T. Kelly)   8. 7
                           Br. colt Stockwell – Lorelei.
0 Mr R. M. Delamere's   KNIGHT OF ERIN (Behan)   8. 7
                           B. colt The Knight of St Patrick – Connemara.

SP 4/5 Angela; 4/1 KYRLE DALY; Evora.
                    Won in a canter by 6 lengths, 2 lengths.
Winner trained by Mr P. Doucie at Mountjoy Lodge, Curragh.

1874

The long-sought amendments to the articles of the Irish Derby became effective in 1874 and though they had their critics, who described the new format as a glorified handicap, they did give the race a new lease of life. The weight range was now a colossal 36lbs, which gave everyone a chance, at least on paper. Unfortunately, the introduction of the 'new look' Irish Derby coincided with the hardest going on the Curragh in living memory. In consequence fields were small throughout the meeting. Top weight was carried by Ben Battle, winner of the Beresford Stakes in his first season and recently second in the Baldoyle Derby, surprisingly beaten by the moderate Bloomfield. Although Tom Connolly was confident that Ben Battle would be much better suited by the galloping Curragh track, the public put their faith, and cash, on Hollywood, who had finished in front of Kildare in the Madrid Stakes. The other fancied runner was James Cockin's Concord. By virtue of never having raced he claimed an additional 14lbs allowance.

From a perfect start Chancellor made the early running ahead of Kildare and Hollywood, with Ben Battle and Concord tucked in behind. After two furlongs Hollywood joined Chancellor and these two shared the lead to the top of the hill, where Ben Battle moved up ahead of Chancellor to dispute the lead, as Concord and Kildare began to lose touch. Approaching the Chains Ben Battle and Hollywood drew right away from the others and the race began in earnest. Holland, the rider of the favourite, was the first to go for his whip, but Hollywood had no answer to the decisive burst of speed which carried Ben Battle clear to a comfortable five lengths victory. Chancellor finished a similar distance further back, with Concord a poor fourth.

Ben Battle's impressive victory confirmed his status as the best of his generation in Ireland. At the same time it made his Baldoyle defeat all the more difficult to understand, for Bloomfield, his Baldoyle conqueror, was little better than selling plate class in England. Ben Battle was destined never to be beaten again. During the remainder of the season he won three Queen's Plates and the Lord Lieutenant's Plate. The following year he again won three Queen's Plates as well as winning the Lord Lieutenant's Plate for the second time. As a five-year-old he broke down while being prepared for the Liverpool Spring Cup and was retired to stud. A powerful, dark brown colt, Ben Battle was distinctly heavy-shouldered, which made him difficult to train. Located initially at the Stand House Hotel on the Curragh, then in England for two seasons and latterly at Brownstown Lodge, Ben Battle became the leading sire in Ireland. Outstandingly his best son was Bendigo, winner of the Cambridgeshire, Lincolnshire, Hardwicke Stakes, Eclipse Stakes, Jubilee Stakes and Champion Stakes, but a stud failure. Theodemir and Tragedy gave Ben Battle the distinction of becoming one of only four Irish Derby winners to sire a winner of the same race, while another of his sons, Ambush II, won the Aintree Grand National, carrying the colours of HRH the Prince of Wales. Ben Battle's immediate victim in the Irish Derby, Hollywood, won the Liverpool Spring Cup and the Lancastrian Handicap at the same meeting and later sired the Irish Grand National winner, Eglantine.

Bred by his owner, Ben Battle was easily the best son of Rataplan, a full-brother of Stockwell and half-brother of King Tom, both champion sires in England. Though not in the same league as his illustrious relations, Rataplan finished fourth in West Australian's Derby, won the Manchester Cup and amassed no less than nineteen Queen's Plates. Ben Battle's heavy shoulders were a legacy of his sire, who also got Austerlitz, winner of the Grand National and Belle, winner of the Galway Plate.

The 'J. W. Denison' in whose name Ben Battle ran, was, as the racing fraternity well knew, John D. Wardell, a prosperous Dublin tea importer and founder of the well-known tea merchants, Baker Wardell. Now part of Irish Tea Merchants, Baker Wardell continues to thrive under the direction of the founder's great-grandson. Although he bred and raced on an extensive scale, John Wardell's bad luck in big races had become a by-word among racing men, who consequently received Ben Battle's success with genuine delight. This happy event would appear to have marked the turning point in Wardell's racing fortunes, for in 1875 he won the Railway Stakes with Maelstrom and the Beresford Stakes with Richelieu. Three years later he won the Irish Derby for the second time with his high-class filly Madame du Barry. By then, however, John Wardell was mortally ill and Madame du Barry's triumph marked his last racecourse appearance. Following his death in September 1878 his bloodstock came under the hammer and his Newtown Stud, Dunboyne, was also sold. It was not long, however, before his son, also J. D. Wardell, re-registered the popular 'Olive green, black cap'.

The second of three training successes in the race for Tom Connolly of Curragh View, Ben Battle was a first Irish Derby mount for Edwin Martin. He was the son of F. Martin, who became private trainer to J. D. Wardell of Brownstone (sic) Lodge, on the Curragh. The same owner also had horses in training with W. Martin at Newmarket. Edwin Martin would not appear to have got much riding outside his own stable, for his only major Irish successes were gained on Richelieu and Maelstrom, carrying the 'Olive green, black cap'.

Wednesday, 24th June, 1874   **£378 10 0**   **5 Ran**   **1½m (Howth Post)**

The Irish Derby Sweepstakes of 20sovs each, 10sovs forfeit and 3sovs only if declared on the 1st May, 1873, 100sovs added by the Turf Club. The second horse to receive 30 guineas and the third to save his stake. For three years old. Colts 8st 4lb; fillies and geldings 8st. The winner of the Angleseys or Railways at the Curragh, or a stake value 400sovs, to carry 7lb extra; of two such stakes 12lb; if one value 300sovs, 5lb; of 200sovs, 3lb. Penalties not accumulative. Horses that have never won a weight-for-age race value 100sovs, allowed 7lb. Horses that have never started, allowed 14lb. Produce of untried sires or mares allowed 3lb. Only one allowance.

(28 subs)

1 Mr J. W. Denison's	BEN BATTLE (E. Martin)	8. 4	T. Connolly
	B/Br. colt Rataplan – Young Alice by Young Melbourne.		
2 Mr J. C. Murphy's	HOLLYWOOD (Holland)	7. 8	
	B/Br. colt Orest – Furze Chat by King Tom.		
3 Mr G. Knox's	CHANCELLOR (Salter)	7.11	
	B/Br. colt Solon – Claret Cup.		
4 Mr J. Cockin's	CONCORD (Realton)	6.11	
	B. filly King Tom – Melody.		
5 Mr J. Lee's	KILDARE (T. Broderick)	7.11	
	B. colt Plum Pudding – Nu.		

SP 6/4 Hollywood; 5/2 BENBATTLE, Concord; 8/1 Chancellor.
Won by 5 lengths. 2m 49s.
Winner trained by Mr Thomas Connolly at Curragh View, Curragh.

1875

In a field of only four quality compensated for quantity and an exciting race appeared in prospect. Maid of Erin, sister and half-sister to two previous winners of the race, was made favourite, on the strength of her defeat of Ingomar in the Madrid Stakes. She was now 11lbs better off. Ingomar had since narrowly beaten Innishowen in the Baldoyle Derby and the latter's recent shock success in the Manchester Cup added spice to their re-encounter. The small but select field was completed by Turco, a son of Selim. Despite rumours that she had recently been lame, Maid of Erin was soundly backed to confirm the form.

Last away from the start, Turco soon led from Ingomar and Innishowen, with Maid of Erin some lengths behind. At a moderate pace Turco and Ingomar led in turn to the entrance to the straight, where the four runners bunched up. As Turco weakened, Kelly dashed Ingomar into a clear lead and immediately had Maid of Erin in trouble. The crowd now began to shout Ingomar home, only to realise that Ashworth had merely been biding his time on Innishowen, from whom he conjured a burst of speed to which Ingomar had no answer. At the line Innishowen was three lengths clear of Ingomar, with Maid of Athens staying on strongly a length further back. Innishowen's success gave James Cockin the distinction of becoming the first man to be directly associated with three winners of the Irish Derby.

Bred by his owner, Innishowen was a chestnut colt by Uncas out of Aneroid, the mare that Cockin had originally purchased to circumvent the rules introduced specifically to prevent his 'farming' of Irish Queen's Plates with his English-based string. Uncas, also bred by Cockin, won no fewer than eleven races as a two-year-old, including the Anglesey, Railway and Beresford Stakes. As a three-year-old Uncas gave King Alfred weight and a sound beating in the Dee Stakes before going wrong. As King Alfred went on to run Blue Gown to half a length in the Epsom Derby, Uncas was, not unreasonably, advertised as 'about the best horse of this year'. He stood his first season in England in 1871 and Innishowen was thus from his first crop. Leased to a Mr Dunne, he stood subsequently at the Royal Hotel stables, Stand-house, Kildare at a fee of 8gns. Uncas became leading sire in Ireland, responsible for three further winners of the Irish Derby, Redskin, King of the Bees and Theologian. Though this prepotent sire did not manage to beget a two-year-old to emulate his own remarkable Curragh treble in the premier juvenile events, he did get Wild Duck, who carried off the Anglesey, Beresford, National Stakes treble in 1874.

Moderate as a two-year-old, Innishowen must have made phenomenal improvement in his second season, for, in winning the Manchester Cup, he beat Marie Stuart, winner of the Oaks at Epsom a year earlier. His reversal of Baldoyle form with Ingomar was attributed by his trainer Job Toon to altered riding tactics. At Baldoyle he had been forced to make all his own running, whereas at the Curragh, despite the slow early gallop, Ashworth had been able to hold his mount up for a late run, using his speed to the full. Sadly, Innishowen lost his form even more dramatically, with the result that in 1879 he found himself bound for South America. Ingomar, also by Uncas, won the inaugural Curragh Cesarewitch, several Queen's Plates and the valuable Croydon Hurdle. Having stood near Balbriggan for a few seasons, he too took to the high seas; to New Zealand. Turco, though he finished last of the four in the Irish Derby, proved the best of the lot in the long run, for he won all sorts of races over the next seven years. While he did not win a Grand National, Turco found Aintree a happy hunting ground, for he won the Liverpool Hurdle (1879), the Sefton 'Chase (1880) and later the same year won the Becher Hurdle and the Craven 'Chase on the same afternoon. Partnered to these successes by the redoubtable Mr Harry Beasley, he was ridden to victory in France by the less well-known M. Duval de Fraville. The race – an Open Military 'chase – was at Croix de Berny and one reads that: 'the prize consisted of the brown horse Bibletto, aged, by Ruy Bles out of Miss Bowen.'! History does not relate whether Bibletto thus avoided the fate common to less favoured racehorses in France. Turco, after his long and honourable racing career received his reward at Richard Stackpoole's stud in Ennis, Co. Clare, where he held sway until 1896.

Innishowen was prepared for his Irish Derby triumph by Job Toon, who, with his lightweight jockey brother, had charge of James Cockin's Hednesford, Staffordshire, stable, to which the winning rider, G. Ashworth, was also attached. He was quite successful in Ireland in the 'seventies, but appears to have ridden little in public after that decade.

Wednesday, 23rd June, 1875   **£281 10 0**   **4 Ran**   **1½m (Howth Post)**

The Irish Derby Sweepstakes of 20sovs each, 10sovs forfeit and 3sovs only if declared on the 1st May, 1874, 100sovs added by the Turf Club. The second horse to receive 30 guineas and the third to save his stake. For three years old. Colts 8st 4lb; fillies and geldings 8st. The winner of the Angleseys or Railways at the Curragh, or a stake value 400sovs, to carry 7lb extra; of two such stakes 12lb; if one value 300sovs, 5lb; of 200sovs, 3lb. Penalties not accumulative. Horses that have never won a weight-for-age race value 100sovs, allowed 7lb. Horses that have never started, allowed 14lb. Produce of untried sires or mares allowed 3lb. One one allowance.

(20 subs)

1 Mr J. Cockin's	INNISHOWEN (G. Ashworth)	8.1	Toon (UK)
	Ch. colt Uncas – Aneroid by Colonist.		
2 Mr N. Ennis's	INGOMAR (T. Kelly)	8.8	
	B. colt Uncas – Wild Deer by Red Hart.		
3 Capt. Gubbins's	MAID OF ERIN (T. Broderick)	8.3	
	Br. filly Solon – Colleen Rhue.		
0 Mr R. M. Delamere's	TURCO (M. Ryan)	7.8	
	Bl/Br. colt Selim – Breda.		

SP 5/4 Maid of Erin; 2/1 INNISHOWEN; 3/1 Ingomar; 5/1 Turco.
3 lengths, 1 length. 2m 54½s.

1876

The eleventh running of the Irish Derby attracted an equine star in Umpire, and an enormous crowd assembled to witness the certain triumph of this unbeaten colt. Though opposed by four hopefuls, Umpire started at long odds-on to confirm his Baldoyle Derby superiority over Richelieu. Axminster, attempting to credit Colleen Rhue with a third Irish Derby winner, was already known to be a sour individual. The Deer was thought unlikely to get the trip by her experienced trainer, while Sweet Thought was only in the field to act as pacemaker for Richelieu.

Sweet Thought failed dismally in his pacemaking role, abdicating this task to The Deer. However, nothing could go fast enough to stay for long ahead of Umpire, who strode to the front and dealt contemptuously with Richelieu's despairing challenge in the straight. The Deer provided the only surprise of the race, when coming with a wet sail to run Richelieu to a head for second place.

A strapping bay colt, Umpire was bred by Mr William Ryan at Ballymany, near the Curragh. He was by Tom King, a half-brother to Solon, that had run second to

Selim in the inaugural Irish Derby. Tom King, who stood at Rathbride Stables, the Curragh, in 1872, was described as a 'Blood bay, 16hh, with great power, excellent formation and plenty of bone.' Umpire inherited the characteristics of his sire rather than of his dam, Acceptance, a shy breeder, whose only other produce of note was Accepted, winner of the National Produce Stakes and three other races in 1879.

Having won his only two races as a two-year-old, Umpire extended his unbeaten sequence to seven when winning the Irish Derby. He was then put by for the Cambridgeshire, in which he finished fourth to Rosebery in a huge field. Returning to Curragh, Umpire won twice at the October meeting, bringing his record to nine victories in ten attempts. As a four-year-old Umpire went through the season undefeated, one of his four successes being in the Dublin Plate. This was in fact the Baldoyle Derby, which, having failed to fill, was re-opened to older horses. Thus it was that Umpire made history as the only horse to win two 'Baldoyle Derbies'. His next race was the Manchester Cup, which he won with top weight. Umpire ran only twice as a five-year-old, on successive days at the Curragh. On the first day he was beaten by Master Kildare over two miles, but avenged this defeat the next day, when giving Master Kildare no less than 37lbs and a beating over three miles. The true merit of this achievement only became apparent when Master Kildare went on to win the City and Suburban Handicap and the Liverpool Autumn Cup. At stud the careers of these two high-class horses diverged; Master Kildare sired the 1885 Epsom Derby winner, Melton, whereas Narraghmore, winner of the Irish Derby in 1891, was the best of Umpire's disappointing progeny. On his owner's death in 1889 Umpire was sold for only 200gns.

Umpire was owned by Mr C. Ryan, whose father had bred the colt at Ballymany, and was prepared for his triumphant racecourse career by a very shrewd trainer, whose name would later be linked with a far, far greater animal . . . Bendigo. Joe French, Newmarket-born and related to the celebrated jockey Tom French, lived and trained for many years on the Curragh. Though his name was generally associated with Rossmore Lodge, it was from Straw Hall, where Eddie Harty has successfully revived the training tradition, that Joe French sent out Umpire to win the Irish Derby.

The Irish Racing Calendar states, with beguiling simplicity, that Umpire was ridden to victory in the Irish Derby by a jockey named Lynch. What makes this disclosure less than satisfactory is the knowledge that there were no fewer than four jockeys of this name riding in Ireland around this time. However, by process of deduction, one can perhaps eliminate the Lynch who was leading jockey in Ireland in 1860 and 1861, riding mainly for Christopher St George, notably on Solon. At the other end of the time scale, W. Lynch had only just begun his riding career in the mid-'seventies. Thus one is left to choose between P. Lynch and M. Lynch. The former appears to have ridden successfully up until 1871, when he had 17 winners, but little thereafter. By contrast, between 1873 and 1879 M. Lynch (shown as Newmarket-based in 1872, when he rode five winners in Ireland), rode good winners for such as Garret Moore, George Knox and Mr C. Ryan (on Umpire's half-sister, Accepted). In conclusion, it seems likely that the Lynch who rode Umpire in the Irish Derby was M. Lynch, who, in 1880, was attached to Thomas Brown's Newmarket stable. Some years later Lynch, whose reputation had become somewhat unsavoury, rode a hot favourite at the invariably fog-bound Manchester finale. The horse finished down the field. As Lynch rode back to unsaddle he was seen looking down anxiously at his mount's forelegs, which led one disgruntled observer to exclaim: 'Never mind his legs, it's his jaw that's broken!' That M. Lynch should shortly afterwards have announced his departure to America was not perhaps entirely coincidental.

Wednesday, 28th June, 1876   **£298 10 0**   **5 Ran**   **1½m (Howth Post)**

The Irish Derby Sweepstakes of 20sovs each, 10sovs forfeit and 3sovs only if declared on the 1st May, 1875, 100sovs added by the Turf Club. The second horse to receive 30 guineas and the third to save his stake. For three years old. Colts 8st 10lb; fillies and geldings 8st 6lb. The winner of the Angleseys or Railways at the Curragh, or a stake value 400sovs, to carry 7lb extra; of two such stakes 12lb; if one value 300sovs, 5lb; of 200sovs, 3lb. Penalties not accumulative. Horses that have never won a weight-for-age race value 100sovs, allowed 7lb. Horses that have never started, allowed 14lb. Produce of untried sires or mares allowed 3lb. Only one allowance.

(20 subs)

1	Mr C. Ryan's	UMPIRE (Lynch)	9. 3	J. French
		B. colt Tom King – Acceptance by Ambrose.		
2	Mr J. W. Denison's	RICHELIEU (E. Martin)	8.13	F. Martin
		Br. colt The Palmer – Strategy.		
3	Mr J. A. Cassidy's	THE DEER (F. Wynne)	7.13	P. Doucie
		B. filly Kidderminster – Gazelle.		
4	Mr W. S. Lyons's	AXMINSTER (T. Broderick)	7.10	
		B. colt Kidderminster – Colleen Rhue.		
5	Mr J. W. Denison's	SWEET THOUGHT (Parry)	8. 3	F. Martin
		Ch. colt Parmesan – Lucilla.		

SP 1/3 UMPIRE; 4/1 Richelieu; 7/1 Bar.
                2 lengths, HEAD. 2m 51½s.
Winner trained by Joseph French at Straw Hill, Curragh.

1877

In line with widespread alterations in the rules and administration of racing in Ireland, the conditions of the Irish Derby had been amended, increasing the basic weights, adjusting the scale of penalties and allowances and increasing the amount of added money for the race. The glorious summer weather attracted an even larger crowd than usual for the occasion, necessitating extra 'race specials' from Kingsbridge. Moreover, the absence of Arbitrator, the expected favourite, gave the race an invitingly open appearance. In place of Arbitrator, Charles Blake was represented by Rebel Chief, trained at Russley by Robert Peck. Claiming all the allowances, and something of a dark horse, Rebel Chief had been accompanied across the Channel by Lord Drogheda's Philammon, from Joseph Dawson's Newmarket stable. Of the home-trained quartet Notus was the prime fancy, despite reservations concerning his stamina. Tyrconnel, winner of the National Produce Stakes, was thought to have too much weight, while Queen of the Bath had run too badly at Baldoyle to have any chance. That left Redskin, the only gelding in the field and recently successful at Cork Park, but now stepping up appreciably in class. In a spirited betting market Rebel Chief, Notus and Philammon each attracted substantial support, with the last-named eventually emerging as the clear favourite.

Queen of the Bath made the running for the first mile, followed by Rebel Chief, Notus and Philammon. At this point Rebel Chief moved upsides Queen of the Bath, only to drop back rapidly. This left the filly again clear as she led into the straight, where she was immediately challenged by Philammon, on whom Lynch struck for home, pursued by Redskin, Tyrconnel and Notus. Two furlongs from home Lynch's tactics looked likely to succeed, for both Notus and Tyrconnel were under severe pressure. However, Redskin could now be seen coming with a strong run and, having got the measure of the flagging favourite inside the final furlong, he drew right away to win by five lengths. Tyrconnel struggled on gamely to finish within a length of Philammon. Though it came as a complete surprise, not least to his connections, Redskin's well-earned success was rapturously received, for he had kept the coveted prize at home, against all the odds.

Bred by his owner, Captain Stamer Gubbins, Redskin was only the second gelding ever to run in the Irish Derby – the previous one had finished last – and after 1880 geldings were barred from entry. By Uncas, Redskin was out of the Kingfisher mare Wild Daisy. Though he lost his form after the Irish Derby, Redskin's stud-book status dictated a lengthy racing career and he remained in training for a further eight seasons, during which he paid his way all over England and Wales, including a double in one day at lovely, long-forgotten Llandrindod Wells, ridden by Mr W. H. 'Willie' Moore. Philammon continued to improve, becoming virtually unbeatable in Queen's Plates, irrespective of weight or distance. As an aged horse he reached his peak, winning the Liverpool Spring Cup and the Esher Stakes in 1882. Boycotted on his retirement to stud in Ireland, by virtue of his ownership, Philammon was transferred to England and subsequently repatriated by Lord Drogheda when the Land League agitation had died down. He rewarded his owner's perseverance by becoming the leading sire in Ireland. One of his many winners was Pet Fox, successful in the Irish Derby in 1887.

Captain Stamer Gubbins, the popular owner-breeder of Redskin, founded his celebrated Knockany Stud in Co. Limerick in 1866. Here he stood Uncas and Xenophon and by the latter he bred Seaman, winner of the Grand National in 1882. Stamer Gubbins raced on an extensive scale, heading the list of winning owners in Ireland in 1874 and 1877. Mountjoy Lodge, which he had rebuilt, he maintained as a private stable, under the charge of Dan Broderick. After his premature death as the result of a riding accident in 1879, he was succeeded at Knockany by his brother John, destined to become even better known on the Turf.

Redskin, in common with the rest of Gubbins horses, was trained at Mountjoy Lodge by Dan Broderick. When Stamer Gubbins rebuilt Mountjoy Lodge around 1860, he offered the ex-jockey free tenure of the premises for life. However, Broderick firmly insisted on paying his generous employer an annual rent of £10. After Gubbins' tragic death, Dan Broderick became a public trainer and employed Phillie Behan as his head lad. Behan subsequently married Broderick's daughter and assumed control of Mountjoy Lodge on his father-in-law's death in 1895.

Francis Wynne, the rider of Redskin, was one of the leading flat jockeys in

Ireland at the time. Born in 1857, Frank was the younger son of Denis Wynne, the Rossmore Lodge trainer. Denny Wynne had won the Grand National on Mathew in 1847 and fifteen years later his elder son, Joe Wynne was killed in the same race, when his mount collided in mid-air. Frank Wynne began his riding career with Mr St George's Rathbride Cottage stable, having his first mount in public at the age of thirteen, when weighing just 4st. Like his father and brother before him, Frank Wynne became champion jockey in Ireland on more than one occasion and rode three Irish Derby winners in four years. Rising weight eventually forced him to follow in the footsteps of his father and brother, riding over fences.

Wednesday, 27th June, 1877   **£340**   **5 Ran**   **1½m (Howth Post)**

The Irish Derby Sweepstakes of 20sovs each, 10sovs forfeit and 5sovs only if declared on the first of the month preceding the race, namely the 1st May, 1877. The minor forfeit to the fund. 150sovs added by the Turf Club. The second horse to receive 20sovs out of the stakes. For three years old. Colts 8st 12lb; fillies and geldings 8st 8lb. Produce of untried sires or mares allowed 3lb, if claimed at entry, only one allowance. The winner of the Angleseys or Railways at the Curragh, or of a stake value 400sovs, 8lb extra; of the Angleseys and Railways or two stakes value 400sovs, 12lb extra; of races collectively value 600sovs, 10lb extra; of one value 300sovs, 3lb extra. Penalties not accumulative. Horses that have never won a race value 100sovs, allowed 6lb. Maidens allowed 12lb. Only one of these allowances can be claimed.

(22 subs)

1 Capt. Gubbins's   REDSKIN (F. Wynne)   8. 2   D. Broderick
Ch. gelding Uncas – Wild Daisy by Kingfisher.
2 Lord Drogheda's   PHILAMMON (Lynch)   8. 0   Joseph Dawson (UK)
Br. colt Solon – Satanella by Wild Dayrell.
3 Mr R. M. Delamere's   TYRCONNELL (J. Connolly)   9. 0   T. Connolly
Ch. colt Lord Ronald – Connemara.
4 Mr T. Dodd's   NOTUS (M. Ryan)   8. 0
B. colt Master Richard – Sea Breeze.
5 Mr J. W. Denison's   QUEEN OF THE BATH (Huxtable)7.10   F. Martin
B. filly Knight of the Garter – Cygnet.
6 Mr C. J. Blake's   REBEL CHIEF (J. M'Donald)   7.11
Ro/Ch. colt Scottish Chief – Dryad by Cape Flyaway.

SP 2/1 Philammon; 5/2 Notus; 3/1 Rebel Chief; 5/1 REDSKIN.
5 lengths, ½ length. 2m 54½s.
Winner trained by Mr Dan Broderick at Mountjoy Lodge, Curragh.

1878

Ever more popular with the public, who thronged both the course and enclosure, the Irish Derby drew a field of six, dominated by the three fillies in the race. Public form appeared to revolve around the Dublin Plate – otherwise the Baldoyle Derby – in which Sisyphus had beaten Venice and Madame du Barry. The second and third on that occasion were now respectively 21lbs and 23lbs better off and the Doucies, father and son, made no secret of their strong fancy for Venice. Immorata, winner of the National Produce Stakes and more recently successful over ten furlongs at Baldoyle, was also well fancied. The third choice in a brisk betting market was Madame du Barry, on whom Frank Wynne had wasted hard to take full advantage of all her allowances. Only reports of recent coughing in her stable kept Madame du Barry at relatively generous odds.

The early running was made by the blinkered Terror, who led from Sisyphus, these two being clear of Venice and King of Trumps, with Madame du Barry in last place. As Sisyphus dropped back and Immorata lost touch, the remainder began to close on Terror, who gave best at the entrance to the straight. Venice now went clear, apparently with the prize at her mercy, and backers of the favourite began to count their winnings. To their growing horror the wily Wynne now played his hand, producing the lightly-weighted Madame du Barry with a relentless run in the middle of the course. Game to the last, Venice responded to Broderick's inimitable urgings. The two battling fillies were now inside the furlong and nothing else mattered. Still the backers of Venice prayed for another Broderick miracle. But Venice was not Maid of Athens and it was not to be. Madame du Barry, having broken her rival's resistance, surged clear to a three-length win. King of Trumps struggled home a tired and distant third. The winner's time was almost three seconds faster than that of the previous record-holder, Ben Battle. Curiously, both carried the colours of 'J. W. Denison'.

Even though she had deprived favourite backers of what had seemed like certain success, Madame du Barry returned to a rousing reception, directed in the main at her courageous and ailing owner, whose popularity was in inverse proportion to his proverbial ill-luck on the Turf. 'J. W. Denison', otherwise John D. Wardell, was also known to be a dying man. As if sensing that this might well be their last opportunity, the essentially intimate racing fraternity sounded their appreciation of a gallant and generous owner to the echo. A poignant and memorable occasion was indeed a final salute, for John Wardell never saw a racecourse again, dying of cancer three months later.

Home-bred at Wardell's Dunboyne stud, Madame du Barry was by the Epsom Derby winner, Favonius, out of Strategy, whose older produce, Richelieu, had finished second in the Irish Derby for Mr Wardell and his private trainer, F. Martin, two years earlier. Favonius, despite dying the previous year at the age of nine, also sired Sir Bevys, winner of the Epsom Derby in 1879.

Following the death of her owner, Madame du Barry was purchased by that hot-tempered Kilkenny sportsman and MP, George Leopold Bryan, for 570gns. Trained for her new owner by Michael Dennehy at French House, she won the Curragh Cesarewitch as a four-year-old and two Queen's Plates the following season. By morbid coincidence George Bryan then died and Madame du Barry featured in a second dispersal sale. She passed into the hands of one Charles Perkins, a North of England owner and her career now began in earnest . . . In the last week of September she carried Perkins' 'Turquoise and violet jacket' no less four times, first past the post on each occasion. Her astonishing record reads as follows: Sept. 25 – Manchester, Autumn H'cap, 1m.4f. – Won; Sept. 28 – Ayr-Glasgow H'cap, 1m.2f. – Won; Sept. 30 – Perth, Breadalbane H'cap, 1m.2f. – Won; Oct. 1 – Perth, Montrose H'cap, 1m.1f. – Won (Disqualified for going the wrong side of a marker). Rested for all of two weeks, Madame du Barry made a winning reappearance at Newmarket on Oct. 13. On Nov. 4 she, was unplaced at Lincoln, but won over two miles the next day. Next stop was Manchester, where on Nov. 24 she won the November Cup over one mile as a prelude to a triumphant finale two days later, when she slaughtered a large field in the valuable Manchester November Handicap. Thus, in the space of eight weeks, Madame du Barry started ten times, winning seven, having traversed the length and breadth of England and Scotland to accomplish these labours of Hercules.

Kept in training as a six-year-old, this remarkable mare won at York, before achieving her most spectacular success, when carrying Jem Snowden to a twenty-length victory in the Goodwood Cup. Placed in five of her other seven starts that year, Madame du Barry's valiant efforts served only to reassure the handicapper that *enough* weight will bring together a Derby winner and a donkey! She was asked to give as much as 49lbs to her opponents. These efforts left their mark, for, on her seasonal debut in 1882, Madame du Barry broke down irreparably and was sent to stud. Having produced seven foals, including Rose du Barry, three times successful as a two-year-old in the colours of Baron de Hirsch, Madame du Barry received not well-earned retirement, but a one-way passage to Austria; an ignominious end to one of the finest fillies in the annals of the Irish Derby.

Wednesday, 26th June, 1878	**£330**	**6 Ran**	**1½m (Howth Post)**

The Irish Derby Sweepstakes of 20sovs each, 10sovs forfeit and 5sovs only if declared on the first of the month preceding the race, namely the 1st May, 1878. The minor forfeit to the fund. 150sovs added by the Turf Club. The second horse to receive 20sovs out of the stakes. For three years old. Colts 8st 12lb; fillies and geldings 8st 8lb. Produce of untried sires or mares allowed 3lb, if claimed at entry, only one allowance. The winner of the Angleseys or Railways at the Curragh, or of a stake value 400sovs, 8lb extra; of the Angleseys and Railways or two stakes value 400sovs, 12lb extra; of races collectively value 600sovs, 10lb extra; of one value 300sovs 5lb extra; of 200sovs, 3lb extra. Penalties not accumulative. Horses that have never won a race value 100sovs, allowed 6lb. Maidens allowed 12lb. Only one of these allowances can be claimed.

(27 subs)

1	Mr J. W. Denison's	MADAME DUBARRY (F. Wynne)	7. 7	Martin
		B. filly Favonius – Strategy by Adventurer.		
2	Mr J. Doucie's	VENICE (T. Broderick)	8. 8	P. Doucie
		B. filly Uncas – Trieste.		
3	Mr C. Ryan's	KING OF TRUMPS (W. Miller)	8. 0	
		B. colt Lord Clifton – Queen Bee by King Tom.		
4	Mr J. G. Blake's	TERROR (M. Miller)	8. 0	
		B. colt Fright – Rose Noble.		
5	Lord Drogheda's	SISYPHUS (J. M'Donald)	9. 3	M. Moneypenny
		B/Br. colt Outcast – Satanella by Wild Dayrell.		
6	Mr G. Knox's	IMMORATA (J. Connolly)	8.13	
		Ch. filly Lothario – Claret Cup.		

SP Evens Venice; 4/1 Immorata; 5/1 MADAME DUBARRY, Sisyphus; 100/15 King of Trumps; 10/1 Terror.

3 lengths, bad third. 2m 46¾s.

1879

Though the Irish Derby of 1879 attracted a field of eight, it was generally regarded as a match between Soulouque and Shinglass, two of the leading juveniles of the previous season. The former had won the Anglesey Stakes on his debut. Unplaced behind Shinglass two days later, he had then won on successive days at the Curragh in October before retiring into winter quarters. Showing tremendous physical improvement as a three-year-old, he had finished a four-length second to Shinglass in the Baldoyle Derby in May, conceding 7lbs. In the meantime Shinglass had twice disappointed at Manchester. His dislike of the prevailing heavy going was public knowledge and the absence of blinkers did nothing to encourage his supporters. Undecided, the rain-sodden crowd made the pair co-favourites, before squelching back to the cover of the Stand House to watch the race.

At the third attempt the starter got them away, headed by Lakeview, who soon gave way to Arras. At an extremely modest gallop Arras led Lord Randolph, Lakeview and Soulouque to halfway. As Lakeview faded, Miser and Soulouque dashed up to Arras, with Shinglass a rapidly improving fourth. Approaching the Chains the two principals drew clear of their struggling rivals. All the way up the long, tiring straight Connolly on Soulouque appeared to have the upper hand and was being hailed as the winner. However, try as he might, he could not shake off the reluctant Shinglass, on whom Ryan never gave up. Only in the last hundred yards did Soulouque manage to get ahead of his rival, passing the post a length to the good, with Refuge a remote third. As Joe French, his trainer, had feared, Shinglass would not give his true running in the heavy ground and it was this, rather than his own superiority, that gave the slowest-ever Irish Derby to Soulouque.

Bred by his owner, Mr William Dunne, Soulouque was an imposing bay colt by Roman Bee out of Tawney, by Ivan. Roman Bee, winner of the Anglesey Stakes in 1862, was out of Queen Bee, whose fortuitous purchase by Mr Dunne's father had brought fame and fortune to the Dunnes of Ballymanus. Bought from a disreputable Dublin solicitor called Copperthwaite for about £30 in 1856, Queen Bee, by Harkaway, bred a host of winners, including Busy Bee, Queen of the Bees, Roman Bee, Russian Bee and Bee Quick. After a successful career at stud, Roman Bee died in 1878, having covered a mare called Gazelle, a prolific dam of winners for James Cassidy of Monasterevan. The resulting produce was Master Ned, destined to credit Roman Bee with his second posthumous Irish Derby winner. Soulouque's dam, Tawney, bred several other winners for the Dunnes, notably Soulouque's own-brother, Cimaroon, also a winner of the Anglesey Stakes, beating Madame du Barry. On two occasions William Dunne had the pleasure of seeing two of the progeny of Tawney and Roman Bee win at the same meeting.

William Dunne JP, of Ballymanus, Queen's County, was elected a member of the Turf Club in 1868, when only twenty-five, an indication of the importance of his family in Irish racing at the time. His father, Michael Dunne MP who became famous as 'the Silent Member', having sat in the House of Commons from 1852 to 1865 without uttering, bred Cortolvin, winner of the Grand National in 1867. Five years earlier Michael Dunne had headed the list of owners in Ireland, largely due to

the success of Roman Bee. In the rolling limestone pastures of picturesque Ballymanus, William Dunne maintained the family tradition by breeding such as King of
the Bees, winner of the Irish Derby in 1880, and the brilliant Queen of the Bees,
winner of the Anglesey, Railway and National Stakes in 1872. This remarkable
treble was in itself sufficient to make her owner-breeder the leading owner in Ireland
that year. Senior Steward for several terms, this brusque but kind-hearted man raced
purely for sport, sparing neither effort nor expense for the general good of his
beloved pursuit. During a lean period in the fortunes of Ballymanus, William Dunne
repeated his father's experience with Queen Bee, when giving 35gns for Armorel.
One of the seven winners that this mare bred was the aptly-named Great Surprise,
winner of the King's Stand Stakes in 1912 and the leading sprinter of his day. The
last horse to carry William Dunne's 'Pink, black cap' was Steep Holm, also out of
Armorel, when successful at Baldoyle in June 1915. Within a week William Dunne
was dead, following an operation. At a meeting of the Stewards on Derby Day at
the Curragh, the Earl of Enniskillen (Senior Steward) proposed that 'We, the
Members of the Turf Club, desire to record our deep regret at the death of our old
and esteemed colleague, Mr W. Dunne, who had been for so many years a staunch
supporter of racing in Ireland, and whose wise counsel, based on long experience,
has always been generously accorded to the Turf Club in its deliberations.'

The last of three Irish Derby winners for trainer Tom Connolly, Soulouque was
the first of four such for John Connolly, then emerging as the outstanding Irish flat
jockey of his era. His uncle, Pat Conolly, had been champion jockey on numerous
occasions in Ireland, before establishing himself as the most successful lightweight of
his day in England, where he won all the Classics, being twice successful in the
Epsom Derby on Plenipotentiary (1834) and Coronation (1841). Unlike the majority
of his contemporaries, John Connolly rode exclusively on the flat, confining his
activities to the principal courses, as they were then: the Curragh, Baldoyle, Cork
Park and Down Royal. Unlike his illustrious uncle, whom English writers described
as having 'an ugly Irish seat', John Connolly was a supremely stylish rider, whose
mastery of the Curragh has seldom been rivalled. The best horse with whom this
brilliant jockey was associated was Barcaldine, unbeaten in Ireland or England.
Barcaldine was trained in Ireland by Tom Connolly (no relation), and he was
assisted by Pat Connolly, a brother of the jockey, who took charge at Curragh View
on the death of Tom Connolly. Having ridden his last big winner on Angelus in the
Railway Stakes two years earlier, John Connolly died in 1896, leaving an orphan
son.

The Irish Derby was unquestionably Soulouque's finest hour. On his reappearance he ran deplorably in the Liverpool Cup, whereupon he vanished for three
years, making a short-lived and inglorious comeback in 1882, when unplaced in a
Hunters' Flat Race at Sandown, ridden by Arthur Coventry. Singlass redeemed his
reputation by winning no less than seven races as a four-year-old and went on
winning for the next two seasons. Refuge found her metier over shorter distances
and later went hurdling and 'chasing with success. Arras won over a mile the day
after the Derby, and kept up the good work for the next two seasons. The Squaw
won the valuable Manchester H'cap 'Chase three years later, ridden by Frank
Wynne, while Lord Randolph, Lakeview and Miser all contributed something to
their keep. Thus it transpired that, though all his victims won subsequently and

endorsed the form, the Irish Derby winner, in achieving his place in the history of the race, attained heights to which he would never again aspire.

Wednesday, 25th June, 1879   **£325**   **8 Ran**   **1½m (Howth Post)**

The Irish Derby Stakes of 400sovs, by subscription of 15sovs, but half only for horses struck out on or before the 2nd September, 1878. The second to receive 50sovs and the third 25sovs out of the stake. For three years old. Colts 8st 12lb; fillies and geldings 8st 8lb. The winner of the Angleseys and Railways at the Curragh, or of two stakes value 400sovs each, 10lb extra; of Angleseys or a stake value 400sovs, or stakes collectively value 600sovs, 7lb extra; of a stake value 200sovs, 3lb extra. Produce of untried sires or mares allowed 3lb, if claimed at entry, but not for both. Horses that have never won a race value 100sovs, allowed 5lb. Maidens allowed 10lb. Only one of these allowances can be taken.

(27 subs)

1 Mr W. Dunne's	SOULOUQUE (J. Connolly)	9. 5	Connolly
	B. colt Roman Bee – Tawney by Ivan.		
2 Mr C. Taaffe's	SHINGLASS (M. Ryan)	9. 2	French
	Ch. colt Stockinger – Lady Lynbury by The Coroner.		
3 Mr J. C. Murphy's	REFUGE* (W. Lynch)	7. 9	
	B. filly Uncas – Madeline.		
4 Lord Drogheda's	ARRAS (J. M'Donald)	8. 0	
	Ch. filly Kidderminster – Swivel.		
5 Mr John Colgan's	THE SQUAW (F. Wynne)	8. 5	
	Br. filly Uncas – Sarsaparilla.		
6 Mr T. Roberts's	LORD RANDOLPH (M. Lynch)	7.13	
	Ch. colt Uncas – Lady Fanny by Lord Clifden.		
7 Mr C. J. Blake's	LAKEVIEW (J. Callaghan)	7.12	
	B. filly Speculum – Lady of the Lake.		
8 Mr J. A. Cassidy's	MISER (T. Broderick)	8.11	P. Doucie.
	B. gelding Solon – Chocolate.		

SP 100/30 SOULOUQUE, Shinglass; 4/1 Arras, The Squaw.
1 length, bad third. 3m 10s.
Winner trained by Mr Thomas Connolly at Curragh View, Curragh.

*Refuge ran un-named.

1880

The richest Irish Derby to date, with a guaranteed prize fund of 550sovs, drew a field of eleven, as well as an enormous attendance, encouraged by delightful summer weather. Principal topic among the racing fraternity was still the sensational race for the Epsom Derby between Bend Or and Robert the Devil, with its even more sensational aftermath. The owner of Robert the Devil had lodged an objection to the Duke of Westminster's winner, on the basis that he was in reality a colt called Tadcaster. Though the Epsom Stewards overruled the objection, at least one of them later expressed grave misgivings on the question. Perhaps overawed by the excellence of the cross-Channel Classic crop, the sun-baked crowd went solidly for the only English-trained runner, Helen Mar. Owned by Mr J. C. Murphy of Osberstown, near Naas, Helen Mar was trained by Hopper at Stourbridge and ridden by the fashionable Newmarket lightweight, A. F. Lemaire. Despite the fact that Helen Mar had never yet appeared in public, she was preferred in the betting to Umpire's half-sister, Accepted, winner of the National Produce Stakes and more recently successful over six furlongs at the Curragh and also to Eyrefield, a winner at the big Baldoyle meeting. Under the conditions of the race, Helen Mar received substantial weight from these two and also from Pioneer, penalised for winning the Waterford Testimonial Stakes. Both Lord Drogheda and Charles Blake, two stalwarts of the Turf Club still seeking their first Irish Derby, were represented, the latter by the quietly-fancied Baron Farney, an unraced son of Cambuslang. The only other runner to figure in the betting was King of the Bees. Having disappointed in the Baldoyle Derby, Dan Broderick's charge had scored a surprise success over six furlongs only the previous day.

The Flirt, ridden by Billy Miller, made the early running from Miss Kate and Kilmachree, with Baron Farney bringing up the rear. Though headed briefly by Miss Kate and Kilmachree, The Flirt regained the lead entering the straight, with the rest of the field closely bunched behind her. In the straight the picture changed rapidly, as King of the Bees, Helen Mar and Baron Farney shot clear of the pack, pursued by Eyrefield and Kilmachree. In an exciting struggle, which had the crowd shouting their respective fancies home, Lemaire tried unsuccessfully to force the favourite through on the rails. Her lack of previous racecourse experience caused her to hesitate and her chance had disappeared. Having effectively disposed of the challenge on his inside, Frank Wynne kept King of the Bees at full stretch to hold off Baron Farney by a length, with Helen Mar half a length further back. Caught for speed in the closing stages, Eyrefield stayed on to finish fourth.

Owned by William Brophy of Herbertstown, King of the Bees was bred by William Dunne, successful in the race twelve months previously with Soulouque. King of the Bees was by the leading sire, Uncas, out of Winged Bee, by Artillery, and thus another good winner from the Dunnes' famous Queen Bee family. He was also the third of four Irish Derby winners sired by the prepotent Uncas, himself a son of 'the Emperor of Stallions', Stockwell. King of the Bees reappeared at the Maze in July, where he failed to win in three attempts. Gelded during the close season, he continued to disappoint as a four-year-old and was later exported to Germany.

Though he credited William Brophy with his only success in the Irish Derby, King of the Bees was by no means the best animal to carry the 'White, rose cap' of one of the leading owner-breeders in Ireland. William Brophy headed the list of winning owners in Ireland in 1887, due largely to the two-year-old triumphs of Miss Pitt and Philomel, winner of the Anglesey and National Produce Stakes. On his death in 1892 William Brophy's bloodstock realised the highest prices ever recorded in Ireland. Star of the sale was the broodmare Chrysalis, a half-sister to King of the Bees, who, together with her foal, yearling, two-year-old and three-year-old realised the then enormous price of 10,850gns. Top-priced of the quintet was Laodemia, subsequently successful in the Derby Cup and the Doncaster Cup. Crystabelle, the three-year-old, had won the Anglesey and Railway Stakes in 1891, before beating her contemporaries Red Prince II and Roy Neil by an astonishing fifty lengths over a mile and a half, an incredible performance by a two-year-old. In addition to breeding Rockdove, still the only animal ever to win both the Curragh and Newmarket Cesarewitches, William Brophy was credited with breeding Rockdove's half-brother, Portmarnock, whose victory in the Irish Derby he did not live to see. Mr Brophy's widow later bred Mayfowl, a champion in India, where he won a record three Viceroy's Cups and deadheated in a fourth.

Baron Farney, besides winning the Curragh Cesarewitch later the same season, developed a partiality for Galway, where he scored a double at the annual meeting in successive years. He became the sire of Miss Georgie, the dam of Lord Rossmore, winner of the Irish Derby in 1903. Helen Mar, having won on the flat at three and four, became an accomplished 'chaser, winning at Croydon and at Punchestown, besides being placed in an Irish Grand National. Eyrefield proved his toughness by winning a three-mile Queen's Plate the very next day. The following year, having finished second in the Sefton 'chase at Aintree, Eyrefield won the Prince of Wales Plate at Punchestown. Accepted became a successful sprinter and subsequently bred The Rejected, winner of the Lincolnshire Handicap in 1890. The Flirt won several springs, while Pioneer went on to win 'chases in France. Not for the first time the Irish Derby proved to be the victor's finest hour, while only a prelude to success for the vanquished.

Charles J. Blake, *one of the founders of modern Irish racing and thrice successful in the Irish Derby. Source:* The Irish Field.

Henry Eyre Linde. *Master of Eyrefield Lodge and outstanding among Irish trainers in the last century. He saddled his own Pet Fox to win the Irish Derby in 1887. Source:* Irish Field.

Wednesday, 23rd June, 1880   **£475**   **11 Ran**   **1½m (Howth Post)**

The Irish Derby Stakes of 550sovs, by subscription of 15sovs each to the fund, but 6sovs only for horses struck out on or before the 2nd September, 1879. The second horse to receive 50sovs and the third 25sovs out of the stake. For three years old. Colts 8st 12lb; fillies and geldings 8st 8lb. The winner of the Angleseys and Railways at the Curragh, or of two stakes value 400sovs each, 10lb extra; of Angleseys or a stake value 400sovs, or stakes collectively value 600sovs, 7lb extra; of a stake value 200sovs, 3lb extra. Horses that have never won a race value 100sovs, allowed 5lb; maidens allowed 10lb; only one of these allowances can be taken. Produce of untried sires or mares allowed 3lb, if claimed at entry, but not for both.

(42 subs)

1	Mr W. Brophy's	KING OF THE BEES* (F. Wynne) 8. 7 B. colt Uncas – Winged Bee by Artillery.		D. Broderick
2	Mr C. J. Blake's	BARON FARNEY (J. Callaghan) 7.13 Br. colt Cambuslang – X L by Polish.		James Dunne
3	Mr J. C. Murphy's	HELEN MAR (Lemaire) 7. 9 B. filly Scottish Chief – Madaline.		UK
4	Mr H. E. Linde's	EYREFIELD (Mr H. Beasley) 8. 9 Ch. colt Uncas – Highland Mary by Solon.		H. E. Linde
5	Mr E. Bourke's	KILMACHREE (J. Connolly) 8. 2 Br. colt Solon – Eva.		
6	Mr C. Ryan's	ACCEPTED (W. Lynch) 9. 1 B. filly Blarney – Acceptance.		French
0	Mr G. Knox's	THE FLIRT (W. Miller) 8. 3 B. filly Uncas – The Beauty.		
0	Mr J. Doucie's	MISS KATE (T. Broderick) 7.12 B. filly Knight of the Garter – Gazelle.		
0	Mr James Power's	PIONEER (M. Ryan) 9. 1 B. colt Uncas – Brunette.		
0	Lord Drogheda's	ST MAUR (A. Hall) 7.13 B. colt Somerset – Rachel by Faugh-a-Ballagh.		
11	Mr G. D. Stokes's	GLANDINE (Miley) 7. 9 Ch. gelding St Ronan – Leda by Dundee.		

SP 7/4 Helen Mar; 100/30 Accepted; 100/15 Eyrefield; 10/1 Baron Farney; 100/8 KING OF THE BEES, St Maur.

1 length, ½ length. 2m 45s.

Winner trained by Mr D. Broderick at Mountjoy Lodge, Curragh.

*King of the Bees ran un-named.

1881

The fifteenth renewal of the Irish Derby resembled an attempt to stage Hamlet without the Prince, for the Classic scene was overshadowed by Barcaldine, unbeaten in his four races as a two-year-old, but never nominated for the Irish Derby. Already he had won the Baldoyle Derby handsomely, when less than half fit. On the day of the Derby he slaughtered the useful Noble Lord in a three-mile Queen's Plate, carrying 8lbs overweight. Unfortunately, Barcaldine's opportunities to prove his greatness were curtailed by the tactics of his unscrupulous owner, George Low, whose activities led to his being Warned Off in October 1881. Barcaldine was later sold by Order of the Sheriff, becoming the property of Robert Peck, in whose hands he remained unbeaten, proving himself one of the outstanding animals of his age and undoubtedly the finest racehorse to emerge from Ireland in the latter part of the last century.

Shorn of the glamour of Barcaldine's majestic presence, the Irish Derby seemed likely to be a mundane affair, dominated by Master Ned and Greenfield. Master Ned had won the Anglesey Stakes, beating Speranza and Faustin and had beaten them again in October, having finished a respectful second to Barcaldine in the interim. Greenfield, a half-brother to Shinglass, the best colt of his generation in Ireland, had won as a two-year-old and had won three races in his second season. The race appeared to be between these two, for they held Faustin and Speranza on form, while Handcuff had only run once and Golden Rose had no worthwhile performance to her credit. The conditions of the race required Master Ned to concede between 7lbs and 24lbs to his rivals and it was doubt about his ability to do this that left him friendless in the Ring. Favourite was Greenfield, with Handcuff and Faustin, a stablemate of Barcaldine, also supported. The race itself requires little description. The two form horses came right away from their field and, in a desperate finish, Master Ned held on to beat Greenfield by a neck. Faustin finished third. It was a fine performance on Master Ned's part to concede weight all round, especially to Greenfield.

Master Ned, a strongly-made bay colt, was bred by his owner, Mr J. A. Cassidy. By the recently-deceased Roman Bee, Master Ned was out of Gazelle, whose dam, Antelope, was a half-sister to Chanticleer. Gazelle bred numerous winners for Mr Cassidy, including The Deer, Master Bob, Melitta, Athy, Salamis and Carmelite. On her death in 1885, Mr Cassidy had her hooves mounted in silver, with a silver plate listing all her foals. Unplaced over a mile on his reappearance, Master Ned won five of his remaining six 'races', including three walk-overs for Queen's Plates. However, his defeat of Lord Drogheda's very good mare, Miriam, at the Curragh in September was a meritorious performance. Over the next two seasons Master Ned ran only three times, scoring his solitary success in a Queen's Plate. Retired to stand at the Compton Stud in England, Master Ned was described as 'likely to beget good hunter stock'. Repatriated to Melitta Lodge, under the care of Pat Doucie, Master Ned failed to make his mark and ended his days as a hunter sire in Co. Cork, where he died in 1901. Of his Irish Derby opponents, Greenfield did best, finishing third in the Liverpool Summer Cup, before being retired to stud in Co. Antrim as a premium sire. Handcuff won the Kirwan Stakes on the day after the Irish Derby and the valuable Becher Hurdle at Liverpool the following year. As Barcaldine went on to confirm his greatness, the utter irrelevance of the Irish Derby of 1881 became ever more apparent.

Named after his owner-breeder's son, Master Ned was the first of two successive Irish Derby winners owned by Mr J. A. Cassidy of Monasterevan, Co. Kildare, a member of the Turf Club and one of the foremost owners of the time. James Archbold Cassidy was the proprietor of the Monasterevan Distillery, built by his grandfather, John Cassidy, in 1784. Burned to the ground within a year of being opened, by a disgruntled employee, Monasterevan Distillery had been rebuilt by

John Cassidy, with the financial assistance of a relation by marriage, Robert Harvey, a Dublin wine merchant. Harvey subsequently moved his business to Bristol, where it achieved worldwide renown through its Bristol Cream. Although Cassidy's Whiskey was not destined to achieve such lasting fame, it was at the peak of its fortunes in the last quarter of the nineteenth century, under the energetic guidance of James Cassidy. A striking and immaculate figure, Cassidy was described as a more handsome man than his friend and neighbour, Lord Drogheda, after whom Cassidy named his winner of the Baldoyle Derby, The Marquis. Besides his business and bloodstock interests – he was leading owner in Ireland in 1873, 1879 and 1882 –James Cassidy was a keen follower of the Kildare Hunt, and it was a near-fatal fall while hunting with the 'Killing Kildares' that obliged Cassidy to disband his stud and stable some time prior to his death, at Cannes, in 1890. The last major victory for the 'Straw-colour and blue' was achieved with Fethard in the Galway Plate in 1888.

Wednesday, 29th June, 1881	**£460**	**6 Ran**	**1½m (Howth Post)**

The Irish Derby Stakes of 550sovs, by subscription of 15sovs each to the fund, but 6sovs only for horses struck out on or before the 2nd September, 1880. The second horse to receive 50sovs and the third 25sovs out of the stake. For three years old. Colts 8st 12lb; fillies 8st 8lb. The winner of the Angleseys and Railways at the Curragh, or of two stakes value 400sovs each, 10lb extra; of Angleseys or a stake value 400sovs, or stakes collectively value 600sovs, 7lb extra; of a stake value 200sovs, 3lbs extra. Horses that have never won a race value 100sovs, allowed 5lb; maidens allowed 10lb; only one of these allowances can be taken. Produce of untried sires or mares allowed 3lb, if claimed at entry, but not for both.

(31 subs)

1 Mr J. A. Cassidy's	MASTER NED (T. Broderick)	9. 5	P. Doucie	
	B. colt Roman Bee – Gazelle by Ivan.			
2 Mr C. Taaffe's	GREENFIELD (F. Wynne)	8.12	J. French	
	B. colt Lothario – Lady Lynbury.			
3 Mr W. Dunne's	FAUSTIN (J. Connolly)	8. 2	Connolly	
	B. colt Roman Bee – Tawney.			
4 Mr James Andrew's	HANDCUFF (M. Ryan)	7.13	J. Gannon	
	Br. colt Outcast – Bracelet.			
5 Mr C. J. Blake's	GOLDEN ROSE (Callaghan)	7. 9	J. Dunne	
	Ch. filly Lothario – Moss Rose by Kettledrum (NOT IN GSB)			
6 Mr R. M. Delamere's	SPERANZA II (F. Connolly)	8. 5	Connolly	
	B. filly King John – Eblana.			

SP 4/6 Greenfield; 5/1 Faustin, Handcuff; 100/15 MASTER NED.
Neck, Third close-up.
Winner trained by Mr Patrick Doucie at Melitta Lodge, Curragh.

1882

Ever-increasing interest in the Irish Derby drew a sufficiently large crowd to the Curragh to warrant three 'race specials' for the Dublin contingent alone. The apparently moderate two-year-old form of the previous season had received a recent and timely boost through the valiant performance of Faugh-a-Ballagh in running the mighty Foxhall to a neck in the Ascot Gold Cup. Favourite on his debut in the Railway Stakes the previous September, Faugh-a-Ballagh had finished behind Melliflor, The Jilt and The Marquis. The last-named had since caused an upset when beating Theorist and Melliflor in the Baldoyle Derby, with Sortie, much better-fancied than his winning stablemate, unplaced. Despite the rumours which abounded concerning his well-being, courage and stamina, Melliflor was preferred in the betting to Garret Moore's Theorist, who had disappointed the touts in a recent gallop. Next in demand was Minnie, unraced that season, but fancied to emulate the success of her owner's King of the Bees two years earlier. The only other fancied runner in the field of nine, not sired by the all-conquering Uncas, was James Cassidy's highly-tried but exasperating colt, Sortie.

From a perfect start the early running was made by the fillies, Minnie and Noble Duchess, who showed ahead of Sortie, Valerie and Melliflor. With a mile still to run Clan Chattan had become tailed off, Merry May was losing touch and Noble Duchess had begun to wilt, giving way to Sortie, who quickly joined and passed Minnie. Entering the straight Sortie held a clear lead, with only Theorist still a threat. Approaching the distance Theorist had reduced Sortie's lead, but only on sufferance. Under the urging of Nicholas Behan, the lightly-weighted leader drew away effortlessly to win by a leisurely four lengths, with Minnie heading the stragglers in third place. Melliflor confirmed his critics' gloomy prognostications, never at any stage looking likely to justify favouritism.

The second successive Irish Derby winner for James Cassidy and the fourth for his trainer Pat Doucie, Sortie was a brown colt by See Saw out of Relief, by Julius. Bred in England by Mr A. Hoole, Sortie was the first produce of his dam, thus qualifying for the 3lbs allowance for the produce of untried mares. As it transpired, he was also her best. See Saw, by Buccaneer, was a good racehorse, winning the Royal Hunt Cup and the Cambridgeshire. Among his best winners were Footstep (Lincolnshire), Upset (Goodwood Cup) and Dog Rose (Stewards' Cup). Through his son, Loved One, See Saw became the grandsire of Gondolette, who produced the Classic winners Ferry and Sansovino, as well as that wonderful broodmare Serenissima.

Pulled out again the following day, Sortie, on whom Frank Wynne replaced Nicholas Behan, failed by four lengths to concede 7lbs to Too Good, ridden by the jockey-in form . . . Nicholas Behan, whose fifth winner of the meeting this was. That Sortie was being asked the well-nigh impossible was confirmed the following year, when Too Good – spontaneously named by Elizabeth, Empress of Austria – won the Grand Steeplechase de Paris. Sortie won twice more as a three-year-old, each time over a mile, besides walking over for a Queen's Plate. He did not run the following season and subsequently reappeared owner-ridden by a Mr S. Kelly, to whom, hopefully, he brought more pleasure than profit. Of those that he beat in the Irish Derby, only Theorist paid the winner any compliment, winning a further nine races, including the Great Lancashire Handicap at Liverpool. Melliflor and Yahboob Khan were exported to Germany, while the remainder vanished into appropriate obscurity.

Nicholas Behan, the winning rider, was the first of no fewer than four brothers to appear on the role of honour of Ireland's greatest race, and the only one to do so as a rider. For though they were all successful jockeys, William, Jack and Phillie had to wait until taking up training before achieving success in the Irish Derby. Nicholas Behan rode his first winner, Countess Hohenembs, at the Curragh April meeting in 1880, weighing barely 5st. Consistently in demand as a lightweight over the next few seasons, he had ridden King of the Bees to a surprise win the day before that colt's success in the Irish Derby. Troubled by increasing weight, he followed his brother Willie into the National Hunt sphere, before relinquishing his licence in 1897.

Wednesday, 28th June, 1882	**£460**	**9 Ran**	**1½m (Howth Post)**

The Irish Derby Stakes of 550sovs, by subscription of 15sovs each to the fund, but 6sovs only for horses struck out on or before the 2nd September, 1881. The second horse to receive 50sovs and the third 25sovs out of the stake. For three years old. Colts 8st 12lb; fillies 8st 8lb. The winner of the Angleseys and Railways at the Curragh, or of two stakes value 400sovs each, 10lb extra; of Angleseys or a stake value 400sovs, or stakes collectively value 600sovs, 7lb, extra; of a stake value 200sovs, 3lbs extra. Horses that have never won a race value 100sovs, allowed 5lb; maidens allowed 10lb; only one of these allowances can be taken. Produce of untried sires or mares allowed 3lb, if claimed at entry, but not for both.

(31 subs)

1 Mr J. A. Cassidy's	SORTIE (N. Behan) Br. colt See-Saw – Relief by Julius.	7.13	P. Doucie
2 Mr G. Moore's	THEORIST (F. Wynne) Br. colt Uncas – Miss Theo.	8. 7	PVT (V. Ahearne)
3 Mr W. Brophy's	MINNIE (T. Broderick) Br. filly Herbertstown – dam by Droumore.	9. 9 (car. 7.10)	D. Broderick
4 Mr H. E. Linde's	VALERIE (Mr T. Beasley) Ch. filly Uncas – Lucy.	8. 8 (car. 8.10)	H. E. Linde
5 Mr W. Dunne's	MELLIFLOR* (J. Connolly) B. colt Uncas – Queen of the Bees.	9. 2	Tom Connolly
6 Mr John Igoe, jnr's	MERRY MAY (Owner) Br. filly Ben Battle – Alba.	7. 9	
0 Mr J. W. Nuttall's	CLAN CHATTEN (Mr H. Nuttall) B. colt Keith – Birds-Eye.	8. 4 (car. 8. 8)	
0 Mr W. Holland's	NOBLE DUCHESS (W. Miller) Ch. filly Uncas – Hetty by Hobbie Noble.	7.12 (car. 8. 1)	
0 Mr James Andrews's	YAKOOB KHAN (Cassidy) Bl/Br. colt Uncas – Claret Cup.	8. 2	James Gannon

SP 6/4 Melliflor; 2/1 Theorist; 4/1 Minnie; 5/1 SORTIE; 8/1 Valerie; 100/2 Bar
4 lengths, poor third.

*Melliflor sent abroad soon after race.

1883

The field of seven for the Irish Derby included May Boy, the best Irish two-year-old of his generation and two English challengers, Ithuriel and Mespilus. However, for many racegoers, the runners were less significant than one of the riders. As long ago as 1873 Joseph Doyle had lost his licence for 'premeditated foul riding' in a race at the Curragh, won by Ben Battle. While few at the time doubted his guilt, as his applications for renewal of his licence were persistently turned down, public opinion began to insist that Doyle had fully atoned for his crime. As the result of a widely-supported petition the Stewards had finally reinstated Doyle in October 1882. A brilliant piece of tactical riding to win on Barbarian the previous day showed that the long years in the wilderness had done nothing to blunt the skills of this dashing lightweight.

Though not eligible for the General Stud Book, May Boy fully merited both top weight and favouritism. Besides winning four races in Ireland, including the Beresford Stakes, he had carried the redoubtable George Fordham to victory in the valuable Sandown Nursery. His shock defeat by Rosa at Baldoyle had landed Eyre Linde and Tommy Beasley before the Stewards, who had accepted their explanation. Beaten in the Baldoyle Derby under a welter weight, May Boy was confidently expected to reverse that running with Captain Arthur and Sylph. Pat Doucie was represented by Captain Arthur, beaten a neck in the Baldoyle Derby, and also by the filly Rosa, bidding to complete a hat-trick in the Irish Derby for James Cassidy and Doucie. The English-trained pair were still maidens, while Charles Blake's filly, Sylph, had failed to fulfil her early promise. In a strong betting market May Boy was preferred to Captain Arthur.

The pace was a scorching one from flagfall, with Ithuriel showing the way to Captain Arthur, Rosa and Mespilus. It soon transpired that the English pair had started something which they could not finish, for both Ithuriel and Mespilus had cried enough by half way, where Captain Arthur took up the running from May Boy and Rosa. The lead remained unchanged into the straight, where Sylph passed the fading Rosa to challenge May Boy and Captain Arthur. Prospects of an exciting, three-cornered struggle died as quickly as they had risen, for the two well-backed colts compounded suddenly, leaving Sylph to race clear to an easy three-length success. Tommy Beasley accepted defeat so emphatically as to throw away second place to Captain Arthur. The breakneck early gallop was held responsible for the rout of the fancied runners and the utterly unexpected success of Charles Blake's filly, ridden by the uncrowned 'King of the Curragh', John Connolly.

The stunned and silent crowd experienced another shock in the following race, which was 'won' by the 4-to-1 ON favourite, Francis Joseph. It then transpired that the judge had not been in his box to place the horses. The Stewards ordered the race to be re-run at the end of the day. To compound the punters' agony Francis Joseph, starting at 5-to-2 ON, could finish only third to Butte des Mortes. The latter belonged to a man who, three years earlier, had found himself in an unenviable position which led to his name becoming part of the English language . . . Captain Charles Boycott.

Though rewarding only to the bookmakers, Sylph's victory was not begrudged by the majority of racegoers, for she carried the 'French grey, scarlet hoop' of that popular and widely-respected stalwart of Irish racing, Charles J. Blake, of Heath House, Maryborough. The younger son of Valentine O'Connor Blake of Towerhill, Co. Mayo, Charles Blake was thus a member of a family whose associations with Galway and the West went back to the twelfth century. Educated at Stoneyhurst and Trinity College, Dublin, Charles Blake took his call to the Irish Bar, though he never practised. Instead, having made his fortune out of supplying wool for uniforms during the Franco-Prussian War, he began to indulge his inherent interest in racing, initially under the aegis of George Henry Moore, becoming a Member of the Turf Club in 1867 and Steward for the first time in 1874. Three years later he formed a lasting friendship with Captain Machell of Bedford Lodge, Newmarket. It was to Bedford Lodge that the Towerhill-bred Arbitrator was sent, having proved his merit in Ireland. He won the Liverpool Cup and the Lancashire Handicap on successive days, later becoming a leading stallion in Ireland.

In 1880 Charles Blake purchased Heath House, near Maryborough, or Portlaoise, as it is now known. A gaunt, early Georgian mansion, overlooking Maryborough Heath, a smaller version of the Curragh and a racecourse in the early part of the nineteenth century. Built in 1727 by Warner Westenra, who represented the Borough of Maryborough in the Irish Parliament from 1727 to 1761 and became the grandfather of the first Lord Rossmore. Having remodelled and refurbished Heath House, using timbers salvaged from a shipwreck on the West coast, Charles Blake laid out his stud and training stable, employing a series of private trainers, James Dunne, Pat Doucie, T. Harris and Sam Jeffrey, formerly in Captain Machell's employ. Although restricted both in terms of horses and patrons, the semi-private Heath House stable won every worthwhile race in Ireland on numerous occasions. Charles Blake headed the list of owners in Ireland in 1886, 1888 and 1896 and was notably successful with the progeny of his own stallion, Arbitrator. A shrewd judge of young bloodstock, Blake purchased Rockdove as a yearling for 220gns and won both Irish and English Cesarewitches with her. Another notable purchase was the St Leger winner, Kilwarlin, whom he passed on to Lord Rodney. But perhaps the best example of his uncanny ability to discern well-disguised potential was the broodmare Excellenza. Having begged Lord Cadogan, then Viceroy, to retain the filly to whom he had taken a violent dislike, Blake then took her over himself. Excellenza went on to breed winners of over £19,000, including Glasgerion.

Bald, bearded, stern-faced and a confirmed bachelor, like so many of his family, Charles Blake took over the mantle of the Marquis of Drogheda as the guiding light and progressive reformer of the Irish Turf. Remaining active as a Steward of the Turf Club up to the time of his death in 1917, Charles Blake handed over the affairs of his six hundred acres to his nephew Charles. Following the latter's premature decease, Blake bequeathed Heath House to another nephew, Isodore, who maintained his uncle's tradition as a progressive member of the Turf Club administration. Isodore's brother, Colonel Arthur J. Blake subsequently took over as trainer at Heath House, with immediate and lasting success.

James Dunne, the trainer of Sylph, would appear to have discovered the elixir of eternal youth, for his racing career seems endless. He served his time with Joseph Osborne, the author of the 'Horsebreeders' Handbook', who, as 'Beacon', supplied the learned and lively racing notes in Bell's Life. Dunne had his first mount in public at Maryborough Heath in 1854. The mare was Rosalba, later to become the dam of the Grand National winner, Salamander. A successful lightweight, James Dunne became private trainer to the Blake family at Towerhill, moving to Heath House with Charles Blake in 1880. Having saddled Sylph and St Kevin to win the Irish Derby for Blake, Dunne moved to England, training at Lewes for a few seasons. 1892 saw him back in Ireland as a public trainer at Stand House, the Curragh. From there he moved to Curragh View and eventually built his own yard on the Little Curragh, naming it Osborne Lodge, in tribute to his first employer. Unrivalled as a trainer of stayers, James Dunne believed in giving his horses all the time they required to realise their potential. In consequence he attracted as owners sportsmen who could afford to wait. His owners invariably remained loyal to the rotund, chirpy, bird-like little man, whose snowy white hair and aura of wistful innocence earned him the nick-name 'Fairy' Dunne. Though he never headed the trainers' list in a long and honourable racing career, the master of Osborne Lodge sent out two further winners of the Irish Derby, three winners of the Irish Oaks and the first three winners of the Irish St Leger. He was eighty-seven when he died in 1927.

Sylph, Rosa and Rolla were all saddled again the next day. Sylph won the Kirwan Stakes, with Rosa last of four. However, Mr Cassidy's filly did not leave the meeting empty-handed, for she had walked over for a Queen's Plate earlier the same day. Improving all the time, Sylph made her next appearance at Galway, where she met May Boy on 14lbs worse terms and beat him again. She completed her four-timer when winning a three-mile Queen's Plate at the Curragh in October. Two days

Wednesday, 27th June, 1883	£460	7 Ran	1½m (Howth Post)

The Irish Derby of 550sovs, by subscription of 15sovs each (to the fund), but 6sovs only for horses struck out on or before the 2nd September, 1882. The second horse to receive 50sovs and the third 25sovs out of the plate. For three years old. Colts 8st 12lb; fillies 8st 8lb. The winner of the Angleseys and Railways at the Curragh, or of two stakes value 300sovs each, 10lb extra; of Angleseys or a stake value 300sovs, or stakes collectively value 600sovs, 7lb extra; of a stake value 200sovs, 3lb extra. Horses that have never won a stake value 100sovs, allowed 6lb; maidens allowed 10lb; only one of these allowances can be taken. Produce of untried sires or mares allowed 3lb (if claimed at entry) but not for both. Any person entering three horses, his own bona fide sole property, can strike out one at the time appointed for declaring forfeit without having to pay the forfeit.

(38 subs)

1 Mr C. J. Blake's	SYLPH (J. Connolly)	7.12	James Dunne
	Ch. filly Solon – Dryad by Cape Flyaway.		
2 Mr Daly's	CAPTAIN ARTHUR (N. Behan)	7.13	P. Doucie
	B. colt Umpire – Claret Cup.		
3 Mr J. Gubbins's	MAY BOY (Mr T. Beasley)	9. 2	H. E. Linde
	Ch. colt Xenophon – May Day (NOT IN GSB)		
0 Lord Ellesmere's	ITHURIEL (W. Faire)	7.13	Charles Archer (UK)
	Ch. colt Lord Ronald – Ithona.		
0 Mr A. H. Smith-Barry's	MESPILUS (A. Giles)	8. 2	(UK)
	B. colt Uncas – Fair Alice.		
0 Mr G. Moore's	ROLLA (Joseph Doyle)	7.12	Private
	B. filly Joskin – Miss Ahna.		
0 Mr J. A. Cassidy's	ROSA* (J. Doucie)	8. 8	P. Doucie
	B/Br. filly Salvator – Grisette (dam of Aegeus)		

SP 2/1 May Boy; 3/1 Captain Arthur; 5/1 Ithuriel, Mespilus, Rolla; 10/1 SYLPH.
3 lengths, bad third.
Winner trained by Mr James Dunne at Heath House, Maryborough.

*Rosa formerly named Sal Volatile.

later, making her racecourse farewell, Sylph renewed rivalry with May Boy once more. The pair were inseparable in the betting and the excitement intense as, in a driving finish, the colt triumphed by a length. The following year Sylph was sold to Germany.

May Boy, successful in two Queen's Plates before his epic third encounter with Sylph, went on to win over hurdles at Liverpool. As a four-year-old he was placed in the Grande Hurdle at Auteuil and won two more Queen's Plates, in one of which he beat the recent Irish Derby winner, Theologian. Despite the stigma of 'half-bred', May Boy was given a chance at stud. In the circumstances he did well, the best of his progeny being Chatterbox (Baldoyle Derby), Chit Chat (National Produce Stakes) and May Thorn. Mespilus was promptly put back to sprinting, to which his running in the Irish Derby had indicated his aptitude, scoring doubles at Warwick and Newmarket. Rosa finally came good as a six-year-old, winning on the flat, over hurdles and over fences. Sylph needed to be no Sceptre to beat this lot. However, they can do no more than win; and win she did.

1884

The biggest Derby Day crowd since Master Ned's year assembled on the Curragh, under cloudless skies, to witness the certain triumph of John Gubbins' high-class filly, Grecian Bend. This daughter of the 1871 Irish Derby winner, Maid of Athens, had already laid claims to be regarded as the best of her generation. Second to Sir Hugh on her debut, she had gone on to run up an unbeaten sequence in the Marble Hill Stakes, the Railway Stakes, the International Foal Stakes at Baldoyle and the Beresford Stakes. In her most recent appearance she had won the Baldoyle Derby in smashing style. Sir Hugh, who had looked very good indeed, until the advent of Grecian Bend, had begun his second season by winning the Batthyany Stakes at Lincoln, but had since been down the field in the Manchester Cup. Sleeping Beauty, a two-year-old winner, had developed that costly complaint called 'seconditis', while Spahi had no worthwhile form. A firm odds-on favourite, John Gubbins' magnificent filly looked unbeatable. Next in the betting came Sir Hugh and then Theologian. Though the latter had been making his racecourse debut in the Baldoyle Derby, he had failed to beat Grecian Bend when in receipt of 24lbs. Now 8lbs worse off at the weights, Theologian would have had to make phenomenal improvement to cause an upset. Confident that Grecian Bend was the one to reverse this tiresome run of beaten favourites at the meeting, the sun-drenched crowd took up vantage points from which to cheer their champion home.

Theologian broke fastest, followed by Spahi and Sleeping Beauty, with Grecian Bend fighting for her head at the rear of the field. The order remained unchanged to the mile post, where Connolly increased the pace on Theologian, going six lengths clear, with Grecian Bend still under restraint at the rear. As Theologian hurtled into the straight, Tommy Beasley unleashed Grecian Bend, who swept past Sleeping Beauty and Spahi in hot pursuit. Sir Hugh she passed as though he were standing still, and the vast assembly rose to acclaim their heroine. Abruptly, the tumultuous welcome choked in a thousand throats, as the awful truth became apparent . . . The crafty Connolly had judged his pacemaking to perfection, nursing Theologian home to win cleverly by a length. Some way back in third place came Sir Hugh. The impossible had happened and a stunned crowd watched in silence and dismay as an ebullient Garrett Moore greeted Theologian and his smiling jockey.

As though to add insult to injury, Theologian never showed remotely comparable form again. Second in two Queen's Plates, he was sold to the Earl of Spencer to go to stud in England, where he sired nothing of any account. Grecian Bend was placed twice at Liverpool at the back-end and made some amends by winning three races the following season. Sir Hugh went 'chasing with success and finished second in the Galway Plate. He stood subsequently in Cork and in England. Sleeping Beauty, a half-sister to Kildare, won good flat races and 'chases for her owner-trainer, Dan Broderick, and later became an excellent broodmare. She featured in the sensational dispersal sale of the late William Brophy's bloodstock in 1892, when she, her yearling and her foal fetched 680gns. The yearling turned out to be Rockdove and the foal Portmarnock, winner of the Irish Derby. She subsequently bred a second winner of the Irish Derby in Carrigavalla. Spahi won twice as a four-year-old at the Curragh April meeting. However, it was not until the following year – 1886 – that he earned his place in Irish racing history when, ridden by Tommy Beasley, he foiled Fred Archer's attempted hat-trick on the great jockey's only appearance in Ireland. Over the subsequent seasons Spahi won the Lancashire 'Chase, two more Queen's Plates, the Manchester 'Chase twice and five other races, before retiring to stud at the age of eleven.

The last of four Irish Derby winners sired by Uncas, Theologian was bred by his owner, Garrett Moore, out of his remarkable mare Miss Theo. Having won thirteen races in England and Ireland, Miss Theo bred Theophrastus, the best hurdler of his day and no less than three Irish Derby winners, a record which is unlikely to be equalled. Garrett Moore, the eldest son of John Hubert Moore, was born in 1851, some years before his father's return from England to train on the Curragh at Jockey Hall. During the 'sixties and 'seventies, strict, stern, rheumatism-racked J. H. Moore successfully established himself as the first professional National Hunt trainer in Ireland. During this time his hard-riding, hell-raising, happy-go-lucky son developed into a very, very good Gentleman Rider. Father and son achieved their finest hour when they combined to win the Grand National in 1879 with The Liberator. Prior to that they had twice taken the Irish Grand National with Scots Grey. Over six feet tall and built in proportion, Garrett Moore's love of the good things in life forced him to retire from race-riding in the early 'eighties, when he took over the training at Jockey Hall.

Having sent out Theologian's half-brother, Theodemir, to win another Irish Derby in 1886, Garrett Moore moved his stables to England, where he remained for the rest of his life. In one of his rare subsequent raids on the Curragh, he carried off a third Irish Derby with Theodolite, the last of Miss Theo's unique triple. Garrett Moore's greatest training feat was accomplished in 1891, when he took over the training of the savage Surefoot. Having won the Two Thousand Guineas the previous season, Surefoot had developed a ferocious temper, which had cost him the Epsom Derby. In the peace and seclusion of the Lambourn downs and woodlands Garrett Moore coaxed and cajoled Surefoot back into a better frame of mind. His efforts were rewarded by a spectacular victory in the Eclipse Stakes. A director of Hurst Park racecourse, Garrett Moore died in 1908, having seen his younger brother, W. H. 'Willie' Moore, train three Grand National winners at Weyhill, where he was succeeded by their nephew, Hubert Hartigan.

In the fashion of the day Gentlemen Trainers did not always choose to hold the trainer's licence in their own names, though this nicety may not have been invariably dictated by social convention. Consequently, William Behan is officially credited with the Irish Derby success of Theologian. Formerly a successful jockey – one of five such brothers – Willie Behan was at the time head lad at Jockey Hall. He thus became the second of four Behans to figure in the annals of the Irish Derby.

Wednesday, 25th June, 1884	£460	5 Ran	1½m (Howth Post)

The Irish Derby of 550sovs, by subscription of 15sovs each (to the fund), but 6sovs only for horses struck out on or before the 2nd September, 1883. The second horse to receive 50sovs and the third 25sovs out of the plate. For three years old. Colts 8st 12lb; fillies 8st 8lb. The winner of the Angleseys and Railways at the Curragh, or of two stakes value 300sovs each, 10lb extra; of Angleseys or a stake value 300sovs, or stakes collectively value 600sovs, 7lb extra; of a stake value 200sovs, 3lb extra. Horses that have never won a stake value 100sovs, allowed 6lb; maidens allowed 10lb; only one of these allowances can be taken. Produce of untried sires or mares allowed 3lb (if claimed at entry) but not for both. Any person entering three horses, his own bona fide sole property, can strike out one at the time appointed for declaring forfeit without having to pay the forfeit.

(32 subs)

1	Mr G. Moore's	THEOLOGIAN (J. Connolly) B/Br. colt Uncas – Miss Theo by Leamington.	8. 2	W. Behan
2	Mr John Gubbins's	GRECIAN BEND (Mr T. Beasley) B/Br. filly Victor – Maid of Athens.	9. 4	H. E. Linde
3	Mr E. Smithwick's	SIR HUGH (T. Harris) B/Br. colt Lord Gough – Querida.	9. 5	James Dunne
4	Mr D. Broderick's	SLEEPING BEAUTY (Joseph Doyle) B. filly Ben Battle – The Beauty.	8. 2	D. Broderick
5	Lord Drogheda's	SPAHI (W. Miller) Ch. colt Ben Battle – Minette.	7.13	M. Moneypenny

SP 4/6 Grecian Bend; 3/1 Sir Hugh; 7/1 THEOLOGIAN.
1 good length, a fair third.
Winner trained by W. Behan, private trainer to owner.

1885

In a far from vintage year nine paraded for the Irish Derby. Top weight was carried by John Gubbins' Jack, on whom Tommy Beasley was determined to wipe out the haunting memory of the previous year. Although Jack's credentials were nothing like as outstanding as those of Grecian Bend had been, he had won the Baldoyle Derby very easily by six lengths and the same from Tice and Madcap. The last-named now had a hefty pull in the weights, on the strength of which he was made an uneasy favourite. Royal Rose carried the hopes of Heath House. Winner of four races as a two-year-old, she was making her seasonal debut and was considered far ahead of her stablemate, St Kevin. The Chicken, despite his success over the course and distance only the day before, with St Kevin in third place, was completely unfancied.

The Rath made the early running on rain-softened ground, ahead of Tice and Runnemede, with St Kevin the backmarker. They had covered only a furlong when Harris, the rider of Royal Rose, felt a leather snap, putting the second favourite out of the race. Having made the running for over a mile, The Rath gave way to Tice and Madcap, with Runnemede, St Kevin and The Chicken close on their heels. Runnemede hit the front in the straight, looking likely to win, only to be challenged immediately by the unconsidered St Kevin. Making the most of his unexpected advantage, Saunders set sail for the line and the race appeared over bar the shouting – of which there was none. Suddenly, when all seemed lost, like an avenging angel, Madcap swept through in the middle of the course. The crowd howled encouragement at the favourite, now closing the gap with every stride. Alas for the popular fancy, the effort of giving away both weight and distance proved too much. St Kevin scraped home by three parts of a length, with Runnemede a good third. While few begrudged Charles Blake his opportunist winner, the general feeling was that Nicholas Behan had done less than justice to the favourite.

St Kevin, a chestnut colt by Arbitrator out of Lady of the Lake, was bred and owned by Charles Blake, a Steward of the Turf Club at the time. Lady of the Lake was the first thoroughbred ever purchased by the master of Heath House. While she lived to a ripe old age, St Kevin's sire unfortunately did not. Foaled in a lakeside field at Towerhill, Co. Mayo, Arbitrator won four times as a two-year-old, culminating in a twenty-length success at Warwick, ridden by Fred Archer. Kept off the course for much of the following season by illness, Arbitrator reappeared to finish fourth in the Cambridgeshire and went on to win the Liverpool Autumn Cup and the Great Lancashire Handicap on successive days. Retired to Towerhill, this son of Solon and True Heart was already firmly established as a leading sire in Ireland when Kilwarlin's success in the St Leger of 1887 brought his sire to the notice of English breeders. Tragically, for his sporting owner in particular and Irish breeding in general, Arbitrator died at Heath House the following year, aged only fourteen. The same year Theodolite became Arbitrator's second winner of the Irish Derby. Next to his owner, Arbitrator had been most consistently patronised by Edmond Smithwick of Kilcreene Lodge, Kilkenny, whose faith had been rewarded by such good two-year-olds as Kilcreene and St Kieran. Still in the possession of Charles Blake's grandnephew is a magnificent silver smoking-piece, modelled on a race-course number board, listing Arbitrator's most notable progeny and incorporating the stallion's silver-mounted hooves, which Smithwick presented to his long-standing friend.

St Kevin made his third appearance at the Derby meeting when pulled out the next day for the Kirwan Stakes, in which The Chicken beat him, for the second time in three days. Having won at Galway and walked over for a Queen's Plate, St Kevin was placed in his remaining three races, being beaten yet again by The Chicken. As a four-year-old St Kevin ran only twice, getting the Wellington Stakes at the Curragh April meeting, on the disqualification of Alcester and finishing fourth to Jack the following day. Madcap and Runnemede, the placed horses in the Irish Derby, were subsequently purchased by Mr H. T. Barclay, the owner of Bendigo, and trained for the Newmarket Autumn Double. Neither posed any threat to that remarkable mare Plaisanterie. The Chicken, Billy Pitt's best son, won over fences before being shipped to America. Tice won the Curragh Cesarewitch, beating The Chicken and St Kevin, while The Rath won five races as a four-year-old. All in all they were a thoroughly moderate lot.

The second Irish Derby winners in three years for Charles Blake and his private trainer, James Dunne, St Kevin was the first winning ride of the season for Henry Saunders, an English-born lightweight attached to Heath House, where he was employed as second jockey to Thomas Harris, the leading jockey in Ireland in 1888 and subsequently trainer to Charles Blake. Saunders may well have considered his chance victory on St Kevin no more than his due, for he had been replaced by John Connolly on Sylph two years earlier. Having scored what proved to be the biggest success of his riding career, Henry Saunders ended the season on a less happy note. Beaten a head on Draco for the valuable National Produce Stakes – by Harris on Conservator – Saunders had his licence withdrawn for foul riding. Though restored to favour the following season, during which he rode a further seven winners, Henry Saunders seems to have faded rapidly from prominence, making progressively less frequent appearances until his retirement in 1896.

Wednesday, 24th June, 1885 £460 **9 Ran** 1½m (Howth Post)

The Irish Derby of 550sovs, by subscription of 15sovs each (to the fund), but 6sovs only for horses struck out on or before the 2nd September, 1884. The second horse to receive 50sovs and the third 25sovs out of the plate. For three years old. Colts 8st 12lb; fillies 8st 8lb. The winner of the Angleseys and Railways at the Curragh, or of two stakes value 300sovs each, 10lb extra; of Angleseys or a stake value 300sovs, or stakes collectively value 600sovs, 7lb extra; of a stake value 200sovs, 3lb extra. Horses that have never won a stake value 100sovs, allowed 6lb; maidens allowed 10lb; only one of these allowances can be taken. Produce of untried sires or mares allowed 3lb (if claimed at entry) but not for both. Any person entering three horses, his own bona fide sole property, can strike out one at the time appointed for declaring forfeit without having to pay the forfeit.

(45 subs)

1	Mr C. J. Blake's	ST KEVIN (H. Saunders)	7.13	James Dunne
		Ch. colt Arbitrator – Lady of the Lake by Lord of the Iles.		
2	Mr P. Colfer's	MADCAP (N. Behan)	8.12	
		B. colt Umpire – Tantrum.		
3	Mr M. Dennehy's	RUNNEMEDE (W. Miller)	8. 2	M. Dennehy
		B. colt King John – Rio.		
4	Mr J. Nolan's	THE CHICKEN (T. Broderick)	8. 3	
		B. colt Billy Pitt – The Pheasant.		
5	Capt. Jones's	TICE (J. Rowan)	7.12	
		B. filly Umpire – Trickstress.		
6	Mr C. W. Thompson's	THE RATH (T. Bailey)	7.13	
		B. colt Hollywood – Pink Domino.		
7	Mr J. Gubbins's	JACK (Mr T. Beasley)	9.2	
		Bl. colt Arbitrator – Valour's dam by Mount Zion.		
8	Lord Drogheda's	ALCESTER (Callon)	8. 2	
		Ch. colt Ben Battle – Wisdom.		
0	Mr C. J. Blake's	ROYAL ROSE (T. Harris)	8. 5	James Dunne
		Br. filly Arbitrator – Moss Rose.		

SP 2/1 Madcap; 4/1 Royal Rose; 6/1 Tice; 8/1 Jack, Runnemede; 100/8 Bar.
¾ length, 2½ lengths.
Winner trained by Mr James Dunne at Heath House, Maryborough.

1886

A prolonged drought had left the going on the Curragh very hard; much too hard for Ashplant, outstandingly the best colt of his generation in Ireland. A winner of five races as a two-year-old and unbeaten in three outings that year, Ashplant had shown signs of imminent leg trouble, leaving his shrewd trainer no choice but to withdraw the assured favourite. This meant that the hopes of Eyrefield Lodge now rested on Sweetness, a rank outsider. In the absence of an obvious favourite, the crowd went for Draco. This half-brother to Maid of Athens and Kyrle Daly had run well at Baldoyle and appeared to have a touch of class, conspicuous by its absence in the opposition. The lightly-weighted Nightmare, though making her seasonal debut, was the subject of strong local rumour, sufficient to see her backed to second favouritism. Theodemir, winner of the Downshire and Waterford Testimonial Stakes, represented owner-trainer Garrett Moore, whose dispersal sale took place before racing. The only other runner with worthwhile public form was Charming Nancy, winner of the Baldoyle Derby on her most recent appearance.

The start was delayed by the antics of Loch Aber, who repaid everybody's patience by bolting off the course when the starter at last got them away. The early running was made by the fillies Sweetness and Charming Nancy, who gave way in turn to Nightmare and Theodemir, with Draco trying to get on terms. The rest had ceased to count by the time the three leaders lined out for home. As they did so Nightmare swung wide, giving John Connolly the chance of seizing the coveted rails berth. Using his advantage to the full, Connolly picked up Theodemir and drove him home in vintage style to beat Nightmare by a hard-fought half-length. Draco stayed on at one pace to take third place. For Garrett Moore, in the process of moving his stable to England, Theodemir's victory provided an unexpected but welcome farewell. It also made him the only man ever to breed, own and train two winners of the Irish Derby.

A brown half-brother to Theologian, by Ben Battle, Theodemir ran only once more in 1886, when unplaced in the Jubilee Prize at Baden Baden. Nightmare walked over at Bellewstown and was then awarded a Queen's Plate on the disqualification of Draco. She later became a successful steeplechaser. Draco won the Kirwan Stakes the following day and continued to make amends over the next two seasons for his disappointing performance in the Irish Derby. Dictator won the Kirwan Stakes in successive seasons and became the sire of a good two-year-old in Fulminator, a half-brother to the Irish Derby winner, Bowline. Charming Nancy became one of the mainstays of Garrett Moore's newly-established Winchester stable, winning numerous 'chases. The 'half-bred' Black Rose improved with age, winning from six furlongs to two miles, besides achieving the doubtful distinction of becoming Fred Archer's only losing mount in Ireland. This occurred in October 1886, when, at Charles Blake's instigation, Archer made his only riding appearance in Ireland. Having won on his other two mounts, he could finish only third on Black Rose, behind Spahi and Lord Chatham.

Three weeks later Archer was dead.

Wednesday, 30th June, 1886   **£460**   **8 Ran**   **1½m (Howth Post)**

The Irish Derby of 550sovs, by subscription of 15sovs each (to the fund), but 6sovs only for horses struck out on or before the last day of the September meeting, 1885. The second horse to receive 50sovs and the third 25sovs out of the plate. For three years old. Colts 8st 12lb; fillies 8st 8lb. The winner of the Angleseys and Railways at the Curragh, or of two stakes value 300sovs each, 10lb extra; of Angleseys or a stake value 300sovs, collectively value 600sovs, 7lb extra; of a stake value 200sovs, 3lb extra. Horses that have never won a stake value 100sovs, allowed 6lb; maidens allowed 10lb; only one of these allowances can be taken. Produce of untried sires or mares allowed 3lb (if claimed at entry) but not for both. Any person entering three horses, his own bona fide sole property, can strike out one at the time appointed for declaring forfeit without having to pay the forfeit.

(38 subs)

1	Mr G. Moore's	THEODEMIR (J. Connolly)	9. 1
		Br. colt Ben Battle – Miss Theo by Leamington.	
2	Mr T. Mathews's	NIGHTMARE (M. Dawson)	7. 9
		Br. filly Umpire – Night Thought.	
3	Mr J. Lyons's	DRACO (Thomas Harris)	9. 1
		B. colt Arbitrator – Colleen Rhue.	
4	Captain G. Maher's	DICTATOR (Henry Saunders)	7.13
		Br. colt Arbitrator – Pinnace.	
5	Mr C. Taaffe's	CHARMING NANCY (T. Bailey)	8.12
		Ch. filly Piersfield – Little Annie.	
0	Mr C. J. Blake's	BLACK ROSE (L. Kelly)	8.11
		Br. filly Arbitrator – Moss Rose.	
0	Mr J. Gubbins's	SWEETNESS (J. Hoysted)	7.12
		B. filly Xenophon – Vanessa.	
L	J. A. Cassidy's	LOCH ABER (P. Ball)	7.9
		Ch. filly Blair Athol – Trumps.	

SP 5/2 Draco; 5/1 Nightmare; 100/15 THEODEMIR, Loch Aber; 7/1 Charming Nancy; 10/1 Bar.

½ length, 4 lengths.

Winner trained by owner at the Hall, Curragh.

1887

The richest prize in the history of Irish racing drew an enormous crowd, who gathered in brilliant sunshine to witness an open race for the Irish Derby. Pride of place on the racecard was held by Kildare, penalised for his successes in the Anglesey and Railway Stakes. Though unplaced in the Manchester Cup earlier in June, Kildare had previously won well over two miles at the Curragh. Despite the advantage which the firm going was expected to give Kildare, many were deterred by his big weight, preferring to support Henry George, whose two recent victories over two miles guaranteed his ability to see out the stiff Curragh twelve furlongs. Next in demand was the unreliable King Milan, a reluctant fourth in the Baldoyle Derby, who now met Holly, the winner of that race, on 31lbs better terms. The

Philistine and Pericles, placed at Baldoyle, also met Holly on better terms, but lacked King Milan's obvious ability. The other fancied runner in the record field of eleven was H. E. Linde's Pet Fox. Though Pet Fox had never run, Linde had resolved to plunge on him in the Irish Derby, until the defeat of his stable companion, Mulberry, the previous day caused Linde to have second thoughts. The public, untroubled by such deliberations, made Pet Fox third favourite.

First to show was Little Widow, who led from King Milan, Pericles and Holly, with Pet Fox bringing up the rear. After half a mile had been covered Little Widow gave way to Early Bird, with Pet Fox taking closer order. At the half way mark Pericles crossed his legs and fell, bringing down Holly. Henry George was badly hampered, as was Kildare, forced to jump the prostrate Holly. Unaffected by the turmoil behind, Early Bird continued to lead from King Milan and Pet Fox, as Kildare and Henry George strove to get back on terms. In the straight Early Bird faded quickly, leaving King Milan narrowly ahead of Pet Fox, with Henry George still making up lost ground. Hitting the front two furlongs out, Pet Fox drew steadily away from King Milan to win by a comfortable three lengths. Third, four lengths further back, came Henry George, the unlucky horse of the race. Brought to a standstill by the fallen Pericles, Henry George had lost much more ground than the amount by which he was ultimately beaten. Moreover, he had only really begun to stride out on encountering the better ground in the straight. However, there could be no gainsaying the authority of Pet Fox's win and his owner-trainer's satisfaction was marred only by his decision not to back his horse as he had originally intended. Fortunately, neither the horses nor their riders involved were injured as a consequence.

By Philammon, beaten favourite in the Irish Derby ten years earlier, Pet Fox was bred by Mr W. Murphy of Ballyshannon, in whose name Pet Fox mistakenly appeared on the racecard. Wild Vixen, the dam of Pet Fox, was bred by Captain Stamer Gubbins. Being by Victor out of Wild Daisy, she was thus a half-sister to Gubbins Irish Derby winner, Redskin. For Mr Murphy Wild Vixen had previously bred Queen of the Vixens, a winner on the flat. Pet Fox was subsequently sent over to Jousiffe's Lambourn stable. His English form was abysmal, his only success being in the run-off of a deadheat over five furlongs at Kempton Park. Repatriated as a five-year-old, Pet Fox promptly showed his appreciation by winning first time out at Baldoyle. Though he won at Punchestown before retiring to stud in 1890, his Irish Derby triumph was by then a distant memory and Pet Fox got few opportunities to prove himself as a stallion.

King Milan was purchased by Mr E. B. Barnard and carried his new owner to victory at Lewes in August, as a prelude to winning a valuable race at Redcar. Henry George, having beaten Draco by a head at the Curragh, after an epic struggle, joined the exodus to England, where he won sprints. Kildare finished third in the Liverpool Autumn Cup, before losing his form completely, just as his younger full-sister, Philomel, emerged as the leader of her generation, winning six of her seven races. Fethard went on to provide James Cassidy with his last major success when winning the Galway Plate as a four-year-old. Little Widow was unbeaten in her four remaining races that season, including the Curragh Cesarewitch. Over the next five years Little Widow ran more times, and to better effect, than the rest of that Irish Derby field combined, becoming one of the best jumping mares of her day. Both Holly and Pericles recovered from their Irish Derby debacle to win races.

Henry Eyre Linde, the owner-trainer of Pet Fox, was the outstanding Irish trainer of the nineteenth century, whose achievements remained unrivalled until the emergence of M. V. O'Brien and P. J. Prendergast over fifty years later. Born in Eyrefield Lodge, his family home, in 1835, Linde joined the Army following a dispute with his father, bought himself out and then joined the Royal Irish Constabulary. On his father's death in 1862 he took over Eyrefield Lodge. The first good animal to come his way was Highland Mary. Scarcely more than a pony, she won numerous races for Linde, including the first of his countless Punchestown triumphs, before breeding the first Eyrefield. There followed a succession of famous 'chasers, such as Empress, Woodbrook, Seaman, Cyrus, Martha, Gamebird, Mohican, Whisper Low and Too Good. Empress and Woodbrook won the Grand National for Linde, while Martha and Cyrus were narrowly beaten in the great race, the latter beaten a short head by Seaman, a Linde cast-off. Equally successful with his schooner-borne raiders in France, Linde carried off the Grand Steeplechase de Paris

Eyrefield Lodge

The Lodge

Eyrefield Lodge, *the most famous stable in Ireland, whose representatives were equally feared at Aintree, Auteuil or the nearby Curragh. Source:* Illustrated Racing.

The Stables

with Whisper Low and Too Good, as well as the Grande Hurdle with Seaman. Eyrefield Lodge representatives carried off every major jumping race in the English and Irish Calendars, while his virtual monopoly of events at Punchestown led Captain Joy to dub him 'Farmer Linde'.

Linde was ever ready to admit that much of the credit for his phenomenal and sustained success was due to the men who rode for him, notably the celebrated Beasley brothers. Harry and Willie lived and trained at nearby Eyrefield House, while Tommy, the most finished rider of them all, held the purely honorary title of assistant trainer at Eyrefield Lodge. In fact Linde's long-serving right-hand man was 'Eyrefield Dan' McNally, who once commented: 'Sure, Mister Tommy mightn't know which end a horse eats with!' Nevertheless it was the schooling from their early days over all types of fences on Linde's private schooling ground, by the brilliant brothers, that made Linde's jumpers so desperately difficult to beat. After the Beasley era Linde was well served in the saddle by Terry Kavanagh, Willie Hoysted and Charlie Whelan, all top-flight horsemen.

Unlike his contemporary rivals, Linde became deeply involved in breeding as well as racing, invariably taking a share in any animal either bred at or bought into Eyrefield Lodge. This policy was responsible for his heading the list of winning owners in Ireland for six years in succession. Though his first love was steeple-chasing – he was never averse to sending a promising flat horse jumping – Linde was equally adept at preparing flat racers. Besides winning the Irish Derby with Pet Fox, he provided three consecutive winners of the Beresford Stakes, while the National Produce Stakes fell to Eyrefield Lodge runners five times in a row.

Tall, severe-looking and invariably top-hatted on the racecourse, Linde pos-sessed a dry wit, which gave rise to an endless fund of anecdotes. One of these concerned a young foreigner, who once rode too close to Linde's string, upsetting the excitable Red Prince II. Astonished at the tirade of abuse which he had thus provoked, the injured innocent retorted that his father was Baron ——. Like a flash came the rejoinder: 'What a pity your mother wasn't barren too!' Though he married twice, Linde had no children. Thus, on his death in 1897, from Bright's Disease, Eyrefield Lodge, which H. E. Linde had worked so hard to restore to its founding family, was put up for auction, being bought by Eustace Loder, in whose family it remains. Henry Eyre Linde was not only the most successful trainer in the history of Irish racing up to modern times, but, by his character, talent and integrity he did more than perhaps any other to elevate the occupation of training groom to the status of a respectable profession for those who followed in his calling.

Although several sources credit Tommy Beasley with the winning ride on Pet Fox in the Irish Derby, the colt was in fact ridden by Terry Kavanagh, a professional jockey attached to the Eyrefield Lodge stable at the time. Better known as a National Hunt rider, Terry Kavanagh rode successfully on the flat for over ten years, before turning his attention fully to the jumping game. His finest hour came in 1897, when he rode Manifesto to the great horse's first Grand National victory, just a week after the death of his former employer, H. E. Linde. A tough, resolute rider, though not perhaps a finished horseman, Terry Kavanagh was recently characterised thus, by an English scribe: 'Kavanagh was the sort of tough customer who didn't argue when told to lose weight. His kind sweated it off by carrying sacks of potatoes, then by sleeping on a manure heap.' Such a fanciful description, revealing as it does more about the author than his subject, would probably not have caused undue distress to a man in Kavanagh's calling, where winners must come before finer feelings. Having shared the training duties at Eyrefield Lodge with Dan McNally, who remained on well after Linde's death, Terry Kavanagh died in Newbridge in January 1908.

Wednesday, 29th June, 1887   **£763**   **11 Ran**   **1½m (Howth Post)**

The Irish Derby of 1000sovs, by subscription of 17sovs each (to the fund), but 8sovs only for horses struck out on or before the last day of the September meeting, 1886. The second horse to receive 150sovs and the third 70sovs out of the plate. For three years old. Colts 8st 12lb; fillies 8st 8lb. The winner of the Angleseys and Railways at the Curragh, or of two stakes value 300sovs each, 10lb extra; of the Angleseys or of a stake value 300sovs, or of stakes collectively value 600sovs, 7lb extra; of a stake value 200sovs, 3lb extra. Horses that have never won a stake value 100sovs, allowed 6lb; maidens allowed 10lb; only one of these allowances can be taken. Produce of untried sires or mares allowed 3lb (if claimed at entry), but not for both. Any person entering three horses, his own bona fide sole property, can strike out one at the time appointed for declaring forfeit without having to pay the forfeit.

(60 subs)

1	Mr H. E. Linde's	PET FOX (T. Kavanagh)	8. 2	Owner
		B. colt Philammon – Wild Vixen by Victor.		
2	Mr S. M. Nolan's	KING MILAN (T. Harris)	9. 1	James Dunne
		Ch. colt Thurio – Empress.		
3	Mr W. Brophy's	HENRY GEORGE (P. Lynch)	8. 9	
		B. colt Philammon – Chrysalis.		
4	Mrs M. Knox's	KILDARE (J. Connolly)	9. 8	Connolly
		B. colt New Holland – The Beauty.		
5	Mr J. A. Cassidy's	FETHARD (T. Broderick)	7.13	
		B. colt Lord Gough – Venice		
6	Mr W. Pallin's	THE PHILISTINE (W. Hoysted)	9. 1	
		B. colt Philammon – Mohican II.		
0	Mr C. J. Blake's	CELESTE* (L. Kelly)	7.12	James Dunne
		B. filly Xenophon – Magdalene.		
0	Mr T. G. Gordon's	THE EARLY BIRD (J. Woodburn)	8. 9	
		Br. colt Albert Victor – Infanta.		
9	Mr A. Tiernan's	LITTLE WIDOW (J. Westlake)	7.12	
		Br. filly Ingomar – Sprite.		
F	Mr J. Lyons's	PERICLES (H. Saunders)	8. 2	James Dunne
		B/Br. colt Arbitrator – Colleen Rhue.		
BD	Mr R. M. Delamere's	HOLLY (M. Dawson)	9. 5	Connolly
		B. colt Hollywood – Sister to Tyrconnell.		

SP 3/1 Henry George; 4/1 King Milan; 6/1 PET FOX; 7/1 The Philistine, Kildare; 100/8 Bar.
                    3 lengths, 4 lengths.
Winner trained by Mr Henry E. Linde at Eyrefield Lodge, Curragh.

*Celeste ran un-named.

1888

If proof were needed of the rock-hard state of the ground on the Curragh in the summer of 1888, it was provided by the crippled survivors of the opening day's racing. In consequence, fields on Derby Day were small. One of the most notable absentees was Primrose League, the early favourite for the feature race. Just before racing began Linde announced that sore shins had necessitated the withdrawal of his Baldoyle Derby winner. Though it came as a disappointment to many, the scratching of Primrose League was music to the ears of William Brophy, whose filly, Miss Pitt, immediately became the new favourite for the race. Brophy's reasons for renewed optimism were two-fold. Firstly, Miss Pitt had looked to be a very good filly in the first half of the previous season, but it had gradually become clear that Primrose League was her superior. Secondly, Brophy was also the owner of Philomel, winner of six of her seven races as a two-year-old and outstandingly the best of her generation in Ireland, but Philomel had never been entered for the Irish Derby. On the opening day of the meeting Philomel had won a Queen's Plate in a canter and proceeded to repeat that performance in the race before the Derby.

With Primrose League out of the way, Miss Pitt did not appear to have much to beat. Though she had not had a race that season, on all known form she had the measure of her home-trained opponents, one of whom, Justitia, had finished second to Primrose League in the Baldoyle Derby. The only conceivable danger seemed to be Theodolite, a bad third in an amateur riders' welter race at Lewes three weeks previously, ridden by his owner, Captain L. Heywood Jones. Fancy for Theodolite stemmed not from his public form, but from the fact that he was bred and trained by Garrett Moore, already twice successful in the race with Theodolite's half-brothers. This massively-quartered bay colt had been stabled since his arrival with the Beasleys at Eyrefield House, and they maintained a non-committal silence concerning the English raider's well-being.

From a ragged start – a feature of that day's racing – Theodolite got away fastest, only to be headed by Rosebud, who went into a clear lead ahead of Justice to Ireland, Miss Pitt and Theodolite. Rosebud maintained a diminishing lead until turning for home, where Hospodar and Theodolite swept past her, with the latter going better. At the Chains Theodolite and Hospodar had the race to themselves and gallantly though Hospodar battled, he was always going to be beaten by the English colt, who won comfortably by three parts of a length. Rosebud straggled in third, ahead of the bitterly disappointing Miss Pitt, whose performance in a slowly-run race suggested that she lacked both speed and stamina. To add to Mr Brophy's chagrin, Philomel completed an historic treble of Queen's Plates on the final day of the meeting.

A triple triumph for trainer Garrett Moore and his wonderful broodmare Miss Theo, Theodolite was a second and posthumous Irish Derby winner for his sire Arbitrator. In common with his half-brothers, Theodolite was far from top-class, but he had been 'laid out' for the Irish Derby. His form subsequently reverted to its previous level and, though placed on the flat, over hurdles and fences, his only other success in three seasons racing as a gelding was gained in the Champion Hurdle at

Kempton Park, ridden by Mr Willie Moore, the trainer's brother. Hospodar won the Curragh Cesarewitch, lost his form completely as a four-year-old, but regained it with a vengeance the following year, winning five good races. He was still winning 'chases in England three years later. Rosebud was bought by Harry Dyas, the owner of Manifesto, who placed her to good effect over hurdles. Justitia went sprinting and beat Philomel by three lengths over six furlongs, as well she might, for she received no less than 14lbs per length! Justice to Ireland, owned by the Knox family, was named after their winner of the Curragh Derby in 1848, the only occasion on which that race was run.

Winning the Irish Derby on Theodolite was yet another step in the rapid rise to prominence of jockey W. 'Billie' Warne. Born in Stockton-on-Tees in 1869, Warne became apprenticed to James Ryan at Creen Lodge, Newmarket and rode his first winner in 1886. The following year he scored his first major success when winning the Ascot Gold Cup on his stable's second string, Bird of Freedom. Weeks prior to his Irish Derby win Billie Warne achieved his only English Classic success, on Briar-root in the One Thousand Guineas. Though 1888 was his best year in these islands, it also included the most galling experience of his riding career, when he rode the strongly-fancied Bismarck in the Stewards Cup at Goodwood. Charles Morton, who was closely associated with the horse, described the episode in his memoirs: '. . . he came over the hill with the race at his mercy. Less than a furlong from home he was leading by ten lengths, when he suddenly swerved right across the course and deliberately put his head over the rails. Something came up and beat him a short head and I could have wept in my mortification.' Like many jockeys before and since, Billie Warne found it difficult to bridge the gap between successful apprentice and established jockey and in 1895 he sailed for Germany. Riding the lightweights for Reg Day's all-conquering stable, he became first jockey to the Kaiser and headed the list of winning riders at Baden Baden for eleven consecutive seasons. Among myriad big race victories were two German Derbies, two St Legers and five Hamburg Grands Prix. Unfortunately, like Fred Winter, Billie Warne did not manage to get out of Germany before World War One. Interned for the duration, he lost everything and returned home penniless and forgotten. He did ride one winner – for Jack Jarvis at York in 1919 – but it was a swansong, not a come-back. Billie Warne died at Exning, near Newmarket, in 1952.

Unlike his half-brothers, Theologian and Theodemir, who ran in the colours of their breeder and trainer, Theodolite carried the 'White, cherry sleeves and white cap' of Captain L. Heywood Jones, a successful owner and amateur rider in England, where his ability in the saddle was highly regarded, as the following excerpt from the Daily Telegraph of December 1905 indicates: 'One of the most brilliant jockeys of his time was Captain "Roddy" Owen and it will be readily conceded that a man required to have developed more than average ability to be able to hold his own with the brothers Beasley, Mr Arthur Coventry, Mr G. Lambton, Captain L. H. Jones and Captain W. B. Morris.' Captain Jones made his first appearance in the story of the Irish Derby as the owner of Tice. By Umpire out of Trickstress, Tice was thus bred for the task, but she could only finish fifth to St Kevin in 1885, in which year his colours were carried successfully by Rapparce, who went on winning until 1888, when Captain Jones, who had since transferred his racing interests to England, made a successful reappearance in the Irish Derby saga via Theodolite. It is through Captain Jones' ownership of Theodolite that due space can be given to achievements of the offspring of Garrett Moore's remarkable mare Miss Theo. Foaled in 1855, Miss Theo was bred by Mr W. McGrane and was by Leamington out of Hebe, by Bandy. Apart from her unique Irish Derby treble with Theologian, Theodemir and Theodolite, she bred no fewer than seven other winners, whose feats form a legend of their own.

Her first produce was Theophrastus (1877), winner of the Beresford Stakes, ridden by M. Lynch. Put to hurdling, he became the best of his era and in six seasons won the most important hurdle races in the English Calendar. One of his most notable victories was gained in the Croydon Grand Hurdle, in which he deadheated with his younger half-sister Theodora, winning the decider by a neck. Theodora (1878) won four races as a three-year-old and subsequently became the dam of the full-brothers Theosophist (1885) and Theophilus (1886). Bred and raced by Captain Jones, these two sons of Arbitrator won no less than twenty races between them. Theosophist won the Great Lancashire Handicap at Liverpool and the Sandown Grand Hurdle, while Theophilus, having won four times as a two-year-old, won the Union Jack Stakes and the St George Stakes at Liverpool. In addition, they combined to provide their enthusiastic owner-breeder with the most satisfying moment of his racing career when winning successive races at Sandown in 1888, crowning a memorable year on the Turf for Captain L. Heywood Jones.

Wednesday, 27th June, 1888　　　　**£560**　　　　**6 Ran**　　　　**1½m (Howth Post)**

The Irish Derby of £700, by subscription of 15sovs each (to the fund), but 6sovs only if struck out on or before the last day of the September meeting, 1887. The second horse to receive 100sovs and the third £25 out of the plate. For three years old. Colts 8st 12lb; fillies 8st 8lb. The winner of Angleseys and Railways at the Curragh, or of two stakes value 300sovs each, 10lb extra; of the Angleseys or a stake value 300sovs, or of stakes collectively value 600sovs, 7lb extra; of a stake value 200sovs, 3lb extra. Horses that have never won a stake value 100sovs, allowed 6lb; maidens allowed 10lb; only one of these allowances can be taken. Produce of untried sires or mares allowed 3lb (if claimed at entry), but not for both. Any person entering three horses, his own bona fide sole property, can strike out one at the time appointed for declaring forfeit without having to pay the forfeit.

(47 subs)

1	Capt. L. H. Jones's	THEODOLITE (W. Warne)	8. 2	G. Moore (U.K.)	
		B. colt Arbitrator – Miss Theoby Leamington.			
2	Mr S. M. Nolan's	HOSPODAR (M. Dawson)	8. 2	James Dunne	
		Ch. colt Camballo – Mayoress.			
3	Mr A. Tiernan's	ROSEBUD (W. Waterson)	7. 9		
		B. filly Rostrevor – Annie M'Gregor.			
4	Mr W. Brophy's	MISS PITT (J. Connolly)	8.11		
		B. filly Philammon – Lady Pitt.			
5	Mr C. J. Blake's	JUSTITIA (H. Saunders)	7.12	James Dunne	
		Ch. filly Lord Gough – Award.			
6	Mrs M. Knox's	JUSTICE TO IRELAND (J. Hoysted)	8. 2	Private	
		B. colt Philammon – The Beauty.			

SP 5/4 Miss Pitt; 5/2 THEODOLITE; 5/1 Justitia; 9/1 Hospodar; 20/1 Bar.
¾ length, very bad third. 2m 50s.

Besides those already mentioned, Miss Theo bred Theorist (1879) winner of nine races and second in the Irish Derby, Theodoric (1884) also successful nine times, Theon (1886) winner of three races, Theodosius (1888) five times successful and Theodosia II a three-time winner. In all Miss Theo bred the winners of fifty-two races, and if the exploits of Miss Theo's offspring seem to have been accorded undue space, it is justifiable on the basis of her astonishing record. Had she bred but one winner of the Irish Derby, much less three, she remains one of the most remarkable matrons in the history of the race.

1889

Yet another glorious summer – as indeed they invariably seemed to be – had baked the Curragh as dry as a bone, resulting in a small but interesting field for the Irish Derby. The 'class' runner was undoubtedly Captain Greer's filly Tragedy. Successful in three of her seven races as a two-year-old and second in three others, Tragedy had won the one mile Cork Derby on her most recent outing. On this form she had the beating of Gawsworth and Lord Fingall, first and second in the Baldoyle Derby. Queen May appeared to be outclassed, leaving Baillie as the only conceivable danger. Like Theodolite the year before, Baillie's English form amounted to very little, yet his long journey from Middleham, Yorkshire, indicated stable confidence in his chance. Moreover, he claimed all the allowances. Anticipating public demand, the bookmakers posted Baillie at 2-to-1 ON, with no shortage of takers, until a heavy run on Tragedy forced the favourite out to 6-to-4 ON.

After two false starts Baillie got away in front, only to be headed by Lord Fingall, with Queen May some lengths adrift. At the mile post Lord Fingall held a clear lead over Baillie, Gawsworth and Tragedy. Coming down the hill Gawsworth joined Lord Fingall, with Baillie running wide. As Lord Fingall and Gawsworth passed the Chains, Baillie swerved right across the course, threatening to run out on to the road. Meanwhile, Tommy Beasley had been stealthily moving Tragedy closer to the leaders. As Gawsworth weakened Beasley pounced, shooting Tragedy past the tiring Lord Fingall, with the race at his mercy. Suddenly, like a bolt from the blue, the forgotten favourite reappeared, rocketing up the stands side with Staunton riding like a man inspired. However, Baillie's earlier aberrations had made his task impossible and while he snatched second place from Lord Fingall, he could not trouble Tragedy, who won in record time.

A bay filly by Ben Battle, who had himself set a record in the race, Tragedy was out of The White Witch, by Massinissa. A wretched racemare, The White Witch proved much better at stud and two years later, after Tragedy's full-sister, Comedy, had won the Cambridgeshire, there was a sudden upsurge of interest in Massinissa, long neglected in the fastnesses of County Down. Tragedy ran three times in rapid succession after her record-breaking performance at the Curragh. Unplaced at Kempton and Newmarket, she finished a bad third in the Midland Derby at Leicester and was promptly taken out of training. At stud she bred Wildfowler,

Captain Sir Henry Greer, *knighted for his services to bloodstock breeding, founder of the National Stud and owner of Gallinule, the most prepotent influence on Irish breeding at the turn of the century. Source:* Irish Field.

Terry Kavanagh, *successful on Pet Fox before gaining greater fame on dual Grand National winner Manifesto. Source:* Irish Field.

winner of the St Leger for his breeder Henry Greer. Following Wildfowler's Classic success, Tragedy was bought by Sir Tatton Sykes for £5,000, an Irish record. Of the four that finished behind Tragedy at the Curragh, Lord Fingall and Gawsworth did most to contribute to their keep. The former won both three-mile Queen's Plates at the Irish Derby meeting in 1890.

Captain T. Gisborne Gordon, the breeder of Tragedy, controlled affairs at Brownstown Lodge, where Tragedy was trained, the licence being held by T. Lewis. Born in the North of Ireland in 1851, T. G. Gordon lost his right arm in a shooting accident while still a young man. Despite this handicap he became an Irish Rugby International, being capped as a three-quarter in 1877 and 1878. His first good horse was The Early Bird, winner of the Madrid Stakes in 1887. Three years later he won the same race with Delamont and in 1892 Loot gave him his most important victory in the Anglesey Stakes. A Member of the I.N.H.S., T. G. Gordon was for many years registrar to the Down Royal Corporation of Horse Breeders, organizers of racing at the Maze.

Tragedy carried the colours of a newcomer to the ranks of ownership, Captain J. H. Greer, who, long before his death in 1934, would become recognized as one of the outstanding contributors to the development of thoroughbred breeding in Ireland. His name would forever be associated with his most famous horse – Gallinule. Born in Moy, Co. Tyrone, in 1855, the eldest son of Lieutenant-General H. H. Greer, Harry, as he was always known, joined the 74th Highlanders. Having served mostly in India, Harry Greer retired in 1890 with the rank of captain. Shortly before resigning his commission he had taken up racing, with instant success, his first runner being Tragedy. At the same time he purchased Gallinule, installing that confirmed bleeder and roarer at his Brownstown Stud. The rest of the Gallinule saga is recorded elsewhere, suffice to say that he became one of the most successful sires in thoroughbred history. After her success in the Irish Derby, Greer sent Tragedy to be trained by Sam Darling at Beckhampton, thus beginning a remarkably successful partnership, which yielded two Classic winners in the 'White, tartan sleeves, cherry cap', Wildfowler and Slieve Gallion.

In 1908 Harry Greer was elected to membership of the Jockey Club, dissolved his partnership with Sam Darling and thereafter concentrated his remarkable energies on breeding. Created Senior Steward of the Jockey Club in 1914 and again in 1915, he was then appointed Director of the newly-created National Stud. After the British Government had sold Russley, the English portion of the stud, Greer concentrated on developing Tully, Co. Kildare on the lines of a high-class private stud, in which he was extremely successful. Having sold Brownstown to Mr W. Parrish during World War One and established Tully to his satisfaction, he undertook the additional challenge of building up and consolidating the Aga Khan's sizeable stud complex around Sheshoon, with equally satisfactory results. Harry Greer received a knighthood in 1925 for services to the nation and was subsequently made a Senator in the Irish Free State Government. Less than a year before his death in August 1934, Sir Harry Greer resigned as Director of the National Stud, owing to ill-health. Deprived of an heir by the death in action of both his sons in 1917, Harry Greer is commemorated by one of the showpieces of the Irish nation; an enduring monument to a remarkable man.

Tragedy, *winner of the Irish Derby for Harry Greer in 1889. Mated with Gallinule, she produced the St Leger winner, Wildfowler.*

Gallinule, *condemned as a 'bleeder' and a 'roarer', he amply repaid Harry Greer's faith in him by siring no fewer than six winners of the Irish Derby in seven years. Gallinule subsequently became the first Irish-based stallion to head the list of winning sires in Britain since his great-great-grandsire, Birdcatcher, half a century earlier. Source:* Irish Field.

Tommy Beasley, the rider of Tragedy, was the eldest of the famous five Beasley brothers, whose collective riding feats will never be surpassed. Equally accomplished on the flat or over fences, Tommy was the most polished rider of the quintet. Taken under the wing of the famous former Corinthian, Allen McDonagh, at Athgarven

Lodge in 1870, Tommy Beasley went on to win the Grand National three times between 1877 and 1892, during which time the race was never run without a Beasley riding in it. In 1879 four of the brothers rode in it – in itself a record. In twelve successive rides Tommy Beasley, who could scale 8st 7lbs with ease, was placed six times and only had two falls. In fact his most serious riding injury occurred when he broke a leg in a fall riding across the Curragh to the Post Office! Besides his Grand National victories, 'Mr Tommy' won two Irish Derbies, two Irish Grand Nationals, two Galway Plates and the Grand Steeplechase de Paris. His Irish Derbies apart, perhaps his most cherished victory on the flat was his defeat of Fred Archer at the Curragh in October 1886, which earned him a reception to rival that which Archer himself had earlier received. Besides being brilliant in silks, Tommy Beasley was an accomplished huntsman, a crack shot and a skilful fisherman. Nominally Assistant Trainer to H. E. Linde for many years, Tommy Beasley retired from the saddle in 1900 and died five years later after a lengthy illness, for which the sudden death of his beloved wife was in part responsible.

Wednesday, 26th June, 1889	**£460**	**5 Ran**	**1½m (Howth Post)**

The Irish Derby of 550sovs, by subscription of 15sovs each (to the fund), but 6sovs only if struck out on or before the last day of the September meeting, 1888. The second horse to receive 50sovs and the third 25sovs out of the plate. For three years old. Colts 8st 12lb; fillies 8st 8lb. The winner of the Angleseys and Railways at the Curragh, or of two stakes value 300sovs each, 10lb extra; of the Angleseys or of a stake value 300sovs, or of stakes collectively value 600sovs, 7lb extra; of a stake value 200sovs, 3lb extra. Horses that have never won a stake value 100sovs, allowed 6lb; maidens allowed 10lb; only one of these allowances can be taken. Produce of untried sires or mares allowed 3lb (if claimed at entry), but not for both. Any person entering three horses, his own bona fide sole property, can strike out one at the time appointed for declaring forfeit without having to pay the forfeit.

(34 subs)

1 Capt. Greer's	TRAGEDY (Mr T. Beasley)	9. 1	T. G. Gordon
	B. filly Ben Battle – The White Witch by Massinissa.		
2 Mr C. J. Cunningham's	BAILLIE (J. Staunton)	7.13	Hall (UK)
	Ch. colt Baliol – Lottie by Solon.		
3 Mr P. M. Saurin's	LORD FINGALL (Mr H. Beasley)	9. 5	H. Beasley
	Ch. colt Rostrevor – Red Berry.		
4 Mr C. W. Bagge's	GAWSWORTH (Foster)	9. 2	F. F. Cullen
	B. colt Favo – Agile.		
5 Mr J. Gubbins's	QUEEN MAY (W. Hoysted)	8. 8	
	Br. filly Philammon – May Day (NOT IN GSB)		

SP 4/6 Baillie; 3/1 TRAGEDY; 6/1 Lord Fingall; 100/15 Gawsworth; 100/8 Queen May.
3 lengths, Head. 2m 43¼s.
Winner trained by Lewis for Mr T. G. Gordon at Brownstown Lodge, Curragh.

1890

In common with its more illustrious Epsom counterpart, the Irish Derby had begun to suffer from lack of owners' support, owing to the failure of the Curragh executive to supplement the prize fund. Whereas the Epsom management had rectified their problems by guaranteeing a minimum stake of £5,000, no such gesture was forthcoming at the Curragh. A direct consequence was an undistinguished field of five, further depleted by the late withdrawal of the likely favourite, Battle Gage. His defection left Rice Meredith's powerful Curragh View stable represented solely by Kentish Fire. Named only that morning, Kentish Fire had run but once as a two-year-old and was making his seasonal debut in the Irish Derby. However, he was rumoured to have beaten Battle Gage in a recent trial and this, if true, fully entitled him to favouritism, for the latter had beaten Goldminer and Fairest Flower at the Phoenix Park. However, the public, understandably sceptical of stories of home gallops, opted for Delamont, unbeaten in his three races that season, albeit over shorter distances. Second favourite was Goldminer, preferred to Kentish Fire, with Fairest Flower and Sunrise ignored.

At a sedate early pace Sunrise showed the way to Goldminer and Kentish Fire, with Delamont and Fairest Flower whipping in. The short-running Sunrise compounded climbing the hill, giving way to Goldminer, who swung into the straight closely pursued by Delamont, Kentish Fire and Fairest Flower. Responding gamely to the urgings of his rider, Goldminer fought off the challenge of Delamont, but had nothing more to give when Dawson produced Kentish Fire with an irresistible run, which carried him four lengths clear at the line, with Delamont a further two lengths in arrears.

Immediately after the race Kentish Fire's jubilant owner-breeder, Mr M. A. Maher, refused Harry Beasley's offer of £1,200 for the winner. Nor was it difficult to see why both parties should entertain such high hopes for Kentish Fire, for was he not a three-parts brother to that Aintree immortal Frigate, twice second in the Grand National under Harry Beasley, second yet again when ridden by Willie Beasley and at last victorious with Tommy Beasley in the saddle in 1889? Like Kentish Fire, Frigate had been bred by Mat Maher at Ballinkeele, near Enniscorthy. Frigate was by Maher's own stallion Gunboat and on that horse's death in 1883 Maher had replaced him with his own son Torpedo, the sire of Kentish Fire. Fair Maid of Kent, beautifully bred by Gladiateur out of a Stockwell mare, though a shy breeder, proved a wonderful servant to Mat Maher, for in addition to Kentish Fire she produced the latter's full-brother Tornado, winner of numerous races under both codes. The success of Kentish Fire drew the attention of other breeders to his sire and the victory of another son, Bowline, in the Irish Derby two years later saw Torpedo confirmed as one of the most popular stallions in the country, a position he retained until his death in 1899.

Descended from an old Tipperary family, that had settled in Ballinkeele towards the end of the Eighteenth century, Matthias Aidan Maher represented the best of sporting owner-breeders, who raced primarily for the love of the sport. Aided by his brother, Captain George Maher, he bred, owned and trained a host of National

Hunt winners, outstanding among them being of course Frigate, whose eventual triumph at Liverpool after so many near misses fully entitled her to the heroine's reception which was accorded her. That she should have started a hot favourite for her first-ever race, a four-mile 'chase at Derby when only a four-year-old, attested to her owner-trainer's reputation in that sphere. Mat Maher was a member of the Turf Club and Senior Steward in 1892. Like his brother, he was also a member of the I.N.H.S. committee. While their National Hunt horses were trained at home in Ballinkeele, the Mahers had their flat runners trained on the Curragh and it was from Rice Meredith's stables that both Kentish Fire and Bowline sallied forth to success in the Irish Derby, bearing the 'Purple, white sleeves'. By the time that Powderlough, also by Torpedo, had become the first dual winner of the Irish Cesarewitch (1896–7), carrying George Maher's colours, the Maher flat racers had accompanied Rice Meredith from Curragh View to Rathbride Manor, where they remained in the care of Michael Dawson up to the time of Mat Maher's death in July 1901.

Kentish Fire was the first of three Irish Derby winners trained by Rice Meredith, the outstanding Irish flat race trainer between the Connolly and Dawson eras. Formerly a well-known gentleman rider, Rice Meredith succeeded the Connollys at Curragh View, where the former Connolly apprentice, Michael Dawson, remained as stable jockey. Rapidly recognized as a shrewd and skilful trainer, whose judgement was rarely proved wrong, in 1891 Rice Meredith moved to Rathbride Manor, which he made into the finest yard in Ireland and whence his runners swept all before them both at home and in England. Alas, in racing triumph and disaster are seldom far removed and at Kilkenny in 1893 Rice Meredith was called before the Stewards to explain the discrepancy in running of Master Joe on successive days. Not satisfied with the explanations of Rice Meredith and his jockey, Malone, the Kilkenny Stewards referred the case to the Turf Club. At the subsequent enquiry several prominent bookmakers were asked to produce their books for examination. The result was that both Rice Meredith and Malone were warned off. Living in enforced and heartbroken retirement at The Rath, Kilsallaghan, Co. Dublin, Rice Meredith broke a leg while out hunting with the Ward Union in November 1897 and suffered a fatal heart attack a month later. Thus ended the sadly abbreviated career of one of the most brilliant trainers in the annals of the Irish Derby.

The son of a jarvey, Michael Dawson was apprenticed to Pat Connolly, a family friend. Under the guidance of the stable jockey John Connolly, the featherweight Dawson had his first ride in public in 1882, riding five winners that year. Able to go to scale at 5st 9lbs, Dawson was in ever-increasing demand and went on to ride the winners of every important race in the Irish Calendar, including three Irish Derbies in four years. On Rice Meredith's disqualification Dawson took over the Rathbride Manor stables, combining riding and training with conspicuous success. Best known of his charges during the transitional period of his career was undoubtedly Winkfield's Pride, winner of the Railway Stakes and three other races in 1895. Transferred to Robinson's Foxhill stable to be prepared for the Cambridgeshire, Winkfield's Pride started favourite and won easily. For good measure he won the Old Cambridgeshire with equal ease two days later. In four outings as a four-year-old, this remarkable colt won the Lincolnshire Handicap, finished second to Persimmon in the Ascot Gold Cup, won the Doncaster Cup and concluded the

Wildfowler, *whose success in the St Leger gained Gallinule acclaim by British breeders. Wildfowler went on to sire an Irish Derby winner in Wild Bouquet. He is shown here with his trainer Sam Darling, handler of the famous half-brothers, Blairfinde, Galtee More and Ard Patrick. Source:* Irish Field.

Mat Maher. *Ballinkeele-based owner-breeder of Irish Derby winners Kentish Fire and Bowline. The former was a three-parts brother to Frigate, successful in the Aintree Grand National in 1889 after three near-misses for Mat Maher. Source:* Irish Field.

season with a resounding triumph in the Prix du Conseil Municipal, one of the most valuable races in France. By the turn of the century Michael Dawson had retired from the saddle to concentrate exclusively on training. Nor was he long about filling any void in the saddle, for in his apprentice, David Condon, he had discovered a jockey of infinite promise, who rode with head, hands and heels in the manner of his master and mentor. The emergence of David Condon coincided with the appearance of the most brilliant horse that Dawson would ever train, St Brendan. Dawson's training career is covered in the chapter on St Brendan, the first of his four training triumphs in Ireland's greatest race.

The field for this running of the Irish Derby has already been described as disappointing and it would be a grave misuse of the language to write in laudatory terms of the subsequent careers of the quintet. Albeit prone to injury, Kentish Fire never fulfilled his promise. Unlike his blood relations, Frigate and Tornado, Kentish Fire did not improve with age. On his only other appearance as a three-year-old he was second to Mervyn in the Irish Cesarewitch. An injury to a hind tendon kept him off the course for the whole of the following season and though he was later placed on the flat and over hurdles he never won again, in a campaign which lasted until a split pastern enforced his retirement as an eight-year-old. Put to stud at Ballinkeele, he failed to carry on his line. Of the others, Goldminer did win several races from six furlongs to two miles over the next two seasons, while Fairest Flower got her head in front at Cork Park later that year. As his running in the Irish Derby indicated, Sunrise did better when brought back to shorter distance. Viewed at this distance the Irish Derby of 1890 remains notable for personalities rather than participants.

Wednesday, 25th June, 1890 £460 **5 Ran** 1½m (Howth Post)

The Irish Derby of 550sovs, by subscription of 15sovs each (to the fund), but 6sovs only if struck out on or before the last day of the September meeting, 1889. The second horse to receive 50sovs and the third 25sovs out of the plate. For three years old. Colts 8st 12lb; fillies 8st 8lb. The winner of the Angleseys and Railways at the Curragh, or of two stakes value 300sovs each, 10lb extra; of the Angleseys or of a stake value 300sovs, or of stakes collectively value 600sovs, 7lb extra; of a stake value 200sovs, 3lb extra. Horses that have never won a stake value 100sovs, allowed 6lb; maidens allowed 10lb; only one of these allowances can be taken. Produce of untried sires or mares allowed 3lb (if claimed at entry), but not for both. Any person entering three horses, his own bona fide sole property, can strike out one at the time appointed for declaring forfeit without having to pay the forfeit.

(38 subs)

1 Mr M. A. Maher's	KENTISH FIRE (M. Dawson)	8. 2	R. Meredith	
	Ch. colt Torpedo – Fair Maid of Kent by Gladiateur.			
2 Mr C. J. Blake's	GOLDMINER (T. Harris)	9. 1	P. Doucie	
	Br. colt Arbitrator – Strike.			
3 Mr T. G. Gordon's	DELAMONT (L. Kelly)	8.12	T. G. Gordon	
	Br. colt Marmion – Tees Treasure.			
4 Mr L. L'Estrange's	FAIREST FLOWER (Doyle)	7. 9	Dennehy	
	Ch. filly York – dam by Haymaker.			
5 Mr J. Brady's	SUNRISE (J. Nolan)	7.13	Dennehy	
	Ch. colt Cassock – Larker.	(car. 8. 0)		

SP Evens Delamont; 5/2 Goldminer; 4/1 KENTISH FIRE; 100/8 Bar.
    4 lengths, 2 lengths.
Winner trained by Mr Rice Meredith at Curragh View, Curragh.

1891

For those most closely involved in the unceasing circus which is Irish racing, Derby Day 1891 opened on a sombre note with the funeral of Pat Doucie, who had trained four winners of the great race. Once again the feature race was distinctly devoid of glamour and the main topic of conversation during the preliminary events was 'the Leopardstown objections'. During the course of the two-day meeting earlier in June there had been no less than four objections, all of which were referred to the Turf Club. As the rules then stood, all bets remained in suspense pending the outcome of the Stewards' deliberations. This chaotic situation had provoked one sporting journalist to describe that particular fixture as 'the worst important meeting ever held in Ireland'. Chief sufferer in 'the Leopardstown affair' was the jockey Joe Foster, whose two winners had eventually been disqualified through incorrect registration of ownership. Out of luck at Leopardstown, Foster had high hopes of compensation in the Irish Derby on Duchess of Fife.

The field of six was dominated by the ex-Irish filly Narraghmore, now trained at Newmarket by Charles Archer. Raced in Ireland in her first season, Narraghmore had finished third on her debut and remained unbeaten in her four subsequent races, though she had not tried conclusions with De Beers or Eyrefield, the leading colts of her generation. Since changing stables she had run only once, when unplaced at the Guineas meeting. Trained especially for the Irish Derby, in which her lessor's father had twice been successful, with Ben Battle and Madame du Barry, Narraghmore had a favourite's chance and was supported accordingly. Those seeking one to beat the odds-on favourite were divided on the relative merits of Duchess of Fife and Rossmore. Though the former had won as a two-year-old, her recent form was uninspiring, while the hard-working Rossmore had twice failed against Narraghmore the previous season. More recently he had finished second in the Baldoyle Derby, taking his revenge on the winner, Chatterbox, the following day. The hard going was thought to be in his favour. Battle Bell had twice finished in front of Rossmore, but had recently flopped badly when favourite for the Baldoyle Derby. If stamina limitations had been responsible for her failure at Baldoyle, the stiff Curragh twelve furlongs would expose her shortcomings even more brutally. Having transferred his flying colt De Beers to England, William Dunne of Ballymanus relied on the filly Kaboonga to repeat his victory with Soulouque twelve years earlier. In receipt of 20lbs from Narraghmore, Kaboonga was quietly fancied to give the Rice Meredith stable a second successive victory in the race. The field of six was completed by Charles Blake's unraced Arbitrator colt, Mediator, whose dam was a full-sister to St Kevin, successful in the race for Mr Blake in 1885.

Though its outcome was perhaps a foregone conclusion, the race itself was full of incident. From flagfall Kaboonga shot into a clear lead, many lengths ahead of Battle Bell and Duchess of Fife, with the favourite lying fourth. To the horror of her supporters Battle Bell galloped straight into the mile post, giving her jockey a dreadful fall. Meanwhile the rest of the field had begun to close up on the tearaway leader, who remained just ahead of Narraghmore as they turned for home. All the way up the long, staring straight the two fillies raced stride for stride until Narraghmore's class finally prevailed, enabling her to pass the post less than a length to the good. Rossmore, having pursued the two fillies from a long way out, finished three lengths away in third place, without ever appearing likely to trouble the principals.

Narraghmore, a bay filly by Umpire out of Cecropia, was bred by William Ashe of Narraghmore, Co. Kildare, out of a mare that had once been exchanged for a cow. By Cecrops out of Bounce by Flatterer, Cecropia was born in 1874, had her first foal in 1881 and produced a further sixteen foals prior to her death in 1906 at the ripe old age of thirty-two. As successful as she was prolific, Cecropia's offspring included the winners Ashplant, Ashstick, Ashburn and General Gordon. Through her daughter Miss Plant she became the grandam of Ambush II, winner of the Grand National in 1900 in the colours of the Prince of Wales.

Victory in the Irish Derby provided Dubliner John D. Wardell with the additional distinction of becoming the first winning owner to follow in father's footsteps, for, racing as 'J. W. Denison', his father had been successful in 1874 with Ben Battle and four years later with Madame du Barry. On his father's death in Madame du Barry's year the family breeding and racing interests were disbanded. However, it was not long before John Wardell re-registered the 'Olive green, black cap', which were also carried successfully by Blancmange, a beneficiary of one of the objections of that ill-starred Leopardstown meeting and subsequently the winner of the Madrid Handicap. John Wardell also won numerous races with General Gordon, a half-brother to Narraghmore by Ben Battle. Narraghmore ran only once more as a three-year-old when unplaced in the Manchester November Handicap. The following year, having finished a close third to the Irish-trained Mervyn in the Liverpool Spring Cup, Narraghmore made her final appearance in the Chester Cup. Retired to the place of her birth, Narraghmore bred several winners for William Ashe, notably the winning two-year-olds Ashdod and O'Cullen, as well as the 'chaser Irish Angel. Those that finished behind Narraghmore in the Irish Derby subsequently did little to add to the lusttre of her name.

Charles Archer, who trained Narraghmore at Ellesmere House, Newmarket, was a younger brother of the famous 'Tinman', having been born in 1858, the year in which his father won the Grand National on Little Charlie. He was a dashing and fearless rider until increasing weight obliged him to turn to training, though not before he had made the painful discovery that his famous brother's affection for him did not extend to the racecourse. On one occasion Charlie had tried to get up his brother's inside, only to find himself put promptly through the rails! Equally as good-looking as Fred, Charlie lacked his brother's natural dignity and it was said of him at the time that the more famous Fred Archer became the more conceited his brother grew. Nonetheless, George Lambton described him as '. . . a fine judge of racing: when he fancied a horse it was good enough for anyone to follow. He betted

---

Wednesday, 24th June, 1891   **£460**   **6 Ran**   **1½m (Howth Post)**

The Irish Derby of 550sovs, by subscription of 15sovs each (to the fund), but 6sovs only if struck out on or before the last day of the September meeting, 1890. The second horse to receive 50sovs and the third 25sovs out of the plate. For three years old; Colts 8st 12lb; fillies 8st 8lb. The winner of the Angleseys and Railways at the Curragh, or of two stakes value 300sovs each, 10lb extra; of the Angleseys or of a stake value 300sovs, or of stakes collectively value 600sovs, 7lb extra; of a stake value 200sovs, 3lb extra. Horses that have never won a stake value 100sovs, allowed 6lb; maidens allowed 10lb; only one of these allowances can be taken. Produce of untried sires and mares allowed 3lb (if claimed at entry), but not for both. Any person entering three horses, his own bona fide sole property, can strike out one at the time appointed for declaring forfeit without having to pay the forfeit.

(35 subs)

1	Mr J. D. Wardell's	NARRAGHMORE (Mr T. Beasley)	9. 1	Archer (UK)
		B. filly Umpire – Cecropia by Cecrops.		
2	Mr W. Dunne's	KABOONGA (J. Doyle)	7. 9	Meredith
		B. filly Necromancer – My Jewel.		
3	Mr T. Donovan's	ROSSMORE (T. Kavanagh)	8. 9	F. F. Cullen
		Ch. colt Baliol – Kitty.		
4	Mr C. J. Blake's	MEDIATOR (T. Doyle)	7.13	
		B. colt Arbitrator – dam by Umpire – Lady of the Lake.		
5	Mr J. Phelan's	DUCHESS OF FIFE (Foster)	7.13 (car 8.0)	
		Br. filly Bay Cardinal – Queen of England.		
F	Captain Richardson's	BATTLE BELL (Taylor)	8. 5	T. G. Gordon
		Br. filly Ben Battle – Ivy by Xenophon.		

SP 4/5 NARRAGHMORE; 5/1 Duchess of Fife, Rossmore; 6/1 Battle Bell; 10/1 Bar.
Won easily by ¾ length, 3 lengths.
Winner trained by Mr C. Archer at Newmarket.

heavily and when he brought off a good thing the Ring knew it.' The best animal he trained was Highland Chief, a leggy, long-striding bay, the property of Lord Elles- mere. Disregarding his brother's opinion, Charlie went for a massive gamble on his charge in the Epsom Derby of 1883. In a pulsating finish St Blaise beat Highland Chief by a neck, with Fred Archer's mount, Galliard, half a length away in third place. Despite Webb's admission that he had ridden an ill-judged race on Highland Chief, the rumours persisted that Fred Archer had thrown the race on Galliard in an effort to save his brother's bet. The scandal-mongers regarded themselves as absolutely vindicated when Lord Falmouth, the owner of Galliard and Fred Archer's long-standing patron, promptly announced his retirement from racing. Undaunted by this reverse and undismayed by its repercussions, Charlie Archer begged and borrowed every penny he could to have on Lowland Chief the following day. Riding one of his finest races, 'Slinky' Webb got Lowland Chief home by a neck, more then recouping Archer's Derby losses. Despite having his permit to train at Newmarket withdrawn at the end of that season, Charlie Archer was soon restored to favour and continued to train with fair success, winning the Lincolnshire Handicap with Wolf's Crag (1893) and Sir Geoffrey (1900). He had retired from training for a number of years prior to his death in 1922. Three years later his son, Frederick Charles Archer, sent out the gift horse, Double Chance, to win the Grand National.

1892

Derby Day got off to a subdued start with the dramatic news of the sudden death in London of the Marquis of Drogheda. Such was the impact of this news that the majority of the huge crowd present at the Curragh fully expected the meeting to be cancelled as a mark of respect. However, the Stewards, having immediately con- vened in the Stand House under the chairmanship of Charles Blake and recorded due tribute to 'the Admiral Rous of the Irish Turf', wisely decided that the show must go on. Shocked by the news of Lord Drogheda's death, disgruntled by the interminable delays at the solitary turnstile in operation, frustrated by the shortage of racecards, those in search of winners could at least console themselves that a recent amendment to the rules governing betting would simplify the problems of collection, should that happy eventuality arise. The new rule stated that: 'All bets on Irish race-courses, whether for ready money or booked bets, shall be paid on the horse that is placed first by the judge, unless an objection be lodged within fifteen minutes after the winner has passed the scales. Any subsequent objection cannot interfere with bets.' Fortified by the successes of the favourites in the preliminary events, the punters set about unravelling the Derby form. Best public form was undoubtedly held by Roy Neil, winner of the Cork Derby, with Detonator third, and by Blancmange, winner of the Madrid Handicap, with Detonator unplaced. How- ever, on this occasion rumoured home trials caught the public imagination, for the crowd made The Dummy a red hot favourite. The Dummy had run only once that season, when successful over five furlongs at Derby in April. However, F. F. Cullen's representative quite outshone the opposition in the paddock. The only other runner to attract any appreciable volume of support was William Brophy's Wordsworth, whose dam was an own-sister to the 1870 Irish Derby winner, Billy Pitt. On his most recent appearance he had beaten General Gordon by a neck in the Baldoyle Derby. Detonator was well held on recent form, War Cloud had not run as a three-year-old and Fanessa, the only filly in the race, had never run at all.

The race got off to a sensational start when Wordsworth shot ahead of his field, only to swerve sharply to his left and out of the race. This left War Cloud ahead of Fanessa and Blancmange, with The Dummy in last place, as they covered the first mile. At this point Fanessa compounded suddenly, as Roy Neil and Blancmange took up the running, pursued by The Dummy, whose supporters prepared to shout home their favourite. The cheering was shortlived, for The Dummy's unproven stamina gave out abruptly, leaving Blancmange and Roy Neil with the race between them. Just as the former looked to have got the better of his rival, he crossed his legs, shooting the startled Mr John Beasley up his neck. Seizing the advantage, Dawson drove Roy Neil clear and despite Beasley's valiant efforts the post came in time for Roy Neil, who won by a length, with The Dummy a remote eight lengths in arrears. The supporters of Roy Neil could count themselves lucky, for Blancmange, who swerved after stumbling, lost far more than the length by which he was beaten. The winner provided Rice Meredith and his stable jockey Michael Dawson, with their second success in the Irish Derby.

Roy Neil was bred by his owner, Dr George Moorhead, a forthright, sporting country doctor of Scottish descent, who maintained a small stud in Tullamore. In accordance with the convention of the day, Dr Moorhead raced under an assumed name: R. M. Delamere. In this guise he and his father had seen their colours carried successfully for many years on Irish racecourses, having won the National Stakes with Prodigal (1871) and Tyrconnell (1876), in addition to the Beresford Stakes with Prospector (1866). Nor has time dimmed the family connection with the Turf, for Dr Moorhead's grandson, a member of the I.N.H.S., bred The Dikler, winner of the Cheltenham Gold Cup in 1973.

Put in training with Rice Meredith, Roy Neil's racecourse debut was delayed until the backend of his two-year-old days, when he won an all-aged Scurry at the Curragh. Pulled out again two days later, he not surprisingly found the twelve furlongs of the Derby course excessive, though the race was in fact won by another two-year-old, Crystabelle, whose winning margin was an astonishing fifty lengths. Before retiring into winter quarters Roy Neil had been shipped to Liverpool, where he won the Duchy Plate over a mile. Having won the Cork Derby and the Irish Derby, Roy Neil's next appearance was in the Great Northern St Leger over ten furlongs at Stockton in August, which he won as an odds-on favourite should. Having finished at the wrong end of the field in Alice's Ebor Handicap, he resumed his winning ways at Manchester and then finished ninth in the Cesarewitch won by Burnaby. After this race he was purchased for 4,000gns by Mr Greenhalgh, who sent him to join Burnaby's trainer E. J. Hobbs at Lambourn. This transaction turned out rather better for Dr Moorhead than for Mr Greenhalgh, for the nearest that gentleman ever got to seeing a return on his investment was Roy Neil's modest third in the Liverpool Summer Cup. Dr Moorhead's desire to repurchase Roy Neil for stud purposes was frustrated by the colt's sudden death while in training. Roy Neil came from the first Irish crop of his sire Kendal, then standing at the Knockany Stud. By Bend Or out of the Macaroni mare, Windermere, Kendal was bred by the Duke of Westminster, who is reputed to have preferred him as a yearling to his contemporary at Eaton, Ormonde. As a two-year-old Kendal won five of his seven races, including the Ham Stakes at Goodwood and the July Stakes at Newmarket, before breaking down irreparably in the Rous Memorial Stakes. Prior to this misfortune Kendal had narrowly beaten the unraced Ormonde in a trial at Kings-clere, thus becoming the first and only animal ever to finish in front of Westminster's magnificent champion. Twelve months later, when John Porter had saddled the invincible Ormonde to win the St Leger, the grateful Duke offered him either £500 or Kendal. Porter promptly chose the latter, leased him as a stallion and two years later sold him to John Gubbins for 3,000gns. The successes of Roy Neil, Crystabelle and Red Prince II enabled Gubbins to re-sell Kendal to Major Platt for 20,000gns, though not before obtaining two colt foals by Kendal from his useless racemare Morganette . . . The elder, Blairfinde, won the Irish Derby, while Galtee More went on to win the Triple Crown in 1897. Galtee More's triumphs resulted in Kendal's interrupting St Simon's reign as leading sire after seven consecutive seasons. Strangely, Kendal's fortunes declined following his repatriation and he was subsequently sold at the age of eighteen to the Buen Ojo Stud in Argentina, for £10,500. Though deprived of his best chance of a tail-male successor by the sale of his outstanding son, Galtee More, to Russia, Kendal's line was vigorously sustained by Tredennis, through his son Bachelor's Double and to a lesser degree by Sir Edgar and Red Prince II. In addition to the Irish Derby victories of his sons Roy Neil and Blairfinde, the successes of Killeagh and Shanballymore maintained the influence of their grandsire on Ireland's greatest race.

If Roy Neil's sire had been bred in the purple, his dam provided the type of outcross which has traditionally emphasised the strength in depth of Irish breeding, in addition to maintaining the wonderful vigour of Irish bloodstock. Sylva, the dam of Roy Neil, was by Sylvanus, an unknown son of the 1855 Epsom Derby winner, Wild Dayrell. The obscurity of Sylvanus is underlined by the fact that the unraced Sylva was his sole representative in the General Stud Book. Bred by Dr Moorhead, Sylva produced eight other modest winners before foaling Rusialka, who, after a serious accident in training, was saved for stud by the primitive ingenuity of Moorhead and his blacksmith. She rewarded their efforts by producing the Grand National winner Shaun Spadah. Thus, by curious coincidence, did the dams of successive Irish Derby winners become grandams of Grand National heroes.

Of those that failed behind Roy Neil in the Irish Derby, the erratic Wordsworth was the first to make amends, winning over three miles the very next day. The luckless Blancmange reputedly became temperamental, which is less than surprising in view of the questions subsequently asked of him. Having won over a mile and a half as a five-year-old at Baldoyle, he was promptly sent back down the course for a six furlong event and finished second! During the following three seasons he was successfully exploited in selling races in England by a group of heavy gamblers headed by Captain Percy Bewicke and known as the Grately Confederacy. The Dummy, having appeared not to stay at the Curragh, ran Detonator to a head over two miles at Down Royal and renewed the challenge the following day over three miles, going down on this occasion by half a length. Sent to England, he was bought out of a seller by Lady Mabel Sievier, wife of the ebullient Bob, for whom he landed a gamble before being shipped to South Africa. The aristocratically-bred War Cloud, whose dam won both the Anglesey and Railway Stakes, proved useless on the flat and eventually made some amends over fences at such bygone fixtures as Athlone, Kells and Baldoyle. Detonator soon recovered the form which had enabled him to win four good races as a two-year-old. Having twice vanquished The Dummy at Down Royal, he went on to win at Leopardstown, the Curragh and Manchester.

Out of luck as a four-year-old, Detonator repeated his double at Down Royal the following season and eventually concluded an industrious career on a note of triumph in the valuable Jubilee Hurdle at Manchester in 1896. If this was not perhaps a memorable Irish Derby, it nevertheless reflected an improvement in the standard of the race, which augured well for the years ahead.

Wednesday, 29th June, 1892 £310 7 Ran 1½m (Howth Post)

The Irish Derby of 400sovs, by subscription of 15sovs each (to the fund), but 6sovs only if struck out on or before the last day of the September meeting, 1891. The second horse to receive 50sovs and the third 25sovs out of the plate. For three years old. Colts 8st 12lb; fillies 8st 8lb. The winner of the Angleseys and Railways at the Curragh, or of two stakes value 300sovs each, 10lb extra; of the Angleseys or of a stake value 300sovs, or of stakes collectively value 600sovs, 7lb extra; of a stake value 200sovs, 3lb extra. Horses that have never won a stake value 100sovs, allowed 6lb; maidens allowed 10lb; only one of these allowances can be taken. Produce of untried sires or mares allowed 3lb (if claimed at entry), but not for both. Any person entering three horses, his own bona fide sole property, can strike out one at the time appointed for declaring forfeit without having to pay the forfeit.

(28 subs)

1	Mr R. M.Delamere's	ROY NEIL (M. Dawson)	9. 1	Meredith
		B. colt Kendal – Sylva by Sylvanus.		
2	Mr J. D. Wardell's	BLANCMANGE (Mr J. Beasley)	8.12	
		B. colt Plutarch or Castlereagh – Farina.		
3	Mr F. F. Cullen's	THE DUMMY (T. Kavanagh)	9. 5	F. F. Cullen
		Ch. colt Favo – Kitty.		
4	Mr C. J. Blake's	WAR CLOUD (J. Hogan)	8. 2	
		B/Br. colt Ben Battle – Sibyl.		
5	Mr M. A. Maher's	DETONATOR (T. Harris)	9. 2	Meredith
		B. colt Torpedo – Songstress.		
6	Mr C. Kilmurray's	FANESSA (Lawlor)	7. 9	James Dunne
		Br. filly Favo or Skylark – Morning Star.		
PU	Mr W. Brophy's	WORDSWORTH (J. Connolly)	9. 5	
		Ch. colt Kendal – Lady Pitt.		

SP Evens The Dummy; 7/2 Blancmange; 5/1 ROY NEIL; 6/1 Wordsworth; 100/7 Bar.
1 length, 8 lengths.
Winner trained by Mr Rice Meredith at Rathbridge Manor, Curragh.

1893

The value of the Irish Derby – more than double that of the previous year – accurately reflected the development of racing in Ireland at the time. Not only were there more horses than ever in training, particularly three-year-olds, but they were racing for more than twice the prize money offered in 1866, the inaugural year of the Irish Derby. Although only eight eventually faced the starter, the number of sub-scriptions – sixty-one – was the highest since the inception of the race. The crowd, which had foregathered under threatening skies, opted unhesitatingly for Baccarat as the likely winner of the main event. Though he stripped light, Harry Beasley's representative was undoubtedly the form horse. Winner of the Railway Stakes, he had finished in front of Loot, the winner of the Anglesey Sakes, when second to The Jew on his most recent outing. The fact that the Curragh maestro, John Connolly, had wasted severely to ride Nollikens, the highly-regarded Beasley second string, only served to increase confidence in Baccarat, ridden by his owner-trainer. Loot and First Flower both appeared to be weighted out of it, while Guestmaster, who carried the 'French grey, scarlet hoop' of the Senior Steward, had finished behind The Jew and Loot in the Baldoyle Derby. Mat Maher's filly, Bowline, carrying Michael Dawson's colours, owing to a bereavement in her owner's family, had shown nothing in public as a three-year-old.

After a delay at the start Guestmaster and Kendal Green made the running for six furlongs. Here Guestmaster dropped back abruptly, leaving Kendal Green just ahead of Nollikens, First Flower and Baccarat. As they entered the straight First Flower and Baccarat swept past the leaders, with Loot making a determined effort to get into the race. Two furlongs out First Flower and Baccarat were joined by the wide-running Bowline, who hit the front at the distance and held on gamely to beat First Flower a trifle cleverly. Baccarat, appearing not to get the stiff twelve furlongs, faded to finish third, just in front of his stable companion, Nollikens. Thus, for the second time in four years the partnership of Mat Maher, Rice Meredith and Michael Dawson had triumphed.

A second Irish Derby winner for Torpedo, Bowline was bred by her owner out of Eline, by Cremorne, winner of the Epsom Derby, Grand Prix de Paris and Ascot Gold Cup. As a four-year-old Eline won a 'chase at Roscommon for Mat Maher, before retiring to the paddocks at Ballinkeele, where she produced a succession of winners remarkable more for their endurance, than brilliance. Her first produce, Aline, scored her first success as a six-year-old at Punchestown, won a Queen's Plate and a Royal Whip, both over four miles the following year and went on winning good 'chases until twelve years of age. Bowline raced until the age of eleven. Carline won the Kildare Hunt Cup as a six-year-old. Doraline won at six and seven, while Eliminator, in contrast, won the valuable International Foal Plate at Leopardstown as a two-year-old in 1896. Having named Eline's first seven foals in alphabetical order, Mat Maher broke the sequence . . . and with it his luck. On his death in 1901 Eline became the property of Mr J. Kavanagh, for whom she bred only one moderate winner. In the meantime Lavelline, by Laveno, maintained the family tradition by winning almost thirty hurdles and 'chases up to the age of thirteen.

Bowline only ran twice more that year, badly on each occasion. As a four-year-old she recovered her form, winning two Queen's Plates at the Derby meeting in June and two other races over a mile. Transferred to Jewitt's stable at Newmarket as a five-year-old, Bowline's only success was in the valuable Markeaton Handicap at Derby in November, a race which she was to make her own over the next two seasons, without, however, winning anything else. In the tradition of her line Bowline was campaigned in England, Ireland and France for a further four years, winning hurdle races at Auteuil and Nice, before eventually being retired to stud, where she produced only three foals prior to her demise in 1905. One of these, Royal Line, was kept for stud and through her Bowline became the grandam of two good colts in Royal Hackle II and Royal Weaver, winner of the National Produce Stakes. Bowline's victims at the Curragh on that Wednesday in June 1893 went on to prove themselves workmanlike rather than brilliant, accurately reflecting the overall standard. Baccarat became a specialist in National Hunt Flat Races, a rare old gambling medium in those days. In this metier he was twice successful when ridden by a rising young man named James J. Parkinson. However, not even his part in that gentleman's prodigious Turf career sufficed to save poor old Baccarat from an ignominious end pulling a carriage in Antwerp.

Wednesday, 28th June, 1893	**£763**	**8 Ran**	**1½m (Howth Post)**

The Irish Derby of 1000sovs, by subscription of 17sovs each (to the fund), but 8sovs only for horses struck out on or before the first Wednesday in September, 1892. The second horse to receive 150sovs and the third 70sovs out of the plate. For three years old. Colts 8st 12lb; fillies 8st 8lb. The winner of the Angleseys and Railways at the Curragh, or of two stakes value 300sovs each, 10lb extra; of the Angleseys or of a stake value 300sovs, or of stakes collectively value 600sovs, 7lb extra; of a stake value 200sovs, 3lb extra. Horses that have never won a stake value 100sovs allowed 6lb; maidens allowed 10lb; only one of these allowances can be taken. Produce of untried sires or mares allowed 3lb (if claimed at entry), but not for both. Any person entering three horses, his own bona fide sole property, can strike out one at the time appointed for declaring forfeit without having to pay the forfeit.

(61 subs)

1	Mr M. A. Maher's	BOWLINE (M. Dawson)	8. 5	Meredith
		Ch. filly Torpedo – Eline by Cremorne.		
2	Mr H. E. Linde's	FIRST FLOWER (W. Hoysted)	9. 5	Linde
		B. colt Favo – Primrose.		
3	Mr H. Beasley's	BACCARAT (Owner)	9. 2	H. Beasley
		B. colt King of Trumps – Bounce by Victor.		
4	Mr H. Beasley's	NOLLIKENS (J. Connolly)	7.13 (car. 8.0)	Beasley
		B. colt Atheling – Vera by The Baron.		
5	Mr T. G. Gordon's	LOOT (Mr T. Beasley)	9. 5	Gordon
		Br. colt Ben Battle – Tees Treasure.		
6	Mr P. J. Hartigan's	KENDAL GREEN (John Doyle)	7. 9	
		Ch. filly Kendal – Buda.		
0	Mr S. M. Nolan's	GUESTMASTER (T. Harris)	8. 2	Dunne
		Ch. colt St Gatien – Bide-a-Wee.		
0	Mr H. E. Linde's	WORSTED (C. Whelan)	7.13	Linde
		B. gelding Kendal – Blue Stockings.		

SP Evens Baccarat; 6/1 Nollikens; 8/1 BOWLINE; 10/1 Guestmaster, First Flower; 100/5 Bar.
½ length, 4 lenths. 2m 50s.
Winner trained by Mr Rice Meredith at Rathbride Manor, Curragh.

1894

The field of ten represented the best of their generation in Ireland and was further spiced by the presence of the solitary English raider, Blairfinde. Prime local fancy was the Linde representative, Ball Coote, winner of four races as a two-year-old and more recently a good third in the Baldoyle Derby under the welter weight of 10st 2lbs. On this form he had the measure of the two who had finished in front of him at Baldoyle, Arline and Gazeteer. Hartstown, a winner at Baldoyle in May and subsequently beaten a neck by Ash Stick at Leopardstown, was strongly fancied by those generally well-informed in these matters. The English challenger, Blairfinde, one of the first horses sent to Sam Darling at Beckhampton by his owner-breeder John Gubbins, had run only twice, both times unplaced as a two-year-old. An over-grown, ungainly animal, he had drawn from Ball Coote's trainer, Eyre Linde, the comment: '. . . a damned coach horse; and if he wins our Derby I will eat him!' Nonetheless, stable confidence in Blairfinde rapidly proved infectious, with the result that he eventually shared favouritism with Ball Coote, Hartstown being the only other to attract any real support. As the runners paraded the huge crowd took up vantage points under cloudless skies to witness Ball Coote and Blairfinde renewing the ancient national rivalry.

Arline and Hebron were first to show, ahead of Blairfinde, Ball Coote and Gauntlet, with the stable companions Ash Stick and Miss Snap bringing up the rear. At the mile post Clayton pushed Hebron clear, with Ball Coote already coming under pressure. Into the straight Hebron led from Gazeteer, with Blairfinde and Hartstown taking closer order behind them. Riding to orders to avoid any threat of interference, Garrett kicked for home on Blairfinde, who immediately surged clear of his struggling rivals. Drawing further ahead with each raking stride, Blairfinde passed the post ten lengths to the good. The awesome ease of his victory surprised even the most ardent among Blairfinde's supporters, to say nothing of its effect on the stunned Ball Coote camp. Hartstown won a good race for second place from the Blake pair, Hebron and Gazeteer. As a delighted Tommy Garrett brought Blairfinde back to the winner's circle, a crest-fallen Eyre Linde offered his congratulations to the quietly triumphant Gubbins and Darling, pronouncing the winner: 'A devil of a fine horse!' Having said his piece, Linde was heard to reflect that John Gubbins, a long-standing friend and patron and currently Linde's house guest, might have at least told his host what the 'coach horse' could do!

Dogged by training difficulties, Blairfinde never appeared on a racecourse again and was retired to stand at Knockany, the place of his birth. Despite receiving extensive patronage, particularly following the Triple Crown triumph of Galtee More in 1897, Blairfinde never really justified his owner's act of faith in refusing an offer of £10,000 for the colt when he retired to stud. Revenue (Liverpool St Leger), Dibs (Ebor Handicap), Demure (Cesarewitch) and Port Blair were about the best of his stock up to and beyond the time of his death from an internal haemorrhage in 1908. Despite the brevity of his racing career, Blairfinde's ability was adequately endorsed by the subsequent exploits of those he had left for dead on that sunny afternoon in June. Hebron won the very next day and went on to win the Woking-

Michael Dawson. *Leading jockey turned trainer, whose three riding successes in the Irish Derby were followed by a similar number as a trainer. Having assumed Linde's role as the outstanding Irish trainer, the master of Rathbride headed the list of Irish trainers ten times since records began in 1906 until his death twenty years later. Source:* Irish Field.

Blairfinde, *'that damned coach horse' ran away with the Irish Derby in 1895. His dam, Morganette, subsequently produced two Epsom Derby winners, Galtee More and Ard Patrick. Shown holding Blairfinde is Tommy Garret, his partner in that cantering Curragh success. Source:* Irish Field.

ham Stakes as a four-year-old. Gazeteer, like good wine, improved with age, winning consistently for a further five seasons, notably in the hands of that astute jockey Charlie Wood. Gauntlet proved an equally prolific winner, successful no less than ten times in one year for Captain Wentworth Hope-Johnstone. Ball Coote went through the rest of the season undefeated, making his failure in the Irish Derby all the harder to understand. Arline and Ash Stick likewise continued to pay their way for many years, the latter winning on the flat at Leopardstown all of seven years later, ridden by no less than Danny Maher.

However, the full significance of Blairfinde's place in the roll of honour of the Irish Derby lies neither in his abbreviated racing career, nor in his disappointing stud record. Rather does he merit remembrance as the forerunner of an unrivalled record of triumph involving an owner, a trainer and a broodmare. The story of the wonderful achievements of the offspring of Morganette, carrying the colours of John Gubbins and trained by Sam Darling is Turf legend.

John Gubbins was a substantial figure in Irish racing, in every sense of the word. Born in the family seat in Limerick in 1839, John Gubbins rapidly achieved renown as a sportsman, being an adept and enthusiastic steeplechase rider, despite his size and weight. Though forced to forsake raceriding for hunting, shooting and salmon fishing, he remained fascinated by steeple-chasing, keeping a succession of notable jumpers with his friend Eyre Linde at Eyrefield Lodge. With these he was never afraid to take on the stars of his elder brother's string, trained by Dan Broderick at Mountjoy Lodge. Another challenge of which John Gubbins was seldom afraid was a tilt at the Ring and he is reputed to have wagered virtually his entire fortune on Linde's Whisper Low when that horse carried off the Grand Steeplechase at Auteuil in 1882. On his brother's tragic death John Gubbins assumed control of Knockany and Bruree and proceeded to turn them into the finest stud complex in Ireland. One of his purchases was an ugly, useless, but beautifully bred mare named Morganette. Having produced one winning filly by the Knockany stallion Kendal, she then produced Blairfinde. Shortly afterwards John Gubbins became so incensed at the abuse of his Limerick Staghounds by the Land League that he forsook hunting in Ireland to concentrate on racing in England, having headed the list of winning owners in his native land in 1883, 1885 and 1889. In line with this decision he transferred his stable from the care of Mr G. W. Lushington to the infinitely capable hands of Sam Darling at Beckhampton. Blairfinde's Irish Derby was only the beginning . . . Three years later Morganette produced another colt by Kendal. Such was the size and presence of the foal that Gubbins promptly named him after the highest peak overlooking his stud: Galtee More. Defeated only twice in his life, Galtee More won the Triple crown and was sold to Russia for £21,000. Five years later Gubbins and Darling struck again with another champion colt out of Morganette. This was Ard Patrick, whose victory in the Derby robbed Sceptre of an unique nap hand in the Classics. To prove that this was no fluke Ard Patrick again beat Sceptre in the Eclipse Stakes in 1903 in what has been described as one of the finest races of the century. Ard Patrick went to Germany for a similar figure and though Morganette bred nothing else of comparable quality, she more than merited her simple epitaph in Knockany, where she shares a headstone with May Day, 'who immortalised this stud'. However, John Gubbins was not spared to write these words, for this martyr to gout had succumbed to bronchitis in 1906, predeceasing his celebrated broodmare by three years.

In Sam Darling Gubbins chose wisely and well, for Morganette's stock were invariably slow to come to hand and no trainer ever exercised greater patience in pursuit of perfection than the master of Beckhampton. Son and grandson of jockeys – his grandfather won the St Leger on Rockingham in 1833 – Sam Darling soon forsook the saddle for training, at which he became recognized as a master of his art. When the Beckhampton horses were ready they carried a gloss of health and vitality which set them apart from their rivals. Striking both in personality and appearance, capable of being taken for a magistrate, Sam Darling ran his large farm and stable with a discipline and efficiency which, allied to a sense of tact and humour, made him the perfect foil to the gout-induced vagaries of John Gubbins. Forced through ill-health to retire just before World War I, Sam Darling lived long enough to see his son Fred follow in his footsteps, becoming champion trainer on numerous occasions and saddling no less than seven Derby winners. His other son, Sam H. Darling, also became a successful trainer and his son-in-law, Richard Marsh, became famous in his own right as the trainer of three Royal Derby winners. Big, bluff John Gubbins and dapper little Sam Darling were alike in many ways, even to their respective dying wishes. John Gubbins stipulated that, as he had always aspired to breed fast horses, so should his hearse be pulled at speed on his final journey. Darling decreed for his part that the streets of Beckhampton be swept and sanded and that his coffin be borne to the graveyard on a freshly painted one of his own farm carts.

If Blairfinde's jockey palls to insignificance beside his formidable owner and trainer, he can scarcely be blamed for that. Tommy Garrett was a member of the staff at Beckhampton, who got little more than the odd mount. Having achieved his finest hour at the Curragh, he rode a few more winners for the stable in the ensuing seasons, though not sufficient to leave him looking anything less than quietly content photographed in his working clothes holding his favourite mount on the gallops at Beckhampton.

Wednesday, 27th June, 1894	**£560**	**10 Ran**	**1½m**

The Irish Derby of 700sovs, by subscription of 15sovs each, but 6sovs only for horses struck out on or before the 6th September, 1893. The second horse to receive 100sovs and the third 25sovs out of the plate. For three years old. Colts 8st 12lb; filies 8st 8lb. The winner of the Angleseys and Railways at the Curragh, or of two stakes value 300sovs each, 10lb extra; of the Angleseys or of a stake value 300sovs, or of stakes collectively value 600sovs, 7lb extra; of a stake value 200sovs, 3lb extra. Horses that have never won a stake value 100sovs, allowed 6lb; maidens allowed 10lb; only one of these allowances can be taken. Produce of untried sires or mares allowed 3lb (if claimed at entry), but not for both. Any person entering three horses, his own bona fide sole property, can strike out one at the time appointed for declaring forfeit without having to pay the forfeit.

(49 subs)

1	Mr John Gubbins's	BLAIRFINDE (W. T. Garrett)	8. 2
		Br. colt Kendal – Morganette by Springfield.	
2	Mr J. Daly's	HARTSTOWN (W. Taylor)	9. 2
		B. colt Atheling – Sunnyside.	
3	Mr C. J. Blake's	HEBRON (W. Clayton)	7.13
		Br. colt Kilwarlin – Seraphine by Hermit.	
4	Mr C. J. Blake's	GAZETTEER (W. Horton)	9. 2
		Ch. colt Gallinule – Award.	
5	Mr H. Beasley's	GAUNTLET (John Doyle)	7.13
		Ch. colt Gallinule – Lady Louisa by Solon.	
6	Mr H. E. Linde's	STARLIGHT III (C. Whelan)	8.12
		Ch. colt Castlereagh – Pink Demine by Lord Ronald.	
7	Mr H. E. Linde's	BALL COOTE (W. Hoysted)	9. 2
		Ch. colt Gallinule – Valerie.	
8	Mr W. Ashe's	ASH STICK (M. Dawson)	9. 1
		B. colt St Gatien – Cecropia.	
0	Col. Thomson's	ARLINE (A. Magee)	
		B. filly Baliol – Bohemian Girl by Balfe.	
0	Mr R. M. Dellamere's	MISS SNAP (J. Westlake)	7.12
		Br. filly Marden – Sylva.	

SP 2/1 BLAIRFINDE, Ball Coote; 6/1 Hartstown; 100/12 Bar.

Won in a canter by 10 lengths, 2½ lengths, ½ length. 2m 42s.

Winner trained by Mr S. Darling at Beckhampton, England.

1895

If strength in numbers meant anything in racing the Irish Derby of 1895 must have been won by a runner sired by the leading sire of the day, the recently-deceased Favo. That it meant as little then as it does now was reflected in the betting market, dominated by the only two runners of the six-strong field not by Favo. The odds-on favourite was Captain Machell's Portmarnock, a good fourth to Victor Wild in the Jubilee Stakes at Kempton six weeks earlier. The only other runner to attract any volume of support in a weak market was 'R. M. Delamere's' Snap. Though this half-brother to the same owner's Roy Neil had no worthwhile public form to recommend him, it was common knowledge that Michael Dawson, the colt's trainer and rider, had wasted for weeks to ride him in the hopes of winning his fourth Irish Derby in six years. Favoloo had won the Baldoyle Derby easily enough, but appeared unlikely to confirm that form with Burnett on vastly altered terms. Threatening skies gave way to thunder and lightning, which, though too late to ease the rock hard going, resulted in a smaller crowd than in recent years.

Dan Mack, the mount of the former crack jockey, George Barrett, went off at a furious pace ahead of Favoloo, Instability and Portmarnock. Still in front at the half way stage, Dan Mack led by a reduced margin from a closely-grouped quartet, with only Snap beginning to show signs of distress. Joined now by Burnett and Favoloo, Dan Mack tore into the straight, with the hot favourite, Portmarnock, poised on the heels of the leaders. Just as Portmarnock swept to the fore, Dan Mack galloped straight into the heels of Favoloo, injuring the latter to such an extent that John Doyle was forced to pull him up. With the only possible danger thus removed, Portmarnock surged away to win by twelve lengths, the longest winning margin in the history of the race. Burnett outstayed Instability to finish a remote second. Immediately after the race John Doyle lodged an objection against George Barrett for foul riding, which the Stewards found was not sustained.

A big dark brown colt, Portmarnock was one of the last animals bred by the late William Brophy of Herbertstown, one of the foremost Irish breeders of his day, who had himself won the Irish Derby with King of the Bees fifteen years previously. The first of no fewer than six Irish Derby winners sired by Gallinule, Portmarnock was out of Sleeping Beauty, whose sire, Ben Battle, had won the Irish Derby in 1874. Bred by George Knox from his mare The Beauty, Sleeping Beauty was a half-sister to Kildare, winner of the Anglesey and Railway Stakes in 1886. Fourth in the Irish Derby and successful both on the flat and over fences for Dan Broderick, Sleeping Beauty reached her zenith as a broodmare in 1895, when Rock Dove, an own-sister to Portmarnock, added the English Cesarewitch to the Irish equivalent she had won a year previously. In addition, her two-year-old, Dosser, won his only race later the same season.

When successful at the Curragh, Portmarnock carried the well-known colours of Captain J. O. Machell, who had recently purchased a half-share in the colt from C. J. Blake and T. L. Plunkett. After the Irish Derby Portmarnock was transferred from Heath House, Maryborough to Bedford Lodge, the Newmarket stable, where James Jewitt trained a very successful string under the overall management of

Captain Machell. Second in the Liverpool Autumn Cup, ahead of Rock Dove, Portmarnock ran only twice the following season, winning the Rous Memorial Stakes at Royal Ascot, Machell's favourite hunting ground. Off the course as a five-year-old, Portmarnock returned to win the Salford Borough Handicap at Manchester in his fifth and final season. Having stood for four seasons at the Kentford Stud, Portmarnock was sent to Germany. Subsequently brought back to stand at Captain Northey-Hopkins' stud in Staffordshire, Portmarnock failed to make a name for himself, fetching a paltry 55gns at his owner's dispersal sale in 1911. His victims in the Irish Derby accomplished little on the racecourse and still less at stud.

Captain James Octavius Machell, part-owner of Portmarnock, was one of the most notable figures in English racing during the last quarter of the nineteenth century. Born in 1838, the son of a Beverley rector, Machell was a descendant of the Machells of Crackenthorpe Hall, Westmoreland, the family seat for more than twenty generations. Commissioned in the Army, Machell resigned in 1863, because he had been refused leave to attend the St Leger. An accomplished athlete, he had for a time been stationed on the Curragh and it was while in Ireland that he once won a substantial wager by springing from the floor onto a high mantlepiece, twisting in mid-air and landing faced towards his incredulous companions, still holding a glass unspilled in his hand. It was during his stay in Ireland that he began to display his uncanny eye for a horse. Though far from affluent on leaving the Army, Machell did own a horse named Bacchus, which he produced for the Prince of Wales's Stakes at Newmarket, backing it to win him £10,000 to £400. In surviving an objection to win, Bacchus 'made' Machell. He then became racing manager for 'The Squire', Sir Henry Chaplin, for whom he won the Epsom Derby with Hermit (1867), winning a fortune for Chaplin and ruining the Marquis of Hastings in the process. The next Derby winner under Machell's astute management was Harvester, who deadheated with St Gatien in 1884. In the meantime Machell's extraordinary genius for realising the potential of a raw young horse had seen him successful in three Grand Nationals, with Disturbance, Reugny and Regal. However, Machell's greatest triumph on the Turf still lay ahead . . . Not only was he directly responsible for the mating which produced Isinglass, but he also masterminded the problem-ridden preparation of that outstanding Triple Crown winner during four seasons in which this brilliant but basically unsound horse was beaten only once.

'The Captain', as he was universally known on the Turf, occupied a position in racing which could scarcely be said to exist today. Established as an unrivalled judge of a horse, a talented trainer (though he invariably employed experts in their own right in this capacity), and an astute and fearless gambler, Machell attracted a succession of wealthy young men anxious to cut a dash on the Turf. Both as mentor and manager, Machell proved generally successful, and if some of his proteges found that racing threatened financial ruin, it was often in spite of Machell's advice rather than because of it. George Lambton, who might be said to have succeeded Machell in the role of introducing 'young bloods' to racing, described the older man thus: 'One could not say that he was a popular man; in fact he was more feared than liked . . . There were two sides to his nature, one cold, hard, calculating and suspicious, the other generous, affectionate, simple as a child's; the contrast was so violent that it was almost impossible to believe him the same man.' In his later years Machell admitted that his suspicious nature had cost him dear, losing him the services of Mr J. M. Richardson, after they had combined to win successive Grand Nationals, and also of 'The Demon', George Fordham, the jockey whom he most admired. However, it was his slighting of Fred Archer, shortly before Archer's suicide, which preyed most on his mind, so much so that he subsequently made two attempts on his own life. A martyr to gout in his latter years, this eminent figure of Victorian racing died in 1902.

The association between Captain Machell and Charles Blake was one of long standing and the closeness of the connection was further emphasized by the position of S. C. Jeffrey as trainer at Heath House, after nearly twenty years in Machell's employment in Newmarket. Hard-working, conscientious, close-mouthed and partial to an occasional gamble, 'Shem' Jeffrey held sway at Heath House for over thirty years. During this period he trained three Irish Derby winners, the winners of all the other Irish Classics, including Soldennis and Lady Violette, successful in the in-augural runnings of the Irish Guineas, and developed Soldennis into the highest stakes winner to date in Irish racing. Though by no means his most successful charge, Jeffrey always regarded Oppressor as the best, if unluckiest horse that he ever trained. In recognition of his years of loyal service, Charles Blake stipulated in his will that Jeffrey be kept on the Heath House payroll for the rest of his days. Unfortunately for himself, Jeffrey did not take kindly to the intervention of Colonel Arthur Blake in the supervision of the stable. Matters came to a head when Jeffrey was called to account for his policy in regard to the flying Fohanaun, on whom he undoubtedly intended to have a 'touch' for himself. Realising that Death does indeed bring changes, Jeffrey sacked himself. After training in the north of Ireland for a short time, Jeffrey retired to his native Newmarket, where he died in 1933, at the age of seventy.

William Clayton, *rider of Port-marnock. The Curragh was to prove the scene of his finest and darkest hours. Source:* Racing Illustrated.

Portmarnock, *the first of six Irish Derby winners sired by the mighty Gallinule. Source:* Racing Illustrated.

William Clayton, the rider of Portmarnock, was also a former Machell employee, before coming to Ireland, where he was immediately successful. At the time of his win in the Irish Derby Clayton was on the crest of a wave, Portmarnock being but one of eight winners to his credit in the course of the three-day meeting. For whatever reason, Clayton's popularity as a jockey declined dramatically at the turn of the century, so much so that in 1904 his only placing from a handful of rides was when third on Mr J. Lonsdale's un-named Copestone filly at the Curragh in April. Whether it was the sight of the same filly winning the Irish Oaks under another that proved the final straw was never revealed . . . Two days later, at the Curragh, the scene of his greatest triumph, William Clayton died by his own hand.

One other aspect of an otherwise unmemorable Irish Derby is worthy of recall. It related to John Doyle's objection against George Barrett on the grounds of foul riding. Though unsuccessful, Doyle's complaint was almost certainly justified, for the unfortunate George Barrett was by then in the grip of insanity, which was to lead to his premature death three years later. A leading rider in England since his youth, Barrett had once been stable jockey for the powerful John Porter stable, winning the Triple Crown on Common in 1891. The following year his extraordinary performance on La Fleche, lagging at the rear of the field and shouting and gesticulating at the other riders until all too late, undoubtedly cost that good mare the Derby. Though he subsequently rode an excellent race to win the St Leger on Orme, beating La Fleche, Barrett's increasingly lunatic behaviour made him a hazard on the racecourse. The hapless John Doyle was destined to be one of the last of poor Barrett's victims.

GALLINULE

In tracing the development of flat racing in Ireland certain events stand out as being of profound significance. Undoubtedly one of these was the advent of Gallinule at Brownstown Stud in 1891. His influence on the standard and status of Irish blood-stock was both immediate and enduring. By Isonomy, out of a durable mare named Moorhen, Gallinule was foaled in England in 1884, when his dam was eleven years old. Raced since she was three, Moorhen won six selling plates in her first season, had a colt foal at five, slipped her foal the following season and was promptly put back in training, winning a further twenty races of every description until finally retired, aged nine. Gallinule won three races as a two-year-old, proving himself just short of top class. In his second season his owner, Lord Savernake, was warned off, whereupon Gallinule became the property of the talented, if misguided young Scottish millionaire and amateur rider, George Alexander Baird. His new owner, who raced as 'Mr Abingdon', soon regretted his £5,100 outlay, for the big, handsome chestnut became both a 'bleeder' and a 'roarer'. After three fruitless seasons Baird retired Gallinule and hawked him around as a potential stallion. He had begun to despair of ridding himself of his good-looking but useless animal when he received a firm offer of 1,000gns from Captain Henry Greer. An astonished Baird was heard to enquire, 'Who's the mug? I hope he's got the money.' The ill-fated Baird did not live to eat his words.

Harry Greer had begun a lasting association with racing in 1888 and moved to live in Ireland shortly afterwards. On purchasing Brownstown, historic home of the legendary Birdcatcher, Greer had courageously embarked on a search for a stallion with the potential to sire Classic winners. Although Irish-breds had won the great English races, they were sufficiently few and far between to be dismissed as freaks. The English racing Establishment did not consider Ireland capable of producing high-class flat horses on a regular basis. Having overcome an initial period of misgiving, during which he failed to sell Gallinule for £300 because of his widely-known infirmities, Greer offered his stallion's services free to approved mares to give Gallinule an opportunity to prove his worth.

As though aware of his owner's enterprising act of faith and conscious of his links with Brownstown through his great-great-grandsire, Birdcatcher, Gallinule sired Portmarnock, winner of the Irish Derby, in only his second crop. He repeated this triumph in the following year with Gulsabark. To set the seal on his merit, his progeny proceeded to monopolise Ireland's premier race between 1898 and 1901. Breeders who had fought shy of Greer's unsound horse now found it necessary to book nominations a year in advance. In 1898 Harry Greer's judgement was vindicated in England when Gallinule's son, Wildfowler, carried Greer's own colours to victory in the St Leger. But even better was yet to come, for in 1904 Gallinule's best daughter, Pretty Polly, swept to victory in the One Thousand Guineas, Oaks and St

Wednesday, 26th June, 1895	**£562**	**6 Ran**	**1½m (Howth Post)**

The Irish Derby of 700sovs, by subscription of 15sovs each, but 6sovs only for horses struck out on or before the 5th September, 1894. The second horse to receive 100sovs and the third 25sovs out of the plate. For three years old. Colts 8st 12lb; fillies 8st 8lb. The winner of the Angleseys and Railways at the Curragh, or of two stakes value 300sovs each, 10lb extra; of the Angleseys or of a stake value 300sovs, or of stakes collectively value 600sovs, 7lb extra; of a stake value 200sovs, 3lb extra. Horses that have never won a stake value 100sovs, allowed 6lb; maidens allowed 10 1lb; only one of these allowances can be taken. Produce of untried sires and mares allowed 3lb (if claimed at entry), but not for both. Any person entering three horses, his own bona fide sole property, can strike out one at the time appointed for declaring forfeit without having to pay the forfeit.

(54 subs)

1	Capt. Machell's	PORTMARNOCK (W. Clayton)	9. 5	Jeffrey
		Br. colt Gallinule – The Sleeping Beauty by Ben Battle.		
2	Mr J. Reid's	BURNETT (W. Hoysted)	9. 1	
		Ch. colt Favo – Valerie.		
3	Mr H. Beasley's	INSTABILITY (A. Behan)	8.12	Beasley
		Ch. filly Favo – Homeless by The Rover.		
4	Mr R. M. Delamere's	SNAP (M. Dawson)	8.2 (car. 8.3)	Dawson
		Br. colt Waif or Coracle – Sylva.		
5	Mr H. E. Linde's	DAN MACK (G. Barrett)	7.13	Linde
		Ch. gelding Favo – Skarte.		
PU	Mr St J. Cambridge's	FAVOLOO (John Doyle)	9. 2	
		Ch. colt Favo – Loo by Arbitrator.		

SP 2/5 PORTMARNOCK; 6/1 Snap; 8/1 Favoloo; 10/1 Bar.

Won in a canter by 12 lengths, 3 lengths.

Winner trained by Mr S. Jeffrey at Heath House, Maryborough.

The Stewards having investigated a complaint of foul riding on the part of George Barrett, made by John Doyle, and having taken the evidence of other jockeys riding in the race, considered that the complaint was not sustained and that no blame attaches to Barrett.

Leger and went on to prove herself one of the great racemares of all time. By now Gallinule commanded the fee of 200gns and underlined his value, even at that figure, by the Classic successes of Night Hawk and Slieve Gallion. Another of his fillies, Hammerkop, won the Cesarewitch before producing the Derby winner, Spion Kop.

By the time of his death at Brownstown, on 9th January 1912, Gallinule had twice been champion sire in England, a feat only once previously achieved by a stallion based in Ireland – Birdcatcher. His progeny won over £250,000, a colossal sum by the standards of the time, and he headed the list of Sires and Broodmares on no less than five occasions. It is entirely appropriate that today the Gallinule Stakes at the Curragh should be a recognized Irish Derby trial, for no stallion contributed more to Ireland's greatest race or to the status of Irish bloodstock.

1896

In contrast to previous years the Irish Derby bore an extremely open appearance, for an undistinguished crop of three-year-olds had so far failed to produce an obvious favourite. For regular racegoers the Irish Derby also lacked another familiar ingredient . . . a runner from Eyrefield Lodge, trained by H. E. Linde. Long acknowledged as the greatest trainer ever to practise in Ireland, Linde had been forced by an illness, which was shortly to prove fatal, to dispose of his horses at the end of 1895. Though he had only once been successful in the race, Linde had scarcely let a year pass without at least one runner in the Irish Derby since 1880. At the time he disbanded his stable Henry Eyre Linde had headed the list of winning owners in Ireland for the sixth successive year, a record which remains unequalled.

Deprived of a form favourite, the huge, sun-baked crowd opted to follow the stable in form. Such was the luck of the Rossmore Lodge stable in recent weeks, the stable cat would probably have won. Accordingly The Mute was installed an easy-to-back favourite to atone for the failure of his full-brother, The Dummy, four years earlier. Other public fancies were Gulsalberk, said to be ahead of his stablemate Glenbower, and Fairy Isle, a good winner at Baldoyle. The latter carried the contagious confidence of his owner, bookmaker John Reese, who had clad his ample figure in his 'Royal blue and white' for the occasion. The Widger brothers, still elated by their Aintree triumph with Wild Man from Borneo, had high hopes of an unusual double with their un-named Buda colt. The only other to attract support, mostly for a 'place' was the gigantic Josephus, a model of consistency and expected to improve upon his length defeat in the Baldoyle Derby.

For more than half the journey the running was made by the outsiders Calyce and Bird of Flight, who only gave way to Conquering Hero on the turn for home. Determined to make the most of his advantage, 'Tommy' Lushington kicked for home on Conquering Hero, now shadowed by Gulsalberk and The Mute. Neither Lushington nor the many backers of The Mute were allowed to hope for long; once in the straight Gulsalberk swept past Conquering Hero and had no difficulty in

John Gubbins, *large both in stature and standing in racing and breeding at the turn of the century, founder of Bruree and Knockany, the home of his fabulous mare Morganette. Source:* Irish Field.

S. C. 'Shem' Jeffrey, *who turned out three Irish Derby winners from the historic Heath House stable. Source:* Irish Field.

repelling the despairing challenge of The Mute all the way to the line. Beaten over seven lengths into third place on Conquering Hero, Mr Lushington promptly lodged an objection against the winning jockey, Alf Aylin, for foul riding. Just as a year earlier, the objection was equally promptly overruled.

A second successive winner of the Irish Derby for his sire, Gallinule and for his trainer, S. C. Jeffrey, Gulsalberk provided Charles Blake with his third success in the race. Senior Steward at the time, this popular and progressive Turf administrator had previously been successful with Sylph (1883) and St Kevin (1835). All three had been bred by their owner, who had, of course, a quarter interest in Portmarnock, successful twelve months earlier. Rosamene, the dam of Gulsalberk, despite the 'touch of the tarbrush', which rendered her ineligible for inclusion in the General Stud Book, proved a good servant to C. J. Blake, winning seven races from five furlongs to two miles, before becoming a successful matron. She was by Arbitrator, already the sire of two Irish Derby winners in St Kevin and Theodolite, and certainly the best horse bred at the Blake ancestral home, Towerhill, Co. Mayo. Regrettably, Gulsalberk failed to fulfil the promise exhibited in the Irish Derby, for he was never again even placed in two seasons. The Mute, Conquering Hero, Bird on the Wing and Fairy Isle all managed to make some contribution to their keep. Josephus, for whom the Irish Derby simply came too soon, eventually filled into his massive frame and went on to win all sorts of races over the next five years. Calyce, cruelly described as the ugliest mare ever to look through a bridle, later confounded her critics by producing Shanballymore, winner of the Irish Derby.

In winning the Irish Derby on Gulsalberk, Alfred Aylin joined the band of jockeys successful at their first attempt. Yet another in a lengthy succession of English riders attached to the Heath House stable, Alf Aylin was the eldest of three jockey brothers. Though he only rode in Ireland for three seasons, and then had to share the stable rides, Alf Aylin won most of the major races in the Irish Calendar at the time. After the 1897 season, in which he won the Irish Oaks on Dabchick, rising weight obliged Aylin to return to England and a new career over fences. He was later followed at Heath House by his brother Clyde, likewise successful in the Irish Derby and Irish champion jockey in 1922, the year of his death.

Wednesday, 24th June, 1896 **£560** **10 Ran** **1½m**

The Irish Derby of 700sovs, by subscription of 15sovs each, but 6sovs only for horses struck out on or before the 4th September, 1895. The second horse to receive 100sovs and the third 25sovs out of the plate. For three years old. Colts 8st 12lb; fillies 8st 8lb. The winner of the Angleseys and Railways at the Curragh, or of two stakes value 300sovs each, 10lb extra; of the Angleseys or of a stake value 300sovs, or of stakes collectively value 600sovs, 7lb extra; of a stake value 200sovs, 3lb extra. Horses that have never won a stake value 100sovs, allowed 6lb; maidens allowed 10lb; only one of these allowances can be taken. Produce of untried sires or mares allowed 3lb (if claimed at entry), but not for both. Any person entering three horses, his own bona fide sole property, can strike out one at the time appointed for declaring forfeit without having to pay the forfeit.

(54 subs)

1	Mr C. J. Blake's	GULSALBERK (Alf. Aylin) B. colt Gallinule – Rosamene by Arbitrator. (NOT IN GSB)	8. 2	Jeffrey
2	Mr F. F. Cullen's	THE MUTE (J. Waterson) Ch. colt Favo – Kitty by Remorse.	8. 6	Owner
3	Mr N. B. Johnson's	CONQUERING HERO (Mr G. W. Lushington) Br. colt Gallinule – Moira.	8.12	Owner
4	Mr J. Reese's	FAIRY ISLE (W. Horton) B. colt Oberon – Glen Isla.	8. 9	Orton
5	Mr John Widger's	BUDA COLT (M. Dawson) B. colt Glenvannon – Buda.	8.3 (car 8.4)	
6	Mr R. Richard's	CALYCE (T. Almack) B. filly Kendal – Calaite.	7.12	
7	Mr S. E. Shirley's	JOSEPHUS (T. Lane) B. colt Favo – Maria Theresa by Kingcraft.	8. 2	
8	Mr E. Smithwick's	GLENBOWER (T. Kavanagh) B. colt Conservator – Niniche.	8.12	Jeffrey
9	Captain Peel's	BIRD OF FLIGHT (J. Wynne) Br. colt Loved One – Barometer.	7.13	
10	Mr M. A. Maher's	ZELNE (F. Widdowfield) Ch. filly Zagazig – Minute Gun.	7. 9	

SP 4/1 The Mute; 5/1 Fairy Isle, Buda Colt; 6/1 GULSALBERK; 100/12 Josephus; 100/8 Bar.
Won cleverly by 2 lengths, 5 lengths.
Winner trained by Mr S. C. Jeffrey at Heath House, Maryborough.

Mr Lushington, rider of the third horse Conquering Hero, lodged a complaint of foul riding against Aylin, rider of the winner Gulsalberk, but it was not sustained.

1897

Not even their most ardent admirers could have compared any of the eight runners to the Irish-bred champion, Galtee More, winner of the Epsom Derby four weeks previously, the middle leg of his Triple Crown. Two-year-old form was represented by Field Day, winner of three races, including the Beresford Stakes, when owned by Lord Fermoy. He was now trained in England, as was Electric Ray, second to him in the Beresfords. Best chances of an Irish victory appeared to lie with Mr W. P. Cullen's Wales, even though he had finished only third to the two expatriates in the Beresford Stakes, receiving weight from both. Electric Ray had not appeared in public in 1897. Field Day had run well in the Royal Hunt Cup two weeks previously. Wales had finished third in the April Stakes, a valuable trial, in which he had been narrowly beaten by a newcomer, The Bereft. Of the other contenders, Cashmere and Head the Trick had won their last races, both at Leopardstown, while Frenchhaven had not been out and White Hackle had achieved nothing. Field Day was installed as favourite, only to be ousted by Wales, who was regarded as the pick on looks. Overnight rain had left the going unusually good as a huge crowd watched the field parade in glorious sunshine.

The start was delayed for twenty minutes by the antics of Frenchhaven, whose unfortunate rider faced suspension for disobedience at the start of an earlier race. When they finally got away, the fractious Frenchhaven immediately shot clear of Wales, White Hackle and Cashmere, with Head the Trick bringing up the rear. At the top of the hill White Hackle moved into second place as the field closed up. Swinging down the hill the pace improved, Frenchhaven compounded and Wales, White Hackle and Electric Ray raced together into the straight, with Field Day and Head the Trick taking closer order. As the leaders struggled for supremacy, first Electric Ray and then White Hackle appeared to have beaten Wales. However the locally-trained colt wore down both challengers to win cleverly by three parts of a length from White Hackle, with the fast-finishing Field Day, baulked in the straight, beating Electric Ray by a head for third place.

Wales was bred in Charleville, Co. Cork, by Mr P. Ryan, who leased him to his trainer, W. P. Cullen, whose 'Black, pink hoop and cap' he carried. He was from one of the few crops sired by Belgrave, a useful handicapper bred by the Duke of Westminster, out of Delilah, by the Duke's Derby winner, Bend Or. Belgrave was stood by A. F. G. Cornelius Jr in Borris-in-Ossory, where he died at the early age of eleven, two years before his son's Derby triumph. Wales' dam, Victoria, bred relatively few foals during a lengthy stud career, of which Wales was the best. Given little time to rest on his laurels, Wales finished last of four in his next race, over five furlongs, second over one mile at Manchester, before winning a three-mile Queen's Plate at the Curragh. Third over a mile at Leopardstown in November, he finished the season by running second over six furlongs at Manchester. Cullen's lease expired in November, which resulted in the horse being sold to Mr W. Liddell, whose Electric Ray had finished fourth in the Derby. Remaining in Cullen's charge, Wales started sixteen times in 1898, winning two hurdle races with his trainer in the saddle, as well as two seven-furlong races and two Queen's Plates over two miles. He

The Cullen Brothers, Willie and Fred, *outstanding gentleman riders and successful owner-trainers, who were associated with successive winners of the Irish Derby. Source:* Irish Field.

remained in training for a further three seasons, after which he was retired to stud in Limerick. Moved subsequently to Yorkshire, he sired nothing of note. Of the other Derby runners, White Hackle had to wait three years to win a Selling 'chase, while Electric Ray, Head the Trick and The Bereft all won small races over the next two seasons.

Trainer and lessee of Wales, William Parke Cullen was the younger of two renowned Galway-born riders and trainers. Having won his first 'chase on The Colonel in 1879, he went on to win the Conyngham Cup on Royal Meath and the Galway Plate, appropriately enough, three times, on Erin's Star (1885), Victrix (1887) and Castle Warden (1896). He had several mounts in the Grand National and only months previously had suffered the greatest disappointment of his riding career when he was 'jocked off' Manifesto at the eleventh hour, yielding the Aintree honour and glory to his compatriot Terry Kavanagh. Willie Cullen began training in Rossmore Lodge in partnership with his brother F. F. 'Fred' Cullen, but soon went out on his own at Rathbride Cottage, where he trained a mixed string. In common with many Irish trainers of the day, W. P. Cullen moved his jumpers to temporary quarters in England for the winter campaign. Frequently acting as his own first jockey, Willie Cullen combined the roles of rider and trainer with consistent success until well past forty years of age. Two animals successfully exploited on both sides of the Channel by 'W.P.' were Killyleagh and What, subsequently the sire and dam of Killeagh, winner of the Irish Derby in 1906. A gentleman and sportsman in the best tradition, Willie Cullen predeceased his brother, dying at Clonkeen, Co. Galway, in 1937.

Tommy Fiely was a prominent lightweight jockey, able to go to scale at 6st 3lbs. At this time he rode exclusively on the flat, confining his activities to the major tracks. He had ridden only one winner during the 1897 season prior to the Derby meeting. In the course of the three days he rode three winners on the opening day, a double on Derby day and one winner on the last day, being placed on three of his remaining four mounts. Such are the fortunes of racing! His nineteen winners that year included the aforementioned Killyleagh and the Derby fourth, Electric Ray. The following year he won the Baldoyle Derby on Split the Wind, one of the last winners sired by Belgrave. From 1903 to 1913 he rode only under National Hunt rules. After his retirement that year he continued to be a regular racegoer until after the Second World War.

Wednesday, 30th June, 1897	£470	8 Ran	1½m (Howth Post)

The Irish Derby of 550sovs, by subscription of 15sovs each, but 6sovs only for horses struck out on or before the 2nd September, 1896. The second horse to receive 50sovs and the third 15sovs out of the plate. For three years old. Colts 8st 12lb; fillies 8st 8lb. The winner of the Angleseys and Railways at the Curragh, or of two stakes value 300sovs each, 10lb extra; of the Angleseys or of a stake value 300sovs, or of stakes collectively value 600sovs, 7lb extra; of a stake value 200sovs, 3lb extra; Horses that have never won a stake value 100sovs, allowed 6lb; maidens allowed 10lb; only one of these allowances can be taken. Produce of untried sires or mares allowed 3lb (if claimed at entry), but not for both. Any person entering three horses, his own bona fide sole property, can strike out one at the time appointed for declaring forfeit without having to pay the forfeit.

(40 subs)

1	Mr W. P. Cullen's	WALES (T. Fiely)	7.13	
		Ch. colt Belgrave – Victoria by Victor or Walter.		
2	Mr East's	WHITE HACKLE (Aylin)	8. 3	
		B. colt Hackler – White Rose (dam Ursula)		
3	Mr W. Clarke's	FIELD DAY (Mr G. W. Lushington)	8.12	(UK)
		Ch. colt Winkfield – Wedding Eve.		
4	Mr W. Liddell's	ELECTRIC RAY (W. Horton)	8. 2	(UK)
		Ch. colt Torpedo – Compromise.		
5	Capt. Murray's	FRENCHHAVEN (T. Almack)	8. 2	
		B. colt Monsieur – Crosshaven.		
6	Mr W. J. Goulding's	HEAD THE TRICK (T. Kavanagh)	8. 8	
		Ch. filly Castlereagh – Loo by Arbitrator.		
7	Mr R. H. Stubbers's	CASHMERE (A. Anthony)	8.12	
		B. colt Marmiton – Deodar.		
8	Mr T. Boylan's	THE BEREFT (M. Dawson)	9. 5	
		Ch. colt Favo-Morning Star.		

SP 4/1 WALES; 5/1 Field Day, Cashmere, Electric Ray; 7/1 Head the Trick, Frenchhaven; 10/1 Bar.

Won cleverly by ¾ length, 1 length, HEAD.

Winner trained by Owner at Rathbride Cottage, Curragh.

1898

Irish Derby Day 1898 fell on the feast of Saints Peter and Paul, a church holiday, which helped to create a record crowd. The railway carried over six thousand racegoers from Dublin alone. Unfortunately the quality of the Derby field scarcely equalled the occasion. The public form of the six runners added up to very little, Lady Flush being the only previous winner among them. However, Kilfintan, whose stable companion, Split the Wind, had won the Baldoyle Derby, was considered superior by his connections. Despite his lack of a race that season, he quickly became a raging hot favourite, being backed to 7-to-4. Only Noble Howard was seriously backed to beat the favourite. This big, gross chestnut son of Gallinule had disappointed in his previous races, but was thought to have overcome his old tendency to break blood vessels. Fulminator was considered safely held on his eight-length second to Split the Wind at Baldoyle. The Ruler had been a further eight lengths away on that occasion. Idolator was an unknown quantity, having only run once in his life, over twelve months previously.

After one false start Lady Flash broke in front of Idolator, with Noble Howard last away. The early pace was sufficiently modest to allow Moran to drive Noble Howard into the lead from Idolator and Lady Flush. Kilfintan was already labouring at the rear of the small field, where, to the consternation of those who had taken the odds about him, he remained. Passing the halfway mark Noble Howard led from Lady Flush, Idolator and Fulminator. Moran quickened the pace from the top of the hill, chased by Idolator, Fulminator and Lady Flash. Supporters of The Ruler and Kilfintan already knew their fate. Clear entering the straight, Noble Howard easily repelled Fulminator's challenge, passing the post three lengths clear, with Idolator six lengths further back. The winner returned to a popular reception, having finally justified his trainer's faith in his ability.

Noble Howard was the third Irish Derby winner sired by Gallinule, whose profound influence on Irish bloodstock has been referred to elsewhere. Mr S. M. Nolan bred the winner from his own mare, Little May, an unraced daughter of Xenophon. During eighteen years in his ownership Little May was a good servant to Mr Nolan, for whom The Arrowed, a full-brother to Noble Howard, finished second in the Irish Derby of 1904. Noble Howard ran only twice after his Derby triumph, unplaced each time, after which no more was heard of him. With the exception of the hard-working Lady Flash, the rest of the Derby runners lapsed into appropriate obscurity.

One interesting aspect of Noble Howard's career concerned his second appearance as a two-year-old, in the celebrated Londonderry Plate at Leopardstown on August 21st 1897, a meeting graced by the presence of the future King George V and Queen Mary. The advertised distance of the race was five furlongs and one of the favourites, Sabine Queen, was trained by Lt. Col. F. F. McCabe. After the race, in which his filly was unplaced, McCabe lodged an unique objection, on the grounds of the course being too short. The local stewards avoided the issue by rejecting the objection because it was lodged after the permitted interval. McCabe appealed to the Turf Club. By then the course had been measured and found to be all of 100yds short. Though the Turf Club upheld the local stewards' ruling, the Leopardstown executive was heavily fined and obliged to correct the distance of the course, at very considerable expense. One result of this extraordinary occurrence was an amendment to the Rules of Racing, stating that in future all objections to aspects of the course must be lodged before the event in question! Sabine Queen, medium of this 'cause celebre', won the Irish Oaks for McCabe in 1898.

Sebastian M. Nolan, the owner-breeder of Noble Howard, was yet another of the

Galwaymen, who seem to have played a disproportionately large role in the saga of Ireland's greatest race. Born in Ballinderry, Tuam, on St Patrick's Day 1846, at the height of the Famine, Sebastian Nolan made his fortune in the guano importing business, acquiring substantial property in and around the city of Galway. He registered his colours in 1885 and three years later scored his other major Turf success when Hospodar won the Curragh Cesarewitch. Well-known during his life both in business and racing circles, Sebastian Nolan became a celebrity after his death, as the result of a heart attack while playing golf on Easter Monday 1907. In a codicil to his will he directed that the bulk of his considerable fortune should go to the Magdalen Asylum in Galway. Understandably incensed by this revelation, his family took an action in the High Court, where the will was proved in favour of the religious order responsible for the asylum for destitute and fallen women. In tribute to their 'kind and generous benefactor', the nuns erected a magnificent celtic cross over his grave in Galway, where they have continued to administer his charitable bequest to the present day.

The most pleased man on the Curragh after Noble Howard's victory was almost certainly his trainer, R. L. Exshaw, who had never lost faith in the colt's ability, despite a series of setbacks and disappointments. Although Rossmore Lodge was controlled by F. F. Cullen, whose brother had won the race with Wales a year previously, the actual training of the inmates had for a number of years been conducted by Robert Lyster Exshaw. Several times leading Gentleman Rider in the

Wednesday, 29th June, 1898	£470	6 Ran	1½m

The Irish Derby of 550sovs, by subscription of 15sovs each, but 6sovs only for horses struck out on or before the 1st September, 1897. The second horse to receive 50sovs and the third 15sovs out of the plate. For three years old. Colts 8st 12lb; fillies 8st 8lb. The winner of the Angleseys and Railways at the Curragh, or of two stakes value 300sovs each, 10lb extra; of the Angleseys or of a stake value 300sovs, or of stakes collectively value 600sovs, 7lb extra; of a stake value 200sovs, 3lb extra. Horses that have never won a stake value 100sovs, allowed 6lb; maidens allowed 10lb; only one of these allowances can be taken. Produce of untried sires or mares allowed 3lb (if claimed at entry), but not for both. Any person entering three horses, his own bona fide sole property, can strike out one at the time appointed for declaring forfeit without having to pay the forfeit.

(38 subs)

1 Mr S. M. Nolan's	NOBLE HOWARD (T. Moran)	8. 2	
	Ch. colt Gallinule – Little May by Xenophon.		
2 Mr M. A. Maher's	FULMINATOR (W. Horton)	7.13	
	Br. colt Dictator – Eline.		
3 Mr C. J. Blake's	IDOLATOR (T. Fiely)	8. 2	
	Ch. colt Enthusiast – Ida.		
4 Mr R. J. Love's	LADY FLUSH (T. Almack)	8.11	
	Ch. filly Enthusiast – Flush.		
5 Mr J. Reese's	THE RULER (A. Anthony)	9. 2	
	Br. colt Isosceles – Brittania.		
6 Mr E. More O'Ferrall's	KILFINTAN (A. Sharples)	7.13	
	B. colt Monsieur – Pride of Eyrefield.		

SP 7/4 Kilfintan; 7/2 NOBLE HOWARD; 6/1 Bar.
Won easily 3 lengths, 6 lengths.
Winner trained by Mr R. Exshaw at Rossmore Lodge, Curragh.

'sixties and 'seventies – the pre-Beasley era – Robert Exshaw had maintained a lengthy string at Hybla House, Monasterevan, where he enjoyed the facility of his own private racecourse as a schooling ground. Besides winning the Galway Plate on Aster in 1871, Robert Exshaw became one of the very few men ever to 'fly' the Big Double at Punchestown successfully when he accomplished this remarkable feat on Red Man in 1870. Some weeks after Noble Howard's Irish Derby Robert Exshaw suffered a heavy fall at Rossmore Lodge and though his injuries were not immediately thought serious, he died as a result of them less than two months later.

Tommy Moran, the rider of Noble Howard, was born at Kildysart, Co. Clare in 1879. On leaving school he became apprenticed to F. F. Cullen at Rossmore Lodge and rode his first winner at the Curragh in 1897. Shortly after his success in the Irish Derby he was forced by increasing weight to begin riding over jumps. The following year he became associated with M. J. Harty's Alston stable and thus with that wonderful 'chaser, Tipperary Boy, on whom he won the Galway Plate in 1899 and 1901, as well as the Irish Grand National. He was champion jockey in 1899, in which year he accomplished the unusual feat of riding the winners of a two-year-old race, a flat handicap, a hurdle and a steeplechase at the same meeting. 1902 saw him riding in Austria-Hungary and in 1906 he rode in England. Having retired from the hazards of steeplechasing to the comparative safety of running a public house in Clonmel, Tommy Moran was killed tragically while shooting cormorants from a boat in Dumore Harbour in 1924.

1899

Derby Day 1899 was marred by thunder and lightning, which reduced the traditionally large crowd. Despite a bigger field than in recent years, the Derby appeared to be a one-horse race, dominated by Mr T. L. Plunkett's Oppressor. This fine big brown son of Gallinule had only run twice in his life. On his only public appearance in 1898 he had scored an impressive success in the Railway Stakes. Put away for the Epsom Derby, he had run an excellent race to finish fifth to the brilliant Flying Fox, having been hampered by the fatal fall of Holocauste. Only two of his nine opponents attracted any support. One of these was Monmouth, winner of his first two juvenile starts and third in the Baldoyle Derby, attempting to give 3olbs to the winner. However, his enthusiasm for racing was already suspect. The other was Green o' My Eye. Peter Purcell Gilpin's gelding had won the International Foal Stakes at Leopardstown in November and was to be ridden by the joint-champion jockey, Tommy Lane. Pick of the field on looks were Oppressor and Elena, while The Mistress and Too Good looked to be out of their depth in this company.

There was little delay at the start and the early leader, Strokestown, set a reasonable pace from Monmouth, with Oppressor prominent. With a mile to race Strokestown led from Monmouth, Millman and Too Good. These four were clear of the rest of the field, headed by the favourite, with The Mistress bringing up the rear. At half-way Too Good began to lose his place, while Green o' My Eye could be seen making ground. Coming down the hill Monmouth took up the running from Strokestown, with the favourite moving into third place, ahead of the hard-ridden Millman, with Green o' My Eye still in touch. In the straight Oppressor drew up to Monmouth, with the race clearly at his mercy. Anthony delayed his challenge until inside the final furlong, where he shook up Oppressor, who quickened like a good horse to go right away to a cantering win. Elena ran on through a tired field to take third place. Rosglas, having taken no part in the early stages, ran on when the race was over to finish fifth. The subsequent form of the beaten runners complimented the winner, for most of them won several times.

By Victor, out of an un-named daughter of Uncas, Oppressor's dam, Moira, was bred by Denis O'Callaghan at Brackenstown, a renowned nursery of good winners. When racing for Mr B. R. Brasier, Moira had won steeplechases at Ballyclough and Cork Park. She then developed an unpleasant tendency to bolt on the way to the start and was hastily retired to her owner's paddocks where her performance was more satisfactory. During her long career at Brackenstown she bred numerous winners, notably General Peace, own-brother of Oppressor and also winner of the Railway Stakes, before winning the Lincolnshire Handicap and Auteuil Hurdle. Denis O'Callaghan had leased Oppressor to Mr Plunkett for the colt's racing career.

Oppressor did not win again as a three-year-old, his best effort being to finish third in the Manchester November Handicap. The following year he started by winning a Queen's Plate over the Derby course in May, flopped in the Chester Cup, finished a very good third to The Grafter at Manchester and finally had to give best to the good filly Glenart at the Curragh. One of the reasons for Oppressor's loss of form was a progressively worsening wind infirmity, a trait that Gallinule was prone to transmit. Tubed as a five-year-old, Oppressor won two races, beating Gallinaria in the second of these, albeit receiving 11lbs from the younger horse. Retired to stud at Julianstown, Co. Meath, to stand alongside General Peace, Oppressor received scant patronage in his early seasons. However, by 1913 it was claimed that of his twenty-one runners, sixteen were winners.. His best winners were Shining Way, winner of the Irish Oaks, Wilkinstown and Redwood. His line survives today through the 1952 Epsom Oaks winner, Frieze, whose fourth dam, Mount Brenda, was by Oppressor.

The third Irish Derby winner in five years trained by S. C. Jeffrey, private trainer at Heath House, Oppressor was owned by Mr T. L. Plunkett, proprietor of a thriving brick factory in Portmarnock, Co. Dublin. Elected to the Turf Club in 1897, following the success of his colt Diavolo in the Anglesea Stakes the previous year, T. L. Plunkett raced extensively both in England and in Ireland, where he was in partnership with Charles Blake in many of the horses trained at the Heath. Among these was Portmarnock, in whom the partners had sold a half share to Captain Machell prior to that colt's Irish Derby success in 1895. Though T. L. Plunkett has frequently been credited with breeding Portmarnock, he in fact purchased the colt in utero at the famous dispersal sale of the late William Brophy's bloodstock. One that he did breed was Baldoyle, also by Gallinule, a good two-year-old winner for Mr Plunkett in England in 1898, when trained by F. Jeffrey, a brother of the Heath House trainer. Having reduced his racing and breeding interests at the outbreak of the First World War, T. L. Plunkett died in 1927.

Algy Anthony, the successful rider, is perhaps better remembered for his steeplechasing exploits, in particular the distinction of becoming the first professional to win

Mr F. O. Ruttledge (left) *and* **Mr R. McK.Waters,** *prominent figures in Irish racing at the end of the nineteenth century. Source:* Racing Illustrated.

the Grand National both as jockey and trainer. Born near Cheltenham in 1872, Algernon Anthony was apprenticed to Sam Darling at Beckhampton and rode his first winner in 1886 for Mr Lea, of Lea & Perrins fame. Towards the end of 1892 he moved to Ireland, joining the Eyrefield Lodge stable, controlled by Noble Johnston and Mr Lushington. Within four years he had become the leading jockey in Ireland, heading the lists for three years in succession. In gaining the second of his championships – 1897 – he rode the highest total of winners till then recorded by a professional jockey in Ireland. In addition to winning both the Irish Derby and the Irish Oaks twice, Algy Anthony scored at least once in nearly all the major two-year-old events, notably on Sirenia and Bachelor's Double. When Eyrefield Lodge ceased to be a training stable Anthony removed to Conyngham Lodge with Mr Lushington, the licence being held by Joe Hunter. It was from Conyngham Lodge that this trio sallied forth to Liverpool with Ambush II for the Grand National in 1900. Carrying the colours of HRH the Prince of Wales, Algy Anthony steered Ambush II to his famous victory, watched by his delighted owner. Three years later the partnerships looked certain to repeat their triumph, only for Ambush II to swerve and fall at the last fence. Later the same year Algy Anthony gained some small compensation when winning the Galway Plate on Hampton Boy. Having repeated that success on Schwarmer six years later, Algy Anthony retired to take up training.

Based at Westenra, where Michael Connolly now trains, Algy Anthony enjoyed equal success as a trainer. Unquestionably his greatest charge was Major Gerrard's slashing great 'chaser Troytown. As a seven-year-old Troytown won the Champion 'Chase at Liverpool and the Grand Steeplechase de Paris at Auteuil, reviving memories of the Linde era. The following year, reportedly carrying half the Sinn Fein war fund, Troytown powered his way to victory in the Grand National, in a manner which led his exhausted rider to describe him as 'more of a steam engine than a racehorse'. One of the greatest horses ever to win the Grand National, Troytown suffered a fatal injury on a return visit to Auteuil. He is commemorated by the Troytown 'Chase at Navan. Algy Anthony did not long outlive his greatest charge, dying after a lengthy illness in 1923.

Wednesday, 28th June, 1899   **£783**   **10 Ran**   **1½m**

The Irish Derby of 1000sovs, by subscrption of 17sovs each, but 8sovs only for horses struck out on or before the 7th September, 1898. The second horse to receive 150 sovs and the third 50sovs out of the plate. For three years old. Colts 8st 12lb; fillies 8st 8lb. The winner of the Angleseys and Railways at the Curragh, or of two stakes value 300sovs each, 10lb extra; of the Angleseys or of a stake value 300sovs, or of stakes collectively value 600sovs, 7lb extra; of a stake value 200sovs, 3lb extra. Horses that have never won a stake value 100sovs, allowed 6lb; maidens allowed 10lb; only one of these allowances can be taken. Produce of untried sires or mares allowed 3lb (if claimed at entry), but not for both. Any person entering three horses, his own bona fide sole property, can strike out one at the time appointed for declaring forfeit without having to pay the forfeit.

(66 subs)

1	Mr T. L. Plunkett's	OPPRESSOR (A. Anthony)	9. 5
		Br. colt Gallinule – Moira by Victor.	
2	Lord Fermoy's	MONMOUTH (John Doyle)	8.12
		B. colt Jacobite – Rose MacDonald.	
3	Mr C. J. Blake's	ELENA (C. Gray)	7. 9
		B. filly Gallinule – Sanctissima.	
4	Mr D. Owen's	STROKESTOWN (T. Archer)	7.13
		Ch. colt Connaught – Madrida.	
5	Mr R. E. Cassidy's	ROSGLAS (G. Kennedy)	7.13
		Ch. colt The Rejected – Carmelite.	
6	Mr P. P. Gilpin's	GREEN O' MY EYE (T. Lane)	9. 5
		Ch. gelding Wiseman – Village Green.	
7	Mr F. F. MacCabe's	MILLMAN (T. Fiely)	7.13 (car 8. 1)
		Ch. gelding Enthusiast – Millcog.	
0	Mr M. A. Maher's	THE MISTRESS (J. Westlake)	7.12
		Br. filly Dictator – White Sleeves.	
0	Mr F. F. Cullen's	SCOTCH ROBBER (T. Moran)	8. 2
		B. gelding Craig Royston – Rosie.	
0	Mr H. Beasley's	TOO GOOD* (J.Walsh)	8. 6 (car 8. 7)
		Br. gelding Ocean Wave – Cipoletta.	

SP 4/7 OPPRESSOR; 8/1 Mormouth, Green o' my Eye; 10/1 Millman; 100/7 Bar.
Won in a canter 2½ lengths, 6 lengths.
Winner trained Privately.

*Too Good ran un-named.

1900

The year of Queen Victoria's Jubilee visit to Ireland saw a field of twelve parade for the Irish Derby on June 27th. Weeks of heavy rain had left the going unusually good for the time of year. Although Dinna Ken and Gallinaria represented the best two-year-old form of the previous season, Cerasus was favoured in the betting, on the strength of his short-head defeat in the Baldoyle Derby by Flying Hackle. Next in demand in an open betting market was Lord Fermoy's Leading Power who ran unnamed. Though the pick of the field on looks, the last-named was still obviously backward. Nevertheless, the conditions of the race greatly favoured the two market fancies, both of whom received 13lbs from Dinna Ken and Gallinaria. Among the large crowd were two interested spectators, Robert Sievier and his trainer, Charles Morton. They had come over to purchase Dodragh, winner of the Waterford Testimonial Stakes the previous day. However the asking price of £2,000 was considered too high.

After a good early gallop Cerasus took up the running down the hill, followed by Likely Bird, Gallinaria and the Leading Power colt. As they turned into the straight this quartet drew clear of the remainder. At the Chains Likely Bird headed Cerasus, leading into the final furlong, where he was overhauled by Gallinaria and the Leading Power colt. After a brief tussle Gallinaria pulled clear of her opponent, reaching the post an easy winner by four lengths from Lord Fermoy's colt, with Likely Bird staying on two lengths further back in third place. Cerasus, Old Brown Bess, Good Time and Lady Valentine followed the principals home in that order. Biggest disappointment of the race was Dinna Ken, beaten at half-way.

Gallinaria's easy victory came as a pleasant surprise to her connections, for she had not regained her two-year-old form and was not expected to stay. Yet another Derby winner sired by Gallinule, Gallinaria was bred by her owner, Captain Eustace Loder, at Eyrefield Lodge and trained there by 'Eyrefield Dan' McNally, under the supervision of Mr G. W. Lushington, who managed the Loder racing interests in Ireland. Winner of the Curragh Grand Prize over five furlongs in October on her fourth and final two-year-old run, Gallinaria had made little physical improvement over the winter, remaining a light-framed, shelly chestnut. She was unplaced in her remaining two races on 1900, as was the runner-up. Likely Bird won two small races, while Cerasus won the valuable New Century Cup at the Curragh in September. The luckless Dinna Ken went on to finish second in four successive races.

As a four-year-old Gallinaria, already in foal to Laveno, won a King's Plate at the Curragh in June, finished second to Oppressor, giving him 11lbs, in a similar event in July and again finished in second place in a King's Plate in September, trying to give 21lbs to Cerasus. Dinna Ken made amends as a four-year-old, winning five of his thirteen races, though finishing second in six others.

Gallinaria's dam, Pierina, by Morgan out of the Galopin mare, Balornock, was bred by one Mr Ellison in 1889. Acquired by Mr Noble Johnson from the Royal trainer, Richard Marsh, in 1896, she produced Gallinaria. Passed on to Major Loder, Pierina produced the winning filly Piano, before being exported to Austria in 1903. Retained throughout her stud career by Major Loder, Gallinaria produced a high-class colt Galvani, winner of the Middle Park Stakes and Champion Stakes before dying while foaling in 1908.

The Irish Oaks, decided over one mile on August 8th, was regarded as a match between Mr Hall-Walker's Lucky Hit and the Eyrefield Lodge filly, May Race. The remaining four runners were ignored. Ridden by the American, Johnny Reiff, Lucky Hit lost a lot of ground at the start. Although she got upsides May Race in the straight, Algy Anthony had merely been biding his time on the leader. In the last fifty yards he asked May Race for her effort, sufficient to land her a clever winner by a head. Sea Goose finished a bad third. Thus the Eyrefield Lodge team completed the Derby-Oaks double. Algy Anthony had amply demonstrated his versatility, having ridden the Curragh-trained Ambush II to victory in the Prince of Wales colours in the Grand National earlier in the year.

Major Eustace Loder, owner of Eyrefield Lodge and, of course, of Gallinaria and May Race, became known in racing circles as 'Lucky Loder'. Between 1900 and 1914 his colours, 'Yellow, dark blue sleeves and black cap', were carried by the winners of £125,875 in stakes. He won the Derby with Spearmint in 1906, having won the Fillies' Triple Crown two years earlier with the peerless Pretty Polly. On Eustace Loder's death in 1914 Eyrefield and Old Connell studs became the property of his nephew, Lieutenant-Colonel Giles Loder. The Loder luck held good, providing Giles Loder with his Derby winner, Spion Kop in 1920. The Loders had bought Eyrefield Lodge from the executors of Henry Eyre Linde, who had trained there with such outstanding success. Shortly afterwards Loder decided to utilise Eyrefield solely as a stud farm. Thereafter the produce retained to race in Ireland was supervised by Mr Lushington at nearby Conyngham Lodge, while the better-class yearlings were sent over to P. P. Gilpin at Newmarket. Overall management of the Loder bloodstock interests devolved upon Mr Noble Johnson, the breeder of Gallinaria.

'Eyrefield Dan' McNally, *licence-holder at Eyrefield Lodge after the death of his long-time employer, H. E. Linde, and thus accredited with the Irish Derby successes of Gallinaria and Carrigavalla. Source:* Irish Field.

Mr G. W. Lushington, *one of only two amateur riders to win the Irish Derby, which he did on Gallinaria in 1900, the same year in which he masterminded the Grand National triumph of Ambush II in the colours of his principal patron, HRH the Prince of Wales in whose silks he appears here. Source:* Racing Annual 1901.

By his victory on Gallinaria Mr G. W. Lushington became only the second and, as it transpired, also the last amateur to win the Irish Derby. Understandably it was the most satisfying of his many successes on the flat. Born at Chilham Castle in Kent in 1860, Graham Wildman Lushington joined the Queen's West Surrey Regiment in 1881, seeing service in Cork and in Belfast, where the regiment was sent to quell rioting. It was while in Belfast that Tommy, as he was familiarly known, rode his first winner under Rules on Lisburn. The same animal subsequently gave him a near-fatal fall, leading to his retirement from the Army. Taking up residence on the

Wednesday, 27th June, 1900	**£783**	**12 Ran**	**1½m (Howth Post)**

The Irish Derby of 1000sovs, by subscription of 17sovs each, but 8sovs only for horses struck out on or before the 6th September, 1899. The second horse to receive 150sovs and the third 50sovs out of the plate. For three years old. Colts 8st 12lb; fillies 8st 8lb. If claimed at time of entry, produce of untried sires or mares allowed 3lb, but not for both. The winner of the Angleseys and Railways at the Curragh, or of two stakes value 300sovs each, 10lb extra; of the Angleseys or of a stake value 300sovs, or of stakes collectively value 600sovs, 7lb extra; of a stake value 200sovs, 3lb extra. Horses that have never won a stake value 100sovs, allowed 6lb; maidens allowed 10lb; only one of these allowances can be taken. Any person entering three horses, his own bona fide sole property, can strike out one at the time appointed for declaring forfeit without having to pay the forfeit.   (66 subs)

1	Capt. Eustace Loder's	GALLINARIA (Mr G. W. Lushington) Ch. filly Gallinule — Pierina by Morgan.	8.12
2	Lord Fermoy's	LEADING POWER* (J. Westlake) Ch. colt Pioneer – Vital Power.	7.13
3	Mr J. C. Sullivan's	LIKELY BIRD (John Doyle) Br. colt Winkfield – Like a Bird.	8. 3 (car. 8. 4)
4	Mr S. E. Shirley's	CERASUS (T. Casey) Ch. colt Cherry Ripe – Felicity.	7.13
5	Mr W. Hall-Walker's	OLD BROWN BESS (W. Horton) B/Br. filly Petronel – Glen Isla.	7.12
6	Mr W. H. West's	GOOD-TIME (Peter Hughes) Br. filly Springtime – Surprise.	7. 9
7	Mr D. G. M'Cammon's	LADY VALENTINE (A. Anthony) B. filly Buckingham – Geology.	8. 5 (car. 8. 6)
8	Hon. A. L. Brabazon's	GOLDEN BAY (L. Byrne) Ch. colt Bend Or – Sea Shell.	8. 2
9	Mr W. P. Cullen's	DINNA KEN (T. Moran) Ch. colt Broxton – Rosie White.	8.12
0	Mr P. P. Gilpin's	GREEN WITCH (F. M'Allister) Ch. filly Wiseman – Village Green.	7.12
0	Mr D. Shanahan's	THE HAWK (John Doyle, jr.) B. colt Hackler – Avisa.	7.13
0	Mr M. A. Maher's	IMPRESSARIO (T. Farrell) B. colt Dictator – Songstress by Van Amburgh.	8. 2

SP 3/1 Cerasus; 4/1 Leading Power; 6/1 GALLINARIA, Likely Bird, Dinna Ken; 7/1 Lady Valentine; 10/1 Bar.

Won easily by 4 lengths, 2 lengths.

Winner trained by Mr D. M'Nally at Eyrefield Lodge, Curragh.

* Leading Power ran un-named.

Curragh with T. G. Gordon at Brownstown Lodge, Tommy Lushington developed into one of the best amateurs of the day. Untroubled by weight, he was more than a match for the professionals on the flat, scoring a notable clean sweep of the three Queen's Plates at a Curragh June meeting on King Ebor. Other good winners ridden by him on the flat were Tragedy and Fiorenza. Riding the last-named, Tommy Lushington won the opening race on that epic day at Liverpool, when Ambush II carried Algy Anthony to triumph in the Grand National. Tommy Lushington had purchased the horse on behalf of his royal patron, endured the disappointment of his early career, ridden him to win his previous race and supervised his training for this supreme moment.

Sometime earlier Tommy Lushington had moved back to England to train for John Gubbins at Telscombe in Sussex. Riding as 'Mr Wildman', he won the Sefton 'Chase at Liverpool and the Grand International 'Chase at Sandown on Battle Royal. However, John Gubbins decided to send his English horses to be trained by Sam Darling at Beckhampton, so Lushington returned to Conyngham Lodge, and Ambush II. Having provided Lushington with the proudest moment of his career, Ambush II proceeded to place him in the trickiest situation any trainer could envisage. In the course of preparation for the Grand National of 1905 Ambush II suffered a massive internal haemorrhage and dropped dead on the Curragh. Having conveyed the doleful news to his royal patron, Lushington had the horse's head and hooves cut off, intending to have them suitably mounted for presentation to his sovereign. One can only imagine his consternation and dismay on receiving the royal command to forward the skeleton to Liverpool Museum! Eventually, by assiduous application of wire and glue the task was accomplished and the skeleton dispatched to the Museum, where it remains. Several years after this episode Lushington received a more pleasant reminder of Ambush II when Colonel Knox sent a yearling son of Fiorenza to be trained at Conyngham Lodge. Impressed by the offspring of his old winning partner, Lushington took a share in the colt. Later named Ballaghtobin, he won the Irish Derby in 1915, providing Tommy Lushington with his last big moment on the Turf. He died in Dublin two years later, after a long and painful illness.

1901

The Irish Derby of 1901 attracted 32 entries. From the original entry nine paraded on 26th June before a large crowd, swollen by a record number of travellers from Kingsbridge. The pick of an exceptionally good-looking field was Royal Winkfield. His stablemate, The Man, was described as being 'almost too tall for anything, but notwithstanding his giant size he wears a most galloping-like appearance'. There were no English runners and two-year-old form of the previous season was best represented by Royal Winkfield, Carrigavalla and Theatre Royal. The first pair had been placed behind Lord Fermoy's un-named flying machine, known as the Eudocia filly. The latter remained unbeaten as a two-year-old and was undoubtedly the fastest of her generation. Theatre Royal had won the Beresford Stakes. On three-year-old form Merrion and Carrigavalla had finished second and third respectively behind Coolock in the Baldoyle Derby. Despite not having appeared in public that season, Royal Winkfield displaced Merrion as Favourite at 2-to-1. Carrigavalla, winner of two handicaps on successive days at the Curragh in April, before finishing a neck behind Merrion at Baldoyle, attracted fair support at 5-to-1.

In a fast-run race, which concerned only the principals, Royal Winkfield and Merrion ran each other into the ground, presenting the race to Carrigavalla. As Thompson, on the favourite, and Harry Buxton on Merrion, battled for supremacy, Algy Anthony could be seen biding his time, waiting to pounce. At the furlong marker he swept the winner to the fore to win cleverly by half a length from Royal Winkfield, with an exhausted Merrion four lengths away in third. Anyone who has ever set out to make it all in a race will understand how John Thompson must have felt. Had the half-length gone the other way, his would have been acclaimed a masterly piece of tactical race-riding. As it transpired, he appeared to have presented the race to the wily Anthony. Royal Winkfield's subsequent form proved that he did not stay beyond a mile in a truly-run race.

The winner, a bay colt by the all-conquering Gallinule, was described thus by the Irish Field correspondent; 'a very pleasing-like colt, and distinctly shows more quality than his black-brown brother Portmarnock, that won the blue ribbon of Irish racing in 1895'. Unmoved by the pedigree and performance of his winner, the pragmatic owner, Mr W. J. Goulding, sold Carrigavalla that same afternoon to a South African, W. J. W. Murray. Transferred to England, Carrigavalla proved the wisdom of Goulding's decision by descending to selling plates. Even when successful in one of these as a five-year-old he failed to attract a bid. The subsequent performances of the other runners proved the lowly standard of the Irish Derby of 1901.

An interesting feature of this otherwise unremarkable Derby meeting was the successful appearance of the two previous winners of the big race. In the opening race on Derby Day Oppressor, ridden by his Derby jockey, Algy Anthony, won a mile handicap. Since his Derby victory two years earlier he had become a roarer, for which complaint he had recently been tubed. The next day it was the turn of Gallinaria to carry Mr Lushington to an easy victory in a two-mile King's Plate.

Carrigavalla was the second consecutive Irish Derby winner sent out from Eyre-

Leading Irish Jockeys. *Alf Aylin won the Irish Derby on Gulsaberk (1896), Algy Anthony was twice successful, on Oppressor (1899) and Carrigavalla (1901), while Tommy Fiely rode Wales to victory in 1897. Tommy Doyle, a member of Ireland's most prolific and successful riding families, was fourth on his only ride in the race. Source:* Irish Field.

field Lodge and thus attributed to Dan McNally as trainer. McNally had been Eyre Linde's head man for many years, remaining at Eyrefield after the property had been purchased by Eustace Loder. In an era when 'gentlemen' did not hold trainers' licences, McNally appeared as the licence-holder at Eyrefield, though stable policy was almost certainly dictated by Noble Johnson and Lushington.

But for the intervention of Tommy Lushington the previous year, Carrigavalla would have provided an unique hat-trick for Algy Anthony in the Irish Derby. For while both John Connolly and Michael Dawson had ridden three winners of Ireland's greatest race, neither had ridden more than two in a row.

Carrigavalla carried the 'Pink, Cambridge Blue cap' of William Joseph Goulding, who was using the assumed name of 'Mr A. Summers' at the time. Previously he had

Wednesday, 26th June, 1901	**£783**	**9 Ran**	**1½m (Howth Post)**

The Irish Derby of 1000sovs, by subscription of 17sovs each, but 8sovs only for horses struck out on or before the 5th September, 1900. The second horse to receive 150sovs and the third 50sovs out of the plate. For three years old. Colts 8st 12lb; fillies 8st 8lb. If claimed at time of entry, produce of untried sires or mares allowed 3lb, but not for both. The winner of the Angleseys and Railways at the Curragh, or of two stakes value 300sovs each, 10lb extra; of the Angleseys or of a stake value 300sovs, or of stakes collectively value 600sovs, 7lb extra; of a stake value 200sovs, 3lb extra. Horses that have never won a stake value 100sovs, allowed 6lb; maidens allowed 10lb; only one of these allowances can be taken. Any person entering three horses, his own bona fide sole property, can strike out one at the time appointed for declaring forfeit without having to pay the forfeit.

(68 subs)

1 Mr A. Summers's	CARRIGAVALLA (A. Anthony)	8.12
	B. colt Gallinule – The Sleeping Beauty by Ben Battle.	
2 Mr J. C. Sullivan's	ROYAL WINKFIELD (J.	8. 2
	Thompson) Br. colt Winkfield – Queen Charming.	
3 Mr J. James's	MERRION (H. Buxton)	9. 1
	B/Br. colt Enthusiast – Dame Fortune.	
4 Mr S. M. Nolan's	JOCKEY OF NORFOLK (J.	8. 2
	Clayton) Ch. colt Gallinule – Little May.	
5 Mr W. Hall-Walker's	WHAT NEXT (W. Lane)	7.13
	Br. colt Dictator or Quidnuno – Veda.	
6 Mr W. Behan's	PRESIDENT STEYN (Peter	7.13
	Hughes) Ch. colt Bailsman or Good Lad – Dutch Rose.	
7 Mr S. E. Shirley's	THEATRE ROYAL (John Doyle)	8. 5
	Ch. filly Florizel – Theatre.	
8 Mr C. J. Blake's	LADY ELECT (T. Casey)	7. 9
	B. filly Beldemonio – Sanctissima.	
9 Mr J. C. Sullivan's	THE MAN (Joseph Doyle)	8. 2
	Br. colt Kilwarlin – Bright Star.	

SP 2/1 Royal Winkfield; 5/2 Merrion; 5/1 CARRIGAVALLA; 6/1 Theatre Royal; 8/1 Lady Elect; 10/1 Bar.

Won cleverly ½ length, 4 lengths.
Winner trained by Mr D. M'Nally at Eyrefield Lodge, Curragh.

Theatre Royal was, with the permission of the Stewards, on payment of fine saddled outside the enclosure.

raced under his real name except for a brief period as 'Mr St J. Cambridge'. A member of a Cork family, Sir William Goulding, as he was to become, was Chairman of the Great Southern Railway – a company founded by his grandfather. Sir William owned two winners of the Irish Oaks – Kosmos and The Kiwi – and was deprived of a similar double in the Irish Derby by the fatal accident to Twenty-third. As a breeder Sir William was also successful notably with Favoloo, winner of the Baldoyle Derby. Elected a member of the Turf Club in 1904, Sir W. J. Goulding eventually served as Senior Steward.

1902

This running of the Irish Derby offered both quality and quantity. Not only had it attracted the Irish two-year-old champion of 1901, but also two English challengers, Port Blair and Fermoyle. The age-old cross-Channel rivalry was lent extra piquancy in this instance, for eight years earlier John Gubbins' English-trained Blairfinde had beaten James Daly's Hartstown in the same race. Now Daly was renewing the challenge with his unbeaten St Brendan. Gubbins relied upon Port Blair, a son of Blairfinde. In sweltering sunshine the huge crowd debated the merits of the two principals to the exclusion of the other nine runners, whose collective form amounted to little. The hope of Ireland, St Brendan, had won his three starts as a two-year-old, concluding with the Railway Stakes, which he won with contemptuous ease. In the course of a busy first season Port Blair had won three of his nine races, run third to Sceptre at Epsom, been beaten a neck in the Coventry Stakes at Royal Ascot and finished third in the Middle Park Stakes. As proof that he had trained on he won twice before finishing fifth to the immortal Sceptre in the Two Thousand Guineas, beaten only five lengths. His owner was attempting an unique Derby double, having won the Epsom Classic with Ard Patrick.

Despite having to concede 3lbs to St Brendan, Port Blair was made a hot favourite. His appearance, allied to his form, outweighed his lack of size. St Brendan's critics said that he looked 'peacocky' and that he had lost his juvenile dash and brilliance. Moreover, it was generally felt that St Brendan's lack of a previous outing might tell against him. In fact his talented trainer had only one reservation about St Brendan. This powerful colt had always taken a strong hold, both at home and in his races. To assist his young jockey in restraining his impetuous mount, Michael Dawson had employed a special running snaffle, constructed in such a way that the harder the horse fought for his head the higher the bit ran up in his mouth. This singularly effective contraption is today in the possession of the Curragh trainer, Michael Connolly, with whose grandfather Michael Dawson served his apprenticeship.

The start, which was somewhat delayed, was obscured from view by some badly-sited tents. When the field appeared Truehaven was in the lead. After only two furlongs St Brendan surged to the front, setting a furious pace. So strong was the gallop that by halfway the field was strung out and only Port Blair, Happy Medium, Fermoyle and Truehaven were within reach of the leader. Truehaven dropped away as St Brendan came down the hill with a clear lead, pursued by Port Blair, on whom Kempton Cannon was making desperate attempts to narrow the gap. St Brendan swept into the straight full of running and two furlongs out, as Cannon put Port Blair under severe pressure, it became clear that the Irish colt would win. Suddenly the crowd began to cheer and there followed one of the most remarkable scenes ever witnessed on an Irish racecourse. As St Brendan neared the line the cheers grew louder and louder and when he passed the post, two and a half lengths ahead of Port Blair, hats were thrown in the air, amidst scenes of general excitement. Almost un-noticed in the jubilation, Fermoyle finished with a very strong run, which would have earned him second place in another fifty yards. As Michael Dawson led in the winner, the cheers broke out again, signifying not only the defeat of the invaders, but also James Daly's popularity with the racing public.

St Brendan was by Daly's own stallion, Hackler. A good racehorse, Hackler was by the Two Thousand Guineas winner, Petrarch, out of a Cambridgeshire winner, Hackness. Hackler, who stood throughout his career at Daly's Hartstown Stud in Clonsilla, was leading sire in Ireland four times before his death in 1907. Among the best of his progeny were the dual Cambridgeshire winner, Hackler's Pride, the speedy Lalla Rookh and Sabine Queen, as well as his two Grand National winners, Jenkinstown and Covercoat. James Daly bought St Brendan's dam, Court Card, together with St Brendan's older own-brother from Mr E. Flannery of Buttevant for £400. Subsequently named Conari, the own-brother won the valuable Leopardstown Grand Prize over five furlongs in August 1902.

On his next appearance St Brendan easily won one of the most important sprints in Ireland at the time, the Drogheda Memorial Stakes. He was then prepared for the St Leger at Doncaster, in which he ran much too freely over a distance far in excess of his stamina, finishing fifth behind Sceptre. His last race of the season saw him score an easy success in the Turf Club Cup over seven furlongs at the Curragh, carrying 10st 7lbs. As a four-year-old he ran only once, finishing unplaced in the Royal Hunt Cup, for which he started favourite. 1904 saw him emulate his older brother in winning the Leopardstown Grand Prize, as well as a mile race at the Phoenix Park. Kept in training as a six-year-old, St Brendan won the Earl of Sefton Plate at Liverpool in March. Ridden by Danny Maher, he beat Otherwise and Chaucer by two necks. His last victory was at Kempton in May. Having run once early in 1906, he was retired to his owner's stud in time to cover a few mares. Despite receiving ample opportunity, St Brendan was not a successful sire. His best runners were Mellifont, winner of the Anglesey Stakes and Wether's Well, winner of the Portland. His daughter, Killeen, became the dam of the Prix Dollar winner and French sire, Cerealiste.

St Brendan was undoubtedly a high-class racehorse with devastating speed, whose stamina limitations were emphasized by his impetuosity. It was his class alone that enabled him to win the Irish Derby. The merit of that performance was confirmed by the previous and subsequent form of Port Blair, winner of over £7,000. War Wolf went on to win the Ebor Handicap in 1904.

James Daly was born in Dundalk and moved to Dublin in 1870. He established a wide reputation as a horse dealer while still a young man, supplying British Army remounts for the Crimean War. Among the hundreds of good horses that passed through his hands were the Grand National winners Comeaway, Why Not, Eremon and Jenkinstown. He purchased Aboyeur as a foal and passed the future Derby winner on to J. H. H. Peard, who sold him to A. P. Cunliffe. His Hartstown Stud was one of the first in Ireland to be run on modern lines. Hackler, Enthusiast and Bushey Park were just three of the high-class stallions that stood there. St Brendan was the best of scores of very good horses to carry his 'Brown, red cap'. Quiet by nature, with a good sense of humour, James Daly possessed an endless fund of stories, which never failed to delight teller and audience alike. He lived to a ripe old age, dying in 1917, firmly established as a doyen of the Irish turf, where he had many times headed the list of winning owners.

St Brendan was the first of four winners of the Irish Derby trained by Michael Dawson, the master of Rathbride Manor. Having assumed control of the stable on the disqualification of the unfortunate Rice Meredith, Michael Dawson went on to prove himself the greatest trainer in Ireland in the first half of this century. Comparisons have frequently been drawn between this small, bearded, secretive genius and his great rival contemporary, J. J. Parkinson. Training records were instituted in Ireland in 1906 and the bare statistics reveal that Dawson headed the lists ten times until his death twenty years later, whereas Parkinson only achieved this distinction on five occasions. However, the real distinction between these two leaders of their profession lay between quality and quantity. Whereas Parkinson won hundreds of races with all types of horses, few of them of outstanding merit, Dawson concentrated on producing high-class animals, capable of winning in the best company. Horses such as Bachelor's Button and Bachelor's Double went on to achieve famous victories in England, having been developed by the master of Rathbride Manor. Though not averse to satisfying the requirements of his gambling patrons, Michael Dawson preferred to train for owners who could afford and were prepared to allow him the time to exercise his patience and skill in developing his charges to their ultimate potential. He was succeeded by his son Joseph and after the latter's early death by his younger son Michael, who trained Sindon to win the Irish Derby in 1958.

Winning the Irish Derby on St Brendan represented the highlight of David Condon's brief career. Apprenticed to Michael Dawson, he had completed his time only months earlier and was already regarded as the most promising young rider to emerge in Irish racing for many years. Although still only seventeen, he combined natural ability with a keen tactical brain. If he still lacked strength in a close finish, time and maturity would remedy this. Between completing his apprenticeship and becoming first jockey at Rathbride, he had ridden briefly in England, coming third in the Lincolnshire on Over Norton. 1902 saw him finish second in the jockeys' championship, only three winners behind the redoubtable John Thompson. A lengthy and successful career seemed assured. The flatracing season of 1903 started well for Michael Dawson and his talented protege, Meldre and Bachelor's Button providing a double at the opening Curragh meeting. One morning towards the end of May David Condon had left Rathbride on his way to the races, only to be recalled to ride a school over hurdles. The horse involved was one Bushmaster, unplaced in St Brendan's Derby, when ridden by John Thompson. That simple instruction bore tragic consequences, for a fall proved fatal to Ireland's most talented jockey. Once again it really did seem true that only the good die young.

Wednesday, 25th June, 1902   **£811**   **11 Ran**   **1½m (Howth Post)**

The Irish Derby of 1000sovs, by subscription of 17sovs each, but 8sovs only for horses struck out on or before the 4th September, 1901. The second horse to receive 150sovs and the third 50sovs out of the plate. For three years old. Colts 8st 12lb; fillies 8st 8lb. If claimed at time of entry, produce of untried sires or mares allowed 3lb, but not for both. The winner of the Angleseys and Railways at the Curragh, or of two stakes value 300sovs each, 10lb extra; of the Angleseys or of a stake value 300sovs, or of stakes collectively value 600sovs, 7lb extra; of a stake value 200sovs, 3lb extra. Horses that have never won a stake value 100sovs, allowed 6lb; maidens allowed 10lb; only one of these allowances can be taken. Any person entering three horses, his own bona fide sole property, can strike out one at the time appointed for declaring forfeit without having to pay the forfeit.

(76 subs)

1	Mr James Daly's	ST BRENDAN (D. Condon)	9. 5	
		Br. colt Hackler – Court Card by Royal Hampton.		
2	Mr J. Gubbin's	PORT BLAIR (K. Cannon)	9. 8	(UK)
		Br. colt Blairfinde – Income.		
3	Mr W. Hall-Walker's	FERMOYLE (Goswell)	8. 2	(UK)
		B. colt Florizel – Deception		
0	Colonel Rynd's	BUSHMASTER (J. Thompson)	7.13 (car 8.0)	
		Br. colt Bushey Park – Madge.		
0	Mr S. E. Shirley's	DRUMBRACKAN (T. Bell)	8. 2	
		B. gelding Wiseman – Kirsche.		
0	Mr S. M. Nolan's	GYNETH COLT* (L. Byrne)	8. 2	
		Bl. colt Gallinule – Gyneth.		
0	Mr Jackson Clark's	HAPPY MEDIUM (H. Buxton)	8.12	
		B/Br. colt Wiseman – Larkaway.		
0	Mr S. E. Shirley's	KILLAIDAN (J. Clayton)	9. 2	
		Br. colt St Aidan – Killarney.		
0	Mr C. J. Blake's	LESLIE (H. Lane)	7.13	
		B. colt Leveno – Moira.		
0	Captain Murray's	TRUEHAVEN (P. Hughes)	8. 3	
		B. colt Troubadour – Crosshaven.		
0	Mr J. C. Sullivan's	WAR WOLF (W. Higgs)	8. 3	
		B. colt Wolf's Crag – Annora.		

SP 11/10 Port Blair; 3/1 ST BRENDAN; 9/1 Fermoyle; 10/1 Happy Medium; 100/8 War Wolf, Bushmaster; 100/7 Leslie, Truehaven; 33/1 Bar.

Won easily by 2½ lengths, same.

Winner trained by Mr Michael Dawson at Rathbride Manor, Curragh.

*Gyneth colt un-named.

1903

In contrast to the previous year the field for the Irish Derby of 1903 did not contain any outstanding animals. Certainly, Lord Rossmore, the sole cross-Channel challenger, was not in the same league as the Triple Crown winner of that year, Rock

Sand. However, undaunted by menacing skies, the crowd attempted to decide between two of the eight-strong field. Lord Rossmore had raced in Ireland as a two-year-old and though his only victory had been gained on a disqualification, he had finished second in both the Railway and Beresford Stakes. Now owned by A. P. Cunliffe and trained on Salisbury Plain by Jack Fallon, his good win at Royal Ascot only the previous week entitled him to strong support. Best of the home brigade appeared to be J. C. Sullivan's lightly-raced Winkfield's Fortune, yet another of Winkfield's progeny, with which Sullivan had enjoyed such success and a full-brother of his Cambridgeshire winner, Winkfield's Pride. Of the others, only Crookhaven had any worthwhile form, which included a win over Lord Rossmore the previous season. In what was regarded as a two-horse race, Lord Rossmore was a marginally firmer favourite.

Having caused a lengthy delay at the start, Crookhaven was first away and made the running for almost a mile, with the favourite apparently labouring at the rear of the field in the early stages. With less than half a mile to race Higgs dashed Winkfield's Fortune into the lead, pursued by Easterling and Rosanule, with Lord Rossmore improving. However, the favourite swung into the straight, giving away ground to the leading trio. This he rapidly regained and just as Winkfield's Fortune had beaten off Easterling and Rosanule, Dillon launched his challenge on Lord Rossmore. The two colts raced head-to-head into the final furlong, where Winkfield's Fortune became unbalanced, giving the advantage to Lord Rossmore. Though Higgs rallied his mount and was gaining with every stride, Lord Rossmore just held on to win by a short head, with Easterling a respectable third in front of Rosanule. Though the second appeared unlucky not to get up and probably lost through inexperience, the winner showed tremendous gameness, for he was conceding all of 14lbs to the runner-up and had been in transit since winning at Ascot less than a week before.

Lord Rossmore was bred by Mr James Grew of Portadown, in whose colours he ran as a two-year-old, before being purchased by J. H. H. Peard on A. P. Cunliffe's behalf. His sire, Cherry Ripe, was owned by Lord Rossmore and stood throughout his career at Rossmore, Co. Monaghan. The fifth Baron Rossmore enjoyed a colourful, if costly career on the Turf, racing under the guidance of Captain Machell, often in the company of the Prince of Wales. His ancestors, whose family name was Westenra, were of Dutch origin and came to Ireland during the reign of Charles the Second. Long associated with racing in Ireland, their name and title are perpetuated in that connection by two famous Curragh training stables. Cherry Ripe, an un-raced son of Sterling, sired Cerasus, Red Heart and the Grand National winner, Drogheda, despite limited opportunities. He died at the age of eighteen, less than a year before his son's triumph. The winner's dam, Miss Georgie, was by Baron Farney, second in the Irish Derby of 1880. In three further outings in 1903 Lord Rossmore finished fifth in the Cesarewitch before coming a close third in the Manchester November Handicap, giving over 14lbs to first and second. He represented Druids' Lodge for a further six seasons, during which he won a number of small races. When Tom Lewis succeeded Jack Fallon at Druids' Lodge he had Lord Rossmore gelded and put to jumping. As a nine-year-old this long-serving Irish Derby winner was put back on the flat and successfully exploited in selling races before being bought by the Epsom trainer, Richard Wootton, who won two more of these lowly but lucrative events with him.

Just at the end of the last century five gentlemen of diverse yet complimentary talents agreed to combine those talents to one end – the extraction of large sums of money from the Ring. Alan Percy Cunliffe was one of this quintet, soon to earn renown as the 'Hermits of Salisbury Plain' or the 'Netheravon Confederacy'. Each member had a role to play. William Purefoy handled all the stable commissions, J. H. H. Peard acted as vet and spotter of talent in Ireland, Frank Forester provided numbers of useful horses, E. A. Wigan acted as the syndicate's spokesman, while A. P. Cunliffe administered stable policy.

Having selected a suitably isolated training establishment, Druids' Lodge, in the middle of Salisbury Plain, their next move was to recruit a trainer. The success of an Irishman campaigning a string of 'chasers in England during the winter months soon attracted their attention. Jack Fallon was accordingly installed in Druids' Lodge, a virtual prisoner, whose excursions were confined to taking horses to racemeetings. W. B. Purefoy held the indentures of an Irish-born apprentice, Joseph Dillon, whose more promising younger brother, Bernard, was imported and groomed as stable jockey. Total secrecy was the keynote of the syndicate's operations. The medium of their first major 'coup' was the three-year-old filly, Hackler's Pride, whose cantering success in the Cambridgeshire of 1902 netted the Confederacy £250,000. Hackler's Pride repeated her Cambridgeshire victory in 1903, while Ypsilanti, bought out of a seller for £300, cost the bookmakers fortunes when winning the Kempton 'Jubilee' in 1903 and 1904.

Although both Fallon and Dillon were becoming rich as a result of their employers' operations, neither could stand the enforced isolation indefinitely. When Fallon broke free in 1906 to become a public trainer he had amassed £70,000. Lacking the guidance of Cunliffe and the financial astuteness of Purefoy, he went broke in 1914. Despite several fresh starts, notably with Jimmy White at Foxhill, Fallon never managed to capitalise on his undoubted flair with horses. For some years prior to his death in 1936 he was supported by a charitable fund administered by Sir John Thursby.

A. P. Cunliffe owned Aboyeur, awarded the 1913 Derby on the disqualification of Craganour. Another good horse to carry his 'White, black seams' was Charles O'Malley, third in the Derby and second in the Gold Cup. While standing at W. B. Purefoy's Greenfields Stud in Tipperary, Charles O'Malley sired Charlebelle, winner of the Oaks in 1920 for Cunliffe. A director of Sandown Park, A. P. Cunliffe outlived Captain Forester, if only by a few days, to become the last surviving member of the Confederacy at the time of his death in September 1942.

Joseph Dillon, a native of Caherina, Co. Kerry, was still an apprentice when winning the Irish Derby on Lord Rossmore, the highlight of his racing career. He never reached the heights of his brother, 'Ben'. The latter, having escaped from the rigid confines of Druids' Lodge, soon became one of the foremost jockeys of the day. Stable jockey to P. P. Gilpin from 1906 to 1908, he rode two winners of the One Thousand Guineas, in addition to the Coronation Cup on Pretty Polly and the Grand Prix de Paris on Spearmint. For Alec Taylor's powerful Manton stable he won the Derby on Lemberg in 1910, dead-heated for the Eclipse Stakes on him and rode him to victory in the Coronation Cup in 1911, his last season to ride. An increasingly frequent visitor to London's West End, his judgement became erratic towards the end of his career. Joe Dillon, steadier, if less talented, than his younger brother, forsook the flat for his first love, steeplechasing. His biggest success in this sphere was winning the Imperial Hurdle on the one-eyed Rosendale, after whom he named his Epsom home. Joe Dillon then went to ride successfully in Austria, until forced to return to England at the onset of the Great War. When peace had been restored he ventured abroad once more, this time to Belgium, where he began training, numbering among his clients the infamous Horatio Bottomley. Wednesday 24th June 1903 was a day to remember not only for Joe Dillon, but also for his father, who had travelled from Kerry to witness his son's moment of glory in the Irish Derby. Overjoyed at his elder son's thrilling short head success, his happiness knew no bounds when he received the news from Newcastle mere minutes later that Ben had ridden Cliftonhall to victory in the Northumberland Plate.

Wednesday, 24th June, 1903   **£783**   **8 Ran**   **1½m (Howth Post)**

The Irish Derby of 1000sovs, by subscription of 17sovs each, but 8sovs only for horses struck out on or before the 3rd September, 1902. The second horse to receive 150sovs and the third 50sovs out of the plate. For three years old. Colts 8st 12lb; fillies 8st 8lb. If claimed at time of entry, produce of untried sires or mares allowed 3lb, but not for both. The winner of the Angleseys and Railways at the Curragh, or of two stakes value 300sovs each, 10lb extra; of the Angleseys or of a stake value 300sovs, or of stakes collectively value 600sovs, 7lb extra; of a stake value 200sovs, 3lb extra. Horses that have never won a stake value 100sovs, allowed 6lb; maidens allowed 10lb; only one of these allowances can be taken. Any person entering three horses, his own bona fide sole property, can strike out one at the time appointed for declaring forfeit without having to pay the forfeit.

(57 subs)

1 Mr A. P. Cunliffe's LORD ROSSMORE (J. Dillon)   9. 2   Fallon (UK)
Ch. colt Cherry Ripe – Miss Georgie by Baron Farney.

2 Mr J. C. Sullivan's WINKFIELD'S FORTUNE (W.   8. 2
Higgs)   Ch. colt Winkfield – Alimony.

3 Capt. Ashmore's EASTERLING (H. Buxton)   7.13
Bl/Br/Gr. colt Lesterlin – Victrix.

4 Mr C. J. Blake's ROSANULE*† (T. L. Miller)   8. 2   (NOT IN GSB)
B. colt Gallinule – Rosanene

5 Capt. Murray's CROOKHAVEN (J. Thompson)   8. 8
B. filly Circassian – Sweethaven.

6 Mr J. Lonsdale's LAUREL VALE (C. Whelan)   7.13
B. gelding Laveno – Copestone.

7 Mr W. Hall-Walker's ESTRAPADE* (Joseph Doyle)   7.13
B. colt Janissary – Ginestra.

8 Capt. Maher's FERNS (F. Morgan)   8. 2
B. gelding St Aidan – Minute Gun.

SP 6/4 LORD ROSSMORE; 7/4 Winkfield's Fortune; 5/1 Rosanule; 10/1 Bar.
Short head, 3 lengths.
Winner trained by Mr J. Fallon at Netherhaven.

*Rosanule and Estrapade were, on payment of the fine, each saddled outside the enclosure.
†Rosanule ran un-named.

1904

In pleasant contrast to the thunderstorms which marred the previous year's event, this Irish Derby was staged on sun-baked ground under cloudless skies, which must have made the touring South African cricket team feel quite at home among the large throng. Such was the crowd in the parade ring that one spectator had a miraculous escape. Kicked simultaneously by two of the runners, he suffered no more than the loss of his hat. An unusual feature of the field of nine was the inclusion of no less than three full-brothers of former Irish Derby winners. Of these the most strongly fancied was Cherry Pip, an own-brother of Lord Rossmore, from the same stable, though carrying the colours of J. H. H. Peard, the Irish-based associate of the 'Hermits of Salisbury Plain'. Cherry Pip had won the Champion Nursery at Hurst Park in November, beating Dean Swift. However, most favoured of the English runners was Glenamoy, a fine big chestnut son of Gallinule, despite his already being fired behind. Equally fancied was the locally-trained Royal Arch. Michael Dawson's representative had only run twice in his life, behind Pretty Polly on his debut and then second to the leading Irish two-year-old, Jean's Folly, in the Railway Stakes. No one any longer doubted Michael Dawson's ability to prepare a horse to win such a race first time out. Both Grey-Green and Leo XIII had been placed behind Jean's Folly as juveniles and despite the latter's second in the Baldoyle Plate, Grey-Green's prospects were more highly regarded.

The start was delayed for all of thirty minutes as the starter sought to get the unruly Christian de Wet and Leopardstown away on equal terms. Their antics upset Royal Arch and The Arrowed in turn. When the ever-patient Mr Blennerhassett finally got them away Grey-Green was the first to show from The Arrowed and Glenamoy. These were clear of the main group, headed by Leopardstown, with Christian de Wet bringing up the rear. Passing the mile mark Glenamoy took up the running from The Arrowed, Leopardstown, the fading Grey-Green and Royal Arch. As they reached the chains McCall became uneasy on the leader, as The Arrowed and Royal Arch closed with him. In the straight The Arrowed and Royal Arch drew clear with the race now between them. Hard as The Arrowed struggled under strong driving, he could not concede 13lbs to Royal Arch, who galloped home amidst tremendous cheering and applause. Glenamoy stayed on to take third place, a head in front of the early leader, Grey-Green.

The winner returned to a reception similar to that which greeted St Brendan two years previously. Although Royal Arch had not captured the imagination of the public in the same manner as St Brendan, he and his very popular owner had once again kept the great race at home in the face of a strong English challenge. In fact such were the scenes of enthusiasm that the master of Liffey Bank had to seek refuge from his well-wishers in the sanctuary of the Press room.

Royal Arch was bred by Miss Knox-Gore of Killala, Co. Mayo from her home-bred mare, Miss Augusta. The latter was out of Ballyroe, purchased from George Low in 1879, when her yearling by Solon was an unknown quantity. He was later to become famous as Barcaldine. Florizel II, sire of Royal Arch, stood at the Heath Stud, Newmarket at the high fee of 100gns. Though a good rather than great racehorse, it was his breeding that made him such an attractive stallion prospect. By the wonderful racehorse and sire, St Simon out of Perdita II, he was thus a full-brother of Persimmon and Diamond Jubilee, both Royal Derby winners. In the same year that Royal Arch was foaled Florizel II's son, Volodyovski, won the Derby. This might in part explain James Daly's willingness to pay Miss Knox-Gore a steep price for six foals, including Royal Arch and Glenamoy. In subsequently choosing which to sell and which to retain, James Daly gave further proof of his shrewd judgement in these matters.

On his next appearance Royal Arch beat two moderate rivals in a King's Plate over two miles at the Curragh in July. His only other successes were gained as a four-year-old, when he won two more such events, defeating a solitary rival on each occasion. His last appearance in public was in a hurdle race at Baldoyle in January 1906. This otherwise mundane affair was distinguished by the performance of one of Royal Arch's Derby victims, Leo XIII. Since re-named Capo Lazarro, he had turned savage and in the course of the race seized an unfortunate jockey by the foot, refushing to release his hold even as he jumped the hurdles. Royal Arch was subsequently retired to stud at Mill House, Knockdrin, near Mullingar, at the modest fee of 5gns. He got scant opportunity to prove his worth, being found dead in his box at the age of seven. The Arrowed went on to win over both hurdles and fences as a four-year-old, before being sold to race in America, where he collapsed and died in a race at Los Angeles, also aged seven. Of the others Grey-Green did best, while Christian de Wet, though successful on the flat and over hurdles, never looked like emulating the standard of his brother, Oppressor.

FRANK MORGAN

One of a famous Waterford family of horsemen, closely related to the Widgers, Hurleys and Murphys, Frank Morgan was one of sixteen cousins riding at the one time, of whom no less than eight were Morgans. He was born in the ancestral home in 1887 and initially apprenticed to his cousin, T. J. Widger. Transferred to J. J. Parkinson, he rode his first winner when weighing only 5st 12lbs. After two years he moved to Michael Dawson, becoming first jockey to James Daly. At the time of his success on Royal Arch he was still an apprentice. Destined by nature to become too heavy for the flat, he soon switched successfully to riding over obstacles, becoming champion jockey in Ireland under both codes in 1917. On one occasion, at Down-patrick, he rode the winner of all six races on the card. After the First World War he turned his attention to training, his first major success in the role being achieved with Clonree in the Galway Plate of 1920, trained and ridden by Frank Morgan. Clonree was only one of three winners of the Grand Sefton sent out from his Curragh stables. However, it was with another of his Grand Sefton winners that this immensely skilful trainer achieved lasting renown. In 1925, when the race was still in its infancy, he saddled Ballinode, a fast, chancy jumper, otherwise known as 'the Sligo mare', to win the Cheltenham Gold Cup. Thus began a family connection with the Gold Cup, for in 1938, Danny Morgan rode the winner, Morse Code, the first and only horse to beat Golden Miller at Cheltenham. For good measure Danny sent out Roddy Owen to win it in 1959, ridden by Bobby Beasley, whose father and great-uncle had ridden winners of the Irish Derby.

Wednesday, 29th June, 1904   **£783**   **9 Ran**   **1½m (Howth Post)**

The Irish Derby of 1000sovs, by subscription of 17sovs each, but 8sovs only for horses struck out on or before the 2nd September, 1903. The second horse to receive 150sovs and the third 50sovs out of the plate. For three years old. Colts 8st 12lb; fillies 8st 8lb. If claimed at time of entry, produce of untried sires or mares allowed 3lb, but not for both. The winner of the Angleseys and Railways at the Curragh, or of two stakes value 300sovs each, 10lb extra; of the Angleseys or of a stake value 300sovs, or of stakes collectively value 600sovs, 7lb extra; of a stake value 200sovs, 3lb extra. Horses that have never won a stake value 100sovs, allowed 6lb; maidens allowed 10lb; only one of these allowances can be taken. Any person entering three horses, his own bona fide sole property, can strike out one at the time appointed for declaring forfeit without having to pay the forfeit.

(58 subs)

1 Mr James Daly's	ROYAL ARCH (F. Morgan)	8. 2	
	Br. colt Florizel – Miss Augusta by Mr Winkle.		
2 Mr S. M. Nolan's	THE ARROWED (H. Buxton)	9. 1	(UK)
	Bl. colt Gallinule – Little May.		
3 Mr L. Robinson's	GLENAMOY (G. M'Call)	8.12	(UK)
	Ch. colt Gallinule – Alice Morgan.		
4 Mr R. Canning's	GREY-GREEN (John Doyle)	7.13	
	Br. colt Grey Leg – Ivy Spray.		
5 Mr G. Hurley's	LEO XIII* (W. Higgs)	8. 2	
	B. colt Laveno – Homeless.		
6 Mr J. Lonsdale's	LEOPARDSTOWN (A. Anthony)	9. 2	
	B. colt Laveno – Mareca.		
7 Mr J. H. Peard's	CHERRY PIP* (J. Dillon)	9. 5	Fallon (UK)
	Ch. colt Cherry Ripe – Miss Georgie.		
8 Mr F. Rock's	RED HEART'S PRIDE (J. M'Quillan) Ch. filly Red Heart – Millrace.	8. 5	
9 Mr C. J. Blake's	CHRISTIAN DE WET (J. Thompson) Br. colt Gallinule – Moira.	8. 2	

SP 5/2 ROYAL ARCH, Glenamoy; 6/1 Cherry Pip, Grey-Green; 10/1 Bar.
Won easily by 3 lengths, same, head.
Winner trained by Mr M. Dawson at Rathbride Manor, Curragh.

*Cherry Pip & Leo XIII were, on payment of the fine, saddled outside the enclosure.

1905

Although it did not include any overseas challengers, the 1905 race was full of interest. The previous season had not produced any outstanding two-year-olds and as a consequence the field of eleven bore a very open appearance. The enthusiastic and extrovert Lord Rossmore had acquired both Silver Wedding and Waddler the year before. Both had won good races as juveniles, but the former was thought to have made the greater progress and accordingly his owner declared to win with Silver Wedding, an own-brother of the 1903 winner. However, the eventual favourite was still a maiden, Jenatzy, purchased as an un-named two-year-old by 'Boss' Croker, and named after the celebrated racing driver, M. Jenatzy, who had won the 1903 Gordon Bennett Trophy at the Phoenix Park, driving a Mercedes-Benz at the incredible average speed of 55mph. Despite being unsuited by the firm ground, Jenatzy displaced James Daly's Galgreina as favourite. The latter had the most impressive recent form, having won over a mile at Sandown in April, ridden by Danny Maher. The only other runner with public form to attract any real support was Frank Morgan's mount, Young Abercorn, recently successful in three races. Adding interest to an already intriguing betting market was the inspired money for the lightly-raced Flax Park, a last-minute booking for fiery Peter Hughes, smarting at being 'jocked off' Velocity, winner of the April Stakes.

Following the customary delay at the start, caused in the main by Young Abercorn, Flax Park and Velocity, all eleven got off to a good start. In the early stages Silver Wedding took them along at a good gallop ahead of Jenatzy and Young Abercorn, with Landgrave and Velocity trailing. Jenatzy took it up with a mile to run, followed by Galgreina and Young Abercorn, with Velocity still in the rear. Approaching the straight Jenatzy dropped back, beaten by the ground, giving way to Silver Wedding, who led into the straight clear of Young Abercorn, Galgreina, The Priory and Waddler, with Flax Park and Velocity improving. The last-named surged to the fore with two furlongs to cover, challenged by Galgreina and Flax Park. These three drew clear, locked in combat, in which Galgreina was definitely hampered. Close home Flax Park got the better of Velocity and ran on well to win by a length, with Galgreina two and a half lengths further back. Chief sufferer in the rugged closing stages was undoubtedly Galgreina and had she finished second Halsey would certainly have objected. However, she was beaten in the end as much by lack of stamina as by interference.

The most curious feature of the race was the running and riding of Velocity. Supposedly a non-stayer, he had lain a long way out of his ground in the early stages, shot suddenly from last to first and only been beaten close home, conceding 17lbs to the winner. His puzzling performance provoked a Stewards' enquiry. His owner's explanation has not been revealed to posterity and we must be content with the knowledge that it was found acceptable by the powers-that-were. Time was to prove Velocity an extremely unlucky loser. Transferred to England, he concluded the season by winning the Cambridgeshire and went on to win the Doncaster Cup, City and Suburban Handicap and Grand Prix d'Ostende, proving himself one of the best of his generation. By contrast, Flax Park, while he won the Liverpool Cup as a four-year-old, accomplished little else and was eventually exported to Denmark in 1908.

Flax Park was bred by his owner, Mr P. J. Dunne of Carrolstown, Trim. His sire, Bushey Park, had an honourable racing career, proving himself a high-class stayer by victories in the Newmarket St Leger, Alexandra Plate, Great Yorkshire Stakes and Liverpool Cup. During his career at the Hartstown Stud, Clonsilla, as the property of James Daly, he was for many years a leading sire, heading the list in 1904. Despite being an out-and-out stayer himself, he was capable of siring very fast animals, notably Bushey Belle, winner of both the Phoenix and National Stakes and the best filly of 1902. Flax, the dam of Flax Park, was bred by P. J. Dunne in 1896. All four of her produce were by Bushey Park, before her early demise in 1907.

Classic success came very late in life to Flax Park's owner. Born in 1833, P. J.

James 'Fairy' Dunne, *doyen of Irish trainers, whose four successes in the Irish Derby spanned a quarter of a century. Source:* Irish Field.

John Thompson, *pioneer of the American crouch in Ireland, nine times Irish champion jockey, whose tragic death in 1913 deprived him of victory in Ireland's greatest race. Source:* Sporting Annual 1901.

Dunne was an owner-breeder, who raced for sport. His early love was steeplechasing and it was in that sphere that he had his first winner, at Punchestown more than thirty years previously. In 1904 his Ascetic's Silver won the Irish Grand National and what might have been a fabulous double for Mr Dunne in 1905 was marred by the fact that while Ascetic's Silver was first past the post at Aintree, he was, alas, riderless. Although the horse made ample amends twelve months later, P. J. Dunne did not live to realize his life's ambition. Already mortally ill at the time of Flax Park's Derby victory, he died the following September. Besides being a member of Meath County Council, P. J. Dunne did an immense amount of work for the poor of Trim, particularly in establishing a school for the children of the workhouse. Following Mr Dunne's death Flax Park was bought by James Daly for 1,400gns and subsequently passed on to Mr P. Cullinan, in whose colours he won the Liverpool Cup, thus emulating his sire. Some years later Mr P. Cullinan won the Railway Stakes with Flax Meadow, also by Bushey Park.

In offering the mount on Flax Park to Peter Hughes, James Dunne secured a jockey with a burning will to win, preferably at the immediate expense of the Jacksons' Velocity. Apparently Hughes had been employed by the Jacksons in their private stable in Roscrea and had learned only the previous day that he did not after all ride Volocity. Furiously upset, Hughes resigned on the spot and took the first train back to Kildare. A chance encounter with James Dunne resulted in his booking for the ride on Flax Park. By his own account Hughes immediately went and bought a new whip for the occasion. When he pulled up Flax Park after winning, he found that only the handle of the stick remained! Though doubtless exaggerated, this anecdote, which he never tired of recounting, gives a fair idea of both his temperament and his riding style. Nevertheless, in an era in which John Thompson, the ultimate 'stick jockey', reigned supreme, Peter Hughes was both popular and successful, though he never headed the list. Having had his best year in 1906, he won his second Irish Derby in 1908 and rode his last major winner on The County in the Madrid Plate in 1915, a race he had won three times previously, since coming to prominence at the turn of the century.

Wednesday, 28th June, 1905	£783	11 Ran	1½m (Howth Post)

The Irish Derby of 1000sovs, by subscription of 17sovs each, but 8sovs only for horses struck out on or before the 7th September, 1904. The second horse to receive 150sovs and the third 50sovs out of the plate. For three years old. Colts 8st 12lb; fillies 8st 8lb. If claimed at time of entry, produce of untried mares allowed 3lb. The winner of the Angleseys and Railways at the Curragh, or of two stakes value 300sovs, each, 10lb extra; of the Angleseys or of a stake value 300sovs, or of stakes collectively value 600sovs, 7lb extra; of a stake value 200sovs, 3lb extra. Horses that have never won a stake value 100sovs, allowed 6lb; maidens allowed 10lb; only one of these allowances can be taken. Any person entering three horses, his own bona fide sole property, can strike out one at the time appointed for declaring forfeit without having to pay the forfeit.

(54 subs)

1	Mr P. J. Dunne's	FLAX PARK (P. Hughes) B. colt Bushey Park – Flax by Hackler.	7.13	Dunne
2	Mr H. V. Jackson's	VELOCITY (J. Smyth) B. colt Speed – Ballast.	9. 2	Balfe
3	Mr James Daly's	GALGREINA (W. Halsey) Br. colt Gallinule – The Interloper.	9. 5	Dawson
4	Lord Rossmore's	SILVER WEDDING (H. Buxton) Ch. colt Cherry Ripe – Miss Georgie.	9. 5	Shanahan
5	Capt. W. Scott's	YOUNG ABERCORN (F. Morgan) Ch. colt Abercorn – Arriot.	8. 6	M'Guire
6	Lord Rossmore's	WADDLER (John Doyle) Br. colt Wildfowler – Raia.	9. 2	Shanahan
7	Mr J. Clune's	THE PRIORY (John Doyle, jr.) Br. colt Desmond – Bodega.	9. 2	Dunne
8	Mr T. K. Laidlaw's	HARE WARREN (G. Butchers) B. colt Bushey Park – Lady Julia.	8. 9	Dawson
9	Mr R. Croker's	JENATZY (J.Thompson) Br. colt Speed – Benedictine.	8. 6	Parkinson
10	Mr John Widger's	AIDANCE (M. Widger) B/Br. colt St Aidan – Miss Corogh Hill.	8. 2	W. Behan
11	Mr C. J. Blake's	LANDGRAVE (F. Hunter) B. colt Portmarnock or Lesterlin – Elflock.	7.13	Private

SP 5/2 Jenatzy; 7/2 Galgreina; 5/1 FLAX PARK, Silver Wedding, Young Abercorn; 100/3 Bar.
1 length, 2½ lengths. 2m 37.4/5s.
Winner trained by Mr J. Dunne at Osborne Lodge, Curragh.

Lord Rossmore declared to win with Silver Wedding.
Velocity was saddled outside the enclosure.
  The Stewards of the Turf Club called on Mr Jackson to explain the previous running of Velocity during the year; and having heard his statement, accepted his explanation.

1906

The field for Irish Derby of 1906 did not appear beforehand to be up to the standard of previous years. Prime pre-race fancies were Juliet II, winner of the Waterford Testimonial Stakes in her first season and Steinhager, the prime contender from Maddenstown Lodge, trained there by J. J. Parkinson for Boss Croker.

This year marked the introduction of a railed parade ring; timely in view of the enormous crowd, which the brilliant sunshine brought flocking in. Parkinson saddled three runners in the field of nine, Steinhager, Gaultier and Bells of Shandon. Michael Dawson was doubly represented by Cascatella and Killeagh, while Phillie Behan saddled Juliet II. The huge crowd made Steinhager favourite at 5-to-2, with Juliet II and Cascatella next in demand. Despite the Irish Field reporter's comments that, 'In the paddock Mr Lowry's colt carried off the palm, and he seemed trained to the hour', Killeagh was largely ignored at 100-7.

After a delayed start Bells of Shandon, the intended pacemaker for Steinhager, was slowly away. In consequence the favourite was forced to make his own running at a false pace. At the top of the hill, with six furlongs to race, Thompson kicked on with Steinhager and appeared to have the measure of Juliet II, as they entered the straight. However, both Killeagh and Veno had been taking progressively closer order. Drawing level with the leader, Killeagh burst ahead at the distance to win cleverly by 1½L., with Veno a short head behind the favourite in third place.

The Irish Field described Killeagh thus: 'He would stand about 15.3 so, like his dam's produce, he is not a big one but is a beautifully balanced, symetrically turned three-year-old, showing quite a lot of quality and in such perfect condition did Michael Dawson send him to the post that he had scarcely turned a hair when he returned to the paddock.'

Clyde Aylin, the rider of Killeagh, was born in England and apprenticed to W. T. Robinson at Foxhill. He moved to Ireland at the turn of the century to ride for S. C. Jeffreys, private trainer to Blakes of the Heath and married to a sister of Jeffrey's wife. He rode subsequently for the Dawson stable and latterly over obstacles for R. H. Walker. In 1906 he finished second in the jockeys table to the peerless John Thompson. Champion jockey in Ireland for the first and only time in 1922 with 70 winners, he was killed riding over fences at the Leopardstown Christmas meeting of that year. His tragic and untimely death deprived Ireland of a very honest and competent rider, besides leaving a widow and six young children. He is buried near the historic Rock of Dunamase, hard by the former Blake establishment on Maryborough Heath.

Within a few weeks of his Derby success Killeagh was sold to the English financier Sir Ernest Cassell, for a price in the region of £4,000. His sale price contrasts sharply to the winner's stake in the Irish Derby of 1906 – £783. Transferred to the care of the Hon. George Lambton at Newmarket, Killeagh raced for a further two seasons, during which he won three times at Newmarket and ran with the distinction in races such as the Ascot Gold Vase and the Manchester Gold Cup.

At the end of his racing career Killeagh was purchased by Dr Kennedy and repatriated to stand in Tullamore. Despite being reasonably priced and extensively

115

promoted, Killeagh did not prove successful as a stallion. By 1918 his fee had fallen to a nominal £5 2s 6d. His only winner of note was The County, winner of the Madrid Free Handicap in 1915, the same year in which Punch, by Killyleagh, won the Irish Grand National.

Of those that finished behind Killeagh in the Irish Derby, Steinhager went on to win several good races, twice beating Flax Park in King's Plates. Juliet II won the Irish Oaks, ridden by Algy Anthony, rider of Ambush II, when the latter won the Grand National of 1900. She was subsequently sold to Boss Croker for 1600gns and amply repaid his investment both on the racecourse and in the paddocks.

Killeagh was bred by W. P. 'Willie' Cullen, the Waterford Lodge trainer and former leading amateur rider. Out of a moderate racemare called What, Killeagh was by the Kendal horse, Killyleagh, trained by Cullen to win the Sandown Grand Prize and subsequently purchased as a stallion by Dr J. M. Kennedy, who stood him

---

Wednesday, 27th June, 1906 **£783** **9 Ran** **1½m (Howth Post)**

The Irish Derby of 1000sovs, for three years old. Colts 8st 12lb; fillies 8st 8lb. If claimed at time of entry, produce of untried mares allowed 3lb. The winner of the Angleseys and Railways at the Curragh, or of two stakes value 300sovs each, 10lb extra; of the Angleseys or of a stake value 300, or of stakes collectively value 600sovs, 7lb extra; of a stake value 200sovs, 3lb extra. Horses that have never won a stake value 100sovs, allowed 6lb; maidens allowed 10lb; only one of these allowances can be taken. The second horse to receive 150sovs and the third 50sovs out of the stake. By subscription of 17sovs each, but 8sovs only for horses struck out on or before the 6th September, 1905. Any person entering three horses, his own bona fide sole property, can strike out one at the time appointed for declaring forfeit without having to pay the forfeit.

(65 subs)

1 Mr J Lowry's	KILLEAGH (C. Aylin)	9. 5	Dawson
	B. colt Killyleagh – What by Oberon.		
2 Mr R. Croker's	STEINHAGER (J. Thompson)	8.12	Parkinson
	B/Br. colt Count Schomberg – Benedictine.		
3 Mr C. Wadia's	VENO (late Cracky Ice) (H.	8. 2	Private
	Robbins) B. gelding Laveno – Iceberg.		
4 Mrs Sadleir-Jackson's	JULIET II (A. Anthony)	8.12	P. Behan
	B. filly Troubadour – Miss Carden.		
5 Mr R. D. Jameson's	CINDER BILL* (Mr G. W.	8.12	Hunter
	Lushington) Br. colt Bill of Portland – Cinder Ellen.		
6 Mr James Daly's	CASCATELLA (P. Hughes)	7. 9	Dawson
	B. filly Hackler – Powerscourt.		
7 Mr John Widger's	GAULTIER (M. Widger)	9. 1	Parkinson
	Ch. colt Wildfowler – Delores by George Frederick.		
8 Mr J. Lonsdale's	CHEVEN (Joseph Doyle)	7.13	W. Behan
	Ch. colt Chevening – Miss Florian.		
9 Mr R. Croker's	BELLS OF SHANDON (F. Hunter)	7.13	Parkinson
	B. colt Amerious – Richfield Belle.		

SP 5/2 Steinhager; 3/1 Juliet; 7/2 Cascatella; 100/8 Veno, Gaultier; 100/7 KILLEAGH; 100/3 Bar.

1½ lengths, Short head.
Winner trained by Mr M. Dawson at Rathbride Manor, Curragh.

*Cinder Bill was saddled outside the enclosure.

at Elmfield, Tullamore. Killeagh was one of only two to race from Killyleagh's first crop. Cullen sold What in foal to Mr W. W. Kilroy for 28gns and Mr Kilroy passed on the subsequent produce to Joseph Lowry of Bachelors Lodge for £50 and a 'fiver' back for luck.

Lightly raced as a two-year-old; in accordance with Dawson policy, Killeagh ran only twice. First time out he finished in the ruck behind Juliet II in the Waterford Testimonial Stakes at the Curragh. On his second and final two-year-old run, ridden by the English jockey George Butchers, he ran the odds-on Dive to a short head in the Beresford Stakes, over one mile in the Curragh in October. Prior to the Derby he ran only once as a three-year-old, when dead-heating with American Boy for the April Stakes over seven furlongs at the Curragh. It was a classic example of Dawson's patience and skill which made him the outstanding trainer of his era. His handling of Killeagh had told both the owner and himself all they needed to know, while revealing virtually nothing to the public. It was no accident that one well-known commission agent was seen to have twenty 'ponies' on Killeagh at 100-to-7.

Michael Dawson, master of Rathbride Manor on the edge of the Curragh, rode three Irish Derby winners before commencing training. In this sphere he was immediately successful, saddling a further four winners of the premier Irish Classic. From 1906, when Irish training statistics were first compiled, until his death in 1925, Michael Dawson was leading trainer no less than ten times and runner-up on a further five occasions.

Killeagh's owner, Mr Joseph Lowry was a long standing patron of the Dawson stable, besides being one of the leading breeders and owners of the period. The story of the fortuitous circumstances which led to his purchase of Tredennis, the champion stallion, is part of Irish racing history. By him Lowry got a whole stream of good horses, such as Bachelor's Button and Bachelor's Double. The former was one of the very few ever to beat Pretty Polly and the latter gave Dawson his fourth and final success in the Irish Derby of 1908.

1907

That the Irish Derby of 1907 was a non-betting event mattered not a damn, they flocked in their thousands to see it. The magnet that drew horsemen from all corners of Ireland was the new four-legged, four-letter national hero – Orby. By his historic triumph in the Epsom Derby – the greatest race in the world – Richard Croker's colt had done more to enhance the prestige of Irish racing than any man or beast before him. By risking his immensely valuable colt in a race of relatively trivial importance, Croker was simply paying tribute to the racing fraternity who had welcomed him with open arms when others had shunned him. The huge crowd cheered Orby when he appeared in the paddock and again as he cantered to the post. Though six took the field against him, including his pacemaker Georgetown, Orby's presence 'quite paralysed speculation and although it was really 100-to-1 on him few cared to lay the 10-to-1 asked by the bookmakers'. The 'race' itself is equally well described by the Irish Field: 'The crack simply lobbed along in third place until making the line for home. Here he shot to the front and practically ambled past the post four lengths ahead of Georgetown, who easily beat Gleg. Apart from when St Brendan beat Port Blair no Irish Derby winner ever received such an ovation.'

Croker's generous and public-spirited gesture, while of incalculable benefit to the status of the Irish Derby, was to prove disastrous to the future racecourse career of his champion. His trainer, Col F. F. McCabe, had begged Croker not to run his weak-jointed colt on the prevailing hard ground, claiming, with good reason, that Georgetown would prove a perfectly capable deputy. Though Orby pulled up sore, Croker felt his decision vindicated and ordered McCabe to train Orby for the St Leger . . . In July Orby finished last of four at Liverpool and a month later the Irish Field reported sadly that: 'Orby has sprained the sub-carpal ligament of his off fore-leg, which practically amounts to a breakdown and so all question of his running in the St Leger is set at rest.' Thus ended the career of the most celebrated winner trained in Ireland up to that time.

The saga of Orby and his colourful connections is a lengthy legend. However, because of its enormous significance in the development of Irish racing, we make no apology for relating it here. The story begins with his extraordinary owner, Richard Croker. Born in Clonakilty, Co. Cork, in 1841, Croker and his parents fled the ravages of the Famine, arriving penniless in New York in 1848. Working his way up from the bottom in Tammany Hall politics, Croker eventually defeated 'Boss' Tweed for control of Tammany Hall, thus becoming the most influential man in New York, henceforth known as 'Boss' Croker. Having begun racing in New York with some success, Croker anticipated the closure of the New York tracks when moving himself and his horses to England, where he employed Charles Morton as his trainer and set out to demonstrate the supremacy of the American thoroughbred.

In his memoirs Morton describes his problems in trying to win races with Croker's American-breds, many of which had been doped while racing in America. The experiment was not a success and Morton was under no illusions as to the reasons: 'Time after time it has been clearly proved that valuable horses never properly acclimatize when transported thousands of miles away.' He goes on to point out that other American owners only achieved success in England when: 'Croker showed them the fatuity of ousting the British thoroughbred with horses reared and trained for nothing but speed.'

When it became obvious that Charles Morton, a quietly determined master of his craft, would not be any man's lackey, Croker decided to transfer operations to Newmarket, headquarters of English racing. To his furious dismay Croker learned that the Jockey Club would not grant permission for his horses to be trained on Newmarket Heath. One of the Stewards who handed down this generally surprising decision was Colonel E. W. Baird. Vowing vengeance, Croker transferred himself and his horses to Ireland, where he purchased and restored Glencairn, outside Dublin, forming a stud there and putting his ever-increasing string in training with J. J. Parkinson on the Curragh. Morton concludes that it was only when Croker abandoned his American-is-best policy and founded his stud in Ireland that he achieved success in the form of Orby. What Morton overlooks is that one of Croker's many imports was a yearling filly named Rhoda B, trained by Morton to win first time out as a two-year-old and finish second in two more good races in 1897. Retired to Croker's stud, she produced two foals to his imported stallions Americus and Dobbins, before foaling a chestnut colt by Orme in 1904.

Subsequently named Orby, the colt ran twice as a two-year-old when trained by Parkinson. Very well tried, Orby made his debut at Leopardstown in August 1906. Starting a red-hot favourite at 3-to-1 ON and ridden by the champion jockey John Thompson, Orby finished only third to Mr Laidlaw's Gleg, ridden by Clyde Aylin. His second and final race as a two-year-old was in the Railway Stakes over six furlongs at the Curragh in September. Starting second favourite, he could finish only third behind Electric Rose and Silver Fowl. The winner, also owned by Croker and ridden by the Maddenstown Lodge apprentice Tom Peare, was completely unfancied.

During the winter of 1906 Croker moved his string, now the largest in Ireland, to Glencairn and appointed Colonel F. F. McCabe as his trainer, the licence being held by James Allen. Orby, who had been transferred from Parkinson to Atty Persse at Stockbridge, was brought back to Glencairn in November. In his first outing as a three-year-old Orby put up an impressive performance in the Earl of Sefton's Plate at Liverpool. Ridden by the stable apprentice Alan Buck, Orby came right around his field to win by three lengths. At last he seemed likely to fulfil his immense promise. Reappearing in the Baldoyle Derby (or Plate as it was that year), Orby was fairly mobbed during the preliminaries. He had never been seen to look so well. Casting aside his two pacemakers, Orby won so easily that he had covered a further two furlongs before Bullock could pull him up. Immediately money began to pour on him for the Epsom Derby and the sheer weight of Irish money forced his price down from 66-to-1 to 100-to-9. Still the English sporting press refused to entertain the possibility that an Irish-trained horse could possibly win the Epsom Derby. Most dogmatic in his disbelief was William Allison of the Sportsman, who wrote: 'The turf in Ireland has no spring in it, the climate is too depressing, and no Irish trainer knows enough to even dare to compete for the greatest race in the world.'

Despite the fact that Orby had won over the full Derby distance at Baldoyle, Croker decided that the colt would not get the trip at Epsom and ordered him to be struck out of the Derby. After a blazing row with McCabe, who pointed out that half the country had backed the horse, Croker agreed to let him take his chance, but insisted that a 'first rate' jockey be engaged. After the names of Maher, Lynham and Halsey had been bandied about, Johnny Reiff was brought over from France for the mount.

A further indication of the prevailing English attitude to Irish-trained horses is provided by the Royal trainer Richard Marsh in his autobiography: 'I was taken to see Orby in his box on the morning of the race. He had done his work at Epsom and was quietly eating his feed. The top half of the door was open and all the windows. A bitter wind was blowing in, and there was Orby, with no clothes on, and looking as though he had never even been dressed over. I could see he was a horse with a magnificent frame, but lacking most conspicuously in muscular development.' Later that morning Marsh remarked to Sam Darling, trainer of the favourite, Slieve Gallion; 'I have seen a beautiful horse this morning, but I never saw one look much worse to run in the Derby.'

In the race itself the favourite hit the front a mile out. At six furlongs he was clear of Benzonian, Galvani, Orby and Wool Winder. Two furlongs from home

Slieve Gallion's stamina gave out and Orby took up the running, with an easy victory apparently in sight. However, he in turn reached the end of his tether, began to hang badly and in the end just lasted home to beat Wool Winder by two lengths. A triumph for Ireland, Orby's victory was Croker's revenge and the fact that Wool Winder belonged to Colonel E. W. Baird made victory seem sweeter still. Orby returned to Ireland to an incredible reception. Bonfires were lit in the streets of Dublin and the astonished animal was paraded through cheering crowds, preceded by a brass band. The elation felt throughout the country was aptly summed up by one old woman's remark to McCabe: 'Thank God and you, Sir, that we have lived to see a Catholic horse win the Derby!'

Richard Croker's impact upon Irish racing must be visualized in a much wider context than the breeding and ownership of the first Irish-trained winner of the Epsom Derby. Writing some years later, Colonel McCabe described Croker's significance thus: 'Irish racing badly needs men (such as Croker) who can afford to race on an extensive scale and who are not always ready to sell to the first, or highest, bidder who comes along' . . . He started to race in the most lordly fashion and was soon head of the list of winning owners in Ireland (1905, 1906 and 1911). He not only refused to sell his own winners, but he insisted upon buying the best that ran against his. Such a man was a Godsend to Ireland, where the Turf was under the government of men, who were, for the most part, just horsedealers and breeders for sale, who elected each other to the Club and to the stewardship of the Club. Mr Croker himself could never understand why, when he owned more horses than any other man in Ireland and ran more and won more races, he should not be a member of the Turf Club. But as the Club is constituted up to the present, Mr Croker had as much chance of being translated up to heaven alive as he had of securing election to the Club. Plus ca change . . . However, Croker's successor as godfather of Irish racing, who, coincidentally, also lived and had his horses trained in Sandyford, would not encounter such resistance.

Lest anyone should have attempted to dismiss Orby's epic victory as a flash in the pan, Croker and McCabe returned later the same season with Orby's half-sister Rhodora, with whom they lifted the valuable Dewhurst Plate, at Newmarket. The following season Rhodora returned to Newmarket to carry off the One Thousand Guineas. Croker's revenge was complete.

Croker and McCabe parted company at the end of the best season that either would ever experience. Allen remained in Croker's employ, until he too was replaced in 1913 by F. Grundy and C. Prendergast. Croker continued to enjoy fair success on the Irish Turf and had the additional satisfaction of seeing Orby establish himself as an excellent stallion. Diadem credited Orby with his first Classic winner when taking the One Thousand Guineas in 1917. A year previously, Croker, having decided to take a prolonged trip to America, sold off most of his bloodstock, including a colt foal by Orby, secured by Lord Glanely for 470gns. Later named Grand Parade, he gave Orby his greatest success when emulating his sire in the Epsom Derby. However, it was a posthumous honour for Orby, who had dropped dead in 1918. His line survives through The Boss, a fast horse who sired another like himself in Sir Cosmo, the sire of Panorama. Through The Boss Orby also became the great-grandsire of that good sprinter and stallion Golden Bridge. The line has always been notable for speed rather than stamina.

'Boss' Croker did not long outlive his favourite horse, dying of thrombosis in April 1922, 'full of years, honours and troubles', as one American writer put it. He was buried in a lakeside mausoleum within sight of Glencairn. His pallbearers included Oliver St John Gogarty, 'Alfie' Byrne and Arthur Griffith, reflecting Croker's quietly influential role in Irish political circles. Ironically, his house is today the British Ambassador's residence, while the stables and gallops belong to the McGrath family. Years after his death Croker's remains were removed to a nearby graveyard. This his spirit appears to resent, for there have been frequent sightings of his burly, bearded, frock-coated figure floating through the house and grounds. In those to whom Croker reappeared, mainly old retainers and their families, his ghost aroused only the most kindly recollections and Gogarty might well have had his friend in mind when he wrote:

> Remark, I shall have worth
> Achieved before Life fades:
> A gentle man on Earth
> And gentle 'mid the Shades.

Colonel F. F. McCabe, 'Boss' Croker's racing manager and trainer at the time of Orby's famous victory, had already packed a lot into his forty-odd years. Born in 1868, he had already achieved a considerable reputation as a racing cyclist and cross-country runner by the time he qualified as a Doctor of Medicine in 1891. He then volunteered for service with the South Irish Horse in the Boer War, returning to Ireland with the rank of Surgeon-Captain. Settling in Park Lodge, Sandyford, he began training racehorses, with a fair share of success, one of his best being the filly Sabine Queen, the medium of his sensational objection to the length of the 'five furlong' course at Leopardstown. She subsequently won the Irish Oaks for him. At the end of the 1906 season, McCabe's neighbour, 'Boss' Croker, though once again leading owner in Ireland, was thoroughly dissatisfied with the performance of his string. One particular cause of this was the public record of Orby. Tried a brilliant horse, Orby could finish only third in the Railway Stakes to stable companion Electric Rose. Though the winner carried Croker's colours, she was in fact leased from her trainer J. J. Parkinson. Under the terms of the lease the prize money went to the lessor . . . For Croker this proved the final straw. In McCabe's own words: 'He turned to his neighbour, who, with a very few horses, was winning a great many races.' Thus began a turbulent association, as short-lived as it was successful. An idea of the scale and intensity of their operation is provided by their participation at the Irish Derby meeting, at which Croker's colours were carried eleven times, winning four races. For good measure, Leucosia, Croker's present to McCabe for winning the Epsom Derby, also won at the meeting. A colourful and opinionated character, McCabe was not disposed to kiss the rod, which Croker's New York experience had accustomed him to wield. Their final falling-out arose over Croker's insistence on selling Hayden, Orby's lead horse, at the end of the season. McCabe contended that the horse, who had more than paid his way, was simply stale after an arduous season. Croker would not be gainsaid and they parted. The following year a refreshed Hayden won the Kempton Jubilee for the Persse stable.

Twelve months after his triumph with Orby, F. F. McCabe featured in an even more romantic and improbable Epsom success. Having split with Croker, McCabe moved to Newmarket, setting up as a public trainer at Queensbury Lodge, with William Bullock as stable jockey. One of McCabe's first patrons was the eccentric Italian Chevalier Ginistrelli, who, to the amusement of the racing fraternity in Newmarket, aspired to win the Epsom Derby with his love-match filly, Signorinetta. Although McCabe has never officially been credited with her preparation, both he and Bullock were closely involved with the filly. In the One Thousand Guineas Signorinetta finished down the field and trainer and jockey must have looked on with distinctly mixed feelings as a beaming 'Boss' Croker led in his winner, Rhodora, ridden by Bullock's successor, the American Lucien Lyne. However, undaunted, the Chevalier insisted on sending Signorinetta to Epsom, where, ridden by Bullock, she astounded the racing world with a smooth success in the Derby. Two days later the same partnership conclusively silenced the sceptics when carrying off the Oaks, in which Rhodora was brought down. To add insult to injury, Croker saw the ecstatic Chevalier being presented to King Edward VII, an honour he had bitterly criticized McCabe for failing to achieve on his behalf a year earlier. Unfortunately Signorinetta's extraordinary Epsom double brought no lasting reward either to Bullock or McCabe, the latter receiving no more than a glass of wine and a cigar.

McCabe later saw service in the First World War and in the Irish Free State Army. Thereafter he combined training with journalism, becoming proprietor of the Irish Field. He was still active in both capacities until shortly before his death at Sandyford in 1954, still the only man to have sent out an Irish-trained winner of the Epsom Derby.

William Bullock, the rider of Orby at Baldoyle and the Curragh, though not at Epsom, came from an old-established North of England racing family. His uncle, Ralph Bullock, rode Kettledrum to win the Epsom Derby in 1861, while his brother, Bertram, better known as George, rode and trained with some success. Apprenticed to Malton trainer Tom Bruckshaw in 1901, William Bullock had ridden only a handful of winners before the declining fortunes of the Bruckshaw stable induced him to try his luck in Ireland in 1905. The following season he began to get the opportunities which his ability merited, finishing well up in the jockeys' table behind John Thompson. Retained by Croker in 1907, he had his best season to date and if he did not get the ride on Orby at Epsom he did have the satisfaction of winning the Dewhurst Plate on Rhodora. Curiously, his Epsom double on Signorinetta seems to have been regarded with the same degree of downright disbelief that greeted his mount and it was a deeply disillusioned young man who eventually set sail for Denmark, where, having survived a near-fatal illness, he became champion jockey for four consecutive seasons, before returning to England. Once again he was disappointed by the lack of demand for his services and accepted a retainer to ride in Germany. Returning home for the final time in 1932, he joined the Elsey stable and scored what proved to be his last major success when winning the Northumberland Plate on the Elsey-trained Leonard in 1933. Now a silent, serious-minded man, William Bullock spent most of the remaining thirty years of his life with the Elsey stable, still bemused by the utter irrelevance of that Derby-Oaks double to the rest of an honest, hard-working career.

Wednesday, 26th June, 1907   **£783**   **7 Ran**   **1½m (Howth Post)**

The Irish Derby of 1000sovs. For three years old. Colts 8st 12lb; fillies 8st 8lb. If claimed at time of entry, produce of untried mares allowed 3lb. The winner of the Angleseys and Railways at the Curragh, or of two stakes value 300sovs each, 10lb extra; of the Angleseys or of a stake value 300sovs or of stakes collectively value 600sovs, 7lb extra; of a stake value 200sovs, 3lb extra. Horses that have never won a stake value 100sovs, allowed 6lb; maidens allowed 10lb; only one of these allowances can be taken. The second horse to receive 150sovs and the third 50sovs out of the stake. By subscription of 17sovs each, but 8sovs only for horses struck out on or before the 5th September, 1906. Any person entering three horses, his own bona fide sole property, can strike out one at the time appointed for declaring forfeit without having to pay the forfeit.

(63 subs)

1 Mr R. Croker's	ORBY (W. Bullock)	9.8	Allen	
	Ch. colt Orme – Rhoda B by Hanover.			
2 Mr R. Croker's	GEORGETOWN (H. Simpson)	8.6	Allen	
	B. colt Teufel – Georgiana.			
3 Mr T. K. Laidlaw's	GLEG (A. Anthony)	9.5	Dawson	
	B. colt Bushey Park – Clever Girl.			
0 Mr C. J. Blake's	ELECTOR (C. Aylin)	8.2	Jeffreys	
	Ch. colt Gallinule – Lady Elect.			
0 Mr J. P. Moore's	DESMOND O'NEILL (M. Colbert)	8.2	Dawson	
	Ch. colt Count Schemberg – Fama.			
0 Mr D. Shanahan's	STRAWBERRY PLANT (P. Quinn) Ch. colt Abercorn – Victoria Plant.	8.2	Owner	
0 Mr G. W. Lushington's	ARDNAGLUE (R. Mortimer)	8.6	Hunter	
	B/Br. gelding Killyleagh – Remember.			

SP 1/10 ORBY; 20/1 Bar.

Won in a canter by 4 lengths, 3 lengths.

Winner trained by Mr J. Allen at Glencairn, Co. Dublin.

1908

The conditions of the Irish Derby continued to arouse controversy, opinion being divided between those who sought to enhance the prestige of the race and those who thought numerical support of prime importance. Edward Kennedy, later to become renowned as the breeder of The Tetrarch, had proposed the adoption of conditions similar to the Epsom Derby, with a guaranteed stake of £3000. Despite promises of support from many leading owners, Kennedy's proposal was rejected by the Stewards of the Turf Club, with the result that the format of the race remained basically unaltered. However, during the preceding months the Stewards had had the course widened. Even in this their wisdom was questioned, for on the opening day of the Derby meeting, two horses collided with the rails at the entrance to the straight, one of them having to be destroyed.

While 1908 had produced no Irish colt to emulate Orby, the One Thousand Guineas success of 'Boss' Croker's Rhodora had served to confirm the merit of her contemporaries. Following her fall in the Epsom Oaks, Rhodora ran badly at Ascot and was subsequently taken out of the Irish Derby. Her defection left Twenty-third the most likely candidate for favouritism. As a two-year-old 'Mr A. Summer's' one-eyed colt had beaten The Convert in the Railway Stakes, prior to the latter's success in the Beresford Stakes. More recently Twenty-third had beaten Rose Cross and Christmas Daisy at the Phoenix Park, before accounting for The Convert and Wild Bouquet in the Baldoyle Derby. Both on looks and form Twenty-third appeared a deserving favourite, with only The Convert and Wild Bouquet even mildly fancied to reverse the form. The only cross-Channel runner was the ex-Irish Carlowitz and though he had won twice in England, one of those successes had been gained in a selling race at Kempton. Arranmore, though twice a winner at two, seemed to be outclassed. The Tower, a huge ungainly individual trained near Cashel by John Dwyer, looked quite out of place in this company. While both The Convert and Wild Bouquet had strengthened in appearance since Baldoyle, the only real danger to Twenty-third seemed to lie in his increasing waywardness at the start.

For those who had taken even money about the favourite, the preliminaries bore a distinctly ominous look. In the parade ring Twenty-third reared up, getting a leg over the rails and skinning it. In the process he appeared to injure his stifle. Once out on the course he stopped dead, remaining stock still for what seemed ages. Eventually, and with great reluctance he proceeded to the start, where it took all the Starter's patience and Clyde Aylin's skill to get him off only ten lengths behind his field. The Tower went into an immediate lead from Rose Cross, pacemaker for Wild Bouquet, Arranmore and Wild Bouquet, with the favourite bringing up the rear. After half a mile The Tower and Rose Cross showed clear of Arranmore and Wild Bouquet, who in turn were clear of Carlowitz and an improving Twenty-third. At the mile post the favourite had closed upon the fading leaders, with the rest of the field in a bunch behind him. Down the hill Arranmore led from Twenty-third, with Rose Cross and The Tower dropping back rapidly. Approaching the straight, where the rails began, Aylin dashed the favourite up on Arranmore's inner. Then disaster struck. Twenty-third galloped straight into the concrete posts. Such was the force of the impact that his off-shoulder and ribs were shattered. Before assistance could reach him, he had bled to death. What had appeared a formality seconds earlier now became anyone's race. As Arranmore weakened, Carlowitz was driven into the lead, with Wild Bouquet in hot pursuit. Behind these The Convert now began to make rapid progress, only to ruin his chance by swerving right across the course. Two furlongs from home Wild Bouquet drew level with Carlowitz. Neck and neck these two courageous colts raced for the line, each answering his rider's every call. Both jockeys were seen at their best, though markedly different in style. Walter Bray, the former crack English apprentice was quietly effective, whereas Peter Hughes rode with a loose rein, arms and legs driving, with his whip singing off his gallant mount, not unlike the later Gordon Richards. Within yards of the post Wild Bouquet wore down his rival to win by a length. The Convert, who would almost certainly have won but for swerving, finished strongly to take third place on the heels of the exhausted leaders.

The general excitement aroused by this thrilling finish soon gave way to speculation about the cause of Twenty-third's dramatic departure from the race and whether he would otherwise have won. His owner, 'Mr A. Summers', actually Sir

William Goulding, lodged a complaint on behalf of his badly shaken jockey against John Doyle, for foul riding. After a lengthy enquiry the Stewards found that, as Twenty-third was well clear of The Tower at the time of impact, any foul riding must have occurred at an earlier stage in the race. Accordingly, they exonerated Doyle. The fact that Twenty-third had only one eye was a more likely cause of his fatal accident, in which Clyde Aylin was fortunate to escape serious injury.

Wild Bouquet, a good-looking chestnut son of Wildfowler, was bred by his trainer, James Dunne. Un-raced as a two-year-old, he had only run three times before the Irish Derby, for which he started as a maiden. On his next appearance he was annihilated by Rhodora in the Champion Prize, run over the Derby course and distance. That was on September 4th. On the previous day Rhodora had carried 10st 7lbs to an equally facile victory over seven furlongs. Even Croker's Classic winners had to work for their keep. After two more unplaced efforts Wild Bouquet was sold to join Atty Persse's stable in England. Despite a tendency to break blood vessels, he developed into a high-class hurdler. His dam, Bunch of Roses, won at two and three years and bred three other modest winners.

Wildfowler, sire of Wild Bouquet, was bred by Captain Henry Greer, who owned the colt in partnership with his trainer, Sam Darling, when Wildfowler won the St Leger of 1898. By Greer's great stallion, Gallinule, out of the Irish Derby winner, Tragedy, Wildfowler became Champion Sire in Ireland, besides getting Llangibby, winner of the Eclipse Stakes. Bought in 1908 by a syndicate of French breeders, Wildfowler proved to be a dismal failure in France. When the syndicate was dissolved in 1916, Wildfowler, Classic winner and leading sire realized a paltry £16.

The success of Wild Bouquet provided compensation for his owner, Sir Ernest Cochrane, who had declined to purchase Flax Park prior to that colt's Irish Derby victory, on account of an inconsequential blemish above the horse's knee. Ernest Cecil Cochrane was an Englishman, who had become involved in racing while serving in Ireland with the Connaught Rangers. His first runner was a winner, Birdcraft in 1905. Elected to the Turf Club in the same year, he soon began to race on an extensive scale, winning the Irish Oaks with Reina in 1907. On that occasion Reina was ridden by Fred Hunter, on whom Sir Ernest had first claim. Hunter's inability to do the weight on Wild Bouquet in the Derby provided Peter Hughes with yet another fortuitous winning mount in the race. In common with many owners before and since, Sir Ernest Cochrane found that his beginners' luck soon deserted him, with the result that his interest in racing rapidly waned. Besides being a director of the well-known mineral water company which bears his name, he established a reputation as a playwright.

Wild Bouquet provided James Dunne with his fourth and final Irish Derby. The veteran trainer had sent out Sylph from Heath House twenty-five years earlier and saddled St Kevin and Flax Park in the interim. For quick-tempered, fiery Peter Hughes, Wild Bouquet was a second lucky mount in the Irish Derby, though in both instances this capable lightweight demonstrated that he received less opportunities than his ability deserved. Of those that finished behind Wild Bouquet in the Irish Derby, Arranmore improved out of all recognition to win the Newbury Spring Cup, before finishing second to Dark Ronald in the Royal Hunt Cup, while The Tower was afterwards second in the Stewards' Cup at Goodwood.

Wednesday, 24th June, 1908   **£783**   **8 Ran**   **1½m**

The Irish Derby of 1000sovs. For three years old. Colts 8st 12lb; fillies 8st 8lb. If claimed at time of entry, produce of untried mares allowed 3lb. The winner of the Angleseys and Railways at the Curragh, or of two stakes value 300sovs each, 10lb extra; of the Angleseys or of a stake value 300sovs, or of stakes collectively value 600sovs, 7lb extra; of a stake value 200sovs, 3lb extra. Horses that have never won a stake value 100sovs, allowed 6lb; maidens allowed 10lb; only one of these allowances can be taken. The second horse to receive 150 sovs and the third 50 sovs out of the stake. By subscription of 17sovs each, but 8sovs only for horses struck out on or before the 4th September, 1907. Any person entering three horses, his own bona fide sole property, can strike out one at the time appointed for declaring forfeit without having to pay the forfeit.

(70 subs)

1 Sir E. C. Cochrane's*	WILD BOUQUET (P. Hughes)	7.13		Dunne
	Ch. colt Wildfowler – Bunch of Roses by Enthusiast.			
2 Mr W. C. Cooper's	CARLOWITZ (W. Bray)		8.12	G. S. Davies (UK)
	Ch. colt Vitez – Carol.			
3 Mr A. Buckley, jr.'s	THE CONVERT (J. Thompson)		8.12	P. Behan
	B/Br. colt Desmond – Eudoxia.			
4 Mr J. Rooney's	SWEET LESTER (E. Charters)		8.12	Parkinson
	B. colt Lesterlin – dam by Sweetheart – Rustle.			
5 Surg.-Capt. MacCabe's	ARRANMORE (W. Bullock)	9. 5		Owner
	B. colt Succoth or Enthusiast – Court Card.			
6 Mr J. R. O'Connor's	THE TOWER (John Doyle)	7.13		Dwyer
	Br. colt Sir Edgar – Pisa.			
7 Sir E. C. Cochrane's	ROSE CROSS (F. Hunter)		8. 6	Dunne
	B. colt Rays Cross – White Rose.			
F Mr A. Summers's†	TWENTY-THIRD (C. Aylin)	9. 5		Dawson
	Ch. colt Wildfowler – Kosmos.			

SP Evens Twenty-third; 6/1 WILD BOUQUET, The Convert; 7/1 Carlowitz, The Tower; 8/1 Arranmore; 20/1 Bar.

1 length, ¾ length. 2m 45s.
Winner trained by Mr J. Dunne at Osborne Lodge, Curragh.

*Sir E. C. Cochrane declared to win with Wild Bouquet.
†Mr Summers, on behalf of C. Aylin, lodged a complaint against John Doyle, and the Stewards having had a full examination decided that, in the absence of corroborative evidence, the complaint was not substantiated.

1909

The Irish Derby of 1909 attracted a field of seven, distinguished by the presence of the leading Irish two-year-old of 1908, Bachelor's Double. Unbeaten in two races the previous season, he had not been seen in public since. His trainer, Michael Dawson, had declared Bachelor's Chance, another of Joseph Lowry's colts, to act as pacemaker for the hot favourite. Though not in the same class as his stable-mate, Bachelor's Chance had finished second in the Baldoyle Derby on his last run, a short head in front of The Phoenician, from whom he had received 20lbs. The Phoenician had won twice before his Baldoyle run, where it was widely felt that a recently indisposed Steve Donoghue had not been able to do him justice. This belief had prompted Major Joicey to pay a large sum for The Phoenician shortly before the big race. The sole English challenger, Electric Boy, had finished well behind Bachelor's Double in the Railway Stakes. Having won at Lincoln in March, he then finished a very creditable sixth behind Minoru in the Epsom Derby. His subsequent failure at Ascot, due to a broken blood vessel, made backers wary of supporting P. P. Peebles raider. Of the others, Garinish Island had won the Madrid Handicap, Legate had won at Thurles only a week previously, while Love's Folly, the only filly in the field, had not run that season. A muted betting market saw Bachelor's Double firmly entrenched at even money, with only mild interest in Electric Boy and The Phoenician.

From a perfect start The Phoenician broke fastest, only to be headed immediately by Legate, these two being followed by Electric Boy, Bachelor's Chance, Love's Folly and the favourite. The failure of Bachelor's Chance to fulfil his pace-making role resulted in a slow early gallop. Passing halfway The Phoenician took it up at a better pace, as Legate and Love's Folly began to fade. Coming down the hill, The Phoenician was clear of Bachelor's Chance, Garinish Island and the favourite, with Electric Boy dropping back, apparently beaten. In the straight The Phoenician seemed to have stolen the race, for the favourite was still well adrift and under pressure. With less than two furlongs to race, Donoghue appeared to have completely outmanoeuvred Sharples. However, the favourite now demonstrated his courage as well as his class. Rallying gamely under pressure, he caught the leader well inside the final furlong to win by a length and a half. Electric Boy recovered well in the closing stages to finish third. The bare result was grossly unfair to the winner, who had suffered from a muddling gallop and a thoroughly bad ride. Had Donoghue's opportunism gained the day, it would have been a travesty, particularly in the light of the winner's subsequent achievements.

Bachelor's Double was bred by his owner, Joseph Lowry, at his Bachelor's Lodge Stud near Navan, by Tredennis out of Lady Bawn. Useless as a racehorse, Tredennis had been bought by Lowry's son, Albert, at Newmarket, for only £100 as a replacement for the deceased Le Noir. From modest beginnings Tredennis got progressively better stock, his fee rose from 5gns to 200gns and he eventually became Champion Sire in Ireland in 1921, at the age of twenty-three. By the time of his death, five years later, he had sired the winners of 480 races, value £147,749, in Britain and Ireland, a remarkable achievement by this unconsidered son of Kendal. In general his colts were better than his fillies and he left no less than nineteen sons at stud in 1926, of whom Bachelor's Double, Soldennis and Golden Myth became Champion Sires in Ireland.

Lady Bawn, dam of Bachelor's Double, was a twin daughter of Milady and thus a half-sister to Bachelor's Button, who, in winning the Ascot Gold Cup, became the only horse ever to beat Pretty Polly in England. Though twins seldom survive and rarely prosper, both Lady Bawn and Lady Black bred numerous good winners. Besides Bachelor's Double, Lady Bawn bred Bachelor's Hope, winner of the Kempton Jubilee and the Irish Derby winner, Bachelor's Wedding, own-brother to Bachelor's Brother.

Having scored a facile success over four-year-olds in a two-mile King's Plate at the Curragh in July, Bachelor's Double suffered his first defeat when unplaced behind Bayardo in the St Leger. However, a cantering success in the Lord Lieutenant's Plate over the Derby course and distance in October enabled him to conclude the season on a winning note. His four-year-old campaign opened on an auspicious note, with an impressive victory in the City and Suburban Handicap at Epsom in April. His immediate victims were Mustapha and Dean Swift, with Minoru unplaced. Returning to Epsom for the Coronation Cup, he ran Sir Martin to a length and a half. Following this high-class performance he was sold to Mr W. W. Bailey for £6000 and transferred to Atty Persse's Stockbridge stable. Born in Ireland, Bailey amassed his wealth comparatively late in life, making a fortune out of the Middle East rubber boom at the turn of the century. He raced on an extensive scale both in England and Ireland and if his eccentric betting exploits exasperated his friends and trainers alike, they provided him with much-needed relief from an acutely painful illness.

On his first appearance in Bailey's colours, Bachelor's Double spreadeagled a good field when winning the Royal Hunt Cup by four lengths. The following day he was saddled for the Gold Cup, over nearly three times the distance, and finished a gallant third to Bayardo. He then won the Atlantic Stakes at Liverpool in July,

Wednesday, 30th June, 1909	**£783**	**7 Ran**	**1½m**

The Irish Derby of 1000sovs. For three years old. Colts 8st 12lb; fillies 8st 8lb. If claimed at time of entry, produce of untried mares allowed 3lb. The winner of the Angleseys and the Railways at the Curragh, or of two stakes value 300sovs each, 10lb extra; of the Angleseys or of a stake value 300sovs, or of stakes collectively value 600sovs, 7lb extra; of a stake value 200sovs, 3lb extra. Horses that have never won a stake value 100sovs, allowed 6lb; maidens allowed 10lb; only one of these allowances can be taken. The second horse to receive 150sovs and the third 50sovs out of the stake. By subscription of 17sovs each but 8sovs only for horses struck out on or before the 2nd September, 1908. Any person entering three horses, his own bona fide sole property, can strike out one at the time appointed for declaring forfeit without having to pay the forfeit.

(61 subs)

1	Mr J. Lowry's*	BACHELOR'S DOUBLE (A. Sharples) Ch. colt Tredennis – Lady Bawn by Le Noir.	9. 5	Dawson
2	Major Joicey's	THE PHOENICIAN (S. Donoghue) B. colt Grebe – The Israelite.	8. 6	Behan
3	Mr E. P. Gall's	ELECTRIC BOY (W. Bray) B. colt Speed – Palotta.	9. 1	Peebles (UK)
4	Mr J. H. H. Peard's	GARINISH ISLAND (W. H. Williams) Ch. colt Wavelet's Pride – Brightness.	8. 3	Owner
5	Mr J. Lowry's	BACHELOR'S CHANCE (J. Clayton) B. colt Apollo – Haply.	8. 2	Dawson
6	Sir E. C. Cochrane's	LOVE'S FOLLY (P. Hughes) Ch. filly Love Wisely – Verdina.	7.12	Dunne
7	Mr J. J. Parkinson's	LEGATE (J. Thompson) B. colt Knight of Malta – Oberland.	9. 1	Owner

SP Evens BACHELOR'S DOUBLE; 9/2 Electric Boy; 6/1 The Phoenician, Garinish Island; 10/1 Love's Folly, Legate; 33/1 Bachelor's Chance.

Won easily by 1½ lengths, 3 lengths.

Winner trained by Mr M. Dawson at Rathbride Manor, Curragh.

*Mr Lowry declared to win with Bachelor's Double.

before running second to Bronzino in the Doncaster Cup. Kept in training as a five-year-old, he had his first run in the Jubilee Handicap at Kempton. It was common knowledge that Persse's stable had been ravaged by coughing, which resulted in Bachelor's Double starting at 100-to-7. Ridden by Donoghue, he bolted in by four lengths, landing a substantial gamble for the stable. This performance led to him starting joint-favourite with Lemberg for the Coronation Cup. In a thrilling finish he went down by less than a length to Lemberg and Swynford. Now firmly established as one of the best and most versatile horses of a particularly talented generation, Bachelor's Double ran once more before retiring with career winnings in excess of £10,000.

Bachelor's Double began his career as a stallion at James Daly's Hartstown Stud, Clonsilla at a fee of £99. Immediately successful, he included Greek Bachelor, Guinea Cap, Comrade, Tut Tut, Love in Idleness, Backwood and Double Life among the best of his progeny. Later transferred to Bailey's widow's Rathbane Stud in Limerick, Bachelor's Double became Champion Sire in Ireland in 1920. He proved equally successful as a broodmare sire, featuring as grandsire of such Classic winners as Call Boy, Scottish Union, Lovely Rosa, and Pillion, as well as the Gold Cup winner Precipitation. His performances both on the racecourse and at stud appear all the more remarkable when it is taken into account that he was by a non-winning sire, out of a non-winning dam, by a non-winning maternal grandsire out of a non-winning granddam. Bachelor's Double ranks with Orby as one of the outstanding winners of the Irish Derby in the first fifty years of its existence.

1910

Undeterred by menacing weather and an apparently undistinguished field for the big race, an enormous crowd thronged the Curragh on Derby Day. Once again the fact of its coinciding with a Church holiday helped to swell the attendance. For the first time the racecard included the pedigrees and trainers of all runners, as well as their owners' colours. Of the nine-strong field only three had won as two-year-olds, with Kilbroney, winner of the National Produce Stakes, boasting the best juvenile form. Both Aviator and Killaidan Park had won at Down Royal, but neither seemed likely to overcome their resultant penalties. Three-year-old form seemed to point to Fomelhault, twice successful at the Phoenix Park, Aviator, winner of the Baldoyle Derby and the temperamental Kilbroney. The last-named had run out with the Baldoyle Derby at his mercy, but had since redeemed himself by winning a King's Plate over fourteen furlongs at Cork Park. Doubts about Aviator's ability to carry top weight and Kilbroney's temperament resulted in J. H. H. Peard's Fomelhault being made favourite. Additional significance was attached to the booking of Steve Donoghue for Fomelhault. Donoghue was then embarking on his long reign as the most successful and sought-after jockey in England. Though Michael Dawson saddled no less than three runners, none appeared to be strongly fancied to add to his record in the race.

As the runners went to the post, the heavens opened, saturating the crowd and forcing the jockeys to seek shelter behind the old stone barracks in the centre of the course. The torrential downpour created instant floods along the track. When the rainstorm abated the start was further delayed by Kilbroney breaking the tapes. First of the sodden runners to emerge through the driving rain was the Dawson-trained Tauranga, who set up a long lead from Killy, Aviator and Fomelhault. Wolfdog had already become tailed off. Passing half way Tauranga still led from Aviator and the improving Kilbroney. Down the hill into the straight Aviator took it up from the fading Tauranga, with Kilbroney a close third and Fomelhault under pressure in fourth place. As Aviator raced up the straight, sending up a shower of spray, he was joined by Kilbroney, these being clear of Fomelhault, Killaidan Park and the rest of the field. The leaders battled up the straight with nothing between them, until Aviator stumbled at the furlong marker, giving a momentary advantage to his rival. Rallied superbly by John Doyle, Aviator fought back courageously to wear down the hard-ridden Kilbroney and win by a neck. Fomelhault finished a remote and exhausted third. The rain-soaked crowd, fired by Aviator's game display in a stirring finish, gave him a hero's welcome, as octogenarian James Lonsdale proudly led in his home-bred winner.

Aviator was a small, but well-made brown colt by Flying Lemur out of Lady Harriett, by Blairfinde. Flying Lemur was a full-brother to the Triple Crown winner, Flying Fox. Though disappointing as a two-year-old, he won the Ascot Derby for the Duke of Westminster and the following day ran Sceptre to a length and a half in the St James's Palace Stakes. Bought by Mr J. Musker and retired to the Cobham Stud in Surrey, he got Aviator in his last season before being sold for 7500gns to go to the Kisber Stud in Hungary, where he died within weeks of arrival. Lady Harriett, by the Irish Derby winner of 1894, also bred the useful Lord Harry, winner of the April Stakes and Curragh Cesarewitch for Mr Lonsdale.

On his reappearance two weeks later, Aviator started at 6-to-1 ON for a King's Plate at the Maze, only to be beaten by his solitary opponent, the five-year-old Warlock. The latter was subsequently beaten twenty lengths by Kilbroney in a similar event at the Curragh. Rested until October, Aviator started favourite for the Curragh Cesarewitch, but could finish only fourth behind Garinish Island, Kilbroney and Killaidan Park. The following year he showed a glimpse of his old form when beaten two short heads by Royal Hackle and General Peace over the Derby course and distance in April. Transferred to Lionel Digby's stable at Whitsbury, Aviator failed to win on the flat in two seasons and eventually regained winning form in a maiden hurdle at Gatwick, ridden by Ivor Anthony. Repatriated as a six-year-old, he made his final appearance when unplaced at Baldoyle. His heroic performance in conceding 6lbs to Kilbroney in the Irish Derby had got to the bottom of the gallant Aviator, for he was never again the same horse. The merit of that performance only became apparent from Kilbroney's achievements as a four-year-old. Trained by Charles Waugh at Newmarket, Kilbroney won the Great Metropolitan Handicap at Epsom and the Goodwood Cup, before running the Epsom Derby winner, Lemberg, to a neck in the Doncaster Cup at level weights. While it would be rash to contend that Aviator would thus have won the Epsom Derby, his victory at the Curragh must rank as a performance of the highest class.

At the end of his racing career the highly-strung Kilbroney was exported to New

Zealand, where he became a most successful sire. Fomelhault became a Phoenix Park specialist – perhaps not surprisingly, in view of his ownership. Later sent over to Tom Lewis at Druid's Lodge, he was the medium of two typically rewarding stable gambles at Ascot and Salisbury. Killaidan Park won over hurdles before being sent to South Africa, while both Kilmarnock and Nemo won in Ireland before going across the Channel. Tauranga, having disappointed when favourite for the Irish Oaks, was retired to stud, where she produced several winners.

James Lonsdale was eighty-six years old when he led in Aviator on Derby Day. Having been prominent in the coursing world for many years, he turned his attentions to the Turf late in life, breeding and racing on a large scale. Successful with Topstone in the Irish Oaks of 1904, he remained actively involved in racing until his death in August 1913, at his residence, The Pavilion, Armagh. Jack Behan, trainer of Aviator, was a former jockey, forced to retire by increasing weight. He then became headman to Denis Shanahan at Strawhall, before moving to assist his

Wednesday, 29th June, 1910	**£620**	**9 Ran**	**1½m**

The Irish Derby Stakes of 700sovs. For three years old. Colts 8st 12lb; fillies 8st 8lb. If claimed at time of entry, produce of untried mares allowed 3lb. The winner of the Angleseys and Railways at the Curragh, or of two stakes value 300sovs each, 10lb extra; of the Angleseys or of a stake value 300sovs, or of stakes collectively value 600sovs, 7lb extra; of a stake value 200sovs, 3lb extra. Horses that have never won a stake value 100sovs, allowed 6lb; maidens allowed 10lb; only one of these allowances can be taken. The second horse to receive 50sovs and the third 15sovs out of the stake. By subscription of 15sovs each, but 6sovs only for horses struck out on or before the 1st September, 1909. Any person entering three horses, his own bona fide sole property, can strike out one at the time appointed for declaring forfeit without having to pay the forfeit.

(54 subs)

1	Mr J. Lonsdale's	AVIATOR (John Doyle)	9. 8	J. Behan
		Br. colt Flying Lemur – Lady Harriett by Blairfinde.		
2	Mr J. Porter Porter's	KILBRONEY (A. Anthony)	9. 2	Hunter
		B. colt The Wag – Innismakil.		
3	Mr J. H. H. Peard's	FOMELHAULT (S. Donoghue)	8. 3	Owner
		Br. colt Aquascutum – Florzella.		
4	Mr J. Browne's	KILLAIDAN PARK (W. Bray)	9. 2	Dawson
		B. colt The Solicitor or Killaidan – Sylvan Park.		
5	Mr W. Dunne's	TAURANGA (A. Sharples)	7.12	Dawson
		Ch. filly Laveno – Tereska.		
0	Mr A. M'Mahon's	KILLY (J. Thompson)	8. 2	Dawson
		Br. colt Killyleagh – Babette.		
0	Sir E. C. Cochrane's	KILMARNOCK (P. Hughes)	8. 2	Dunne
		Ch. colt Ayrshire – Early to Bed.		
0	Mr R. Croker's	NEMO (J. Clayton)	8. 2	Allen
		Ch. colt The Solicitor – Nara.		
0	Sir W. J. Goulding's	WOLFDOG (M. Colbert)	7.13	Bacon
		B/Br. colt Speed – Knocknabreagh.		

SP 5/2 Fomelhault; 7/2 Kilbroney; 9/2 AVIATOR; 6/1 Kilmarnock; 100/12 Killaidan Park, Tauranga, 100/6 Bar.

Neck, 6 lengths. 3m 42.5s.

Winner trained by Mr J. Behan at Waterford Lodge, Curragh.

brother, Philip, at Mountjoy Lodge. At the end of the 1909 season he became private trainer to Mr Lonsdale at Waterford Lodge, resigning months before his employer's death four years later. His other notable training triumph was with Kircubbin in the Irish St Leger of 1921.

Aviator's rider, John Doyle, descended from generations of jockeys. His father, John, and uncle Denis both had long and successful careers in the saddle. He was apprenticed to Michael Dennehy at French House in 1888, when only twelve and rode his first winner that year. Soon noted for his strength and judgement, he was brought to England for a season by that shrewd judge, Captain Machell to ride the stable lightweights and received wide acclaim for his winning ride on Burnaby in the Cesarewitch of 1892. By the time of his victory on Aviator he was already regarded as a veteran, through experience rather than age. Twice runner-up to John Thompson in the Irish jockeys' table, he shared the title with Thompson in 1911, the year in which he purchased Rossmore Lodge. In 1916 a serious fall at Baldoyle ended his riding career. Though he subsequently sent out numerous winners from those historic stables, he never had the good fortune to train a high-class animal. However, he more than adequately maintained the family tradition of producing good jockeys, with the result that he had five sons riding in 1928. John Jnr won the Irish One Thousand Guineas on Moucheron in 1928 and on Petoni in 1932. James won the same Classic on Voltoi in 1924, while Joseph rode Dog Fox to win the Irish Grand National in 1925. A kindly, good-humoured man, with a fund of amusing stories, John Doyle died after a long illness at Rossmore Lodge in January 1942.

1911

The 1911 renewal could justly be termed 'the small man's Derby', for it was won by a humbly-bred colt, owned by a small farmer and trained in the depths of County Tipperary.

As a two-year-old Shanballymore won twice in four attempts. He made a winning debut at Cork Park in July, finished well behind the speedy Hornet's Beauty at Leopardstown, won again at Cork Park and concluded his first season by running unplaced behind Better Still at the Curragh in October. Also unplaced in this race was Short Grass. Though not regarded among the leaders of his generation, Shanballymore had beaten Cigar decisively over five furlongs at Cork Park in September, at level weights. Cigar won both the Railway Stakes and the National Produce Stakes. Other prominent juveniles in 1910 were Clonbern, winner of the Phoenix Stakes and the unbeaten Hornet's Beauty.

During the winter Hornet's Beauty was sold to England, where he ran up the remarkable sequence of fourteen victories as a three-year-old. Better Still was another of his generation to cross the Irish Sea, to join the Hartigan stable. Having run unplaced in the Madrid Free Handicap and finished second at Limerick, Shanballymore then ran Short Grass to three lengths at the Phoenix Park in May, giving the Dawson runner 14lbs.

Derby Day saw a field of twelve parade for the big race before a huge crowd in dull, dry weather. Favourite at 7-to-4, Short Grass had recently been purchased by Mr G. A. Prentice for £2500 and transferred to the care of Joe Hunter at Conyngham Lodge. Second favourite at 4-to-1 was Drinmore, undefeated in two races. Bracketed with Shanballymore at 6-to-1 was Clonbern, half-brother to Orby and Rhodora. Drinmore and Clobern were regarded as being the pick of the field on looks, though it was noted that Shanballymore appeared heavier and more muscular than ever before.

From flag-fall the outsider, Tullynacree made the running at a good gallop until her stamina gave out passing the six furlong mark. Seizing his opportunity, John Doyle slipped Shanballymore through on the inside to lead from Drinmore, Clonbern and St Melruan, with the favourite tracking this quartet. With three furlongs to run Drinmore and Shanballymore drew clear of the remainder and after a prolonged struggle the latter wore down his opponent to win cleverly, rather than easily, by two and a half lengths. Better Still ran on late to get within three parts of a length of the runner-up, a neck ahead of Short Grass, with St Melruan and Clonbern fifth and sixth. The recorded time for the race was 2m 43.2secs, though the Irish Field here sounded a note of caution: 'the eccentricities of the watch in the matter of racing are past praying for and need not be seriously considered'.

Shanballymore returned to a great ovation from the large Tipperary contingent, who had travelled up to the Curragh to support their local champion. After the race the bizarre origins of the winner began to come to light. His sire, Popoff, was an own-brother to the good steeplechaser Romanoff. Bred by Colonel Murphy, Popoff was given away as a yearling, owing to his having a dropped hip. Sold to a short-sighted farmer for £25, he was later raffled for 6d. tickets, played for in a card game as a thirty shilling stake and exchanged for a barrel of porter! Shanballymore's dam, Calyce, was an ugly, useless mare bred by Richard Bull and purchased by John Kelly for £6. When the produce of this unprepossessing pair was a yearling, a Tipperary bookmaker, Bryan O'Donnell, offered Kelly 100-to-1 against his ugly duckling one day winning the Derby. Kelly accepted his offer . . . Partly for this reason Kelly refused several attractive offers for his colt prior to the Derby.

On his next appearance the Derby winner beat his solitary opponent in a two-mile King's Plate at the Curragh. Sold thereafter to Mr J. E. Drake, Shanballymore raced for a further four seasons in the North of England, winning at York as a five-year-old and at Stockton in his final season. Retired to stud at Middleham, Yorkshire, he was not a successful sire. For John Kelly, a modest farmer from Cappawhite, Co. Tipperary, the 1911 Derby was a fairytale come true, while for John Dwyer, the small-time trainer from the shores of Loughferoda (Lake of the Weaver), near Cashel, it provided the highlight of a lifetime's devotion to racing.

John Doyle, rider of Shanballymore, was one of a family of celebrated Irish jockeys. Successful in the Cesarewitch on Burnaby almost twenty years earlier, he was winning his second consecutive Irish Derby. In later years he had no less than five sons all riding as jockeys, one of whom now trains in the North of England. John Doyle also rode two winners of the Irish Oaks and invariably finished high in the list of winning jockeys, sharing the championship honours with John Thompson in 1911 and finishing second to him in the following year. In December 1911 Doyle purchased Rossmore Lodge for £1300, where he trained successfully for many years.

In more recent years Paddy Prendergast has upheld the tradition of this famous establishment.

Of the other runners in Shanballymore's Derby, Tullynacree won the Irish Oaks next time out, while Drinmore won the very next day after the Derby and later won three races in England for Paddy Hartigan's stable. St Melruan won the King's Plate the day after the Derby and, together with Better Still, won races in England. Short Grass found his true metier in sprints, while Killaman and Flying Comet both won as four-year-olds. Clonbern failed to live up to the standards of his illustrious relations, winning but one moderate race in his third season. Not perhaps an outstanding Irish Derby, but far from being one of the worse renewals, as the subsequent performances of most of the runners repeatedly demonstrated.

Though it was hardly surprising that the humbly-bred Shanballymore should have

Wednesday, 28th June, 1911   £783   **10 Ran**   1½m

The Irish Derby Stakes of 1000sovs. For three years old. Colts 8st 12lb; fillies 8st 8lb. If then entitled and claimed at time of entry, produce of untried mares allowed 3lb. The winner of the Angleseys and Railways at the Curragh, or of two stakes value 300sovs each, 10lb extra; of the Angleseys or of a stake value 300sovs, or of stakes collectively value 600sovs, 7lb extra; of a stake value 200sovs, 3lb extra. Horses that have never won a stake value 100sovs, allowed 6lb; maidens allowed 10lb; only one of these allowances can be taken. The second horse to receive 150sovs and the third 50sovs out of the stake. By subscription of 17sovs each, but 8sovs only for horses struck out on or before the 7th September, 1910. Any person entering three horses, his own bona fide sole property, can strike out one at the time appointed for declaring forfeit without having to pay the forfeit.

(56 subs)

1	Mr J. Kelly's	SHANBALLYMORE (John Doyle)	8. 6	Dwyer
		B. colt Popoff – Calyce by Kendal.		
2	Mr J. H. Taylor's	DRINMORE (J. Thompson)	8. 6	Dawson
		B. colt General Symons – Marcellad.		
3	Mr P. Cullinan's	BETTER STILL (C. Aylin)	8.12	Persse (UK)
		Br. colt Flying Hackle – Ethelreda.		
4	Mr G. A. Prentice's	SHORT GRASS (P. Hughes)	8. 3	Hunter
		B. colt Laveno – Outburst.		
5	Mr James Daly's	ST MELRUAN (M. Colbert)	8. 2	Dawson
		B. colt Persimmon – Meldhre.		
6	Mr R. Croker's	CLONBERN (F. Hunter)	9. 5	Allen
		Ch. colt Clonmell – Rhoda B.		
7	Mr J. A. B. Trench's	KILLAMAN (R. Bona)	8. 2	Owner
		B. colt Killyleagh – Saucy Lass.		
8	Mr J. Hutton's	TULLYNACREE (G. Maynard)	7.12	Dawson
		Br. filly Fowling-piece – Atlanta.		
9	Mr D. O'M. Leaby's	KILSHANE (S. Hill)	7.12	Owner
		B. colt The Solicitor – Bal Austa.		
10	Mr W. A. Wallis's	FLYING COMET (A. Douglas)	8. 5	Harrison
		Br. filly Flying Hackle – Corona.		

SP 7/4 Short Grass; 4/1 Drinmore; 6/1 SHANBALLYMORE, Clonbern; 10/1 Bar.
2½ lengths, ¾ length. 2m 43.1/5s.
Winner trained by Mr J. Dwyer at The Commons, Cashel, Co. Tipperary.

proved a failure at stud, two of his Derby victims were destined to make their mark in this sphere. Having proved himself one of the best handicappers in England, Drinmore retired to stand in Mullingar, where he became a leading sire of jumpers, including the lion-hearted Thomond and Southernmore. Short Grass, after a relatively undistinguished racing career in England, was bought by an American breeder, Ernie Hertz. Sent across the Atlantic in 1914, he won no less than eleven races in the States before becoming a successful stallion, based in Lexington.

1912

The Irish Derby of 1912 was remarkable principally for the paucity of contenders and for the first appearance in Ireland of the American jockey, Danny Maher, then at the height of his fame in England. That the field should number only five was understandable in part by the meagre prize money. At £620 to the winner the race was worth less than in any year since 1898, save 1910, when Aviator netted the same sum for Mr Lonsdale. Of the leading two-year-olds of the previous year only Gael Rhu took part. He had beaten Far and Wide and Simon Lass at the Phoenix Park in April 1911. Together with Wise Symon and the unbeaten Croker filly, Amsterdam, these represented the best of their generation.

Pre-race opinion regarded the Derby as a mere formality for Gael Rhu, who had run second on his seasonal debut at the Curragh, with Kithogue unplaced. He confirmed this form in the Baldoyle Derby, where he gave Kithogue 16lbs and a handsome beating. Third at Baldoyle was Civility, beaten just over three lengths, receiving 4lbs from the winner. Though winner of the Marble Hill Stakes from five starts at two, Civility did not appear to be in the same class as Gael Rhu. The latter was bought after his Baldoyle success by Mr G. A. Prentice, specifically to win the Irish Derby, just as he had bought Short Grass the year previously. Of the remainder Tickler had no form to recommend him, while Whistling Duck completed the quintet as pacemaker for Kithogue. The betting market was completely dominated by Gael Rhu, backed by his new owner with £1400 to win £800 and again with £1000 to win £500. This ensured his being firmly entrenched at 2-to-1 ON. Next in demand was Civility. The booking of Maher, added to the owner's conviction that, differently ridden. Civility would have won at Baldoyle, resulted in his being preferred in the betting to Kithogue and Tickler, ridden by Steve Donoghue.

In the race itself, run in fine weather before a huge crowd, Tickler made the early running, giving way after two furlongs to Whistling Duck, who led the small field at a very strong gallop to the top of the hill. Here, the pacemaker, ridden by young Joseph Doyle, was passed by his stablemate, Kithogue, ridden by the youngster's father, John Doyle, bidding for a hat-trick in the Derby. Meanwhile, Maher could be seen sitting motionless in last place, though never more than twelve lengths off the leader. As they swung into the straight Gael Rhu and Tickler challenged Kithogue in a three-way battle for the lead. Whistling Duck, having fulfilled his role, dropped away as Maher stealthily moved Civility closer to the struggling trio in front. With less than two furlongs to run, the favourite had shot his bolt, whereupon Maher shook up the long-striding Civility, to coast away from his toiling opponents and score an utterly decisive success. The Judge's verdict was two and a half lengths, with Kithogue eight lengths further back in third place.

The crowd gave Civility a tremendous reception as he was led in by a jubilant John Reese. Much of the applause was undoubtedly for Danny Maher, who had just provided a perfect example of artistic and restrained race-riding, allowing his opponents to cut each other's throats, before swooping to administer the coup de grâce. Despite alarming his employers by his flat refusal to walk the course, being content to survey it from the top of the grandstand, Maher was particularly anxious to make his first ride in Ireland a winning one, for his parents had emigrated to America from Nenagh.

John Reese had moved from his native Manchester to Cork some thirty years previously. Having established a chain of betting offices, he then became a prominent member of the Ring, making a book at all the major Irish meetings. In 1890 he established his Civility Stud at Ballincurrig, on the outskirts of Cork city. This venture did not reward Reese's enterprise, for the land involved had been reclaimed from marsh and required a system of sluices to keep it drained. Its total unsuitability was confirmed by Henry Ford & Co., who purchased the stud in 1915, to house the employees of their assembly plant, recently constructed on the site of the former Cork Park racecourse. The houses that were built there soon began to subside, obliging Fords to abandon the property. A keen fruit farmer, Reese for many years distributed his 'Civility strawberries' at the Curragh on Derby Day. His Derby triumph was not undeserved, for his 'Royal blue, white sleeves and cap' had been sported on Irish racecourses for many years. Civility went wrong after the Derby. Though put back in training as a four-year-old, he was never any use subsequently, nor was his stud career in any way rewarding to his adoring owner. John 'Civility' Reese spent the last years of his life travelling the world to improve his failing health, once again without any great success.

'Civility' Reese came by his unusual nickname as the result of his intercession in another bookmaker's dispute with a client during a racemeeting. The other bookie, not content with refusing to settle a disputed wager, was roundly abusing his client. Furious at Reese's intervention, the other layer turned on the would-be referee, mockingly addressing him as 'Mr Civility'. Tickled by this title, Reese promptly adopted 'Civility' as his telegraphic address, later reinforcing the image by calling his stud by the same name.

For Bartholemew 'Batt' Kirby, Civility's success provided a great advertisement in his first year as a public trainer. A native of Knocklong, Co. Limerick, Kirby began training in his home town and had only moved to the Curragh within the previous year. In awe of no man, Batt Kirby had an unfortunate tendency to allow expenditure to exceed income, which led to the premature decline of a promising career. Following his return to Limerick he bred Knocklong Boy, a notable sprinter in Ireland in the 'Twenties.

Civility was bred at his owner's Civility Stud near Cork city. He was by the resident stallion, Grebe, By Bend Or, Grebe was a half-brother to Eager, winner of twenty races. Grebe's early stud career showed sufficient promise to encourage his owner to relocate him to the Curragh in 1910. Notwithstanding Civility's triumph,

Grebe's early success was not sustained and he was sold as a hunter stallion in 1917. Despite the later decline in Grebe's status, his line survives through one of his better offspring. In his first season at the Curragh he got Willbrook, winner of the Doncaster Cup and second in the Ascot Gold Cup. Though this fine stayer died after only one season at stud, he did sire St Joan, dam of the Cambridgeshire winner and famous foundation mare, Double Life. The Israelite, bred by Reese in 1896, was a half-sister to The Jew, winner of many races for Eyre Linde. She had bred two previous winners, also by Grebe, one of these, The Phoenician, had finished second in the Irish Derby of 1909. Reese had in fact sold The Israelite to Lord Rossmore in 1910 for only 26gns. Unfortunately for Lord Rossmore, never the luckiest of owners, The Israelite became a shy breeder.

As the most notable visiting jockey to grace the Curragh since Fred Archer in 1886, Danny Maher deserves particular mention here. Born in Connecticut, Maher made his name in America, where he rode 350 winners in three seasons. Only nineteen when he arrived at Newmarket in 1900, Maher remained apart from his countrymen, whose doping and gambling activities were causing such a furore in English racing cirles at the time. Unequalled in his handling of two-year-olds, Maher was soon riding for the most powerful stables in the land, including those of George Lambton, Percy Peck and Alec Taylor. Victories in the Derby and St Leger on Rock Sand in 1903, established Maher's reputation as a Classic jockey. Two further Derbies followed on Cicero and Spearmint. Despite delicate health and perennial weight problems, he was champion jockey in England in 1908 and 1913. Befriended

Wednesday, 26th June, 1912   **£620**   **5 Ran**   **1½m**

The Irish Derby Stakes of 700sovs. For three years old. Colts 8st 12lb; fillies 8st 8lb. If then entitled and claimed at time of entry, produce of untried mares allowed 3lb. The winner of the Angleseys and Railways at the Curragh, or of two stakes value 300sovs each, 10lb extra; of the Angleseys or of a stake value 300sovs, or of stakes collectively value 600sovs, 7lb extra; of a stake value 200sovs, 3lb extra. Horses that have never won a stake value 100sovs, allowed 6lb; maidens allowed 10lb; only one of these allowances can be taken. The second horse to receive 50sovs and the third 15sovs out of the stake. By subscription of 15sovs each, but 6sovs only for horses struck out on or before the 6th September, 1911. Any person entering three horses, his own bona fide sole property, can strike out one at the time appointed for declaring forfeit without having to pay the forfeit.

(44 subs)

1	Mr J. Reese's	CIVILITY (D. Maher)	8.12	Kirby
		B. colt Grebe – The Israelite by Isosceles.		
2	Mr G. A. Prentice's	GAEL RHU (F. Hunter)	9. 2	Hunter
		B. colt Earla Mor – Katarina.		
3	Mr J. Lonsdale's	KITHOGUE (John Doyle)	8. 2	J. Behan
		B/Ch. colt Morganatic – Copestown.		
4	Mr W. Dunne's	TICKLER (S. Donoghue)	8. 2	Dawson
		Br. colt General Symons – Tereska.		
5	Mr J. Lonsdale's	WHISTLING DUCK (Joseph	7.12	J. Behan
		Doyle) Ch/Br. filly Soliman – Mareca.		

SP 1/2 Gael Rhu; 5/1 CIVILITY; 7/1 Tickler, Kithogue; 100/1 Bar.
Won in a canter by 2½ lengths, 8 lengths. 2m 51s.
Winner trained by Mr B. Kirby at Curragh View, Kildare.

by Lord Rosebery, to whom he remained intensely loyal, Maher regarded his dead-heat with Lemberg on Rosebery's Neil Gow for the Eclipse Stakes of 1910 as the finest performance of his career. Bane of the handicapper through his preference for winning by the minimum necessary margins, Maher, unlike his arch-rival Frank Wootton, never favoured the rails as the shortest way home. Forced to retire through ill-health in 1913, he made a short-lived comeback two years later, prior to his premature death in 1916. If notable for no other reason, the Irish Derby of 1912 remained a treasured memory by those fortunate enough to witness the virtuoso performance of Daniel Aloysius Maher, one of the greatest jockeys of all time.

1913

Prize money for the major races in Ireland increased dramatically in 1913, the Derby becoming worth over £1000 to the winner. This had the effect of awakening cross-Channel interest to such an extent that the Irish Derby was destined to be won by English-trained horses no less than nineteen times between 1913 and 1940.

The merit of the Irish two-year-olds of 1912 was confirmed by the subsequent performances in England of two in particular, Happy Fanny and Bachelor's Wedding. The former, purchased for an English owner by Steve Donoghue after he had won the Phoenix Plate on her, proved herself a very successful sprinter. Other leading juveniles of that year included Lyonesse, Sleipner and Royal Weaver. In March 1913 Bachelor's Wedding was purchased by Sir William Nelson for £4000 and transferred from Michael Dawson to Atty Persse at Stockbridge. Nelson had refused to buy Happy Fanny despite Donoghue's entreaties and bought Bachelor's Wedding instead. Unplaced in the 2000 Guineas, Bachelor's Wedding won at Newmarket before running a very good race in the sensational Epsom Derby, which resulted in the disqualification of Craganour in favour of the rank outsider, Aboyeur.

Meanwhile, in Ireland, Sleipner, having won at the Curragh on his seasonal reappearance, had failed by six lengths to concede 20lbs to Count Anthony in the Baldoyle Derby. Sadly, Sleipner proved to be John Thompson's last ride in public. Count Anthony, a late foal, had finished third to Royal Weaver in the National Produce Stakes on the last of his three juvenile appearances. On that occasion Bachelor's Wedding had finished behind both. Of the other Derby runners only the Parkinson representative, Fainne Geal, had won as a three-year-old, while Chadville, a full-brother of Shanballymore, had shown no public form.

Derby day dawned bright and clear, bringing the usual large crowd, additionally excited by rumours of a repetition of the Suffragette protest, which had so dramatically and fatally occurred during the Epsom Derby. Though three intended runners had travelled over from England, both Croker horses, Knight's Key and Josh, were announced as non-runners. Pick of the field on looks were Bachelor's Wedding, Count Anthony and Royal Weaver. This consensus was reflected in the market, which made Persse's charge a steady 6-to-4 favourite followed by Count Anthony at 2-to-1 and Royal Weaver at 9-to-2. There was a little support for Sensitive Symons at 8-to-1 while the remainder were ignored.

Of the eight who faced the starter only Faria, the rank outsider, was slowly away. The early running was made by Count Anthony, who took them along at a moderate gallop to the top of the hill, where he was joined by Sensitive Symons, Royal Weaver and the favourite. These four swung down the hill and into the straight in a line abreast followed by Arizona Beau. First to crack was Sensitive Symons, whereupon Clyde Aylin kicked for home on Count Anthony. As Royal Weaver dropped away Donoghue could be seen poised motionless behind the hard-ridden leader. At the distance Donoghue asked Bachelor's Wedding to go on about his business, which he did readily, winning by a very comfortable length and a half from Arizona Beau, who had put in a late but unavailing challenge. Two lengths further back came Count Anthony, a long way in front of Chadville, Sensitive Symons, Fainne Geal, Royal Weaver and Faria. Biggest disappointment of the race was Royal Weaver, even more inconvenienced by the hard state of the going than Count Anthony.

The winner, a powerful chestnut, was bred by Joseph Lowry of Oatlands Stud, Navan and provided yet another advertisement for Lowry's wonderfully successful stallion. Tredennis. Bachelor's Wedding was the third high-class product of the union between Lowry's home-bred Lady Bawn and Tredennis. Foaled in 1902, Lady Bawn was a twin and had never raced. Her first foal was Bachelor's Double, unbeaten as a two-year-old, winner of the Irish Derby in 1909 and then of the City and Suburban, the Royal Hunt Cup and the Jubilee Handicap. Two years later Lady Bawn produced Bachelor's Hope, also a winner of the Jubilee Handicap. Then came Bachelor's Wedding, for whom the Irish Derby proved to be the highlight of his racecourse career in these islands. Third to Tracery and Louvois in the Eclipse Stakes on his next appearance, he then finished down the field in the St Leger and only managed to win one small race at York in his third and final season. However, when exported to India, he regained his best form, winning the Viceroy's cup in 1914 and again in 1917.

Those who finished behind Bachelor's Wedding enjoyed mixed fortunes in their subsequent careers. Arizona Beau managed to win only one small race for military riders, ridden by Sir John Tichbourne. Count Anthony won the newly-instituted Northern Derby at Down Royal, but could only finish third in the Northern St Leger at the same venue. Royal Weaver was sold to England where he won four modest races for the Persse stable as a four-year-old. Neither Faria nor Fainne Geal made any contribution to their keep. However, Chadville, though disappointing on the flat, was unbeaten over hurdles as a four-year-old. Most successful of all was Sensitive Symons. After winning on the flat in England he set up an unbeaten sequence over hurdles for the Paddy Hartigan stable, ridden each time by the greatest of all hurdle jockeys, George Duller. He was subsequently just as successful over fences, ridden by Mr Jack Anthony, one of the trio of celebrated steeplechase jockeys and himself victorious in three Grand Nationals.

Though this was the first occasion since he had commenced training that Michael Dawson was not represented in the Irish Derby, he did have the satisfaction of having developed the winner as a two-year-old. Moreover, Dawson had handed Bachelor's Wedding over to a fellow-Irishman, Henry, Seymour Persse, member of a famous old Galway sporting family and owners of the Nun's Island Distillery. After a successful career as an amateur rider, Atty Persse began training in the Phoenix Park before moving to England. Starting as a trainer of jumpers, Persse had his first major flat successes with Bachelor's Double. However, he will always be remembered as the trainer of The Tetrarch, probably the best two-year-old ever seen in England. This 'Spotted Wonder', as the precocious mottled-grey colt became known, remained unbeaten throughout 1913, his only season to race. Persse won his first Classic with the American-bred Sweeper II in the 2000 Guineas of 1912, repeated this success with Tetratema and Mr Jinks and won the fillies' equivalent with Silver Urn. Never reluctant to plunder prizes in his native land, he won two successive Irish Derbies, two Irish Oaks, one 2000 Guineas and the 1000 Guineas twice. He was champion trainer in England in 1922 and again in 1930.

Although his 'White, red, white and blue sash, red cap' might indicate otherwise, Sir William Nelson was Irish by birth. He made a fortune from both the meat trade and his steamship company, the Nelson Line. Shortly after the turn of the century he virtually retired from his business concerns and concentrated on his breeding and racing interests. His horses raced mainly in England, except during World War I.

| **Wednesday, 25th June, 1913** | **£1165** | **8 Ran** | **1½m** |

The Irish Derby Stakes of 1000sovs. For three years old. Colts 8st 12lb; fillies 8st 8lb. If then entitled and claimed at time of entry, produce of untried mares allowed 3lb. The winner of the Angleseys and Railways at the Curragh, or of two stakes value 300sovs each, 10lb extra; of the Angleseys or of a stake value 300sovs, or of stakes collectively value 600sovs, 7lb extra; of a stake value 200sovs, 3lb extra. Horses that have never won a stake value 100sovs, allowed 6lb; maidens allowed 10lb; only one of these allowances can be taken. The second horse to receive 75 sovs and the third 25sovs out of the stake. By subscription of 5sovs each for horses struck out on or before the 5th June, 1912, with 10sovs extra for those then remaining in and 10sovs additional for those not struck out on or before the 1st January, 1913. Any person entering three horses, his own bona fide sole property, can strike out one at the time appointed for declaring minor forfeit without having to pay the forfeit.

(68 subs)

1	Sir Wm. E. Nelson's	BACHELOR'S WEDDING (S. Donogoue) Ch. colt Tredennis – Lady Bawn by Le Noir.	9. 1	Persse (UK)
2	Mr H. S. Gray's	ARIZONA BEAU (W. Williams) B. colt Arizona – Ashbelle.	8.12	P. Behan
3	Mr C. J. Blake's	COUNT ANTHONY (C. Aylin) Br. colt Santoi – Mary Hamilton.	9. 5	Jeffrey
4	Mr J. Kelly's	CHADVILLE (Joseph Canty) B. colt Popoff – Calyce.	8. 2	Dwyer
5	Mr J. H. Taylor's	SENSITIVE SYMONS (Joseph Doyle, jr.) Ch. colt General Symons – Sensible.	8. 2	Fetherston
6	Mr P. Murphy's	FAINNE GEAL (J. Patman) Ch. filly His Majesty – Stella.	8. 8	Parkinson
7	Mr P. Cullinan's	ROYAL WEAVER (John Doyle) B. colt Flying Hackle – Royal Line.	9. 8	J. Dunne
8	Mr W. A. Wallis's	FARIA (T. Bennett) (car 8. 1) B. filly Fariman – Royal Ia.	7. 9	Harrison

SP 6/4 BACHELOR'S WEDDING; 2/1 Count Anthony; 9/2 Royal Weaver; 8/1 Sensitive Syons; 20/1 Arizona Beau; 33/1 Fainne Geal; 50/1 Chadville; 200/1 Faria.

Won in a canter by 1½ lengths, 2 lengths. 2m 43.3/5s.

Winner trained by Mr H. S. Persse, at Stockbridge, England.

When racing was suspended by Government Order in 1917, the prohibition included Ireland. It was largely due to the efforts of Sir William Nelson that Ireland was exempted and racing allowed to continue. In recognition of his services The Irish Horse Breeders, Owners & Trainers Association made him its first president. His bloodstock operation was based at Clonbarron, Co. Meath, where he maintained a large establishment. The best horse he owned was Tangiers, winner of the Kempton Jubilee and Ascot Gold Cup in 1920, trained by Dick Dawson, one of Sir William's succession of trainers. Lady Nelson became the first woman to own a Grand National winner when Ally Sloper carried her colours to victory in 1915.

1914

This year saw a further dramatic increase in prize money for the Irish Derby. Having exceeded £1000 to the winner in the previous year for the first time in the history of the race, the prize fund doubled in 1914. Encouraged by his success the previous year, Atty Persse determined to repeat his raid on Ireland's premier prize. The colt chosen for this mission was one Land of Song. In his first season Land of Song had run three times. On his racecourse debut he won the Windsor Castle Stakes at Royal Ascot. Next time out he finished second to Black Jester in the Richmond Stakes at Goodwood, completing the season by running the unbeaten Aldford to a head at Newbury. As a three-year-old he finished fourth to Kennymore in the 2000 Guineas, only to disappoint in his next two races.

Meanwhile, in Ireland, the leading two-year-old of 1913, Mellifont, had not yet run. Of the other prominent two-year-olds Irish Chief scored an impressive success at the Curragh in April, which resulted in his being sold to race in England, while Righ Mor, finished a well-beaten third to Irawaddy in the Baldoyle Derby. Hornet's Treasure, conquerer of Mellifont in the National Produce Stakes was being kept to sprinting, while Lonely Lady and Lough Foyle had been sold to race in England. King's Common, owned and trained by J. J. Parkinson, winner of the Railway Stakes as a two-year-old, had won the seven-furlong April Stakes on his only run in 1914. Killeigh had also won this race prior to his Derby success in 1906.

As the Derby drew near the English challenge appeared formidable. Among the intended raiders were Marten and Peter the Great. Marten, trained by Fred Darling at Beckhampton, had won the Prince of Wales Stakes at Ascot after being badly away in the Epsom Derby. Peter the Great, trained by Fred Withington, having finished third at Epsom to Durbar II, went on to win the Hardwicke Stakes at Ascot easily from Corcyra. The Irish defence to this awesome challenge appeared to rest entirely upon King's Common. The last-named was considered much superior to his stablemate, Irawaddy.

As it transpired, neither Marten nor Peter the Great were despatched to the Curragh and hopes of keeping Ireland's greatest prize at home began to rise accordingly. Although June 24th dawned dull and overcast, this proved no deterrent to the largest crowd ever witnessed at the Curragh since St Brendan's year. The Parkinson stable had struck form with a vengeance the previous day, winning five of the six races on the card. Three of these had been ridden by the new stable jockey, Colin Barrett and the other two by the trainer's gifted son, Mr W. J. Parkinson. The only race to elude Parkinson on the opening day was the Waterford Testimonial Stakes, won by Joe Hunter's charge, Butterfly Belle. The Irish Field noted in relation to the last-named, 'It is said that Ballaghtobin, (undefeated in three races already), is a good two stone in front of the Waterford Testimonial winner. If this is the case he must be something very extra indeed'. Prophetic words; as events were to prove.

In the field of six only King's Common and Land of Song were seriously fancied. The conditions of the race required the English colt to concede 7lbs to King's Common and the latter was regarded by connections as a certainty to give Parkinson his first Irish Derby. While the Irish colt was backed to 6-to-4 ON, Land of Song remained easy to back at 3-to-1. The timidity of his supporters was based upon both his light-framed and washy appearance and Persse's widely-reported doubts about Land of Song's ability to stay the stiff Curragh twelve furlongs. Righ Mor was only mildly fancied at 6-to-1. The second Michael Dawson representative, Bachelor's Jap, was a very big colt, still patently backward. Neither of the remaining pair, Schultz and Rockbellew, appeared to possess sufficient class.

The race was run at a very fast gallop from flagfall, with Joe Canty forcing the pace on Bachelor's Jap. Only at the two furlong marker did he surrender the lead to King's Common, who was challenged immediately by Donoghue on Land of Song. As the latter inched ahead Barrett was seen to become distinctly uneasy as his mount failed to match strides with the English colt. At the Lord Lieutenant's Gate Land of Song appeared a certainty, but Barrett suddenly conjured such a dramatic response from King's Common that in a driving finish they failed by only a head to catch Land of Song. Although Donoghue afterwards stated that he had won comfortably, majority opinion held that the winner had been lucky to last home and that the post had come just in time for him. Righ Mor finished a respectful four lengths behind the principals, followed by Bachelor's Jap and the two outsiders. The time was a very good 2m 35.6secs.

Land of Song was a medium-sized, light-framed chestnut colt by Llangibby out of Aliena, a mare by Mackintosh, who bred three other modest winners. Aliena had been picked up at a 'flapping' meeting near Newcastle by the shrewd Scottish trainer John McGuigan. A winner of three races as a two-year-old, Aliena had descended to the lowest levels of racing, but the wily McGuigan knew that she traced to that very good filly, Superba, winner of seven in a row at two and placed in both the Oaks and St Leger. McGuigan passed her on to Mr Simons Harrison, who resold her to Major Wise. From her Major Wise bred Land of Song. Sent over to Doncaster as a yearling, Land of Song made 640gns to the bid of Mr Temple Patterson. In carrying the Patterson 'Black, white chevrons, scarlet sleeves and cap' to victory at the Curragh, the colt provided a timely tonic for his owner, then recovering after a serious operation.

On his next outing in England Land of Song easily upset the odds on the high-class Sir Eager at Salisbury. Immediately afterwards he was purchased by Messrs Robinson and Clark for £4000 and exported to Australia as a stallion. Good colt though he undoubtedly was, Land of Song had received no less than 28lbs from The Tetrarch in a trial before the 2000 Guineas and been beaten out of sight. Of those who followed him home at the Curragh, both King's Common and Righ Mor were promptly sold to race in England, with little success, while Schultz developed a costly habit of starting favourite only to finish perpetually second or third. Rockbellew won several small races over the next few seasons. Thus concluded the last Irish Derby before the clouds of war darkned over Europe and the flower of nations' youth became cannon fodder in Flanders' trenches.

Wednesday, 24th June, 1914   **£2040**   **6 Ran**   **1½m**

The Irish Derby Stakes of 2000sovs. By subscription of 50sovs each, half forfeit for those struck out on or before the 7th January, 1914, but 5sovs only for those struck out on the 4th June, 1913. For three years old, colts 8st 12lb; fillies 8st 8lb. If then entitled and claimed at time of entry, produce of untried mares allowed 3lb. The winner of the Angleseys and Railways at the Curragh, or of two stakes each value 500sovs, or of one value 700sovs, 7lb extra; of a stake value 300sovs, or of stakes collectively value 600sovs, 3lb extra. The second horse to receive 100sovs and the third 50sovs out of the stake. The nominator of the winner to receive 100sovs, of the second 50sovs and of the third 25sovs from the stake. Any person entering three horses, his own bona fide sold property, can strike out one at the time appointed for declaring minor forfeit without having to pay the forfeit.

(92 subs)

1	Mr E. Temple Patterson's	LAND OF SONG (S. Donoghue)	9. 5	Persse (UK)
		Ch. colt Llangibby – Aliena by Mackintosh.		
2	Mr C. T. Garland's	KING'S COMMON (C. Barrett) 8.12		Parkinson
		Ch. colt William Rufus – Miss Common.		
3	Mr James Daly's	RIGH MOR (F. Hunter) 9 5		Dawson
		Br. colt Desmond – dam by Timothy – Florence Montgomery.		
4	Mr A. Lowry's	BACHELOR'S JAP (Joseph Canty) 8. 9		Dawson
		Br. colt Tredennis – Japanese Doll.		
5	Mr J. R. Markey's	ROCKBELLEW (W. Earl) 8. 9		Dawson
		Bl. colt Aquascutum – Signora.		
6	Mr N. J. Kelly's	SCHULTZ (James Canty) 8.12		P. Behan
		Bl. colt Aquasutum – Ballistite.		

SP 4/6 King's Common; 3/1 LAND OF SONG; 6/1 Righ Mor; 20/1 Bar.
Head, 4 lengths. 2m 36.3/5s.
Winner trained by Mr H. S. Persse at Stockbridge, England.

1915

The full consequences of World War I were slow to make themselves felt by the Irish racing community. The first hint of official recognition came in February when the Stewards granted permission for the abandonment of the Fermoy meeting, 'owing to the course being in occupation of the military'. However, in May, following the suspension of all racing in England, other than at Newmarket, the Stewards and Members of the Turf Club held a conference 'for the purpose of considering the question of the continuance of racing in Ireland'. After lengthy debate it was decided, 'That racing should be continued in Ireland for the present'. The Stewards justified their decision on three premises: the effect on the horsebreeding industry which such a discontinuance of racing would bring about, the conditions which led to a curtailment of racing in England did not apply in Ireland, they would order the suspension of racing in Ireland should the Government intimate that racing inter- ferred in any way with the Public Service. At the same meeting it was agreed to grant licences to English jockeys under certain conditions. Already a drift from England to Ireland by racing personnel was becoming evident. One of the first Englishmen to apply for a trainer's licence was one J. T. Rogers.

Ballaghtobin made his seasonal appearance at the Curragh April meeting, where he finished last of four to the four-year-old Aquafortis. His next race was the Baldoyle Derby in May. Carrying top weight of 9st 5lbs, he gave Carnwherry 12lbs and beat him by a neck, with Ulster Man, Red Branch Knight and La Poloma behind. This was generally regarded as an excellent performance by such a long- striding colt on this sharp course. It was his last run in preparation for his major target, the Irish Derby.

Of the other good Irish juveniles of 1914, Offaly had been sold to race in South America, Herodius had died during the winter, St Cuimin had run twice unplaced, La Poloma had failed to impress at Baldoyle, while Butterfly Belle had joined R. W. Armstrong in England. With the strongest-ever English raiding party in prospect, it appeared that hopes of keeping the Derby at home rested on Ballaghtobin, 'Bat' Kirby's Red Branch Knight and Phillie Behan's representative, Carnwherry.

On June 30th, amid torrential showers, a smaller crowd than usual saw a field of thirteen parade for the Irish Derby. The inclusion of Lady Prim, formerly owned and nominated by the recently-deceased William Dunne, provided the first instance of the amended rule, whereby the death of its nominator no longer rendered an animal ineligible for those races for which the deceased had entered it. Of the English challengers, Achtoi, a medium-sized brown colt trained by G. S. Davies at Michel Grove in Sussex, seemed to have outstanding claims. Prior to finishing fourth to Pommern in the New Derby at Newmarket, he had won the Dee Stakes at Chester. Atty Persse had sent over the lightly-raced Llangibby colt, Cromdale, to attempt a hat-trick for the Stockbridge stable. In the face of strong support for these two, Ballaghtobin, though looking magnificent, eased in the market to 7-to-2. Achtoi hardened to become clear favourite at 7-to-4, while Cromdale attracted substantial support at 6-to-1. Fitzorb, despite a hefty wager by his owner, eased to 8-to-1, with Red Branch Knight and The Revenge the only others in demand. The last-named, twice successful in England, was ridden by Edwin Piper, who had shot from obscurity to short-lived fame as rider of Aboyeur, awarded the sensational 1913 Derby on the controversial disqualification of Craganour.

From flag-fall Lady Prim made the running ahead of Ballaghtobin. After four furlongs St Cuimin fell, almost bringing down Carnwherry, on whom John Doyle made a miraculous recovery. Achtoi was also badly hampered, while Joe Harty, rider of St Cuimin was thrown so high in the air that one bystander wondered whether he would ever come down! Lady Prim continued to lead to the four furlong mark, where she was headed by Ballaghtobin. The new leader was promptly joined by Achtoi, with Cromdale, The Revenge and Fitzorb next in order. Meanwhile the badly hampered Carnwherry could be seen making headway behind these. The leaders Ballaghtobin and Achtoi swung into the straight racing stride for stride, where Barrett on Ballaghtobin was first to go for his whip. 'Hellfire Jack' Trigg then set about the favourite, forcing him ahead at the Lord Lieutenant's Gate. Under severe pressure from Barrett, Ballaghtobin fought back level and then inched ahead to win by a neck in a desperate finish, in which both horses and jockeys gave their all. Four lengths further back came Cromdale, followed by The Revenge, Fitzorb. Ulster Man and Carnwherry. The last-named had recovered a prodigious amount of ground and must have been counted most unlucky not to have been placed, though the connections of Achtoi were equally entitled to feel that the interference caused by the fall of St Cuimin had cost them the race. The time recorded was a very good one at 2mins 39secs.

The winner returned to a tremendous ovation, reflecting not only the popularity of Ballaghtobin and his connections, but also their successful repulsion of the English invasion. Fiorenza, the dam of the winner, was bred in England by one Mr B. B. Sapwell. By the Bend Or horse, Orvieto, Fiorenza won two small races before going to stud, where she bred seven winners for the well-known North of England trainer, Captain Percy Bewicke. In 1912 she was purchased by Colonel Chaloner Knox, a member of the Turf Club, for 55gns, in foal to Morganatic. The produce of this mating was Ballaghtobin, the eighth and last winner out of Fiorenza, who died foaling in 1914. After Ballaghtobin's successful debut in 1914 Lord Decies paid £4000 for a half-share in the colt, thus becoming a joint-owner with Colonel Knox and Mr G. W. Lushington, now racing manager for the Loder family. Thereafter Ballaghtobin carried the 'Scarlet, scarlet and green quartered cap' of Lord Decies, who had been elected a Steward of the Turf Club less than three months before his Derby triumph.

Joe Hunter, who trained at Conyngham Lodge under the aegis of Tommy Lushington, was a remarkably gifted member of his profession, who had prepared Ambush II to win the Grand National for the Prince of Wales in 1900. While never having the good fortune to train a really outstanding animal, Joe Hunter consistently figured within the top six trainers in Ireland, heading the lists in 1915, 1920 and 1921. Willie Barrett, the rider of Ballaghtobin, came, with his jockey brothers Michael and Anthony, from the West of Ireland. After an unspectacular start to his career, he came suddenly to prominence in 1912, when finishing fourth in the jockeys' table to John Thompson. Equally as strong in a finish as his more famous rival, Barrett favoured riding his horse out with hands and heels, whereas Thompson was more lavish in his use of the whip. Willie Barrett headed the list of professional jockeys in 1914, ahead of Colin Barrett, to whom he was not related. Though now firmly established as the best jockey riding in Ireland, Barrett experienced increasing weight problems, which eventually forced him to retire in 1922. Shortly afterwards his weight had risen to over twelve stone. More than ten years were to elapse before Hubert Hartigan induced Barrett to spend the winter months breaking yearlings for him. Within months his weight had fallen to 8st 7lbs. Hartigan then persuaded the former champion to apply for his licence again. Immediately successful on this occasion, he continued to ride good winners until his final retirement at the end of World War II. An accomplished boxer, Willie Barrett was a much better jockey than either of his brothers. Anthony, while regarded as a stylish rider, lacked that vital dash.

Martin Quirke, himself champion jockey in 1923 with a record-breaking 87 winners, nominates Willie Barrett as the jockey he least liked to see near him in a finish. While restrained in his use of the whip, he could use it to equal effect in either hand. His technique at the start was extremely deceptive, for he invariably stood his mount right up against the tapes, encouraging his opponents to assume that he would be slowly away when the tapes rose. Irrespective of what advantage they tried to obtain, he was seldom headed out of the gate.

The Right Honourable John Graham Hope de la Poer Beresford, Fifth Baron

---

Wednesday, 30th June, 1915   **£2430**   **13 Ran**   **1½m**

The Irish Derby Stakes of 2,000sovs. By subscription of 50sovs each, half forfeit for those struck out on or before 6th January 1914, but 5sovs only for those struck out on 3rd June 1914. For three years old. Colts, 8st 12lb; fillies, 8st 8lb. If then entitled and claimed at time of entry, produce of untried mares allowed 3lbs. The winner of two stakes, each value 500sovs, or of one value 800sovs, 7lb extra; of a stake value 300sovs, or of stakes collectively value 700sovs, 3lb extra. The second to receive 100sovs and the third 50sovs out of the stake. The nominator of the winner to receive 100sovs, of the second 50sovs and of the third 25sovs from the stakes. Any person entering three horses his own bona fide sole property can strike out one at the time appointed for declaring minor forfeit, without having to pay the forfeit.

(80 subs)

1 Lord Decies's	BALLAGHTOBIN (W. Barrett)	9. 5	Hunter
	B. colt Morganatic – Fiorenza by Orvieto.		
2 Mr A. M. Singer's	ACHTOI (C. Trigg)	9. 5	Davies (UK)
	Br. colt Santoi – Achray.		
3 Mr A. F. Bassett's	CROMDALE (S. Donoghue)	8. 9	Persse (UK)
	Ch. colt Llangibby – Goldscleugh.		
4 Mr W. J. Tatem's	THE REVENGE (E. Piper)	8.12	De Mestre (UK)
	B. colt The White Knight – St Flora.		
5 Mr M. Fitzgerald's	FITZORB (F. Hunter)	8.12	Morton (UK)
	Ch. colt Orby – Glaze.		
6 Mr J. W. Widger's	ULSTER MAN (Mr W. J.	9. 1	Parkinson
	Parkinson) Ch. colt Aquascutum – Kilgobbin Maid.		
7 Mr H. S. Gray's	CARNWHERRY (John Doyle)	8.12	P. Behan
	Ch. colt Arizona – Lady Egremont.		
8 Mr A. Lucas's	LORD WAVELET (C. Ringstead)	8.12	
	Ch. colt Wavelet's Pride – Lady Maude.		
9 Mr B. Kirby's	RED BRANCH KNIGHT (M.	8.12	Owner
	Colbert) B. colt The White Knight – Red Bell.		
10 Mr G. H. Dennehy's	LADY PRIM (Joseph Canty)	8. 8	
	B. filly Earla Mor – Mechante.		
11 Mr A. M'Cann's	SAILOR'S LASSIE (J. Rose)	8. 5	Jeffrey
	B. filly Eminent – Black Eyed Susan.		
PU Col. W. Hall Walker's	ROMUS (C. Barrett)	8.12	
	Ch. colt White Eagle – Bella Roba.		
F Mr W. J. Parkinson's	ST CUIMIN (Joseph Harty)	9. 5	Parkinson
	B. colt St. Monans – Verdant Isle.		

SP 7/4 Achtoi; 7/2 BALLAGHTOBIN; 6/1 Cromdale; 8/1 Fitzorb; 10/1 The Revenge, Red Branch Knight; 100/8 Ulster Man; 100/6 Lady Prim, Carnwherry; 66/1 Romus, Sailor's Lassie; 100/1 Bar.

Neck, 4 lengths. 2m 39s.
Winner trained by Mr J. Hunter at Conyngham Lodge, Curragh.

Decies, had a distinguished military career in two South African campaigns prior to succeeding his brother to the title in 1911. A noted all-round sportsman, he represented Great Britain on showjumping tours of North and South America, besides making his reputation as a polo player and yachtsman. He was appointed Military Press Censor in 1916, holding the position until it was disbanded three years later. Lord Decies' colours had not been seen for many years prior to his death in 1944, aged seventy-eight.

Ballaghtobin reappeared in a King's Plate over two miles at the Oaks meeting in July. Opposed only by the six-year-old, General Symons, he won in a canter by twenty lengths. He was then sent over to Sam Darling to be prepared for the Cesarewitch, for which he received 8st 4lbs, a high weight for a three-year-old. Ridden as always by Willie Barrett, Ballaghtobin ran a tremendous race, until the weight proved too much over such a distance. The race was won in record time by Sir Abe Bailey's wonderful stayer, Son-in-Law. As a four-year-old Ballaghtobin won three races in Ireland and finished unplaced at Newmarket on his only appearance in 1917.

Achtoi was rested after his valiant effort in the Irish Derby, not appearing until September, when he finished third to Pommern in the New St Leger at Newmarket. He subsequently gained some compensation by winning the Newmarket St Leger. Cromdale ran twice after his Curragh debut, winning each time. With the exception of Fitzorb, who won his next race, the remainder of those that finished behind Ballaghtobin achieved nothing of note during the remainder of the season.

Ballaghtobin's subsequent career makes sorry reading. Because of the curtailment of racing in England in 1917, he was sent out to India, to return three years later. Sold for only 105gns in July 1920, he rewarded his new owner by finishing last in a selling race at Derby. Retired to stud he begot nothing remotely as good as he had once been himself. With the benefit of hindsight, it seems tragic that Ballaghtobin was ever trained for long-distance events, for he possessed brilliant speed, in addition to an unmistakable touch of class. Achtoi fared much better at stud, heading the Irish list in 1928. Prior to his death in 1940 he had sired the winners of five Irish Classics, two Cesarewitch winners and two Champion Hurdle victors in Blaris and Insurance.

1916

The historic events of Easter Monday 1916, when Padraig Pearse proclaimed the birth of the Irish Republic, from the steps of the General Post Office in Dublin, were destined eventually to lead to the Ireland that we know today. A more direct consequence of the Easter Rising, in this context, was the suspension of all racing in Ireland until early June. This, added to the drastic reduction of racing in England owing to the War, made the Derby picture very obscure. Nor was Irish two-year-old form of much assistance, for of the leading lights Vera Cruz was being kept to sprinting, while Ayn Hali would not see a racecourse until July. Of the seven

Irish-trained runners, Brendan, Cimarron and Captive Princess had the best juvenile form. Brendan had finished second to Captive Princess at Leopardstown before winning impressively at the Curragh in July, those being his only runs. Captive Princess had not won after beating Brendan, but had run Cimarron to two lengths in the Curragh Grand Prize in October. Of the three English challengers, only Furore had shown any worthwhile two-year-old form. Trained then by S. H. Darling, he had been placed in four of his six races.

In the only major Derby trial, the Baldoyle Derby, Brendan had been soundly beaten by the outsider Mountain Park, who received 16lbs. Behind these two came Roi Petit, Captive Princess, Zefus and the hot favourite, Cimarron. This result made nonsense of previous form, for at the Curragh in early April Cimarron had given Mountain Park 20lbs and beaten him into fourth place. It was generally felt that such inconsistent form indicated that the home-trained runners were a moderate lot. Consequently the search for a favourite concentrated on the English trio. Furore had twice demonstrated his gameness when getting up in the last stride to win over the distance at Gatwick. In his final race before the Derby he had finished a respectable third to Valais at level weights. Valais had finished fourth in the New Derby. King Robert had won only the first of his four races that year, in which he beat Valais cleverly by half a length, with Gilbert the Filbert back in fourth place. Though Furore appeared to be held by King Robert on a line through Valais, he was thought to have made the greater improvement. This was reflected in the betting market, where Furore replaced King Robert as favourite. Hopes of an Irish victory were pinned on Brendan and Cimarron, for Bachelor's Image, though an own-brother to Bachelor's Double and Bachelor's Wedding, patently needed more time to fulfil his undoubted potential.

After only a brief delay the field got off to a good start, headed by Roi Petit, who led from Brendan, Captive Princess, Bachelor's Image and Cimarron, with the favourite in last place. This order was maintained for six furlongs, with Furore apparently labouring at the rear of the field. As they swung right-handed down the hill King Robert came with a smooth run to take the lead, followed by Cimarron, Gilbert the Filbert, Brendan and an improving Furore. Bachelor's Image had already fallen away, beaten, while the early leaders, Roi Petit and Captive Princess were losing ground. Racing into the straight King Robert began to draw away from Cimarron and Brendan and was already being hailed as the winner. However, the joy of his supporters was short-lived, for the favourite was now in full flight. Furore overhauled his compatriot a furlong out and, after a brief tussle, drew steadily away to win by a comfortable three lengths, with Brendan a similar distance away in third place. By running on again in the closing stages to finish fourth, Captive Princess indicated her potential as a stayer.

Furore, a medium-sized brown colt, was bred in Ireland by Captain Henry Greer and sent up for sale as a yearling at Newmarket, where he made 200gns to the bid of Mr H. Ellis, a Virginian planter, whose first venture into ownership this was. Fugleman, sire of Furore, was by the Epsom Derby winner Persimmon and took up duties at Greer's Brownstown Stud in 1910. He sired nothing else of note and was later transferred to Co. Limerick as a country stallion. Furore's dam, Rappel, was a useful racemare, who won under both rules and raced for eight seasons before being retired to stud. The day after the Derby Mr Ellis bought her foal by Earla Mor.

Named Furious, he won the Lincolnshire Handicap in 1920. In addition to these, her best, Rappel bred five other winners.

The success of Furore completed a wonderful day for his trainer Victor Tabor, who had won the opening race with the ageless stable favourite, Mustapha, now nine years old and successful every season since his two-year-old days. Charles Victor Tabor, son of an Essex farmer, came into racing as an amateur rider, winning numerous races on horses trained by Herbert Lines. On commencing training himself in 1907 he quickly became respected for ability to exploit two-year-olds in selling races, a highly specialized activity at that time. However, this preoccupation did not make him any less effective in producing winners of better-class races, as his Cesarewitch record indicates. He won this marathon handicap with Furore (1917), Arctic Star (1928) and Punch (1937). Equally proficient under National Hunt rules, 'Vic' Tabor trained that spectacular Irish-bred 'chaser, Airgead Sios, to win thirteen of his twenty-six races, including the Champion 'Chase, Grand Annual 'Chase and the Becher 'Chase twice during the 'thirties. Airgead Sios had been bought from an Irish priest by Mrs Tabor, sister of the celebrated jockey and trainer Percy Woodland. Victor Taber retired in 1946 and died five years later, aged seventy-seven.

Herbert Robbins had received a thorough grounding in his profession, for his indentures extended over eleven years. Born in 1877, he served his time successively with Herbert Randall, Sceptre's jockey, Charles Peck and John Hallick. Initially quite successful, he experienced several lean years, including a spell in Ireland, before joining Victor Tabor's Epsom stable in 1911. Able to go to scale at 7st, he soon began to achieve recognition as a good lightweight and 1912 yielded 55 winners, placing him seventh in the jockeys' championship. That year he won the Ascot Stakes on The Policeman and the following year was credited with the Lincolnshire on Berrilldon, upon the disqualification of Cuthbert. On his Irish Derby winner he won the Cesarewitch of 1917 for his retaining stable and three years later he won the Lincolnshire on Furore's half-brother, Furious, for Tabor's brother-in-law, Percy Woodland. 1920 also saw him victorious in the Manchester Cup and November Handicap on George Dundas' Pomme de Terre. His last major successes were on Double Hackle in the Ascot Stakes and Northumberland Plate for Joe Cannon. Herbert Robbins rode his last winner in 1925, dying two years later at Lambourn from an internal complaint. He was described as a grave and reserved man, with a strong vein of carefully suppressed tenderness and sentimentality.

Furore did not win again until succeeding in the Cesarewitch the following season. As his career progressed he became increasingly inclined to drop himself out in the early stages of a race, frequently leaving himself an impossible amount to do. Kept in training for a further three seasons, he won once as a five-year-old and walked over for the Whip at Newmarket in the two succeeding seasons, before retiring to stud in Wales and into obscurity.

Those that finished behind Furore at the Curragh, with one exception, did little to enhance the form or to enrich their owners. Bachelor's Image belied both his name and family reputation and was banished to stud in Wales. King Robert was deported to Brazil. Sprig of Mint went to stud in Limerick, where he did better than any but his owner could possibly have expected. The shining exception in this morass of mediocrity was Captive Princess. On her next run she showed tremendous gameness in getting up on the line to win the Irish Oaks. Then followed an utterly convincing success in the Irish St Leger, where she proved herself to be a high-class staying filly. At stud she bred four winners, including the good sprinter Lord Wembley. Though 1916 will never be forgotten in the wider context of Irish history, it merits a low rating in the annals of the Irish Derby.

Wednesday, 28th June, 1916   **£2910**   **10 Ran**   **1½m**

The Irish Derby Stakes of 3000sovs. By subscription of 50sovs each, half forfeit for those struck out on or before 5th January, 1916 but 5sovs only for those struck out on 2nd June, 1915. For three years old. Colts, 8st 12lb; fillies, 8st 8lb. If then entitled and claimed at time of entry, produce of untried mares allowed 3lb. The winner of two stakes each value 500sovs, or of one value 800sovs, 7lb extra; of a stake value 300sovs, or of stakes collectively value 700sovs, 3lb extra. The second to receive 100sovs and the third 50sovs out of the stake. The nominator of the winner to receive 100sovs, of the second 50sovs and of the third 25sovs from the stakes. Any person entering three horses his own bona fida sole property can strike out one at the time appointed for declaring minor forfeit, without having to pay the forfeit.

(144 subs)

1	Mr H. Ellis's	FURORE (H. Robbins)	8.12	Tabor (UK)
		Br. colt Fugleman – Rapel by Rapallo.		
2	Col. W. Hall Walker's	KING ROBERT (Walter Griggs)	9. 1	Waugh (UK)
		Br. colt Royal Realm – Burnt Almond.		
3	Mr J. Daly's	BRENDAN (F. Hunter)	8.12	Behan
		Br. colt St Brendan – Lady Ina.		
4	Mr W. A. Wallis's	CAPTIVE PRINCESS (T. Burns)	8. 8	Dunne
		B. filly Captivation – Princess Eager.		
5	Mr J. J. Parkinson's	ZEFUS (Joseph Harty)	8. 9	Owner
		Ch. colt William Rufus – Zefa.		
6	Mr C. J. Blake's	CIMARRON (S. Donoghue)	8.12	Jeffrey
		B. colt Symington – Caspia.		
7	Mr J. W. Burton's	GILBERT THE FILBERT (E. Wheatley) B. colt Earla Mor – Rainproff.	8.12	H. Lines (UK)
8	Mr A. H. Ledlie's	SPRIG OF MINT (R. Crisp)	8.12	Parkinson
		B. colt Spearmint – Palotta.		
9	Mr P. Cullinan's	ROI PETIT (M. Beary)	8.12	Dunne
		B. colt Roi Herode – Little May II.		
10	Mr A. Lowry's	BACHELOR'S IMAGE (W. Barrett) Ch. colt Tredennis – Lady Bawn.	8.12	Dawson

SP 2/1 FURORE; 11/4 King Robert; 6/1 Cimarron, Brendan; 7/1 Bachelor's Image; 8/1 Zefus; 20/1 Sprig of Mint, Gilbert the Filbert; 33/1 Bar.

Won easily by 3 lengths, same.

Winner trained by Mr C. V. Tabor at Epsom, Surrey.

1917

By this time racing in England had been brought practically to a standstill. However, largely due to the efforts of Sir William Nelson, plans to halt racing in Ireland had been modified and although the fixture list had been reduced, racing continued. Sir William had interceded successfully with the Government on the basis that Ireland was not a Manufacturing country, but was heavily dependent on the breeding industry and, in consequence, any cessation of racing would have a disastrous effect upon this vital sector of the Irish economy. Symptoms of a country at war were everywhere in evidence; from the numbers of racegoers in khaki and the women collecting for the Red Cross to the crop of oats growing incongruously on the gallops opposite the stands.

As a result of the most prolonged winter in recent years and the curtailment of racing, the form of the ten runners for the Irish Derby was somewhat sketchy. However, it was generally thought that the winner would come from the English-trained quintet. Of these the most strongly fancied were Argosy and Kingston Black. The former had won his two races at Newmarket in impressive style and neither his trainer's misgivings about the horse's fitness nor his heavily bandaged forelegs deterred the public, who backed him to favouritism. Kingston Black, ridden by the ageless Otto Madden, was backed on the strength of his home trials, rather than his racecourse form. Of the home-trained runners, First Flier, second to Lisnalinchy in the Baldoyle Derby, seemed to have the best prospects of repelling the English challenge.

For many the race was ruined at the start, where Kingston Black refused to jump off with the others, effectively taking no part in the proceedings. The early running was made by Prince Lionel, who led from First Flier, Argosy and Dresden, with Kingston Black tailed off. First Flier took it up five furlongs out and thereafter never really looked like losing, though challenged briefly in the straight by Argosy. Beaten by a facile five lengths, Argosy finished four lengths ahead of his compatriot, Dresden, with Prince Lionel a further length away in fourth place. First Flier returned to a rapturous reception, reflecting both the popularity of his owner-trainer and the public's patriotic pleasure in seeing the raiders repulsed.

Bred in England by Mr Musker, First Flier was a bay colt by Henry the First out of Grey Flier, a coarse-looking daughter of the good hurdler, Friary. Sent up to the First July Sales at Newmarket in 1915, First Flier had been bought by J. J. Parkinson for only 35gns, even less than the miserable average of 53gns realised by the Musker draft. For a further 120gns Parkinson had picked up three more Musker yearlings, and, mid-way through the 1917 season, they had won £3549 between them. Henry the First, by Melton, was an own-brother to Whistling Rufus and Galloping Simon. Successful in four of his six races as a two-year-old, including the Dewhurst Plate, Henry the First finished second to Pretty Polly in the St Leger and twice beat St Amant, to whom he finished fifth in the Epsom Derby. Leased by Mr Musker at the end of his racing career, Henry the First stood in France for three seasons, returning to Musker's stud in 1909. Though his progeny did well on the Continent, Henry the First was neglected by English breeders on his return, achieving little of note prior to his death in 1916. Grey Flier, for whom Argosy's owner, Sir William Tatem, paid 1650gns after the Irish Derby, bred only one other small winner.

The day after the Irish Derby, Lisnalinchy, First Flier's conqueror at Baldoyle, won easily over two miles. Both these colts were then nominated for the re-opened New Derby and sent to Newmarket. In the event neither ran, Lisnalinchy because of hock trouble and First Flier because he completely lost his form. Brought back to Maddenstown, First Flier started odds-on for the Irish St Leger, but was beaten easily by Double Scotch. A week later he was sent to Limerick for a two-mile amateur riders' race. Once again he started odds-on and once again he was beaten. Sold for 1150gns at the Newmarket Sales in January 1918, having won £3086, First Flier went to India, where he rediscovered his best form, dead-heating with the ex-Irish Mordennis in the Aga Khan Cup and winning the Viceroy's Cup in 1919. Having raced successfully for a further three seasons, he broke a leg and was destroyed in 1922.

Argosy, a high-class colt, handicapped by splint troubles throughout his career, never ran again after the Irish Derby. Retired to J. J. Parkinson's stud, Argosy sired Embargo, winner of the Irish Two Thousand Guineas and Derby in 1926, enabling Argosy to head the list of sires in Ireland. That year he was bought by Mrs W. W. Bailey to replace Bachelor's Double. Within months of taking up duties at Rathbane Stud, Co. Limerick, Argosy dropped dead, to the dismay of Irish breeders, who had belatedly realised his great potential. That Argosy should have taken as long as he did to achieve recognition was largely due to Parkinson's practice of selling so many horses abroad and it is interesting to note that ten years after his death Argosy still ranked sixth in the table of winners in India by Irish and English-based sires.

Dresden (later renamed Chinaman), Prince Lionel and Crom Abu all went on to win races of some description. The last-named, one of the very last foals sired by Desmond, became something of a selling hurdle specialist for Victor Tabor. Geraldina, a three-time winner as a two-year-old, but of little account thereafter, suddenly soared in value when her half-brother, Grand Parade, won the Epsom Derby in 1919. However, she bred only one small winner. Kingston Black's behaviour in the Irish Derby brought back painful memories of his half-brothers identical performance twelve years earlier. When 14-to-1 ON for the Lavant Stakes at Goodwood, Black Arrow had refused to start. Ridden by Tommy Burns, Kingston Black finished sixth in the New Derby, later running second to Gay Crusader in the Substitute St Leger.

First Flier's victory rectified one glaring omission in the annals of the Irish Derby: 'Winner trained J. J. Parkinson'. Born in Tramore, Co. Waterford in 1870, J. J. 'Jim' Parkinson was almost certainly the most successful trainer in the history of Irish racing, on the basis of sheer numbers of races won. Having qualified as a veterinary surgeon at London Veterinary College, he spent some time as understudy to Michael Dennehy, before starting to train in his own right in the old Stone Barracks, which overlooks the Irish Derby course. Having fallen foul of the authorities in his capacity as amateur rider, Jim Parkinson went to the United States, where he was immediately struck by the advantages of the riding style with which Tod Sloan would soon revolutionise European jockeyship. On his return to Ireland Parkinson began training again, with immediate success. Undoubtedly the best 'horse' in Parkinson's yard in those early days was his crack apprentice, John Thompson. Born in Bunclody, Co. Wexford, Thompson joined his master in about 1898 and under Parkinson's tutelage became the first Irish jockey to employ the ridiculed, but devastatingly effective 'monkey-on-the-stick' style. Ironically, Thompson's first major success came when he rode Berrill to foil Sloan's massive gamble on his own mount, Codoman, in the Cambridgeshire of 1900.

John Thompson remained with Parkinson at Maddenstown Lodge until his tragic death, as the result of a fall while schooling, in 1913. At the time of his death Thompson had been champion jockey in Ireland for nine of the past eleven years.

His championships had been gained largely on winners trained by Jim Parkinson. From the time that training records were first kept in 1905, Parkinson was leading trainer on six occasions, second eight times and third nine times. These statistics were, of course, based on stake money won, rather than numbers of races. On the latter basis Parkinson reigned supreme. His 134 winners in one year (1923) remains an all-time Irish record, approached in recent years only by Dermot Weld.

Parkinson's great rival was Michael Dawson, who trained on the other side of the Curragh. Overall, it has to be said that Dawson won bigger races and higher stakes with fewer but more select horses. For this reason he has been held the greater trainer of the two. However, the fundamental approaches of the two men to their profession could not have been more dissimilar and this must be taken into account when attempting to compare the two men who dominated the ranks of Irish trainers for over a quarter of a century. Dour Michael Dawson trained horses to realise their potential and win the best races of which they were capable. He was not a betting man, though some of his patrons undoubtedly were. In complete contrast, the volatile, dynamic Jim Parkinson trained on a turnover basis: 'Buy them in, have them win and sell them on.' In consequence, he rarely had less than one hundred horses in training – the largest string in Europe – backed up by hundreds more awaiting either training or shipment to the Americas, India or the Antipodes. Twice leading owner in stakes won, he topped the league in terms of races won on a record twenty occasions. If his horses seemed to be most successful on courses where a Dawson-trained runner was rarely seen, there was an excellent reason for this. For many years a race at a country track was worth less than £21 to the winner; that (well-backed) winner could be sold to England as a maiden . . .

However, J. J. Parkinson could train a good horse every bit as well as a moderate one, as his record shows: two Irish Derbies, four Irish Oaks and all the major two-year-old races. One of his most notable feats was to take five runners to the Epsom Derby meeting in 1909. Four of them won, while the fifth was beaten a head, having jumped the road. All five were ridden by John Thompson. Other leading riders associated with Maddenstown Lodge included Michael Beary, Martin Quirke, Harry and Rufus Beasley, Colin and Billy Barrett, Frank Morgan and Fred Hunter. Billy Parkinson, the trainer's son, headed the list of jockeys in Ireland as an amateur in 1915 and 1916, the only full seasons during which he rode. His 72 winners in 1915 constituted an Irish record, which was only surpassed in 1923, by another Maddenstown Lodge rider, Martin Quirke.

Besides administering his vast string, quartered in three separate yards, Jim Parkinson was an active director of Tramore and Limerick Junction racecourses, Goff's Bloodstock Sales and Tote Investors Ltd. He was also a Free State Senator from 1922 until 1936. His re-election to the Irish Senate in 1937 moved the British Bloodstock Breeders' Review to marvel at Parkinson's astonishing energy and diversity: 'How he finds time to give attention to politics is a mystery.'

One of the less pleasant actions of this extraordinary man's career was his leading role in breaking the stable lads' strike in 1924. But, by the same token he is still remembered in Maddenstown as an unstinting benefactor of the poor and needy, when times were bad. Unlike Michael Dawson, Parkinson was not an easy man to ride for; if a jockey were not first out of the gate he was suspected of stopping his horse, apprentices were expected to work for next to nothing, morning exercise was chaotic, his only means of correspondence was by telegram, and still the 'winner machine' rolled on . . . Parkinson's last years were marred by ill-health, which was undoubtedly responsible for his increasingly erratic behaviour. He died in 1948, aged seventy-eight, and was succeeded by his son Emmanuel, still living in Maddenstown. J. J. Parkinson's grandson, Tony Sweeney, is probably the most knowledgeable and eloquent racing journalist in Ireland.

Wednesday, 27th June, 1917 £2725 **10 Ran** 1½m

The Irish Derby Stakes of 3000sovs. By subscription of 50sovs each, half forfeit for those struck out on or before 3rd January, 1917, but 5sovs only for those struck out on 7th June, 1916. For three years old. Colts, 8st 12lb; fillies 8st 8lb. If then entitled and claimed at time of entry, produce of untried mares allowed 3lb. The winner of a race value 1000sovs, or of two races each value 5000sovs, 7lb extra. The second to receive 100sovs and the third 50sovs out of the stakes. The breeder of the winner to receive 100sovs, of the second 50sovs and of the third 25sovs from the stakes. Any person entering three horses his own bona fide sole property can strike out one at the time appointed for declaring minor forfeit, without having to pay the forfeit.

(106 subs)

1 Mr J. J. Parkinson's	FIRST FLIER (W. Barrett)	8. 9 (car 8.10)	Owner
	B. colt Henry the First – Grey Flier by Friary.		
2 Sir W. J. Tatem's	ARGOSY (S. Donoghue)	8.12	De Mestre (UK)
	B. colt Bachelor's Double – Fragrant.		
3 Mr M. Singer's	DRESDEN (C. Trigg)	8. 9	Davies (UK)
	B. colt Santo – Betsy Jane.		
4 Mr J. Reid Walker's	PRINCE LIONEL (T. Burns)	8.12	J. Rogers
	B. colt Chaucer – St Clare.		
5 Mr J. Daly's	CROM ABOO (F. Hunter)	8.12	Behan
	Br. colt Desmond – Lady Car.		
6 Mr W. Raphael's	ROCHETTO (R. Watson)	8.12	Persse (UK)
	Ch. colt Rock Sand – Bobbin.		
7 Mr W. T. de Pledge's	GERALDINA (J. Thwaites)	8. 5	Fetherston'
	Br. filly Denneford – Grand Geraldine.		
8 Mr C. J. Blake's	PENDRAGON (J. Clark)	8. 9	Jeffrey
	Ch. colt Glasgerion – Elfland.		
9 Lord Carnarvon's	THEODOSIUS (R. Cooper)	8.12	R. C. Dawson (UK)
	B. colt Valens – Cambrae.		
L Col. W. Hall Walker's	KINGSTON BLACK (O. Madden)	8.12	C. Waugh (UK)
	Br. colt Royal Realm – Black Cherry.		

SP 2/1 Argosy; 5/2 Kingston Black; 6/1 FIRST FLIER; 7/1 Pendragon; 100/8 Rochetto, Dresden, Geraldina; 100/6 Crom Aboo; 20/1 Prince Lionel; 50/1 Bar.
Won in a canter by 5 lengths, 4 lengths. 2m 39s.
Winner trained by Mr J. J. Parkinson at Maddenstown Lodge, Curragh.

1918

The final year of the Great War saw racing in Ireland thriving in the face of adversity. Not only was fodder in desperately short supply – racehorses being limited to 13lbs per day – but Sinn Fein, the Irish Republican Party, had declared a policy of disrupting fixtures. Despite these difficulties, the Irish Derby was worth over £3000 for the first time in its history and attracted four English challengers. Outstanding among these, and firm ante-post favourite was King John, a white-splashed chestnut, reminiscent of his grandsire, Gallinule. Having won as a two-year-old and over the Derby distance at three, Giles Loder's colt had made the running in the New Derby until headed by Gainsborough, to whom he eventually finished fourth. His credentials appeared outstanding in an otherwise undistinguished field and the last-minute withdrawal of the Perrse-trained Sheerup made King John seem a racing certainty. His compatriots Shenley Boy, a half-brother to Tagalie, and Chicago were both still maidens and any support for the latter was due solely to his being ridden by Steve Donoghue. Best-fancied of the home-trained quartet was Z.Z., twice a winner at two and though unraced at three, being ridden by Joe Childs, successful in the first two legs of the English Triple Crown on Gainsborough. Of James Dunne's two runners, the filly Sari Bahr was thought more likely to stay the distance than Empire Maker.

The early running was made at a fast gallop by the unconsidered Navarre, who led from Sari Bahr, King John and Chicago. Navarre remained clear until reaching the mile post, where the field began to close. Entering the straight King John, Z.Z. and Sari Bahr drew ahead of Navarre, with the race apparently between them. Z.Z. was the first to weaken, thus allowing Sari Bahr her brief moment of glory. Her supporters hopes were short-lived, for, passing the two furlong marker, she was challenged by the long-striding King John, who simply cruised away to win by an effortless eight lengths from Sari Bahr, with Navarre staying on doggedly to take third place. Those who had taken the price about the odds-on favourite never had a moment's worry and, though it looked to have been a thoroughly mediocre contest, King John could scarcely have been asked to do more than to win as he did.

King John was bred by his owner by Roi Herode out of Miranda, herself a full-sister of the fabulous Pretty Polly. Though she did manage to win over five furlongs as a three-year-old, Miranda never promised to rival her relation's achievements on the racecourse. However, in terms of producing winners, she was numerically more successful. King John's sire, Roi Herode, was bred and trained in France, where he was little more than a good staying handicapper. However, he happened to represent the Herod line, then almost extinct in Britain and Ireland. The Irish breeder Edward 'Cub' Kennedy had long been anxious to revive the Herod line and accordingly purchased Roi Herode for £2000 after he had finished second in the Doncaster Cup of 1909 and installed him at his Straffen Stud in Co. Kildare. The very first mare covered by Roi Herode was Vahren . . . the result was The Tetrarch and thus Roi Herode's reputation as a stallion was sealed at one stroke. Not surprisingly Roi Herode found it impossible to sustain such a standard of excellence. Throughout a lengthy career he only got one other of possibly equal brilliance, another grey flying machine called Milesius, who unfortunately became disenchanted with racing. Roe Herode sired three other Irish Classic winners in Judea and Cinq à Sept (Irish Oaks) and St Donagh (Irish Two Thousand Guineas).

Captain Giles Loder, the winning owner-breeder, had inherited Eyrefield Lodge in 1914 on the death of his uncle Eustace Loder, who in addition to Pretty Polly and Spearmint, owned a winner of the Irish Derby, Gallinaria. Though he could not know it at the time of King John's Curragh triumph, not far away in the Eyrefield paddocks Giles Loder had a yearling colt destined for far greater things; Spion Kop. Besides winning the Epsom Derby with Spion Kop, Giles Loder won the One Thousand Guineas with Cresta Run, while in Ireland Spike Island and Zodiac each won two Classics and Spelthorne and Sea Symphony one each. Later in life his colours were carried with distinction by The Cobbler and Arctic Explorer. A distinguished military career gave way to a lifetime of discerning devotion to breeding and racing. Assisted successively by Noble Johnson and Peter Burrell, Giles Loder progressively culled the Eyrefield bloodlines until the Admiration family reigned supreme, a policy which rewarded him with a constant succession of high-class winners up to the time of his death in 1966 at the age of eighty-two. He had been a member of the Turf Club since 1918 and of the Jockey Club since 1924. Unmarried, his recreations in later life were gardening and golf.

Eustace 'Lucky' Loder once declared that: 'You may put all the brains you have into racing, but you will be nowhere unless you have luck.' That both he and his nephew possessed that vital element in abundance can scarcely be denied, but it must also be said that in Peter Purcell Gilpin they found a trainer capable of capitalising their good fortune to the full, for he was one of the supreme exponents of his profession. Born at Pau in the French Pyrenees in 1858 of Irish parents, Peter Purcell joined the 5th Lancers in 1881, became an accomplished Gentleman Rider and in 1883 married Miss Meux-Smith, niece of Sir Richard Gilpin, upon whose death Purcell assumed the name Gilpin, under the terms of his wife's inheritance. After some years training in Ireland, P. P. Gilpin moved to Blandford in Dorset, pulled off a notable 'coup' with Clarehaven in the Cesarewitch of 1900 and with the proceeds built Clarehaven in Newmarket. Over the next quarter of a century this tall, immaculate and faintly forbidding Irishman turned out such champions as Pretty Polly, Comrade and Spion Kop, the best of a galaxy of good winners whose exploits earned their trainer the title The Wizard of Clarehaven. Interested only in the preparation of high-class horses, P. P. Gilpin (known as Two Peas to distinguish him from P. P. Peebles, Three Peas), had no superiors in discovering the particular talents of the animals entrusted to his care. In keeping with his autocratic mien, P. P. Gilpin had very definite ideas about the place of jockeys and consequently remained impervious to the persuasive wiles of Steve Donoghue. He was leading trainer in England in 1904 and 1915, in which year one of his principal patrons, Mr L. Neumann headed the owners' list. Besides masterminding Clarehaven, P. P. Gilpin maintained a successful stud at Dollanstown, Co. Kildare, where he died in 1928. He was succeeded by his son Victor, who carried on the family tradition until his retirement at the outbreak of the Second World War.

That King John's rider, H. H. Beasley, should have been a successful rider was not only natural but almost inevitable, for he was a member of a famous Irish racing family. His father, also Harry, won the Grand National on Comeaway, having three times finished second in the Aintree epic and last donned silks at the age of eighty-three. Young Harry, having headed the list of riders in Ireland in 1918, joined the Persse stable in Stockbridge, winning the Two Thousand Guineas on Mr Jinks in 1927. Other big races to fall to his ice-cool judgement were the Cambridgeshire on Forsetti and the Coronation Cup on Condover and Apelle. In Ireland he won a second Irish Derby on Zionist and the Two Thousand Guineas on Fourth Hand. When the McCalmont horses left Stockbridge so did Beasley, who continued to figure in the first flight until his retirement before the Second World War. Extremely reserved in manner, Harry Beasley was nonetheless positively garrulous in comparison to his brother Pat 'Rufus' Beasley, for a time first jockey to Cecil Boyd-Rochfort and now training in Yorkshire. Tall for a flat jockey, Harry Beasley earned this tribute from Sam Darling: 'If I were having a selling-plate gamble, Harry Beasley would be the jockey for me. I do not think he would raise even an eyelid if I told him I had £10,000 on, and it would certainly not cause him to ride other than in the usual steady fashion.'

On his retirement he became head man to C. A. 'Charlie' Rogers, dying after a long illness in 1959. His son H. R. 'Bobby' Beasley, having been champion jockey in Ireland in 1960, rode with great success in England, where he became one of the

Wednesday, 26th June, 1918 **£3100** **7 Ran** **1½m**

The Irish Derby of 3500sovs, being 3000sovs nett to the winner, 100sovs to the breeder of the winner, 50sovs to the breeder of the second, 200sovs to the owner of the second and 100sovs to the owner of the third. By subscription of 50sovs each, half forfeit for those struck out on or before 2nd January, 1918, but 5sovs only for those struck out on 6th June, 1917. For three years old. Colts and geldings, 8st 12lb; Fillies, 8st 8lb. If then entitled and claimed at time of entry, produce of untried mares allowed 3lb. The winner of a race value 1000sovs, or of two races each value 500sovs, 7lb extra.

(125 subs.)

1 Capt. Giles Loder's	KING JOHN (H. H. Beasley)	8.12	Gilpin (UK)
	Ch. colt Roi Herode – Miranda by Gallinule.		
2 Capt. Shirley's	SARI BAHR (F. Fox)	8. 5	Dunne
	Ch. filly Oppressor – Merry Shields.		
3 Mr J. J. Parkinson's	NAVARRE (E. M. Quirke)	8.12	Owner
	Ch. colt William Rufus – Zefa.		
4 Mr W. Raphael's	SHENLEY BOY (W. Barrett)	8.12	Dewhurst (UK)
	Gr. colt Lemberg – Tagale.		
5 Mr J. C. Sullivan's	Z.Z. (J. Childs)	8. 9	Behan
	Ch. colt Zria – Zingarella.		
6 Mr W. A. Wallis's	EMPIRE MAKER (M. Beary)	8.12	Dunne
	B. colt Rhodesian – Princess Eager.		
7 Sir E. Cassell's	CHICAGO (S. Donoghue)	8. 9	Halsey (UK)
	B. colt Cylgad – Lady Americus.		

SP 1/3 KING JOHN; 6/1 Z.Z.; 100/12 Sari Bahr; 100/8 Chicago, Shenley Boy; 20/1 Navarre; 50/1 Empire Maker.

8 lengths, 4 lengths. 2m 41.2/5s.
Winner trained by Mr P. P. Gilpin at Clarehaven Lodge, Newmarket.

select band to have won the Grand National, Gold Cup and Champion Hurdle. Unlike his father, Bobby suffered from nerves, lost and won his battle with the bottle and made a triumphant comeback to win another Gold Cup on that exciting enigma Captain Christy.

King John's subsequent career was interrupted by the onset of rheumatism, which kept him off the course for the rest of that season. The following year he won the Great Yorkshire Handicap, only to be disqualified for bumping and boring. Strongly fancied for the Cesarewitch, for which he started second favourite, King John ran badly, but redeemed himself with a runaway success in the last big race of the season, the Manchester November Handicap, ridden by Elijah Wheatley. Kept in training as a five-year-old, King John only ran once before leg trouble put an end to his career. He was then sold to a French breeder for £6000, only to be 'spun' by a London vet on account of a cataract, the legacy of an injury sustained during his yearling days. He was eventually sold for a paltry £1200 to go to New Zealand, whence he departed in 1921. Sari Bahr, second to King John at the Curragh, finished fourth in the Irish St Leger, won an amateur flat race at the same venue when ridden by his owner and subsequently bred three minor winners. Navarre found his way to South Africa, while Shenley Boy, having won twice, sailed for Egypt. Z.Z., after finishing a remote third to Dionysus in the Irish St Leger, was gelded before embarking on a lengthy career in 'sellers' for that selling plate specialist, George Poole. The good-looking but bad-tempered Empire Maker, a half-brother to the Irish St Leger winner Captive Princess, won several races when trained by Frank Morgan, successful in the Irish Derby in 1904 on Royal Arch. Chicago found his metier over fences, continuing to win 'chases until eleven years of age.

1919

The aftermath of the 'war to end all wars' saw a boom in racing in England, with the Derby, restored to its rightful home, drawing a record crowd. But, while England rejoiced at the return to peacetime conditions, the struggle for independence in Ireland grew more intense. Political activity had caused the abandonment of the most important two jumping meetings of the year at Fairyhouse and Punchestown. Though this type of disruption had ceased on the release of the Irish political prisoners held in English gaols, a new threat to racing had emerged in the form of a coal shortage, effecting rail services. However, neither political activity nor fuel shortages served to detract from the prospect of a fascinating race for the richest-ever Irish Derby. Not even the strike which prevented the printing of racecards deterred a huge crowd, who eagerly gave up to ten shillings for a single sheet listing the runners. Rumours that the Epsom Derby winner, Grand Parade, was to attempt the double previously achieved only by Orby was superseded by word that he was lame and thus out of the race.

The field of eight was distinguished by the presence of The Panther, winner of the English Two Thousand Guineas, and Glanmerin, narrowly beaten at Ascot by the Irish-bred Grand Parade. These two high-class colts had been accompanied from Newmarket by the maiden Cheap Popularity. For The Panther this was a vital retrieving mission. Top-priced yearling of his generation, head of the Free Handicap, winner of the Two Thousand Guineas, The Panther had captured the public imagination to such an extent that he had started a raging hot favourite for the Epsom Derby. Excited in the parade, he had behaved abominably at the start, got left, charged through his field and run himself into the ground, eventually trailing in nearer last than first. With Donoghue now replacing the unfortunate Cooper, The Panther was once again entrusted with favouritism. Glanmerin, who had beaten a stale Grand Parade as a two-year-old, had recently run the Epsom Derby winner to three-quarters of a length in a match for the King James's Palace Stakes at Ascot. However, he bore visible signs of a rough crossing from England and, as at Ascot, he was to be ridden by the gifted but notoriously erratic Cornelius Foy. The home team was headed by Snow Maiden, Loch Lomond and Ballyeaston, who had finished in that order in the Baldoyle Derby. Though beaten five lengths at Baldoyle, Loch Lomond had clearly failed to act on that sharp track, in addition to being hampered by the ungenerous Ballyeaston. Immediately after that race he had been transferred to J. J. Parkinson's Maddenstown stable. Equipped for the first time with blinkers to sharpen him up and avoid problems at the start, Loch Lomond appeared most likely of the Irish runners to keep the prize at home.

Both The Panther and Loch Lomond caused trouble at the start and when the field finally got away Ballyeaston whipped around, losing twenty lengths. The early running was made by Loch Lomond and one of the rank outsiders, Sir William. After three furlongs Loch Lomond drew clear of Sir William, The Panther, Cheap Popularity, Snow Maiden and Glanmerin, with Ballyeaston still trailing. Loch Lomond continued to force the pace to such effect that he was ten lengths clear at half way, with the favourite already under pressure. Coming down the hill Loch Lomond still held a clear lead from Snow Maiden and Cheap Popularity, with the rest already in trouble. Although Beary got Snow Maiden into a challenging position in the straight, one left-hander was all Loch Lomond required to carry Martin Quirke clear for a decisive six-length victory. Apart from the fiasco of the favourite, the surprise of the race was the showing of the maiden Cheap Popularity, who ran on strongly in the dying stages to take second place from Snow Maiden. Even allowing for an element of patriotic bias it was an immensely popular victory and Miss Cowhy, the first successful woman owner in the history of the race, led her colt in amid prolonged cheering.

Loch Lomond, a massive, heavy-topped bay-brown, was bred by Mr J. Cowhy of Buttevant, Co. Cork, by Lomond out of Mary Melton. The dam had been purchased as a yearling by Mr Cowhy at the Musker dispersal sale in 1906. By Lord Melton out of Bonnie Duchess, her third dam, Mitherless Bairn, was a half-sister to the Irish Derby winner, Ben Battle. Unraced till she was five years old, Mary Melton won two modest flat races, at Fermoy and Charleville. Despite the affectionate perseverance of her grateful owner, Mary Melton bred only one other winner during nearly thirty years in Buttevant. Lomond, a high-class son of Desmond, was a leading two-year-old, winning the New Stakes at Ascot and the Gimcrack Stakes at York.

He had been bought by Lord Dunraven to succeed Desmond at Fort Union and became leading sire in Ireland in 1919, due mainly to the exploits of Loch Lomond. Lomond was exported to the Argentine in 1924 in a deal which brought Buen Ojo, subsequently to become the maternal grandsire of two Irish Derby winners, to Ireland. Mr Cowhy died in the latter part of 1918 and, had the 'nominations void' rule not been deleted from the Rules of Racing in Ireland, Loch Lomond would automatically have been deprived of the chance to prove himself the best of his generation in Ireland and arguably superior to his cross-Channel contemporaries, Grand Parade and Buchan.

Put in training with Michael Dawson, Loch Lomond had been brought along slowly and given every chance to fill into his immense frame. Dawson, as befitted the outstanding trainer of his era, never rushed his more promising charges. Thus Loch Lomond did not appear in public till July 1918, when he had a quiet introduction at the Curragh, followed by another educational outing in the Phoenix Plate in August. His third and final run as a two-year-old saw him finish a respectable third to Daylight Saver and Corn Sack in the one mile Beresford Stakes, the first public indication of his Classic potential. After an early outing in March of the following year, Loch Lomond won over a mile at the Phoenix Park in May and again over twelve furlongs at Leopardstown later the same month, ridden on each occasion by Arthur Langford, an Australian lightweight recently retained by Dawson. His final race before the Irish Derby was to be the Baldoyle Derby, for which Miss Cowhy, who had inherited Loch Lomond on the death of her brother, was anxious to book Martin Quirke, the leading apprentice. Dawson was adamant that the colt should be ridden by the stable jockey . . . Utterly unable to act on the course, Loch Lomond was beaten by Snow Maiden and although it was obvious that no jockey alive could have got him home in front that day, Martin Quirke found himself escorting Loch Lomond back J. J. Parkinson's stable that same evening. The difference in approach between the two leading Irish trainers is illustrated by the fact that Parkinson spent the remaining two weeks 'sharpening up' his new charge. Whether Parkinson's tactics contributed to Loch Lomond's success remains a moot point. Nevertheless, while Loch Lomond is inscribed in the annals of the Irish Derby as 'trained Parkinson', the lion's share of the credit for his victory belonged to the master of Rathbride, deprived of a record seventh Irish Derby.

Loch Lomond's subsequent racecourse career was as short-lived as it was disastrous. The following month he was asked to give weight to the flying four-year-old filly Tut Tut over five furlongs. Totally unsuited by the going and distance, Loch Lomond finished a gallant second, broke down in the process and never ran again. Quite why such a question should have been asked of an Irish Derby winner is a mystery and his rider's recollection that he ran simply because he happened to have been entered reflects little credit upon his connections. Retired to the Maddenstown Stud in 1921 and subsequently to his birthplace in Co. Cork, Loch Lomond achieved fair success as a sire of stayers and jumpers, Old Orkney, perennial rival of Brown Jack, Loch Leven and Coolern being about the best of his progeny. On his death in 1936, his owner, who had subsequently become Mrs E. M. Crofts, replaced Loch Lomond with Flamenco, a very successful National Hunt sire.

Deprived of the opportunity to confirm his undoubted ability, Loch Lomond was paid repeated compliments by his Irish Derby victims. Cheap Popularity ran away with the Irish St Leger, before falling prey to the heel bug which ended his career. On her next appearance Snow Maiden easily defeated the Ascot winner Tetrarchia in the Irish Oaks and went on to win two races over a mile carrying welter weights. Glanmerin won the Sussex Stakes at Goodwood next time out. The following year he won the Stewards' Handicap at Nottingham, having finished second in the Royal Hunt Cup. As a five-year-old he again finished second in the Royal Hunt Cup, beaten a head by Illuminator, besides winning three valuable handicaps, culminating in an easy victory in the Portland Handicap at Doncaster. At stud initially in England and latterly in Ireland, Glanmerin sired numerous winners. Rested until October following his Curragh failure, The Panther flopped once again in the Champion Stakes and was sold to Argentine for £15,000. There he sired the winners of £58,000, before being purchased by a syndicate and repatriated in 1929. The Panther died suddenly two years later, the post mortem revealing a badly diseased heart, which may have accounted for his rapid deterioration as a three-year-old. Ballyeaston, having collected two fortuitous walkovers, showed his true colours in the Irish St Leger, in which he capitulated without even a token struggle. Both Sir William and King Eber went on to win under both codes, the latter taking the Galway Hurdle as a four-year-old.

Loch Lomond's success in the Irish Derby assured James J. Parkinson of his fourth Irish training championship. It also confirmed the arrival of his star apprentice Martin Quirke in the top flight of Irish jockeys. When interviewed after the Derby, the winning rider confessed that the only moment of danger had occurred when Loch Lomond had attempted to pull up at the point where the racecourse crossed the gallops on which he had been regularly worked by his erstwhile trainer and where he had become accustomed to easing up. Born in Lattin, Co. Tipperary, Martin was spotted by Colonel Charles Moore, a Steward of the Turf Club and later Racing Manager to King George VI, who lived at nearby Mooresfort. At Moore's instigation young Quirke joined Phillie Behan's patriarchal establishment at Mountjoy Lodge. Quick to realise that Behan's policy offered little opportunity for an apprentice, Quirke returned home. At his second attempt he had much better luck, joining Parkinson's stable, then one of the largest in Europe. He had his first success on his master's Spanish Knight at Leopardstown in November 1916 rapidly becoming leading apprentice. A quiet, stylish rider, particularly effective on two-year-olds, he was never one of the whip-waving school. According to his brother Denis, who also rode for Parkinson and later in France for Lord Derby, Martin was an unmistakable pursuer, hissing forcefully through his teeth as he pushed his mount along in the closing stages of a race. Following his abrupt departure from Parkinson, vowing never to ride again, he rode successively for Michael Dawson, Colonel Blake and Roderick More O'Ferrall, who provided him with a winning swansong at Naas in 1946. Champion jockey in 1923 with a record 87 winners on the flat, he won eight Irish Classics, including no less than five victories in the Irish Two Thousand Guineas. One of these was gained on Khosro, whom he regarded as second only to Loch Lomond of the many high-class horses he rode during his thirty years in the saddle. On the death of his original mentor, Phillie Behan, Martin Quirke purchased Mountjoy Lodge, whence he sent out Jack Ketch to win the Irish Two Thousand Guineas in 1957. In 1962 he handed over to his son Stephen, who won the same Irish Classic in successive years with Atherstone Wood and Mistigo.

Wednesday, 25th June, 1919   **£3550**   **8 Ran**   1½m

The Irish Derby of 4000sovs, being 3400sovs to the owner of the winner, 200sovs to the breeder of the winner. 100sovs to the breeder of the second, 200sovs to the owner of the second, and 100sovs to the owner of the third. By subscription of 50sovs each, 30sovs for those struck out on 1st January, 1919, but 10sovs only for those struck out on 5th June, 1918. For three years old. Colts and geldings 8st 12lb; Fillies 8st 8lb. If then entitled and claimed at time of entry, produce of untried mares allowed 3lb. The winner of a race value 1000sovs, or of two races each value 500sovs, 7lb extra.

(126 subs)

1	Miss Cowhy's	LOCH LOMOND (E. M. Quirke)	8. 9		Parkinson
		B./Br. colt Lomond – Mary Melton by Lord Melton.			
2	Mr A. Lowry's	CHEAP POPULARITY (J. Ledson)	8. 9		Powney (UK)
		Ch. colt Tredennis – Eager Bess.			
3	Mr J. J. Maher's	SNOW MAIDEN (M. Beary)	8. 8		Behan
		Gr. filly The Tetrarch – Snoot.			
4	Lord H. Vane's	GLANMERIN (C. Foy)	8.12		Pickering (UK)
		Ch. colt Orby – Bridewain.			
5	Sir A. Black's	THE PANTHER (S. Donoghue)	9. 5		Manser (UK)
		Br. colt Tracery – Countess Zia.			
6	Sir T. Dixon's	BALLYEASTON (W. Barrett)	8. 9		Hunter
		B. colt Marcovil – Minstrelsy. (car. 8.13)			
7	Mr J. H. H. Peard's	KING EBER (H. H. Beasley)	8. 9		Owner
		B. colt Ulster King – Green Gown.			
8	Mr P. Cullinan's	SIR WILLIAM (T. Burns)	8.12		Dunne
		Br. colt Juggernaut – Miss Clytie.			

SP 5/4 The Panther; 3/1 LOCH LOMOND; 4/1 Snow Maiden; 6/1 Ballyeaston; 8/1 Glanmerin; 25/1 Cheap Popularity; 100/1 Bar.

6 lengths, ½ length. 2m 43s

Winner trained by Mr J. J. Parkinson at Maddenstown Lodge, Curragh.

1920

Racing in Ireland had survived relatively untouched the growing armed struggle for independence, master-minded by Michael Collins and countered by two para-military bodies, whose conduct was a disgrace to the Crown – the Black and Tans and the Auxiliaries. Though Punchestown was again abandoned, owing to a General Strike in support of the political prisoners on hunger strike in Mountjoy, racing at the Curragh continued to prosper. A survey commissioned by the Turf Club revealed that stake money at the Curragh had trebled since 1913 and concluded that owners raced with better prospects in Ireland than elsewhere in the British Isles. Possibly in anticipation of such findings, the Stewards had already decided to proceed with the building of a new grandstand, mooted years previously, but postponed owing to the war. Though work was in progress, the new stand had not been completed by Derby Day. Once again the highlight of the Irish racing calendar

attracted an enormous crowd, which overflowed the existing stands and even resorted to clambering on the framework of the new structure. During the winter the
hill in the centre of the course had been levelled, greatly improving visibility from
the enclosures.

The overall mediocrity of the Classic crop was reflected in the field of eight,
though the presence of two English-trained runners inevitably gave the race added
interest. Better-fancied of the pair was the Newmarket-trained He Goes. A high-
class and consistent two-year-old winner of Royal Ascot and Newmarket, He Goes
had only run once as a three-year-old, finishing tenth in the Epsom Derby, won in
record time by Spion Kop. Pick of the paddock, He Goes dwarfed his compatriot,
the grey Prince Herod. Unbeaten in his first four races as a juvenile, Prince Herod
had won his last race, over a mile at Epsom on Derby Day, ridden by the indomitable Steve Donoghue, feared dead when Abbot's Trace fell with him in the Derby
less than an hour earlier. Despite their credentials, the English pair were forced to
give pride of place in the betting to Michael Dawson's representative Wily Attorney.
Bred by his owner, Albert Lowry, out of a half-sister to the Irish Derby winners
Bachelor's Double and Bachelor's Wedding, Wily Attorney had been asked little as
a two-year-old. But, with characteristic Dawson care, he had developed into a
Classic colt, winning his only two races that season with consumate ease. The form
of the other fancied runners revolved around a very rough race for the Baldoyle
Derby, in which Aeroplane and Kirk-Alloway had deadheated a short head behind
Royal Ashe, with Michaelis Liber half a length away in fourth place. Kirk-Alloway,
on whom Billy Barrett had put up 7lbs overweight at Baldoyle, was strongly fancied
to avenge his ill-luck on that occasion, though once again Barrett was putting up
overweight. A surprise runner was Lombard, a narrow winner of the final race on
the previous day, ridden by Martin Quirke.

After a lengthy delay they were off, with Lombard setting a scorching gallop
ahead of Wily Attorney, Michaelis Liber and He Goes. The order was maintained to
half way, where Aeroplane struck into the heels of Red Rhetoric, losing several
lengths. At the top of the hill Lombard gave way to Wily Attorney, who led from
Prince Herod, Aeroplane and He Goes. Approaching the straight Aeroplane,
hustled by Beary to recover lost ground, showed ahead briefly from Wily Attorney,
who immediately regained the lead. Both suffered from the jostling which ensued,
giving way to Prince Herod and He Goes. Canty then forced Wily Attorney through
on the rails to join issue with Prince Herod in the centre and He Goes on the stands
side. At the distance the three horses came very close together, with the hard-ridden
Prince Herod squeezing Wily Attorney against the rails. Inside the final furlong He
Goes got his head in front, only to swerve violently towards the rails, impeding the
hapless Wily Attorney. Though the latter challenged strongly, He Goes held on to
pass the post a length to the good, with a tired Prince Herod half a length further
back.

From the stands Wily Attorney looked to have been desperately unlucky, having
been the chief sufferer. A Stewards' Enquiry was widely anticipated and its absence
caused general dismay. However, Canty, rider of Wily Attorney, promptly lodged
an objection to He Goes on grounds of crossing, bumping and boring. While this
was expected, Donoghue's intervention was not. He objected to He Goes for
crossing and to Wily Attorney for bumping. Further consternation was caused by the

announcement that the Stewards had overruled both objections, though both Canty's and Donoghue's deposits were returned. The only conclusion seemed to be that, though the Stewards appreciated that serious interference had taken place, they were unable to apportion blame and thus felt it best to allow the result to stand.

He Goes was bred by his owner at his stud in Co. Meath, by Prince Palatine out of Feronia. Prince Palatine, the greatest racehorse bred by Colonel Hall Walker at what is now the Irish National Stud, won the St Leger, Coronation Cup, Eclipse Stakes and Ascot Gold Cup, twice. After a disappointing start at J. B. Joel's Childwick Bury Stud, Prince Palatine was sold to France and thence to America, where he perished in a stable fire in Lexington in 1924. Though he sired such as Prince Galahad, He Goes and Rose Prince, Prince Palatine, in view of his breeding, physique and racecourse record, was a sad failure as a sire. His line survives through Rose Prince's Derby-winning grandson, Arctic Prince and also through Prince Galahad's Irish Classic winners, Knight of the Grail and Smokeless. Feronia, dam of He Goes, never ran, but descended from a dam line of prolific winner-producers. Her grandam, Cherry Duchess bred Enthusiast, winner of the Two Thousand Guineas and Sussex Stakes in 1889 and a successful sire in Ireland. La Carolina, Feronia's dam, also bred Lady Car, third in the Phoenix Plate in 1902, during the visit to Ireland of her Royal owner-breeder. Feronia bred two further winners in Iron Hand, own-brother to He Goes, and Iron Band, by Captivation. The former, trained by Jock Fergusson, won the Ebor Handicap in 1920 and became the sire of the dual Galway Hurdle winner, Kuckleduster.

Having finished unplaced in Caligula's St Leger, He Goes then trailed in fifteen lengths behind Kirk-Alloway and Aeroplane in the Irish equivalent. Transferred from Newmarket to Jock Fergusson's Delamere Forest stables, He Goes was sent hurdling to restore his interest. Though twice successful in this sphere, he never won again on the flat. Retired to the Hartstown Stud in Clonsilla in 1924, He Goes later moved to Co. Wexford, proving a total failure as a sire. Wily Attorney won his only other race that season in a common canter and won again as a four-year-old, before going to stud in Co. Meath, standing for only one season before being sent to Poland, where he proved successful. Kirk-Alloway, having won the Gold Cup at the Curragh by a short head, won the Irish St Leger by a similar margin and later retired to stud in Northern Ireland. Aeroplane never really recovered the injuries sustained when he struck into Red Rhetoric in the Irish Derby. He replaced his short-lived sire, Sleipnir, at the Blackditch Stud in Clondalkin in 1922. Red Rhetoric won both his remaining races at the Curragh and returned to his favourite track the following year to win the Gold Cup at 16-to-1 ON. He later sired Macross, winner of the Naas November Handicap. At the time He Goes was regarded as the most fluky and least deserving winner of the Irish Derby since Flax Park had beaten Velocity in 1905. The subsequent careers of the participants merely served to confirm the mediocrity of the Classic crop of 1920.

Captain Henry Whitworth's 'Cardinal and black hoops, black sleeves and cap' were familiar on Irish racecourses for many years. Joint Master of the Galway Blazers in 1902/3, Harry Whitworth then hunted the Westmeath hounds for five seasons before moving to Yorkshire to take on the York and Ainsty. Besides his hunting, breeding and racing interests he was a keen polo player. John Fairfax-Blakeborough, the noted Turf historian, recalled Harry Whitworth as being one of the earliest advocates of the benefits of weighing horses regularly and gauging their progress by their increase in weight while in work. Vera Cruz, one of the leading Irish two-year-olds of 1915, carried his wife's colours and though he reduced his racing interests in Ireland after the First World War, he continued to keep sufficient in training to enable him to top the owners' table in 1920. The last good animal to carry his colours in Ireland was Golden Oracle, a leading Irish sprinter in the mid 'twenties.

Just as He Goes' victory in the Irish Derby signalled the end of his owner's association with flat racing in Ireland, so also did it herald the close of a long and distinguished training career for the master of Kremlin House – dapper, courtly Joseph Butters. Born at Knowsley, Lancashire, in 1847, Joe Butters was apprenticed to the legendary John Scott at Malton and subsequently to James Waugh, whose daughter he married. In 1873 he went to Austria, where he became leading jockey, before starting to train for such as Baron Springer, Count Kinsky and Mr Baltazzi. He returned to England in 1903 to train for Prince Soltykoff and though he won many races, including the 1910 Victoria Cup with Senseless and the 1911 City and Suburban with Mushroom, he never saddled the winner of an English Classic. His nearest miss in this respect came with Nassovian in the 1916 Derby. At the owner's insistence, stable jockey Nathan Spear was replaced by Frank O'Neill, who arrived from New York only on the morning of the race. In a close finish Nassovian went down by a neck and a head to Fifinella and Kwang-Su. By the time of his retirement in 1926 Joe Butters had seen his sons Frank and Fred successfully established. The former was destined to become leading trainer no less than seven times while training for Lord Derby and later for the Aga Khan. Both sons turned out winners at the Epsom Derby, while Frank saddled four winners of the Irish Derby for good measure.

The sense of swansong surrounding the success of He Goes was completed by his rider's retirement at the end of the season. Frederick George Templeman bore one of the oldest names in the history of English jockeys. His grandfather, Sim Templeman, was one of the outstanding riders of the mid-nineteenth century, who rode Cossack and Surplice to successive victories in the Epsom Derby in 1847–8. Apprenticed to John Hallick at Lambourn, Fred Templeman rode his first winner at Gatwick, where he later came close to ending his career. Riding Dutch for Paul Nelke, Templeman was hugging the rails so closely that he collided violently with the winning post. Severe head injuries kept him out of the saddle for some time. Having twice finished second in the Derby, Fred Templeman emulated his ancestor when successful on Grand Parade in 1919, carrying Lord Glanely's second colours. Yet again a stable jockey, in this case Arthur Smith, had opted for the wrong one. Another great public favourite with whom Fred Templeman was associated was Irish Elegance, on whom he won the Royal Hunt Cup under a record 9st 11lbs. On retiring from the saddle he began training at Lambourn, where he also farmed extensively. Equally sound and consistent a trainer as he had been a jockey, Fred Templeman sent out Diolite and Lambert Simnel to win the Two Thousand Guineas and Chatelaine to win the Oaks. His brother, Arthur, who rode Velocity to win the Cambridgeshire in 1905, later became a successful trainer in India. Fred Templeman gave up training in 1956, but remained active as an owner and breeder until his death in 1973 at the age of eighty-three.

Wednesday, 23rd June, 1920   **£4790**   **8 Ran**   **1½m**

The Irish Derby of 4000sovs, being 3400sovs to the owner of the winner, 200sovs to the breeder of the winner. 100sovs to the breeder of the second, 200sovs to the owner of the second, and 100sovs to the owner of the third. By subscription of 50sovs each, 30sovs for those struck out on 7th January, 1920, but 10sovs only for those struck out on 4th June, 1919. For three years old. Colts and geldings 8st 12lb; Fillies 8st 8lb. If then entitled and claimed at time of entry, produce of untried mares allowed 3lb. The winner of a race value 1000sovs, or of two races each value 500sovs, 7lb extra.

(152 subs)

1 Capt. H. Whitworth's   HE GOES (F. Templeman)   9. 5   J. Butters (UK)
Br. colt Prince Palatine – Feronia by Fariman.

2 Mr A. Lowry's   WILY ATTORNEY (Joseph Canty) 8.12   M. Dawson
Ch. colt Tredennis – Bachelor's Berrill.

3 Mr James White's   PRINCE HEROD (S. Donoghue) 9. 5   M. Hartigan (UK)
Gr. colt Roi Herode – Egglestone.

4 Mr T. K. Laidlaw's   KIRK-ALLOWAY (W. Barrett) 8.12   Hunter
Bl. colt Tracery – Cantrip. (car. 9.0)

5 Mr W. C. Carr's   MICHAELIS LIBER (J. Dines) 8. 9   M. Reidy
Br. colt Charles O'Malley – Los Angelos.

6 Mr D. J. Cogan's   AEROPLANE (M. Beary)   8. 9   M. Rice
B. colt Sleipner – Consilio.

7 Capt. E. Shirley's   RED RHETORIC (H. H. Beasley) 8. 9   J. T. Rogers
Ch. colt William Rufus – Lady Cicero.

8 Mr W. F. Power's   LOMBARD (E. M. Quirke)   8. 9   J. J. Parkinson
B. colt Myram – Boda.

SP 5/2 Wily Attorney; 3/1 HE GOES; 4/1 Kirk-Alloway; 6/1 Aeroplane; 7/1 Michaelis Liber; 10/1 Prince Herod, Red Rhetoric; 100/1 Lombard.
1 length, ½ length. 2m 40s.
Winner trained by Mr J. Butters at Newmarket.

Objections to He Goes on the grounds of bumping, boring and crossing, and to Wily Attorney for bumping were overruled and the deposits returned.

1921

Though the probable outcome remained impossible to predict, there were definite signs that the struggle for Irish independence was nearing a conclusion. The wave of assassination and reprisal had struck directly at racing when the Senior Steward, the Right Honourable Frank Brooke, was shot dead in his Dublin office for no apparent motive. He was replaced in office by the retired Percy La Touche, one of the most able administrators in the history of the Turf Club. The loss to Irish racing was compounded by the death of La Touche in March 1921. Wearied by the tensions of undeclared war, frustrated by the skeleton train service, an enormous crowd none-theless made the annual pilgrimage to the Curragh, encouraged by the prospect of a high-class race for the ever more valuable Irish Derby. Such was the quality of the field that the absence of English-trained runners was unimportant.

The 'talking horse' of the Classic generation was Mr P. W. Shaw's Belsize. This chestnut son of Captivation had gone through his first season unbeaten in four races and was regarded by J. J. Parkinson as the best he had trained since Orby. Though he had not appeared in public as a three-year-old, he was reported to have been working in brilliant fashion at home. Any reservations about his stamina were offset by the state of the going, the hardest in living memory. His connections had backed him heavily and the public, following the stable money, made Belsize favourite. His closest market rival was Soldennis, trained on The Heath by Sam Jeffrey. As a two-year-old he had beaten both Kircubbin and Ballyheron in the valuable National Produce Stakes at the Curragh. Second at Liverpool on Grand National Day, he had since won the April Stakes and the Irish Two Thousand Guineas, in which he again beat both Kircubbin and Ballyheron. Crowdennis, winner of two of his juvenile races, had been beaten by Shaw's Bridge in his only outing as a three-year-old. However, he had been forced to check by a stray dog and was fancied to avenge that defeat. Tremola, winner of his most recent race over a mile at Kempton, when trained by Harry Powney, had since joined the Irish Derby specialist, Michael Dawson, who was hoping to make up for his ill-fortune with Loch Lomond and Wily Attorney. Kircubbin and Ballyheron completed the list of fancied runners. The former was something of a surprise runner, having been reserved for the Irish St Leger. Ballyheron, talented but temperamental as a two-year-old, had disgraced himself when finishing last in the National Produce Stakes behind Soldennis. Pulled out again the next day, Ballyheron was saddled outside the enclosure and, wearing blinkers, won the Beresford Stakes, despite trying to duck out. His ability was unquestioned, but his temperament was not, and he was once again saddled outside the enclosure. Westview and Keredern were in the field to act as pacemakers for Soldennis and Tremola respectively, while the remaining runner, Knock Brack, started friendless at 100-to-1.

The preliminaries were protracted by Tremola spreading a plate. During the delay Belsize began to get excited and became even more upset at the start, where Tremola caused further problems. When the starter finally got them away both Belsize and Tremola were slow to break. Crowdennis, on whom Canty got a 'flier', immediately went into a clear lead from Westview and Soldennis. As the race developed Shaw's Bridge and Kircubbin took closer order behind Crowdennis, as Westview dropped back. After a mile Shaw's Bridge, Kircubbin and Crowdennis shared the lead ahead of Ballyheron and Soldennis, with Belsize and Tremola making up ground. Coming down the hill Shaw's Bridge dropped out, leaving Ballyheron tracking Crowdennis and Kircubbin, with Belsize and Tremola still improving. As the leaders swung into the straight Ballyheron joined Kircubbin and Crowdennis ahead of the wide-running Tremola. Crowdennis was the first to weaken, as Ballyheron began to wear down Kircubbin. Behind them Tremola was in full cry and making ground with every stride. Inside the final furlong Wing pushed Ballyheron clear of Kircubbin and kept him going straight to pass the post ahead of the flying Tremola. Behind them Kircubbin stayed on to hold Soldennis out of third place. In a race which highlighted the art of raceriding Wing was seen at his brilliant best, whereas the hapless Brennan, narrowly beaten at Epsom for the second time weeks previously, had clearly overdone his waiting instructions on Tremola. It was equally true that Canty had made too much use of Crowdennis. However, neither

Aylin nor Quirke could be held responsible for the eclipse of Soldennis and Belsize, both of whom simply failed to stay.

Ballyheron was bred by his owner, Colonel R. B. Charteris, a member of the Turf Club. By Santoi, Ballyheron was out of Anxious, purchased in 1915 for a modest 72gns. By Eager out of Mint Agnes, Anxious won once as a two-year-old. She bred four other winners, of whom Glasheen, by Bachelor's Double, was the best. Santoi, by Queen's Birthday out of Merry Wife, was bought as a yearling by Mr George Edwardes, who named him after a musical, San Toy, that he was then staging in the West End. Slow to reach his peak, Santoi came good as a four-year-old, winning the Kempton Jubilee and the Ascot Gold Cup. As a five-year-old he defeated the Epsom Derby winner, Volodyovski, then four, over a mile and a half. Fired by the success of his 190gns purchase, Edwardes decided to stand his hot-tempered champion at stud. To achieve this end, Edwardes bought and completely refurbished Ballykisteen in Co. Limerick. Here the irascible Santoi, placated by his beloved donkey companion, held sway for twenty seasons, proving himself to be a sire of tough, sound, if highly-strung stayers. Best of his get was the 'half-bred' Shogun, decidedly unlucky in the Epsom Derby of 1913. Santorb emulated his sire in winning the Ascot Gold Cup. Lord Glanely's, he won the Coronation Cup, while China Cock, Morny Wing's favourite horse, won four Liverpool Cups. Santoi's record in the Cesarewitch remains quite remarkable in that he was responsible for no less than four winners of that marathon handicap: Yentoi, Fiz-Yama, Sanctum and Yutoi. Dono and Woodland Lass were two winners of the Irish equivalent sired by Santoi, who was succeeded at stud by his son Achtoi, second in the Irish Derby in 1915 and leading sire in Ireland in 1928.

Ballyheron's next race was to be the Irish St Leger, from which he was a surprise absentee, when found to be coughing on the eve of the race. Transferred to England for his four-year-old career, Ballyheron finished third in both the Coronation Cup and the Ascot Gold Cup, but failed to win again. Kept in training as a five-year-old, he broke down while being prepared for another attempt at the Gold Cup. He was subsequently sold to Poland, where he did well as a sire. Havinging finished second to Polemarch in the Great Northern St Leger, Tremola finished only fifth behind the same rival in the final Classic at Doncaster. Winner of three more races over the next two seasons, Tremola retired to stud near Newmarket and became the sire of the good sprinter, Stingo. Exported to Sweden in 1933, he died three years later. Kircubbin beat Crowdennis over a mile next time out, prior to winning the Irish St Leger in a canter, principally at the expense of Soldennis. Sold to France at the end of the season for £4000, Kircubbin proved himself to be a high-class horse when defeating the French crack, Ksar, in the Prix du President de la Republique. Champion sire in France in 1930, this humbly-bred horse sired Château Bouscaut, winner of the Prix du Jockey Club and sire of The Phoenix and Chanteur, through whom his line survives, despite the failure at stud of Chanteur's best son, Pinza.

If the merit of Ballyheron's victory was boosted by Kircubbin, its excellence was confirmed by the subsequent career of Soldennis. Kept in training for a further three seasons, Soldenis won the April Stakes twice more, won two Drogheda Memorials, two Turf Club Cups and the Ayr Gold Cup. A great favourite with racegoers, Soldennis thrived on work and tended to lose his form if rested. He retired to stud at The Heath in 1925 the winner of twenty-four races, nine in his final season, and

£13,046 in prize money, an Irish record. Soloptic and Sol de Terre credited him with three Irish Classics, while Solenoid and Solerina both won the Stewards' Cup at Goodwood. Champion sire in Ireland in 1930, Soldennis was transferred to Newmarket in 1934 and two years later sired more winners than any other stallion in Britain and Ireland.

Crowdennis, yet another son of the prepotent Tredennis, proved himself second only to Soldennis as a sprinter. In 1922 he won five of his six races, being beaten by Soldennis in the other. The following year he won the Wokingham Stakes at Ascot and the Great Surrey Handicap at Epsom, before being sold to go to Australia, where he made his mark as a sire. Shaw's Bridge finished second in the Irish Cambridgeshire, but later met with an accident and had to be destroyed. Belsize was brought back to sprinting and won a further ten races before taking up stud duties in Co. Cork in 1927. Of the last three to finish in the Irish Derby of 1921 only Keredern failed to win subsequently. The performances of Kircubbin, Soldennis and Crowdennis suggest that Ballyheron beat an above-average field in the Irish Derby.

Ballyheron's success contributed to Joseph Hunter's third and final Irish training championship. More significantly, it marked the entry into the annals of the Irish Derby of the most successful jockey in the history of the race . . . Morny Wing. Born in Doncaster, where he was christened after his horse-dealing father's jockey idol, Mornington Cannon, Morny Wing served his apprenticeship with Alfred Sadler Jr at Newmarket. Having ridden his first winner in 1911, he finished third to Steve Donoghue in the English jockeys' table only three years later and went on to ride winners in India and Spain, before crossing to Ireland in 1917 to ride two for Bert Lines. Both won, as did Wing's next three Irish mounts. Like Donoghue a decade earlier, Morny Wing fell in love with Ireland and the Irish racing scene, which he proceeded to adorn for the next forty years. Associated successively with the stables of Joe Hunter, Sam Jeffrey, Phillie Behan, Darby Rogers, Colonel Blake, Michael Collins and Hubert Hartigan, he rode a record number of Irish Classic winners, including six Irish Derbies, seven Irish One Thousand Guineas and seven Irish St Legers. Outright champion jockey nine times, he headed the list of flat jockeys on no less than fifteen occasions. Unlike his formidable opponents, Burns and Canty, he did not ride under National Hunt rules.

Not since the tragic death of John Thompson had any jockey so completely dominated Irish flat race riding. Like his predecessor, Wing came as near as makes no odds to being invincible in short distance races, giving rise to the adage, 'Never leave Wing out in a sprint!'. Brilliant at the gate, Wing could change his stick faster than any man alive and this, coupled with his exceptional strength, pulled countless races out of the fire in a career total of over two thousand winners. Having once gone through the card in India, Morny Wing rode a five-timer in Ireland on three occasions, but could never get that elusive sixth winner. That he should once have been forced to forgo the opportunity by somewhat startling instructions is another story . . . He did, however, once ride eight consecutive winners at a three-day meeting at Tramore.

Stocky, square-faced and unsmiling, Morny Wing was a by-word for integrity in an era when such tended to be the exception rather than the rule in racing. While Windsor Slipper was outstandingly the best horse he ever rode – unbeaten either at home or in public – he never displaced China Cock in Morny Wing's affections. This great Liverpool specialist, on whom he won both the Spring and Autumn Cups, as well as the Queen's Prize, was the horse that brought him to prominence. Notwithstanding the galaxy of high-class horses that he subsequently rode, it was China Cock's portrait which occupied pride of place in Rosewell, his Curragh home. Morny Wing retired in 1949, appropriately on a winning note, and began training at Rosewell. Among the many tributes to mark his retirement was this one from F. F. McCabe, who had supervised the Epsom triumph of Orby more than forty years earlier, 'I would rather have Wing on any two-year-old of mine than any of the great ones presently riding in England. He wins by persuasion and not by the whip.'

Like many another jockey-turned-trainer, he had little taste for the humdrum worries of the stable yard and in this respect he was fortunate to have the assistance of his brother-in-law, Kevin Bell, subsequently to prove himself a shrewd and resourceful trainer in his own right. Wing's solitary Irish Classic success was

---

Wednesday, 22nd June, 1921   **£4935**   **10 Ran**   1½m

The Irish Derby of 4500 guineas, being 4000sovs to the owner of the winner, 200sovs to the breeder of the winner, 200sovs to the owner of the second, 150sovs to the breeder of the second, 100sovs to the owner of the third, and 75sovs to the breeder of the third. By subscription of 50sovs each, 30sovs for those struck out on 5th January, 1921, but 10sovs only for those struck out on 2nd June, 1920. For three years old. Colts and geldings, 8st 12lb; Fillies 8st 8lb. If then entitled and claimed at time of entry, produce of untried mares allowed 3lb. The winner of a race value 1000sovs, or of two races each value 500sovs, 7lb extra.

(169 subs)

1 Col. R. B. Charteris's	BALLYHERON* (M. Wing)	8.12	Hunter
	B. colt Santoi – Anxious by Eager.		
2 Mr A. Lowry's	TREMOLA (J. Brennan)	8.12	Dawson
	Ch. colt Tredennis – Bachelor's Beauty.		
3 Major Dixon's	KIRCUBBIN (M. Beary)	8.12	Behan
	B. colt Captivation – Avon Hack.		
4 Mr C. L. Mackean's	SOLDENNIS (C. Aylin)	9. 5	Jeffrey
	Ch. colt Tredennis – Soligena.		
5 Mr P. Cullinan's	CROWDENNIS (Joseph Canty)	8. 9	Doyle
	Br. colt Tredennis – Crowden.		
6 Mr D. W. Barnett's	SHAW'S BRIDGE (J. Dines)	8. 9	Rankin
	B. colt Bridge of Earn – Chaleureuse.		
7 Mr P. W. Shaw's	BELSIZE (E. M. Quirke)	9. 5	Parkinson
	Ch. colt Captivation – Chancery.		
8 Mr N. J. Grene's	KNOCK BRACK (J. Moylan)	8. 9	Moss
	Ch. colt Prince Hermes – dam by Sir Edgar – Lady Norah.		
0 Mr James Conway's	KEREDERN (H. Jameson)	8.12	Dawson
	B. colt Bridge of Earn – Volage.		
0 Mrs Heney's	WESTVIEW (H. H. Beasley)	8. 9	Jeffrey
	Bl. colt Kroonstad – Dooneen.		

SP 3/1 Belsize; 4/1 Soldennis; 5/1 Crowdennis; 6/1 Tremola; 7/1 BALLYHERON; 8/1 Shaw's Bridge, Kircubbin; 10/1 Westview; 20/1 Keredern; 100/1 Knock Brack.
2½ lengths, ½ length.
Winner trained by Mr J. Hunter at Conyngham Lodge, Curragh.

*Ballyheron saddled outside the enclosure.

achieved with Do Well in the St Leger of 1951, ridden by a proming young jockey Liam Ward. Morny Wing died in 1965, predeceased many years by his son Wally, whose immense promise in the saddle had ended with his tragically early death while riding in India.

An interesting sidelight on Ballyheron's Irish Derby arose some years later when the Revenue Commissioners took Morny Wing to the High Court, claiming that his £400 winners present from Colonel Charteris was liable to tax. A majority verdict ruled that it was not.

1922

The Irish Derby of 1922 was staged in an atmosphere of extreme political tension. Following the creation of the Irish Free State the previous year, those who aspired to nothing less than a republic withdrew from the process of democratic government, seized key buildings in Dublin and began the inexorable process of civil war. Less than a week before the Derby a General Election had been held, which, despite grave doubts as to the accuracy of the electoral register, gave a clear mandate to the Government, who began immediate action against the dissenters. Notwithstanding the air of national tension, a large crowd gathered on the Curragh to witness a field of twelve parade for Ireland's premier prize. As has always happily been the case, political considerations were set aside in the search for the likely winner. Despite the fact that he had beaten little in the Irish Two Thousand Guineas and was not a certain stayer, the Newmarket-trained Spike Island was entrusted with favouritism. Next in demand was the unbeaten King David, with whom Joe Hunter and Morny Wing were confident of repeating their success of the previous year. Although the firm ground had hampered his preparation, he had been trained especially for this race and was easily the pick of the paddock on looks. Monserrat, trained by Richard Marsh for the King's cousin, Lord Lascelles, had finished fifth in the Royal Hunt Cup a week previously. Of the others, only Highlandmore, who needed to be ridden from behind, and Galway Prince were seriously supported. The 'Half-bred' O'Dorney, though out of La Poloma, winner of the inaugural Irish St Leger, was by the sprinter Flying Orb and thus thought unlikely to stay the stiff Curragh mile and a half.

After a considerable delay at the start, caused by the rider of Brother Charles breaking a leather, the field got away, headed by Soliman's Orb and King David. At half way Soliman's Orb led from King David, these two being clear of Spike Island, Valiant and O'Dorney. Down the hill the field closed behind the leaders, with Soliman's Orb, Spike Island, O'Dorney and Monserrat all vying for the lead, closely followed by Highlandmore and Galway Prince. As Highlandmore weakened the final stages concerned Soliman's Orb, O'Dorney, Spike Island and Monserrat. Approaching the distance Archibald went for his whip on Spike Island, who responded gamely to repel the persistent challenge of O'Dorney by a length and a half, with Monserrat a neck away in third place and Soliman's Orb a similar distance further back. Despite the slow early gallop there were no excuses proffered for the beaten horses and Archibald's post-race verdict that Spike Island was the only true stayer in the field was a fair summary of the race.

Named after a military post in Cork harbour, Spike Island was bred by his owner at his nearby Eyrefield Lodge Stud and was by Spearmint out of Molly Desmond. Spearmint, winner of both the Epsom Derby and Grand Prix de Paris when trained by P. P. Gilpin, was the best racehorse sired by the Melbourne Cup winner Carbine. Though not outstandingly successful at stud, Spearmint did sire Spion Kop, as well as Royal Lancer, winner of both the English and Irish St Legers in 1922, in which year Spearmint headed the list of winning sires in Ireland. Following his death in 1924 his sons Zionist and Spelthorne won the Irish Derby and Irish St Leger respectively. Molly Desmond, the dam of Spike Island, was the best daughter of the 'peerless' Pretty Polly. Having won the Cheveley Park Stakes, she produced in Spike Island and Zodiac the winners of three and a half Irish Classics.

Afflicted by the troublesome forelegs from which Spearmint had himself suffered and which he transmitted to many of his progeny, Spike Island went wrong soon after the Irish Derby, with the result that he never ran again. Sold as a stallion to the Argentine for £4000 the following year, Spike Island eventually found his way to Italy, where he became a leading sire. Mated with Donatello's dam, Delleana, he begot Dossa Dossi, winner of the Italian One Thousand Guineas and Oaks in 1933. She became the third dam of the Epsom Derby winner Psidium, who in turn sired Sodium, winner of the Irish Sweeps Derby in 1966. O'Dorney, Spike Island's immediate victim at the Curragh, subsequently emulated his dam by winning the Irish St Leger, but became disenchanted with racing and suffered the ignominy of being gelded. Whether or not this demoralised the rest of the participants in the Irish Derby of 1922, none achieved much of note afterwards . . .

Success in the Irish Derby was nothing new to either Major Giles Loder or to Peter Purcell Gilpin, they having combined to win it four years earlier with King John. However, Spike Island's victory continued the triumphal debut in England and Irish racing of that excellent, though tragically shortlived American rider, George Archibald. In contrast to many of his compatriots who crossed the Atlantic to ride, George Archibald might be described as 'the quiet American'. Born at Oaklands, San Francisco in 1890, he became a leading jockey in his own country before going to ride for Baron Oppenheimer in Germany, where he headed the list. Interned in Austria during the First World War, he was eventually released through diplomatic influence and resumed his career in Switzerland. Racing on the snow in St Moritz, Archibald rapidly realised that horses could not quicken on such a surface and profited accordingly from his consequent pillar-to-post tactics.

After a further successful spell in Spain, George Archibald arrived in England in 1922 to ride for P. P. Gilpin's Clarehaven stable. Success was immediate and included the Two Thousand Guineas on St Louis, the City and Suburban on Paragon and the Irish Two Thousand Guineas and Derby on Spike Island. In 1923 he came close to repeating his Two Thousand Guineas success on Knockando in a very tight finish with Ellangowan. The judge made an error in identifying the placed horses and when Lord Jersey intervened, asking Archibald where he had finished, the quick-witted American replied, 'I won it, my lord!' His best year in these islands was 1924 when he rode 52 winners in England, in addition to two further Irish Classic successes with Spike Island's half-brother, Zodiac. Very popular, despite his reserved manner, George Archibald was regarded as a most capable horseman, equally effective on either sluggish or temperamental animals. Constantly beset by weight problems, he spent the winter of 1926 riding in India, in an effort to keep his weight down to ride for Sir Abe Bailey during the following season in England. On the opening day of the Craven meeting he rode in five races, despite complaining of severe abdominal pain, was rushed home having completed his engagements and died two hours later, his constitution weakened through excessive wasting. His son later became a trainer in Newmarket.

Wednesday, 21st June, 1922   **£4715**   **12 Ran**   **1½m**

The Irish Derby of 5000 guineas, Being 4500sovs to the owner of the winner, 200sovs to the breeder of the winner, 200sovs to the owner of the second, 150sovs to the breeder of the second, 100sovs to the owner of the third, and 100sovs to the breeder of the third. By subscription of 50sovs each, 30sovs for those struck out on 4th January, 1922, but 5sovs only for those struck out on 1st June, 1921. For three years old. Colts and geldings, 8st 12lb; Fillies, 8st 8lb. The winner of a race value 1000sovs, or of two races each value 500sovs, 10lb extra.

1	Major Giles Loder's	SPIKE ISLAND (G. Archibald)	9. 8	P. P. Gilpin (UK)
		B. colt Spearmint – Molly Desmond by Desmond.		
2	Mr D. Sullivan's	O'DORNEY (C. Aylin)	8.12	Jeffrey
		Ch. colt Flying Orb – La Paloma. NOT IN GSB.		
3	Lord Lascelles's	MONTSERRAT (H. Jones)	8.12	Marsh (UK)
		Br. colt Coriander – Monossa.		
4	Lord Kenmere's	SOLIMAN'S ORB (T. Burns)	9. 8	Dawson
		B. colt Orby or Willaura – Soliman's Star.		
5	Miss Cowhy's	HIGHLANDMORE (M. Beary)	8.12	Rankin
		Ch. colt Lomond – Gargamelle.		
6	Mr G. Barclay's	GALWAY PRINCE (J. Evans)	8.12	Barclay Jr
		Ch. colt Orby or White Eagle – Queen Mother.		
7	Mr T. K. Laidlaw's	KING DAVID (M. Wing)	8.12	Hunter
		B. colt Righ Mor – Minstrelsy.		
8	Mr T. J. O'Neill's	BACHELOR'S HEIR (Joseph Canty)	8.12	Coombs
		B. colt Tredennis – Bachelor's Berrill.		
9	Mr T. J. O'Neill's*	DOUBLE FIRST (J. Patman)	8.12	Coombs
		Ch. colt Tredennis – Alexa.		
10	Major Cape's	VALIANT (H. H. Beasley)	8.12	Jeffrey
		Ch. colt Orpiment – Soligena.		
11	Mr F. F. M'Donogh's	BROTHER CHARLES (D. Ward)	8.12	Owner
		B. colt Melleray – Lass o' Gowrie.		
12	Capt. C. Moore's	RACHEL (E. M. Quirke)	8. 8	Behan
		Gr. filly Roi Herode – Sacrifice.		

SP Evens SPIKE ISLAND; 7/2 King David; 6/1 Highlandmore; 7/1 Galway Prince; 10/1 Montserrat; 25/1 Soliman's Orb, Valiant, Double First; 33/1 Rachel; 50/1 O'Dorney, Bachelor's Heir; 100/1 Brother Charles.

1½ lengths, neck. 2m 39.1/5s.

Winner trained by Mr P. P. Gilpin at Clarehaven Lodge, Newmarket.

*Mr O'Neill declared to win with Double First.

1923

In the absence of any outstanding contender the Irish Derby drew a large if undistinguished field, which included three English-trained runners. Though the summer to date had been by no means good, the going at the Curragh remained very firm. Favourite was Mr Dan Sullivan's Soldumeno, winner of three of his previous races. Having won the Madrid Handicap and a King's Plate at the Curragh in April, Soldumeno ran disappointingly in the Baldoyle Derby, where he was slowly away. However, his most recent run had resulted in a half-length success in the Irish Two Thousand Guineas, where he had beaten Clonespoe, Buacaill Breah, Darragh, Tara Hill, King Dennis and Orpine at level weights. With the exception of Darragh, all of these renewed rivalry with Soldumeno on more favourable terms. The second favourite was Jackdaw of Rheims, owned by Jimmy White, the theatrical impresario. Though a good two-year-old, Jackdaw of Rheims had only run once in his second season and looked short of peak condition. Best fancied of the English challengers was Waygood, winner of his only race that season over the Derby distance at Birmingham. Trained at Newmarket by William Halsey, Waygood had been stabled with J. T. Rogers at Crotanstown for the past fortnight, impressing those who had seen him on the gallops. Lord Queenborough's Greek Bachelor had also been successful on his most recent attempt, winning over a mile at Sandown in April. The third English contender, Darragh, had been a high-class two-year-old when trained on the Curragh by Joe Hunter, winning the National Stakes and the Railway Stakes. Now trained at Newmarket by Lord George Dundas, Darragh had beaten Pharos, subsequently second in the Epsom Derby, over a mile in April. However, since then he had run very badly in the Irish Two Thousand Guineas and was known to dislike hard ground.

After the tapes had been broken twice, the fifteen runners got away to a level start, headed by Jackdaw of Rheims and Waygood, who shared the lead ahead of Beech Hill, Clonespoe and King Dennis. Soldumeno, having jumped off sideways, brought up the rear with Melra. After they had covered six furlongs Jackdaw of Rheims began to drop back, leaving Waygood clear of Simon Orb and Tara Hill, with Soldumeno and Melra improving. Down the hill Burns brought Soldumeno to challenge the long-time leader and excitement mounted as this pair raced into the straight clear of Toy Label, Simon Ross and Simon Orb. Halfway up the straight Waygood came under pressure as Soldumeno appeared to get the upper hand. However, Morny Wing quickly put down his whip and, riding with hands and heels, drove Waygood clear inside the final furlong to win easily in the end by four lengths from Soldumeno. Three lengths further back, Greek Bachelor stayed on strongly to be third, while Darragh, appreciating the easier going in the straight, ran through tired horses to finish fourth. The time of 2mins 39.8secs was better than average.

Waygood, a bay colt, was bred in England by his owner, Walter Raphael, a wealthy London stockbroker. He was by August Belmont's American-bred Tracery, a son of the Triple Crown winner Rock Sand. Owing to the closure of the New York racetracks by anti-betting legislation, Tracery had been shipped to England as a yearling and proved himself a high-class racehorse. Unraced as a two-year-old,

Tracery made his racecourse debut in the Epsom Derby of 1912, finishing third to Walter Raphael's grey filly Tagalie. Unbeaten during the remainder of that season, he won the St James's Palace Stakes, the Sussex Stakes and the St Leger. As a four-year-old he won the Eclipse Stakes and the Champion Stakes, having been brought down in the Ascot Gold Cup by a lunatic brandishing a revolver in one hand and a flag in the other. Retired to stud in 1914, Tracery sired The Panther, Transvaal, Flamboyant and Cottage, before being exported to Argentina in 1920, whence he was hastily repatriated by an English syndicate following the Derby win of Papyrus. The success of Waygood meant that Tracery became the first horse to sire the winners of the English and Irish Derbies in the same season, though his maternal grandsire, Orme, had been responsible for Orby, winner of both races in 1907. Tracery died from colic in August 1924. Ascenseur, dam of Waygood, bred three other winners, including La Voiture. Unfortunately for Mr Raphael, Ascenseur had broken her leg in a paddock and had to be destroyed only a week before Waygood's victory at the Curragh.

Waygood only ran once more that season when unplaced in the St Leger behind Tranquil and Papyrus. Also unplaced in a race full of incident were Parth, Soldumeno and Ellangowan. As a four-year-old Waygood lost his form completely, finishing unplaced in races such as the Coronation Cup, Ascot Gold Cup and Cambridgeshire. Trained by J. Crawford at Ogbourne as a five-year-old, Waygood did much better, his four successes including the valuable Sandown Anniversary Handicap under top weight. At the end of the 1925 season Waygood was exported to America, having earned recognition as a good, honest, hard-working handicapper.

Soldumeno, second in the Irish Derby, went on to win a Curragh Biennial in which he beat Glenshesh, winner of the Irish One Thousand Guineas. His habit of breaking slowly became more pronounced with age and cost him a Kempton Jubilee, in which he failed by two short heads to catch Parth and Verdict. Those that finished behind him on that occasion included Pharos, Brownhylda, Twelve Pointer, Polyphontes and Waygood. Retired to stud in 1926, Soldumeno was exported to South Africa in December of the same year. His half-sister, Resplendent, having won the Irish One Thousand Guineas and Oaks for her owner-breeder Dan Sullivan, became the dam of the Epsom Derby winner Windsor Lad. Greek Bachelor, third in the Irish Derby, won the City and Suburban Handicap at Epsom as a five-year-old. Retired to Captain Dixon's New Abbey Stud in Kilcullen in 1927, Greek Bachelor became a leading sire of two-year-olds in Ireland, heading this category in 1931 and 1935. Among the best of his progeny were The Greek, Dark Greek and Grangemore. Darragh, a gelded son of Captivation out of the Irish Oaks winner Latharna and thus a full-brother to the 1927 Irish St Leger winner, Ballyvoy, went on winning on the flat until 1927, in addition to winning several hurdle races. Clonespoe proved a wonderfully consistent servant to the Moss stable. As a four-year-old he narrowly failed to achieve an unique Irish Autumn Double, finishing second in the Irish Cesarewitch before beating Soldennis in the Irish Cambridgeshire. Trained in England as a five-year-old, Clonespoe won the Brighton Cup before eventually retiring to stud in Ireland as the winner of thirteen races. Jackdaw of Rheims, having won three times in Ireland as a two-year-old, was leased by Jimmy White, for whom he won twice as a four-year-old before a leg injury necessitated his retirement to the Hanover Stud in Co. Carlow, where he had been bred by his owner Mr Oliver

Slocock. Prior to his death in 1944, Jackdaw of Rheims had become an established National Hunt sire, responsible for the Irish Grand National winners Alice Maythorn (1936) and Jack Chaucer (1940), in addition to Silent Prayer (Galway Plate).

Walter Raphael was a member of a wealthy Jewish family of financiers of Dutch extraction, who inherited his father's racing interests on the latter's death in 1899. Having seen his Louviers narrowly beaten by Minoru in the Derby of 1909, he was soon rewarded by the successes of Tagalie in the One Thousand Guineas and Derby of 1912, which enabled him to take second place in the list of winning breeders and third in the list of owners in that year. The following year his Louviers, having been placed first by the judge in the Two Thousand Guineas, was eventually placed second in the controversial Derby, which resulted in the disqualification of Craganour. Bettina became Walter Raphael's third home-bred Classic winner, when scoring a surprise victory in the One Thousand Guineas. Tall in stature and portentious in appearance, Walter Raphael suffered the misfortune of having his wallet stolen at the Curragh the day after the Derby. The temporarily penniless millionaire, obliged to seek the loan of a fiver, no doubt reflected anew on the ups and downs of racing! During the last ten years of his life he reduced his racing interests, which were modest in scale at the time of his death in 1938.

William Halsey, trainer of Waygood, had been a leading jockey before retiring to take up training at Newmarket. Born in 1867, he had begun riding under National Hunt rules at the age of thirteen and finished second in the Grand Nationals of 1890 and 1900. One of the first jockeys to ride with simultaneous success under both codes, he won the Two Thousand Guineas on Handicapper in 1901 and the St Leger on Wool Winder in 1907, besides being placed in the Derby of 1903 on Flotsam. Though never champion jockey, he finished second in the list in 1902 and was third in 1903 and 1907. As a jockey he will always be associated with that racecourse champion and stud failure, The White Knight, on whom he won successive Coronation Cups and and Ascot Gold Cups in 1907 and 1908. The Gold Cup of 1907 was in many respects a sensational affair, as The Irish Field reported at the time: 'The hundredth year of the Ascot Gold Cup will long be memorable. The extraordinary achievements of the thieves who in broad daylight and from under the nose of a policeman pilfered the trophy was in a sense a fitting prelude to the deadheat between the French and Irish representatives, The White Knight and Eider and the mutual attempts of the pair to savage each other in the last hundred yards, while the climax came with the disqualification of Eider.' To add to the excitement, Halsey objected to George Stern, rider of Eider, for catching hold of his leg and trying to shove him off. Though Stern was exonerated, Eider was disqualified for boring.

A forceful and determined rider, William Halsey was rare among jockeys in his readiness to admit to having ridden a bad race. Regarded as totally honest, he guarded his reputation with a useful pair of fists and a tongue like a lash. On retiring from the saddle he trained Hapsburg to finish second in the Derby of 1914 and later to win the Eclipse Stakes for Sir Ernest Cassell, his principal patron. Waygood was his last major winner prior to his retirement in 1924. Married to the daughter of another top-class jockey, John Watts, William Halsey was succeeded by his son Claude, who, having ridden against his father for several seasons, trained with success in France between the Wars and subsequently in England until his death in 1955, predeceasing his father by six years.

Wednesday, 27th June, 1923   **£4650**   **15 Ran**   **1½m**

The Irish Derby of 5000gns. Being 4500sovs to the owner of the winner, 200sov to the breeder of the winner, 200sovs to the owner of the second, 150sovs to the breeder of the second, 100sovs to the owner of the third, and 100sovs to the breeder of the third. By subscription of 50sovs each, 30sovs for those struck out on 3rd January, 1923, but 5sovs only for those struck out on 7th June, 1922. For three years old. Colts and geldings, 8st 12lb; Fillies, 8st. The winner of two races each value 500sovs, or of a race value 800sovs, 4lb extra; of two races each value 800sovs, or of a race value 1500sovs, 7lb extra, of a race value 4000sovs, 10lb extra.

(149 subs)

1	Mr W. Raphael's	WAYGOOD (M. Wing) B. colt Tracery – Ascenseur by Eager.	8.12	Halsey (UK)
2	Mr D. Sullivan's	SOLDUMENO (T. Burns) B. colt Diadumenos – Sunbridge by Bridge of Earn.	9. 5	Jeffrey
3	Lord Queenborough's	GREEK BACHELOR (G. Archibald) Ch. colt Bachelor's Double – Mitylene.	9. 2	P. P. Gilpin (UK)
4	Sir T. Dixon's	DARRAGH (H. Jelliss) Ch. colt Captivation – Latharna.	9. 5	Dundas (UK)
5	Miss M. Hayes's	BUACAILL BREAH (A. Barrett) Ch. colt Willaura – Barile.	8.12	J. Hartigan
6	Mr A. M'Cann's	KING DENNIS (Joseph Canty) Br. colt Tredennis – Diavolezza.	8.12	M. Dawson
7	Mr N. J. Grene's	CLONESPOE (J. Moylan) Ch. colt Prince Hermes – dam by Sir Edgar – Lady Norah.	8.12	Moss
8	Mr T. G. O'Brien's	SIMON ORB (E. M. Quirke) Ch. colt Flying Orb – Simon's Rose.	8.12	Hunter
9	Mr B. O'Donnell's	TOY LABEL (James Doyle) B. colt Santoi – Blue Label.	8.12	J. Doyle
10	Mr Thomas Clarke's	SIMON ROSS (M. Colbert) Ch. colt Captain Ross – Simon's Lawn.	8.12	M. Dawson
11	Mr C. F. Kenyon's	ORPINE (J. Patman) B. colt Orpiment – Elevation.	8.12	McKenna
0	Mr J. S. Lowry's	BEECH HILL (J. Dines) Bl. colt Morena – Sodiska.	8.12	Prendergast
0	Mr James White's	JACKDAW OF RHEIMS (H. H. Beasley) Br. colt Jackdaw – Amaryllis.	8.12	Ward
0	Mr H. M. Hartigan's	TARA HILL (James Canty) Gr. colt Junior – Prosperpine.	8.12	Behan
15	Mr James Daly's	MELRA (D. Ward) Br. filly Corcyra – Melmond.	8. 8	Owner

SP 5/2 Soldumeno; 9/2 Jackdaw of Rheims; 6/1 WAYGOOD; 8/1 King Dennis, Greek Bachelor; 10/1 Clonespoe; 100/6 Darragh, Simon Ross, Simon Orb; 20/1 Buacaill Breah, Orpine; 40/1 Tara Hill, Melra, Beech Hill; 100/1 Bar.
                    4 lengths, 3 lengths. 2m 39.4/5s.
Winner trained by Mr W. Halsey at Newmarket.

1924

The decreased prize money for this year's Irish Derby reflected the currently depressed state of racing in Ireland, which had resulted in the collapse of several of the smaller country racecourses. Speaking at the annual meeting of the Turf Club in May, Mr T. K. Laidlaw, the retiring Steward, attributed the decline in racecourse attendances to unfavourable weather, the unsettled state of the country and the depression in trade. While it was generally agreed that there was also too much racing, no one was prepared to propose an equitable means of achieving the necessary reduction. In 1921 770 races had been run for a prize fund of £145,151. Two years later a record 980 races had been staged for stakes totalling £128,312. An additional problem had arisen in the international rates of exchange, which had the effect of making Irish bloodstock more than usually expensive to foreign buyers. In response to an owners' campaign for reduced training charges, Curragh trainers took the drastic step of cutting their stable lads' wages. Understandably, this provoked a strike, resolved, only after a bitter struggle, in the trainers' favour.

To add to the woes of the Irish racing fraternity, the biggest prize of the year – the Irish Derby – appeared destined for export. In the Irish Two Thousand Guineas the Newmarket-trained Grand Joy had given weight and a beating to the much-vaunted Vesington King, with Zozimus in fourth place. To make matters worse, Mignault, who had scored a runaway win in the Baldoyle Derby, with Zozimus a remote fourth, had not even been entered for the Irish Derby. Consequently the three home-trained runners looked to have little chance of repelling the English quartet. Best hopes of a local victory lay with Lady Conyngham's Illyrian, third over ten furlongs on his previous outing. Neither Jehangir nor Churchtown, both down the field in the Irish Two Thousand Guineas, was at all fancied. The English challenge was, in the circumstances, formidable. Outstanding among them was Haine, a powerful and improving colt, who had won the Bessborough Stakes at Ascot only a week previously. Although his three two-year-old victories meant that he had to concede weight all round, he was still made a firm even-money favourite. Next in demand was the common-looking Zodiac, owned by Major Giles Loder and trained by P. P. Gilpin at Newmarket. This half-brother to Spike Island, though still a maiden, had finished second to Polyphontes in the recent Ascot Derby. Neither Bridge of Cahir nor Bucks Yeoman could boast comparable credentials. Bucks Yeoman had fallen in the Epsom Derby, while Bridge of Cahir showed signs of being as temperamental as his half-brother, Ballyheron.

From a perfect start, Haine, fighting hard for his head, made the running from Zodiac, Jehangir and Bucks Yeoman. After a very slow early gallop the pace quickened suddenly at the top of the hill, causing Jehangir to lose his place. Swinging down the hill towards the straight Zodiac joined Haine at the head of affairs, followed by Bucks Yeoman, Illyrian and Churchtown. Entering the straight Churchtown dropped back and Bucks Yeoman came under pressure as Zodiac and Haine forged clear, apparently with the race between them. Suddenly Harry Beasley got an opening on the rails and dashed Illyrian through to challenge the leaders. Inside the distance Canty on Haine found himself sandwiched between Illyrian on

First Dead Heat for the Irish Derby. *Joe Canty forces Haine up to share victory with Zodiac (George Archibald) on the right. Illyrian (H. H. Beasley), on the rails, finished third. Source:* Irish Field.

Ballyheron, *the first of six Irish Derby winners for jockey Morny Wing. Source:* Irish Field.

the rails and Zodiac on his outside. So tightly bunched were they that Canty could not use his whip. Just as Zodiac was being shouted home the winner Illyrian weakened, leaving Canty with room to manoeuvre. Seizing this last-second opportunity, Canty conjured a final desperate burst from Haine to snatch a deadheat on the line. Illyrian finished three-quarters of a length off the inseparable principals.

The connections of both Haine and Zodiac were quick to make excuses for their respective charges. However, it was generally agreed that Haine had been extremely unlucky not to have won outright. Handicapped by having to make all the running, he had been deprived of Canty's unique inspiration in the vital stages of a thrilling finish. The excited crowd experienced further drama when it became known that J. H. H. Peard, authorised agent for Lady Conyngham, owner of Illyrian, had objected to Haine being declared the winner. However, public suspense was short-lived, for Peard's objection was quickly overruled. It transpired that Peard had contended that Mrs Davis, wife of Haine's trainer, was a Disqualified Person, residing at the time with her husband, Captain Davis. The Stewards, having investigated the objection, promptly overruled it and, considering it to be frivolous, fined Mr Peard 25sovs. To have done otherwise would have reduced an occasion of spectacle and drama to the level of pure farce.

Haine was bred in Co. Limerick by Mr Dan Hederman and was by Hainault out of Almond, by Lomond. Although she did not win herself, Almond's two previous offspring had both been winners. Her grandam, Weeping Ash, was the dam of Earla Mor, while her dam, Commission, was an own-sister to Letterewe, third dam of Blue Dun, Teresina and Westward Ho. Hainault, a half-brother to Phalaris, by Swynford, won six races from a mile to two miles in a career dogged by a knee injury. Purchased from Lord Derby by Lord Dunraven, he joined Lomond at the Fort Union Stud and quickly made his mark as a sire. 1924 was the high point of Hainault's all-too-brief stud career, when Haine, Mignault and Amethystine (Irish Oaks) contributed to his becoming leading sire in Ireland. Amethystine went on to win a Kempton Jubilee, while Haintoinette credited him with another Irish Oaks in 1928. Unfortunately the latter success was posthumous, for an infinitely promising stud career ended abruptly with Hainault's death in 1926, aged only twelve. His name survives in modern pedigrees through such as Nimbus, Phil Drake, Grey Sovereign and Hardicanute. Very much more recently Hainault's name has come to the fore in the pedigree of Roland Gardens.

Haine was bought at Doncaster as a yearling for 420gns by Mr C. F. Kenyon, who sent him to one of his private trainers, Harold Bazley at Highfield, Malton. Successful in his first two races, Haine then joined another of Mr Kenyon's private trainers, Captain Davis, at Tern Hill in Shropshire, for whom he won the valuable Prince of Wales's Nursery at the Doncaster St Leger meeting. On his reappearance after the Irish Derby Haine was unplaced behind Pharos in the Liverpool Cup in July. His final run as a three-year-old saw hin finish fourth at Stockton, then, following the death of his owner, Haine was sold at Newmarket in October for 1050gns to Mr E. C. Sykes. Now trained at Doncaster by F. D. Cole, Haine won only once as a four-year-old when scoring in the Spring Handicap at Newcastle. Purchased by Viscount St Davids, Haine was retired to the Landwade Hall Stud near Newmarket as the winner of six races value £6645. Despite being modestly priced at 18gns, Haine failed to attract much custom and consequently sired nothing of note. In view of his breeding and the recent demise of his sire, it seems reasonable to assume that Haine would have proved more attractive to Irish breeders.

At the time of his Irish Derby deadheat, Haine carried the 'White, green and white sleeves and cap' of one of the largest owners then racing in terms of sheer numbers of horses in training. Charles Frederick Kenyon was a Manchester businessman, who had amassed a fortune through speculating in rubber. Interested initially in hackneys, which he bred on a large scale, he began racing in 1919 under the assumed name of Mr K. Tilstock. Plunging in at the deep end, Mr Kenyon purchased the Blink Bonny Stud and the Highfield stables from Sir John Thursby. Through extensive and frequently expensive purchases he built up a staggering collection of racehorses, employing three trainers in England and one, McKenna, in Ireland. In 1924 he won no less than 56 races in England and 13 in Ireland up to the time of his death in September, as a result of which all his bloodstock was sold at public auction. Among the best of an essentially moderate fleet of horses to carry his ubiquitous colours were Sir Greysteel, Audlem, winner of the Gold Vase and Haine. Charles Kenyon raced purely for sport, having no interest in betting and simply loved to see his colours to the fore as frequently as possible. In recording the death of this remarkable owner, the Bloodstock Breeders Review paid him this tribute: 'One wonders what Mr Kenyon would have made of his racing and breeding venture if his life had been prolonged a few more years. We have seen nothing quite like it for a very long time.'

Hain's Irish Derby was the highlight of 'Bob' Davis' training career. Born in Melbourne, Charles Lukin Davis served with the 17th Lancers during the Boer War, before going to live in France. Re-enlisting at the outbreak of the Great War, he found himself attached to a cavalry regiment stationed in Dublin, where a Turf career of frequently fluctuating fortunes led to his becoming well-known in Irish circles. It was after an abortive 'coup' at Manchester that a fortuitous meeting with

Mr Kenyon soon saw Bob Davis training a large string in splendid style at Tern Hill, where he could do little wrong during the four years of his benefactor's lavish patronage. Following Mr Kenyon's untimely demise, Bob Davis trained for a time for Sir Edward Elgar, having charge of the record-priced 'chaser Silvo. He then moved to the North of England to train for Mr J. Settle. However, his irascible nature and violent temper were no asset to Bob Davis in a profession which calls for patience and forbearance. During the last years of his life Bob Davis was seldom seen racing, spending much of his time at the Cavalry Club, where he was held more in awe than affection by his fellow-members. He died in 1942 at the age of sixty-six.

Zodiac, half-brother to Spike Island and representing the same team of owner, trainer and jockey as successful two years earlier with the latter, was by the Epsom Derby winner Sunstar. Unfashionably-bred, Sunstar showed only fair ability as a two-year-old, but improved out of all recognition during the following winter, astonishing even his phlegmatic trainer Charles Morton. Having won the Two

Wednesday, 25th June, 1924   **£4350**   **7 Ran**   **1½m**

The Irish Derby of 5000sovs. Being 4200sovs to the owner of the winner, 200sovs each to the breeder of the winner and owner of the second, 150sovs each to the breeder of the second and owner of the third, and 100sovs to the breeder of the third. By subscription of 50sovs each, 30sovs for those struck out on 2nd January, 1924, but 5sovs only for those struck out on 6th June, 1923. For entire colts and fillies foaled in 1921. Colts, 8st 12lb; Fillies, 8st 8lb. The winner of two races each value 500sovs, or of a race value 800sovs, 4lb extra; of two races cash value 800sovs, or of a race value 1500sovs, 7lb extra; of a race value 4000sovs, 10lb extra; of a race value 6000sovs, 12lb extra. Any surplus on entrance fees will be divided as follows: 75% to the owner of the second and 25% to the owner of the third.

(93 subs)

1	Mr C. F. Kenyon's	HAINE (Joseph Canty)	9. 2	Capt. C. Davies (UK)
		B. colt Hainault – Almond by Lomond.		
2	Major Giles Loder's	ZODIAC (G. Archibald)	8.12	P. P. Gilpin (UK)
		B. colt Sunstar – Molly Desmond by Desmond.		
3	Lady Conyngham's	ILLYRIAN (H. H. Beasley)	8.12	Peard*
		B. colt Corcyra – Illia.		
4	Sir A. Bailey's	BUCKS YEOMAN (M. Beary)	8.12	R. Day (UK)
		B. colt Son-in-Law – Bracelet.		
5	Mrs E. M. Croft's	CHURCHTOWN (E. M. Quirke)	8.12	M. Dawson
		Br. colt Bachelor's Double – Brown Betty.		
6	Col. Charteris's	BRIDGE OF CAHIR (T. Burns)	8.12	Boyd-Rochfort (UK)
		B. colt Bridge of Earn – Anxious.		
7	Mr F. Clarke's	JEHANGIR (J. Moylan)	8.12	Fetherston'
		B. colt My Prince – Minway.		

SP Evens HAINE; 3/1 ZODIAC; 7/1 Bucks Yeoman; 10/1 Illyrian; 20/1 Bar.
Dead-heat, ¾ length. 2m 46.3/5s.
Stakes divided
Haine trained by Captain C. Davies.
Zodiac trained by Mr P. P. Gilpin at Clarehaven Lodge, Newmarket.

*Mr J. H. H. Peard, authorised agent for Lady Conyngham (owner of Illyrian), objected to Haine being declared the winner, on the grounds that Mrs Davis, wife of Captain Davis (the trainer of Haine) was a Disqualified Person and resided with Captain Davis. The Stewards having investigated the objection, considered it frivolous, overruled it and fined Mr Peard 25 sovs.

Thousand Guineas and Newmarket Stakes, Sunstar developed into a raging hot favourite for the Derby. Less than ten days before the big race he strained a suspensory ligament . . . Morton's care and skill, the artistry of George Stern and the colt's own raw courage saw him win the Derby on the three legs. He never ran again. Retired to Jack Joel's Childwick Bury Stud, Sunstar sired numerous high-class horses, notably Craig an Eran and Buchan, in addition to Galloper Light, Alan Breck and Somme Kiss. His line survives through Craig an Eran's son Admiral Drake, founder of an important bloodline in France. Zodiac's next race was in the St Leger at Doncaster, where, starting at 100-to-1, he finished only eleventh behind Salmon Trout. One week later he maintained his record of success at the Curragh when winning the Irish St Leger by a head from Zarope, to whom he was conceding 14lbs. Purchased by Donald Fraser, Zodiac was retired to the Tickford Park Stud at Newport Pagnell, where he stood for three seasons, prior to being exported to Uruguay at the end of the covering season in 1927. Though Zodiac left nothing behind him to perpetuate his name in Europe, he went on to become champion sire in Uruguay.

1925

After months of what had come to seem like endless winter, the Irish Derby was staged in delightful summer weather, which drew a large crowd, including the Governor-General, Tim Healy and the Free State President, W. T. Cosgrave. The track itself had been improved by the removal of the old stone posts which had marked the Derby course. These had been replaced by oak uprights and the going, for the first time that year, rode fast. Only one of the last five runnings of the Irish Derby had been kept in Ireland and the credentials of the English-trained quartet, comprising half the field, gave every indication that cross-Channel dominance was to be continued. The raiding party was headed by the Aga Khan's Zionist, trained by Dick Dawson at Whatcombe. Second to Manna in the Epsom Derby, Zionist had then swerved badly in his most recent race at Ascot, allowing Warminster to beat him by a neck, receiving 12lbs. Meeting his rival on level terms, Zionist was confidently expected to make amends. However, Zionist had to share favouritism with his compatriot Sparus. Winner of the Greenham Stakes, Sparus had finished down the field in the Epsom Derby, but had since divided Solario and Manna in the Ascot Derby. Thought certain to relish the firm ground, Sparus attracted substantial support. Both Warminster and Foxlaw appeared held by the joint favourites. Irish hopes rested squarely on St Donagh, unbeaten since his final race as a two-year-old, the Curragh Grand Prize. Revelling in the bog-like conditions, St Donagh had run out an easy winner of the Irish Two Thousand Guineas. More recently he had won a very rough race for the Baldoyle Derby, with Larkspur, Lisworney and Brighter London behind him and though he had been coughing in the meantime, his trainer, E. Fordred was confident that Mr A. B. Coyle's colt was fit enough to do himself justice, Lisworney, destined to be champion trainer Michael Dawson's last runner in the race he had won more times than any other trainer was friendless at 50-to-1.

From the start Warminster made it a rattling gallop, followed by St Donagh, Sparus and Zionist, with Foxlaw and Lisworney the backmarkers. After they had covered a mile both Sparus and St Donagh had had enough, leaving Zionist to go in pursuit of the leader. These two turned into the straight with the race between them. Warminster hung on bravely to the distance, where he was overhauled by Zionist, who, showing no signs of his earlier waywardness, ran on resolutely to win by one and a half lengths. Brighter London, having appeared hopelessly beaten over half a mile from home, plugged on under Joe Canty's driving to take third place, six lengths further back. Though Zionist thus added to the growing list of English-trained winners of the Irish Derby, he was in almost every other respect Irish, being bred, trained and ridden by Irishmen.

A bay son of Spearmint, whose suspect knees he inherited, Zionist was bred by Captain Charles Moore at Mooresfort, Co. Tipperary, whose colours he carried in the Irish Derby, owing to the Aga Khan's silks having been left behind at Whatcombe. The mandatory fine of 2sovs for wrong colours scarcely diminished the Aga Khan's pleasure at collecting this, the first of a record five Irish Derbies. Purchased as a yearling for 2400gns, Zionist was unbeaten in his first three races as a two-year-old, concluding with the Dewhurst Stakes. Hailed as the best colt of his generation, he had then flopped badly behind Diomedes in his final race as a two-year-old. Unraced after his success in the Irish Derby, Zionist was 'laid out' for the Lincolnshire, for which he started favourite and failed by only a head to concede 4lbs to King of Clubs, ridden by young Pat Donoghue. He then resumed his mischievous habit of swerving, which cost him his next and final two races. Retired to stud in France, he proved disappointing. His sire, Spearmint, who had died a year previously, was also the sire of Spike Island, winner of the Irish Derby in 1922. His dam Judea, by Roi Herode out of Sacrifice, was an excellent racemare, winning the Beresford Stakes and Irish Oaks for Captain Moore. Judea also bred Dumas, third in the Cambridgeshire and one of those involved in the celebrated triple deadheat at Windsor in 1923.

Zionist was the first of three Irish Derby winners trained by R. C. Dawson, to which must be added two Irish Oaks and three Irish St Legers. However, these successes were almost incidental to the career of one of the outstanding trainers of this century. Richard Cecil Dawson was born in Ireland in 1865, the son of a trainer and breeder. On leaving Trinity College, Dublin, he began training at Cloghran near Dublin, scoring his first notable success with Castle Warden in the Galway Plate of 1896. The following year, having seen Castle Warden beaten by Drogheda in the same race, Dick Dawson bought the winner in partnership with Mr G. C. Adams and took him to England, where he established his stable at Whatcombe in Berkshire. Nor was Dawson long in making his presence felt in England, for Drogheda won the Grand National at his first attempt in 1898. Thereafter he turned his attentions increasingly to flat racing, winning the Royal Hunt Cup in 1902 with The Solicitor and the Stewards Cup with Mauvezin. Robert le Diable, Missovia, Valens and Buckwheat were other good winners for the Whatcombe stable prior to the First World War, though none of these made such a lasting impression on his trainer's memory as the wretched Mustapha, second in three successive Cambridgeshires.

At the beginning of the Great War Dick Dawson moved to Newmarket, where he trained for two seasons for the newspaper magnate Sir Edward Hulton, winning the Cambridgeshire with Silver Tag and a substitute Derby and Oaks with her younger half-sister, Fifinella. This highly successful partnership ended when Dawson insisted that he could not continue to train the Hulton horses on fifty shillings per week! Returning to Whatcombe, Dawson won the Kempton Jubilee and Ascot Gold Cup with Sir William Nelson's Tangiers. In 1921 Dick Dawson secured the most important owner of his lengthy career when taking charge of the Aga Khan's top-class string, on the recommendation of George Lambton. During the next ten years Dawson produced Diophon (Two Thousand Guineas), Salmon Trout (St Leger) and Blenheim (Derby) for his principal patron, in addition to the flying filly, Mumtaz Mahal. During the same period he also won the Derby with Trigo and the Oaks with Brownhylda. In 1931, as the result of a blazing row, the Aga Khan transferred his horses to Frank Butters, among them the two-year-olds Dastur, Firdaussi and Udaipur, destined to win the Derby, St Leger and Oaks respectively. For the Aga Khan Dick Dawson bought Friar's Daughter in 1922 as a yearling for 250gns. She produced Dastur and Bahram. But Dick Dawson's most notable purchase was unquestionably Blandford, for whom he gave 730gns as a yearling. This brilliant but unsound racehorse met Malva in his first trial: their next encounter produced Blenheim. Retired to stud at Cloghran, Blandford became the leading sire of his age. Champion trainer in England in 1916, 1924 and 1929, Dick Dawson in the latter year became only the second trainer to have turned out the winners of both the Grand National and the Epsom Derby. The first was Dawson's good friend George Blackwell, both men favouring searching preparations, which many thought unnecessarily severe. In the same year Dawson's stakes winnings of £74,754 exceeded all previous totals save that of George Dawson in 1889. With his moustaches and pince nez Dick Dawson appeared anything but a racehorse trainer, much less the popular vision of an Irish trainer, for he was almost totally devoid of a sense of humour. As though deliberately to emphasize the improbability of his calling, Dick Dawson never saddled his own runners. Having married late in life and produced numerous children, this unlikely master of his profession retired in 1945 and died ten years later, when in his ninetieth year.

That Zionist was a good if wayward racehorse was confirmed by the subsequent performances of those that finished behind him at the Curragh. Warminster, having finished third to Salario in the Coronation Cup, ran fourth behind the same champion of his generation in the Ascot Gold Cup. Brighter London, an own-brother to Jackdaw of Rheims, finished second to the five-year-old Waygood at Sandown, before running Spelthorne to a neck in the Irish St Leger, with Flying Dinah, winner of the Irish One Thousand Guineas, five lengths away in third place. He went on to win in England as a four-year-old before retiring to stud in Co. Wexford, where he became the sire of numerous winners, including the high-class hurdler Knight O'London. St Donagh unfortunately never recovered from the jarring he received in the Irish Derby and was retired to stud at Co. Meath. Sparus won the Liverpool Cup as a four-year-old. But the best of those unplaced behind Zionist was undoubtedly Foxlaw, totally unsuited by the early gallop in the Irish Derby. Beaten a short head in the Jockey Club Cup by Bucellas, with both Plack and Sansovino behind him, Foxlaw trained on to win both the Northumberland Plate and the Jockey Club Stakes, in which he beat his stable companion Solario by a neck. Kept in training as a five-year-old, this game son of Son-in-law emulated his sire by winning the Ascot Gold Cup. Despite dying when only thirteen, Foxlaw sired two Gold Cup winners in Foxhunter and Tiberius.

| **Wednesday, 24th June, 1925** | **£4350** | **8 Ran** | **1½m** |

The Irish Derby of 5000sovs. Being 4200sovs to the owner of the winner, 200sovs each to the breeder of the winner and owner of the second, 150sovs each to the breeder of the second and owner of the third, and 100sovs to the breeder of the third. By subscription of 50sovs each, 30sovs for those struck out on 7th January, 1925, but 5sovs only for those struck out on 4th June, 1924. For entire colts and fillies foaled in 1922. Colts 8st 12lb; Fillies, 8st 8lb. The winner of two races each value 500sovs, or of a race value 800sovs, 4lb extra; of two races each value 800sovs, or of a race value 1500sovs, 7lb extra; of a race value 4000sovs, 10lb extra; of a race value 6000sovs, 12lb extra. Any surplus on entrance fees will be divided as follows: 75% to the owner of the second and 25% to the owner of the third.

(143 subs)

1	HH Aga Khan's*	ZIONIST (H. H. Beasley)	9. 5	R. Dawson (GB)
		B. colt Spearmint – Judea by Roi Herode.		
2	Mrs W. Raphael's	WARMINSTER (G. Archibald)	9.5	G. Sadler (GB)
		Ch. colt Louvois – Lomelie.		
3	Mr B. M. Slocock's	BRIGHTER LONDON (Joseph Canty) B/Br. colt Jackdaw – Amaryllis.	9. 5	T. Coombs
4	Mr A. B. Coyle's	ST DONAGH (J. Dines)	9. 5	E. Fordred
		B. colt Roi Herode – Simon Tit.		
5	Mr W. P. Gill's	LARKSPUR (A. Clarke)	8.12	J. T. Rogers
		B. colt Spearmint – Laragh.		
6	Mr W. M. G. Singer's	SPARUS (F. Bullock)	9. 5	A. Taylor (GB)
		B. colt Gainsborough – Flying Spear.		
0	Sir A. Bailey's	FOXLAW (J. E. Evans)	9. 2	R. Day (GB)
		Br. colt Son-in-Law – Alope.		
0	Lord Kenmare's	LISWORNEY (James Doyle)	9. 2	M. Dawson
		B. colt Prospector – Fantoi.		

SP 5/2 ZIONIST, Sparus; 5/1 St Donagh; 8/1 Warminster, Foxlaw; 100/8 Brighter London, Larkspur; 50/1 Lisworney.

1½ lengths, 6 lengths. 2m 39.4/5s.
Winner trained by Mr R. C. Dawson at Whatcombe, Berkshire.

*Owner of Zionist fined 2sovs for wrong colours.

1926

Although the introduction of the Totalisator to Irish racecourses had been debated in the Dail, its benefits to the sport remained firmly in the future. Of more immediate import were the recently-introduced Betting Tax and the effects of the industrial unrest in England on the Irish economy. As had been widely predicted, the combination of the Betting Tax and the Entertainment Tax, in a time of economic depression, had an immediate and disastrous effect on racecourse attendances. However, none of this deterred an ever large than usual English raiding party for the Irish Derby, nor indeed a huge attendance for the feature event. So great was the crowd that the railing on the left of the grandstand collapsed, fortunately without injury to those concerned. Of the English-trained sextet, Embargo had already won the Irish Two Thousand Guineas and had since finished second in the Royal Hunt Cup, beaten a neck by Cross Bow. Bulger, unbeaten as a two-year-old and twice successful in his second season, had failed in his only attempt beyond a mile. Resplendent, winner of the Irish One Thousand Guineas, had finished second in the Epsom Oaks. Glen Albyn and Tenacity had both won over a mile. Of the three home-trained hopefuls, only White Orb, winner of the Baldoyle Derby, appeared to have the qualifications to repel the invaders. Silver Lark, prior to finishing third in the Irish Two Thousand Guineas, had crashed through the rails in the Madrid Plate and subsequently developed an understandable tendency to hang away from the 'fence'. Although Embargo and Steve Donoghue were always firm favourites to supplement their Irish Two Thousand Guineas success, there was strong support for Bulger in a market spiced by a red-hot tip for the maiden Waterkoscie.

First to show was Lord Wembley, who led from White Orb, Waterkoscie, Embargo and Resplendent. Under orders not to make the running, Wing restrained Lord Wembley, allowing Geraint to take it up at a steady pace. With a little over half a mile to run Geraint began to lose his place, the pace quickened suddenly and a new leader emerged in Resplendent, pushed along by Jack Moylan and pursued by Embargo, Silver Lark, Lord Wembley and Bulger. In the straight Resplendent gave way to the wide-running Silver Lark, who was challenged in turn by Bulger on the rails and Embargo. In an exciting three-cornered struggle Embargo showed his unmistakable touch of class when quickening near the line to beat Silver Lark by half a length. Bulger, on whom Smirke had found himself with little room on the rails, finished a similar distance away, almost falling as he passed the post. Embargo thus became Steve Donoghue's third Irish Derby winner and the one with which he might be said to have been most intimately associated. Happily acknowledging the congratulations of his legion of admirers and well-wishers, the hero of the hour avoided the ignominy of his fellow-jockeys who rode in the next race, declared void by the Stewards owing to the farcical pace at which it was first walked and then run.

Embargo, a brown colt, was bred by Mr W. F. Power at the Rathcannon Stud, Kilmallock, Co. Limerick and was bought as a yearling at the Doncaster Sales by Sam Darling, the Newmarket trainer, for 600gns. He was by Argosy, second in the Irish Derby, out of the Marco mare, Elland, who bred three other winners, though none of comparable merit. Consistent if luckless in his first season, Embargo won once, at Newmarket, and was several times beaten by narrow margins when well supported. As a three-year-old he had been beaten a head in the Greenham Plate, finished fourth to Colorado in the Two Thousand Guineas and thrown away the Royal Hunt Cup by swerving close home when beaten a neck by Cross Bow. Reverting to shorter distances after the Irish Derby, he finished third to Oojah in the Select Stakes at Newmarket, ran disappointingly in the Cambridgeshire, in which Bulger finished second to Insight II, and concluded a busy season by deadheating with Inca at Derby in November on the disqualification of Abbot's Smile. Trained as a four-year-old by F. R. G. Scott, Embargo made a winning reappearance when justifying favouritism in the City and Suburban at Epsom. Second in the Kempton

Jubilee, Embargo then ran Coronach to a length in the Coronation Cup, with Foxlaw eight lengths away in third place. Unplaced behind the latter in the Ascot Gold Cup, Embargo won the valuable Grand International d'Ostend in August and concluded his racecourse career when third to Colorado in the Champion Stakes. Purchased by J. J. Parkinson, Embargo was installed at his owner's First Flier Stud near the Curragh, where he sired numerous winners under both codes, though none to approach his own undoubted class. His best winners on the flat included Hands Off, British Quota, Control and Spot Barred, while under National Hunt rules Honor's Choice, Pongo and Prince Blackthorn kept his name to the fore up to the time of his death in 1944. On the balance of his form Embargo deserves recognition as a high-class racehorse, who, on his run against Coronach, laid claims to be considered among the best of his generation.

In winning the Irish Derby with Embargo and the Epsom Derby with Windsor Lad, HH the Maharaja of Rajpipla achieved the unique distinction of winning both races at the first attempt. Ruler of the State of Rajpipla in the Presidency of Bombay, the Maharaja registered his colours in England for the first time in 1924, though he was already extensively involved in racing in his own country, having won the Indian Derby in 1919. One of his first purchases in England was Embargo, the second best horse to carry his colours in a lengthy career, which lasted until his death in 1951. Good horse that he was, Embargo was outshone by a truly great colt in Windsor Lad, one of the best horses to race in England between the two World Wars. The exploits of Windsor Lad brought fame and popularity to his colourful owner, known to the racing world as 'Mr Pip'. Marcus Marsh, who trained Windsor Lad, described his owner thus: '. . . the prototype of all Oriental playboys . . . small, dark and handsome and possessed of considerable charm'. Addicted to glamorous women and the good life, 'Mr Pip' installed himself in a Victorian mansion near Windsor, where, reminiscent of the Great Gatsby, he threw endless parties at which champagne flowed and chorus girls abounded. To celebrate Windsor Lad's Derby success 'Mr Pip' gave a party at the Savoy at which a young elephant, garlanded in his colours of purple and cream, was paraded round the dance floor. Though endlessly lavish in his entertaining, 'Mr Pip' marred his own enjoyment of racing by excessive caution, amounting to meanness, allied to an enduring suspicion of trainers and jockeys whom he employed. Ignorant of and curiously uninterested in horses, ill-advised by a succession of unsavoury hangers-on, 'Mr Pip' could never understand why his remarkable early success on the Turf could not be sustained, though he did win the Stewards Cup with First Consul towards the end of his life. In common with another Eastern potentate then racing in England, the Maharaja of Rajpipla had another side to his character, which revealed him as an able and enlightened administrator of his Indian territory, where he wrought many improvements for the benefit of his subjects, notably in the areas of communications, health and education.

While the records show that Embargo was trained to win the Irish Derby by Charles Bartholemew, this was only partly true. Though Charlie Bartholemew, son of a well-known French trainer of the same name, held the licence at Elston House, Shrewton, the home of Eleanor, Lady Torrington, it was an open secret that the horses there were effectively supervised by 'Nellie' Torrington and the man in her life – Steve Donoghue. Having run away from home to make a career on the stage, the striking and ambitious Eleanor Souray had captivated and married Lord Torrington, wealthy heir to title and property, former Page of Honour to Queen Victoria and counting among his ancestors the ill-fated Admiral Byng. Lady Torrington and Steve Donoghue became acquainted during a voyage to South Africa during the First World War. As soon as the war was over Lady Torrington became separated from her husbaand, not long after Donoghue had divorced his first wife, Brigid Behan. In 1919 Lady Torrington purchased Elston House, Shrewton, comprising a mansion, stud farm and racing stable. Formerly the property of John Porter, Elston House had at one time been leased to Bob Sievier, primarily to prepare his wonderful filly Sceptre. Set in the heart of the Wiltshire countryside, with all of Salisbury Plain on which to work horses, yet convenient to the bright lights of London's West End, Elston House provided the perfect setting for Lady Torrington to indulge her

Wednesday, 23rd June, 1926   **£4350**   **10 Ran**   **1½m**

The Irish Derby of 5000sovs. Being 4200sovs to the owner of the winner, 200sovs each to the breeder of the winner and owner of the second, 150sovs each to the breeder of the second and owner of the third, and 100sovs to the breeder of the third. For entire colts and fillies foaled in 1923. Colts, 8st 12lb; Fillies, 8st 8lb. The winner of two races each value 500sovs, or of a race value 800sovs, 4lb extra; of two races each value 800sovs, or of a race value 1500sovs, 7lb extra; of a race value 4000sovs, 10lb extra; of a race value 6000sovs, 12lb extra. Entrance 5sovs for yearlings entered on July 23rd. Second entry at 20sovs on 8th October, 1924. Horses not struck out on 3rd June, 1925, pay 25sovs extra, and those not struck out on 6th January, 1926, pay 20sovs in addition. Any surplus on entrance fees will be divided as follows: 75% to the owner of the second and 25% to the owner of the third.

(144 subs)

1	Maharajah of Rajpipla's	EMBARGO (S. Donoghue) Br. colt Argosy – Elland by Marco.	9. 5	Bartholomew (UK)
2	Mrs C. L. Mackean's	SILVER LARK (T. Burns) Br. colt Silvern – Laverock.	8.12	Blake
3	Mrs T. Carthew's	BULGER (C. Smirke) Br. colt Bridge of Earn – Black Gem.	9. 2	Wootton (UK)
4	Mr D. Sullivan's	RESPLENDENT (J. Moylan) B. filly By George! – Sunbridge.	8.12	Persse (UK)
5	Mr W. Barnett's	WHITE ORB (E. M. Quirke) Ch. colt White Eagle – Mercy. NOT IN GSB.	9. 2	J. T. ROGERS
6	Mr D. Frames's	WATERKOSCIE (J. Dines) Br. colt Kosciusko – Waterproof.	8.12	Killalee (UK)
7	Mr A. Hood's	GLEN ALBYN (G. Archibald) B. colt Bridge of Earn – Alarmed.	8.12	Peacock (UK)
8	Mr A. B. Coyle's	GERAINT (Joseph Canty) Ch. colt Orpiment – Gerenda.	8.12	Fordred
9	Lord Glanely's	TENACITY (J. Thwaites) B. colt Gay Crusader – Decagone.	8.12	Archer (UK)
10	Mr W. A. Wallis's	LORD WEMBLEY (M. Wing) Br. colt Tredennis – Captive Princess.	8.12	Staunton

SP 4/5 EMBARGO; 3/1 Bulger; 10/1 Waterkoscie; 100/8 Silver Lark, White Orb, Resplendent; 100/6 Glen Albyn; 20/1 Tenacity; 100/1 Bar.
½ length, same. 2m 41.1/5s.
Winner trained by Mr Charles Bartholomew at Shrewton.

hobby of training racehorses and her passion for entertaining high society, with Donoghue, then at the peak of his career, as her constant companion. Combining the good life with a fair measure of racecourse success, Elston House was just the establishment to appeal to the fun-loving young Maharaja of Rajpipla. However, despite winning the Lincoln with the reformed rogue Tapin and the successes of Embargo and others, the Elston House establishment could not support the improvident expenditure of its inhabitants, nor were their attempted betting 'coups' any help. Eventually Elston House was put on the market, its contents sold and Lady Torrington declared bankrupt. This domineering, colourful, capricious and ultimately unfortunate woman committed suicide in very reduced circumstances in 1931. Thus the saga of Steve Donoghue's personal life continued, for genius though he undoubtedly was on a horse, off one he was a delightful, gullible, ill-fated fool.

1927

The 1927 renewal of the Irish Derby was staged against a background of growing political unrest, public resentment of the Betting and Amusement taxes and widespread conviction that the result of many races was being arranged beforehand. In these circumstances it seemed all too likely that the recent domination of the Derby by English-trained horses would continue. The defeat of Archway, leading Irish two-year-old the previous season, by the English colt, Fourth Hand, in the Irish Two Thousand Guineas convinced many Irish owners and trainers of the futility of contesting Ireland's richest races. Thus the field of six included only two local defenders, Archway and the outsider Coinage. The latter had been decisively outclassed by Archway both as a two-year-old and more recently in the first of the Classics. On a line through Fourth Hand, Archway appeared to have little chance of containing either Chantrey or Knight of the Grail.

The formidable raiding party was headed by Chantrey, from the mighty Manton stable of Alec Taylor. Unraced as a two-year-old, this son of Gainsborough had run the Epsom Derby second, Hot Night, to a short head at York before running away with the Prince of Wales Plate at Royal Ascot by fifteen lengths. Nor were Knight of the Grail's credentials any the less impressive. In his first season he had made a winning debut in the Coventry Stakes at Ascot and then finished a close second in the Dewhurst Stakes. Down the field in the Two Thousand Guineas at Newmarket, he then looked like springing a major surprise in the Epsom Derby, where he led in the straight, only to fade into seventh place behind Call Boy. That confirmed expatriate pot-hunter, Atty Persse, sent over Lavengro, disappointing since his success in the Railway Stakes, when trained by Michael Dawson. The sole Newmarket representative, King Herald, though a winner on his local course, looked out of his depth in this company. The aura of certain success surrounding Chantrey and his connections encouraged the public to make him a hot favourite, ahead of Knight of the Grail, while the partisan element trusted in the genius of Joe Canty to save the day on Archway.

The six runners were quickly dispatched, headed by Lavengro at a moderate pace in front of Chantrey, King Harald and Knight of the Grail. This order was maintained to the top of the hill, where Harry Beasley tried to slip his field on the leader, but without success, for he was soon overhauled by Chantrey. As Lavengro weakened, Chantrey led into the straight from King Harald, Knight of the Grail and an improving Archway on the rails. Both King Harald and Knight of the Grail challenged the leader over the final two furlongs. King Harald was first to crack, leaving Chantrey and Knight of the Grail to battle to the line. With fifty yards to run Beary forced Knight of the Grail's head in front to win by a neck. Archway, finishing fastest of all, was only a head further back in third place. The result aroused raging controversy, centering around the luckless Archway. Twice thwarted in trying for his accustomed position on the rails, Canty had finally got there, only to find himself pocketed by the fading King Harald. By the time he had extricated Archway and come on the outside the race was lost. To add to the heated post-mortem, backers of the favourite claimed that Jelliss's acceptance of the slow early gallop had robbed his proven stayer of certain victory.

Knight of the Grail, a medium-sized bay colt, was bred by Mr F. B. O'Toole at his Rathmoyle Stud near Edenderry and sold three times as a yearling, initially to Mr P. Day, a Dublin horsedealer, for 85gns. Mr Day passed him on at a profit to Andrew Young of Naas, who sent the colt to the Newmarket sales. Led out of the ring unsold at 400gns he was subsequently purchased privately by Sir Delves Broughton for 350gns. Two years later Mr Young successfully sued the purchaser for a further 600gns, due under a contingency of the sale. His sire, Prince Galahad, was unbeaten as a two-year-old in 1919, winning the Chesham Stakes and Dewhurst Plate. Based at the Greenfields Stud in Tipperary, he also sired Knight Error, winner of the Lincolnshire and Smokeless, winner of the Irish One Thousand Guineas and Oaks. Due almost entirely to Knight of the Grail's Derby success, Prince Galahad was Champion Sire in Ireland in 1927. On his next appearance Knight of the Grail won a good handicap at Hurst Park. Though placed in the Royal Hunt Cup, he failed to win as a four-year-old, but made amends the following season when he won the Liverpool Summer Cup. He was then trained by Walter Earl for Solly Joel.

Chantrey gained prompt compensation for his Curragh defeat when hacking up in the Welsh Derby at Chepstow in July. His death shortly afterwards was a bitter blow to Mr Singer and to Alec Taylor. Archway's luckless record in the Irish Classics continued in the Irish St Leger, where he could finish only third to Ballyvoy and West Indies. Trained in England as a four-year-old by Major A. W. Molony, Archway ran his contemporary, Brown Jack, to a head at Windsor and finished a close third in the Bessborough Handicap at Ascot, before finally getting his head in front at Goodwood in August. King Harald ran only once more before being retired to stud by his optimistic owner. Reverting to his true metier of sprinting, Coinage showed his true ability when winning the important Drogheda Memorial Stakes at the Curragh in July, beating that wonderful weight-carrier, Knocklong Boy, favourite even with over eleven stone on his back. Coinage was afterwards exported to India.

The winning owner, Sir Henry John Delves Broughton, was the eleventh incumbent of a baronetcy created by a grateful Charles II, following the Restoration. Extensively involved in the rubber trade in East Africa, he served as a major in the Irish Guards during World War One and subsequently began racing on a substantial scale, winning eighty-six races over twenty-two seasons with such good horses as the sprinter Pheidon. His solitary success with Knight of the Grail sufficed to make him the leading owner in Ireland in 1927. Becoming interested in breeding, he produced numerous winners from his Doddington Stud in Cheshire. He was only fifty-nine at the time of his death in 1942, resulting from a riding accident on his estate in Kenya.

Knight of the Grail's trainer was a man of vast and varied experience, to whom this success came in the twilight of a lifetime's devotion to the Turf. Born in 1855 into an ancient and distinguished Dorset family, Ronald James Farquharson spent many years riding as an amateur in India. On riding his first winner at Colombo in 1877, he received a gold chain from the grateful owner, which he wore as a talisman throughout his life. He returned to England in 1906, bringing with him two good New Zealand-breds, with which he established his reputation as a trainer. From his secluded stables at Tileshead in Wiltshire he sent out a steady, if unspectacular stream of winners, invariably making the best use of material entrusted to his care.

Firmly established in the top flight of jockeys in England during a period when standards of jockeyship had seldom been higher, Michael Beary was no stranger to Irish racecourses. Born in Tipperary thirty-two years earlier, he was originally apprenticed to Colonel McCabe on the Curragh, before transferring to Atty Persse. While with Persse he rode his first winner, at Bath in 1913, through the good offices of Steve Donoghue, then stable jockey at Stockbridge. Beary completed his apprenticeship in Ireland with J. J. Parkinson, becoming Irish champion jockey in 1920. Returning once again to England, he finished third in the jockeys' table to Donoghue and Charlie Elliott in 1922 and soon became recognised as a brilliant rider of two-year-olds, much in the style of his idol, Danny Maher. Prior to his success on Knight of the Grail he had won the Irish Oaks three years in succession, as well as the Irish St Leger on Kircubbin. Though he had yet to win an English Classic, he had already achieved his greatest riding performance when winning the Cambridgeshire of 1923 on Verdict, beating the mighty French colt Epinard. That year also saw the first of Beary's two suspensions, this time for foul riding. Two years later he had his licence withdrawn for involvement in betting, from which he was later exonerated. His appointment as first jockey to the Aga Khan brought him into increasing conflict with his compatriot, Dick Dawson. Their clash of personalities led to the Aga Khan's string being transferred from Dawson to Frank Butters and began a long-lasting feud between Dawson and Beary. A lengthy and successful career, highlighted by victory in the Epsom Derby on Mid-day Sun, failed to bring financial stability to this inconsistent and irrepressible Irishman. Obliged in consequence to continue riding until well over fifty, he became known as the Peter Pan of racing. Belated retirement to take up training brought instant and fleeting success when Ki Ming won the Two Thousand Guineas for him in 1951. Continuing financial difficulties forced him to resume riding until his final retirement in 1955, at the age of sixty. He lived only a year longer, dying in London after a short illness. Despite his undoubted ability and abundant personal charm, Michael Beary did not endear himself to all members of the racing fraternity, which led one sporting journalist to liken him to oysters . . . either you love them or you loathe them.

Wednesday, 22nd June, 1927   **£4350**   **6 Ran**   **1½m**

The Irish Derby of 5000sovs. Being 4200sovs to the owner of the winner, 200sovs each to the breeder of the winner and owner of the second, 150sovs each to the breeder of the second and owner of the third, and 100sovs to the breeder of the third. For three years old entire colts and fillies. Colts, 8st 12lb; fillies, 8st 8lb. The winner of two races each value 500sovs or of a race value 800sovs, 4lb extra; of two races each value 800sovs or of a race value 1500sovs, 7lb extra; of a race value 4000sovs, 10lb extra; of a race value 6000sovs, 12lb extra. Entrance 5sovs for yearlings entered on 22nd July, 1925. Second entry at 20sovs on 12th October, 1925. Horses not struck out on 2nd June, 1926, pay 25sovs extra, and those not struck out on 5th January, 1927, pay 20sovs in addition. Any surplus on entrance fees will be divided as follows: 75% to the owner of the second and 25% to the owner of the third.

1	Sir Delves Broughton's	KNIGHT OF THE GRAIL (M. Beary) B. colt Prince Galahad – Magical Music by Radium.	9. 5	Farquharson (UK)
2	Mr W. M. G. Singer's	CHANTREY (H. Jelliss) B. colt Gainsborough – Chancery.	9. 5	Taylor (UK)
3	Mr C. Wadia's	ARCHWAY (Joseph Canty) Ch. colt Arch-Gift – Linger Longer Lucy.	9. 2	J. T. Rogers
4	Mr W. Raphael's	KING HARALD (J. Marshall) B. colt Juggernaut – Deborah.	8.12	S. Darling (UK)
5	Mr J. T. Milton's	COINAGE (T. Burns) Ch. colt Tredennis – Bank Note.	8.12	F. Grundy
6	Mr D. Sullivan's	LAVENGRO (H. H. Beasley) B. colt Happy Warrior – Sunbridge.	8.12	Persse (UK)

SP 4/6 Chantrey; 3/1 KNIGHT OF THE GRAIL; 5/1 Archway; 10/1 Lavengro; 100/8 King Harald; 50/1 Coinage.

Neck, Head. 2m 43.2/5s.

Winner trained by Mr Ronald J. Farquharson at Tileshead, Wiltshire.

1928

Although the unprecedented cancellation of the Phoenix Park April meeting had goaded the Government into revoking the Amusement tax, the financial position of Irish racing remained gloomy. The effects of the tax, added to the Turf Club's continued failure to restore public confidence in the integrity of racing, had resulted in racecourse attendances being halved since 1925. The multiplicity of off-course betting shops had become regarded as an even greater social evil than alcohol and the Promised Land of the Totalisator seemed as far away as ever. Nonetheless, the prospect of seeing Athford and Wavetop, the best of what had been rated an exceptional crop of Irish two-year-olds, attempting to keep Ireland's premier prize at home drew a larger crowd than for some years past.

Athford, the first produce of that wonderfully successful union between Bland-ford and Athasi, had won both the Phoenix Plate and Anglesey Stakes, before spreadeagling a good field in the National Produce Stakes. On his only three-year-old appearance he had finished fourth to Baytown in the Irish Two Thousand

Guineas, when not strongly fancied. Wavetop, the other leading juvenile, had finished a close second to Baytown in the first colts' Classic, before running Elton to a neck in the Baldoyle Derby, conceding 15lbs to the winner. The Railway Stakes winner, Cardinal's Ring, appeared to be held by Wavetop, having finished behind him both at the Curragh and Baldoyle. Neither Silver Work, a stablemate of Wavetop, nor Wondrous had any chance on form, though both had won recently. The home-trained quintet faced a numerically equal challenge from across the Irish Sea, headed by O'Curry and Baytown. Bracknell Home, Appledore and Physician completed the raiding party, but did not appear good enough in an above-average year. When trained by Phillie Behan, Baytown had won his first two races, before finishing fourth to Athford in the Phoenix Plate. Since winning the Irish Two Thousand Guineas he had won at Kempton, before finishing a disappointing fifth to O'Curry over one mile at Royal Ascot. O'Curry, a half-brother to O'Dorney out of a winner of the Irish St Leger, had finished third to Flamingo in the English Two Thousand Guineas and won at Newbury, prior to beating Baytown at Ascot. Recent rain had left the ground right for O'Curry, who became a firm favourite.

Having caused some delay at the start, Athford got away quickly, unlike Physician, Bracknell Home and Silver Work. The early running was made by the rank outsider Wondrous from Athford, O'Curry and Baytown. After they had covered half a mile O'Curry and Athford, both doubtful stayers, took it up from Cardinal's Ring, Wavetop, Wondrous and Appledore. Turning into the straight, Athford's stamina gave out, leaving O'Curry to go clear of Cardinal's Ring, Wavetop and Bracknell Home, with Baytown still well off the pace. Two furlongs out O'Curry cried enough, whereupon Wavetop and Appledore joined battle for the lead, pursued by Bracknell Home and the rapidly improving Baytown. No sooner had Wavetop mastered Appledore and been hailed as the winner, than Fox delivered his challenge on Baytown. In the ensuing struggle Wavetop faltered within yards of the line, giving the verdict to Baytown by a neck in a finish which had the crowd roaring with excitement. Bracknell Home stayed on to be third, without ever appearing likely to win. Both Athford and O'Curry patently failed to stay.

Baytown, a lengthy, attractive grey colt, was bred by Charles T. Wallis at his Vesington Stud in Meath. Poor health had prompted Mr Wallis to accept Sir Charles Hyde's offer of £6000 for his unbeaten colt prior to the Phoenix Plate. After that race Baytown had been transferred to Whitsbury, where Norman Scobie acted as private trainer for Sir Charles Hyde. One of the leading breeders in Ireland, Charles Wallis also bred Vesington Star and Prince Meteor, both leading two-year-olds of their respective generations. Encouraged by Baytown's successes, Sir Charles Hyde paid £5000 for his yearling half-brother, who proved a disappointment. Mr Wallis only just lived long enough to see Baytown win the Derby, dying in October of the same year. Baytown's sire, Achtoi, had finished second to Ballaghtobin in the Irish Derby before becoming a successful stallion, while his dam, Princess Herodias, by the French-bred Poor Boy, was a half-sister to Prince Meteor, the leading two-year-old in Ireland in 1928.

Returning in September to the scene of his Classic triumphs, Baytown narrowly missed becoming the first Irish Triple Crown winner, when failing by only a length to concede 6lbs to Law Suit in the Irish Leger. An easy win at Nottingham preceded two really high-class runs at Newmarket. In the first of these Baytown was a close third to the St Leger winner, Fairway, in the Champion Stakes, beating Invershin, winner of the Ascot Gold Cup. Two weeks later Baytown was narrowly beaten in the Cambridgeshire by the Frenchman, Palais Royal. The following day he gained an easy win in the Free Handicap, his twelfth and final race of the season. He raced for a further two seasons, winning three times, before being retired to stud by Sir Charles Hyde, who had refused £20,000 for him as a four-year-old. A sound, tough and consistent racehorse, though some way short of top-class, Baytown was not a success at stud and it was only after his death that his quality as a broodmare sire became apparent. His daughter Kong bred the brilliant sprinter Grey Sovereign, as well as Nimbus, winner of the Epsom Derby. Through Grey Sovereign's prowess at stud Baytown's name appears in many modern pedigrees. Baytown's immediate Curragh victim, Wavetop, became unsound after winning his next race. He later proved himself a good sire of steeplechasers, notably Knight's Crest, whom Cyril Harty saddled to defeat the might Prince Regent in the 1944 Irish Grand National. As a four-year-old Athford was trained by Dick Dawson to win the Newbury Spring Cup, Kempton Jubilee and Doncaster Cup, in the same season that his younger brother, Trigo, won the Epsom Derby, as well as both English and Irish St Legers.

Sir Charles Hyde had been created a baronet of Birmingham in 1922 in recognition of his contributions to medical and educational institutions. As proprietor of the Birmingham Mail and Birmingham Post he was widely respected throughout the newspaper industry and became chairman of the Press Association. Immediately successful upon entering racing in 1923, he used the victory of his filly, Game Shot, in the Gimcrack Stakes as an opportunity to make one of the most pertinent, constructive and memorable speeches yet heard at the historic Gimcrack dinner. Throughout his twenty years in racing he had only one trainer, Norman Scobie. Following his sudden death in 1942, at the age of sixty-six, his Whitsbury Manor Stud was bought by William Hill. The purchase included Sir Charles' home-bred Kong, winner of the Wokingham Stakes. For Hill this daughter of Baytown bred Nimbus and Grey Sovereign.

Norman Scobie was the son of Australia's best-known trainer, James Scobie, who trained four Melbourne Cup winners and no less than eight winners of the Victoria Derby before his death in 1940 at the age of eighty. After a successful start as a trainer in his native land, Norman Scobie emigrated to England at the suggestion of Frank Bullock. He experienced a lean time before becoming private trainer to Sir Charles Hyde, for whom he won many good races with perfectly-prepared horses. Following his employer's sudden death, Norman Scobie became a public trainer. By the time of his retirement in 1956, when he handed over to his jockey son-in-law, Douglas Gunn, he had saddled at least one winner on every course in Britain except Goodwood.

Though Freddie Fox did not ride any Irish Classic winner other than Baytown, he had long been established as one of the leaders of his profession in England. Apprenticed to Fred Pratt, for whom he won the One Thousand Guineas on Atmah in 1911, this intelligent and articulate lightweight went on to be champion jockey in England in 1930, beating Gordon Richards by one winner. Though Atmah's success was followed by almost twenty years of Classic frustration, Freddie Fox gained ample compensation, winning the Two Thousand Guineas on Diolite, the Derby on Cameronian and the St Leger on Firdaussi. His final Classic winner was undoubtedly the best horse he ever rode, Bahram, unbeaten winner of the Triple Crown. Having retired in 1936, this popular and widely-respected Justice of the Peace, known locally as the 'Lord Mayor of Wantage', was killed in a motor accident in 1945.

Wednesday, 27th June, 1928   **£4350**   **10 Ran**   **1½m**

The Irish Derby of 5000sovs. Being 4200sovs to the owner of the winner, 200sovs each to the breeder of the winner and owner of the second, 150sovs each to the breeder of the second and owner of the third, and 100sovs to the breeder of the third. For three years old entire colts and fillies. Colts 8st 12lb; fillies, 8st 8lb. The winner of two races each value 800sovs, or of a race value 800sovs, 4lb extra; of two races each value 800sovs, or of a race value 1500sovs, 7lb extra; of a race value 4000sovs, 10lb extra; of a race value 6000sovs, 12lb extra. Entrance 5sovs for yearlings entered on 21st July, 1926. Second entry at 20sovs on 13th October, 1926. Horses not struck out on 1st June, 1927 pay 25sovs and those not struck out on 4th January, 1928, pay 20sovs in addition. Any surplus on entrance fees will be divided as follows: 75% to the owner of the second and 25% to the owner of the third. One mile and a half.

(158 subs)

1	Sir Charles Hyde's	BAYTOWN (F. Fox)	9. 5	Scobie (UK)
		Gr. colt Achtoi – Princess Herodias by Poor Boy.		
2	Mr A. B. Coyle's	WAVETOP (H. H. Beasley)	8.12	F. Grundy
		B. colt Spearmint – Wavinta.		
3	Mr Siegmond Cohen's	BRACKNELL HOME (F. Winter)	8.12	Tabor (UK)
		B. colt Star and Garter – Inversnaid.		
4	Mrs C. L. Mackean's	CARDINAL'S RING (E. M. Quirke)	9. 2	Blake
		Br. colt Jackdaw – Bernsone.		
5	Mr W. Barnett's	ATHFORD (M. Wing)	9. 5	J. T. Rogers
		B. colt Blandford – Athasi.		
6	Mr D. Sullivan's	O'CURRY (P. Beasley)	9. 5	Persse (UK)
		Ch. colt Abbots Trace – La Paloma. NOT IN GSB.		
7	Lord Glanely's	APPLEDORE (G. Richards)	9. 2	Hogg (UK)
		B. colt Silvern – Grania.		
8	Mr F. S. Myrescough's	SILVER WORK (J. Moylan)	8.12	F. Grundy
		Ch. colt Silvern – Tut Tut.		
9	Sir A. Bailey's	PHYSICIAN (J. Childs)	8.12	R. Day (UK)
		B. colt Son-in-Law – Pharmacie.		
10	Capt. R. B. Brassey's	WONDROUS (James Canty)	8.12	H. Hartigan
		Gr. colt Captivation – Blue Wonder.		

SP   6/4 O'Curry; 4/1 BAYTOWN; 6/1 Wavetop, Athford, Appledore; 8/1 Bracknell Home; 100/7 Cardinal's Ring; 50/1 Physician; 100/1 Bar.

Neck, 4 lengths. 2m 46s.

Winner trained by Mr Norman Scobie at Whitsbury.

1929

Though the state of racing in Ireland showed little sign of recovery, the Irish Derby drew a good-class field and attracted a record crowd. An interesting innovation this year was a broadcast commentary on the races, the commentator being Mr M. P.

Byrne. Hopes of keeping Ireland's richest race at home had risen as a result of Salisbury's repulsion of the invaders in the Irish Two Thousand Guineas. One Irish owner who looked forward to the race with mixed feelings was John, Count McCormack. He had owned Star Eagle, one of the leading fancies, as a two-year-old. When the colt went wrong, Count McCormack had sold him cheaply to Mr F. S. Myerscough, for whom Star Eagle recovered sufficiently to win the Madrid Plate and the Baldoyle Derby before finishing third in the Irish Two Thousand Guineas. Foiled in his attempt to repurchase Star Eagle, McCormack determined to replace him. Acting on the advice of Michael Beary, he gave Lord Astor £13,000 for Cragadour, second in Two Thousand Guineas at Newmarket, but since then a disappointing seventh to Trigo at Epsom, just ahead of N.P.B. These two carried the main Irish hopes. However, the leading market fancy was the Newmarket-trained Kopi, winner of the March Stakes at Newmarket before falling at Tattenham Corner when going well in the Epsom Derby. Walter Earl had turned him out to perfection for this consolation prize. So confident were Kopi's connections of victory that his owner had brought a party over on his yacht, which lay at anchor in Kingstown harbour.

Apart from the principals there was strong support for the Aga Khan's representative, Grand Terrace, winner of the Champagne Stakes at Salisbury and one of the leading two-year-olds of his year, recently successful at Newbury. Adding further to the apparent openness of the race was the widespread racecourse tip for Red Clover, the mount of the ill-fated John Harty. Red Clover was regarded as a certain stayer, yet speedy enough to have made most of the running in the Irish Two Thousand Guineas. N.P.B., ridden by Steve Donoghue's son, Pat, did not appear good enough, nor did the recent winners Crafty Captain and Alne Forest, while Song of Essex, winner of the Marble Hill Stakes, had not run that season. Only hours before the race Star Eagle was found to be lame and, though allowed to take his chance, could not be plated. Pick of the field on looks was undoubtedly the hot favourite, Kopi.

In the race itself Crafty Captain set a very fast early gallop, building up a commanding lead from Star Eagle and Kopi. With just over four furlongs to run Crafy Captain surrendered the lead to Kopi and Star Eagle. Entering the straight Winter seized the rails on the favourite and thereafter the race became a procession. Kopi passed the post an easy winner, five lengths clear of Star Eagle, with the non-staying Cragadour a further four lengths away in third place. The victory of the favourite was well received by the crowd and was widely regarded as confirmation of the belief that only his unfortunate fall had robbed him of success at Epsom. Kopi's delighted owner, who had had £1000 on his horse, declared that he had never experienced such a sporting reception in his life.

The winner was bred near the scene of his triumph by Lieutenant-Colonel Giles Loder, by his Derby winner, Spion Kop, out of Suncroft, A Sunstar mare, who traced to Admiration, the dam of Pretty Polly. In this instance 'Lucky' Loder's fortune had deserted him. Disappointed with Suncroft's previous progeny, he had sold the mare in 1926 and sent Kopi to Ballsbridge yearling sales, where he had been bought by Mr H. Arnold, acting on behalf of James Burns, for 350gns. On being put into training on the Curragh, Kopi was soon discovered to be out of the ordinary and was sold, unraced, to Mr S. B. Joel for £3000. As a two-year-old he fulfilled his early promise, winning at Newbury and Manchester. Kopi only ran once after his Curragh success, being beaten at York in August, when long odds-on. Subsequently retired to stud in France, he achieved nothing. Spion Kop, winner of the Epsom Derby in 1920, became one of the few winners of that race to have a son follow in his footsteps when Felstead triumphed in 1928. Though consistently belittled as a stallion, Spion Kop sired the winners of six Irish Classics and was Champion Sire in Ireland in 1932. Another of his successful colts was The Bastard, who became one of the foremost sires ever imported into Australia, though not before the Australians, with unaccustomed delicacy, renamed him The Buzzard.

Solomon Barnato Joel, familiarly called Solly, had made his fortune in the diamond fields of South Africa, where he and his brother, J. B. Joel, were directors of De Beers. His initial success in racing came with the purchase of that high-class Irish colt, Bachelor's Button, who carried his colours to victory over Pretty Polly in the Ascot Gold Cup. Perhaps his most fortuitous purchase was Polymelus in 1906. Having won his owner a fortune when successful in the Cambridgeshire, Polymelus went on to sire Pommern and Polyphontes. The former carried Joel's 'Pink and green stripes' to win the Two Thousand Guineas and New Derby, while the latter became a dual winner of the Eclipse Stakes. Long Set, bought out of a selling race by Joel for 500gns, won the Doncaster Cup, Cambridgeshire, Royal Hunt Cup and Lincolnshire. Despite this impressive record and the large breeding and training establishments maintained by him, Solly Joel never enjoyed the same Turf success as his brother Jack. Besides his business interests he produced plays in Drury Lane and was an enthusiastic yachtsman. His health failed at a comparatively early age, leading to his death in 1931, when only sixty-five. Six years earlier his daughter made racing history when becoming the first woman to ride the winner of the historic Newmarket Town Plate.

As befitted such a lavish supporter of racing, Solly Joel employed a private trainer, at this time Walter Earl. Earl had been born in Bohemia in 1890, of English parents. His father, a former jockey, trained in Austria-Hungary for more than forty years. When only fourteen, Walter was sent to England to become apprenticed to Willie Waugh, who just then succeeded John Porter at Kingsclere. He rode his first winner at Goodwood in 1906, but soon became to heavy to ride on the flat, whereupon he joined Ivor Anthony's jumping stable as second jockey. A bad fall forced him to retire in 1918 and turn to training, his first patron being Bob Sievier. In 1924 he was appointed private trainer to S. B. Joel at Newmarket. The death of his patron in 1931 led to his becoming a successful public trainer up to the time of his succeeding the recently deceased Colledge Leader as private trainer to Lord Derby. Within four seasons he won each of the five Classics, in addition to preparing that great stayer Alycidon for his memorable triumph in the Ascot Gold Cup. A brilliant judge of yearlings, he saw his judgement confirmed by the Classic successes of Airborne and Chamossaire, both bought by him for former patrons. He was leading trainer in 1945, when he saddled Sun Stream to win the One Thousand Guineas and Oaks. Shortly afterwards he began to suffer from ill-health and died in 1950. Curiously, this talented trainer's early ambition had been to become a surgeon.

First jockey to the powerful Joel stable at this time was Fred Winter, then nearing the end of his riding career. Frederick Neville Winter was born in 1894 and served his apprenticeship with Felix Leach at Newmarket. Having had his first mount in public in 1909, he finished fourth in the jockeys' table only two years later, when scoring his only English Classic success on Cherimoya in the Oaks. In 1914 he went to Germany to ride for the Graditz Stud, only to find himself interned for the duration of the war. Four years enforced absence from the saddle effectively ended any hopes of a long career on the flat, for his weight had increased to such an extent that it required a full season's riding over hurdles for Frank Hartigan to reduce it sufficiently to enable him to accept the post with Solly Joel. The Irish Derby was Fred Winter's last major riding success, for he retired at the end of the 1929 season to be in training. During the latter part of his sadly interrupted riding career he was regarded as a strong and forceful rider, well capable of holding his own in any circumstances. During a lengthy training career, successively at Epsom, Southfleet and Newmarket, he trained such good winners as Medway, Strathcarron, Golden Planet and Spaniards Close. On his death in 1965 he was succeeded at Newmarket by his son John, while his other son, Fred, based at Lambourn, has been as

Wednesday, 26th June, 1929　　　　**£4335**　　　　**9 Ran**　　　　**1½m**

The Irish Derby of 5000sovs. Being 4200sovs to the owner of the winner, 200sovs each to the breeder of the winner and owner of the second, 150sovs each to the breeder of the second and owner of the third, and 100sovs to the breeder of the third. For three years old entire colts and fillies. Colts, 8st 12lb; Fillies, 8st 8lb. The winner of two races each value 500sovs, or of a race value 800sovs, 4lb extra; of two races each value 800sovs, or of a race value 1500sovs, 7lb extra; of a race value 4000sovs, 10lb extra; of a race value 6000 sovs, 12lb extra. Entrance 5sovs for yearlings entered on 20th July, 1927. Second entry at 20sovs on 12th October, 1927. Horses not struck out on 6th June, 1928, pay 25sovs and those not struck out on 3rd January, 1929 pay 20sovs in addition. Any surplus on entrance fees will be divided as follows: 75% to the owner of the second and 25% to the owner of the third. One mile and a half.

1	Mr S. B. Joel's	KOPI (F. Winter)	9. 5	Earl (UK)
		Br. colt Spion Kop – Suncroft by Sunstar.		
2	Mr F. S. Myerscough's	STAR EAGLE (M. Wing)	8.12	F. Grundy
		Ch. colt White Eagle – Herod's Joy.		
3	Count McCormack's	CRAGADOUR (H. Wragg)	9. 2	More O'Ferrall
		B. colt Craig an Eran – Pompadour.		
4	HH Aga Khan's	GRAND TERRACE (M. Beary)	9. 5	R. C. Dawson (UK)
		B. colt Grand Parade – Teresina.		
5	Sir T. Dixon's	CRAFTY CAPTAIN (Joseph Canty)	8.12	Parkinson
		B. colt Captivation – Lough Carra.		
6	Major Shirley's	SONG OF ESSEX (E. M. Quirke)	8.12	J. T. Rogers
		Br. colt Essexford – Cradle Song.		
7	Mr M. Cunningham's	RED CLOVER (J. H. Harty)	8.12	Owner
		Br. colt Cottage – Red Cloak.		
8	Sir E. Eley's	N.P.B. (P. Donoghue)	9. 2	G. Pugh (UK)
		Ch. colt Stratford – Ethel H.		
9	Captain H. Whitworth's	ALNE FOREST (J. Moylan)	8.12	Ussher
		Br. colt Stratford – Queen Elf.		

SP 4/5 KOPI; 5/1 Star Eagle, Cragadour; 6/1 Grand Terrace; 8/1 Red Clover; 10/1 N.P.B.; 50/1 Crafty Captain, Song of Essex; 100/1 Alne Forest.
　　　　　　　　5 lengths, 4 lengths. 2m 36.1/5s.
Winner trained by Mr Walter Earl at Newmarket.

successful in the training of National Hunt horses as he was riding them and one cannot say more than that!

Those left bobbing in Kopi's wake at the Curragh paid scant compliment to the form. Though Star Eagle did win his next race, at prohibitive odds, Cragadour exemplified John McCormack's luck on the Turf by showing progressive disimprovement. Grand Terrace suffered the double ignominy of being gelded and exported, while Crafty Captain, having won a King's Plate at Galway, had to go to Wales to win again. In fact the only subsequent success story belonged to Song of Essex, who became a high-class hurdler in England, where he beat such horses as Insurance, dual winner of the Champion Hurdle. In view of the subsequent careers of Kopi and Trigo, those who plunged on the winner at the Curragh, believing him to have been robbed at Epsom, could count themselves more lucky than shrewd, for their reasoning was patently incorrect. Many years were to elapse before any horse who had proved his ability to win the Epsom Derby laid his reputation on the line in the Curragh equivalent, and then not always with success.

1930

The sixty-fifth renewal of the Irish Derby saw the Pari-Mutuel in action. Introduced at the Fairyhouse Easter meeting and subsequently at all the major courses, it had proved a popular attraction and had so far confounded those sceptics who doubted its ability to remain solvent. More importantly, it had forced the bookmakers to quote more generous odds across the board. As part of the campaign to restore public confidence in the integrity of Irish racing, the Board of Control stipulated that for all flat races runners from the same stable in each race should be coupled for win betting purposes. Although far from record proportions, a sizeable crowd had assembled to witness a depleted home side attempt to break the cross-Channel stranglehold on the Irish Derby.

Once again it seemed that the Fates had conspired against the defenders, for Glannarg, winner of the Irish Two Thousand Guineas from Rock Star and Freighter, had not been entered for the Irish Derby. To make matters worse, Sol de Terre, regarded by Colonel Blake as superior to his Guineas winner, strained a muscle in his hip and was forced to miss the race. Thus Irish hopes hinged mainly on Freighter, Charlie Rogers' colt had won the Madrid Plate and finished a close third to Glannarg and Rock Star in the Guineas, before being beaten a short head by Glannarg in the Baldoyle Derby, albeit in receipt of 12lbs. His chances were not improved when he was found to have injured himself in his box on the eve of the big race. Though the other four home-trained hopefuls had all won races, their prospects were accurately reflected in the betting, in which they were quoted at prices ranging from 25-to-1 to 200-to-1.

The English assault was formidable both in quality and quantity. Least fancied were Atty Persse's Bennachie, second in the Dewhurst Stakes, but recently disappointing and Mrs Edgar Wallace's Adlon, trained and ridden by the brothers Beary.

His six-length success in a mile maiden at 'Ally Pally' hardly seemed good enough. The early favourite was Christopher Robin. Victor Gilpin's charge had won the Greenham Stakes and the St James' Palace Stakes at Ascot, beating Rustom Pascha, Illiad and Singapore. As Illiad had been beaten only a length by Blenheim in the Epsom Derby, this was first-class form. Somewhat surprisingly, Christopher Robin was displaced as favourite by Seer, who, notwithstanding his impressive appearance in the paddock, had finished only sixth at Epsom. Lord Astor's impeccably-bred Writ had won the Craven Stakes and been short-headed in the Dee Stakes before swerving away his chance in his most recent race at Newmarket. Fourth in the betting was the unfashionably-bred maiden, Rock Star, only fourth in the Greenham to Christopher Robin, but subsequently second in the Irish Two Thousand Guineas, caught on the line by Glannarg, having made all the running.

From a level break Inniskeen made the early running from Rock Star, Black Admiral, Pitched Battle, Freighter and Christopher Robin, with Seer trailing, despite the slow gallop. At half way Joe Canty dashed Freighter to the front, pursued by Grey Bachelor. This pair led into the straight, with Rock Star, Writ and Christopher Robin taking closer order behind them. Two furlongs out Freighter weakened, leaving Grey Bachelor ahead of Rock Star, Writ and Christopher Robin. As soon as Wing made his challenge on Rock Star the race was over, for the latter sprinted clear to win decisively from Writ and Christopher Robin. The one-paced Seer stayed on to pass the faltering Grey Bachelor for fourth place. Dispirited patriots attempted to console themselves in the face of this rout by reflecting that the winner and the third were at least Irish-bred.

Rock Star, a plain but workman-like bay colt, was bred by Denis Flynn in the South of Ireland and sold as a foal to Mr E. F. Barry, proprietor of the Ballinahown Stud, where stood the sire, Sherwood Starr. Mr Barry passed the colt on privately to Sir Matthew Wilson. Sherwood Starr, by Sunstar, had scored his solitary racecourse success when winning the Jersey Stakes at Royal Ascot for his breeder, Sir Abe Bailey. Rock Star came from his first crop, his fee at the time being a modest 19gns. Apart from Robber Chief, own-brother to the Irish Derby winner, Sherwood Starr sired nothing else of note prior to his demise at an early age in 1935. Rock Star's dam, Rockmills, was bred by Major Lionel Holliday and sold as a yearling at Ballsbridge for a mere 16gns. She was by Mushroom, so called because of a mushroom-shaped growth on his forehead. Put to stud, unraced, Rockmills also bred Tor, winner of the Irish Cesarewitch in 1929 and Robber Chief, winner of eleven races, including the Manchester Cup.

Rock Star did not run again that season, but was kept busy as a four-year-old, running ten times, always in the best company. Though he did not win, he was second in both the Coronation Cup at Epsom and the valuable John Porter Stakes, besides finishing fourth to Trimdon, Singapore and Salmon Leap in the Ascot Gold Cup. As a five-year-old he won at Lingfield and finished second in the Newbury Summer Cup. The following season he was transferred to Major 'Vandy' Beatty's Newmarket stable and won at Epsom before scoring a surprise win in the Bessborough Stakes at Royal Ascot. This long-serving campaigner did not win in the next two seasons, but did score a final success at Bath in 1936, when trained by Fred Pratt. Writ, runner-up at the Curragh, retired to stud in Ireland and sired Voltus, before being exported to Russia in 1936. Christopher Robin, beaten a short head in the Kempton Jubilee, with Ut Majeur, Rustom Pascha and Diolite behind him, became temperamental and joined the equine emigrés to Australia. Though Rock Star won his Irish Derby on merit and proved himself a good horse then and afterwards, he was fortunate in that Sol de Terre could not take part. The latter reappeared after a five-month absence to win the Irish St Leger with contemptuous ease and went on to emphasize his class and versatility when carrying the welter burden of 10st to victory in the Irish Cambridgeshire a month later.

Wednesday, 25th June, 1930   **£4350**   **12 Ran**   **1½m**

The Irish Derby of 5000sovs. Being 4200sovs to the owner of the winner, 200sovs each to the breeder of the winner and owner of the second, 150sovs each to the breeder of the second and owner of the third, and 100sovs to the breeder of the third. For three years old entire colts and fillies. Colts, 8st 12lb; Fillies, 8st 8lb. The winner of two races each value 500sovs, or of a race value 800sovs, 4lb extra; of two races each value 800sovs, or of a race value 1500sovs, 7lb extra; of a race value 4000sovs, 10lb extra; of a race value 6000sovs, 12lb extra. Entrance 5sovs for yearlings entered on 25th July, 1928. Second entry at 20sovs on 10th October, 1928. Horses not struck out on 5th June, 1928, pay 25sovs and those not struck out on 1st January, 1930 pay 20sovs in addition. Any surplus on entrance fees will be divided as follows: 75% to the owner of the second and 25% to the owner of the third. One mile and a half.

(160 subs)

1	Sir Mathew Wilson's	ROCK STAR (M. Wing)	8.12	W. Nightingall (UK)
		B. colt Sherwood Starr – Rockmills by Mushroom.		
2	Lord Astor's	WRIT (R. Dick)	9. 2	Lawson (UK)
		Br. colt Papyrus – Popingaol.		
3	Lt-Col. Giles Loder's	CHRISTOPHER ROBIN (P. Beasley) Br. colt Phalaris – Dutch Mary.	9. 8	V. Gilpin (UK)
4	Mr G. Peck's	SEER (H. Jelliss)	8.12	J. Cannon (UK)
		B. colt Farman – Disillusion.		
5	Mr A. Lowry's	GREY BACHELOR (E. M. Quirke) Gr. colt Poltava – Bacherlor's Fort.	8.12	H. Powney (UK)
6	Mrs B. M. Webster's	FREIGHTER (Joseph Canty)	8.12	C. A. Rogers
		B. colt Argosy – Impudent Ally.		
7	Mr J. T. Rogers's	WILD CORN (E. Gardner)	8.12	Owner
		Ch. colt Essexford – Wild Wheat.		
8	Mrs Edgar Wallace's	ADLON (M. Beary)	8.12	J. Beary (UK)
		Ch. colt Zria's Charm – Linggi.		
9	Lord Wavertree's	BENNACHIE (H. H. Beasley)	9. 2	Persse (UK)
		Bl. colt Papyrus – Mountain Light.		
10	Major Shirley's	INNISKEEN (P. Fitzgerald)*	8.12	J. T. Rogers
		B. colt Hainault – Sari Bahr.		
11	Mr H. I. Ussher's	BLACK ADMIRAL (J. Moylan)	8.12	Owner
		Bl/Br. colt Jackdaw – Short Line.		
12	Mr S. Vlasto's	PITCHED BATTLE (T. Burns)	8.12	More O'Ferrall
		B. colt Battle-axe – Happen.		

SP 3/1 Seer; 7/2 Christopher Robin; 4/1 Writ; 5/1 ROCK STAR; 10/1 Freighter; 100/8 Grey Bachelor; 25/1 Bennachie, Wild Corn, Adlon; 40/1 Pitched Battle; 66/1 Inniskeen; 200/1 Black Admiral. TOTE (2/- unit) 17/. Places 5/6, 4/6, 5/6.
2½ lengths, 3 lengths. 2m 41.3/5s.
Winner trained by Mr W. Nightingall at Epsom.

*Mr P. F. Cannon (Starter) reported P. Fitzgerald for disobedience at the start, the Stewards fined him 5sovs. and severely cautioned him as to his future conduct.

Rock Star's owner, Sir Matthew Wilson, was a Yorkshireman, descendant of an old-established North-country family. Born in 1875, Colonel Sir Matthew Richard Henry Wilson DSO 4th Baronet, had a distinguished military career as Military Secretary to the British Commander-in-Chief in India, where he won the Indian Grand National with Kaffiopan. He retired from the Army in 1912 and two years later became Unionist MP for Bethnal Green. At the outbreak of the 1914–18 war he rejoined the Army and was awarded the DSO for his services in Egypt. In partnership with Lady Curzon of Kedleston he owned Arctic Star, winner of the Goodwood Stakes and Cesarewitch in 1928. Though Sir Matthew Wilson lived until 1958, Rock Star was the last good horse to carry his 'Cerise, bronze cap'.

Despite having held a trainer's licence for only three seasons, Walter Nightingall was already firmly established among the leaders of his profession. Born in 1895, he was the son of William Nightingall, jockey and trainer, who he succeeded in 1926 as master of South Hatch, Epsom. His uncle, Arthur Nightingall, had ridden three winners of the Grand National. Walter Nightingall never gave promise of becoming a successful jockey, but rapidly proved his ability as a trainer, saddling almost one hundred winners within twelve months of succeeding his father. During a career spanning more than forty years he trained such good horses as Straight Deal, winner of the Derby in 1944, Colonist II, High Hat and Vienna, all high-class winners for Sir Winston Churchill and Niksar, winner of the Two Thousand Guineas in 1965, three years before his trainer's death. Throughout his career he was assisted by his sister and after his death the yard was taken by the former Champion Jockey, 'Scobie' Breasley. Particularly partial to Park courses, Walter Nightingall became celebrated for his Saturday winners. Over the years he employed Tommy Carey, Tommy Gosling and Duncan Keith as stable jockeys. On retiring to take up training, each demonstrated the benefit of his experience at South Hatch with this most astute and consistent of trainers.

1931

This year's Irish Derby showed a marked drop in prize money, being worth over £1000 less to the winner than ten years earlier. This reflected the continuing decline in the fortunes of Irish racing, which imminent political developments would soon accentuate. The second 'Irish Sweep' had been held on the Aintree Grand National in March 1931, the winning ticket being worth a stupendous £354,724 to one Emilio Scala, a Battersea cafe proprietor. However, another thirty years were to elapse before the sponsorship by the Irish Sweep would transform the Irish Derby into a race of international significance.

In contrast to the previous year, there was only one English challenger for Ireland's premier prize. Trained at Middleham by the leading Northern trainer, veteran M. D. Peacock, Sir Edward Hanmer's Gallini was regarded as the best colt in the North of England for many years. Winner of two of his juvenile starts and fourth in the Gimcrack Stakes, he had gone lame in the paddock before the Epsom

Derby. Having been hurriedly replated, he made the running for ten furlongs before losing a front plate, eventually finishing a close and unlucky fifth to Cameronian. Mindful of the fact that English raiders had won the last nine runnings of the Irish Derby, few cared to oppose Gallini, who, despite being bandaged in front, started at slight odds-on. He was opposed by five Irish-trained runners, among them Double Arch, narrow winner of the Irish Two Thousand Guineas, but thought to be unsuited by the dead going. Both Sir Walter Raleigh and Beaudelaire had shown winning form, though nothing comparable to that of Gallini. The field was completed by Sea Serpent and his pacemaker, Knight of the Mist. Trained by Phillie Behan at Mountjoy Lodge, Sea Serpent had only seen a racecourse twice in his life, winning on each occasion. On his solitary appearance as a two-year-old he had won the Railway Stakes, beating Bayard, rated the best colt of his generation in Ireland. Making his three-year-old debut at the end of May, Sea Serpent had won the Baldoyle Derby convincingly from Beaudelaire and Soliped, despite running green. Notwithstanding his unbeaten record and the services of the champion jockey, Joe Canty, Sea Serpent was not widely expected to alter the dismal record of home-trained runners in the Irish Derby.

From a perfect start Knight of the Mist went into an immediate lead, ten lengths clear of Double Arch, Sea Serpent, Beaudelaire, Gallini and Sir Walter Raleigh. After they had covered two furlongs Gallini moved into second place behind the pacemaker. At the half way mark, Knight of the Mist, a short runner, gave way to Gallini, who began to force the pace from Double Arch and Sea Serpent, with Sir Walter Raleigh improving. Down the hill, Double Arch and Sir Walter Raleigh drew abreast of Gallini, who rapidly came under pressure. Sir Walter Raleigh and Double Arch led into the straight, closely pursued by Sea Serpent and Beaudelaire, as the favourite fell back, clearly beaten. Two furlongs out, Double Arch compounded, leaving Sir Walter Raleigh in the lead from Sea Serpent and Beaudelaire. At the distance Canty delivered his characteristic coup de grâce on Sea Serpent, who sprinted away to win easily from the staying Beaudelaire and Sir Walter Raleigh. The winner returned to an enthusiastic reception, immediately being acclaimed the leader of his generation on a line through Gallini, beaten further than he had been at Epsom. This somewhat optimistic assessment overlooked the fact that the hapless Gallini had broken down before the straight had been reached.

Ironically, Sea Serpent was the only English-bred member of the field, having been bred by his owner at his Gog Magog Hills Stud in Cambridgeshire, by Golden Myth out of the Spearmint mare, Seabloom. By Tredennis, Golden Myth was a

Mr. J. H. H. Peard. Count McCormack. Mr. More O'Ferrall. Mr. F. Harold Clarke. J. Canty. E. Gardner.

Some of the Principals in the Irish Derby of 1931. Source: Irish Field.

Embargo, *one of five Irish Derby winners ridden by Steve Donoghue, who was also closely involved with the colt's preparation at Shrewton, where Donoghue then lived with Eleanor, Lady Torrington. Source:* The Irish Horse.

Phillie Behan, *pictured here holding Sea Serpent, his solitary winner of the Irish Derby. Five times leading trainer in Ireland, Phillie Behan had no equal as a trainer of two-year-olds. His appearance belies the fact that Steve Donoghue's father-in-law once went to scale at 4st 7lbs. Source:* Irish Field.

high-class racehorse, winning both the Gold Vase and Ascot Gold Cup in 1922, both in record times, before reverting to middle distances to win the Eclipse Stakes. By these performances Golden Myth established Jack Jarvis' reputation as a trainer and also launched Jarvis' apprentice, Charlie Elliott into the racing limelight. In his autobiography Sir Jack Jarvis paid tribute to Golden Myth as the horse that earned him recognition as a trainer, before going on to explain how the same horse was almost the ruination of his stable. On his retirement to stud at Mentmore, Golden Myth was extremely well patronised, with the result that his erstwhile trainer soon found his yard full of Golden Myth's stock. Unfortunately, Golden Myth proved to be an utter failure as a sire. Jarvis' rueful description of his stock is as follows: 'Apart from the painful fact that most of them just could not go, they declined to do even the little of which they were capable.' Sea Serpent was the only good horse sired by Golden Myth in over twenty seasons at stud. Seabloom, herself winner of three races, bred five other winners, including Sea Crag, winner of the Esher Cup and Britannia Stakes in 1928.

Sea Serpent was subsequently found to have wrenched himself when winning at the Curragh and consequently did not run again that year. Transferred to the care of Dick Dawson, he was expected to prove himself a champion as a four-year-old. Regrettably, these expectations were not realised, for having finished second to Salmon Leap at Newmarket on his initial outing, he finished last in the Coronation Cup before his final appearance in the Newbury Summer Cup, again down the field behind Anna and Rock Star, the previous winner of the Irish Derby. Retired to his owner's stud the following season, Sea Serpent failed to sire anything of note in his

Joe Canty, *widely regarded as the greatest Irish jockey of them all. Seven times Irish champion, his record of 117 winners in one year (1925) remains unchallenged half a century later. Source:* Irish Field.

Sir Harold Gray, *owner-breeder of the 1931 Irish Derby winner, Sea Serpent. He bred two further Irish Derby winners, Mondragon (1939) and Zarathustra (1954). Source:* Irish Field.

first few crops and was later transferred to the Loughbrown Stud on the Curragh. In 1939 he suddenly hit the headlines through the Irish Classic successes of Mondragon and Serpent Star, which resulted in his heading the list of sires in Ireland that year. However, his fortunes plummeted as suddenly as they had risen, with the result that this possibly high-class racehorse ended his days in the fastnesses of County Cavan.

Beaudelaire went on to win the Irish St Leger, thus providing a welcome change of luck for Count McCormack, but then broke down. After four seasons at Kildangan Stud, he was sent to Russia. Sir Walter Raleigh won four races in England, trained by Cecil Boyd-Rochfort. Retired to the Brownstown Stud, he sired the ill-fated New Comet, who died within weeks of winning the Phoenix Stakes. An own-brother to the dual Irish Classic winner, Smokeless, Sir Walter Raleigh also sired King of the Jungle, twice winner of the Galway Hurdle and subsequently a successful National Hunt sire. Sir Walter Raleigh appears in latter-day pedigrees as the maternal great-grandsire of Roman Warrior and Wolver Hollow. Gallini broke down irreparably in the Irish Derby and was put to stud in Shropshire. Double Arch won in England for Colledge Leader, before being shipped to India, while the gelded Knight of the Mist won three times as a four-year-old. By curious coincidence, just as Sea Serpent's sire had established one great trainer's reputation, so the seventeen victories of his son, Pelorus, in the late 'forties, signalled the emergence of a rising star in the ranks of Irish trainers . . . P. J. Prendergast.

Mr (later Sir) Harold Gray was born in County Down and though he lived mostly in England, raced principally in the land of his birth, where he headed the list of winning owners in 1931, due largely to the successes of Sea Serpent. He registered his 'Red, white sash' for the first time in 1892 and saw them carried successfully in England, Ireland and France up to the time of his death in the latter country in 1951. Besides Sea Serpent, he bred Nenette, winner of the National Produce Stakes in 1919 and Mondragon, winner of the Irish Derby in the colours of P. J. Ruttledge. Harold Gray did not live to see the best horse he ever bred, Zarathustra, triumph in the Irish Derby and St Leger in 1954, when owned by his son, Mr Terence Gray.

Sea Serpent was the first and only winner of the Irish Derby trained by Phillie Behan, the greatest two-year-old trainer of his era. Born in 1866, Philip Behan was one of seven brothers, all of whom were jockeys. Apprenticed to Joseph French at Rossmore Lodge, he quickly emerged as the leading lightweight jockey in Ireland, being able to go to scale at 4st 7lbs. However, he was soon beset by weight problems, which obliged him to follow in his brothers' footsteps, riding over fences, until his retirement in 1891. His first training post was as private trainer to J. C. Sullivan, for whom he won the celebrated Cambridgeshire of 1900. The outcome of this race led to the abrupt ending of Tod Sloan's riding career in England. Learning of Sloan's attempts to arrange the result of the race so as to ensure the success of his own mount, Codoman, J. C. Sullivan instructed Behan to bring over the best apprentice he could find, conceal his identity until the last possible moment and thus thwart Sloan's scheme. Behan chose well, for the boy selected was none other than John Thompson, who rode an impeccable race to win from Sloan's mount. Sloan's

Wednesday, 24th June, 1931	**£3762 10 0**	**6 Ran**	**1½m**

The Irish Derby of 5000sovs. The winner will receive 75%, second 15%, third 10% of the stakes after deduction of bonuses of 200sovs to the owner (at entry) of the winner, 150sovs to the owner (at entry) of the second and 100sovs to the owner (at entry) of the third. For three years old entire colts and fillies. Colts, 8st 12lb; Fillies, 8st 8lb. The winner of two races each value 500sovs, or of a race value 800sovs, 4lb extra; of two races each value 800sovs, or of a race value 1500sovs, 7lb extra; of a race value 4000sovs, 10lb extra; or a race value 6000sovs, 12lb extra. Entrance 5sovs for yearlings entered on 24th July, 1929. Second entry at 20sovs 9th October, 1929. Horses not struck out on 4th June, 1930 pay 25sovs extra and those not struck out on 7th January, 1931 pay 25sovs in addition. One mile and a half.

(187 subs)

1 Mr H. S. Gray's   SEA SERPENT (Joseph Canty)   8.12   P. Behan
Ch. colt Golden Myth – Seabloom by Spearmint.

2 Count McCormack's   BEAUDELAIRE (T. Burns)   8.12   More O'Ferrall
Ch. colt Argosy – Morgan le Fey.

3 Mr J. H. H. Peard's   SIR WALTER RALEIGH   8.12   Owner
    (H. H. Beasley)   B. colt Prince Galahad – Smoke Lass.

4 Sir Edward Hanmer's   GALLINI (J. Taylor)   9. 2   Peacock (UK)
B. colt Spion Kop – Chicken Pie.

5 Mr J. T. Rogers's   DOUBLE ARCH (E. Gardner)   9. 5   Owner
B. colt Arch-Gift – Twincat.

6 Mr W. J. Kelly's   KNIGHT OF THE MIST (M. Wing)8.12   P. Behan
Ch. colt, Knight of the Garter – Mountain Mist.

SP 10/11 Gallini; 5/2 SEA SERPENT; 100/16 Sir Walter Raleigh; 100/12 Beaudelaire; 10/1 Double Arch; 500/1 Knight of the Mist. TOTE (2/- unit) 8/-. Places 3/6, 7/6.
2½ lengths, 2 lengths. 2m 45.2/5s.
Winner trained by Mr Philip Behan at Mounjoy Lodge, Curragh.

abusive behaviour towards Thompson after the race was reported to the Stewards, which led to the whole unsavoury story being revealed. Sloan never rode in England again.

Prior to his retirement from the saddle, Phillie Behan married the daughter of Dan Broderick, master of Mountjoy Lodge. On the death of his father-in-law, Behan assumed control of these historic stables and trained there with unbroken success until less than a year before his death in 1938. He was Champion trainer in Ireland on four occasions and saddled the winners of six Irish Classics. However, he is best remembered as a brilliant trainer of two-year-olds, invariably the greater part of his string. He trained Grand Parade to win the Anglesey and National Stakes, prior to that colt's success in the Epsom Derby. Grand Parade was only one of seven Behan-trained winners of the National Stakes, in addition to six winners of the Anglesey Stakes and five each of the Railway Stakes and Phoenix Stakes, these comprising the most important juvenile races in Ireland at the time. It was Phillie Behan who gave his future son-in-law, Steve Donoghue, his first major break as a jockey. He was succeeded at Mountjoy Lodge by Martin Quirke, whose son Stephen now trains there.

1932

As a popular attraction the Irish Derby of 1932 had to compete with the Eucharistic Congress, held in Dublin during the last week in June to mark the 1500th anniversary of St Patrick's arrival in Ireland. As a prelude to the biggest public festival since the founding of the Free State, a General Election had been held in February, which resulted in Eamon de Valera's Fianna Fail party being returned to power for the first time. In keeping with his opposition to the Treaty of 1921, Mr de Valera abolished the Oath of Allegiance to the King, dispensed with the office of Governor General and withheld the payment of Land Annuities to the British Government. This last action provoked British sanctions against Irish produce, including bloodstock. The consequences for the Irish breeding and racing industries were to prove calamitous.

Against this ominous background the Irish Derby attracted only one English challenger. However, this was sufficient to strike despondency into Irish hearts, for the solitary raider was none other than Dastur, second in both the Two Thousand Guineas and Epsom Derby, where he had been narrowly beaten by April the Fifth. On his last outing he had won the King Edward Stakes at Ascot in a common canter. Of the home side, Lindley had won the Irish Two Thousand Guineas, beating Hill Song and Solicitous at level weights, with Call Him and Kingsmere unplaced. Lindley had since proved difficult to train, owing to the prevailing hard ground, and Hill Song, now 7lbs better off for his half-length defeat, was the more strongly fancied. Gold Amulet had won the Baldoyle Derby, with Corcy in third place, but as the latter had since finished a somewhat remote fourth at Epsom, the form did not appear good enough to pose any real threat to Dastur. The Aga Khan's colt was always odds-on, with only Hill Song seriously backed to beat him, despite doubts concerning his courage.

The early running was made by Trapper and Kingsmere, who raced clear of Lindley, with Dastur and Corcy the backmarkers. At half way Kingsmere began to run out of steam, leaving Trapper many lengths ahead of his field. Down the hill Trapper maintained his long lead from Hill Song, Call Him, Lindley and Dastur. Entering the straight Trapper could be seen to falter, as Hill Song and Dastur began to close upon him. Inside the last two furlongs Hill Song drew level with the longtime leader, with Dastur tucked in behind this pair on the rails. With barely a furlong to run Trapper weakened suddenly, hampering Dastur. Having extricated the favourite, Beary then realised that Hill Song was still going ominously easily. With desperate urgency he drove Dastur in pursuit of Hill Song. Neck-and-neck the two colts raced for the line. As had been feared, Hill Song showed little inclination to struggle, yielding in the last few strides to Dastur, who won by a head, with Trapper staying on gallantly to be third. A new record for the Irish Derby of 2mins 35.6secs indicated the merit of Dastur's performance.

Dastur, a well-made brown colt, was bred by HH the Aga Khan from that wonderfully successful broodmare Friar's Daughter, then located at Sheshoon Stud, managed for the Aga Khan by Sir Henry Greer. Bought as a yearling for 250gns, Friar's Daughter won as a two-year-old and bred eight winners of twenty-six races, worth over £57,000. The best of her progeny was unquestionably Bahram, unbeaten winner of the Triple Crown in 1935. Dastur was by Solario, winner of the St Leger and Ascot Gold Cup for Sir John Rutherford. An immediate success at stud, Solario realised the then enormous price of 47,000gns on the death of his owner in 1932. He headed the list of sires in 1937 and sired two Derby winners prior to his death in 1945. Having won a two-horse race for the Sussex Stakes, Dastur then finished second to his stable companion Firdaussi in the St Leger, thus achieving the unfortunate distinction of finishing second in each of the Triple Crown races. As a four-year-old he won the Coronation Cup and dead-heated with the three-year-old Chatelaine in the Champion Stakes, before being retired to the Egerton Stud. After

Dastur, *winner of the Irish Derby in 1932 and runner-up in the three Triple Crown races. Three years later his half-brother, Bahram, carried off the coveted Triple Crown for their owner-breeder, the Aga Khan. Source:* The Irish Horse.

an unspectacular start to his stud career, he was transferred to the Old Connell stud, near Newbridge in 1940. From his first Irish crop came Suntop, whose successes in the Irish One Thousand Guineas and Oaks contributed to his heading the list of sires in Ireland in 1943. His best winner was Umiddad, second in the Epsom Derby and winner of the Gold Cup. More successful as a sire of broodmares, Dastur was responsible for the dams of Diableretta, Darius and The Cobbler, in addition to siring Dasaratha, dam of the Irish Classic winners Do Well and Nashua. Though he did not leave a successful son at stud in these islands, Dhoti in Australia, Gold Nib in New Zealand and Dharabanga in Sweden all proved influential sires in their respective territories.

Dastur was the first of four Irish Derby winners trained by Frank Butters for the Aga Khan, who described him in his memoirs as 'the greatest trainer of all'. Joseph Arthur Frank Butters came from a racing background. He was born in Vienna in 1879 to Joe Butters, a respected former jockey and prominent trainer, who had married Janet Waugh, daughter of his former master, James Waugh, the Newmarket

Wednesday, 29th June, 1932	**£3557 10 0**	**10 Ran**	**1½m**

The Irish Derby of 5000sovs. The winner will receive 75%, second 15%, third 10% of the stakes after deduction of bonuses of 200sovs to the owner (at entry) of the winner, 150sovs to the owner (at entry) of the second and 100sovs to the owner (at entry) of the third. For three years old entire colts and fillies. Colts, 8st 12lb; fillies, 8st 8lb. The winner of two races each value 500sovs, or of a race value 700sovs, 4lb extra; of two races each value 700sovs, or of a race value 1400sovs, 7lb extra; of a race value 4000sovs, 10lb extra. Entrance 5sovs for yearlings entered on 23rd July, 1930. Second entry at 20sovs 8 October, 1930. Horses not struck out on 3rd June, 1931 pay 25sovs extra and those not struck out on 6th January, 1932 pay 25sovs in addition. One mile and a half.

(140 subs)

1 HH Aga Khan's	DASTUR (M. Beary)	9. 5	Butters (UK)
	B. colt Solario – Friar's Daughter by Friar Marcus.		
2 Major Shirley's	HILL SONG (E. Gardner)	8.12	J. T. Rogers
	Br. colt Spion Kop – Cradle Song.		
3 Mr J. Johnson's	TRAPPER (John Doyle)	8.12	Collins
	B. colt Hurstwood – Gorse.		
4 Major Dixon's	CALL HIM (Joseph Canty)	8.12	Behan
	Br. colt Call Boy – Trefoil.		
5 Capt. G. F. Dunne's	LINDLEY (M. Wing)	9. 5	Blake
	Br. colt Spion Kop – Teplitz.		
6 Mr R. S. Croker's	CORCY (E. M. Quirke)	8.12	C. Brabazon
	B. colt Achtoi – Babs.		
7 Mr H. S. Gray's	GOLD AMULET (T. Burns)	9. 2	Behan
	B. colt Golden Myth – Nennette.		
8 Mrs C. L. Mackean's	SOLICITOUS (J. Moylan)	8.12	Blake
	Ch. colt Soldennis – Cascatel.		
9 Hon Mrs Brinsley Plunket's	GRAND ECART (B. Curran)	8.12	More O'Ferrall
	Bl. colt Grand Parade – Camargo.		
10 Mr C. Odlum's	KINGSMERE (A. Barrett)	8.12	Blake
	B. colt Roi Herode – Ladoga.		

SP 4/7 DASTUR; 4/1 Hill Song; 10/1 Gold Amulet, Corcy; 100/6 Lindley; 20/1 Call Him, Solicitous; 50/1 Trapper, 500/1 Bar. TOTE (2/- unit) 4/-. Places 3/-, 2/6, 11/6.
Head, 2 lengths, 2m 35.3/5s.
Winner trained by Mr Frank Butters at Newmarket.

trainer. Educated in England, Frank Butters assisted his father in Austria-Hungary, before becoming private trainer to Mautrer de Markham, one of the country's leading owners. Having been interned during World War One, Frank Butters moved to Italy, where he won all the Classics with horses from the Bellata stable. In 1926 he accepted a four-year contract with Lord Derby to take over from the Hon. George Lambton, who became Lord Derby's racing manager. During that period he saddled the winners of four Classics and was leading trainer on two occasions. The worldwide economic depression meant that Butters' contract was not renewed, George Lambton being reinstated as trainer at Stanley House. Thus, at the age of fifty-two, Frank Butters found himself forced to embark upon a new career as a public trainer, setting up at Fitzroy House. One of his first patrons was Sir Alfred Butt, followed soon afterwards by the Aga Khan, who had parted company abruptly with Dick Dawson. Between 1932 and his enforced retirement, as the result of a road accident in 1949, Frank Butters was leading trainer no less than six times, winning a further eleven Classics with such as Mahmoud and Bahram, the greatest horse he ever trained. Frank both in name and nature, he was an enthusiastic gardener and budgerigar fancier, keeping upwards of one hundred birds, each of which he knew by name. Of all the top-class jockeys to ride for him during his long and distinguished career, he nominated the Australian 'Brownie' Carslake as his favourite. This dignified and conscientious master of his profession died on the last day of 1957, having lived in retirement since his accident eight years previously.

Hill Song gained some compensation for his narrow defeat when winning the Irish St Leger on his next appearance, beating Trapper and Lindley. In doing so he set an example for his full-brother, Battle Song, who followed an identical progress in the Irish Classics of 1936. Trapper was bought by the Hon. Dorothy Paget, for whom he won several small races, without ever threatening to displace Golden Miller as the object of her affections. Both Call Him and Lindley won their share of races. Corcy was exported to India at the end of his three-year-old career. Kingsmere and Grand Ecart accomplished little, while Solicitous never showed anything of the ability of his full-brother Sol de Terre, the best older horse in Ireland at the time. Out of luck in the English Classics, Dastur would have been misfortunate indeed not to have won the Irish Derby.

1933

The effects of the Economic War had quickly made themselves felt by the racing and breeding industries in Ireland. The cream of Irish bloodstock had been speedily transferred to England to avoid the 40 per cent import duty imposed by the British Government. Attendances at racemeetings, which had only just begun to show signs of recovery, dwindled again. As a result, with the exception of the Derby meeting, Curragh fixtures were limited to two-day affairs. The prospect of continuing unprofitability compelled the Turf Club to announce that the value of the 1934 Derby would be reduced. However, none of these gloomy factors served to diminish the customary English challenge for Ireland's greatest race.

Most formidable of the three challengers appeared to be the Aga Khan's Shamsuddin, second to the Epsom Derby winner Hyperion in both the Chester Vase and the Prince of Wales's Stakes at Ascot. He was accompanied by Harinero, own-brother to Trigo and winner of the Greenham Stakes, prior to running unplaced in both the Two Thousand Guineas and Derby. The English trio was completed by Myosotis, winner of the Lingfield Derby Trial, but unplaced behind Hyperion at Epsom. Of the five home-trained runners, only Count McCormack's Franz Hals possessed comparable form. This Gainsborough colt had finished seventh at Epsom, ahead of both Harinero and Myosotis. These four dominated the betting, with Shamsuddin slightly preferred to Franz Hals. The remainder, including Rock Star's half-brother Golden Glen, were dismissed as rank outsiders.

From a level break Swindon Light showed the way to Franz Hals, Golden Glen and Shamsuddin, with Harinero the back-marker in the early stages. After four furlongs Swindon Light held a clear lead from Franz Hals, Golden Glen, Shamsuddin and Harinero, with Matona bringing up the rear. This order was maintained past half way and down the hill, where Swindon Light compounded rapidly, giving way to Shamsuddin and Franz Hals, with Golden Glen and Harinero in close pursuit. In the straight Beary kicked for home on Shamsuddin, chased by Golden Glen and Harinero, with Franz Hals dropping back. In contrast to the previous year, Beary now found himself in the role of the mouse rather than the cat. A hasty backward glance caused him to ride for dear life, for the cat was Cecil Ray, who produced Harinero with a long, smooth, irresistible run, which saw him sweep past the struggling Shamsuddin to win comfortably by a length and a half. Golden Glen finished a length further back in third place, ahead of the non-staying Franz Hals. Beary reported that Shamsuddin had simply failed to stay the stiff twelve furlongs.

Bred at the Cloghran Stud by his owner, Harinero was a bay colt by Blandford, the outstanding sire of his era, out of Athasi. Blandford was by Swynford out of Blanche, one of the foundation mares of the National Stud at Tully. As a foal he contracted pneumonia so severely as to prevent his being sent up for sale with the main draft of Tully yearlings. Submitted later at the Newmarket December Sales, he was bought for 730gns by Dick Dawson, in partnership with his brother Sam, proprietor of the Cloghran Stud. Difficult to train, Blandford ran only four times, winning three of his races and being beaten only a short head in the other. A bowed tendon necessitated his retirement to the Cloghran Stud. Despite his brief race-course career, Blandford was considered by his astute trainer to be the equal of his contemporary Captain Cuttle, winner of the Epsom Derby and likewise chronically unsound. Despite being slow to cover his mares, Blandford was an instant and outstanding success at stud, siring four winners of the Epsom Derby, in addition to the outstanding French racehorse Brantome. In 1934 he headed the list of winning sires for the first time, with winners of 57 races worth £75,700, thus beating the record created by Stockwell sixty-eight years previously. Shortly after Harinero's victory at the Curragh Blandford joined the exodus of Irish bloodstock, being moved to Dick Dawson's stud at Whatcombe, another casualty of the Economic War and sad loss to Irish breeders. Blandford died of pneumonia in 1935, after only ten seasons at stud, but already secure in his reputation as one of the most successful stallions in the history of the thoroughbred.

Whereas Blandford's success as a sire could be related to his pedigree, conformation and racecourse ability, the qualifications of Athasi, his most famous mate, to breed anything of merit were much more difficult to foresee. Bred in 1917 by Peter Murphy of Poulaphouca, out of his Irish Oaks winner Athgreany, Athasi was sold as a yearling, following the death of her breeder. The purchaser was David 'Jubilee' Barnett, a Belfast grain importer. Though he did not claim clairvoyance as an excuse for his actions, the groom entrusted with the safe delivery of Mr Barnett's fortuitous purchase became so hopelessly intoxicated in the course of his journey as to result in his being put in gaol for the night, accompanied by the future dam of an Epsom Derby winner and two dual Irish Classic winners. As a racemare Athasi showed little ability, winning two long-distance handicaps in Scotland. Despite her modest record and uninspired pedigree, Athasi was given every chance at stud when mated with Blandford. To him she bred Athford, winner of the Phoenix Stakes, Newbury Cup, Doncaster Cup and Kempton Jubilee. Repeated matings with Blandford produced Trigo, winner of the Derby, St Leger and Irish St Leger, Harinero, winner of the Irish Derby and Irish St Leger, Primero, winner of the same two Irish Classics, Centeno, grandam of Quare Times, Harina, grandam of Tulyar and finally Avena, winner and dam of winners. In addition this marvellous mare bred two winners by Umidwar and one by Cygnus.

Harinero finished third to Statesman at Hurst Park on his reappearance in August. He then ran fourth to King Salmon at York, before running an excellent race to be fifth to Hyperion in the St Leger at Doncaster. His final race that season was the Irish St Leger, which he won by a head from Golden Glen in a thrilling finish. This success concluded a wonderful Irish season for his connections. Mr Barnett headed the list of winning owners, while Dick Dawson, also successful in the Irish Oaks with his own filly Salar, headed the trainers' table. Cecil Ray, besides his Classic wins on Harinero and Salar, won the valuable Phoenix Stakes on His Reverence, trained by 'Ginger' Wellesley. The following year Harinero won the Rosebery Memorial at Epsom, before being exported to Australia, where he proved quite successful as a stallion. Of those that finished behind Harinero little need be said. Shamsuddin won his next race, the Welsh Derby at Chepstow, before being sent to the West Indies, while Matona won the Irish Cambridgeshire as a six-year-old gelding. Though by no means an outstanding winner of the Irish Derby, Harinero, in winning two Irish Classics, proved himself a worthy member of his illustrious family.

Harinero was bred and owned by Mr William Barnett, chairman of W. & R. Barnett Ltd, a Belfast firm of grain importers. In 1925, following the death of his brother, Mr Barnett purchased Athasi from his estate and subsequently boarded her at Cloghran Stud, with marvellous results, as earlier related. In 1933 Mr Barnett transferred both Athasi and Trigo to the Aston Park Stud near Oxford, which he had recently acquired from Clarence Hailey. The success of this venture was reflected by the very high prices obtained for the Aston Park yearlings in 1946, the year in which both Mr Barnett and Trigo died. Aside from his business and bloodstock interests, this cheerful sportsman was a staunch supporter of many charitable institutions in his native Belfast, where he died at the age of seventy-seven. Relative to the scale on which he raced – Trigo was one of his only two runners in 1929 – William Barnett must be counted one of the most fortunate owners of his era.

Though born in England, Cecil Ray made his reputation in South Africa, where he was apprenticed to the Johannesburg trainer, T. P. Johnson. There he rode more than 700 winners, before returning to the land of his birth to ride for Eddie de Mestre. Some time later he became associated with Dick Dawson's stable, as first jockey to Lord Caernarvon. His principal winners in England included Plantago in the Coronation Cup and Caymanas in the Royal Hunt Cup, while the closest he came to Classic renown was when the favourite, Diolite, faded to finish third in the 1930 Derby. A rider of wide and varied experience, Cecil Ray seldom volunteered an opinion, but could be eloquent if asked his views. Despite his apparent reserve he took a keen interest in the progress of apprentices, whom he was ever willing to advise.

At the end of the 1934 season, just as his record of consistent if unspectacular success looked likely to promote him to the first flight, Cecil Ray fell foul of authority in a somewhat curious way. Having finished second in a race at Liverpool, Ray lodged an objection to the winner, owned by Lord Derby. For reasons never revealed, the local Stewards not only overruled his objection and withheld his deposit, but referred the matter to the Jockey Club, with the extraordinary result

Wednesday, 21st June, 1933   **£3557 10 0**   **8 Ran**   **1½m**

The Irish Derby of 5000sovs. The winner will receive 75%, second 15%, third 10% of the stakes after deduction of bonuses of 200sovs to the owner (at entry) of the winner, 150sovs to the owner (at entry) of the second and 100sovs to the owner (at entry) of the third. For three years old entire colts and fillies. Colts, 8st 12lb; Fillies, 8st 8lb. The winner of two races each value 500sovs, or of a race value 700sovs, 4lb extra; of two races each value 700sovs, or of a race value 1400sovs, 7lb extra; of a race value 4000sovs, 10lb extra. Entrance 5sovs for yearlings entered on 22nd July, 1931. Second entry at 20sovs 14th October, 1931. Horses not struck out on 1st June, 1932 pay 25sovs extra and those not struck out on 4th January, 1933 pay 25sovs in addition. One mile and a half.

(99 subs)

1 Mr W. Barnett's	HARINERO (C. Ray)	9. 2	R. C. Dawson (UK)
	B. colt Blandford – Athasi by Farasi.		
2 HH Aga Khan's	SHAMSUDDIN (M. Beary)	8.12	F. Butters (UK)
	Br. colt Solario – Firouze Mahal.		
3 Capt. G. A. Boyd-	GOLDEN GLEN (J. Moylan)	8.12	Ussher
Rochfort's	B. colt Tolgus – Rockmills.		
4 Count M'Cormack's	FRANZ HALS (T. Burns)	8.12	More O'Ferrall
	Ch. colt Gainsborough – Needle Eye.		
5 Mrs K. Kelly's	MATONA (G. Lester)	8.12	Collins
	B. colt Spion Kop – Molly Adare.		
6 Mr W. M. G. Singer's	MYOSOTIS (F. Fox)	8.12	Lawson (UK)
	B. colt Phalaris – Scarlet Martagon.		
7 Mr J. A. Mangan's	SWINDON LIGHT (Joseph Canty)	8.12	Owner
	B. colt Swindon – Shannon Fairy.		
8 Mr J. T. Rogers's	SOJOURNER (E. Gardner)	8.12	Owner
	Ch. colt Soldennis – Ragusa.		

SP 6/4 Shamsuddin; 9/4 Franz Hals; 4/1 HARINERO; 9/2 Myosotis; 33/1 Matona; 50/1 Golden Glen; 100/1 Bar. TOTE (2/- unit) 10/-. Places 3/6, 3/6, 9/-.
1½ lengths, 1 length. 2m 40.1/5s.
Winner trained by Mr Richard C. Dawson at Whatcombe, Berks.

that his licence was withdrawn. Four years later he was granted a licence to train. Based initially at Epsom and then at Grove Cottage, Malton, he sent out many winners, of whom Lady Electra, successful in a war-time Lincoln at Pontefract, was the best. In 1946 he again incurred the displeasure of the Jockey Club, losing his trainer's licence. Subsequently allowed to attend racemeetings, Cecil Ray had just made yet another start as a bloodstock agent when he died in 1948, aged only fifty-five. Reviewing the career of a man who was twice deprived of his livelihood by a process reminiscent of Star Chamber, one is obliged to question the likelihood of the Jockey Club being permitted to retain control over the administration of racing, irrespective of any belated concessions to the fundamentals of commerce or justice.

1934

The Irish Derby of 1934 carried significantly reduced prize money, reflecting the depressed state of the national economy in general and the racing industry in particular. The field of only six was dominated by four English-trained runners, opposed by two long-shots from the Parkinson stable. A regrettable absentee was the Phillie Behan-trained Cariff. This high-class winner of the Irish Two Thousand Guineas had met with a setback in training. The betting market concerned only the English horses, three of whom had run unplaced in the Epsom Derby behind Windsor Lad. Charlie Smirke, rider of Windsor Lad, said afterwards that, rounding Tattenham Corner, Primero had seemed to be his principal danger. Primero had then faded badly, finishing between two of the other raiders, Patriot King and Rathmore. However, William Barnett, recently elected to the Turf Club, was confident that Primero would emulate his own-brother's success of the previous year. Like Primero, Rathmore was still a maiden, but this half-brother to the Irish Oaks and Cesarewitch winner Nitsichin had run well to finish a luckless third in the Ribblesdale Stakes at Ascot. Being by the stayer Achtoi, himself narrowly beaten in the Irish Derby, Peter Thrale's charge could be expected to improve with age and seemed sure to relish the stiff Curragh course. While both Primero and Rathmore were expected to improve on their previous form, the public preferred the chances of the two proven performers, Patriot King and Autumn, inseparable in the betting. Patriot King had won the Wood Ditton Stakes, prior to finishing in front of Primero and Rathmore at Epsom. Autumn, trained by Irishman Cecil Boyd-Rochfort at Newmarket, had won twice as a two-year-old and more recently finished third at Ascot. He was owned by Joseph Widener, vice-chairman of the New York Jockey Club, who raced on a large scale in America, France and England. Neither Gipsy George nor Molino were given even a remote chance of keeping the prize at home.

    The early running was made by the home-trained pair, several lengths clear of the English quartet. After they had covered half a mile Molino began to lose his place, as Primero closed up with the pacemaking Gipsy George. Down the hill into the straight Primero, Patriot King and Autumn swept past Gipsy George, with Primero showing narrowly in the lead. In the straight a tremendous struggle devel-

Only the second dead heat to date in the Irish Derby, *Patriot King (nearest camera) just fails to snatch outright victory from Primero (rails), third prize going to Autumn. Source:* Irish Field.

oped between Primero and Patriot King, with Autumn a close third. Entering the final furlong it appeared that Patriot King had got the better of Primero, whereupon Joe Childs asked Autumn for a winning effort. Autumn hesitated as though ungenuine, was switched to the outside and forfeited his chance. Meanwhile Primero had fought back to regain a narrow lead, only to face a final desperate rally by Patriot King in the last few strides. The latter, finishing faster, seemed to many to have snatched the race on the line. However, the judge, from his vantage point, declared it a deadheat; certainly the fairest outcome of an epic struggle, in which each gave his all. Autumn, in response to vintage Childs pressure, kept on to be third, two lengths off the winners. The first three were all owner-bred and their respective owners had travelled from America, England and Northern Ireland to witness the second deadheat in sixty-nine runnings of the Irish Derby.

Primero, an own-brother to Athford, Trigo and Harinero, won the Great Northern St Leger at Stockton, prior to his return visit to the Curragh, when he emulated Trigo and Harinero in winning the Irish St Leger. He was subsequently sold to Japan, where he became a leading sire, getting Kurinohana, winner of the Japanese Derby. Patriot King, bred at his owner's stud near Aylesbury in Buckinghamshire, was from the first crop of the unknown resident stallion, Bolingbroke. Like Blandford, Bolingbroke was a son of Swynford, though there the similarity ended. Having won two small races for James de Rothschild, Bolingbroke was retired to his owner's stud, where he sired The Old Pretender, winner of the Woodcote Stakes, Rondo, winner of the Ascot Gold Cup and Bimco, who sired the Grand National winner, Teal. Patriot King raced for a further four seasons, winning only one modest race.

In contrast to those connected with Primero, who were all widely-known figures to the racing public, the Patriot King team was very much a private enterprise, headed by 'Jimmy' Rothschild. French by birth, James de Rothschild, elder son of Baron Edmond de Rothschild, the millionaire banker, enlisted in the British army in the First World War, winning the DCM. After the war he became a British citizen, representing the Isle of Ely as Liberal MP from 1929 until 1945, during which time he came to be regarded as the spokesman for Jewish interests in the House of Commons. He entered racing in 1903 and became a member of the Jockey Club in 1922. His early years in racing were characterised by a series of massive tilts against the Ring and although he moderated his gambling in later years, this aspect of racing always interested him more than the development of high-class horses. Despite his somewhat forbidding appearance and autocratic manner, 'Jimmy' Rothschild possessed a sense of humour, as evidenced after a gamble on his Snow Leopard had failed ignominiously. The following week's Calendar announced that the animal's name had been altered to Slow Leopard. During a racing career which lasted for more than half a century his colours were borne by some very good horses, notably Atmah, Beppo and Bombay and latterly Sunny Brae. An indication of his intensely independent outlook is to be found in his maintenance of a private stable from 1914 till his death in 1957, during which time he employed only two trainers.

The first of J. A. de Rothschild's trainers was F. C. Pratt, who held that position from 1914 until his retirement in 1949. Born in Cheltenham in 1876, Frederick Charles Pratt was christened after his famous uncle, Fred Archer. Apprenticed to James Ryan at Newmarket, he had his first ride when aged only eleven and rode his solitary Classic winner for his former master when winning the One Thousand Guineas on Galeottia in 1895. Two years later he went to Austria to ride, soon became too heavy and commenced training in 1902, settling in Lambourn. Some

Wednesday, 27th June, 1934   **£2167 10 0**   **6 Ran**   1½m

The Irish Derby of 5000sovs. The winner will receive 75%, second 15%, third 10% of the stakes after deduction ot bonuses of 200sovs to the owner (at entry) of the winner, 150sovs to the owner (at entry) of the second and 100sovs to the owner (at entry) of the third. For three years old entire colts and fillies. Colts, 8st 12lb; Fillies, 8st 8lb. The winner of two races each value 500sovs, or of a race value 700sovs, 4lb extra; of two races each value 700sovs, or of a race value 1400sovs, 7lb; of a race value 4000sovs, 10lb extra. Entrance 5sovs for yearlings entered on 20th July, 1932. Second entry at 20sovs 12th October, 1932. Horses not struck out on 7th June, 1933 pay 25sovs extra and those not struck out on 3rd January, 1934 pay 25sovs in addition. One mile and a half.

(108 subs)

1	Mr J. A. de Rothschild's	PATRIOT KING (G. Bezant)	8.12	F. C. Pratt (UK)
		B. colt Bollingbroke – Grandissima by Clarrissimus.		
1	Mr W. Barnett's	PRIMERO (C. Ray)	8.12	R. C. Dawson (UK)
		B. colt Blandford – Athasi by Farasi.		
3	Mr J. E. Widener's	AUTUMN (J. Childs)	8.12	C. Boyd-Rochfort (UK)
		B. colt Stefan the Great – Spring III.		
4.	Major V. H. Parr's	RATHMORE (M. Beary)	8.12	P. Thrale (UK)
		B. colt Achtoi – Latium.		
5	Mr J. J. Parkinson's	GIPSY GEORGE (M. Barrett)	8.12	Owner
		B. colt Salmon Trout – Gipsy Lass.		
6	Mr J. J. Sullivan's	MOLINO (W. Howard)	8.12	Parkinson
		Ch. colt Beresford – L.L.O.		

SP 2/1 PATRIOT KING, Autumn; 5/2 PRIMERO; 4/1 Rathmore; 33/1 Gipsy George; 100/1 Molino. TOTE (2/- unit) Patriot King 4/-. Place 5/-. Primero 3/6. Place 4/6.
Dead Heat, 2 lengths. 2m 39.1/5s.
STAKES DIVIDED
PATRIOT KING trained by Mr Fred Pratt at Lambourn, Berks.
PRIMERO trained by Mr Richard C. Dawson at Whatcombe, Berks.

time later James de Rothschild began racing, under the influence of Lord Rosebery. Besides being a heavy gambler, de Rothschild was a good judge of men, who was quick to appreciate Fred Pratt's ability to produce a horse for the occasion and profit accordingly. Thus began a long-lasting partnership, subsequently to result in Pratt becoming de Rothschild's private trainer. Their only English Classic success was achieved with Atmah in the One Thousand Guineas of 1911, ridden by Pratt's former apprentice, Freddie Fox. Beppo won the Manchester Cup and Hardwicke Stakes for them, while Bomba won the Ascot Gold Cup. Their victories in the Cambridgeshire with Brigand (1919) and Milenk (1921) netted fortunes for the stable. Fred Pratt's younger brothers, Willie and Charlie, were also successful trainers, the former in France for many years and the latter at Lambourn. Having retired in 1949, this shrewd and dedicated trainer died a year later.

In keeping with the independent spirit of his racing operations, Jimmy de Rothschild was content to entrust the ride of Patriot King to a member of the stable. G. H. Bezant, a little-known jockey, who rarely even got an outside ride. Apprenticed to Fred Pratt, George Henry Bezant rode a total of five winners before coming out of his time in 1927. With negligible prospects of emulating the erstwhile Pratt apprentice, Freddie Fox, George Bezant remained attached to the stable throughout his career. Patriot King was his only notable success prior to his enforced retirement in 1942 as the result of an arm injury. He subsequently became the proprietor of an hotel in Hungerford.

1935

A singularly weak English challenge reflected the excellence of the Irish three-year-olds of 1935, particularly those trained at Crotanstown by J. T. Rogers. Both Irish Guineas had already fallen to Rogers' representatives, the colts' Classic going to his third string, Museum, a rank outsider at 100-to-1 and the fillies' equivalent to the brilliant Smokeless, winner of the Anglesey and Phoenix Stakes and outstanding filly of her generation. Since then African Lily had added the Baldoyle Derby to the Crotanstown haul, beating Chirgwin and Coup de Roi. Listoi, trained by M. D. Peacock at Middleham and the sole English challenger in the field of eight, had refused to start in the Irish Two Thousand Guineas, but had since won at Redcar. Ted Gardner, Rogers' stable jockey, chose to ride Smokeless in preference to stable companions African Lily, Museum and Parisian. As in the Irish Two Thousand Guineas, Museum was only the stable's third string, relatively unfancied, despite the booking of ageing maestro, Steven Donoghue. Donoghue's arrival on the Curragh by private plane before racing had caused much more excitement than his prospects in the big race.

The race itself was dominated by Rogers' runners, African Lily making the early running from Parisian, Listoi and Museum, with the favourite, Smokless, in last place. After they had gone a mile Parisian weakened as Listoi, Coup de Roi, Cabinteely and Museum closed upon African Lily, with Smokeless tracking this group. Entering the straight African Lily gave way to Cabinteely, who was immediately challenged by Museum. It was at this point that Donoghue's opportunism won the race for Museum, who, having got first run, battled all the way to the line to hold the sustained challenge of Listoi by a length, with Smokeless a neck away in third place. Having recovered from the surprise of seeing Museum confound the experts once again, the crowd gave the winner a rousing reception, much of which was directed at his irrepressible partner, now fifty-one years old, who had won his first Irish Derby more than twenty years earlier.

Museum was bred in England by the trawler magnate, Sir Alec Black, best remembered as the owner of The Panther, and purchased in utero by Sir Victor Sassoon, who gave Sir Alec 10,000gns for Imagery and Jennie Deans. In 1931 Sir Alec had sent Imagery, a full sister to the St Leger and Ascot Gold Cup winner Salario, to be covered by Phalaris, who died almost immediately afterwards. This resulted in Imagery being re-covered by Sir Alec's own stallion, Legatee, who is generally accepted as the sire of Museum, his only offspring of note. By the war-time Triple Crown winner, Gay Crusader, Legatee headed the two-year-old Free Handicap in 1925 and was unbeaten the following season. Having stood for several seasons at Newmarket, Legatee was subsequently transferred to the Curragh, failing to sire anything remotely comparable to Museum. Imagery subsequently bred Phideas, also a winner of the Irish Derby for Sir Victor Sassoon. Originally named Papist, Museum won once as a two-year-old, prior to his shock victory in the Irish Two Thousand Guineas, ridden by Martin Quirke. Reflecting on his Classic success on this spare ride, Quirke explained that for a long time Museum's connections were deceived by the colt's extreme indolence on the gallops, with the result that he was gravely underrated. On his reappearance Museum won the valuable Ebor Handicap at York and concluded a triumphant season by winning the Irish St Leger, ridden each time by Donoghue. Museum thus became the first winner of the Irish Triple Crown, besides completing a clean sweep of the Irish Classics for J. T. Rogers, who had saddled Smokeless to win the two fillies' races. Retired to stud the following season, Museum was a failure as a stallion and was exported to Scandinavia in 1946.

Sir Ellice Victor Sassoon, Third Baronet, had begun racing in India, where his vast business interests were centred. There he raced as Mr Eve, which name he used subsequently for his bloodstock enterprise in England. In 1925 he made a spectacular entry into racing in England, outspending even the Aga Khan, when laying out over £50,000 to found what was to become one of the most powerful breeding and racing empires in the land. In 1937 he headed the lists of winning owners in both England and Ireland, winning the One Thousand and Oaks with Exhibitionist. But it was not until after the Second World War that his enormous outlay on bloodstock was rewarded, and then with interest. Between 1953 and 1960 he won the Epsom Derby no less than four times, with Pinza, Crepello, Hard Ridden and St Paddy. Pinza cost only 1500gns as a yearling, while Hard Ridden cost the derisory sum of 270gns to Sir Victor's own bid at Ballsbridge. By contrast, Crepello and St Paddy were products of a breeding and racing operation which cost an estimated £200,000 a year to maintain. Quite naturally, this astute businessman and great benefactor of British racing was never made a member of the Jockey Club. During the last years of his life he reduced his business interests in India and transferred his centre of operations to the Bahamas, where he died in 1961, within hours of his colt, Prince Poppa winning the Phoenix Stakes.

John T. Rogers, trainer of Museum, was an Englishman, who had moved to Ireland in 1915, following the reduction of racing in England during the First World War. Formerly a National Hunt jockey, he missed the winning mount on Kirkland in the 1905 Grand National owing to an eye injury. Before moving to Ireland he had trained a small but successful string at Cheltenham, whence he sent out Broxted to win the Stewards Cup at Goodwood in 1911. Instantly successful in his adopted country, Jack Rogers built up a large stable at Crotanstown, on the Curragh, besides developing an excellent stud at Athgarven Lodge. He was leading trainer in Ireland in 1935, 1936 and 1937, handing over to his son Bryan in the latter year. In 1940, as a result of his son being killed in action, Jack Rogers resumed training, only to die himself that same year, when returning to the Curragh after saddling a winner at Limerick Junction. Though prone to hasty remarks, as quickly retracted, Jack Rogers lived for his profession, at which he excelled to an extent unparalleled by any 'foreign' trainer in Ireland before or since. He trained the winners of eleven Irish Classics and won the Phoenix Stakes five times in ten years. One of these Phoenix Stakes winners was Trigo. As Mr Barnett's colt was leaving Crotanstown at the end

Wednesday, 26th June, 1935	**£2485**	**8 Ran**	**1½m**

The Irish Derby at 3500sovs. The winner will receive 75%, second 15%, third 10% of the stakes after deduction of bonuses of 150sovs to the owner (at entry) of the winner, 100sovs to the owner (at entry) of the second and 50sovs to the owner (at entry) of the third. For three years old entire colts and fillies. Colts, 8st 12lb; Fillies, 8st 8lb. The winner of two races each value 700sovs, or of a race value 1400sovs, 7lb extra; of a race value 4000sovs, 10lb extra. Entrance 5sovs for yearlings entered on 19th July, 1933. Second entry at 20sovs 11th October, 1933. Horses not struck out on 6th June, 1934 pay 25sovs extra and those not struck out on 2nd January, 1935 pay 20sovs in addition. One mile and a half.

(104 subs)

1 Sir Victor Sassoon's	MUSEUM (S. Donoghue)	9. 5	J. T. Rogers
	B. colt Phalaris or Legatee – Imagery by Gainsborough.		
2 Sir T. Dixon's	LISTOI (J. Taylor)	8.12	M. D. Peacock (UK)
	B. colt Achtoi – Lisvarna.		
3 Mr R. J. Duggan's	SMOKELESS (E. Gardner)	9. 1	J. T. Rogers
	B. filly Prince Galahad – Smoke Lass.		
4 Mr Joseph McGrath's	CABINTEELY (J. Moylan)	8.12	Ussher
	Gr. colt Son and Heir – Testaway.		
5 Major Shirley's	AFRICAN LILY (Joseph Canty)	9. 2	J. T. Rogers
	Ch. colt Spion Kop – Flower Book.		
6 Mr J. T. Rogers's	PARISIAN (M. Wing)	8.12	Owner
	B. Colt Cri de Guerre – Twincat.		
7 Mr J. B. Magennis's	WITHOUT BENEFIT (T.	8.12	Ussher
	(Whitehead) Gr. colt Son and Heir – Joan Haste.		
8 Sir Percy Loraine's	COUP DE ROI (T. Burns)	8.12	More O'Ferrall
	Br. colt Winalot – Sky Royal.		

SP 5/4 Smokeless; 2/1 African Lily; 8/1 Coup de Roi; 100/8 MUSEUM, Listoi, Parisian; 25/1 Cabinteely; 100/1 Without Benefit. TOTE (2/- unit) 25/6. Places 5/6, 5/-, 3/-.
1 length, Neck. 2m 44.1/5s.
Winner trained by Mr J. T. Rogers at Crotanstown, Curragh.

of his two-year-old career, en route to Dick Dawson's Whatcombe stable, Rogers cautioned his travelling head lad, Manuel, to take particular care of 'the best colt that has ever left Ireland'. This talented trainer is commemorated by the J. T. Rogers Memorial Handicap, run at the Curragh in October.

Trained by Matt Peacock, who had taken over the stable following the death of his father in September 1935, Listoi won the Churchill Stakes at Ascot as a four-year-old and was later exported as a stallion to Turkey. Based at the Turkish National Stud, Listoi became one of the most successful stallions ever to stand in that country. Smokeless went on to win the Irish Oaks for Richard Duggan, then mortally ill. Before he died Dick Duggan offered his brilliant filly to his close friend Joe McGrath, a co-founder of the Irish Sweepstakes. McGrath declined his dying friend's offer, promising instead to buy her at public auction. True to his word, McGrath subsequently gave a record 4000gns for her at Ballsbridge. Though Smokeless was comparatively unsuccessful at stud, she could be said to have inaugurated what was to become the most powerful racing and breeding establishment in Ireland. Of the others that finished behind Museum, Cabinteely went on to win the Irish Cambridgeshire later the same season, while Coup de Roi, transferred to Dick Dawson as a four-year-old, won the Northumberland Plate and the Newbury Autumn Cup. Thus, while it would be presumptuous to compare Museum to his illustrious contemporary, Bahram, winner of the English Triple Crown, Museum was undoubtedly a high-class colt.

1936

This year saw the English back in force, with the raiding quintet headed by the Aga Khan's Bala Hissar, a high-class two-year-old, that had been winter favourite for the Epsom Derby. His second season's form had been somewhat disappointing and although he had made the running to Tattenham Corner, he had faded badly to finish well behind the record-breaking grey, Mahmoud, also owned by the Aga Khan. Walter Nightingall's charge, Barrystar, had won the Lingfield Derby Trial, before finishing eighth at Epsom, ahead of Raeburn, winner of the Column Produce Stakes at Newmarket. The remaining English colts, Dytchley and Squadron Castle seemed to have been sent over more in hope than confidence. Though outnumbered by the invaders, the home side contained the favourite, Battle Song. Trained by the all-conquering J. T. Rogers, Battle Song had been beaten only by a head in the Irish Two Thousand Guineas by Hocus Pocus, who was also in the field. Since then Battle Song had run out an impressive winner of the Champion Stakes at Baldoyle, beating Sundown and Cabinteely. An own-brother to Hill Song, winner of the Irish St Leger, Battle Song was thought certain to stay the stiff twelve furlongs. To ensure a true test of stamina, Battle Song's connections had arranged to have the outsider African Spoil act as pacemaker. Hocus Pocus had not been seen in public since his Guineas victory, when it had appeared that a mile was as far as he cared to go. Golden Lancer, the remaining runner, looked to be out of his class.

A cool, cloudy morning had given way to a humid, sultry afternoon, with the result that an over-dressed and consequently uncomfortable crowd watched African Spoil set up an immediate ten-length lead from Hocus Pocus, Bala Hissar, Squadron Castle and Barrystar. Having set a blistering pace to half way, African Spoil surrendered his lead to Hocus Pocus, followed by Barrystar. These two led down the hill from Battle Song, Raeburn, Bala Hissar and Squadron Castle. In the straight a three-cornered struggle developed between Hocus Pocus on the rails, Barrystar and Battle Song on the stands side. Two furlongs out, Battle Song bored in on Barrystar, who bumped Hocus Pocus. The chief sufferer in this scrimmaging was Barrystar, whom Wing was forced to pull back and switch to the outside. Meanwhile, almost unnoticed, Tommy Burns brought Raeburn with a long, smooth run on the outside to tackle Battle Song, then the narrow leader from Barrystar and Hocus Pocus. Once again Battle Song swerved off a straight line, bumping Raeburn. Never one to be easily denied, Tommy Burns got Raeburn balanced again in a flash to pass the winning post one and a half lengths clear of the erratic favourite, with Hocus Pocus running on to take third place ahead of the luckless Barrystar. Though the race had been marred by the sustained barging match in the closing stages, nothing could detract from Raeburn's worthy and convincing success. The force of the initial collision was indicated by the injury to Joe Canty's leg, gashed by Morny Wing's stirrup.

By the champion sire Solario, Raeburn was bred in England by Lord Furness and purchased as a yearling by Mr S. D. Hollingsworth for 5600gns. Harpy, the dam of the winner, had previously bred Orpen, second in all three colts' Classics in 1931. Raeburn ran unplaced at York next time out and then finished last in the St Leger behind Boswell. As a four-year-old he was trained especially for the Ascot Gold Cup, in which he broke down very badly, failing to finish behind Precipitation. Subsequently retired to stud, Raeburn died at an early age, without siring anything of note.

Raeburn was the first runner in Ireland of Mr S. D. Hollingsworth, founder of the Arches Hall Stud in Hertfordshire. From his foundation mare Felsetta, he bred Felucca, who in turn produced Ark Royal, Kyak and Cutter, all winners of the Park Hill Stakes at Doncaster. This very successful stud has been maintained by Mr Hollingsworth's son, who has bred a stream of high-class winners to carry his inherited 'Crimson, silver braid'.

Joe Lawson, trainer of Raeburn, had started life as a farm labourer in his native County Durham. After a brief career in the saddle, curtailed by rising weight, he joined Alec Taylor's famed Manton stable, becoming head lad and then assistant. On Taylor's retirement in 1926, Lawson took over the stable and four years later became champion trainer, with a record stakes total of £93,899, which was only bettered by Noel Murless in 1957. His second training championship was achieved in 1936, though with little help from Raeburn. Having saddled the winners of ten English Classics, Joe Lawson forsook Manton for Newmarket in 1947. In 1954 he realised his life's ambition when winning the Derby with Never Say Die, ridden by a youthful Lester Piggott. Never Say Die went on to win the St Leger, ridden by Charlie Smirke in place of Piggott, then under suspension for reckless riding. Having retired in 1957, after thirty years as a trainer, Joe Lawson died at Newmarket in 1964, at the age of eighty-three.

Raeburn provided Scotsman Tommy Burns with his first and only success in the Irish Derby. Having ridden his first winner at the age of twelve, Tommy came to Ireland in 1914 with his father, who had accepted the post of trainer to Colonel Hall Walker. Undeterred by his employer's belief in the influence of astrology on the performance of his horses, James Burns turned out numerous winners for Lord Wavertree, as Hall Walker had become, before returning to his native Ayr, where he continued to train until his retirement in 1932. Tommy, known familiarly as 'The Scotchman', remained in Ireland, where he headed the list of professional Jockeys in 1916 and rode the winners of nine Irish Classics, before retiring in 1928 to train at Lumville, on the Curragh. After one season he resumed riding, as first jockey to the More O'Ferrall stable. In a riding career which lasted until 1953, Tommy Burns became Irish champion jockey in 1932 and rode a further twelve Irish Classic winners, his overall total being surpassed only by Morny Wing. While the latter was without peer in spring races, there were many who considered Burns the better jockey over a distance. Having retired briefly before the Second World War to give

Wednesday, 24th June, 1936 **£2500** **9 Ran** **1½m**

The Irish Derby of 3500sovs. The winner will receive 75%, second 15%, third 10% of the stakes after deduction of bonuses of 150sovs to the owner (at entry) of the winner, 100sovs to the owner (at entry) of the second and 50sovs to the owner (at entry) of the third. For three years old entire colts and fillies. Colts, 8st 12lb; Fillies, 8st 8lb. The winner of two races each value 500sovs, or of a race value 700sovs, 4lb extra; of two races each value 700sovs, or of a race value 1400sovs, 7lb extra; of a race value 4000sovs, 10lb extra. Entrance 5sovs for yearlings entered on 25th July, 1934. Second entry at 20sovs 10 October, 1934. Horses not struck out on 5th June, 1935 pay 25sovs extra and those not struck out on 8th January, 1936 pay 25sovs in addition. One mile and a half.

(105 subs)

1	Mr S. D. Hollingsworth's	RAEBURN (T. Burns) B/Br. colt Solario – Harpy by Swynford.	9. 2	J. Lawson (UK)
2	Major Shirley's	BATTLE SONG (E. Gardner) Br. colt Spion Kop – Cradle Song.	8.12	J. T. Rogers
3	Mr H. S. Gray's	HOCUS POCUS (Joseph Canty) Br. colt Mascot – Henna Girl.	9. 5	P. Behan
4	Mr F. W. Shenstone's	BARRYSTAR (M. Wing) B. colt Sherwood Starr – Royal Shoot.	8.12	W. Nightingall (UK)
5	HH Aga Khan's	BALA HISSAR (C. Smirke) B. colt Blandford – Voleuse.	9. 5	F. Butters (UK)
6	Mrs W. P. Ahern's	SQUADRON CASTLE (H. H. Beasley) Gr. colt Mr Jinks – Laverock.	9. 5	W. Higgs (UK)
7	Mr R. Tree's	DYTCHLEY (P. Beasley) B. colt Blandford – Valediction.	8.12	Boyd-Rochfort (UK)
8	Mrs E. McGrath's	AFRICAN SPOIL (M. Barrett) Ch. colt Spion Kop – Emolument.	8.12	Parkinson
0	Mr Joseph Maher's	GOLDEN LANCER (M. Curran) Ch. colt Golden Chalice – Royal Favour.	8.12	Slocock

SP 5/2 Battle Song; 3/1 Bala Hissar; 8/1 RAEBURN, Barrystar, Hocus Pocus, Squadron Castle; 25/1 Dytchley; 100/1 Bar. TOTE (2/- unit) 22/6. Places 4/6, 3/6, 4/6.
1½ lengths, 2 lengths. 2m 43.2/5s.
Winner trained by Mr J. Lawson at Thanton, Wilts.

his sons a chance, as he put it, he resumed riding following the death in action of his son James. Doyen of Irish trainers, the Scotchman continues to train a small but rewarding string at Lumville. Not given to regarding geese as swans, Tommy rarely lets one run loose and remains the bane of bookmakers and handicappers alike. His biggest training success was achieved with Vimadee in the Irish St Leger in 1961, ridden by his son, T. P. Burns, a talented jockey, who, like his father before him, was equally proficient under National Hunt rules.

Battle Song, having finished third to the Newmarket-trained Black Domino in the Ulster Derby, emulated his full-brother, Hill Song, when winning the Irish St Leger. Transferred to F. P. Gilbert's East Ilsley stable the following season, Battle Song ran consistently, but without success. In 1940 he was exported to New Zealand as a stallion. Regarded as getting very slow-maturing stock, Battle Song was later sold to Australia, where he did a little better. Squadron Castle, having descended to selling plates and become branded as a rogue, sprang a surprise when winning the Lincolnshire as a six-year-old. Dytchley improved with age, deadheating for the Newbury Autumn Cup, before being shipped to South Africa, where he was joined by African Spoil. Barrystar, Hocus Pocus and Golden Lancer went to America, India and Norway respectively. Both then and now the Irish Derby of 1936 could not be described as anything other than a sub-standard affair.

1937

The new stand in the General Enclosure had been completed in time for the Irish Derby meeting. Providing a view of the Derby course from start to finish, it was well received by the sizeable crowd, enticed by delightful summer sunshine and entertained by the National Army Band. Adding to the general air of enjoyment was the presence of an apparently unbeatable home-trained contender for the big race. Successful two years previously with the Irish Triple Crown winner, Museum, the same combination of Sir Victor Sassoon, J. T. Rogers and Steve Donoghue was represented by Museum's half-brother, Phideas. Successful in the Phoenix Stakes on his final appearance as a two-year-old, Phideas had remained unbeaten in the Madrid Handicap and the Irish Two Thousand Guineas. This odds-on favourite was opposed by two English-trained colts, Senor and Tolman, both still maidens. The remaining three runners were stable companions of the favourite. One of these, Nettleweed, in the Sassoon second colours, was to act as pacemaker. Although Senor, a son of Trigo, was mildly supported, few cared to challenge Phideas' ability to give weight and a beating to moderate opponents.

Nettleweed made the early running from Strong Current, Flaxman and Tolman, with Senor and Phideas bringing up the rear. This order was maintained until the approach to the straight, where Senor, Tolman and Strong Current swept past the weakening pacemaker, tracked by Phideas. The two English colts went clear of Strong Current, with the hot favourite still well adrift. At the distance Senor got the better of Tolman and for a moment it looked as though an upset was on the cards.

However, within the final hundred yards, Donoghue set Phideas alight to such effect that he passed the post a length clear of Senor, without knowing that he had had a race. Tolman plugged on to be third. The result was a personal triumph for Steve Donoghue, now in his final season. Though not as stylish in the saddle as when at his peak, being forced by an old shoulder injury to adopt a more upright stance, the former champion had lost none of his dash, as he had demonstrated by winning the One Thousand Guineas and Oaks on Exhibitionist, also owned by Sir Victor Sassoon. As if sensing a swan-song, the crowd gave a rousing reception to the feckless, reckless, puckish little genius, whom they had, many years earlier, adopted as their own, captivated by his charm and dazzled by his brilliance. A measure of the extent to which the devil-may-care Donoghue had captured the affections of Irish racegoers is indicated even today by those on the Curragh who point with pride to Steve Donoghue's 'birthplace'.

Bred by his owner, Phideas could not be trained after the Irish Derby, owing to the state of the ground, which remained firm for the rest of the season. Though kept in training as a four-year-old, Phideas never ran again and was retired to the Wood Ditton Stud at Newmarket, at a fee of 49gns. After several moves, he was located finally at the Hunsley House Stud, near Hull, where his fee was raised to 98gns in 1945, at which it remained until his death in 1954. Like both himself and Museum, his stock were generally slow to mature, not reaching their best until three or over. Phideas was by Pharos, second to Papyrus in the Derby and winner of the Champion Stakes as a four-year-old, beating Parth and Salmon Trout. Pharos proved very

Wednesday, 23rd June, 1937 £2500 **6 Ran** 1½m

The Irish Derby of 3500sovs. The winner will receive 75%, second 15%, third 10% of the stakes after deduction of bonuses of 150sovs to the owner (at entry) of the winner, 100sovs to the owner (at entry) of the second and 50sovs to the owner (at entry) of the third. For three years old entire colts and fillies. Colts, 8st 12lb; Fillies, 8st 8lb. The winner of two races each value 500sovs, or of a race value 700sovs, 4lb extra; of two races each value 700sovs, or of a race value 1400sovs, 7lb extra; of a race value 4000sovs, 10lb extra. Entrance 5sovs for yearlings entered on 24th July, 1935. Second entry at 20sovs 9th October, 1935. Horses not struck out on 3rd June, 1936 pay 25sovs extra and those not struck out on 6th January, 1937 pay 20sovs in addition. One mile and a half.

(101 subs)

1 Sir Victor Sassoon's	PHIDEAS (S. Donoghue)	9. 5	J. T. Rogers
	B. colt Pharos – Imagery by Gainsborough.		
2 Mr W. Barnett's	SENOR (T. Burns)	8.12	R. C. Dawson (UK)
	B. colt Trigo – Wish Maiden.		
3 Mrs James Corrigan's	TOLMAN (P. Beasley)	8.12	Boyd-Rochfort (UK)
	B. colt Tolgus – Mandoline.		
4 Mr J. T. Rogers's	FLAXMAN (W. Howard)	8.12	Owner
	Ch. colt Schiavoni – New Abbey.		
5 Mr W. Barnett's	STRONG CURRENT (M. Wing)	8.12	J. T. Rogers
	B. colt Stingo – Sunny Seas.		
6 Sir Victor Sassoon's	NETTLEWEED (H. H. Beasley)	8.12	J. T. Rogers
	B. colt Hotweed – Maralga.		

SP 4/7 PHIDEAS; 7/2 Senor; 5/1 Tolman; 10/1 Nettleweed; 20/1 Bar. TOTE (2/- unit) 3/6. Places 2/6, 3/6.

1 length, Same. 2m 40.1/5s.
Winner trained by Mr John T. Rogers at Crotanstown, Curragh.

successful at stud in England and later in France, getting such as Cameronian and Firdaussi in England as well as the unbeaten French and Italian champions, Pharis and Nearco. Phideas' victory ensured that his owner, trainer and sire headed their respective lists in Ireland for that year.

Senor went on to win the St George Stakes at Liverpool, beating Tolman, before finishing second to Owenstown in the Irish St Leger. The following season he won the Queen's Prize at Kempton and the Ormonde Stakes at Chester. He was exported to Argentina as a six-year-old. Tolman won three races after the Irish Derby, while Flaxman, Nettleweed and Strong Current all paid their way, the last-named winning the Naas November Handicap as a four-year-old. Phideas could perhaps be described as a good, rather than great winner of the Irish Derby.

1938

Cold, depressing weather and steady rain dampened the spirits of the Derby Day crowd and dulled the appearance of the newly-painted stands, as the field of nine paraded for the big race. Of the three English-trained runners, Golden Sovereign, winner of the Newmarket Stakes, ninth in the Epsom Derby and third to Scottish Union at Ascot, was most fancied. This Newmarket-trained colt had created an Irish record for a yearling, when submitted at Ballsbridge by Lord Fingall, making 2700gns to the bid of Sir Abe Bailey. Although neither of the other raiders, Valedictory and Manorite, had any worthwhile form, both attracted market support. Outstanding among the home-trained colts was Mr Dan Sullivan's Rosewell. As a two-year-old this son of Orwell had won his only two races, the Railway and Beresford Stakes, in the style of a future champion. Regarded as a certainty for the Irish Two Thousand Guineas, Rosewell had met with a setback at the last moment, leaving the way clear for Nearchus. Though he had not in consequence appeared in public for nine months and was rumoured to be working badly at home, Rosewell, looking magnificent in the paddock, shared favouritism with Golden Sovereign. None of the remaining quintet, including the excitable Honor's Choice and the blinkered Lugnamedon, was even mildly fancied.

From flagfall Honor's Grace went into an immediate lead, clear of Manorite, Solan, Valedictory and Rosewell, with Golden Sovereign bringing up the rear. Passing halfway, Rosewell and Manorite joined the weakening Honor's Choice in the lead, followed by Golden Sovereign. As the leaders swung down the hill, Wing made his move on Rosewell, going clear of Manorite and the improving Golden Sovereign. A long way from home it became obvious that, despite Tommy Weston's most strenuous efforts on Golden Sovereign, neither he nor anything else was going to trouble Rosewell. At the distance, Wing looked over his shoulder at his struggling opponents, before going on to ease Rosewell past the post a facile winner, amidst loud cheering. Golden Sovereign and Manorite plugged on to fill the minor placings, with the winner's stablemate, Solan, in fourth place.

An handsome brown colt, his coat flecked with grey, Rosewell was out of Bower of Roses, second in the Irish Oaks and subsequently successful in seven long-distance handicaps, including the Irish Cesarewitch, for Captain Herbert Dixon. In foal to Orwell, Bower of Roses was bought at Newmarket for 500gns by Captain 'Ossie' Bell, who was thus credited with breeding Rosewell. The latter was submitted at Newmarket as a foal, where Mr Frank Tuthill bought him for 480gns on behalf of Mr Sullivan. The following year Mr Sullivan secured Bower of Roses for 730gns at the same sales. She bred three other minor winners. Rosewell's sire Orwell, a brilliant two-year-old, won the Two Thousand Guineas, before going wrong, and was regarded by Joe Lawson as the best horse he ever trained. However, he proved disappointing as a sire. Prevented from running again that season by hock trouble, Rosewell was sent to England to be trained for his four-year-old career. However, misfortune struck again, this time in the form of a split pastern, which resulted in his being retired, unbeaten in his only three races, to the Hilltown Stud at Consilla, under the management of John Oxx. Reasonably successful as a sire of stayers, Rosewell got such as Do Well (Irish St Leger), Distel (Champion Hurdle) and Linwell (Cheltenham Gold Cup), before being exported to Australia in 1950, where he died from a twisted gut, shortly after his arrival.

Isidore and Arthur Blake, *guardians of their family tradition on the Irish Turf; Isidore as breeder and Turf Club Steward and Arthur as consistently successful trainer, who added two further Irish Derbies to the Heath House tally. Source:* The Irish Horse.

Golden Sovereign, Manorite and Valedictory all went on to win races, while Solan, a half-brother to the Irish Two Thousand Guineas winner, Glannarg, retired to stud in Cornwall. Honor's Choice won the Galway Hurdle as a four-year-old and later became the sire of Kerstin, one of only three mares ever to win the Cheltenham Gold Cup. Aclint Bridge went to Denmark and Lugnadmedon to South Africa. Rosewell's success in the Irish Derby was sufficient to make Dan Sullivan the leading owner in Ireland and contributed to Colonel A. J. Blake's third trainers' championship, consolidated by the victories of Ochiltree (Irish St Leger), Summer Soldier (Ulster Derby), as well as those of the leading two-year-olds, Rose of Portugal and Summer Solstice. Rosewell's abbreviated career on the racecourse makes him a difficult horse to evaluate. However, on the basis that a racehorse cannot be asked to do more than win easily, irrespective of the calibre of his opponents, Rosewell was almost certainly a better colt than the bare details of his brief career might indicate.

Dan Sullivan, a Dublin victualler, had a long and successful career on the Turf, both as an owner and breeder. His first good winner was Courier Belle, who cost him only 155gns and won the Phoenix Stakes in 1913. Even more successful was his next filly, La Poloma, winner of the inaugural Irish St Leger in 1915 and dam of O'Dempsey, O'Curry and seven other winners. For some years Dan Sullivan raced mainly in England, his horses being trained by his compatriot, Atty Persse, who saddled Resplendent to win the Irish One Thousand Guineas and Oaks, besides finishing second in the Epsom Oaks. From this good filly Mr Sullivan bred the Epsom Derby winner, Windsor Lad, whom he sold as a yearling, contrary to the

Wednesday, 22nd June, 1938	£2500	9 Ran	1½m

The Irish Derby of 3500sovs. The winner will receive 75%, second 15%, third 10% of the stakes after deduction of bonuses of 150sovs to the owner (at entry) of the winner, 100sovs to the owner (at entry) of the second and 50sovs to the owner (at entry) of the third. For three years old entire colts and fillies. Colts, 8st 12lb; Fillies, 8st 8lb. The winner of two races each value 500sovs, or of a race value 700sovs, 4lb extra; of two races each value 700sovs, or of a race value 1400sovs, 7lb extra; of a race value 4000sovs, 10lb extra. Entrance 5sovs for yearlings entered on 22nd July, 1936. Second entry at 20sovs 14th October, 1936. Horses not struck out on 2nd June, 1937 pay 25sovs extra and those not struck out on 5th January, 1938 pay 20sovs in addition. One mile and a half.

(96 subs)

1 Mr D. Sullivan's	ROSEWELL (M. Wing)	8.12	Col A. J. Blake	
	Br. colt Orwell – Bower of Roses by Roseland.			
2 Sir A. Bailey's	GOLDEN SOVEREIGN (T. Weston) Br. colt Monarch – Fleche d'Or.	9. 5	Cottrill (UK)	
3 Mr D. S. Kennedy's	MANORITE (F. Hunter, jr.)	9. 5	P. Thrale (UK)	
	B. colt Manna – Wedding Favour.			
4 Mr I. J. Blake's	SOLAN (J. Moylan)	8.12	Col A. J. Blake	
	B. colt Soldennis – Glannagalt.			
5 Mr J. H. Whitney's	VALEDICTORY (P. Beasley)	8.12	Boyd-Rochfort (UK)	
	B. colt Blandford – Valediction.			
6 Major Shirley's	ACLINT BRIDGE (H. H. Beasley)	8.12	B. Rogers	
	B. colt Bosworth – Saracen's Song.			
7 Mr H. I. Ussher's	DUNLOE (E. Gardner)	8.12	Owner	
	B/Br. colt Apron – Gilford.			
8 Mr H. S. Gray's	LUGNADMEDON (E. M. Quirke)	8.12	Canty	
	Ch. colt Sea Serpent – Lemnahye.			
9 Mr Michael M'Donough's	HONOR'S CHOICE (M. Barrett)	8.12	J. J. Parkinson	
	Br. colt Embargo – Thistle Lass.			

SP 2/1 ROSEWELL, Golden Sovereign; 4/1 Valedictory; 6/1 Manorite; 20/1 Bar. TOTE (2/- unit) 5/6. Places 2/6, 2/6, 3/6.
2 lengths, ¾ length. 2m 43.1/5 s.
Winner trained by Colonel A. J. Blake at The Heath, Maryborough.

advice of his trainer. In addition to Resplendent, O'Dempsey and Rosewell, Dan Sullivan's remarkable record in the Irish Classics was supplemented by Soldumeno in the Irish Two Thousand Guineas and Sol Speranza in the Irish One Thousand Guineas and Oaks. Though he was in ill-health at the time of Rosewell's Derby triumph, Dan Sullivan's death, when it occurred in Dublin two years later, was unexpected.

Colonel Arthur J. Blake, trainer of Rosewell, was a nephew of Charles Blake, one of the founders of modern racing in Ireland, whom he succeeded as master of The Heath, Maryborough, where Sam Jeffrey had for many years acted as trainer. From this famous stable, with its gallops incorporating a former racecourse, Colonel Blake sent out a record seventeen Irish Classic winners. He was leading trainer in 1930, 1931 and 1938. Martin Quirke, stable jockey for many years, regarded Colonel Blake as the most encouraging trainer for whom he ever rode, whose quiet confidence and implicit trust in his jockeys inspired them to win races for the master of The Heath, which they would not have won for another trainer. Behind the stable yard at The Heath there remains the steep, walled chute, down which the Blake two-year-olds were taught to jump off, which makes it easy to understand why they invariably broke fast and ran straight! In the latter part of his long and distinguished career, Colonel Blake trained the produce of the Irish National Stud, leased to race in the colours of HE the President. The last of these was Sail Cheoil, winner of the Irish Champion Stakes and Colonel Blake's last runner, when unplaced in the Washington International, ridden by Michael Kennedy, a former Blake apprentice.

1939

The last Derby before World War Two was staged in an atmosphere of general unrest, both in European and domestic affairs. Though the Economic War had ended, IRA outrages in England had led to the introduction in the Dail by the Minister of Justice, P. J. Ruttledge, of the Offences against the State Bill. This was followed by the institution of Special Criminal Courts, the declaration of a State of Emergency and the creation of a Military Court. Despite the Munich Agreement, it was becoming increasingly evident that Europe was moving inexorably towards a state of war, in anticipation of which Mr de Valera proclaimed Ireland's neutrality. However, as far as the fortunes of Irish racing were concerned, the outlook was brighter than for many years. A scheme for the allocation of the Government grant of £10,000, 'for the benefit of Irish racing', had been agreed by the Turf Club and the INHS Committee. The thirty-three recognised racecourses had been divided into three categories and the funds, in the form of added stakes, allocated accordingly. In return for this long-sought aid, each course had to agree to pay the carriage of runners in subsidised races and to submit audited accounts annually to the Turf Club.

June 21st saw an enormous crowd, the likes of which had not been recorded on the Curragh for thirty years, throng the enclosures as the field of nine paraded for the feature. Mr William Barnett, bidding for a third Derby success, was doubly represented by sons of his Epsom Derby winner, Trigo. More fancied of the pair was Cornfield. Trained at Middleham in Yorkshire by Sam Armstrong, Cornfield had already justified favouritism in the Irish Two Thousand Guineas, where the Blake-trained Solo Flight had been denied a clear run. Reported to have done extremely well since his previous visit, Cornfield was made hot favourite. Mr Barnett's other representative was Crushed Corn, one of the leading juveniles of his year. Trained locally by Brian Rogers, he had won impressively at Baldoyle and shared second favouritism with the only other English runner, Kenilworth. Trained at Manton by Joe Lawson, Kenilworth, though still a maiden, had run well at Ascot and had the services of the perennial English champion, Gordon Richards. Morny Wing, Richards' counterpart in Ireland, had chosen Solo Flight in preference to Colonel Blake's other runner, Summer Solstice, winner of the Beresford and Madrid Stakes and third in the Irish Two Thousand Guineas. The only other runners to attract any support were the speedy Wonersh, recently purchased by Miss Dorothy Paget, and Mondragon, owned by the Minister for Justice, P. J. Ruttledge. Having won the Marble Hill Stakes in the style of a good colt, Mondragon had fallen prey to the equine 'flu, which had ravaged James Canty's yard in 1938. While the prevailing hard ground had hindered the preparation of Solo Flight and Summer Solstice, it had produced rapid improvement in both Crushed Corn and Mondragon.

Solo Flight broke fastest, but was soon headed by Fairwargor, who made the running from Solo Flight, Kenilworth, Summer Solstice, Wonersh and Cornfield. After they had covered four furlongs Solo Flight regained the lead only to surrender it to Wonersh, who dashed ahead entering the straight, to the consternation of all who had dismissed him as a sprinter. Challenged in turn by Cornfield and Crushed Corn, Wonersh clung on tenaciously, looking likely to cause a surprise. All the while, Joe Canty had been bringing Mondragon ever closer to the battling leaders. Inside the final two furlongs Wonersh compounded, leaving Cornfield looking the likely winner. Desperately tired, Cornfield stumbled and almost fell, giving the advantage to Crushed Corn. Having seemed certain of victory with first Cornfield and then Crushed Corn, Mr Barnett had his hopes dashed by the famous flourish of Joe Canty, which landed Mondragon first past the post, with half a length to spare over Crushed Corn. Cornfield, too obviously exhausted to be considered unlucky, finished a length away in third place.

Mondragon, a handsome, strongly-made chestnut, was bred by Sir Harold Gray at his Gogmagog Stud in Cambridgeshire. By Sir Harold's Irish Derby winner, Sea Serpent, Mondragon was out of Far Day, a winner of three races as a two-year-old and the dam of four other winners. Having won the Marble Hill Stakes in the colours of his breeder, Mondragon had been purchased by Mr P. J. Ruttledge prior to running as a three-year-old. On his reappearance two weeks later, in the Ulster Derby at Down Royal, Mondragon was set to concede 7lbs to Crushed Corn. As the latter had won the Tipperary Derby at Limerick Junction in the meantime, he was strongly fancied to gain his revenge. In a thrilling finish to a rough race, Mondragon came with a similar late flourish to beat Summer Solstice and Crushed Corn by a neck and a short head. Once again Joe Canty's artistry made it impossible to assess Mondragon's superiority. That was the last that was seen of either of the Derby principals, for both Mondragon and Crushed Corn were exported to India, where the former proved successful as a sire. In their absence the Irish St Leger was won by Skoiter, from Red Shaft, who went on to win the Galway Hurdle as a four-year-old.

Patrick J Ruttledge TD had been an enthusiastic supporter of both racing and coursing for many years before achieving his greatest success with Mondragon, whose two victories were very largely responsible for making Paddy Ruttledge the leading owner in Ireland in 1939. When elected to membership of the Turf Club in the previous year P. J. Ruttledge had become the first Minister of a Free State Government to achieve this distinction, although W. T. Cosgrave had been an honorary member since 1928. Mondragon's Derby success came as a timely tonic for his owner, whose health had suffered greatly due to the pressures particular to his position as Minister for Justice. Later made Minister for Local Govenment and Health, this sporting owner died in 1952.

1939 was the most successful year in James Canty's career as a trainer. In addition to Mondragon he also turned out Serpent Star to win the Irish Oaks for her owner-breeder, Sir Harold Gray, compensation for the sale of Mondragon and the completion of a wonderful double for Sir Harold's own stallion, Sea Serpent, leading sire in Ireland in that year. Overshadowed as a jockey by his brilliant brother, James Canty began training on the Curragh in 1930. Based at Ruanbeg and Curragh Glebe, he continued to turn out a steady succession of well-supported winners until his retirement in the early 'sixties. He was succeeded by his son Phil, who upheld the family tradition when winning the Irish St Leger on Morning Madam in 1950. Now a capable and respected trainer in Ireland, Phil has capitalised on the situation whereby his brother John is equally successful in the winter circuit in California to exploit some of his Irish string in sunnier climes, during the close season in Ireland.

In concluding the story of the Irish Derby of 1939, one is tempted to observe that in no other sport is the element of luck so highly prized in racing; appropriately indicated by the significance subsequently attached by the brothers Canty to their discovery of a horseshoe while walking the course prior to Mondragon's Derby. Their luck continued throughout that season, when Monster Light won the Railway Stakes and Overall the Irish Cambridgeshire. The following season the Canty stable was wiped out by that stableman's nightmare – strangles.

Mondragon was the second outright Irish Derby winner for his rider Joe Canty, the only Irish-born member of a celebrated trio of jockeys, whose names were already part of Irish racing legend: Canty, Burns and Wing. Their combined expertise set a standard of jockeyship in Ireland, which many feel has never been equalled. The youngest of eighteen children, some of whom he never met, Joe Canty was born in 1895 in Knocklong, Co. Limerick, where his family were farmers and shopkeepers. From an early age he demonstrated tremendous natural riding ability and had won scores of Donkey Derbies and 'flappers' before following his older brother Jimmy to Rathbride Manor, to become apprenticed to Michael Dawson, his future father-in-law, in 1910. Two years later he rode his first winner, besides giving an indication of things to come, when riding Queen of the Brush to upset the favourite, ridden by brother Jimmy, in the Marble Hill Stakes at the Curragh. By 1914 he had lost his claim and five years later he won the first of seven Irish jockeys' championships, achieved under both Rules, for rising weight had obliged him to start riding over fences, at which he proved equally adept, with a treble at Punchestown and two victories in the Leopardstown 'Chase.

Combined with the physical qualities of hands and strength, Joe Canty had a keen riding brain, which did not function solely on horseback. In the years between the wars, when prize money was pitifully small, most jockeys attempted to supplement their meagre riding fees by betting. Canty's betting ability matched his riding skill. Moreover, he took great pains to ensure that the odds were in his favour as far as possible. To this end he always attempted to ride schooling on his jumping mounts before riding them in public. He then took care to walk the course before racing, noting the best ground and, sometimes, taking the additional precaution of 'encouraging' the groundsmen to loosen the outside hurdles in the final two flights. Having, as usual, 'fallen asleep' in the early stages of the race, he then produced his mount at the entrance to the straight, coming with a rush on the outside of his rivals, secure in the knowledge that the final two flights would prove no obstacle!

As an inveterate gambler, equally proficient at poker and billiards, it was natural that Canty should have ridden for gambling trainers, the first of these being Phillie Behan, who specialised in two-year-olds, on which Canty excelled, having no superiors at the gate. In the days before the draw for positions, Canty, riding a fancied runner, would deliberately be last out of the paddock, canter slowly down along the favoured rails, forcing his waiting rivals to make room for his arrival, exactly where he wanted to be. Nor did the introduction of a draw for starting positions cause him any problems. At that time each jockey drew a number from a bag held beside the scales as he weighed out. On the occasions when he felt it mattered, Canty simply bribed the man holding the bag to secrete the desired number in an agreed corner of the bag! However, wiles alone did not make Joe Canty the great jockey he was and his all-time record of 117 winners in Ireland in 1925 provided enduring proof of his ability, more especially as the lightest weight he drew all year was 8st 4lbs.

Not long after he had ridden his fourth winner of the coveted Galway Hurdle (Shrewd King in 1929), Joe Canty suffered a serious back injury in a fall. While it ended his career over fences, his injury caused him to lose sufficent weight to resume a full-time career on the flat and it was around this time that Joe Canty began to ride for Hubert Hartigan, an equally ardent gambler and a talented trainer, who was to provide six of Canty's seventeen Irish Classic winners. Champion trainer for three years in succession, Hartigan remains, along with Harry Ussher, one of the most notable Irish trainers, although he never saddled a winner of the Irish Derby. Despite Canty's allegiance to Hartigan and the many 'coups' in which they combined, he was not averse to having a 'touch' for himself. On one occasion at the Curragh Hartigan ran two in the same race, one ridden by Canty and the other by Morny Wing, whose talents were devoted more to riding winners than to backing them. On the strength of home trials Hartigan backed Wing's mount. After Canty had won on the 'wrong one', Hartigan lamented loudly: 'I have the two best jockeys in Ireland riding for me. One never loses a trial and the other never wins one!'

Canty's lifestyle began to take its toll in the post-war years and when he realised that even his 'reviver' – the ever-present flask of black coffee and brandy – was no longer having the required effect, he retired from the saddle, a comparatively wealthy man, to begin training. In a career which spanned almost forty years, Joe Canty had ridden innumerable winners – seven National Stakes, seven Railway Stakes and nine Irish Guineas – many of them now mere names in the Racing

Calendar. However, some stand out as great popular favourites of their day. King Richard, on whom he won the Galway Hurdle in 1924, was one of the best-known horses in Ireland at the time and won no few than ten races that year. Another was olf Poolfix, the Curragh sprint specialist, whose win in the Rockingham Handicap under 9st 12lbs was acclaimed as Canty's greatest riding performance. Knight's Caprice provided him with a winning debut at Goodwood, where Canty had him out of the gate so fast that he was able to cross the entire field and win the Stewards' Cup pulling up. Then of course there was The Phoenix, the greatest horse he ever rode and whom he suspected of suffering from diabetes when he lost his unbeaten record in the Irish St Leger.

Just as Jimmy Canty, an indifferent jockey, became an excellent trainer, so Joe Canty, a brilliant jockey, proved a mediocre trainer, though he turned out a number of winners in the ten years before his retirement from racing. Of far greater interest to him was passing on his vast store of riding knowledge to aspiring jockeys, among

Wednesday, 21st June, 1939	£2500	9 Ran	1½m

The Irish Derby of 3500sovs. The winner will receive 75%, second 15%, third 10% of the stakes after deduction of bonuses of 150sovs to the owner (at entry) of the winner, 100sovs to the owner (at entry) of the second and 50sovs to the owner (at entry) of the third. For three years old entire colts and fillies, Colts, 8st 12lb; Fillies, 8st 8lb. The winner of two races each value 500sovs, or of a race value 700sovs, 4lb extra; of two races each value 700sovs, or of a race value 1400sovs, 7lb extra; of a race value 4000sovs, 10lb extra. Entrance 5sovs for yearlings entered on 20th July, 1938. Second entry at 20sovs 13th October, 1937. Horses not struck out on 27th July, 1938 pay 25sovs extra and those not struck out on 1st March, 1939 pay 20sovs in addition. One mile and a half.

(108 subs)

1	Mr P. J. Ruttledge's	MONDRAGON (Joseph Canty)	8.12	James Canty
		Ch. colt Sea Serpent – Far Day by Fariman.		
2	Mr W. Barnett's	CRUSHED CORN (J. Moylan)	8.12	B. Rogers
		Ch. colt Trigo – Cedarhurst.		
3	Mr W. Barnett's	CORNFIELD (T. Burns)	9. 5	F. Armstrong (UK)
		B. colt Trigo – Arena.		
4	Miss Dorothy Paget's	WONERSH* (H. H. Beasley)	8.12	Hilliard
		Br. colt Mascot – Paula D.		
5	Capt. D. W. Daly's	RED SHAFT (E. M. Quirke)	8.12	More O'Ferrall
		B. colt Scarlet Tiger – Fleche d'Or.		
6	Mrs C. L. Mackean's	SOLO FLIGHT (M. Wing)	8.12	Blake
		Ch. colt Soldennis – Sky Royal.		
7	Lord Astor's	KENILWORTH (G. Richards)	8.12	Lawson (UK)
		B. colt Bosworth – Keener.		
8	Major H. C. Robinson's	SUMMER SOLSTICE (W. Barrett)	8.12	Blake
		Ch. colt Soldennis – Early Summer.		
9	Mr Joseph McGrath's	FAIRWARGOR (Herbert Holmes)	8.12	Parkinson
		B. colt Fairway – Argoeuves.		

SP Evens Cornfield; 6/1 Kenilworth, Crushed Corn; 8/1 Solo Flight; 10/1 Wonersh; 100/8 MONDRAGON; 25/1 Bar. TOTE (2/- unit) 26/6. Places 4/-, 3/6, 2/6.
½ length, 1 length. 2m 38s.
Winner trained by Mr James Canty at Ruenbeg, Curragh.

*Wonersh saddled outside the enclosure.

them his son, J. M. Canty, now a successful trainer at Curragh Glebe. His whole raceriding philosophy was contained in his favourite dictum: 'There's only one place to be in front in a race – at the post.' The greatest 'Kidder' of them all died in 1971.

1940

By now the Nazi onslaught upon Europe had proved the deposed English Prime Minister, Neville Chamberlain, disastrously mistaken in his statement that 'Hitler has missed the bus'. Following the route of the Allies at Dunkirk, Winston Churchill had declared on behalf of the beleaguered British people that: 'We shall fight on the beaches . . . in the fields and in the streets; we shall fight in the hills; we shall never surrender.' As the British nation fought for its life, racing in England had come almost to a standstill, though a substitute New Derby had been staged at Newmarket, in which Pont l'Eveque had beaten Turkhan, with the Aga Khan's better-fancied Stardust unplaced. Considered unlucky at Newmarket, Turkhan appeared to be a certainty for the Irish Derby. He was accompanied from Newmarket by Golden Tiger, tenth in the New Derby, and Claudius. The home-trained quartet was headed by the Blake-trained pair, Teasel and Tobago. Though the former had won the Irish Two Thousand Guineas, Tobago was the choice of stable jockey Morny Wing, and consequently better fancied. Chico, half-brother to Trigo and twice a winner over the distance, represented Mr William Barnett, while the outsider, Antrim, carried the colours of Sir Percy Loraine, British Ambassador in Rome until two weeks earlier, when Italy had declared war on Britain. Even their most ardent supporters gave Turkhan's opponents only a remote chance of defeating the odds-on favourite.

Slowly away, Golden Tiger trailed the field, as Chico made the early running from Tolago, Antrim, Turkhan and Claudius. Despite the fast going, the pace was sufficiently slow to allow Golden Tiger to make up the leeway by the time the field had reached half way, where Chico was joined in the lead by Antrim. Coming down the hill, Smirke allowed the favourite to assert his superiority. Chased into the straight by Golden Tiger and Claudius. Turkhan had now assumed complete control and went on to win with insulting ease from his compatriots. Tolago disappointed his connections by finishing only fifth, one place behind his unconsidered stablemate, Teasel, who never managed to supplement his Guineas success.

Disappointed, though not surprised by the eclipse of the home side, racegoers consoled themselves that Turkhan was at least wholly Irish-bred. This elegant bay colt had been foaled at the nearby Sheshoon Stud, as had both his sire and his dam. By the Triple Crown winner, Bahram, Turkhan was out of Theresina, winner of the Irish Oaks and Jockey Club Stakes. She bred five other winners, including the useful Shahali and Ujiju. Bahram, having proved himself a brilliant racehorse in an unbeaten career, spent five seasons at stud in Newmarket, where he sired Big Game and Persian Gulf. At the outbreak of war, the Aga Khan, having sought the safety of neutral Switzerland, found himself relatively short of negotiable assets. To relieve his unaccustomed penury, he incurred the wrath of British breeders by selling both

Bahram and Mahmoud to the United States, whence they departed, via Ireland, in the latter months of 1940. Strangely, Bahram did not appeal to American breeders and was sold to the Argentine in 1945, where he died eleven years later. Despite his relative lack of success in the Americas, perhaps attributable to changes of climate and lack of time to adjust to these, Bahram's departure represented a severe loss to British and Irish breeders. Turkhan, winner of the Coventry Stakes at Ascot as a two-year-old, went on to win the oft-postponed and much-altered wartime St Leger at Thirsk in November, beating his owner's Stardust. Retired to the Old Connell Stud in Newbridge as a four-year-old, Turkhan distinguished himself as a sire of fillies, among them Ella Retford and Linaria, winners, respectively, of the Irish One Thousand Guineas and Oaks in 1946, in which year he headed the list of sires in Ireland. Having been syndicated for 50,000gns in 1945, Turkhan was exported to France in 1952.

Turkhan was the first of two Irish Derby winners for 'Cheeky Charlie' Smirke, arguably the greatest big-race jockey of his era. Born in London and originally destined to be a boxer, Charlie Smirke was a product of Stanley Wootton's celebrated 'apprentice academy' at Epsom. Having ridden his first winner in 1922, Smirke rapidly established himself in the top flight, though not without incurring the suspicion of the Stewards, who rightly suspected him of betting. In 1928 he lost his licence as a result of the mount, Welcome Gift, getting left at the start at Gatwick. Exonerated by the subsequent behaviour of his ungenerous mount, Smirke had his licence restored after four heartbreaking years in the wilderness. Having relented, Dame Fortune made ample amends when Windsor Lad carried Smirke to a triumphant comeback in the Epsom Derby in 1934. Two years later he rode Mahmoud to his record-breaking Derby success. Many years later Tulyar and Hard Ridden confirmed Smirke's mastery of Epsom as well as his temperament on the big occasion.

In the meantime, Charlie Smirke, having spent the War in the Eighth Army, became instrumental in securing the appointment of his old ally, Marcus Marsh, to succeed the incapacitated Frank Butters as trainer to the Aga Khan and his punting son, the Aly Khan. For Smirke the change was a welcome relief. Butters had always nursed a suspicion of his self-assertive, brash, gambling jockey, whereas Marsh had stated his implicit confidence in Smirke by entrusting him with the greatest horse with whom either were ever to be associated, Windsor Lad. Marsh's faith was promptly reaffirmed by a virtuoso performance on Smirke's part to land Palestine first past the post in the Two Thousand Guineas. Two years later trainer and jockey relived their finest hour when Tulyar triumphed at Epsom, giving rise to a characteristically appalling Smirke quip, 'What did I Tulyar?'. Tulyar was out of Neocracy, whose dam, Harina, was an own-sister to Trigo, Harinero and Primero.

As he entered the twilight of a long and brilliant career, Smirke found himself riding for Alec Head in France, for Marcus Marsh had been thrown over through his failure to work miracles with inferior stock. In the circumstances the relationship was doomed to failure. Deprived of his favourite trainer, discarded by his favourite patron, ageing and troubled by weight, Smirke appeared to have reached the end of a colourful career, punctuated by troubles and triumphs, but never mundane. All that remained was an unwavering belief in his own supreme ability. Divorced, remarried, sustained only by victory in the Irish Two Thousand Guineas, Smirke considered retiring in 1957, content to reflect upon ten English and eight Irish Classic successes. Revitalised by a winter in the Caribbean, he responded with alacrity to the invitation from J. T. Rogers's grandson, Mickey Rogers, to ride an improving ugly duckling called Hard Ridden. A narrow, if comfortable victory in the Irish Two Thousand Guineas for the partnership formed the prelude to a tilt at the Epsom Derby. The last-minute withdrawal of Alcide threw the 1958 Derby open to all-comers. Thus did this unconsidered son of a sprinter provide Charlie Smirke with a faity-tale ending to a turbulent career. Having signed off with characteristic defiance on Hard Ridden, this exasperating character, to some enraging, to many more endearing but to all and sundry incapable of being ignored, retired to the tranquility of the golf course, whence he has resisted all attempts to lure him back to the scenes of his many triumphs and tribulations. Though never in need of others' esteem, Charlie Smirke could scarcely fail to respond to the tribute paid to him by Morny Wing. Invariably silent on the merits of his fellow-riders, Wing was only once provoked into naming his most formidable opponent. The long-sought verdict was swift, emphatic and final: Charlie Smirke.

Wednesday, 26th June, 1940	**£2500**	**7 Ran**	**1½m**

The Irish Derby of 3500sovs. The winner will receive 75%, second 15%, third 10% of the stakes after deduction of bonuses of 150sovs to the owner (at entry) of the winner, 100sovs to the owner (at entry) of the second and 50sovs to the owner (at entry) of the third. For three years old entire colts and fillies. Colts, 8st 12lb; Fillies, 8st 8lb. The winner of two races each value 500sovs, or of a race value 700sovs, 4lb extra; of two races each value 700sovs, or of a race value 1400sovs, 7lb extra; of a race value 4000sovs, 10lb extra. Entrance 5sovs for yearlings entered on 20th July, 1938. Second entry at 20sovs 12th October, 1938. Horses not struck out on 26th July, 1939 pay 25sovs extra and those not struck out on 6th March, 1940 pay 20sovs in addition. One mile and a half.

(105 subs)

1	HH Aga Khan's	TURKHAN (C. Smirke)	9. 5	F. Butters (UK)
		B. colt Bahram – Theresina by Diophon.		
2	Sir Humphrey de Trafford's	GOLDEN TIGER (J. Moylan)	8.12	Boyd-Rochfort (UK)
		Br. colt Scarlet Tiger – Fleche d'Or.		
3	Sir A. Bailey's	CLAUDIUS (M. Beary)	8.12	Lawson (UK)
		Br. colt Tiberius – Doryse.		
4	Col. A. J. Blake's	TEASEL (G. Wells)	9. 5	Owner
		Ch. colt Pharian – Chardon.		
5	Mr C. Odlum's	TOLAGO (M. Wing)	8.12	Blake
		B. colt Tolgus – Lagonda.		
6	Sir Percy Loraine's	ANTRIM (E. M. Quirke)	8.12	More O'Ferrall
		Br. colt Trimdon – Annabel.		
7	Mr W. Barnett's	CHICO (T. Burns)	8.12	D. Rogers
		B. colt Umidwar – Athasi.		

SP 4/11 TURKHAN; 11/2 Tolago; 10/1 Chico, Claudius; 100/8 Golden Tiger; 20/1 Bar. TOTE (2/- unit) 3/6. Places 2/6, 6/-

2 lengths, Same. 2m 41.4/5s.
Winner trained by Mr Frank Butters at Newmarket.

1941

As the War raged on, Ireland, though neutral in principle became progressively more involved in practice. Early in the year rationing came into force. Adding to the problems faced by this divided and essentially defenceless island were outbreaks of IRA activity and foot-and-mouth. The latter epidemic caused the cancellation of racing from the end of March until early May, when a sympathetic Government sanctioned its limited resumption. An immediate beneficiary was Sir Percy Loraine, whose Khosro scored a convincing success in the Irish Two Thousand Guineas, thereby confirming his two-year-old promise. In the Irish Derby Khosro was again opposed by Apocalypse, Etoile de Lyons, Sol Oriens and Tiverton, who had followed him home in that order in the Guineas. The two English challengers, Easy Chair and Lynch Tor, had little to recommend them, neither having won beyond a mile. Doubts about Khosro's stamina, allied to rumours concerning his soundness, caused the large crowd to prefer two sons of the prepotent Hyperion, Apocalypse and Sol Oriens, both in receipt of 7lbs from their Guineas conqueror. The behaviour of Etoile de Lyons in the paddock made it abundantly clear that the duties of the stud rather than the racecourse were infinitely more to his taste. Pick of the field on looks was Sol Oriens, whom Colonel Blake had turned out looking magnificent.

After a short delay at the start, caused by the antics of Khosro and Etoile de Lyons, the ten runners got away, headed by Cardinal Wolsey, pacemaker for Sol Oriens, and a first Derby mount for the promising young T. P. Burns. With less than a mile to run, George Wells sent Sol Oriens up to pass his fading pacemaker and lead down the hill from Apocalypse, Khosro, Etoile de Lyons and Tiverton. In the straight, Khosro drew level with Sol Oriens, with Etoile de Lyons, ill at ease on the firm ground, struggling to stay in touch. None of the others counted now. All the way up the long straight these two courageous colts gamely responded to the urgings of their riders, first one and then the other appearing likely to win. Just as Khosro, under stylish Martin Quirke, seemed to have got the upper hand, Sol Oriens, on whom Geogie Wells was riding like a man possessed, wore down the topweight to win a great race by a length, with Etoile de Lyons four lengths further away. It was a particularly brave performance by Khosro, who had all but broken down in the closing stages.

Sol Oriens, an attractive chestnut colt, was bred by Mrs J. J. Maher and purchased privately by A. P. Reynolds, who raced under the nom de course of 'Mr J. Dillon'. By the Derby and St Leger winner, Hyperion, Sol Oriens was out of Silver Mist, who traced to Sterling Balm, grandam of the English Classic winners, Silver Urn and St Louis. In siring the winners of both the English and Irish Derbies in 1941, Hyperion emulated Tracery, sire of Papyrus and Waygood and also Blandford, who achieved the double with Windsor Lad and Primero. Retired to stud in 1935, the pony-sized Hyperion became leading sire in England in 1940, 1941, 1942, 1945, 1946 and 1954. Only Hermit, St Simon and Stockwell have headed the list on more occasions. Prior to his death at the great age of thirty, Lord Derby's wonderful little horse had established a worldwide dynasty, guaranteed to perpetuate his fame as one of the most influential stallions in the history of the thoroughbred.

Sol Oriens and Etoile de Lyons renewed their rivalry in the Irish St Leger, by which time the ground had eased considerably, allowing Etoile de Lyons to display his true ability. The moment of truth came as the two principals turned into the straight with the race between them. Hit once by Canty, Etoile de Lyons rocketed away to beat Sol Oriens by an extending five lengths. Admittedly, the Derby winner had been plagued with the cough since his triumph in June. Nonetheless, on the balance of their form, it would appear that Khosro and Etoile de Lyons were superior racehorses, so much so that, had the going not been rock hard on Derby Day, Sol Oriens would have finished no better than third. However, that, as the saying goes, is horse racing. Retired to stud as a four-year-old, Sol Oriens got little of note, though he appears as grandsire of Indigenous, who established a new world record over five furlongs on Epsom's downhill sprint course and retired to stud in Ireland, advertised, naturally enough, as 'the fastest horse in the world'. Sol Oriens was destroyed at the Lismacue Stud in Tipperary in 1956. The gallant Khosro, retired to the Kildangan Stud, got Cambyses as his very first foal and seemed set for a sensational stud career, only to die in 1947.

The second of Colonel Blake's two Irish Derby winners, Sol Oriens appeared on the racecard as the property of 'J. Dillon', otherwise A. P. Reynolds, a prominent public figure at that time. Trained as an accountant, Percy Reynolds had exhibited a flair for transport administration, which had induced his friend Sean Lemass to appoint him Chairman of CIE, the newly-formed state transport monopoly. In his single-minded pursuit of the impossible – a profitable state monopoly, symbolised by the celebrated 'flying snail' – Reynolds had made himself thoroughly unpopular in many quarters, hence the pseudonym. Regarded always as singularly lucky owners, Reynolds and his wife scored other notable successes with Linaria in the Irish Oaks and Lady's View, his particular favourite, in the Phoenix Park '1500'. These two fillies were trained by Dick McCormick, who had joined Reynolds as manager of his Clonbarron Stud in Co. Meath. McCormick had previously worked with Steve Donoghue and earlier still he had shared with Donoghue the distinction of being the only men to ride The Tetrarch. Though elected to the Turf Club and to the board of the Irish National Stud Percy Reynolds rapidly lost interest in racing, progressively became disenchanted with politics, and returned to his first love – accountancy.

George H. Wells, the successful rider, began his riding career with James Russell at Mablethorpe in Lincolnshire, becoming a leading apprentice. On completing his time with Hubert Hartigan, to whom his indentures had been transferred, Georgie Wells was an instant success in Ireland, winning both Irish Guineas for Colonel Blake on Teasel and Milady Rose. Subsequently equally successful under National Hunt rules, he took out a trainer's licence for the first time in 1955. Success came just as quickly in his new role, for Umm credited him with the Irish Grand National and the Galway Plate that same year. More recently King's Sprite, ridden by Arthur Moore, son of his fellow-trainer and friend of long standing, Dan Moore, landed a second Irish National for the Wells stable, when beating l'Escargot, trained by Dan Moore. Preferring always to train a limited number of decent horses, George Wells turned out scores of winners for his principal patron, Dick McIllhagga, among them the Galway Plate winner, Terossian. A feature of his horses has always been their versatility; a Wells-trained 'jumper' could never be ignored in a flat race, as layers frequently rediscovered to their cost. Endowed with that particular type of English humour which has always been offensive to Irishmen and thus not universally popular in his adoptive country, Georgie Wells has nevertheless earned the respect, if not the affection of the racing community. Having entered racing with nothing, he can now confidently claim that he has never had cause to regret his choice of calling. And that, in infinitely more lurid language, is how George H. Wells would answer his critics.

Wednesday, 25th June, 1941	**£2500**	**10 Ran**	**1½m**

The Irish Derby of 3500sovs. The winner will receive 75%, second 15%, third 10% of the stakes after deduction of bonuses of 150sovs to the owner (at entry) of the winner, 100sovs to the owner (at entry) of the second and 50sovs to the owner (at entry) of the third. For three years old entire colts and fillies. Colts, 8st 12lb; Fillies, 8st 8lb. The winner of two races each value 500sovs, or of a race value 700sovs, 4lb extra; of two races each value 700sovs, or of a race value 1400sovs, 7lb extra; of a race value 4000sovs, 10lb extra. Entrance 5sovs for yearlings entered on 18th July, 1939. Second entry at 20sovs 14th October, 1939. Horses not struck out on 24th July, 1940 pay 25sovs extra and those not struck out on 3rd March, 1941 pay 20sovs in addition. One mile and a half.

1	Mr J. Dillon's	SOL ORIENS (G. Wells)	8.12	Blake
		Ch. colt Hyperion – Silver Mist by Craig an Eran.		
2	Sir Percy Loraine's	KHOSRO (E. M. Quirke)	9. 5	More O'Ferrall
		B. colt Sir Cosmo – Straight Sequence.		
3	Mr H. M. Hartigan's	ETOILE DE LYONS (Joseph	8.12	Owner
		Canty) Ch. colt Coup de Lyon – Rose of Jericho.		
4	Mr H. S. Gill's	TIVERTON (J. Moylan)	8.12	D. Rogers
		Br. colt Apron – Spiora.		
5	Mr Grant A. Singer's	LYNCH TOR (T. Burns)	8.12	Lawson (UK)
		B. colt Trimdon – Leighton Tor.		
6	Lt-Col. H. Boyd-Rochfort's	EASY CHAIR (W. Nevett)	8.12	C. Boyd-Rochfort (UK)
		B. colt Easton – Aryan.		
7	HH Maharaja of Kashmir's	RAO RAJA (R. Cartwright)	8.12	R. More O'Ferrall
		B. colt Dastur – Indira.		
8	Mr C. Odlum's	CARDINAL WOLSEY (T. P. Burns) Br. colt His Reverence – Lagonda.	8.12	Blake
9	Mr Joseph McGrath's	APOCALYPSE (M. Wing)	8.12	Collins
		B. colt Hyperion – Quadriga.		
10	Mr F. S. Myerscough's	ARABIAN CHIEF (J. Taylor)	8.12	Walker
		Br. colt Spion Kop – Arabella.		

SP 9/4 SOL ORIENS; 3/1 Khosro, Apocalypse; 5/1 Easy Chair; 8/1 Etoile de Lyons; 100/6 Lynch Tor, Tiverton; 50/1 Bar. TOTE (2/- unit) 6/-. Places 3/-, 4/-, 4/6.
1 length, 4 lengths. 2m 37.1/5s.
Winner trained by Colonel A. J. Blake at The Heath, Maryborough.

1942

Despite the shortage of transport and even of forage, racing continued in Ireland during the dark days of 1942, albeit in a limited and centralised manner. Transport restrictions in England prevented the participation of any cross-Channel runners in the Irish Derby. In any one of the last forty-odd renewals of Ireland's greatest race the absence of English-trained raiders would not have caused widespread regret, this year it was regarded as an absolute calamity. This dramatic change of heart had been occasioned by the performances of the greatest colt to be kept in training in Ireland since Orby. His name was Windsor Slipper. In three appearances as a two-year-old Joseph McGrath's lightly-framed racing machine had slaughtered his contemporaries to win the Waterford Testimonial, the Railway and the Beresford Stakes, each victory being more devastating than the last. Oldtimers compared him to St Brendan, the highest praise they could bestow. Windsor Slipper made his three-year-old debut in the Irish Two Thousand Guineas, winning with disdainful ease from Grand Inquisitor and Cara Koosh. His few remaining critics thought at the time that Windsor Slipper looked to be trained to his peak and that Michael Collins had left himself little on which to work. Collins provided the most eloquent answer possible on Derby Day, when Windsor Slipper appeared in the paddock, epitomising the power, the quality and the symmetrical perfection to which most involved in the production and preparation of racehorses can only aspire, for rarely is it realised. The only conceivable danger to the prohibitively-priced favourite appeared to be the fitness of his jockey, Morny Wing, riding with a badly swollen hand, the result of a poisonous sting.

The early running was made by Agamemnon, who showed clear of Bengal, Grand Inquisitor, Ceylon and Windsor Slipper, with Coromyth in sixth place. The order remained much the same until, approaching the half-mile post, Grand Inquisitor, Coromyth and Windsor Slipper drew clear of their rivals. Down the straight, Grand Inquisitor and Coromyth engaged in a prolonged struggle, with Windsor Slipper poised on their heels. With two furlongs to run, Wing pulled the favourite out from behind the battling leaders. In a few strides Windsor Slipper sprinted away, leaving the others bobbing like corks in his wake. Eased at the line, he still passed the post six lengths clear, setting a new course record, until them held by Dastur. His performance was reported thus by one of the national newspapers: 'Nothing more impressive than Windsor Slipper's Irish Derby win has been seen on an Irish racecourse for a long number of years, and yesterday's huge crowd fairly gasped when the champion sprinted away from Grand Inquisitor and Coromyth in the last quarter of a mile.'

Windsor Slipper's triumphant owner, Joe McGrath, immediately issued a challenge to the owners of the best three-year-olds in England to try conclusions with his brilliant colt over the Irish Derby course. Transport restrictions made this impossible. Consequently, Windsor Slipper was prepared for the Irish St Leger, despite the coughing epidemic which swept through the Curragh stables during the summer. While the Irish Triple Crown appeared to be a formality, Joe McGrath had no intention of seeing his champion lose his unbeaten record through the after-effects of the cough. Shortly before the final Irish Classic, Windsor Slipper was galloped, inside the racecourse, over the full St Leger distance with the best that Collins had in his yard, as well as a sprinter, jumped in to extend the colt over the final five furlongs! Having accomplished more in the trial than the race itself could possibly demand, Windsor Slipper went to the post at 100-to-8 ON, winning in a common canter by ten lengths. In doing so, he became only the second and almost certainly the last winner of the Irish Triple Crown. Frustrated in his attempt to prove Windsor Slipper's supremacy over his English contemporaries, McGrath decided to retire his unbeaten colt to stud. Installed at the historic Brownstown Stud, which McGrath had purchased in 1941, Windsor Slipper was immediately booked full at 300gns and seemed certain to revive the former glories of Birdcatcher and Gallinule.

Bred by Lord Furness, Windsor Slipper was the fifth foal of Carpet Slipper, already the dam of the ill-fated Godiva, winner of the English One Thousand Guineas and Oaks in 1940. Having purchased Windsor Slipper privately as a yearling from the executors of the late Lord Furness, Joe McGrath demonstrated the courage of his convictions when paying a record 14,000gns for Carpet Slipper in October 1941. A product of the National Stud at Tully, Carpet Slipper was a half-sister to Charles O'Malley, third in the Derby and sire of the Oaks winner Charlebelle. Windsor Slipper was outstandingly the best colt sired by Windsor Lad in that horse's short and interrupted stud career. Bred in Ireland by Dan Sullivan, Windsor Lad won the Derby for the Maharaja of Rajpipla, after which he became the property of the bookmaker Martin Benson, in whose colours he was never beaten, winning the St Leger, Coronation Cup, Rous Memorial Stakes and Eclipse Stakes. Plagued by sinus trouble and infertility, Windsor Lad had to be put down in 1943, aged only twelve. The exploits of his most brilliant son made him leading sire in Ireland in 1941 and 1942.

Windsor Slipper's stud career got off to a flying start. His first crop included Royal Barge, winner of the King George Stakes at Goodwood and Dublin Town, winner of the Railway Plate. His second crop produced that brilliant sprinter The Cobbler, as well as Solar Slipper, winner of the Champion Stakes. Windsor Slipper did not cover in 1945. However, the sprinting victories of Reminiscence, twice winner of the Portland Handicap, assured the success of his comeback to active service the following year. Thereafter he got little of note and from 1954 until his death in 1960 he covered very few mares. Although the average winning distance of his progeny was a mile, they tended to be either sprinters, such as The Cobbler, or stayers, like Solar Slipper. The export of The Cobbler to New Zealand, Royal Barge to Spain and Solar Slipper to the USA meant that Windsor Slipper's only noteworthy son at stud in these islands was Windsor Sun, winner of the Jersey Stakes. However, his line remains secure through Panaslipper, sired by Solar Slipper, prior to his departure to America in 1957.

Lack of racecourse competititon, allied to a somewhat chequered stud career have tended to militate against Windsor Slipper's standing among the racecourse champions of this century. He was ridden in all his races by Morny Wing, many times Irish champion jockey, a vastly experienced rider, a shrewd judge and not given to hyperbole. He described his best mount thus: 'Windsor Slipper may have been the horse of the century, but it is certain that he was the greatest horse of the century in Irish racing'. Furthermore, as stable jockey at Conyngham Lodge, Wing knew what Windsor Slipper had accomplished at home. Before his two-year-old debut, Windsor Slipper gave 14lbs to his contemporary Rounders in a trial and beat him easily. Rounders had already won three races. When sold to the United States, Rounders went on to beat the mighty Whirlaway. Comparisons between horses of different eras tend to be misleading, if not completely meaningless. Consequently, it is perhaps best to describe Windsor Slipper, along with Blue Peter and Pharis as three champions, deprived by circumstances of the opportunity to confirm their greatness by beating allcomers.

Of those who attempted unsuccessfully to deprive Windsor Slipper of his unbeaten record, the best was probably Grand Inquisitor, winner of twelve races, including the Liverpool Spring Cup as a seven-year-old, in a lengthy career, restricted and protracted by the War. By the predominantly National Hunt sire, His Reverence, Grand Inquisitor was eventually retired to the Gartlandstown Stud near Mullingar, where, mated with the twenty-one-year-old Duchess of Pedulas, he sired Mr What. Unfortunately, Grand Inquisitor got very few opportunities at stud prior to his death in 1955, three years before his most famous son's Grand National victory. Another of his sons, Take Time, finished second in an Irish Grand National, while his daughter, Inquisitive Rose, became the dam of Wrekin Rambler.

Windsor Slipper was the first and finest Irish Classic winner to carry the all-conquering 'Green, red seams and cap' of Joseph McGrath, already established as the largest and most successful owner in the history of Irish racing. Born in 1895, Joe McGrath sold newspapers on the streets of Dublin, before getting employment in a chartered accountant's office. This he forsook to join the Irish Transport and General Workers' Union, bringing him in close contact with Labour leader James Larkin during the bitter General Strike of 1913. By 1916 he was a member of the Irish Republican Brotherhood and was imprisoned after the Rising, becoming a trusted aide of Michael Collins, who once confided that: 'Joe is 100 per cent reliable, and he thinks quickly in a tight corner.' Elected to the British Parliament as a member of Sinn Fein, McGrath devoted his considerable energies and talents to the Dail, the underground Irish Parliament, which lurked in readiness to administer the country when the British should at last withdraw from Ireland. Intimately involved in the treaty negotiations, which led to the formation of the Irish Free State, McGrath stood firmly on the side of the signatories, who opted for less than a 32-county Republic, rather than risk the threat of renewed British repression. As the British withdrew and a disgruntled de Valera prepared to plunge the country into civil war, McGrath was chosen by W. T. Cosgrave as Minister for Labour.

Large in stature and standing, endowed with boundless energy and a talent for figures, McGrath found time from his demanding position to start the Irish Hospitals Sweepstakes, with Richard Duggan and Spencer Freeman. The story of the Sweep merits a book to itself, which has already been recognised. Its incalculable benefit to Irish racing in general and to the Irish Derby in particular is of particular relevance in this context. After one false start and some spectacularly successful political lobbying, McGrath and his partners finally got Government sanction in 1930 to launch the Irish Hospitals' Sweepstakes, since when it has gone from strength to strength, making untold fortunes for its founders and prospering around the world in the face of ever-increasing competition from envious imitators.

Through his association with Dick Duggan, enthusiastic owner as well as successful bookmaker, Joe McGrath became involved in racing. Beginning in a modest way in 1933, he paid an Irish record price for Duggan's dual Irish Classic heroine, Smokeless, following her owner's death in 1935. Never afraid to back his judgement, McGrath bought wisely and well, Carpet Slipper being a case in point. Having bought Nasrullah for £20,000 from the Aga Khan and recouped the purchase price in stud fees, he sold this phenomenally successful stallion to an American syndicate for a staggering £132,857 in 1949. Two years later Joe McGrath achieved his most spectacular and poignant triumph, when his Arctic Prince came home first in the Epsom Derby, resulting in the former IRA 'gunman' being presented to the Queen and Princess Elizabeth. It was a moment that 'Boss' Croker, McGrath's predecessor at Glencairn, would have savoured. In many ways these two great benefactors of Irish racing were remarkably alike. Now owner of one of the largest racing and breeding operations this side of the Atlantic, McGrath admitted in a rare disclosure that his racing cost him £10,000 a year, adding that: 'I should have quit if I didn't breed and sell horses to the United States.' Sales such as that of Arctic Prince in 1956, for a reputed £315,000, helped to balance the books. And there was the Irish Sweep, literally a licence to print money.

When over sixty, his reputation and personal fortune secure, the highest peak of business, politics and racing conquered, Joe McGrath decided that the time had come to link the Irish Sweep to Irish racing. The vehicle chosen was the Irish Derby, approaching its centenary, but still insignificant in the theatre of international racing. As the most powerful figure in Irish racing and an administrator of the Turf Club, McGrath had little difficulty in securing the agreement of the authorities to allow the Irish Derby to become the Irish Sweeps Derby, in return for an initial sponsorship of £30,000. The organisational and promotional genius of Spencer Freeman ensured that, from its inception, the Irish Sweeps Derby attained its status as a race of international significance. Run for the first time in 1962, the Irish Sweeps Derby has achieved general recognition as a fairer and finer test of Europe's best Classic colts than its age-old Epsom counterpart. Moreover, it has had the effect of raising the overall standard of racing in Ireland. Overnight Ireland was transformed from a backwater of European racing into an arena of cosmopolitan competition of the highest standard, with consequent benefit to all involved in the sport and industry so ideally suited to Ireland and Irishmen.

The immensity of Joe McGrath's contribution to Irish racing by means of the Irish Sweep has tended to overshadow his contribution as an owner and breeder on a colossal scale. Leading owner in Ireland on a record eight occasions, five of them consecutively, he revived the former glories of Brownstown, having purchased that historic stud in 1941. As a commercial breeder he rivalled the Aga Khan, with the important difference that, whereas the Aga Khan's involvement in bloodstock breeding in Ireland was one of expediency, McGrath's was one of total commitment. Brownstown became one of the finest studs in Europe, achieving a prominence in international circles which promoted the reputation of Irish bloodstock breeding in general.

Ever content to allow his accomplishments to speak for themselves, McGrath shunned personal publicity, concentrating on the consolidation of industrial and bloodstock dynasties which have survived their founder, flourishing in the capable hands of his sons, Patrick, Joseph and Seamus. On his death in 1966 tributes to the magnitude of this extraordinary man's achievements included those from President de Valera and his political rival, Liam Cosgrave. However, the accolade which he himself would probably have valued most came from his surviving partner, Spencer Freeman, who said simply: 'He was a glutton for work.' Paperboy, trade unionist, gunfighter, politician, emperor of industry, colossus of Irish racing, Joe McGrath became a legend in his lifetime; a legend that will endure as long as Irishmen breed and race thoroughbreds.

Michael Collins provided the training talent to complement the wealth of Joe McGrath and the riding genius of Morny Wing, forming a combination which demonstrated its awesome power through the medium of Windsor Slipper. Born in Mallow, Co. Cork, Michael Collins served his apprenticeship with Michael Dawson at Rathbride Manor. Having begun training in his home town, Collins went to America for several years and on his return ventured to the Curragh, where he commenced with a string of only three at Osborne Lodge, built by James 'Fairy' Dunne. Before long horses trained by Collins and ridden by the rejuvenated Billy Barrett began to command the respect of the Ring. His first major success was achieved when New Comet won the Phoenix Stakes for J. H. H. Peard on the latter's own track. It was a bitter blow to this aspiring young trainer when this speedy filly, having proved herself to be the fastest of her generation, died only weeks later. However, she had brought her trainer to the fore and subsequent 'touches' with His Highness in the Irish Cambridgeshire and Cameron in the Irish Lincolnshire convinced Joe McGrath that this keen-eyed Corkman had the judgement and the ability to take charge of McGrath's ever-increasing string. Now installed in Conyngham Lodge, Collins immediately sought the services of the best available jockey . . . When asked his advice, Colonel Blake sportingly advised Morny Wing, at that time his stable jockey, to accept the proffered retainer, far in excess of anything that he himself could afford. Thus was formed the 'Unholy Alliance', bane of Irish bookmakers for the next five fantastic years. Although Collins' new allegiance cost him an Irish Derby with Sol Oriens, transferred, appropriately, to Colonel Blake, compensation came quickly, in the form of Windsor Slipper. At the end of their first season Collins and Wing headed their respective lists, with prospects apparently unlimited.

The winning trail continued in 1942, when Windsor Slipper's Triple Crown was supplemented by the juvenile triumphs of Stop It, with six consecutive wins, and Fabulous, the first Brownstown-bred runners to carry the 'Green, red seams and cap'. On this occasion all three principals headed their respective categories. 1943 saw the story repeated. Arctic Sun proved to be the best two-year-old filly seen in Ireland for many years, Edvina and the Irish Derby second, Solar Prince, were' among the leading three-year-olds, while Molly's Choice and Greek Star added to the bookmakers' anguish. Once again the 'terrible trio' reigned supreme. Nor was 1944 very different, for although Collins relinquished his trainers' title to Bob Fetherstonhaugh, the three two-year-old fliers, Mafosta, Bazooka and Panastrid, sufficed to keep owner and jockey supreme in their spheres. Panastrid trained on well to win the Irish One Thousand Guineas and this Classic success, supplemented by the gains of Imaal, Three Rock and Stop It, restored Michael Collins' training title. Once again the triumverate dominated the Irish racing scene.

Having come to prominence, affluence and apparent security through the support of Joe McGrath, in 1946 Michael Collins suffered the galling experience of suddenly being deprived of the patronage of the man he had served so well. Bloodied but unbowed, Collins set about filling his empty boxes, unconsoled by the fact that McGrath's fortunes on the racecourse went into spectacular decline following the split. Nor had Collins long to wait before the Irish Two Thousand Guineas success of Mr R. A. Duggan's Solonaway, who went on to further triumphs in the Cork and Orrery Stakes and Diadem Stakes at Ascot. Solonaway subsequently stood at

Collins' Lisieux Stud on the Curragh, as the joint property of Mr Duggan and his erstwhile trainer. Before being exported to Japan in 1958, Solonaway sired Lucero, winner of the Irish Two Thousand Guineas and Sweet Solera, winner of the One Thousand Guineas and Oaks in 1961. Having been succeeded at Conyngham Lodge by his son, Con, himself a shrewd and talented trainer, particularly of sprinters, Michael Collins died in 1961.

Thursday, 25th June, 1942	**£1621 5 0**	**13 Ran**	**1½m**

The Irish Derby of 2250sovs. The winner will receive 75%, second 15%, third 10% of the stakes after deduction of bonuses of 100sovs to the owner (at entry) of the winner, 50sovs to the owner (at entry) of the second and 25sovs to the owner (at entry) of the third. For three years old entire colts and fillies. Colts, 8st 12lb; Fillies, 8st 8lb. The winner of two races each value 500sovs, or of a race value 700sovs, 4lb extra; of two races each value 700sovs, or of a race value 1400sovs, 7lb extra; of a race value 4000sovs, 10lb extra. Entrance 5 sovs on 25th September, 1940. Second entry at 15sovs on 30th October, 1940. Horses not struck out on 23rd July, 1941 pay 15sovs extra and those not struck out on 4th March, 1942 pay 15sovs in addition.

(90 subs)

1	Mr Joseph McGrath's	WINDSOR SLIPPER (M. Wing) B. colt Windsor Lad – Carpet Slipper by Phalaris.	9. 2	Collins
2	Mrs H. G. Wellesley's	GRAND INQUISITOR (G. Cooney) Ch. colt His Reverence – High Prestige.	8.12	E. McGrath
3	Mr D. Frame's	COROMYTH (G. Wells) B. colt Coronach – Diomyth.	8.12	W. J. Byrne
4	Miss Dorothy Paget's	FORT OSWAY (T. Burns) B. colt Windsor Lad – Osway.	8.12	C. A. Rogers
5	HH Aga Khan's	DODOMA (E. M. Quirke) B. filly Dastur – Mumtaz Begum.	8. 8	H. M. Hartigan
6	Mr G. J. Ellis's	MILLER (T. McNeill) B. colt Trigo – Aberystwyth.	8.12	Ussher
7	Mr P. J. Flemming's	AGAMEMNON (W. Hamill) Ch. colt Coronach – Messaline.	8.12	Lenehan
8	Mr W. M. Shawe Taylor's	KILMACDUAGH (J. Tyrrell) Ch. colt Mr Jinks – Fairy Godmother.	8.12	Ussher
9	Major D. McCalmont's	QUEEN EYOT (J. Moylan) Br. colt Windsor Lad – Queen of the Nore.	8.12	Fetherstonhaugh
0	Major J. J. Hilliard's	BENGAL (T. P. Burns) B. colt Mascot – Paula D.	8.12	C. A. Rogers
0	Mrs K. Kelly's	CARA KOOSH (Joseph Canty) Ch. colt Knight of the Garter – Gay Caprice.	8.12	W. J. Kelly
0	Mr G. J. Ellis's	CEYLON (W. Howard) B. colt Colombo – Pompeia.	8.12	Ussher
13	Sir Percy Loraine's	THUNDERBOLT (F. McGiff) B. colt Noble Star – Straight Sequence.	8.12	More O'Ferrall

SP 2/7 WINDSOR SLIPPER; 8/1 Cara Koosh; 100/6 Grand Inquisitor, Dodoma; 25/1 Miller; 50/1 Coromyth, Queen's Eyot; 100/1 Fort Osway; 200/1 Ceylon, Kilmacduagh, Bengal; 300/1 Thunderbolt; 500/1 Agamemnon. TOTE (2/- unit) 2/6. Places 3/-, 4/-, 7/-.

6 lengths, head. 2m 35s.

Winner trained by Mr M. C. Collins at Conyngham Lodge, Curragh.

1943

Undeterred by the total absence of private motor transport, a huge crowd converged on the Curragh to see The Phoenix win the Irish Derby. The outstanding two-year-old of his generation, Fred Myerscough's home-trained colt had extended his unbeaten sequence in the Irish Two Thousand Guineas, his only outing so far in 1943. In a thrilling race The Phoenix had rallied late to beat Solferino and Solar Prince. Solferino had since been held up in his work by an attack of heel-bug, while the prevailing hard ground had caused problems for Michael Collins in preparing Solar Prince. Of the remaining six runners, only Crackerjack, fourth in the Guineas, was even mildly fancied. Since his hard race in the Guineas The Phoenix had been brought back to the Curragh for an exercise spin, designed to obliterate any unpleasant memories of that race. His impressive appearance and calm behaviour in the paddock confirmed the success of that stratagem and the public supported him eagerly at 5-to-2 ON.

Skyline, pacemaker for The Phoenix, found himself redundant from the Off, for The Phoenix pulled his way to the front almost immediately, followed by Skyline, Begorra, Solar Prince and Solferino. The first challenge came from Crackerjack, whose short-lived effort was delivered half way up the straight. Solferino then took on the favourite, whom Canty roused inside the distance, keeping him going to withstand the later flourish of Solar Prince. In a fast-run race the first four home ran true to Guineas form.

Bred by Mrs H. G. Wellesley at the Killarkin Stud, Dunboyne, The Phoenix was a handsome bay colt by Chateau Bouscaut and the Firdaussi mare Fille de Poete, whose first foal he was. His third dam, Friar's Daughter, bred Bahram and Dastur. Chateau Bouscaut was by Kircubbin, winner of the Irish St Leger and afterwards a leading racehorse and sire in France, where he begot Chateau Bouscaut, winner of the Prix Robert Papin, the Prix Morny and the Prix de la Foret, making him the leading two-year-old in France in 1929. Subsequently successful in the Prix Gladiateur, the Prix du Jockey-Club (French Derby) and the Prix du Cadran (French Gold Cup), Chateau Bouscaut became a prolific sire of winners in France, among them Longthank, winner of the French One Thousand Guineas, Dornot and Chanteur 11, while outside France The Phoenix was outstandingly his best representative, Fille de Poete, a three-year-old winner at Baldoyle, also bred Tennyson, winner of four races in 1949.

Bought as a yearling for 290gns by his owner-trainer, Fred Myerscough, The Phoenix had made a winning debut at the Phoenix Park, appropriately. On his next appearance, at the Curragh in July, he had caused a major upset when scuttling the McGrath 'hot pot', Fabulous. This performance sufficiently impressed the vastly experienced Joe Canty as to make him wonder aloud whether this mightn't be the first real racehorse he had ever ridden. Having won the Phoenix Plate in the style of a champion, The Phoenix went into winter quarters and did not appear again in public until successful in the first leg of the Irish Triple Crown. The manner of his victory in the second leg suggested that here was a worthy successor to the mighty Windsor Slipper. The Irish St Leger seemed to be a formality. Opposed only by the gallant Solferino and two no-hopers, The Phoenix was unbackable at 8-to-1 ON. As he had in the Irish Derby, The Phoenix set off at a scorching pace, running his rivals off their feet for the first mile and a half. Inside the last two furlongs Jackie Power managed to get Solferino into a challenging position. Then, to the stupefied amazement of everyone present, The Phoenix capitulated without a struggle and was beaten five lengths. The impossible had happened. Solferino had upset the hottest favourite for an Irish Classic since Orby. Whether The Phoenix, as Canty claimed, was not at his best, whether Canty had made too much use of him, or whether Solferino had only now reached his peak; it did not really matter. The sad fact was that a public hero had been humbled, had sacrificed his unbeaten record and dashed the Triple Crown from his grasp.

Retired to the Ballykisteen Stud, recently purchased by David Frame, The Phoenix became a successful sire, particularly of two-year-olds. In 1949 he was syndicated for the European record of 160,000gns, having got Ash Blonde (Cheveley Park Stakes) and Morning Wings (Irish One Thousand Guineas) in his first crop. Lady Senator credited him with another Irish Guineas winner, while Prince Hansel in Ireland, Bramhall Phoenix in South Africa and Rising Flame in Japan were the best prospects to perpetuate a tenuous bloodline by the time of The Phoenix death in Ballykisteen in 1960. Because of the Ballykisteen policy of using almost exclusively the resident stallions to cover their own mares, The Phoenix became involved in a very successful 'nick' as a broodmare sire, which involved another Ballykisteen stallion, the younger Will Somers. So successful was this cross, that, in Ireland in the 'sixties, every aspiring bloodstock agent reassured wavering clients that in the offspring of Will Somers and a Phoenix mare lay the 'sovereign remedie' for all the ills of ownership!

Solferino, whose dam, Sol Speranza, won the Irish One Thousand Guineas and Oaks, retired to his owner's Woodpark Stud, Dunboyne, and sired Solonaway, before being exported to Holland in 1956. Solar Prince, dogged by hard ground, won at the Curragh as a four-year-old, before being retired to stud in Kildare. Solar Flower, his full-sister, was placed in the English One Thousand Guineas and Oaks and bred Arctic Sun, the leading Irish two-year-old of 1943, who became in turn the dam of Arctic Prince, winner of the Epsom Derby for Joe McGrath in 1951.

The success of The Phoenix in the Irish Derby was the highlight of a marvellous year for owner-trainer Fred Myerscough and jockey Joe Canty. In addition to their Classic successes with The Phoenix they combined to win the Baldoyle Derby with Scotch Guard and the Naas November Handicap with King Kling. Canty also won the Irish Oaks on Suntop. Frederick Spencer Myerscough was born in Rochdale, Lancashire, in 1881 and came to Ireland at the age of sixteen to join the Patriotic Insurance Company. He subsequently founded the firms of Messrs Coyle and Company (Brokers) Ltd, Messrs Coyle and Company (Insurance) Ltd, the Argosy Insurance Co. and the Irish Bloodstock Agency, becoming managing director of each. Turning his business acumen and technical knowledge to racing, he bought that brilliant sprinting mare Tut Tut. She was followed by Diomedes, Prince Meteor and Star Eagle, while St Donagh, carrying the colours of his business partner Mr A. B. Coyle, gave him his first success in an Irish Classic in 1925. In 1941 he won the Irish One Thousand Guineas with Milady Rose, becoming leading owner that year. However, it was not until he began to supervise the training of his own horses at his home, Clonard, Dundrum, Co. Dublin, that he achieved his most notable success through the medium of The Phoenix. Having resigned through ill-health as chairman of Goffs, a company which he had taken over and revitalised in the 'twenties, Fred Myerscough, one of the best-known personalities in Irish racing, died at Clonard in 1954. He was succeeded by his son, Cyril Myerscough, to whom must go much of the credit for the recent and dramatic development of Goffs into one of the most dynamic blood-stock sales companies in the world today.

Thursday, 24th June, 1943　　　　　**£1438**　　　**9 Ran**　　　**1½m**

The Irish Derby of 2000sovs. The winner will receive 75%, second 15%, third 10% of the stakes after deduction of bonuses of 75sovs to the owner (at entry) of winner, 40sovs to the owner (at entry) of the second and 25sovs to the owner (at entry) of the third. For three years old entire colts and fillies. Colts, 8st 12lb; fillies, 8st 8lbs. The winner of two races each value 500sovs, or of a race value 700sovs, 4lb extra; of two races each value 700sovs, or of a race value 1000sovs, 7lb extra; of a race value 1500sovs, 10lb extra. Entrance 5sovs for yearlings entered on 23rd July, 1941. Second entry at 12sovs on 8th October, 1941. Horses not struck out on 22nd July, 1942 pay 15sovs extra and those not struck out on 3rd March, 1943 pay 12sovs in addition.

(80 subs)

1	Mr F. S. Myerscough's	THE PHOENIX (Joseph Canty)	9. 5	Owner
		B. colt Chateau Bouscaut – Fille de Poete by Firdaussi.		
2	Mr Joseph McGrath's	SOLAR PRINCE (M. Wing)	8.12	Collins
		Ch. colt Solario – Serena.		
3	Mr J. McVey, jr's	SOLFERINO (John Power)	8.12	Oxx
		B. colt Fairway – Sol Speranza.		
4	Lt-Col. Sir Cecil S. King-Harman's	CRACKERJACK (E. M. Quirke)	8.12	Blake
		B. colt Coronach – Frantic.		
5	Mr D. Malone's	VICTOR HUGO (G. Wells)	8.12	Owner
		Ch. colt Mieuxce – Badr-ul-Molk.		
6	Mr F. S. Myerscough's	SKYLINE (J. Ussher)	8.12	Owner
		Br. colt Felicitation – Painted Cloud.		
7	Mr E. A. Robinson's	ST VALENTINE (T. P. Burns)	8.12	Blake
		B. colt Umidwar – Appointment.		
8	Sir T. Dixon's	CAVEHILL (A. Brabazon)	8.12	Brabazon
		B. colt Berwick – Quay Hill.		
9	Mr W. Willis's	BEGORRA (W. Barrett)	8.12	E. Parkinson
		B. colt Fairway – Begum.		

SP 2/5 THE PHOENIX; 5/1 Solferino; 6/1 Solar Prince; 100/8 Crackerjack; 50/1 Bar. TOTE (2/- unit) 2/6. Places 2/6, 3/-, 2/6.
1 length, ¾ length. 2m 37.4/5s.
Winner trained by Mr F. S. Myerscough at Clonard, Dundrum, Co. Dublin.

1944

Racing continued to survive the exigencies of war remarkably well, the single greatest handicap being the shortage of transport, which necessitated the transfer of certain Curragh fixtures to the Phoenix Park. The Classics, unaffected by these switches, suddenly assumed a much more open appearance following the enforced retirement of the brilliant filly, Arctic Sun. However, by the time the Irish Derby came up for decision a clear favourite had emerged in the shape of Slide On. In dead-heating with Good Morning in the Irish Two Thousand Guineas, Major McCalmont's colt had beaten Derby rivals Pacifier, Brave Boy, Greek Star, Hyperina and Sir Gabriel. In a driving finish Slide On had shown great courage to overcome repeated interference and was thought unlucky not to have won outright from a fitter Good Morning. The only other runner in the Irish Derby was Water Street. Successful as a two-year-old, Charlie Rogers' charge had won over seven furlongs at the Curragh earlier in June and was the only one even tentatively supported to beat the odds-on favourite.

Brave Boy was the first to show, ahead of Pacifier and Sir Gabriel, with Slide On at the back of the field. The order remained unchanged until the seven runners turned for home, where Slide On and Water Street began to move closer to Brave Boy. As this pair drew level with the long-time leader it looked as though the favourite was going to come home at his leisure. The three horses came very close together and Slide On suddenly faltered, allowing Water Street to take the lead. As Wells made the best of his way home on Water Street a major surprise seemed in prospect. However, Moylan at last got the favourite straightened out and, well inside the final furlong, Slide On got to grips with Water Street, wearing him down in the gamest possible fashion to win by a head. As in the Guineas, it appeared that Slide On had caused a lot of his own difficulties, making unduly heavy weather of what should have been a formality.

One man who felt strongly that such was not the case was the winning jockey, Jack Moylan. Once inside the weighroom he expressed his views in most forceful fashion by flooring George Wells with a blow. Following a complaint to the Stewards by Charlie Rogers an enquiry was held into the incident. One of the Stewards concerned was none other than the winning owner Dermot McCalmont, who had the invidious experience of fining his jockey £10 and severely cautioning him as to his future conduct. On reflection Charlie Rogers would appear to have regarded Moylan's action as justly provoked, for he sportingly reimbursed Jack Moylan's 'tenner'.

Bred by his owner at the Mount Juliet Stud in Co Kilkenny, Slide On was an attractive, medium-sized bay colt by Bobsleigh out of Ojala, by Buen Ojo. Bobsleigh, by the wartime Triple Crown winner Gainsborough, out of the Oaks winner Toboggan, was bred by Lord Derby. A very promising two-year-old, Bobsleigh never lived up to expectations, either on the racecourse or at stud. Slide On, from Bobsleigh's first crop, turned out to be his only Classic winner. Otherwise the best of his progeny were Lake Placid, a good handicapper, Bob Cherry, a first-class sprinter and Oxo, winner of the Grand National. Despite his failure to live up to his illustrious parentage, Bobsleigh assured himself of a place in Classic pedigrees for many years to come by becoming the maternal grandsire of Mossborough, an outstanding sire. Buen Ojo, the sire of Ojala, was a racecourse champion in his native Argentina, whence he was imported to Ireland in 1924 in part exchange for Lomond. Unfortunately, Irish and English breeders fought shy of a horse whose racing record meant nothing to them and whose pedigree – he was supposedly by Craganour – was also suspect. From the handful of runners that he did get Buen Ojo

1944. Slide On, *(Jack Moylan) just gets up to head Water Street (George Wells), nearest to the rails. Not content with beating Wells on the racecourse, Moylan continued the combat in the weighroom. Source:* The Irish Horse.

F. S. Myerscough, *owner-trainer of the Phoenix, robbed of his unbeaten record when failing in the final leg of the Irish Triple Crown. A more enduring monument to Fred Myerscough is Goffs Bloodstock Sales. Source:* The Irish Horse.

sired an extremely high percentage of winners, among them Lindos Ojos. Ojala won the Britannia Stakes at Ascot and bred three good winners prior to Slide On.

Unplaced in the Curragh October Handicap on his only other appearance in 1944, Slide On went on to prove himself a good horse both in Ireland and in England as a four-year-old. Despite being harshly treated by the handicapper, he finished second in the Royal Hunt Cup and third in the Kempton Jubilee, in addition to winning twice at the Curragh. Having won again as a five-year-old, Slide On was bought for 7000gns by the BBA, acting on behalf of the Swedish National Stud, where he took up duties as a stallion. In four seasons this honest, hard-working horse won eight races, with a mere £2880, reflecting wartime stakes, rather than any lack of ability on his part. Water Street, having gone so close in the Irish Derby, gained compensation in the Irish St Leger, beating Lancer and Brave Boy. Greek Star, successful in the Phoenix Plate as a two-year-old, went on winning until 1947 and later sired No Comment, third in the Irish Derby, and Anglo, winner of the Grand National.

Slide On's owner-breeder was one of the most consistently successful sporting owners to race either in Ireland or England during almost half a century of seeing his colours carried by a host of high-class horses. Born in 1887, Dermot Hugh Bingham McCalmont inherited the bulk of the fortune left by Colonel Harry McCalmont, the owner of Isinglass, the champion of his age. However, Dermot, having inherited a similar passion for horses, was destined to own an even greater public idol – The Tetrarch. Bought by his cousin Atty Persse as a yearling, 'the Rocking Horse' was passed on to McCalmont, whose colours he carried unbeaten in his first and only season. Steve Donoghue, his only rider, claimed that The Tetrarch had been on this earth before, while his worshipping public christened him 'the Spotted Wonder'. Retired to McCalmont's Ballylinch Stud in Co. Kilkenny, The Tetrarch became leading sire in 1919. The following year his son Tetratema gave McCalmont his first Classic success when winning the Two Thousand Guineas. Nine years later Tetratema's son, Mr Jinks, gave his owner his second Classic success when following in his father's footsteps. In Ireland McCalmont won Classics with Fourth Hand, Slide On, Avoca, Lapel, Piccadilly, Cassock, Circus Lady and Queen of Sheba.

More respected than liked among the racing community, 'the Major', as he was known, had a somewhat brusque manner, frequently mistaken for aloofness. However, as those who did get to know him discovered, his peremptory manner disguised an extremely shy nature. This is perhaps appropriately illustrated by an episode which occurred at Loughbrown one evening. The Major was being taken on a tour of inspection by his trainer, 'old Bob' Fetherstonhaugh. As each immaculate animal was presented, gleaming, for his inspection, the Major merely grunted and moved to the next box. When the two men had returned to the house, old Bob, unable to contain himself any longer, asked whether the Major had found everything to his satisfaction. McCalmont replied: 'Why yes, Bob, they look magnificent.' 'Then why the Hell couldn't you have said so!' exclaimed his relieved trainer. McCalmont then revealed that as a young man he had been taken on a similar tour of his horses by Atty Persse and had made some comment, promptly evoking a tirade from Persse to the effect that if he, McCalmont, had nothing intelligent to say, would he be so good as to refrain from saying anything at all: advice that the Major still heeded almost forty years later. A member of the Jockey Club, the Turf Club and the INHSC, Major McCalmont was also Master of the Kilkenny Hounds, with whom he continued to hunt until a year before his death, which occurred while on holiday in Rhodesia in 1968. He was succeeded by his son, Major Victor McCalmont, who has carried on his father's tradition in racing, breeding and hunting with conspicuous success.

Though the Classic success of Slide On and Avoca (Irish Oaks) were not enough to enable Major McCalmont to interrupt Joe McGrath's reign as Ireland's leading owner, they made an important contribution to Bob Fetherstonhaugh's first training championship, achieved in the twilight of a long and colourful career on the Turf. Born in 1873, Bob Fetherstonhaugh came of an old Westmeath sporting family, whose family seat was Carrick House. His early years were spent in surroundings of horses and hunting, in which racing played a very small part. However, when the family fortunes declined somewhat abruptly, in true Westmeath tradition, young Bob decided to make his own life in racing and duly absconded to join the Heath House establishment under Sam Jeffrey. Having survived living conditions which defy belief today, he found his next post, assistant trainer to the martinet Atty Persse, positively pleasant. From these experiences grew a sense of discipline and a painstaking pursuit of perfection which he was to retain throughout his life. Returning eventually to Carrick, Bob Fetherston' began to assemble what was to become one of the most powerful jumping stables in Ireland, trained on gallops laid out at nearby Gaybrook which was second to none. Ballyboggan (1918) and Dog Fox (1925) credited him with two Irish Grand Nationals, while the former also won the Leopardstown 'Chase and finished second to Poethlyn in the English Grand National, ridden by Willie Head. The sudden loss of his gallops through the intervention of the Land Commission forced him to seek stables on the Curragh and in 1924 he moved to Loughbrown Cottage, overlooking the racecourse. At this stage he began to apply his meticulous talents to flat racing, though successive victories in the Galway Plate with Symaethis (1938) and Pulcher (1939) served to show that his 'jumping hand' had lost none of its cunning.

Notwithstanding a couple of Classic successes, Bob Fetherston' would most likely be remembered as a National Hunt trainer, had it not been for the outbreak of the Second World War and the consequent embargo on the movement of horses from Ireland to England. Many years earlier, during his time with Atty Persse, Bob Fetherston' had become friendly with Dermot McCalmont, Persse's cousin and client. As a result McCalmont had promised that, in the unlikely event of his ever having horses in training in Ireland, Bob Fetherston' would train them. Thus it was that Slide On came to Loughbrown Cottage, followed by Avoca, Piccadilly, Cassock and Circus Lady, all destined to win Irish Classics in the 'Light blue and scarlet quartered, white cap'. Sunlit Ride's victory in the Irish One Thousand Guineas in 1949 completed Bob Fetherston's tally of 8½ Irish Classics. All were ridden by his stable jockeys, to whom this crusty old tyrant remained unswervingly loyal. They in turn exhibited a devotion to the horses in the stable, which occasionally reached heights of which 'Old Bob' remained happily unaware. A talented trainer and superb raconteur, whose warm heart he was ever at pains to conceal, Bob Fetherston-haugh died in 1950, missed by all who knew and respected him as a stalwart of standards to which few in his profession can nowadays aspire. He was succeeded by his son R. N. 'Brud' Fetherston', a former leading amateur on the flat and fear-somely effective as a gambling rider. Ably assisted by his charming sister Connie, Brud maintained the family association with the McCalmonts, notably with those high-class fillies Agar's Plough and Mesapotamia.

Jack Moylan, the successful rider of Slide On, completed a vastly experienced combination of owner, trainer and jockey, whose collective ages exceeded two hundred years! Born in Churchtown, Co. Cork, the eldest of three jockey brothers, Jack Moylan served his apprenticeship with P. F. Hartigan in England, riding a fair few winners before seeing service in France during World War One. Returning to Ireland to ride for the Moss stable in Limerick, Jack rode Fly Mask to finish second in the Aintree Grand National in 1924. What made that performance particularly remarkable was that he had spent the previous two weeks in hospital and tipped the scales in colours at 7st 12lbs. Two years later he headed the list of winning jockeys in Ireland with 98 successful mounts. Better known at that stage as a jump jockey, Jack Moylan was then retained by Harry Ussher. That shrewd judge, realising that Moylan's remarkable strength relative to his weight could be employed to better effect on the flat, insisted that he restrict his activities to that sphere, thereby inducing his jockey to add a flat-race finish to his other established attributes of hands and judgement. Now recognised as a horseman on a par with Canty, Burns and Quirke, Jack Moylan's height, combined with recurring knee trouble, obliged him to ride with a length of leather which made him look perhaps less of a jockey than the others, though he had no superiors in persuading a sluggish horse to give of his best. In addition to successive Irish Derbies he rode the winners of a further five Irish Classics. Bedevilled by worsening asthma in the latter years of his career, Jack Moylan died in 1949, within a very short time of his retirement. His son, Michael, friend, confidant and father-confessor to generations of jockeys, became one of the most popular valets to appear in an Irish weighroom.

Wednesday, 21st June, 1944 **£1099 10 0** **7 Ran** **1½m**

Irish Derby of 1500sov. The winner will receive 75%, second 15%, third 10% out of the stakes after deduction of bonuses of 50sovs to the owner (at entry) of the winner and 20sovs to the owner (at entry) of the second. For three years old entire colts and fillies. Colts, 8st 12lb; Fillies 8st 8lb. The winner of two races each value 400sovs, or of a race value 700sovs, 4lb extra; of two races value 700sovs, or of a race value 1000sovs, 7lb extra; of a race value 1500sovs, 10lb extra. Entrance 5sovs for yearlings entered on 26th August, 1942. Second entry at 8sovs on 14th October, 1942, Horses not struck out on 21st July, 1943 pay 10sovs extra and those not struck out on 1st March, 1944 pay 8sovs in addition.

(79 subs)

1	Major D. McCalmont's	SLIDE ON* (J. Moylan)	8.12	R. Fetherstonhaugh
		B. colt Bobsleigh – Ojala by Buen Ojo.		
2	Mr M. S. Carroll's	WATER STREET (G. Wells)	8.12	C. A. Rogers
		B. colt Early School – Nigella.		
3	Sir Harold Gray's	BRAVE BOY (Joseph Canty)	8.12	J. Canty
		B. colt Fearless Fox – Lucky Girl.		
4	Mr J. McVey, jr's	HYPERINA (John Power)	8.12	J. Oxx
		Br. colt Hyperion – Solerina by Soldennis.		
5	Mr Joseph McGrath's	GREEK STAR (M. Wing)	9. 2	M. C. Collins
		Ch. colt Hyperion – Nebular.		
6	Mr F. S. Myerscough's	PACIFIER (J. Eddery)	8.12	Owner
		B. colt Pactolus – Golden Lullaby.		
7	Mr Patrick J. Ryan's	SIR GABRIEL (Herbert Holmes)	8.12	W. J. Byrne
		B. colt Rosewell – Lady Gabriel.		

SP 4/7 SLIDE ON; 7/2 Water Street; 7/1 Brave Boy; 8/1 Greek Star; 20/1 Hyperina; 25/1 Pacifier; 50/1 Sir Gabriel. TOTE (2/- unit) 3/6. Places 2/6, 3/6.
Head, 1½ lengths. 2m 39s.
Winner trained by Mr Robert Fetherstonhaugh at Loughbrown Lodge, Curragh.

*Slide On saddled outside the enclosure.

1945

A wartime record crowd watched a field of eight parade for the Irish Derby, run on a Saturday for the first time. It was generally regarded as being a three-horse race, dominated by the topweight Stalino. On his only appearance as a two-year-old Colonel Blake's charge had won the Beresford Stakes in impressive fashion. On the strength of this performance he had started clear favourite for the Irish Two Thousand Guineas, despite his known aversion to firm ground. Though slowly away, Stalino had handled the hard going sufficiently well to beat Coup de Myth and Roussel Water. Covent Garden, Redbay and Bramford had finished well behind Stalino on that occasion and had done nothing in the meantime to suggest that they might turn the tables now. The principal dangers to the heavily bandaged favourite seemed to be Roussel Water and Coup de Myth. The former, representing the all-conquering McGrath-Collins-Wing team, had recently run out an easy winner over ten furlongs over the Derby course. Coup de Myth, purchased by Dublin bookmaker P. J. Kilmartin after his second in the Guineas, was backed from 7-to-1 to less than half those odds, attracting much more active support than Stalino, whose appearance suggested a troubled preparation. Piccadilly, a strongly-made, flashy chestnut, had done nothing to indicate that he was capable of emulating his half-brother Slide On. Both Roussel Water and Piccadilly sweated up during the preliminaries, a characteristic of their respective sires.

At a moderate pace Covent Garden and Coup de Myth led from Piccadilly, Redbay and Roussel Water, with the favourite already showing signs of ill-ease on the firm ground. The order remained unchanged until half a mile from home, where Stalino dropped back, clearly beaten. Coup de Myth, Covent Garden and Redbay swung into the straight locked in a three-way struggle for supremacy, stalked by the patiently-ridden Piccadilly. At the distance Coup de Myth got the better of Redbay and Covent Garden, but, no sooner had he done so than Jack Moylan swooped on Piccadilly, who surged past to win by a length, a head and a neck. A photograph taken from behind the judge's box suggested that the winning margin was in fact closer to four lengths and it was generally felt that a stronger gallop would have resulted in an even more clearcut success for Major McCalmont's home-bred colt. This surprise success provided Piccadilly's connections with more than ample compensation for the narrow defeat of Slide On an hour earlier.

By Fairway out of Ojala, Piccadilly had only run three times previously, and only once that season, when third to Covent Garden over a mile at the Curragh in April. Since then he had shown his shrewd trainer nothing at home, and if the public were astonished at the improvement he had suddenly shown they could derive some consolation from the fact that those connected with the colt were equally amazed. Slide On and Piccadilly thus emulated William Barnett's home-bred pair, Harinero

Piccadilly, *cruising home ahead of Coup de Myth and Redbay to credit owner, trainer and jockey with their second consecutive Irish Derby in 1945. The improvement shown by Piccadilly to emulate his half-brother owed perhaps more to Jack Moylan than his peppery old employers ever realised. Source:* The Irish Horse.

Piccadilly, *being led in by Mrs McCalmont after his surprise success. Source:* The Irish Horse.

and Primero, in winning the Irish Derby in successive years. The economic strictures of wartime racing were reflected in the fact that Major McCalmont's two winners of the Irish Derby netted no more for their wins than Primero's deadheat had earned for Mr Barnett eleven years earlier. Nevertheless, just as he had done a year previously, Major McCalmont donated £100 to the Drogheda Memorial Fund, the trust set up to assist those involved in racing who had fallen on hard times.

Fairway, the sire of Piccadilly, was a brilliant racehorse. Unplaced only twice in fifteen races, his victories included the Coventry, July and Champagne Stakes, the Eclipse and Champion Stakes (twice) and the St Leger. His most costly lapse occurred in the Epsom Derby, for which he started a red-hot favourite, got thoroughly upset in the parade and ran deplorably. Retired to Lord Derby's Woodland Stud in 1931, where he replaced his equally accomplished full-brother Pharos, Fairway became leading sire in England on four occasions and twice leading sire of broodmares. His best son was Blue Peter, winner of the Two Thousand Guineas and Epsom Derby in 1939, while Watling Street credited him with a wartime Derby. Other English Classic winners by Fairway were Pay Up, Kingsway, Garden Path and Tideway. Like many successful stallions, Fairway stamped his stock, frequently

Saturday, 23rd June, 1945　　　　**£1099 10 0**　　　　**8 Ran**　　　　1½m

Irish Derby of 1500sovs. The winner will receive 75%, second 15%, third 10% out of the stakes after deduction of bonuses of 50sovs to the owner (at entry) of the winner and 20sovs to the owner (at entry) of the second. For three years old entire colts and fillies. Colts, 8st 12lb; Fillies, 8st 8lb. The winner of two races each value 400sovs, or of a race value 700sovs, 4lb extra; of two races value 700sovs, or of a race value 1000sovs, 7lb extra; of a race value 1500sovs, 10lb extra. Entrance 5sovs for yearlings entered on 18th August, 1943. Second entry at 8sovs on 13th October, 1943. Horses not struck out on 1st July, 1944 pay 10sovs extra and those not struck out on 7th March, 1945 pay 8sovs in addition.

(77 subs)

1 Major D. McCalmont's	PICCADILLY (J. Moylan)　　B. colt Fairway – Ojala by Buen Ojo.	8.12	R. Fetherstonhaugh
2 Mr P. J. Kilmartin's	COUP DE MYTH (Joseph Canty)　Ch. colt Coup de Lyon – Diomyth.	8.12	M. Byrne
3 Mr R. L. Banker's	REDBAY (A. Barrett)　　Ch. colt Walvis Bay – Rosebud.	8.12	R. More O'Ferrall
4 Lord Talbot de Malahide's	COVENT GARDEN (J. Tyrrell)　B. colt Concerto – Orange Blossom.	8.12	A. J. Blake
5 Mr Joseph McGrath's	ROUSSEL WATER (M. Wing)　B. colt Bois Roussel – Cattewater.	8.12	M. C. Collins
6 Mr John J. Blake's	STALINO (J. Eddery)　　Br. colt Stardust – Inkling.	9. 2	A. J. Blake
7 Mr S. A. Poonawalla's	BRAMFORD (T. Burns)　　B. colt Mieuxce – Yasna.	8.12	R. More O'Ferrall
8 Sir Percy Loraine's	HYRCANIA (E. M. Quirke)　Ch. filly Hyperion – Kyloe.	8. 8	R. More O'Ferrall

SP 6/4 Stalino; 9/4 Roussel Water; 3/1 Coup de Myth; 25/1 PICCADILLY; 50/1 Bar. TOTE (2/- unit) 104/-. Places 10/-, 4/-, 36/6

1 length, Neck. 2m 44.1/5s.

Winner trained by Mr Robert Fetherstonhaugh at Loughbrown Lodge, Curragh.

transmitting his own characteristics of temperamental behaviour, sweating freely and training up very light, which may explain why his colts tended to hold their form for longer than his fillies. On his death in 1948 Fairway's line was already assured by the stud success of his sons Blue Peter, Watling Street, Fair Trial, Fair Copy and Pay Up.

Piccadilly never reproduced to devastating form which he had shown on the day it mattered most, finishing unplaced in the Irish St Leger behind that much-improved gelding Spam, the last of his kind to win an Irish Classic. Transferred to Atty Persse for his four-year-old career, Piccadilly failed to win again and was sold to go to South Africa. Coup de Myth, out of luck in two Irish Classics, gained scant compensation in selling hurdles at Southwell, but years later gained a different kind of fame as the sire of the Cheltenham Gold Cup winner What a Myth. Redbay became champion racehorse in India in 1948. Stalino, whose half-brother Bright News was destined to succeed where he had failed in an Irish Derby, became the sire of the Cesarewitch winner Three Cheers, while Hyrcania, a daughter of the Irish One Thousand Guineas winner Kyloe, redeemed her Irish Derby running in the paddocks, where she bred four winners. 1945 saw the end of the long-standing 'glorified handicap' type of Irish Derby, the establishment of the Racing Board and the birth of the Irish National Stud. It was another milestone in the history of Irish racing.

1946

The 'new look' Irish Derby, in which colts carried 9st and fillies 8st 10lbs, coincided with the end of wartime austerity and confirmed a new era in Irish racing. The occasion was marked by a high-class field and an uncomfortably large attendance. The presence of Royal Tara, the first English-trained challenger since 1941, added further interest to the outcome of Ireland's premier race. No longer distracted by the problems of penalties and allowances, the vast army of punters opted firmly for the Irish Guineas form. In the first of the Irish colts' Classics the blinkered Claro had beaten Cambyses and Royal Tara in a close finish. First and second on that occasion now shared favouritism ahead of the Beary brothers' representative, Royal Tara, whose stamina was suspect. Bracketed in the betting with Royal Tara was the McCalmont–Fetherstonhaugh candidate, Skylighter, whose sire and grandam had already combined to produce Piccadilly. An impressive winner over Grand Inquisitor earlier in the season, Skylighter would have attracted strong support were it not for Jack Moylan's decision to ride Cassock, reputedly better than his stable companion at home. Of the four quoted at 100-to-8, Invertown and Bright News seemed to possess most potential. Despite the fact that Bright News had shown little on the racecourse and even less at home, Darby Rogers sensed that his charge had the ability to win and in booking Morny Wing he had got the jockey most likely to persuade this lazy colt to give of his best.

Having exhibited remarkable patience with the unruly outsider Aquarius, the

Turf Club Stalwarts. *Major McCalmont, Lt-Col. Shirley and Sir Cecil Stafford King-Harman, successors of the 'self-electing horsedealers and breeders for sale', who had barred 'Boss' Croker from the Turf Club in the twilight of Imperial rule. Source:* The Irish Horse.

Roderic More O'Ferrall and Sir Percy Loraine, *whose numerous attempts to win the Irish Derby came closest to success with Khosro, beaten a length by Sol Oriens in 1941, having broken down in running. Source:* The Irish Horse.

starter got the field away, with Cassock the first to show. However, he was immediately headed by J. J. Parkinson's En Garde, in true Maddenstown Lodge tradition. At the half way stage the race began to assume more definite shape, as En Garde and Khyber Pass gave way to Skylighter, who yielded in turn to Claro. Having gambled on Claro's stamina in going on early to secure the favoured rails berth, Joe Canty faced strong challenges from Cambyses and Royal Tara, while Wing shadowed the leaders on Bright News. In a rough encounter Royal Tara came off worst, leaving Cambyses locked in combat with Claro. Inside the final furlong Cambyses cracked and Canty's gamble seemed likely to succeed . . . then Bright News took off 'on the Wing'. Galvanised to produce a devastating last-second burst, Bright News hit the front fifty yards from the line to win by half a length, with Cambyses less than two lengths back in third place.

A bemused and breathless crowd recovered sufficiently to give Morny Wing a rousing reception for his brilliant feat of tactical raceriding. It was his sixth and final victory in the Irish Derby and in a rare interview given after his retirement he revealed that his record-breaking sixth Irish Derby had given him more personal satisfaction than any of his previous winners; Ballyheron (1921), Waygood (1923), Rock Star (1930), Rosewell (1938) and Windsor Slipper (1942). Bright News as an incorrigibly idle colt, who had suddenly responded to the electric atmosphere of the big occasion. Sensing the startling ability this change revealed, Wing had concentrated on outsmarting his great rival. His satisfaction at having succeeded in such spectacular style remained a cherished memory of a distinguished career.

Bred by Lt. Col. E. Shirley in Co. Monaghan, Bright News fetched 1300gns at Ballsbridge as a yearling, a price which reflected the recent Beresford Stakes win of his own-brother Stalino. Their dam, Inkling, won once in 1935 before being bought by Lt. Col. Shirley for 380gns. In addition to her two Irish Classic winners, she produced King Kling (Irish Cesarewitch) and Panama Star, sold at Ballsbridge in 1946 for 6,200gns, an Irish yearling record. Stardust, the sire of Stalino and Bright

News, was a leading two-year-old in 1939 and placed in a wartime Guineas and St Leger. Another of his sons, Star King (re-named Star Kingdom) became a leading sire in Australia. His best daughter to race in Ireland was Pantomime Queen, winner of the Irish One Thousand Guineas and Oaks in 1954.

Bright News was owned by James McVey Jr, a Scottish-born businessman, with extensive interests in Ireland. Sufficiently wealthy to be able to breed and race on a scale which merited the employment of a private trainer, James McVey had engaged John Oxx in that capacity for the 1943 season, being rewarded by Solferino's shock defeat of The Phoenix in the Irish St Leger. Oxx had been replaced by 'Australian Tim' O'Sullivan, a man of very different methods. At the end of the 1945 season Mr McVey disbanded his private stable at Summerseat, while retaining the Woodpark Stud, and sent his horses in training to Captain Darby Rogers at Curragh Grange, among the draft being the winning two-year-old Bright News.

The younger son of the legendary J. T. Rogers, Darby Rogers had made his reputation as a rider in England, where he began training some years before the Second World War. Following the death in action of his elder brother Bryan and the subsequent death of his father the same year, Darby Rogers returned to Ireland in 1940 to supervise the dispersal of the family stable at Crotanstown. Having decided to remain in Ireland, he commenced training at nearby Curragh Grange and was immediately successful, winning the Irish St Leger with Mr William Barnett's Harvest Feast, thereby continuing the Barnett – Rogers association which had produced Trigo. A further seven Irish Classic winners included Sir Winston Churchill's Dark Issue in the Irish One Thousand Guineas in 1955. That particular owner-trainer association had resulted from Darby Rogers' elder son, Tim, being appointed ADC to Churchill following his defeat as Conservative Prime Minister in the first post-war General Election. Mainly for security reasons, Churchill never fulfilled his wish to see his horses run in Ireland.

Always a staunch supporter of Irish-based jockeys, Darby Rogers caused general surprise by putting young Martin Molony up on Desert Drive in the Irish Oaks in 1947. Win or lose – and Desert Drive won – Rogers had shown himself to be no less a judge of a jockey as he was of a horse. Four years later he sent out Signal Box to win the Irish Two Thousand Guineas and finish third in the Epsom Derby, ridden by the same Martin Molony, by then acclaimed as one of the most brilliant Irish jockeys of all time. For all his Classic winners, Darby Rogers' favourite horse was not one of these. Pride of place in his affections belonged to that durable old campaigner Heron Bridge, whose numerous successes included the Champion Stakes at the Curragh, a race which Rogers made virtually his own, winning it no fewer than nine times. Heron Bridge's English forays brought victories in the Churchill Stakes at Ascot and the Chester Cup. Generally successful at reasonable odds, Heron Bridge did many a good turn for his connections at a time when stake money in Ireland was at an all-time low. Bright News' Irish Derby was worth £1099. Less than twenty years later one of Darby Rogers' sons would send out Santa Claus to win over fifty times that amount in the Irish Sweeps Derby, while another son would receive even more for a yearling from his Airlie Stud. Having retired from training in the same year that his son, Mickey Rogers, won the Epsom Derby with Hard Ridden, this tall, distinguished and very dignified old soldier died in 1970.

Reappearing at the Curragh July meeting, Bright News won the Champion Plate, beating the Irish Oaks winner Linaria. Sold to Hector McDonald, a London book-maker, Bright News was forced to miss the Irish St Leger through illness. He was then sent over to Jack Reardon at Epsom and ran an excellent race to finish second to Souverain in the two-mile King George VI Stakes at Ascot in October, with the dual Classic winner Airborne behind him in third place. Though kept in training as a four-year-old, Bright News never ran again. Retired to the Woodpark Stud, Dunboyne, Bright News died as a result of pleurisy and pecarditis at the early age of ten, before making a name for himself. However, his name seems reasonably certain

Wednesday, 26th June, 1946	**£1099 10 0**	**14 Ran**	**1½m**

Irish Derby of 1500sovs. The winner will receive 75%, second 15%, third 10% out of the stakes after deduction of bonuses of 50sovs to the owner (at entry) of the winner and 20sovs to the owner (at entry) of the second. For three years old entire colts and fillies. Colts, 9st; Fillies, 8st 10lb. Entrance 5sovs for yearlings entered on 16th August, 1944. Second entry at 8sovs on 25th October, 1944. Horses not struck out on 18th July, 1945 pay 10sovs extra and those not struck out on 6th March, 1946 pay 8sovs addition.

(101 subs)

1	Mr J. McVey, jr's	BRIGHT NEWS (M. Wing)	9.0	Capt. D. Rogers
		B. colt Stardust – Inkling by Son-in-Law.		
2	HH Aga Khan's	CLARO (Joseph Canty)	9.0	H. M. Hartigan
		B. colt Colombo – Clovelly.		
3	Mr D. Morris's	ROYAL TARA (M. Beary)	9.0	J. Beary (GB)
		B. colt Mieuxce – Scotch Gold.		
4	Sir Percy Loraine's	CAMBYSES (E. M. Quirke)	9.0	R. More O'Ferrall
		Ch. colt Khosro – Mizzenette.		
5	Major D. McCalmont's	CASSOCK (J. Moylan)	9.0	R. Fetherstonhaugh
		Ch. colt Casanova – Lapel.		
6	Lord Fitzwilliam's	LIBERTY LIGHT (E. C. Elliott)	9.0	W. J. Byrne
		B. colt Signal Light – Libertine II.		
7	Mr F. S. Myerscough's	CAMPAIGNER (B. Duffy)	9.0	Owner
		B. colt Dastur – Traverse.		
8	Major D. McCalmont's	SKYLIGHTER (Herbert Holmes)	9.0	R. Fetherstonhaugh
		Ch. colt Fairway – Oracion.		
9	Sir T. Dixon's	INVERTOWN (J. Tyrrell)	9.0	Col. A. J. Blake
		Gr. colt Owenstown – Laharna by Loaningdale.		
10	Mr R. McIlhagga's	MOMENTUM (T. Burns)	9.0	B. Nugent
		Ch. colt Starmond – Grisilla.		
11	Mr J. J. Parkinson's	EN GARDE (M. Barrett)	9.0	Owner
		Ch. colt Challenge – Night Wind.		
12	Mr Terence J. S. Gray's	PYTHON (P. Powell, jr)	9.0	R. More O'Ferrall
		B. colt Sea Serpent – Forest Maid.		
13	Mr Hugh M. Ryan's	AQUARIUS (M. Molony)	9.0	Owner
		Br. colt Dragonnade – Maytide.		
14	Sir Percy Loraine's	KHYBER PASS (A. Barrett)	9.0	R. More O'Ferrall
		B. colt Khosro – Yasna.		

SP 4/1 Cambyses, Claro; 8/1 Skylighter, Royal Tara; 100/8 Invertown, Cassock, BRIGHT NEWS, Liberty Light, Momentum; 33/1 En Garde, Campaigner; 100/1 Bar. TOTE (2/- unit) 24/6. Places 6/-, 4/6, 4/6.

½ length, 1½ lengths. 2m 37.1/5s.

Winner trained by Captain Darby Rogers at Curragh Grange, Curragh.

to survive through the exploits of Scottish Rifle and Caterina, whose maternal grandsire he was destined to become.

The merit of Bright News' Irish Derby success was handsomely upheld by the subsequent achievements of those that finished behind him that day. Claro was transferred to the care of Frank Butters, for whom he proved consistent in high-class company. Having beaten the St Leger second, Murren, over one and a half miles at Newmarket in July, he then won the Great Foal Stakes over the same course, ran Sayani to a head in the Cambridgeshire and then finished second to Honeyway in the Champion Stakes. Exported to Argentina, Claro became the sire of El Chama, a shock winner of the Washington DC International, in which he represented Venezuela. Royal Tara, third in the Irish Derby, won the Kempton Jubilee twice in succession and just failed to concede 24lbs to Sterope in the Cambridgeshire of 1948, before being exported to the United States. Cambyses won the March Stakes and the Burwell Stakes at Newmarket as a four-year-old. Retired to Kildangan, he proved a failure as a sire. Cassock rewarded Jack Moylan's faith in his ability when winning the Irish St Leger in the absence of Bright News. Cassock was later exported to New Zealand as a stallion. Despite limited opportunities – he was located on the South Island – he sired a top-class stayer in Great Sensation. The renewal of international competition provided this Classic crop to prove itself one of the best in Ireland for many years. However, such an assessment is not intended to detract in any way from the undoubted brilliance of those wartime champions Windsor Slipper and The Phoenix, prevented only by circumstances from achieving international acclaim.

1947

The post-war boom in racecourse attendances and betting had begun to make a substantial contribution to the Racing Board through the levy scheme. The benefits were reflected in the 150 per cent increase in the value of the Irish Derby. This badly-needed financial boost had also been used to finance a new series of semi-Classic races, such as the Gallinule, Blandford, Tetrarch, Pretty Polly and Athasi Stakes. The Gallinule Stakes was intended, appropriately enough, as an Irish Derby trial. A combination of the effects of the longest and most severe winter of the century and the necessity to win what was now a prestige race had induced Sam Armstrong to send Sayajirao over from Newmarket for the race. While welcomed by the public, this news struck a chill of fear into the hearts of Irish owners and trainers. Third in both the English Two Thousand Guineas and Derby, Sayajirao had won the Lingfield Derby Trial and was believed by his young trainer to be only now approaching his best . . . Of the home-trained ten, only Grand Weather was seriously fancied to keep the prize at home. A cantering winner of the Irish Two Thousand Guineas, Grand Weather had since finished behind Sayajirao at Epsom, but was patriotically hoped to have made the greater improvement. Esprit de France, a winner at Epsom on Derby Day, and Sans Tache, successful in the

Gallinule Stakes, were lightly supported, more in hope than confidence. The biggest crowd to assemble on the Curragh for years scrambled for vantage points from which to witness another renewal of the age-old battle with the Saxon. Old-timers recalled the epic confrontation between St Brendan and Port Blair and hoped for a similar outcome.

Michael Beary riding the Aly Khan's pacemaker, Woodland Star, took them along at a moderate gallop in the sticky ground. Joined at the Chains by Peat Smoke, Woodland Star still held his lead turning into the straight, tracked by Sans Tache, Grand Weather, Esprit de France and Sayajirao. Hopes of a famous local victory soared as Tommy Burns dashed Grand Weather to the front two furlongs out, only to die as quickly, for once Edgar Britt unleashed Sayajirao the race was over. An electrifying burst of speed carried the Newmarket colt clear to an easy length and a half success, with Esprit de France a similar distance away in third place. The time – six seconds slower than Windsor Slipper's – reflected both the state of the ground and the winner's total superiority. Edgar Britt subsequently confirmed that he had never had an anxious moment throughout the race. Setting patriotic feelings aside, the crowd thronged the winner's enclosure, mobbing the unruffled winner so enthusiastically that a police escort had to be summoned to secure the colt's safe removal.

Bred in Yorkshire by Sir Eric Ohlson, Sayajirao was an own-brother to Sir Eric's wartime Derby winner Dante. Offered at Newmarket as a yearling, Sayajirao had realised a record 28,000gns. By the champion racehorse and sire, Nearco, Sayajirao was out of Rosy Legend, a middle-distance winner in France and now the dam of two Derby winners. By Dark Legend, Rosy Legend traced on her dam's side to Gallinule, thus maintaining that great stallion's influence on the race that his stock had done so much to dignify.

Considered astonishing at the time, Sayajirao's purchase price was a mere trifle to his new owner, whose personal income was reputed to exceed two million pounds per annum: Yuvarajah Shrimant Pratapsinha Gaekwar of Baroda. The Gaekwar had become popularly known in England during the War through his contribution of £50,000 to the Spitfire Fund. Immediately after the War it became obvious that this Indian potentate intended to rival the Aga Khan for supremacy in British racing. To achieve this ambition the Gaekwar bought Warren Place in Newmarket, into which Sam Armstrong moved from Middleham, with carte blanche to buy the best yearlings in the land. To complete the team he flew in the Australian jockey, Edgar Britt, his contract rider in India and one of the leading jockeys in that country. The successes of Sayajirao, named after one of his sons, enabled the Gaekwar of Baroda to finish second to the Aga Khan in the list of winning owners in England. The following year My Babu carried off the Two Thousand Guineas and once again Baroda took second place only to the Aga Khan. By then, however, Edgar Britt had been replaced by his mortal enemy Charlie Smirke and in 1949 Sam Armstrong found himself suddenly out of favour. But, whereas both Britt and Armstrong survived and prospered, Baroda did not. His extravagant exploits on the Turf found little favour in his native province, where his subjects were literally starving to death. Pensioned off by the Indian Government in 1949 on a niggardly £14,000 a year, the Gaekwar was officially deposed two years later, being replaced by his son. The racing empire was disbanded, the Baroda Stud on the Curragh transferred to

HH the Maharani and the dreams of outshining the Aga Khan disappeared forever. Though he later renewed his association with Sam Armstrong – helped by the sale of My Babu for over £200,000 – the Gaekwar of Baroda was a fading memory on the British Turf at the time of his death in 1968.

Frederick Lakin Armstrong – invariably called Sam to avoid family confusion – became the youngest trainer in England when he took out his licence in the 'twenties. Having moved from Middleham to Ireland and back, he transferred operations to Newmarket at Baroda's behest and there remained after the rift. A consistently successful trainer, who saddled over 1500 winners in a long and honourable career, Sam Armstrong will always be remembered for his 'apprentice academy', which produced such accomplished jockeys as Willie Snaith, Wally Swinburn, Josh Gifford and Willie Carson. The last really good horse to pass through his hands was the top-class miler Petingo, ridden to many successes by Armstrong's son-in-law, Lester Piggott. On his retirement in 1973 he was succeeded by his son Robert, while his mantle as the mentor of riding talent passed to 'Frenchie' Nicholson.

Edgar Britt arrived in England in 1945 an unknown quantity. By the time of his retirement and departure in 1959 he had become recognised as the forerunner of 'the Australian invasion' and an exceptional advertisement for the riders from 'down under'. Having ridden his first winner in Sydney in 1930 and gained valuable experience in America, Britt accepted an offer to ride in India in 1935. It was here that he made his initial reputation, riding successively for the Maharajahs of Kohalpur, Kashmir and Baroda, the last-named being the means of his moving to England, with two burning ambitions; to ride a winner for the King of England and to win the Epsom Derby. Britt's quiet, persuasive style and cool, tactical approach rapidly gained him many admirers, with the result that his break with Baroda at the end of 1947 saw him in immediate demand. The following year he rode 148 winners, including a second successive St Leger and Black Tarquin, though none of this made up for his disappointment at seeing Charlie Smirke, whom he regarded as having stolen his job with Baroda, throw away the Derby on My Babu. Britt waited a long time to get even with Smirke and, having done so, insisted that they shake hands and regard that chapter as closed. Having ridden that long-sought winner in the Royal colours, Britt moved North to ride as stable jockey for Captain Charles Elsey, with whom he shared in the Classic triumphs of Musidora, Frieze and Nearula. His last Classic winner was Honeylight in 1956 and three years later this quiet, unassuming master of his craft returned to the land of his birth. Sayajirao was the only Irish Classic winner that Edgar Britt rode and in his autobiography he related how Sayajirao's gargantuan appetite nearly cost him the race. Fortunately, Britt had arrived over to the Curragh three days before the race, just in time, through galloping and muzzling, to get the gross and greedy colt back into racing trim.

Now that Sayajirao had come to hand, he proceeded to confirm his trainer's belief that only the exceptionally prolonged winter had deprived him of the Epsom Derby. Having won the Warren Stakes at Goodwood, he was then prepared for the St Leger, which he won after a thrilling duel with the French colt, Arbar, winner of the Prix du Cadran, King George VI Stakes and Ascot Gold Cup. Placed at the top of the three-year-old Free Handicap, Sayajirao reappeared the following season to win the Hardwicke Stakes at Ascot. That was his last victory, for he was then beaten by Alycidon, a defeat which subsequently proved to have been no disgrace. Sayajirao's final race was the Eclipse Stakes, over a distance well short of his best. In a desperate finish he failed by inches to catch Petition, with Noor and Mogoli behind. Though neither the first or second ran again, the subsequent performances of Noor in America and Migoli in the Arc de Triomphe underlined the merit of Sayajirao's swansong. Retired to the Baroda Stud, he sired a succession of high-class fillies, notably Gladness, Lynchris, Dark Issue and Zenobia, but no outstanding colt, until the advent of Indiana, winner of the St Leger in 1964, second to Santa Claus in the Epsom Derby and to White Label in the Grand Prix de Paris. From his next crop Sayajirao produced I Say, third in the Epsom Derby and winner of the Coronation Cup. At the time of his death in 1966 he had become an established sire of broodmares, besides emerging as an excellent National Hunt sire, notably through

Wednesday, 25th June, 1947   **£2523 15 0**   **11 Ran**   1½m

The Irish Derby of 3500sovs. The winner will receive 75%, second 15%, third 10% of the stakes after deduction of bonuses of 100sovs to the owner (at entry) of the winner, 50sovs to the owner (at entry) of the second and 25sovs to the owner (at entry) of the third. For three years old entire colts and fillies. Colts, 9st; Fillies, 8st 10lb. Entrance 5sovs for yearlings entered on August 15th. Second entry at 15sovs on October 24th. Horses not struck out on 24th July, 1946, pay 20sovs extra, and those not struck out on 5th March, 1947, pay 25sovs in addition. One mile and a half.

(111 subs)

1	HH Maharaja of Baroda's	SAYAJIRAO (E. Britt) Br. colt Nearco – Rosy Legend by Dark Legend.	9.0	F. Armstrong (UK)
2	Mr Y. J. Kirkpatrick's	GRAND WEATHER (T. Burns) B. colt Dastur – Morning Dew.	9.0	E. McGrath
3	Prince Aly Khan's	ESPRIT DE FRANCE (M. Wing) Ch. colt Epigram – Francille.	9.0	H. M. Hartigan
4	Mr J. McLean's	SANS TACHE (Joseph Canty) Ch. colt Stardust – Movzelle.	9.0	H. M. Hartigan
5	Mr R. McIlhagga's	IMPECCABLE (W. Howard) Gr. colt His Highness – Mairi Bhan.	9.0	B. Nugent
6	Mr Joseph McGrath's	PEAT SMOKE (J. Eddery) B. colt Khosro – Smokeless.	9.0	M. C. Collins
7	Mr F. S. Myerscough's	SIGNAL CORPS (P. Powell, jr) B. colt Signal Light – Auchmor.	9.0	Owner
8	Prince Aly Khan's	WOODLAND STAR (M. Beary) B. colt Stardust – Woodside.	9.0	H. M. Hartigan
9	Major. D. McCalmont's	SUSPENDER (J. Moylan) Ch. colt Scottish Union – Lapel.	9.0	R. Fetherstonhaugh
10	Sir Harold Gray's	MAGNIFIQUE (J. G. Canty) Ch. colt Drap d'Or – Magnanimous.	9.0	J. Canty
11	Mr Patrick J. Ryan's	ARRANMORE (W. T. Wells) Br. colt Rosewell – Expensive Lady.	9.0	Owner

SP Evens SAYAJIRAO; 9/4 Grand Weather; 10/1 Esprit de France; 100/8 Sans Tache; 20/1 Woodand Star, Suspender; 40/1 Peat Smoke; 100/1 Bar. TOTE (2/- unit) 4/-. Places 2/6, 3/-, 3/-.
1½ lengths, same. 2m 41.1/5s.
Winner trained by Mr F. Armstrong at Warren Place, Newmarket.

Sempervivum, The Spaniard and latterly Brown Lad, three-time winner of the Irish Grand National.

Of those that followed Sayajirao home on the Curragh, Grand Weather was beaten a neck by Heron Bridge in the Ulster Derby and was retired to stud in Ireland after a luckless four-year-old campaign. Sunrise, winner of the Zetland Gold Cup, was the best animal sired by Grand Weather prior to his export to Greece in 1954. Esprit de France, third in the Irish Derby, won the Jockey Club Stakes at Newmarket and the Irish St Leger and was subsequently successful in America before retiring to stud. Impeccable won the City and Suburban Handicap and carried a record-breaking 9st 12lbs to a six-length success in the Chesterfield Cup at Goodwood. Retired to stud in 1950, he sired a top-class sprinter in Right Boy.

1948

The continuation of the post-war boom in Irish racing was confirmed by the Totalisator returns, nearly five times greater per meeting than in 1938. In accordance with their policy of up-grading Irish racing, the Racing Board and the Turf Club had allocated £4000 in added money for the Irish Derby. Coupled with entry fees, this created a prize fund of £9285, making it the most valuable race ever staged in Ireland. Such a prize inevitably attracted English interest, no fewer than five of the twelve runners coming from Newmarket. In the enforced absence of Beau Sabreur, brilliant winner of the Irish Two Thousand Guineas, the invaders dominated the betting. The favourite was Dorothy Paget's Aldborough, a son of her wartime Derby winner Straight Deal. Already successful three times that season, Aldborough had enjoyed a trouble-free journey by air from Newmarket, in contrast to his compatriots, who had endured a stormy crossing by sea. Of these Nathoo represented the formidable combination of the Aga Khan and Frank Butters, bidding to resume where they had left off with Turkhan in 1940. Successful at the Epsom Derby meeting, this elegant grey had been sent over in preference to Noor, third in the Epsom Derby. Nathoo was the first mount in Ireland for the Australian ace Rae Johnstone, bidding for an unique nap hand of English, French and Irish Derbies in the space of three weeks. Star of Gujrath, a 16,000gns yearling, represented the Baroda–Armstrong alliance, successful twelve months previously with Sayajirao. This highly-strung colt was ridden by Charlie Smirke, the new stable jockey. Of the home-trained hopefuls, only Wild Johnnie, one of Bob Fetherstonhaugh's two runners and the mount of stable jockey Herbert Holmes, attracted any support. Barfelt, a three-time winner as a two-year-old but subsequently disappointing, was a first Irish Derby runner for a young trainer named Vincent O'Brien.

After a delay at the start caused by the antics of Star of Gujrath and Barfelt, the starter got the field away, headed by Knight of the Roses, who led from Aldborough, Fair Ashton and Oppidian, with the two trouble-makers bringing up the rear. At the halfway mark Aldborough hit the front, while Nathoo could be seen making progress from the rear of the field, tracked by Star of Gujrath. Once they

1946. Bright News *(M. Wing) swoops to snatch victory from Claro (Joe Canty), providing Morny Wing with what he described as the most satisfying of his six successes in the race. Source:* The Irish Horse.

1948. Nathoo *(W. R. Johnstone), one of four Irish Derby winners owned by the Aga Khan and trained at Newmarket by Frank Butters. Photographed being led in by the ill-fated Aly Khan, Nathoo is followed by the ubiquitous Andy, in his own very different way an equally well-known and popular figure on the Irish racing scene of the time. Source:* The Irish Horse.

turned into the straight the race became a procession. Nathoo hit the front two furlongs out, brushed Aldborough aside and won easily from Star of Gujrath and the fast-finishing Soodani, also owned by the Aga Khan. The ever-popular Aly Khan led in his father's winner to a warm reception, and if Rae Johnstone looked less than ecstatic, as he explained in his amusing autobiography, that was simply because he felt he had done too little to deserve any part of the popular applause. He returned to the weighroom to discover that some thoughtful thief had removed £15 from his pocket, considerately leaving him a fiver. Such restraint impressed Johnstone, who wrote later that: 'The carefree atmosphere among the Irish horse enthusiasts made riding there almost a greater pleasure than anywhere else.' Charlie Smirke's feelings on this occasion have not been recorded, but his £50 fine for attempting to anticipate the start must have seemed the final straw. Crossing over to ride in the Irish Two Thousand Guineas his plane had been struck by lightning. Second in that race, he had since been beaten on My Babu in the Epsom Derby and widely criticised for that performance. Now second yet again, he had to endure a severe reprimand and a fine!

Bred by the Aga Khan at nearby Sheshoon, Nathoo was a blood-like dark grey by the talented but temperamental Nasrullah out of Taj Shirin, by Gainsborough out of Taj Mahal by The Tetrarch, the source of Nathoo's colour. Taj Shirin had previously bred Taj Akbar, second to Mahmoud in the Epsom Derby of 1936. Nasrullah, also bred in Ireland by the Aga Khan, was by the magnificent Nearco out of Mumtaz Begum. The leading two-year-old of his generation, Nasrullah was subsequently rated only 1lb behind Straight Deal, to whom he finished third in the English Derby. Retired to stud in England, Nasrullah had been purchased after one season by the Nasrullah Syndicate, comprising Gerald McElligott and Bertie Kerr, who passed the horse on to Joe McGrath for £19,000. Immediately successful as a sire, Nasrullah begot the English Classic winners Never Say Die, Nearula, Musidora and Belle of All, heading the list of sires in England in 1951. By this time the American successes of Noor and Nathoo had prompted 'Bull' Hancock of Claiborne Farms to pay 370,000 dollars for Nasrullah. From his first American crop Nasrullah sired Nashua, the greatest stakes winner in the world at the time of his retirement in 1956, prior to which he had been sold for £466,000, also a world record. Leading sire in the United States in 1955, '56, '59, '60 and '62, Nasrullah thus created yet another record by becoming the first stallion ever to head the lists on both sides of the Atlantic. Besides Nashua he sired such as Bold Ruler, Nadir, Bald Eagle and Fleet Nasrullah. Two of these in particular, Bold Ruler and Fleet Nasrullah, emulated their sire's phenomenal success, thus ensuring his place as one of the most influential stallions in thoroughbred history. The last mare covered by Nasrullah prior to his death in 1959 was La Mirambule II. The resulting produce was a colt named Nasram II, who was destined to cause such a shock when defeating the dual Derby winner Santa Claus in the King George VI and Queen Elizabeth Stakes at Ascot in 1964.

Nathoo finished last of three to the outsider Hatchik at Newmarket next time out, before winning the Gordon Stakes at Goodwood and walking over at Liverpool. He then returned to the Curragh to contest the Irish St Leger, in which he renewed rivalry with Riding Mill, Wild Johnnie, Soodani and Barfelt. Also in the field was Beau Sabreur, whom Cecil Brabazon had brought back to fitness after bouts of coughing and lameness. Ridden on this occasion by Morny Wing, Nathoo joined Riding Mill two furlongs out and was immediately challenged by Tommy Burns on Beau Sabreur. In a thrilling finish Beau Sabreur won by a short head and survived an objection for crossing, thereby proving himself the best three-year-old to race in Ireland in 1948. Nathoo was then sent over to the United States to run in the International Gold Cup at Belmont Park. Unplaced in that race, he was sold to a Mr Charles S. Howard to race in California. Having boosted the stock of his sire by his racecourse performances on the west coast, Nathoo was retired to stud in 1951 and sired many winners, though none as good as himself.

Star of Gujrath never raced again after finishing second in the Irish Derby. Purchased by the Italian Bloodstock Agency for 3100gns, he became the first son of Nearco to return to his sire's native land, where he became a leading stallion. Soodani, having won the Ulster Derby at Down Royal, joined Noor and Nashua among the Aga Khan's sales to America that year. Aldborough developed into one of the best stayers in training in England, winning the Queen Alexandra Stakes and the Doncaster Cup, only to die suddenly from intestinal trouble. Barfelt, having finished third in the Irish St Leger, went racing under Pony Club Rules. Riding Mill, only once out of the first four in twenty races, beat Black Tarquin in the Newmarket Stakes and also won the Churchill Stakes. Retired to stud at Kildangan, he was moved to England and thence to Russia. The ultimate destinations of those prominent in this good-class Irish Derby field indicated the ominous drain on English and Irish bloodstock reserves, which was to have such dramatic consequences less than twenty years later.

At the time that Nathoo provided Rae Johnstone with a winning debut in Ireland his luck was such that, as a friend observed: 'If you fell out of bed you'd land on a winner!' Born in New South Wales, a mixture of Irish, German, Portuguese and Welsh blood, William Raphael Johnstone rode his first winner at the age of fifteen and became champion jockey in Sydney in 1931. The following year he accepted a contract to ride in France for Pierre Wertheimer, thus commencing an association with French racing which lasted until his death in 1964. Immediately successful in France, Johnstone headed the jockeys' stable in three of his first six seasons. Known in Australia as 'Togo', owing to his resemblance to a Japanese general at that time, he was rechristened 'Le Crocodile' by French racing fans, enchanted by his famous late rushes to devour the opposition. In 1934 he accepted a retainer to ride for Lord Glanely, then one of the leading owners in England, for whom he immediately won the Two Thousand Guineas on Colombo. A controversial defeat on that red-hot favourite saw Johnstone return to France, embittered by his brief experience of English racing. The very next year Johnstone suffered a similar experience, this time with a French-trained filly, Mesa. Having won the One Thousand Guineas, the partnership started favourite for the Oaks. In a slowly-run muddling race Johnstone got himself hopelessly boxed in on the rails, extricating himself when the race was over to finish a flying third. Johnstone had a long wait to avenge those Epsom debacles. Imprisoned by the Germans when France was overrun, he made a successful comeback after the war when winning the Arc de Triomphe on Nikellora. Reappearing in England in 1947 he made it a case of third time lucky when winning the One Thousand Guineas and Oaks on Imprudence, a prelude to his greatest season. His telegram to the Press Club Derby Luncheon in 1948 read: 'Bon Apetit. My Love to All.' Two days later My Love erased the memory of that disastrous Derby fourteen years earlier. On the same colt he won the Grand Prix de Paris, while Bey in the Prix du Jockey Club and Nathoo in the Irish Derby made it an unforgettable year. Beaten a short head on Amour Drake in the first-ever photo finish for the Epsom Derby in 1949, he had yet another golden year in 1950. Galcador won the Epsom Derby, Asmena the Oaks, Scratch II the St Leger and the Prix du Jockey Club, Camaree the One Thousand Guineas and Corejada the Poule d'Essai des Pouliches and the Irish Oaks – seven Classics in one year.

Rae Johnstone's wonderful run of success was directly related to the post-war dominance of French horses. As their supremacy began to wain, so did the fortunes of 'Le Crocodile', though the Classic successes of Talma II in the St Leger, Sun Cap in the Oaks and Lavandin in the Derby enabled Johnstone to relish his altered reputation in England for several more years and it was in England that he enjoyed his swansong in the saddle on what he regarded as his favourite horse – Hugh Lupus. Robbed by injury of what his rider regarded as certain success in the Epsom Derby, Hugh Lupus made amends as a four-year-old. Ridden each time by Johnstone, he won the March Stakes, Hardwicke Stakes, Scarborough Stakes and Champion Stakes. In 1957 Rae Johnstone retired from the saddle, bowing out at Longchamp, the scene of so many spectacular, come-from-behind triumphs for his unorthodox but supremely effective jockey. He then began training in France, though without much success. A rumoured riding comeback never materialised and he died suddenly, following a heart attack in Paris in 1964. Strong, stylish in his own inimitable way and possessing the temperament of a great big-race rider, as his record shows, Rae Johnstone must rank among the greatest jockeys to grace the roll of honour of the Irish Derby.

Wednesday, 23rd June, 1948   **£6882 10 0**   **12 Ran**   1½m

The Irish Derby. A sweepstakes of 5sovs each for yearling entered on 26th June, 1946, or of 15sovs for those entered on 9th October, 1946, 20sovs extra for all if not struck out on Wednesday, 29th October, 1947, and 25sovs additional for all if not struck out on Wednesday, 26th May, 1948, with 4000sovs added to be contributed by the Turf Club and the Racing Board. The winner will receive 75%, second 15%, and third 10% of the whole stakes after deduction of the bonuses of 100sovs to the owner (at entry) of the winner, 50 sovs to the owner (at entry) of the second and 25sovs to the owner (at entry) of the third. For three years old entire colts and fillies. Colts, 9st; Fillies, 8st 8lb. One mile and a half.

(214 subs)

1 HH Aga Khan's — NATHOO (W. R. Johnstone) 9. 0 — F. Butters (GB)
Gr. colt Nasrullah – Taj Shirin by Gainsborough.

2 HH Maharaja of Baroda's — STAR OF GUJRATH (C. Smirke)* 9. 0 — F. Armstrong (GB)
Ch. colt Nearco – Eleanor Cross.

3 HH Aga Khan's — SOODANI (M. Wing) 9. 0 — H. M. Hartigan
Ch. colt Stardust – Fakhry.

4 Miss Dorothy Paget's — ALDBOROUGH (A. Brabazon) 9. 0 — H. Jelliss (GB)
Ch. colt Straight Deal – Pilch.

5 Mr J. Skeffington's — BARFELT (G. Wells) 9. 0 — M. V. O'Brien
B. colt Birikan – Silver Felt.

6 Sir Percy Loraine's — RIDING MILL (M. Molony) 9. 0 — H. Wragg (GB)
Ch. colt Devonian – Compress.

7 Mrs E. J. King's — WILD JOHNNIE (Herbert Holmes) 9. 0 — Fetherstonhaugh
Ch. colt Challenge – Wild Amye.

8 Miss Vera James's — FAIR ASHTON (Joseph Canty) 9. 0 — B. Thorpe
Ch. colt Fairhaven – Gay Caprice.

9 Lord Portal's — FAIR RAY (M. Beary) 9. 0 — C. Boyd-Rochfort (GB)
Ch. colt Fairway – Dawn Ray.

10 Mr L. P. Freedman's — KNIGHT OF THE ROSES (W. Howard) 9. 0 — R. Fetherstonhaugh
B. colt Knight of the Garter – Fair Rosie.

11 Lt-Col. E. Shirley's — WINDSOR WHISPER (M. Hartnett) 8.10 — M. C. Collins
B. filly Windsor Slipper – Inkling.

12 Mr J. McVey, jr's — OPPIDAN (J. Eddery) 9. 0 — K. Bell
Br. colt Felstead – Fair City.

SP 3/1 Aldborough; 7/2 NATHOO; 5/1 Star of Gujrath; 8/1 Riding Mill; 10/1 Fair Ray; 100/8 Wild Johnnie, Knight of the Roses; 100/6 Windsor Whisper; 20/1 Barfelt; 25/1 Soodani, Fair Ashton; 100/1 Bar. TOTE (2/- unit) 15/6. Places 7/-, 5/-, 12/-.
5 lengths, neck. 2m 37.4/5s.
Winner trained by Mr Frank Butters at Fitzroy House, Newmarket.

*Charles Smirke severely reprimanded and fined 50sovs for attempting to anticipate the start.

1949

Yet another record prize attracted two Epsom Derby disappointments in Brown Rover and Hindostan, each seeking a consolation Derby. The other English-trained runner, Transatlantic, had run surprisingly well to finish second to Solonaway in the Irish Two Thousand Guineas, but was not expected to savour the extra four furlongs. Of the Irish colts, Birdwatcher, an impressive winner of the ten-furlong Gallinule Stakes, was most strongly fancied, although Tribal Song, his conqueror at the Curragh in April, was quietly fancied to confirm that form, despite his poor showing in the first of the Irish colts' Classics. Hindostan, a winner over thirteen furlongs at Liverpool, represented the owner-trainer-jockey combination successful a year earlier with Nathoo. Known to prefer some give in the ground, which the Curragh would certainly not provide, Hindostan, the pick of the paddock, wore

Wednesday, 22nd June, 1949 £7505 **12 Ran** 1½m

The Irish Derby. A sweepstake of 5sovs each for yearlings entered on 25th June, 1947, or of 15sovs for those entered on 8th October, 1947, 20sovs extra for all if not struck out on 27th October, 1948, and 25sovs additional for all if not struck out on 25th May, 1949, with 4000sovs added to be contributed by the Turf Club and the Racing Board. The winner will receive 75%, second 15%, and third 10% of the whole stakes after deduction of the bonuses of 100sovs to the owner (at entry) of the winner, 50sovs to the owner (at entry) of the second and 25sovs to the owner (at entry) of the third. For three years old entire colts and fillies. Colts, 9st; Fillies, 8st 8lb. One mile and a half.

(271 subs)

1	HH Aga Khan's	HINDOSTAN (W. R. Johnstone)	9.0	F. Butters (UK)
		B. colt Bois Roussel – Sonibai by Solario.		
2	Mr Wm. Woodward's	BROWN ROVER (W. H. Carr)	9.0	Boyd-Rochfort (UK)
		B. colt Fighting Fox – La Rose (BRED IN USA).		
3	Mr T. Donnelly's	PINK LARKSPUR (P. Canty)	9.0	J. Oxx
		Br. colt Epigram – What-a-Lark.		
4	Mr A. L. Hawkins's	FLASH ARIN (M. Wing)	9.0	P. J. Prendergast
		Br. colt Mazarin – Fuel Flush.		
5	Lt-Col. E. Shirley's	BIRD WATCHER (T. Burns)	9.0	M. Collins
		Br. colt The Phoenix – Inkling.		
6	Mr Joseph McGrath's	NOVA HERCULIS (J. Eddery)	9.0	S. McGrath
		Ch. colt Nasrullah – Smokeless.		
7	Prince Aly Khan's	SOLAR (A. Brabazon)	9.0	P. Beary
		B. colt Mid-day Sun – Dorinda II.		
8	Mr T. Donnelly's	SOME BLOOM (John Power)	9.0	J. Oxx
		B. colt Full Bloom – Aerial Lass.		
9	Mr A. W. Gordon's	TRIBAL SONG (M. Molony)	9.0	D. Rogers
		B. colt Coup de Lyon – Frontier Song.		
10	Mr D. S. Kennedy's	TRANSATLANTIC (T. Hawcroft)	9.0	P. Thrale (UK)
		B. colt Colombo – Water Rose.		
11	Mr N. Galway-Greer's	BIRO (Herbert Holmes)	9.0	M. V. O'Brien
		B. colt Birikan – Fair Trick.		
12	Mr P. J. Fleming's	COUNT FLEET (W. Howard)	9.0	O. T. V. Slocock
		Ch. colt Rosolio II – Sanguinole.		

SP 5/2 Brown Rover; 5/1 Bird Watcher; 11/2 Transatlantic; 7/1 HINDOSTAN, Tribal Song; 100/8 Flash Arin; 100/6 Some Bloom; 20/1 Solar; 25/1 Nova Herculis, Biro; 33/1 Pink Larkspur; 100/1 Count Fleet. TOTE (2/- unit) 24/6. Places 7/6, 4/6, 14/-.

1¾ lengths, 2½ lengths. No time taken.
Winner trained by Mr Frank Butters at Fitzroy House, Newmarket.

heavy protective bandages in front. Neither the Aga Khan, the Aly or Frank Butters had travelled over for the race. However, Rae Johnstone, smarting at the Press criticism of his luckless ride on Amour Drake in the Epsom Derby, was confident of Hindostan's ability to beat the favourite Brown Rover, winner of a moderate Lingfield Derby Trial.

In spite of the firm ground the early pace was slow, as Flash Arin led Nova Herculis, Pink Larkspur and Brown Rover. The order remained much the same until Nova Herculis went on at half way, where he was immediately challenged by Pink Larkspur, on whom Phil Canty kicked for home fully five furlongs out. Pink Larkspur still led passing the two-furlong post, where he gave way to Brown Rover, who looked likely to justify favouritism. Once again the crowd on the Curragh were thrilled and horrified as 'Le Crocodile' came snapping after Brown Rover. Bringing Hindostan to challenge the favourite at the distance, Johnstone kept his tiring mount going with hands and heels to win cleverly by less than two lengths. Pink Larkspur stayed on to take third place, followed by Flash Arin, the first runner in an Irish Derby for trainer P. J. Prendergast and the last mount in the race for Morny Wing, who had so often made it his own. With Johnstone signifying his genuine pleasure, the crowd gave the winner a warm welcome.

One more in a seemingly endless succession of Classic winners from his owner-breeder's Sheshoon Stud, Hindostan was by the 1938 Epsom Derby winner Bois Roussel, out of Sonibai, a winning daughter of Solario. Hindostan proved to be the best of her offspring. Bois Roussel only raced three times in his life, winning the Prix Juigne at Longchamp in April for his breeder, M. Leon Volterra and the Epsom Derby for Peter Beatty. On his final appearance he finished third to Nearco in the Grand Prix de Paris. By the French Guineas winner Vatout, Bois Roussel was out of the famous broodmare Plucky Liege, whose twelve foals all won races. Sir Gallahad III won the French Guineas and the Lincolnshire Handicap, before becoming leading sire in North America four times. Bull Dog was almost as successful as a sire in America, while Admiral Drake won the Grand Prix de Paris and sired Phil Drake. Bois Roussel was bought by the Aga Khan in 1946 and became leading sire in England in 1949, where Tehran, Ridge Wood and Migoli were his best colts. The Irish Derby successes of Hindostan and Fraise du Bois II enabled him to head the Irish lists in 1949 and 1951. Through his son Tehran and grandson Tulyar, Bois Roussel achieved a partial renaissance of the St Simon line in these islands, for which breeders depended upon him so much. He became the maternal grandsire of such as Petite Etoile, St Paddy, Paddy's Sister and English Prince.

Difficult to train, like many Bois Roussels, Hindostan ran only once more, finishing a distant fifth to Djeddah in the Eclipse Stakes. He was then retired to stud in Ireland, where he attracted so little patronage that he was exported to Japan in 1955, becoming the most successful sire in the history of Japanese racing. Leading sire every year between 1961 and 1967, with the exception of 1966, when he finished second, he was stuffed after his death and put on display at one of the principal racecourses over there. Brown Rover, caught close home in the Irish Derby, returned to the Curragh to contest the Irish St Leger. Having finished second to Moondust, also ridden by Johnstone, Brown Rover was awarded the race following a successful objection by Harry Carr. Four years later Harry Carr was to become involved in another controversial Curragh Classic, with less satisfactory results for him. Pink Larkspur won the Desmond Stakes and then provided Yorkshire-born Johnny Longden, the world's most successful jockey, with his first winner in Europe, when winning another semi-Classic, the Blandford Stakes. The other proved to be of little account and 1949 cannot be rated as a particularly distinguished Irish Derby.

1950

The field of eight included the first French challenger for an Irish Derby. This was Pardal, a maiden half-brother to Ardan from the all-conquering Boussac stable, recently successful in the Epsom Derby and Oaks with Galcador and Asmena. Ridden by Rae Johnstone, also on the crest of a wave, Pardal started a slightly better favourite than Mighty Ocean, impressive winner of the Irish Two Thousand Guineas. There appeared to be little confidence behind the Aga Khan's Eclat, trained by Frank Butters' successor, Marcus Marsh, and ridden by Marsh's favourite jockey, Charlie Smirke. By contrast, Paddy Prendergast was openly optimistic that the improving Dark Warrior would provide him with success in the Irish Derby at only his second attempt. Turkish Prince was in the field to ensure a strong gallop for Dark Warrior. The other three runners were ignored.

Fulfilling his role, Turkish Prince set a blistering gallop ahead of Albus Superbus, Cecil Francis and Dark Warrior. Pardal began to take closer order passing the half way stage, where both Dark Warrior and Mighty Ocean were already under pressure, whereas Eclat appeared to be only cruising. Entering the straight Dark Warrior took the lead from his fading pacemaker, with only Eclat still a danger, for Pardal had come under severe pressure and was making no headway. Approaching the distance the hard-ridden Eclat drew level with Dark Warrior and the two colts battled grimly to the line, with Dark Warrior responding gamely to Thompson's whip and spurs. Fifty yards from the line Eclat cracked and Dark Warrior held on to win by a hard-fought half length. Pardal, for whom Johnstone offered no excuse, finished a further three lengths further back, ahead of the non-staying Mighty Ocean. The time of 2mins 37.3/5secs was the fastest recorded since Windsor Slipper had won the middle leg of his Irish Triple Crown eight years earlier. Mrs More O'Ferrall led in her husband's winner to a raucous reception, signifying the first locally-trained winner of the Irish Derby for four years.

A workman-like brown colt, Dark Warrior was bred by Miss E. C. Laidlaw at the Abbey Lodge Stud and purchased at Ballsbridge as a yearling by P. J. Prendergast for 775gns. Unfashionably bred, Dark Warrior was by the defunct Fairhaven out of Dunure, an unbroken daughter of Umidwar and a Kirk-Alloway mare. By Fairway out of Drift, Fairhaven was an own-brother to the English One Thousand Guineas winner Tideway. Their dam also produced Heliopolis and the dual wartime Classic winner Sun Stream. A winner of four races in three seasons, Fairhaven had been retired to stud in Maynooth, Co. Kildare, where his only two winners of any note were Sea Symphony, who was successful in the Irish One Thousand Guineas in 1947, and Dark Warrior, whose two victories gave Fairhaven the posthumous honour of heading the list of sires in Ireland in 1950. Coincidentally, Fairhaven's half-brother, Heliopolis, by Hyperion, headed the list of Stallions in the United States in the same year.

Frank More O'Ferrall, the winning owner, was a member of an old-established Irish racing family, besides being founder and chairman of the Anglo-Irish Blood-stock Agency, which he started back in 1928. A very prominent agency at one time, the Anglo-Irish was responsible for negotiating the purchases of both Vaguely Noble and Noblesse, in addition to arranging the lease of Ribot to the United States, a piece of high-level political bargaining which made Jimmy Carter's part in the Egyptian-Israeli peace pact appear commonplace! Prior to his association with Paddy Prendergast, Frankie More O'Ferrall had his horses in training with his brother Roderic at the family home, Kildangan, Co. Kildare. Together with their other brother, Rory, all three had the distinction of either, breeding, owning or training Irish Classic winners. Besides Dark Warrior, through whom he headed the list of winning owners in Ireland in 1950, Frankie More O'Ferrall owned that high-class sprinter Democratic and that fast filly Blue Butterfly. A prominent and popular figure in the bloodstock world, Frankie More O'Ferrall was widely mourned following the news of his death on St Leger Day 1976.

It has often been said that, while flat jockeys rarely become successful trainers, the opposite is true of former jump jockeys. Though the precedents were numerous, there was precious little to suggest that Patrick Joseph Prendergast's undistinguished riding career, terminated by a broken neck, destined him for greatness as a trainer. Finished as a jockey, Paddy Prendergast, familiarly known as 'Darkie', returned from England with his young family at the outbreak of the Second World War. Going back to England with the intention of enlisting in the RAF, he was turned down as a result of old riding injuries, arrested on suspicion of being connected with an I.R.A. scare in Liverpool and promptly deported! With little prospects and less money, he applied successfully for a trainer's licence in 1943, as did M. V. O'Brien and J. Oxx. Beginning with one horse, stabled in Michael Collins' yard, Paddy Prendergast was a familiar figure cycling across the Curragh with food for that horse in the basket of his bicycle. The horse turned out to be Pelorus, winner of no less than eighteen races . . . There was no looking back. Displaying an uncanny ability to spot potential pigeon-catching two-year-olds, Paddy Prendergast took post-war Goodwood by storm when Port Blanc pulled off a massive gamble in 1946. Port Blanc was followed by a succession of fliers: The Pie King, Windy City, Royal Duchy, Sixpence and Sarissa. Later on came such as Paddy's Sister, Floribunda, La Tendresse and Young Emperor. His juveniles monopolised the Phoenix Park '1500' from 1950 to 1956 and between 1950 and 1965 a Prendergast-trained two-year-old topped the Irish Free Handicap on twelve occasions.

In the early 'sixties Paddy Prendergast made a conscious decision to divert his proven genius with two-year-olds into the more prestigious Classic arena. Four Irish Derbies, eight Irish Guineas, one Irish Oaks and three Irish St Legers complete P. J. P.'s Irish Classic total to date and include four of the five Irish Classics in 1963, when he came closer than any trainer before or since to emulating J. T. Rogers' historic clean sweep of the Irish Classics with Museum and Smokeless in 1935. Seven times leading trainer in Ireland, Paddy Prendergast made history in 1963 when becoming the first Irish-based trainer ever to head the list in England, an achievement he repeated for the next two seasons. In 1963, that epic year, Paddy Prendergast created another, even more unusual record. When his brilliant filly, Noblesse, won the Epsom Oaks in a canter she not only became the first Irish-trained winner of that race, but also the only Irish-trained winner of an English Classic never to appear on an Irish racecourse.

For many years an ardent advocate of Australian jockeys, of whom Jackie Thompson was the first, Paddy Prendergast has in recent years placed his faith in his former apprentice Christy Roche, and seen his trust amply justified by an Irish champion jockey, whose increased stature is still no barrier against the occasional barracking from the man who made him what he is today. In between came Ron Hutchinson, whose first ride in Europe was on the Prendergast-trained Martial, successful in the Two Thousand Guineas, Garnet Bougoure and that erratic genius Des Lake. One of very few who have made real money out of training – and kept it – Paddy Prendergast can reflect with pride on having launched his sons, Kevin and Paddy Jnr to follow successfully in his footsteps. A gifted and compelling raconteur, Paddy Prendergast exemplifies Kipling's paragon in his ability to walk with Kings,

Wednesday, 21st June, 1950	**£6957 10 0**	**8 Ran**	**1½m**

The Irish Derby. A sweepstakes of 5sovs each for yearlings entered on 23rd June, 1948, or of 15sovs for those entered on 13th October, 1948, 20sovs extra for all if not struck out on 26th October, 1949, and 25sovs additional for all if not struck out on 31st May, 1950, with 4000sovs added to be contributed by the Turf Club and the Racing Board. The winner will receive 75%, second 15% and third 10% of the whole stakes after deduction of the bonuses of 100sovs to the owner (at entry) of the winner, 50sovs to the owner (at entry) of the second and 25sovs to the owner (at entry) of the third. For three years old entire colts and fillies. Colts, 9st; Fillies, 8st 11lb. One mile and a half.

(266 subs)

1	Mr F. More O'Ferrall's	DARK WARRIOR (J. W. Thompson) Br. colt Fairhaven – Dunure by Umidwar.	9.0	P. J. Prendergast
2	HH Aga Khan's	ECLAT (C. Smirke) B. colt Stardust – Eclair.	9.0	M. Marsh (GB)
3	M. Marcel Boussac's	PARDAL (W. R. Johnstone) B. colt Pharis II – Adargatis (BRED IN FRANCE).	9.0	C. Semblat (FR)
4	Mr A. W. Gordon's	MIGHTY OCEAN (A. Brabazon) Ch. colt Coup de Lyon – Fylgia.	9.0	Capt. D. Rogers
5	Mr R. McIlhagga's	TURKISH PRINCE (M. Molony) Ch. colt Turkhan – Taimone.	9.0	P. J. Prendergast
6	Mr Joseph McGrath's	EDWARDSII (R. Quinlan) B. colt Nasrullah – Cattewater.	9.0	S. McGrath
7	Mr B. Kerr's	CECIL FRANCIS (Herbert Holmes) Ch. colt Donatello II – Conversation.	9.0	P. J. Higgins
8	Mr Joseph McGrath's	ALBUS SUPERBUS (J. Eddery) Br. colt Bois Roussel – Katushra.	9.0	S. McGrath

SP 13/8 Pardal; 2/1 Mighty Ocean; 4/1 DARK WARRIOR; 7/1 Eclat; 10/1 Albus Superbus; 20/1 Turkish Prince; 50/1 Edwardsii; 100/1 Cecil Francis. TOTE (2/- unit) 11/-. Places 3/-, 4/6, 3/-.
½ length, 3 lengths. 2m 37.3/5s.
Winner trained by Mr P. J. Prendergast at Rossmore Lodge, Curragh.

1949. Hindostan *(W. R. Johnstone):* '*le Crocodile's beaming countenance reflects the satisfaction of success against all the odds. Source:* The Irish Horse.

1950. Dark Warrior, *with his happy owners Frankie and Anne More O'Ferrall, soon to make headlines of a more sensational, if less satisfying sort. Source:* The Irish Horse.

without losing the common touch. Long since a living legend at Epsom, Ascot and the Curragh, he has never ceased to look more thoroughly happy at home than braving the elements that are so much a part of what was his first love, and so nearly his Nemesis, the National Hunt.

Jackie W. Thompson became the first of an endless stream of Australian jockeys of dramatically differing abilities to be retained by an Irish stable when coming to ride for Rossmore Lodge in 1950. Though tall for a flat jockey, this stylish and likeable rider could scale 7st 7lbs. He had already ridden over 600 winners in his native land and, despite a successful season with 39 winners, he returned to Australia, subsequently refusing several offers to ride in Europe again. 'Thomo', as he is known in his native land, is still riding successfully in Sydney despite being nearly sixty years old.

Dark Warrior ran only once more that season, when sixth to Morning Madam in the Irish St Leger. Transferred to Harry Wragg's Newmarket stable to avail of the greater opportunities open to a four-year-old in England, he got no closer than second in the Queen Alexandra Stakes at Ascot and was later exported to Brazil as a stallion. Eclat, regarded by Marcus Marsh as being somewhat below true Classic standard, was just caught by Flocon in the Eclipse Stakes and disappointed thereafter. Pardal, having failed again as favourite in the Irish St Leger, made amends as a four-year-old, when winning the Princess of Wales' Stakes, the Great Yorkshire Stakes and the Jockey Club Stakes. A successful sire, he got Psidium, Firestreak, Eudaemon, Parbury and Pardallo II. Mighty Ocean finished third in the Ulster Derby and subsequently proved successful both as a racehorse and a stallion in Venezuela. Edwardsii wound up in Australia, where he sired Lord Fury, winner of the Melbourne Cup. Turkish Prince won the Ulster Derby, while Albus Superbus and Cecil Francis won over short and long distances respectively.

1951

A record field for the Irish Derby attracted a record crowd to the Curragh, surprisingly little inconvenienced by the major renovation of stands and enclosure, begun the previous winter, but as yet incomplete. The betting market was dominated by the Irish Two Thousand Guineas winner Signal Box, recently third in the Epsom Derby. Next in demand was the Harry Wragg-trained Fraise du Bois II, one-time ante-post favourite for the Epsom Derby, in which he had got himself hopelessly left at the start. The last-minute withdrawal of Rocklighter, the Irish Guineas runner-up, who had got cast in his box, gave it the appearance of a two-horse race, though one who hoped otherwise was Joe McGrath, whose Arctic Prince had sprung a surprise by his easy win in the Epsom Derby. McGrath's hopes of a double rested on Chadwick Manor, winner of the Gallinule Stakes and Ocean Echo, disappointing since his third in the Irish Two Thousand Guineas. Signal Box remained a firm favourite until a flood of last-minute support for Fraise du Bois II saw him share favouritism.

The early leader was the Prendergast pacemaker Laurie Henton, who took them along at a good gallop until rounding the turn at the top of the hill, where he gave way to Fair Contact and Magic Slipper, with Signal Box, Chadwick Manor, Faux Pas and Fraise du Bois II most prominent of the remainder. Once in the straight Martin Molony set sail for home on Signal Box, with only Bolivar and a reluctant Fraise du Bois II presenting any apparent threat. Bolivar's challenge was short-lived and Molony looked like gaining compensation for his Epsom third when Smirke finally persuaded Fraise du Bois II to put his best foot forward. Inside the final furlong Fraise du Bois drew level with the faltering Signal Box and, despite hesitating on hitting the front, went on to win by three parts of a length. Bolivar finished four lengths further back, ahead of the other English challenger Faux Pas and Chadwick Manor. The irrepressible Smirke claimed afterwards that on good ground his reluctant mount would have won by six lengths.

Those who had backed Fraise du Bois II down to favouritism for the Irish Derby had Charlie Smirke to thank for their winnings. His performance evoked this comment from the Irish Independent: '. . . no tribute can do full justice to the riding of Smirke, whose riding tactics and then his "kidding" of the winner to give his best near home will long be remembered.' Even more to the point, it was Smirke who had made the final decision to let the colt take his chance on the firm ground. Neither the owner nor Harry Wragg had made the journey to the Curragh and even after Fraise du Bois II had been successfully schooled through the Irish single-strand starting gate that morning, Wragg's representative remained undecided whether to run or not until Smirke had convinced him to do so.

A sickle-hocked and excitable son of Bois Roussel, Fraise du Bois II was foaled in France and purchased by the Begum Aga Khan for 8000gns from his breeder, Sir Alfred Butt. His dam Sugar Hills, by the sprinter Coroado, was bred by Major Lionel Holliday at his Cleaboy Stud in Co. Westmeath. Among the leading English two-year-olds of his generation, Fraise du Bois II won the Erroll Stakes and the Royal Lodge Stakes at Ascot and finished second in his other two races. Third in the

1951. Fraise Du Bois II, *owed his success to the judgement and genius of Charlie Smirke.* Source: The Irish Horse.

Joe McGrath, *whose vision made the Irish Derby what it is today, photographed here with the Epsom Derby trophy that he won with the unconsidered Arctic Prince in 1951.* Source: The Irish Horse.

Dee Stakes at Chester, giving weight to the winner, Sybil's Nephew, he had then thrown away his chance at Epsom, before finishing third to Supreme Court and the Derby second, Sybil's Nephew, at Ascot, having once again been slowly away. Following his Irish Derby success Fraise du Bois II was prepared for the St Leger, in which he finished second to the runaway winner Talma II. Unplaced behind Tulyar in both the Eclipse Stakes and the King George and Queen Elizabeth Stakes as a four-year-old, Fraise du Bois II renewed rivalry with Talma II in the Doncaster Cup, broke a leg in running and had to be destroyed. Like so many of Bois Roussel's stock, he was both talented and temperamental, in unpredictable measure.

HH the Begum Aga Khan was the fourth and last wife of the third Aga Khan, one of the most successful owners and breeders in international racing this century. Born in the South of France, the daughter of a bus conductor, six-foot brunette Yvette Blanche Larbousse had been a beauty queen prior to her marriage to the Aga Khan in 1944. Three years later she registered her colours and raced thereafter with a fair measure of success, her best horses being Fraise du Bois II, Neron and Lavandrier, all trained by Harry Wragg. The latter had opted to remain in Newmarket, where racing took place for most of that week. His forbearance was rewarded by a double later in the week, one of his winners being the Begum Aga Khan's Nightman, ridden by Charlie Smirke.

Sheffield-born Harry Wragg was the eldest and most successful of three jockey brothers, the others being Arthur and Sam. Apprenticed to Bob Colling, Harry Wragg gained rapid recognition as a consistent and level-headed rider, whose clarity of thought and action earned him the weighroom nickname of 'Brains', a form of address used for the most part by rival riders less well-endowed in that department. He won his first Epsom Derby on Felstead in 1928, employing to perfection the delayed challenge tactics, which earned him the title of 'the Head Waiter'. By proving that the Derby could be won from behind Harry Wragg did much to discredit the theory, popularised by Steve Donoghue, that the Derby could only be won from the front and thereby restored a measure of sanity to Derby riding. Two further Derbies on Blenheim and Watling Street were included in a career total of thirteen English Classics and one riding championship, prior to his retirement to

Wednesday, 27th June, 1951 £7081 5 0 **16 Ran** 1½m

The Irish Derby. A sweepstakes of 5sovs each for yearlings entered on 22nd June, 1949, or of 15sovs for those entered on 12th October, 1949, 20sovs extra for all if not struck out on 25th October, 1950, and 25sovs additional for all if not struck out on 30th May, 1951, with 4000sovs added to be contributed by the Turf Club and the Racing Board. The winner will receive 75%, second 15%, and third 10% of the whole stakes after deduction of the bonuses of 100sovs to the owner (at entry) of the winner, 50sovs to the owner (at entry) of the second and 25sovs to the owner (at entry) of the third. For three years old entire colts and fillies. Colts, 9st; Fillies, 8st 11lb. One mile and a half.

(244 subs)

1	HH Begum Aga Khan's	FRAISE DU BOIS II (C. Smirke)	9.0	H. Wragg (GB)
		B. colt Bois Roussel – Sugar Hills by Coroado.		
2	Mr F. W. Dennis's	SIGNAL BOX (M. Molony)	9.0	Capt. D. Rogers
		Ch. colt Signal Light – Mashaq.		
3	Mr B. Kerr's	BOLIVAR (E. Smith)	9.0	P. J. Higgins
		Br. colt Birikan – Book Debt.		
4	Mrs R. Foster's	FAUX PAS (W. H. Carr)	9.0	J. Lawson (GB)
		B. colt Mieuxce – Rose Bertin.		
5	Mr Joseph McGrath's	CHADWICK MANOR (J. Eddery)	9.0	P. J. Prendergast
		B. colt Nasrullah – Winged Victory by Colombo.		
6	Lt-Col. H. Boyd-Rochfort's	LOUGH ENNEL (A. Brabazon)	9.0	R. McCormick
		Br. colt Precipitation – Lady of the Lake.		
7	Mr J. P. Mallick's	SHORTGRASS (T. P. Burns)	9.0	Owner
		Gr. colt Pylon II – Celtic Bride.		
8	Miss Dorothy Paget's	FAIR CONTRACT (M. Hartnett)	9.0	C. A. Rogers
		Ch. colt Straight Deal – Fairy Deal.		
0	Mr R. S. Clark's	ANTHONY WAYNE (Herbert Holmes)	9.0	M. C. Collins
		B. colt Windsor Slipper – Bonnie Brae.		
0	Lady Fitzwilliam's	CLAUDIUS (D. Page)	9.0	R. Warden (UK)
		Ch. colt Caracalla – The Golden Girl.		
0	Mr A. L. Hawkins's	LAURIE HENTON (J. Mullane)	9.0	P. J. Prendergast
		B. colt Rockefella – Gauch.		
0	Mrs E. King's	MAGIC SLIPPER (P. Powell, jr)	9.0	M. Arnott
		Ch. colt His Slipper – Polina.		
0	Mr Joseph McGrath's	OCEAN ECHO (R. Quinlan)	9.0	S. McGrath
		B. colt Ocean Swell – Eastern Echo.		
0	Mr N. W. Waddington's	OLD NAPOLEON (John Power)	9.0	S. Murless
		Ch. colt Legend of France – Tattoo II.		
0	Mr T. I. Breen's	SECOND VIEW (T. Burns)	9.0	P. Oakes
		B. colt Turkhan – First Telegram.		
0	Mr W. R. Porter's	SIGNAL PRINCE (K. Gethin)	9.0	P. J. Higgins
		Ch. colt Signal Light – Princess Mine.		

SP 5/2 FRAISE DU BOIS II, Signal Box; 8/1 Chadwick Manor; 9/1 Faux Pas; 100/7 Bolivar; 20/1 Claudius, Fair Contract; 25/1 Magic Slipper; 33/1 Signal Prince; 40/1 Lough Ennel; 50/1 Laurie Henton, Ocean Echo; 100/1 Bar. TOTE (2/- unit) 7/-. Places 3/6, 3/-, 4/6.
¾ length, 4 lengths. 2m 33s.
Winner trained by Mr H. Wragg at Abington Place, Newmarket.

take up training in Newmarket in 1947. Bringing the same qualities of dedication and progressive thinking to bear, Harry Wragg was immediately successful in his new career. A near miss in the Epsom Derby with Fidalgo, owned by his long-standing patron Gerry Oldham, was soon rectified by the shock success of the rank outsider Psidium, on whom Roger Poincelet carried Wragg's waiting tactics to the extreme, being last around Tattenham Corner. Following the tragic death of his son-in-law Manny Mercer at Ascot in 1959, Harry Wragg has employed mainly Australian riders, masters like himself of the waiting game.

Of those that finished behind Fraise du Bois II in the Irish Derby little was subsequently heard. Signal Box never won again and died shortly after retiring to stud. Bolivar finished second to Do Well in the Irish St Leger and Chadwick Manor won the Ulster Derby. All in all, they merely served to confirm the gloomy truth that, for the time being, the French reigned supreme.

1952

The completion of the new grandstand, weighroom and enclosure at the Curragh coincided with another record year in Irish racing. The ever-increasing popularity of the Tote and the introduction of overnight declarations were two of the main factors in broadening the popular appeal of racing in Ireland. Ironically, in this year of records, Irish racing was conducted in enforced isolation, caused by the outbreak of foot-and-mouth disease in England, which prevented cross-Channel challengers until late in the season. In the absence of any English or French contenders the field for the Irish Derby looked distinctly short of quality, class being represented only by the Irish Two Thousand Guineas winner, D.C.M., and Blue Chariot, prevented by injury from contesting the first Irish Classic. Windy Torrent, second in the Irish Two Thousand Guineas and since successful in the Gallinule Stakes, needed some give in the ground, as did Morny Wing's recent Phoenix Park winner, Prince of Fairfield. Besides saddling the blinkered co-favourite, Blue Chariot, leading trainer Paddy Prendergast was also represented by Mr A. L. Hawkins' pair, Thirteen of Diamonds and Royal Coach. Though neither seemed fancied by either owner or trainer, there came inspired support from some quarter for Thirteen of Diamonds.

Royal Coach was the first to show, going into a clear lead from Mighty High, Prince of Fairfield and Windy Torrent, with Blue Chariot also prominent. At the half way mark the pacemaker faltered, giving way to Thirteen of Diamonds, on whom Jimmy Mullane set sail for home, with never a backward glance in search of his better-fancied stable companion. Behind him the hapless Blue Chariot was already in trouble on the bone-hard ground. Although Prince of Fairfield gave chase, he never looked remotely like catching the runaway Thirteen of Diamonds, who rattled up the straight to win by eight lengths in record time. The non-staying D.C.M. struggled on to take third place, while the luckless Blue Chariot, having broken down in the running, was dismounted immediately after passing the post. 'Corky' Mullane declared cheerfully that he had always considered his mount

1952. Thirteen of Diamonds, *whose success appeared to surprise most people, though not his jockey, Jimmy Mullane. Source:* The Irish Horse.

1952. P. J. Prendergast and A. L. Hawkins, *their phenomenal success would seem to have yielded more lasting benefit to one than to the other. Source:* The Irish Horse.

superior to his stable mate, Blue Chariot, adding that he fully expected the latter to break down. The contrasting countenances in the winner's enclosure made it perfectly clear that the inspired late support for the winner had not been initiated by either the owner or trainer, who was overheard to utter an ill-concealed vow that not only would his ebullient jockey never ride another horse in his yard, but that the only horses with which young master Mullane would ever again be associated would be the four employed to tear him limb from limb in as many different directions!

Credit for breeding Thirteen of Diamonds was accorded to Mr Fred Best, owner of the Boxmore Stud, Lurgan, Co. Down, who had given Lord Glentoran 300gns for the unraced Pharian mare Florrie, then in foal to Mustang. Six months before she was due to foal Florrie had injured herself so badly that Mr Best had been advised to have her put down. However, the painstaking efforts of the staff at the Veterinary College had eventually saved both the mare and her foal, Thirteen of Diamonds. Purchased for 470gns as a foal at Ballsbridge by Mr A. L. Hawkins, Thirteen of Diamonds had run seven times as a two-year-old, winning over a mile at Dundalk and running Grand Morning to a short head in the Beresford Plate, in which his stablemate, Blue Chariot, had started an odds-on favourite and finished only fourth. Prior to his success in the Irish Derby he had run three times, finishing second at the Phoenix Park on his most recent outing. On his reappearance Thirteen of Diamonds won the Blandford Stakes over the Derby course, before running the Newmarket-trained Judicate to less than a length in the Irish St Leger.

As a four-year-old Thirteen of Diamonds resumed his winning trail through the rather unlikely medium of an amateur riders' flat race at Worcester, ridden by Gordon Richards' son Peter, before running Hilltop to a short head in the Chesterfield Stakes at Goodwood under top weight. He was then second to the brilliant but wayward Zucchero at York, where his trainer carried off the Convivial Stakes with Moonlight Express and the Gimcrack Stakes with The Pie King. As Ireland's representative in the Washington DC International at Laurel Park Thirteen of Diamonds finished sixth to Worden. Purchased by Alberta Ranches, he won the Washington Birthday Handicap on the new grass track at Santa Anita, before being retired to stud. Unsuccessful as a stallion in the United States, Thirteen of Diamonds was repatriated to stand in Co. Wicklow in 1961. On his death four years later he left behind him a reasonable quota of predominantly National Hunt winners.

Mustang, who outlived his only Classic-winning son by one year, typified the best multi-purpose Irish stallions. Bred by the legendary English trainer Fred Darling, this stoutly-made son of Mieuxe defeated Rockefella as a two-year-old, finished third to Hycilla in the Champion Stakes, and won the Gordon Carter Handicap at Ascot in his third and final season. Retired to stud in Ireland, he sired Southborne, a leading Irish two-year-old, in his first crop, which also included Tangle. Having caused a major upset when beating Abernant in the King's Stand Stakes at Ascot, Tangle became a prominent National Hunt sire. Munch, Mustavon and Indigenous – the fastest horse in the world – were other good winners on the flat by the versatile Mustang, who also begot the gallant roman-nosed Quita Que, trained by Dan Moore to win the Two Mile Champion 'Chase at Cheltenham, besides finishing second in successive Champion Hurdles. As a sire of broodmares Mustang proved equally accomplished, and Arctic Melody, the best three-year-old filly of 1965, was out of a Mustang mare. Thirteen of Diamonds' two victories in 1952 enabled Mustang to head the list of sires in Ireland, with a record total of £9589.

For Paddy Prendergast and his English-born patron, Mr A. L. Hawkins, 1952 was a remarkable year. They won 31 races in Ireland, including the Irish Oaks with Five Spots, who also clocked a record time for that Classic. Prendergast's total Irish winnings of £31,527 comfortably exceeded the record, which he had set himself two years earlier, while Mr Hawkins' 18 winners netted £19,163, beating the record set by the Aga Khan in 1948. A former champion lightweight boxer, A. L. Hawkins had hotel and brewery interests in England, besides owning Devon and Exeter racecourse and the Hamwood Stud in Dunboyne, Co. Meath. In addition to his two Irish Classic winners, Hawkins owned three of P. J. Prendergast's seven consecutive winners of the Phoenix Park '1500', the race which traditionally decided the two-year-old sprint champion in Ireland. Leading owner again in 1953, Hawkins parted company with his trainer the following year, considerably reducing his racing interests in Ireland. In the remaining two years of his life he continued to keep horses in training with George Beeby and R. C. Ward in England. A distinctly colourless character, A. L. Hawkins retains his place in the history of Irish racing through his role in the rise to fame of his talented trainer. And if he found this a rather pricey privilege, he could scarcely attribute that to lack of success.

Harum-scarum Jimmy Mullane came from the County Cork and thus, though totally devoid of the business acumen for which his countrymen are justly celebrated, became known in the racing world as 'Corky'. Stable jockey to P. J. Prendergast's Rossmore Lodge stable while still a teenager, he enjoyed a similarly brief spell in the limelight as A. L. Hawkins, in whose 'Scarlet, scarlet and green hooped sleeves, scarlet cap' he scored his principal successes. Having come to prominence in 1951, Corky Mullane headed the list of Irish flat jockeys the following year with 55 winners, finishing second only to Pat Taaffe in the combined table. Superceded at Rossmore Lodge by Liam Ward, Mullane never achieved similar success, although he did win the Irish Two Thousand Guineas in 1954 on Arctic

Wind, trained by Mickey Rogers, who described him as an excellent rider over short distances, where skill at the gate counts for so much. His last major winner in Ireland was in 1959, when he rode Farney Fox in the Naas November Handicap. Moving to the North of England, he made a brief comeback in 1963, showing a glimpse of his old ability as a brilliant rider of two-year-olds, still characterised by his curious knack of holding a hard-pulling animal with his toes pointing downward. His riding career was ended by a road accident in 1974; yet another of whom it could fairly be said that success had come too soon.

Wednesday, 25th June, 1952   **£7418 15 0**   **10 Ran**   **1½m**

The Irish Derby. A Sweepstakes of 5sovs each for yearlings entered on 21st June, 1950, or of 15sovs for those entered on 11th October, 1950, 20sovs extra for all if not struck out on 31st October, 1951, and 25sovs additional for all if not struck out on 28th May, 1952, with 4000sovs added to be contributed by the Turf Club and the Racing Board. The winner will receive 75%, second 15%, and third 10% of the whole stakes after deduction of the bonuses of 100sovs to the owner (at entry) of the winner, 50sovs to the owner (at entry) of the second and 25sovs to the owner (at entry) of the third. For three years old entire colts and fillies. Colts, 9st; Fillies, 8st 11lb. One mile and a half.

(300 subs)

1	Mr A. L. Hawkins's	THIRTEEN OF DIAMONDS (J. Mullane) Ch. colt Mustang – Florrie by Pharian.	9.0	P. J. Prendergast
2	Mr D. P. Tyndall's	PRINCE OF FAIRFIELD (N. Brennan) Br. colt River Prince – Golden Ash.	9.0	M. Wing
3	Mrs John Thursby's	D.C.M. (L. Ward) Ch. colt Distingue – E.G.K.	9.0	J. M. Rogers
4	Mr Joseph McGrath's	BEECHPARK (J. Eddery) B. colt Nasrullah – Panastrid.	9.0	S. McGrath
5	Prince Aly Khan's	ROYAL BLUE (P. Canty) Ch. colt Royal Charger – Turkoise.	9.0	H. M. Hartigan
6	Mr P. Kieran's	BLUE CHARIOT (C. Smirke) Ch. colt Blue Train – Lanai.	9.0	P. J. Prendergast
7	Lt-Col. W. M. E. Denison's	WINDY TORRENT (R. E. Lawson) Ch. colt Torbido – Windway.	9.0	R. J. McCormick
8	Mr A. L. Hawkins's	ROYAL COACH (P. Powell, jr) Ch. colt Royal Charger – Four-in-Hand.	9.0	P. J. Prendergast
9	Mr M. V. O'Brien's	ILLYRIC (Herbert Holmes) Ch. colt Dante – Titanic.	9.0	Owner
10	Mr S. J. Parr's	MIGHTY HIGH (M. Hartnett) B. colt Magic Red – Topmost.	9.0	M. Hurley

SP 5/2 D.C.M., Blue Chariot; 4/1 Windy Torrent; 6/1 Prince of Fairfield; 10/1 THIRTEEN OF DIAMONDS; 100/8 Royal Blue; 100/6 Illyric; 20/1 Beechpark; 33/1 Royal Coach; 50/1 Mighty High. TOTE (2/- unit) 30/-. Places 5/6, 3/6, 3/6.
8 lengths, 6 lengths. 2m 31.2/3s.
Winner trained by Mr Patrick J. Prendergast at Rossmore Lodge, Curragh.

1953

In the year of An Tostal the Earl of Dunraven, in his concluding address as outgoing Senior Steward of the Turf Club, referred to the completion of the new grandstand at the Curragh, which had been formally opened by HE the President at the April meeting. Combined with other alterations and improvements within the enclosure, this signified the dawn of a new era at the Curragh. Gone was the century-old grandstand, built by the Railway Company in return for Turf Club cooperation in letting the railway cross the Curragh. Gone also was the old acceptance of Irish racing as a cosy, stagnant backwater of its English counterpart. All that now remained for Ireland to take its place among the leading racing nations was a truly international race, and that was closer to becoming a reality than many people could have dreamed. If not yet international, this renewal of the Irish Derby was certainly destined to become controversial.

Once again a large field was promptly narrowed down to two likely winners, the Irish colt Chamier and his Newmarket-trained rival Premonition. Chamier had finished a close second to Sea Charger in the Irish Two Thousand Guineas, in which King of the Tudors, fourth in the English equivalent, had finished third. Ridden by his big-race jockey Bill Rickaby, Chamier had scored a narrow but decisive revenge in the Gallinule Plate, in which Sea Charger had appeared not to stay. Premonition, having started co-favourite with Pinza in the Epsom Derby, had run deplorably, finishing miles behind his stable-companion Aureole. However, the galloping Curragh track, with its premium on stamina, was thought likely to suit Premonition much better. The other two cross-Channel challengers, Timberland and Victory Roll, scarcely looked good enough, while Sea Charger's ability to get the trip was doubted by all but his immediate connections.

The rank outsiders, Lissoy and Jungle Landing, were fastest out of the gate and the former went into a clear lead, until passed by Chamier at the entrance to the straight. Harry Carr, the rider of Premonition, immediately moved in pursuit of what he regarded as his only serious rival. In doing so he brought Premonition sharply in towards Chamier, crossing his field and causing a severe scrimmage, in which Sea Charger and Ardent Lover appeared to be the principal sufferers. Locked in combat, Chamier and Premonition battled stride for stride all the way up the long, staring straight, neither giving an inch, as the frenzied crowd howled for their respective fancies. In their unremitting struggle both colts rolled off a straight line, touching more than once. Just as Chamier appeared to have got the upper hand, Carr conjured a last desperate rally out of Premonition, which saw him past the post a head to the good in a photo-finish, the first in the history of the race. Almost unnoticed in the general excitement, Sea Charger had come with a blistering late run, failing by less than two lengths. Rae Johnstone was quick to contend that, given a clear run, his mount would have won.

As Rickaby brought Chamier back to unsaddle, Vincent O'Brien rushed up to ask his jockey whether he felt there were grounds for an objection to the winner. Rickaby replied that, while he had definitely been impeded, as both he and Carr were visiting jockeys and this was the Irish Derby, he would prefer not to object. Undismayed by such niceties, O'Brien conferred with his owners and then got Rickaby's consent to an objection on his behalf, on grounds of boring. The official record read as follows: 'Irish Derby – the Stewards enquired into the objection lodged by W. Rickaby (rider of Mrs F. L. Vickerman's Chamier) to Brigadier W. P. Wyatt's Premonition being declared the winner of this race on the grounds of boring. Having heard the evidence of Rickaby and W. H. Carr (rider of Premonition) who admitted that the horses touched on more than one occasion, also of the Stewards' Secretary, the Stewards sustained the objection and awarded the race to Chamier, placed Sea Charger second and Clonleason third.' Irish Racing Calendar, 3rd July 1953.

The first successful objection in the history of the Irish Derby caused pandemonium when the decision was finally announced, with the turbulent crowd bitterly divided on the merits of the Stewards' ruling. It subsequently transpired that the evidence of the Stewards' Secretary, who had watched the race from the far side of the course, had proved critical in determining the verdict. An irate Harry Carr, who claimed that the Stewards had not only acted unjustly, but that they had abused him as well, cancelled his remaining rides at the Curragh. Captain Boyd-Rochfort, who had watched the race from the stands with his owners and seen nothing wrong was so incensed that he ordered that the newsreel film of the race be shown repeatedly in the Newmarket cinema for an entire week. Moreover, it was to be more than ten years before he relented sufficiently to run another horse in his native land. What the whole unfortunate affair underlined more than anything was the absolute necessity for the introduction of the head-on film patrol camera on all racecourses.

Still a vivid memory for those present, the Chamier controversy raged on for years afterwards. Each of the jockeys concerned referred to it in their respective autobiographies and their starkly contrasting recollections make it easy to appreciate just why the Stewards' decision aroused the controversy that it did. In his book 'First to Finish' Rickaby wrote: 'There is no doubt that Premonition bored in on me in the vital stages, and he was running so close to me that I was unable to draw my whip, which was in my left hand.' In his memoirs Carr wrote that, having seen the newsreel film of the race, he was more than ever convinced that: 'So far from barging Chamier out of my way as I came through, the camera showed that I had so much room on either side that I could swing my whip without causing interference.' While any attempt to pronounce on the case is obviously pointless at this stage, it is interesting to note that Michael Moylan, who acted as Rickaby's valet that day, recalls that Rickaby's right boot was streaked with whitewash, which he would scarcely have contracted by Chamier hanging left-handed into Premonition . . .

A chestnut colt by Chamossaire, Chamier had been purchased in utero by his trainer Vincent O'Brien, acting on behalf of the Vickermans. Therapia, whose first produce Chamier was, had been sold as a yearling for 1200gns, re-sold as a maiden for 900gns, covered and purchased by O'Brien for 520gns. Her dam Silvonessa was out of Silvonah, who bred the winners of forty-seven races and traced to a union between the dual Derby winner Orby and an Irish Oaks winner Blakestown. A shy breeder, Therapia produced two other moderate winners. Chamossaire, winner of a war-time St Leger, revived briefly the struggling Matchem line, which is again threatened with extinction in these islands on the premature death of Chamossaire's greatest son Santa Claus. Other good horses sired by Chamossaire included Your Highness, Cambremer and Le Sage. His was leading sire in Ireland on three occasions, the last of these being 1964, the year of his demise.

Having suffered a setback in training following his controversial success at the Curragh, Chamier reappeared to finish a disappointing fourth in the Blandford Plate. Sent to Doncaster to renew rivalry with Premonition, Chamier could finish no nearer than sixth to that dour stayer in the St Leger. This was generally, though quite unfairly, taken as evidence that Premonition had beaten Chamier on merit at the Curragh, by virtue of being the better stayer. A surprise last-minute acceptor for the Washington DC International, Chamier finished unplaced behind Worden II. Transferred to Noel Cannon's stable in England, Chamier remained in training for two further seasons, winning the Coronation Stakes at Sandown in each of them. On the first occasion Chamier scored a notable victory over Aureole, King of the Tudors and Souepi. Retired to stud in Ireland, Chamier got off to a flying start, siring Chamour and Prince Chamier in his first crop and Light Year in his second. This rate of success he found impossible to sustain and Chamier departed these shores to Denmark in 1966.

Writing in Racing Review in January 1952 Geoffrey Gilbey, the most respected racing journalist of the time, had this to say: 'If anyone was to ask us what is the most amazing happening in racing under N.H. Rules since the war, I imagine we should at once think of the achievements of Vincent O'Brien.' At that time this remarkable young Corkman had already saddled Cottage Rake and Hatton's Grace to score hat-tricks in the Cheltenham Gold Cup and Champion Hurdle respectively. Eighteen months after that article was written O'Brien had sent out Knock Hard to win him a fourth Gold Cup, while Early Mist had become the first of his three consecutive winners of the Aintree Grand National. His feat in adding to this tally an Irish Derby with Chamier, while still not forty years of age, prompted many to wonder whether this slight, unassuming and intensely introspective little man would not come lay claim to be regarded as the outstanding Irish trainer of all time. Some years later, having twice headed the list of National Hunt trainers in England, O'Brien decided to concentrate exclusively on the flat. The triumphs of Gladness and Ballymoss established his greatness beyond all doubt, and that was to prove only the beginning . . .

Mr and Mrs Frank L. Vickerman, the owners of Chamier, were among the earliest patrons of their phenomenally successful trainer. In fact it was for Frank Vickerman, a British businessman living in Dublin, that O'Brien saddled his first winner over fences, when Panay won at Thurles in 1945. Ridden by Aubrey Brabazon, Panay ran in the colours of 'Mr D. G. B. O'Brien', Vickerman's nom de course at the time. Having persuaded the Vickermans to buy Cottage Rake, for what seemed a high price for a horse that 'made a noise', O'Brien amply repaid their trust in his talent by saddling 'the Rake' to win a Naas November Handicap, an Irish Cesarewitch, Emblem 'Chase, King George VI 'Chase and three Gold Cups, a record which gave rise to this anonymous tribute:

> Aubrey's up, the money's down,
> The frightened bookies quake.
> Come on, my lads, and give a cheer
> Begod, 'tis Cottage Rake.

William 'Buster' Rickaby, the man at the centre of the Chamier controversy, was born for the business of winning Classic races, though not the type who sought to win in the Stewards' Room what he had failed to win on the course. Born in 1917, he was the younger son of Fred Rickaby, who, like his father before him, was stable jockey to Lord Derby until his death in action in the closing stages of the First World War. Apprenticed to his uncle Walter Griggs, as was his brother Fred, Buster

The Irish Derby

Wednesday, 24th June, 1953　　　　£6758 15 0　　　　13 Ran　　　　1½m

The Irish Derby. A sweepstakes of 5sovs each for yearlings entered on 20th June, 1951, or of 15sovs for those entered on 10th October, 1951, 20sovs extra for all if not struck out on 29th October, 1952, and 25sovs additional for all if not struck out on 27th May, 1953, with 4000sovs added to be contributed by the Turf Club and the Racing Board. The winner will receive 75%, second 15%, and third 10% of the whole stakes after deduction of the bonuses of 100sovs to the owner (at entry) of the winner, 50sovs to the owner (at entry) of the second and 25sovs to the owner (at entry) of the third. For three years sold entire colts and fillies. Colts, 9st; Fillies, 8st 11lb. One mile and a half.

(269 subs)

1	Mrs F. L. Vickerman's	CHAMIER (W. Rickaby)	9.0	M. V. O'Brien

Ch. colt Chamossaire – Therapia by Panorama.

2　Mr Martin F. Molony's　SEA CHARGER (W. R. Johnstone) 9.0　　K. Kerr
Ch. colt Royal Charger – Sea Flower by Walvis Bay.

3　Mr A. L. Hawkins's　CLONLEASON (L. Ward)　9.0　　P. J. Prendergast
Ch. colt Chamossaire – Cache.

4　Mrs L. McVey's　ARDENT LOVER (A. Breasley)　9.0　　M. Hurley
B. colt Precipitation – Lucky Girl.

5　Mrs E. J. King's　SUNNY SLIPPER (P. Powell, jr)　9.0　　J. Oxx
Br. colt His Slipper – Coramere.

6　Mr F. W. Dennis's　TIMBERLAND (G. Littlewood)　9.0　　H. Peacock (GB)
B. colt Bois Roussel – Par Excellence.

7　Mr R. S. Clark's　WE DON'T KNOW (J. Mullane)　9.0　　M. C. Collins
B. colt Nasrullah – Marie Galante.

8　Mr J. H. Thursby's　BLUE NOTES (T. P. Burns)　9.0　　J. M. Rogers
Ch. colt Blue Peter – Syncopation by Rhythm.

9　Mr Joseph McGrath's　JUNGLE LANDING (John J.　9.0　　S. McGrath
Eddery)　Ch. colt Airborne – Tracked Down.

10　Mr J. Olding's　VICTORY ROLL (M. Beary)　9.0　　Persse (GB)
Br. colt Nasrullah – Chinese Puzzle.

11　Mr W. J. Kelly's　LISSOY (John Power)　9.0　　K. Bell
Ch. colt The Solicitor – Brusque.

12　Mr T. S. Reeves's　TREETOPS HOTEL (T. Burns)　9.0　　D. Rogers
Br. colt Fairwell – Lady's View.

D　Brigadier W. P. Wyatt's　PREMONITION* (W. H. Carr)　9.0　　C. Boyd-Rochfort
B. colt Precipitation – Trial Ground by Tetratema.　(GB)

SP 5/4 CHAMIER; 2/1 Premonition; 100/9 Ardent Lover; 100/7 Sea Charger, Timberland; 100/6 Clonleason, Victory Roll; 25/1 We Don't Know, Treetops Hotel; 33/1 Blue Notes; 50/1 Sunny Slipper; 100/1 Lissoy, Jungle Landing. TOTE (2/- unit) 5/-. Places 3/-, 5/-, 4/6.
PHOTO FINISH.
Winner trained by Mr. M. V. O'Brien at Churchtown, Co. Cork.

*Premonition won by a head from Chamier, with Sea Charger a length away third, Clonleason was placed fourth. The Stewards enquired into the objection lodged by T. Rickaby (rider of Chamier) to Premonition being declared the winner of this race on the grounds of boring. Having heard the evidence of Rickaby and Carr (rider of Premonition) who admitted that the horses touched on more than one occasion, also of the Steward's Secretary, the Stewards sustained the objection and awarded the race to Chamier, placed Sea Charger second and Clonleason third.

joined the Stanley House stable as lightweight jockey following the death of his uncle and thereby continued the long-standing Rickaby association with the 'Black, white cap', then the most famous colours on the English Turf. Buster Rickaby's boisterous behaviour cost him his job at Stanley House and his war service – he emerged as Major Rickaby – appeared to have cost him his livelihood in a business where memories are frighteningly short. However, having got the opportunities to demonstrate that his innate skill and the style that he had consciously modelled on that of 'Brownie' Carslake had not diminished, Rickaby was signed to ride for Jack Jarvis and thus for Lord Rosebery. Thereafter there was no looking back and by the time of his retirement in 1968 he had ridden over a thousand winners on English Courses, including three Classics, notably the One Thousand Guineas and Oaks on Sweet Solera, thus realising a lifelong ambition to follow in the footsteps of his father and grandfather. He regarded Busted, on whom he won the Eclipse Stakes in the twilight of his career, as the greatest horse he rode. Having retired to take up a position as Stipendiary Steward in Hong King, he was involved in a motor accident, which left him permanently incapacitated, an utterly unjust fate for this eloquent, educated and humourous horseman, for whose absence racing is the poorer.

Premonition, having obtained revenge in the St Leger, was involved in a very rough race in the Prix de l'Arc de Triomphe. Trained for the Cup races as a four-year-old, Premonition won the Yorkshire Cup before controversially beating his pacemaker Osborne, ridden by Premonition's lad who made no effort to win, a short head. That was the end of Premonition, who never won again, whereas Osborne turned out to be a top-class stayer. Sea Charger, having won the Irish Two Thousand Guineas and been singularly unlucky in the Irish Derby, won the Irish St Leger, before going to stud in the United States. Clonleason, promoted to third place in the Irish Derby, won the Desmond Plate and was then beaten by Ardent Lover in the Ulster Derby. Ardent Lover won the Blandford Plate and the Great Yorkshire Stakes. He subsequently went to stud in Australia. Treetops Hotel, last past the post in the Irish Derby, finished second in the Irish St Leger and won the Irish Cambridgeshire. The fact that the 1953 Irish Derby involved some high-class horses made it all the more regrettable that the race could not have been decided purely on their merits.

1954

The ups and downs of racing were vividly illustrated by the suspension of Ireland's leading trainers, P. J. Prendergast and M. V. O'Brien. O'Brien had lost his licence for three months from April 2nd, following an INHS Committee enquiry into inconsistencies in the running of his star 'chasers, Royal Tan, Lucky Dome, Knock Hard and Early Mist. O'Brien, who had just sent out Royal Tan to follow up Early Mist's success in the Aintree Grand National, issued the following statement to the Press: 'I am completely in the dark as to what, if any, offence I am *alleged* to have been guilty'. A quarter of a century later the words 'O'Brien' and 'Alleged' would reverberate around the racing world in a far happier context. Paddy Prendergast had had his licence withdrawn in Britain over the running of Blue Sail. However, the Irish authorities had found no justification for extending that disqualification to Ireland and Rossmore Lodge, the largest public stable in Europe, continued on its winning way.

While the Irish Derby had attracted two cross-Channel runners, Court Splendour and Sharragh, neither seemed up to Classic standard and both were freely available at 20-to-1. The betting market was dominated by Hubert Hartigan's representative, Tale of Two Cities, owned by the successful Scottish gambler James McLean Jr, who had brought over the North of England champion, Willie Nevett, for the ride. Successful in the Madrid and Tetrarch Plates, Tale of Two Cities had also started odds-on for the Irish Two Thousand Guineas, in which he had been thought unlucky not to overhaul Arctic Wind, with whom he was confidently expected to reverse that form. The only other runner even mildly fancied was the John Oxx-trained Hidalgo, an easy winner of the Gallinule Plate, in which he had finished miles ahead of Zarathustra.

From the start Town's Wall raced into a clear lead, tracked by Hidalgo and Zarathustra. Coming down the hill these two closed with the leader and as they did so all three swung wide into the straight, allowing Willie Nevett to seize the coveted rails berth on Tale of Two Cities. However, the favourite's advantage proved short-lived, for neither he nor Town's Wall could resist the challenge of Hidalgo, who stormed clear, looking certain to credit John Oxx with his first Irish Derby. Worse still was in store for an incredulous crowd, who gaped in silence as Paddy Powell brought the long-striding Zarathustra sweeping smoothly up the centre of the course to win by a length and a half, with the non-staying favourite half a length further back in third place. As a smiling Paddy Powell brought his handsome black mount back to unsaddle, people could be heard cursing their folly for condemning a good horse on the strength of one bad run, albeit his most recent one.

The third Irish Derby winner bred by the late Sir Harold Gray, Zarathustra was by the Coronation Cup winner Persian Gulf out of Salvia, an unraced daughter of Sansovino, and the dam of four other winners. Successful in three of his five two-year-old races, Zarathustra had finished a promising fifth in the Irish Two Thousand Guineas on his seasonal reappearance, and had been noted by many as a likely Derby colt. However, his performance in the Gallinule Plate had been so dismal that he had since been ignored, as his starting price – the longest in the history of the race – clearly confirmed. In his two subsequent races Zarathustra repeated his win over the course and distance in the Desmond Plate, beating Arctic Way, and then beat both Arctic Way and Hidalgo for a very easy victory in the Irish St Leger. A foot injury frustrated plans to prove Zarathustra's ability in international competition in the Prix de l'Arc de Triomphe and the Washington DC International and Zarathustra retired for the season as merely the best of his age in Ireland. His owner and trainer, who headed their respective lists, could congratulate themselves on having refused an offer of £8000 for their champion the previous winter, for his three victories had netted £11,748 and his prospects seemed excellent in the Cup races. The late Sir Harold Gray headed the list of winning breeders, Persian Gulf headed the list of winning sires and Paddy Powell failed by only four winners to complete an unique nap hand by heading the list of winning jockeys.

As a four-year-old Zarathustra was asked to prove himself in the highest class. Beginning with a victory at the Guineas meeting at Newmarket, he then finished third to Narrator and Darius in the Coronation Cup. Though only seventh behind Vimy in the King George VI and Queen Elizabeth Stakes, where five lengths covered the first six home, Zarathustra ended the season as he had begun it, with a victory, beating that year's Irish St Leger winner, Diamond Slipper by a neck in the Royal Whip. Kept in training a further season, Zarathustra was transferred to the care of Cecil Boyd-Rochfort in Newmarket. Unrivalled as a trainer of high-class stayers, Boyd-Rochfort proceeded to prove Zarathustra to be the best stayer in these islands, by his victories in the Ascot Stakes, Sandown Stayers' Stakes, Goodwood Cup and Shakespeare Stakes. These performances indicated that Zarathustra would almost certainly have won the Ascot Gold Cup, had he been entered. Accordingly, he remained in training as a six-year-old, with the supreme accolade of stayers as his sole objective. Boyd-Rochfort's preparation for that race invariably commenced at Christmas, after which not a day's work could be lost. Fourth in the Yorkshire Cup, and again at Hurst Park, Zarathustra was then ready to face the best stayers in Europe for what was to be his final and fiercest test. With the Freemason Lodge team in invincible form – Retrial won the Royal Hunt Cup, Almeria the Ribblesdale Stakes and Pall Mall the New Stakes – the stage was set. Stable jockey Harry Carr opted to ride Boyd-Rochfort's other runner, Atlas, in the Royal colours, and so the ride on Zarathustra went to young Lester Piggott, fresh from his Classic successes on Crepello. Carr set out to make all the running on Atlas, who led into the straight for the last time, where he was headed by the French Gold Cup winner, Cambremer. Once in line for home, Piggott produced Zarathustra with an irresistible run, which saw him surge past Cambremer and the Italian champion Tissot. By this smooth success Zarathustra had proved himself the best stayer in Europe. Some weeks later Mr Gray announced that his champion had been purchased for syndication by the Curragh Bloodstock Agency and would stand at the Ballylinch Stud in Co. Kilkenny. His stud career can only be described as disappointing and Zarathustra was subsequently exported to Japan.

Hidalgo, third to Zarathustra and Arctic Way in the Irish St Leger, defeated the

1954. Zarathustra, *the longest-priced winner in the history of the Irish Derby went on to prove himself the best stayer in Europe. Source:* The Irish Horse.

latter in the Royal Whip, before dropping dead at exercise. Tale of Two Cities, fourth to Blue Sail at York – Blue Sail was one of four York winners celebrating Paddy Prendergast's triumphant return to English racing – won the Doonside Stakes at Ayr. Transferred to Jack Fawcus, Tale of Two Cities scored his greatest success in the Zetland Gold Cup at Redcar two years later, establishing a course record. Arctic Wind, opportunist winner of the Irish Two Thousand Guineas, was exported to America. Judged on his subsequent career, Zarathustra deserves recognition as one of the better winners of the Irish Derby.

Described as owner-bred by Mr Terence Gray, Zarathustra was, in fact, the result of a mating arranged by Mr Gray's late father, Sir Harold Gray, who had won the Irish Derby back in 1931 with his home-bred colt, Sea Serpent. Sea Serpent in turn became the sire of Mondragon, bred by Sir Harold Gray and also successful in

Wednesday, 23rd June, 1954 **£7096 5 0** **11 Ran** **1½m**

The Irish Derby. A sweepstakes of 5sovs each for yearlings entered on 18th June, 1952, or of 15sovs for those entered on 8th October, 1952, 20sovs extra for all if not struck out on 28th October, 1953, and 25sovs additional for all if not struck out on 26th May, 1954, with 4000sovs added to be contributed by the Turf Club and the Racing Board. The winner will receive 75%, second 15%, and third 10% of the whole stakes after deduction of the bonuses of 100sovs to the owner (at entry) of the winner, 50sovs to the owner (at entry) of the second and 25sovs to the owner (at entry) of the third. For three years old entire colts and fillies. Colts, 9st; Fillies, 8st 11lb. One mile and a half.

(260 subs)

1	Mr Terence J. S. Gray's	ZARATHUSTRA (P. Powell, jr) Bl. colt Persian Gulf – Salvia by Sansovino.	9.0	M. Hurley
2	Mr E. V. Kelly's	HIDALGO (John Power) Br. colt Arctic Star – Senora.	9.0	J. Oxx
3	Mr J. McLean, jr.'s	TALE OF TWO CITIES (W. Nevett) B. colt Tehran – Merida.	9.0	H. M. Hartigan
4	Mr Owen Barry Walshe's	TOWN'S WALL (L. Ward) B. colt Rockefella – Ella.	9.0	M. C. Collins
5	Captain D. Rogers's	KINGSLEY (P. Canty) B. colt Kingsway – First Blush.	9.0	Owner
6	Mrs E. J. King's	IRISH SLIPPER (D. Page) Ch. colt His Slipper – Coramere.	9.0	H. Nugent
7	Mr J. H. Thursby's	ARCTIC WIND (J. Mullane) Br. colt Arctic Star – Cave of the Winds.	9.0	J. M. Rogers
8	Mrs T. Lilley's	COURT SPLENDOUR (W. Snaith) B. colt Prince Chevalier – Forecourt.	9.0	C. F. N. Murless (GB)
9	Mr N. S. Macnaughton's	BEAU SEJOUR (T. P. Burns) Ch. colt Beau Sabreur – Lyric.	9.0	J. Oxx
10	Mr Joseph McGrath's	SHARRAGH (K. Gethin) B. colt Solar Slipper – Panastrid.	9.0	W. Stephenson (GB)
11	Mr B. Kerr's	CALVERO (W. R. Johnstone) B. colt Stardust – Mogila.	9.0	K. Kerr

SP 8/15 Tale of Two Cities; 6/1 Arctic Wind; 8/1 Hidalgo; 9/1 Calvero; 20/1 Court Splendour; 25/1 Sharragh, Irish Slipper; 50/1 ZARATHUSTRA and Bar. TOTE (2/- unit) 150/6. Places 19/-, 3/6, 3/-.

1½ lengths, ½ length.
Winner trained by Mr Michael Hurley at Osborne Lodge, Curragh.

an Irish Derby. Though based in Monte Carlo, Terence Gray and his wife, the Princesse d'Imeretie Mrs Gray, were long-standing patrons of Curragh trainer Michael Hurley. A former steeplechase jockey, Michael Hurley began training in 1928 and had moved into Osborne Lodge shortly before Zarathustra's surprise success. Other good winners trained by Michael Hurley for the Grays included Engulfed, Saint Denys and Stupor Mundi.

The best horse trained by Michael Hurley in the latter part of his lengthy career was Giolla Mear. Bred by the Irish National Stud, Giolla Mear carried the Presidential colours during his excitable and unpredictable racecourse career. Ironically, having provided Paddy Powell with the biggest win of his career, Michael Hurley also provided him with the winner that ended his life as a jockey – Giolla Mear. Having passed the post in front in the Gallinule Stakes in 1968, the temperamental Giolla Mear threw Paddy Powell, fracturing his thigh and, as it turned out, ending his career. On his retirement Michael Hurley handed over to his son Dermot. After a few seasons the latter decided that it made more sense to have his horses trained by someone else and handed in his licence. Osborne Lodge became the property of that first-class National Hunt jockey, Dessie Hughes.

Paddy Powell, officially P. Powell Jr to distinguish him from his father, a formidable jump jockey, served his apprenticeship with Roderic More O'Ferrall and with Colonel Dick Warden. Having ridden his first winner on Airey Prince in 1943 at the Curragh, his favourite course, Paddy Powell caused quite a stir when moving to England to complete his apprenticeship with Warden at Newmarket, where his quiet, determined horsemanship gained him many mounts. Having ridden over sixty winners as an apprentice, Paddy Powell returned to Ireland, where he cites Zarathustra as the best horse he rode and a four-timer at the Phoenix Park, highlighted by the Phoenix Stakes on My Beau, as the finest riding feat of his career. Equally adept over hurdles, he rode the winners of the Spa and County Hurdles at Cheltenham, as well as winning the Galway Hurdle on Antigue II and Ticonderoga. His aversion to flying cost him the French St Leger on Sicilian Prince, while another riding accident meant that he forfeited an Irish Guineas on Paveh. The latter was ridden by T. P. Burns, his long-time friend, who shared with Paddy Powell that priceless ability to get two-year-olds relaxed and running straight. On his retirement Paddy Powell became an official of the Turf Club, in which capacity this likeable and universally popular character has resolved many difficult situations by good-humoured tact and understanding. When not involved in racing affairs, Paddy Powell indulges in his passion for hunting, as hunstman to the Naas Harriers.

1955

This year's Irish Derby aroused greater interest and speculation than any since the War, for it promised to resolve all the arguments which raged over the respective merits of Panaslipper, second in the Epsom Derby, and Hugh Lupus, a last-minute withdrawal from that race. Hugh Lupus had won the Irish Two Thousand Guineas very impressively and his experienced rider, Rae Johnstone, was adamant that he would have beaten Phil Drake at Epsom, had injury not prevented him from running. A long way down the field in Hugh Lupus' Irish Guineas, Panaslipper had started a rank outsider at Epsom, where he had looked certain to spring a major surprise until caught close home by Phil Drake. Despite the speed with which Phil Drake had come to snatch victory, many felt that had he been ridden with more restraint and judgement, Panaslipper would have had sufficient in reserve to contain the challenge. As Phil Drake went on to win the Grand Prix de Paris, there could be no doubting the value of the form. However, such was the air of mystique surrounding Hugh Lupus that he was backed down to even money, with the Epsom runner-up available at 4-to-1. The only others even remotely fancied to finish better than third were Daemon, Paddy Prendergast's Chester Vase winner and Epsom flop and Tara, an own-brother to the luckless Hidalgo.

Lough Ine and Beau Soleil took them along at a cracking gallop and were still clear approaching the halfway mark, where Aubrey Brabazon suddenly shot Ann's Kuda into a clear lead, tracked by Hugh Lupus. As Hugh Lupus joined Ann's Kuda two furlongs out, Eddery brought Panaslipper to challenge the leaders. These three raced uncomfortably close together until Panaslipper forged ahead to win by two lengths and the same from Hugh Lupus and Ann's Kuda, the surprise packet in the race. Johnstone declared afterwards that the favourite had been beaten on fitness and not on merit. Certainly the firm ground on the Curragh had hindered Jimmy Lenehan in his efforts to get Hugh Lupus back to his best following his Epsom mishap. However, in view of the greater test of stamina which the Curragh imposes, it was significant that Panaslipper's time was fully two seconds faster than Phil Drake's at Epsom.

Bred by Joe McGrath at nearby Brownstown Stud and trained by the owner's son Seamus, Panaslipper represented the very best of Brownstown blood. By the Champion Stakes winner Solar Slipper, a son of Windsor Slipper and Solar Flower, Panaslipper was out of the Irish One Thousand Guineas winner Panastrid. A good-looking bright chestnut, Panaslipper had won three of his six two-year-old races, including the valuable National Produce Stakes. By his victory in the Irish Derby he not only established his superiority over Hugh Lupus, the colt they said would have won the Epsom Derby, but also atoned for the failure of his own-brother Sharragh in the same race twelve months previously.

Shortly after his victory in the Irish Derby it was announced that the Irish National Stud had purchased Panaslipper for £45,000 and that the colt would finish out his three-year-old career before retiring to take up stud duties at Tully. Transferred to the care of Paddy Prendergast, Panaslipper carried the colours of HE the President for the remainder of a muddled and luckless career. Sent to Doncaster, apparently to contest the St Leger, Panaslipper ran instead in the one-mile Scarborough Stakes, in which he was narrowly beaten by a high-class older horse in Tip the Bottle, Worse still, he was injured in running and thus forced to miss the Irish St Leger – his principal objective. In an effort to redeem his reputation he was started for the Champion Stakes, in which he finished an unlucky third to Hafiz II and Darius in a falsely-run race. It was then announced that Panaslipper would run in the Washington DC International. In response to a Press campaign to employ an Irish jockey, Tommy Gosling was stood down and the ride given to Belfast-born

1955. Panaslipper, *atoning in clearcut fashion for his luckless defeat at Epsom. Source:* The Irish Horse.

T. M. Burns. Panaslipper did best of the European contingent, finishing fourth to the Venezuelan pair El Chama and Prendase. Kept in training as a four-year-old, Panaslipper was eventually retired to stud without racing again. As if disillusioned by the whole unsatisfactory state of affairs, Panaslipper proved disappointing at stud, getting nothing better than Hot Brandy and London Gazette prior to his departure to Japan in 1964.

Success in the Irish Derby, though nothing new to Joe McGrath, was gratifying for two reasons in particular. Panaslipper had been bred by him, being by a son of his previous Irish Derby winner Windsor Slipper and, even more importantly, the colt had been trained by his son Seamus, who had taken over the family string from Michael Collins. Employing the facilities at Glencairn, where Orby had been prepared for his Derby double. Though Panaslipper had narrowly failed to emulate that feat, he did follow in the footsteps of Zionist, Dastur and Turkhan in going one better at the Curragh. All three, coincidentally, were owned by the Aga Khan, whose dominance of English racing was rivalled by that of the McGraths in Ireland. Two years later Seamus would experience the agony of seeing another Epsom Classic snatched from his grasp when Silken Glider was just touched off in the Oaks by an inspired Lester Piggott on the Queen's Carrozza. Like Panaslipper, Silken Glider also gained compensation in the Irish equivalent. Leading trainer in Ireland in 1955 and three times subsequently, Seamus McGrath has continued in his quiet way to turn out an endless succession of top-class horses, notably Le Levanstell and his even greater son Levmoss. However, almost twenty years were to elapse before Seamus McGrath achieved his most coveted training success. That came in 1973, when his own colt, Weavers' Hall won a vastly different Irish Derby, now called the Irish Sweeps Derby – a monument to his late father.

Jimmy Eddery, the rider of Panaslipper, was the most successful of several riding brothers from Doneraile, Co. Cork. Having gone to England to serve his apprenticeship with Atty Persse, Eddery returned to Ireland after the outbreak of World War

Two and was immediately successful, notably for owner-trainer Fred Myerscough. He hit the headlines in 1944 when dead-heating in both the Irish Two Thousand Guineas and the Irish Cambridgeshire and the following year scored his first outright Classic success when winning the Irish Two Thousand Guineas on Stalino. His success in Ireland brought Eddery to the attention of the authorities in England, who regarded his abrupt departure from war-ravaged England as misplaced patriotism. However, the timely intercession of an infinitely better-known Cork patriot resolved that particular difficulty and in 1946 Jimmy Eddery succeeded Morny Wing as first jockey to the powerful McGrath stable. A greater contrast would have been difficult to imagine. Lacking any of his predecessor's artistry and finesse, Eddery

Wednesday, 22nd June, 1955   **£6387 10 0**   **13 Ran**   **1½m**

The Irish Derby. A sweepstakes of 5sovs each for yearlings entered on 24th June, 1953, or of 15sovs for those entered on 7th October, 1953, 20sovs extra for all if not struck out on 27th October, 1954, and 25sovs additional for all if not struck out on 25th May, 1955, with 4000sovs added to be contributed by the Turf Club and the Racing Board. The winner will receive 75%, second 15%, and third 10% of the whole stakes after deduction of the bonuses of 100sovs to the owner (at entry) of the winner, 50sovs to the owner (at entry) of the second and 25sovs to the owner (at entry) or the third. For three years old entire colts and fillies. Colts, 9st; Fillies, 8st 11lb. One mile and a half.

(210 subs)

1	Mr Joseph McGrath's	PANASLIPPER (J. Eddery)	9.0	S. McGrath
		Ch. colt Solar Slipper – Panastrid by Panorama.		
2	Lady Ursula Vernon's	HUGH LUPUS (W. R. Johnstone)	9.0	J. Lenehan
		B. colt Djibel – Sakountala. (FOALED IN FRANCE).		
3	Dr John Dennehy's	ANN'S KUDA (A. Brabazon)	9.0	C. Brabazon
		Ch. colt Niccolo Dell'Arca – Superlative.		
4	Mr E. V. Kelly's	TARA (John Power)	9.0	J. Oxx
		B. colt Arctic Star – Senora.		
5	Mrs E. J. King's	DIAMOND SLIPPER (D. Page)	9.0	H. Nugent
		Br. colt His Slipper – Narina.		
6	Mrs E. McGrath's	ARCTIC TIME (P. Powell, jr)	9.0	S. McGrath
		B. colt Arctic Star – Dancing Time.		
7	Mr B. M. Mavroleon's	DAEMON (L. Ward)	9.0	P. J. Prendergast
		B. colt Niccolo Dell'Arca – Kyands.		
8	Mr J. J. Thompson's	LISNASKEA (T. P. Burns)	9.0	K. Bell
		B. colt Solar Slipper – Panama's Star.		
0	Mr R. Sullivan's	BEAU SOLEIL (P. Sullivan)	9.0	J. Oxx
		B. colt Beau Sabreur – Sol Speranza.		
0	Mrs L. McVey's	BRIGHT MOMENT (R. Fawdon)	9.0	T. Farmer (GB)
		B/Br. colt Bright News – Solifa.		
0	Mr J. H. Thursby's	GOLDEN CREST (P. Canty)	9.0	J. M. Rogers
		B. colt Auralia – Glossy Ibis.		
0	Mr D. J. Coughlan's	LOUGH INE (J. O'Sullivan)	9.0	M. Hurley
		Br. colt Arctic Star – Mindy.		
0	Mr S. Myler's	PAUL'S CROSS (M. Kennedy)	9.0	M. Hurley
		B. colt Bright News – Solvada.		

SP Evens Hugh Lupus; 4/1 PANASLIPPER; 11/2 Arctic Time; 100/8 Daemon; 100/7 Tara; 22/1 Diamond Slipper; 50/1 Ann's Kuda; 66/1 Bar. TOTE (2/- unit) 14/6. Places 4/-, 3/-, 17/-.
2 lengths, same. 2m 37.84s.
Winner trained by Mr Seamus McGrath at Glencairn, Sandyford, Co. Dublin.

rode his winners by force rather than persuasion. His rough-riding tactics and over-use of the stick were both a bad example to young riders and a woeful advertisement for the stable that retained him. After his sudden retirement from the saddle in 1959 he remained with the Glencairn stable as assistant, in company with his brother Connie, a former hurdle jockey, who was then travelling head lad. Against his employers' advice Eddery went into the licenced trade in Kildare, with unfortunate results. Having gone back to England and a life with horses, Jimmy Eddery had the satisfaction of seeing his son Pat succeed where he had so narrowly failed in the Epsom Derby, which the first-ever Irish born English champion flat jockey won on Grundy.

Hugh Lupus reappeared in the star-studded King George VI and Queen Elizabeth Stakes, where he got a belated opportunity to try conclusions with Phil Drake, the odds-on favourite. In a thrilling race victory went to another French colt, Vimy, who held off Acropolis by a head, with Hugh Lupus a close fifth, ahead of Phil Drake and Zarathustra. Transferred to Noel Murless to maximise his opportunities as a four-year-old and also to overcome his aversion to travelling, Hugh Lupus proceeded to justify Rae Johnstone's faith in his ability. Never out of the first three in eight races, Hugh Lupus rounded off a triumphant season with a convincing success in the Champion Stakes. Lady Ursula Vernon then retired her elegant colt to her Bruree Stud in Co. Limerick.

Of the others that ran in the 1955 Irish Derby, Ann's Kuda never reproduced similar form, Tara won in England as a four-year-old and Arctic Time, only sixth at the Curragh, upset that form when finishing fourth to Vimy at Ascot. This immaculately-bred colt was then retired to stud. Daemon won the Cumberland Lodge Stakes and the Ormonde Stakes later the same season and became one of Sir Gordon Richards' first winners as a trainer when beating Hugh Lupus at Newmarket as a four-year-old. Diamond Slipper eventually reaped the reward of his consistency when beating Cobetto in a close finish for the Irish St Leger, thus confirming the overall merit of an above-average Irish Derby.

1956

The French were back in force, represented by Prince Aly Khan's Chief III and the Willie Clout-trained Vaudemont. The sole English challenger was Talgo, representing the Oldham-Wragg-Mercer alliance, already successful in the Irish Two Thousand Guineas with Lucero. However, for once it appeared that the overseas challenge could be safely contained by a home-trained colt. This was Roistar, third to the French pair, Lavandin and Montaval at Epsom and an odds-on favourite to provide the McGraths and Jimmy Eddery with a successful sequel to Panaslipper. Talgo, trained specifically for this race, had won three of his four preparatory races, though without beating very much and his suspected sore shins did little to encourage his supporters. No Comment, the unfashionably-bred winner of the Gallinule Stakes, beating Vaquero and Beau Chevalet, was not thought certain to get the trip and only an avalanche of money for Chief III caused any weakening in Roistar's price.

Souverlone, pacemaker for Roistar, set a scorching pace ahead of Chief III, Talgo and Maelsheachlainn, with Roistar and No Comment bringing up the rear. Joined by Chief III coming down the hill, Souverlone still led at the final turn, where he gave way to Vaquero and Talgo. Once in the straight Talgo set sail for home, pursued by No Comment and Roistar. The last-named, chopped for speed and hampered on the final bend, now emerged as the only possible danger to the leader. However, this was one leader who was not going to be caught. Never slackening his relentless gallop, Talgo surged to a six-length success in a new record time for the race. No Comment plugged on gamely to keep third place ahead of the disappointing Frenchmen, while Milesian, by staggering in in seventh place, showed clearly that he did not stay.

Bred by Brigadier C. M. Stewart at the Dowdstown House Stud, Talgo was a good-looking bay colt by the young stallion Krakatao out of Miss France, a non-winning member of the family responsible for the 1950 Epsom Derby winner Galcador. Krakatao, a high-class miler and yet another son of Nearco, was retired to stud in Ireland in 1951, but exported to France in 1957, having sired Talgo, Garden State and Sovrango. It was Talgo's performance in finishing second to the mighty Ribot in the Prix de l'Arc de Triomphe that determined the French to possess Krakatao at all costs. Though he never won again, Talgo competed consistently in the highest class and his run behind Ribot saw him rated the best of his age in England, albeit in a year of total domination by the French. Retired to stud in Ireland, he sired Ticonderoga and Tacitus before being exported to Mexico in 1963 in 1963, the year before his son Biscayne won the Irish St Leger.

1956 was undoubtedly 'Wragg time' in Ireland. Having captured the Irish Two Thousand Guineas and Derby for his principal patron, the master of Abingdon Place sent over his own filly, Garden State, to win a thrilling race for the Irish Oaks. Gerry Oldham headed the list of winning owners in Ireland, while Harry Wragg emerged as leading trainer. Sharing in their triumph was that unrivalled judge of a yearling, Bertie Kerr, who bought Lucero, Talgo and Garden State on the same day at Ballsbridge. Costing a total of 3900gns, their Irish winnings alone amounted to £13,537. To complete Wragg's happiness, all three were ridden by his son-in-law Emmanuel 'Manny' Mercer.

Next to Lester Piggott, Bradford-born Manny Mercer was rated the most talented English jockey to emerge since the War. He had shot into the limelight when winning the Lincoln on the 100-to-1 outsider Jockey Treble in 1947, less than a year after riding his first winner. Over the next decade his flat-backed, flying finish became a familiar sight on English racecourses, bringing him success in both Newmarket Classics on Darius and Happy Laughter. American racegoers received a devastating introduction to this sallow-faced, quiet-spoken, tactical genius when he rode the George Colling-trained Wilwyn in the inaugural Washington DC International in 1952. As Lester Piggott would remind the Americans by his handling of Sir Ivor in the same race many years later, races in America can be won from behind, which Mercer's riding of Wilwyn proved quite dramatically. Poised patiently behind as the local hero, Eddie Arcaro attempted to run the field into the ground, Mercer swooped on Wilwyn for an historic victory, as emphatic as it was unexpected. Manny

Mercer's only other Irish Classic success was also achieved for his father-in-law, on Discorea in 1959. Two months later he was thrown at Ascot by Priddy Fair, kicked on the head and killed; a tragic end to a career which had already yielded so much but promised so much more. His younger brother, Joe Mercer, was to become one of the most stylish and effective jockeys riding in England, while his daughter Carolyn, a successful rider in the style of her father and grandfather, married Pat Eddery.

Though only thirty years old at the time of his first Irish Classic successes, international financier G. S. 'Gerry' Oldham was already a well-known owner in England, where his 'Chocolate and white hoops' have been borne by a succession of high-class horses. Fidalgo, second in the Epsom Derby, Miralgo, winner of the Timeform Gold Cup and Intermezzo, winner of the St Leger, are just three from a long list of winners which Harry Wragg has trained for Gerry Oldham. Just as his colts' names invariably end in 'o', so do those of his fillies end in 'a'. One of these, Cynara, became the fastest two-year-old filly of her generation. During the past decade Gerry Oldham, now domiciled in Geneva, has had the majority of his horses trained in France, notably Sagaro, whose unique treble in the Ascot Gold Cup, will hopefully be kept in mind by support at stud. While his racing interests have largely been concentrated in France of late, Gerry Oldham's connection with racing and breeding in these islands is strongly maintained by his Citadel Stud Establishment, based at Kildangan, where Miralgo was bred.

Roistar finished fifth to the invicible Ribot in the King George VI and Queen Elizabeth Stakes on his next outing and then disappointed in the Irish St Leger. Once again accompanied by his pacemaker Souverlone, he could finish only fourth to Magnetic North. The latter's victory meant that all five Irish Classics went abroad, a total of almost £20,000. This plunder, added to the Government's decision to impose a duty of £140,000 on the Racing Board Levy, hitherto completely reinvested in Irish racing, augured badly for the industry, already affected by falling attendances. Kept in training as a four-year-old, Roistar won three in a row in Ireland, none by more than a head. No Comment, by the handicapper Greek Star out of a point-to-point mare, went on to win the Tote Investors' Cup at Haydock and the historic Lanark Silver Bell. Later in his career he won a Gloucester Hurdle at Cheltenham. The immaculately-bred Chief III, by Nearco out of a Prix de l'Arc de Triomphe winner, went to stud in Germany having won the valuable Prix Ganay as a six-year-old. Maelssheachlainn won the Newbury Autumn Cup and retired to stud in Ireland, while Vaquero won the Irish Cambridgeshire. Leaving aside the runaway winner, it looked a thoroughly moderate Irish Derby and the truth of the matter was quite simply that, while the English Classic crop was bad, its Irish counterpart was worse. However, there was one other potentially high-class colt in the Irish Derby field. His name was Milesian, and in straggling in seventh he merely made the point that he should never have been asked to run over a distance twice beyond his best.

Second at the Curragh and Goodwood in his first two starts, Milesian then scored by six lengths in the valuable Imperial Produce Stakes at Kempton, earning second rating in the Irish Free Handicap, only 1lb below Roistar. Having made an impressive reappearance in the Tetrarch Stakes, Milesian then finished fourth in the Irish Two Thousand Guineas, after which he lost his form completely. Brought back to sprinting as a four-year-old, Mrs More O'Ferrall's good-looking colt showed his appreciation by winning the Salford Borough H'cap at Manchester and the Rocking-ham Stakes at the Curragh, finishing fourth in the Victoria Cup and the Stewards' Cup, his only other runs. Retired to his owner's Palmerstown Stud, this great-grandson of the celebrated Athasi proved wonderfully successful as a sire. His innumerable winners included such as Mystery, Ionian, Western Wind, Falcon, Tandy, Lucky Finish, Partholon and Lanzerote.

Wednesday, 27th June, 1956	**£6256 5 0**	**10 ran**	**1½m**

The Irish Derby. A sweepstakes of 5sovs each for yearlings entered on 23rd June, 1954, or of 15sovs for those entered on 3rd November, 1954, 20sovs extra for all if not struck out on 26th October, 1955, and 25sovs additional for all if not struck out on 30th May, 1956, with 4000sovs added to be contributed by the Turf Club and the Racing Board. The winner will receive 75%, second 15%, and third 10% of the whole stakes after deduction of the bonuses of 100sovs to the owner (at entry) of the winner, 50sovs to the owner (at entry) of the second and 25sovs to the owner (at entry) of the third. For three years old entire colts and fillies. Colts, 9st; Fillies, 8st 11lb. One mile and a half.

(207 subs)

1 Mr G. A. Oldham's	TALGO (E. Mercer)	9.0	H. Wragg (UK)
	B. colt Krakatao – Miss France by Jock II.		
2 Mr Joseph McGrath's	ROISTAR (J. Eddery)	9.0	S. McGrath
	Br. colt Arctic Star – Roisin.		
3 Mr F. N. Shane's	NO COMMENT (P. Powell, jr)	9.0	G. Robinson
	B. colt Greek Star – dam said to be Tiger's Bay.		
4 M. le Comte Roland de Chambure's	VAUDEMONT (W. R. Johnstone)	9.0	W. Clout (FR)
	Ch. colt Verso II – Colette Baudoche. (FOALED IN FRANCE.)		
5 Prince Aly Khan's	CHIEF III (R. Poincelet)	9.0	C. Semblat (FR)
	B. colt Nearco – Nikellora.		
6 Mr N. S. Macnaughton's	BEAU CHEVALET (T. P. Burns)	9.0	J. Oxx
	Gr. colt Beau Sabreur – Chain Bridge.		
7 Mrs R. More O'Ferrall's	MILESIAN (L. Ward)	9.0	M. Dawson
	B. colt My Babu – Oatflake.		
8 Mr B. Kerr's	VAQUERO (D. Page)	9.0	K. Kerr
	B. colt Mustang – Albany Isle.		
9 Mr Terence J. S. Gray's	MAELSHEACHLAINN (P. Matthews)	9.0	M. Hurley
	B. colt Erno – Maighdean Mara.		
10 Mr Joseph McGrath's	SOUVERLONE (J. Wright)	9.0	S. McGrath
	B. colt Souverain – Lonely Maid.		

SP 4/5 Roistar; 9/2 TALGO; 7/1 No Comment; 8/1 Chief III; 100/8 Vaudemont; 100/7 Beau Chevalet; 100/6 Vaquero; 25/1 Milesian; 33/1 Souverlone; 50/1 Maelsheachlainn. TOTE (2/- unit) 14/-. Places 3/6, 2/6, 3/6.

6 lengths, 3 lengths. 2m 30.92s.

Winner trained by Mr H. Wragg at Abington Place, Newmarket.

1957

In pleasing contrast to the previous year, the Irish Classic crop included some high-class animals. Angelet, third in the One Thousand Guineas, and Silken Glider, narrowly beaten in the Epsom Oaks, provided a strong supporting cast to the star of his year – Ballymoss. In finishing second to Crepello in the second fastest time recorded for the race, Ballymoss had done enough to win nine out of any ten Epsom Derbies. Immediately after that performance Vincent O'Brien had made it known that Ballymoss would contest the Irish Derby. This was enough to frighten off any English or French challengers. It then became known that Jack Ketch, stylish winner of the Irish Two Thousand Guineas, would not be risked on the prevailing hard ground. With that the race took on the appearance of a 'Ballymoss benefit', which only a small crowd braved the wind and rain to witness. Of the seven that eventually opposed the odds-on favourite, only Hindu Festival, third in the Irish Two Thousand Guineas and a subsequent winner over the Derby distance at Chester, was given any chance of upsetting the 'hot pot'. As if to confirm the certainty of the outcome, Ballymoss' American owner, John McShain, had come over for the race. He had not travelled to Epsom, having been advised by O'Brien that Ballymoss was not at his best on that occasion . . .

Bugle and Star Prince took them along at a modest pace to the top of the hill, where Valentine Slipper suddenly shot from last to first in an attempt to slip his field. Paddy Powell's initiative never really looked likely to succeed, for Hindu Festival and Ballymoss moved smoothly in pursuit. Having collared the leader, Hindu Festival made a brave but equally unavailing attempt to hold off Ballymoss. Ranging alongside the leader at the distance, T. P. Burns had only to change his hands to send Ballymoss cruising away to a ridiculously easy success. Valentine Slipper deservedly held on to take third prize, while the rest might just as well have stayed at home.

A well-made, medium-sized chestnut, Ballymoss was by Mossborough out of Indian Call. Bred by Lord Derby, Mossborough was by Nearco out of a three-parts sister to Hyperion. Though not quite Classic standard, Mossborough won five races, including the Churchill Stakes. In a lengthy career at stud he sired such good performers as Star Moss, Craighouse, Cavan, Noblesse and Yelapa. Mainly due to the achievements of Ballymoss, Mossborough headed the list of sires in Britain in 1958. Indian Call, by the St Leger winner Singapore out of a Yorkshire Oaks

1956. Talgo, *coming home alone to crown an incredible year in Ireland for his Newmarket trainer Harry Wragg. Source:* The Irish Horse.

1957. Ballymoss, *his cantering success in the Irish Derby was only a prelude to proving himself the outstanding colt in Europe. Source:* The Irish Horse.

winner, was bred by Lord Glanely and purchased at Newmarket in 1939 by Irish breeder Richard Ball for only 15gns. Prior to breeding Ballymoss, for whom he received 4500gns as a yearling at Doncaster, Richard Ball had bred the dual Grand National winner Reynoldstown and the Gimcrack Stakes winner Star King at his stud in Naul, Co. Dublin.

Ballymoss ran four times as a two-year-old, winning once. As a three-year-old he had beaten Chevastrid over one and a half miles at Leopardstown before going to Epsom. Although his preparation had been held up by a poisoned foot, Ballymoss was backed with Irish money from 100-to-1 down to 33-to-1 for the Derby. Hitting the front two furlongs out, Ballymoss had looked like pulling off that gamble until cut down close home by Crepello. As Crepello remains one of the outstanding Derby winners in the last thirty years, Ballymoss could be said to have been unfortunate not to have been born twelve months earlier or later, when victory must have been his. On his next appearance Ballymoss was beaten in soft ground at York by Brioche, but still became ante-post favourite to gain his revenge in the St Leger at Doncaster. A reoccurrence of the soft ground that he quite obviously disliked caused his price to drift on the day of the race. However, having hit the front a quarter of a mile out, Ballymoss was not seriously troubled to beat Court Harwell and Brioche, thus becoming the first Irish-trained winner in one hundred and eighty runnings of the oldest Classic race in the world.

Rated second, 5lbs below the retired Crepello, in the English Three-year-old Free Handicap, Ballymoss remained in training as a four-year-old. Second to Doutelle on his reappearance around the tight Chester track, he was destined to go through the remainder of his European campaign unbeaten, establishing himself as the best racehorse in Europe. Ridden by 'Scobie' Breasley in place of the injured T. P. Burns, Ballymoss scored an easy success in the Coronation Cup at Epsom. Prior to that race Ballymoss and Hard Ridden had worked together up the Curragh; quite a spectacle for those privileged to witness it! On his next visit to England Ballymoss made hacks of his opponents in the Eclipse Stakes, repeating the performance a week later in the King George VI and Queen Elizabeth Stakes. After that race Breasley immediately proclaimed Ballymoss the best horse he had ever ridden. On their next and final European outing horse and jockey combined to beat the best on this side of the Atlantic in the Prix de l'Arc de Triomphe. By this victory Ballymoss became not only the first-ever Irish-trained winner of that race but also the highest stakes winner in European racing. At the wish of his owner Ballymoss made his racecourse farewell in the Washington DC International. Unable to act on the tight, turning track, Ballymoss did well to finish third to Tudor Era and Sailor's Guide. In announcing the retirement of his champion John McShain expressed his desire to stand Ballymoss in Europe at a valuation far below offers he had received in his own country.

Following protracted negotiations, which involved the English National Stud, Ballymoss was finally syndicated at a value of £250,000 to stand at the Banstead Manor Stud near Newmarket, with Mr McShain retaining ten shares and the remaining thirty being guaranteed by Sir Victor Sassoon and William Hill. All those involved saw their faith rewarded when, three years later, Ballymoss became the leading first-season sire in Britain. Two years after that Ballymoss sired his first Classic winner when Ancasta, trained by O'Brien, won the Irish Oaks, a race that fell to another daughter of Ballymoss when Merry Mate won in 1966, the year which saw the long-awaited Classic colt by Ballymoss. In Royal Palace Ballymoss had at last sired a colt in the same class as himself, as he proved by victories in the English Two Thousand Guineas, Derby, Eclipse Stakes and King George VI and Queen Elizabeth Stakes. Sadly, having sired one worthy successor, Ballymoss got nothing of note thereafter. So low did his stock sink that rumours spread of his imminent departure to the land of the Rising Sun. The vehemence of public reaction to such an idea – even after all those years – served as a reminder of what a popular idol Ballymoss had been back in the late 'fifties, when, to every schoolboy each passing dray horse became 'Ballymoss!'

John McShain, usually described as 'a millionaire builder from Philadelphia', was president of the construction company responsible for building the Pentagon. The red B emblazoned back and front on his white colours stood for Barclay Stable, the name under which he raced on a substantial scale in America. In 1958 he made history by becoming the first American ever to head the list of winning owners in Britain. In that unforgettable year he was represented not only by Ballymoss, but also by that wonderful mare Gladness, saddled by O'Brien to win the Ascot Gold Cup, Goodwood Cup and Ebor Handicap. Other good horses to carry his distinctive

Wednesday, 26th June, 1957	**£6790**	**8 ran**	**1½m**

The Irish Derby. A sweepstakes of 5sovs each for yearlings entered on 22nd June, 1955, or of 15sovs for those entered on 2nd November, 1955, 20sovs extra for all if not struck out on 24th October, 1956, and 25sovs additional for all if not struck out on 29th May, 1957, with 4000sovs added to be contributed by the Turf Club and the Racing Board. The winner will receive 75%, second 15%, and third 10% of the whole stakes after deduction of the bonuses of 100sovs to the owner (at entry) of the winner, 50sovs to the owner (at entry) of the second and 25sovs to the owner (at entry) of the third. For three years old entire colts and fillies. Colts, 9st; Fillies, 8st 11lb. One mile and a half.

(210 subs)

1 Mr J. McShain's   BALLYMOSS (T. P. Burns)   9.0   M. V. O'Brien
Ch. colt Mossborough – Indian Call by Singapore.

2 Mr C. F. Myerscough's HINDU FESTIVAL (W. R.   9.0   P. J. Prendergast
Johnstone)   B. colt Hindostan – Nasturtium.

3 Mrs E. J. King's   VALENTINE SLIPPER   9.0   H. Nugent
(P. Powell, jr)   Br. colt His Slipper – Sandra.

4 Miss E. R. Sears's   AMPLEFORTH (L. Ward)   9.0   C. A. Rogers
Br. colt Arctic Star – Rising Fair.

5 Mr Joseph McGrath's STAR PRINCE (J. Eddery)   9.0   S. McGrath
B. colt Prince Chevalier – Starullah.

6 Lady Bury's   POLAR PRINCE (P. Canty)   9.0   D. Rogers
Ch. colt Arctic Prince – Ramiflora.

7 Mr Joseph McGrath's SOLARTICKLE (J. Wright)   9.0   S. McGrath
Ch. colt Solar Slipper – Ballytickle.

8 Lady Ainsworth's   BUGLE (M. Kennedy)   9.0   D. Ainsworth
B. colt Royal Charger – Fleur Bleue.

SP 4/9 BALLYMOSS; 4/1 Hindu Festival; 8/1 Ampleforth; 100/7 Star Prince; 20/1 Valentine Slipper; 50/1 Polar Prince; 66/1 Solartickle; 100/1 Bugle. TOTE (2/6 unit) 3/6. Places 3/-, 3/-, 5/-. 4 lengths, 1 length. 2m 39.12s.
Winner trained by Mr M. V. O'Brien at Ballydoyle, Co. Tipperary.

colours in Ireland included Courts Appeal and Barclay, winner of the Irish St Leger in 1959. However, it was after McShain had split with O'Brien that he achieved his most satisfying moment as an owner-breeder. That came when the John Oxx-trained Merry Mate won the Irish Oaks in 1966, for she was, after all, by Ballymoss out of Gladness.

Ballymoss was ridden throughout his three-year-old career by one Thomas Pascal Burns, known to all and sundry as 'T.P.'. The younger son of Tommy 'the Scotch-man' Burns, T.P. rode his first winner at the Curragh in 1938, at a time when his father had retired 'to give the boys a chance'. The death of T.P.'s jockey brother James saw their father back in the saddle and T.P. moved to England, apprenticed to Steve Donoghue. In 1940 he returned to Ireland, riding mainly for Colonel Blake. Increasing weight dictated a National Hunt career, and it was in that sphere that he became associated with the all-conquering O'Brien stable, riding no fewer than eight Gloucester Hurdle winners. Serious spinal injures, incurred in a fall in 1952, obliged him to stop riding over fences, though he continued to mix flat and hurdle riding to such effect that he headed the list of Irish jockeys in 1954, 1955 and 1957, when Ballymoss gave him the first of six Irish Classic successes as well as his only English Classic.

Though overshadowed during that lengthy period when it was considered almost mandatory that every aspiring trainer in Ireland retain an Australian jockey, T.P. nonetheless remained riding with consistent, if unspectacular success until 1975, by which time he had assumed his father's role as the doyen of Irish jockeys. Ever willing to ride work and advise accordingly, T. P. Burns was always in demand by smaller trainers as their 'stroke jockey' at country meetings, where his vast experience of the sharp, turning tracks made him virtually unbeatable when the money was down. Not that his expertise was purely provincial, for his familar, hunched style was never seen to better effect than at Leopardstown, where he had no peers. Never renowed as a big spender, T.P. joined forces once again with Vincent O'Brien on his retirement. The estimation in which O'Brien held his assistant became apparent when he gave much of the credit for the Arc de Triomphe successes of Alleged to T. P. Burns.

1958

If the previous year had been a good one for Irish racing, 1958 was a great one. Highlighted by the performances of Ballymoss and Gladness, Irish fortunes reached their zenith with the Epsom Derby triumph of Hard Ridden, sent out by young J. M. Rogers to become the first Irish-trained winner of that race since Orby fifty-one years earlier. To complete the Gaelic glee on that occasion Hard Ridden had been followed home by another Irish-trained colt in Paddy's Point. Hard Ridden had never been an intended runner in the Irish Derby and in his absence Paddy's Point was made favourite to confirm his superiority over the Newmarket-trained Nagami, third in the Epsom Derby. Two factors prevented Paddy's Point starting an even shorter-priced favourite. He had shown a tendency to hang at Epsom and this, if repeated in a small field on such a wide, sweeping course, would prove disastrous. Moreover, Nagami was expected to be much better suited to the galloping Curragh course than he had been to turns and gradients of Epsom. Of the other ten runners, Lorenzo was considered vastly inferior to his stablemate Nagami, Royal Highway seemed unsuited by the soft ground and Sindon had disappointed since dividing Hard Ridden and Paddy's Point in the Irish Two Thousand Guineas. However, it was just the sort of wet, miserable day on which upsets occur . . .

Lorenzo was the first to show, leading from Royal Highway, Mesembryan-themum and Kentucky Sun, with Paddy's Point, Irish Penny and Sindon being waited with at the rear of the field. At the half-way stage Advance Guard attempted to justify his name, passing the fading Lorenzo, only to be passed in turn by Royal Highway, who led into the straight, chased by Nagami and Sindon. Meanwhile, having been denied an opening on the rails, Willie Robinson had been forced to bring Paddy's Point around his field, before setting off in pursuit of Sindon, who had caught and beaten Royal Highway. Having hit the front on a supposedly doubtful stayer, Liam Ward could do little other than pray for the winning post to come before something else did. That something else was Paddy's Point, whose blistering late run took him level with Sindon inside the final furlong. Ward went for his whip and the two colts flashed past the post together, amid scenes of tremendous excite-ment. Some way back Royal Highway held off Nagami for third place. Although the judge called for a photograph, the bookmakers quotes suggested that Sindon had just held on and when Willie Robinson was seen to take Paddy's Point into the enclosure reserved for the second, the camera was merely required to confirm that Sindon had won by a head and four lengths.

Bred by Mr J. Clarke at the Dunderry Stud, near Navan, not far from Hard Ridden's birthplace, Beauparc, Sindon was an attractive, scopy chestnut by Hyper-bole out of Cotton Wool. In common with Hard Ridden, Sindon boasted a pedigree calculated to confound the purists of Classical breeding. His sire Hyperbole, though by Hyperion, was a high-class handicapper, whose nine successes included the Jersey Stakes and the Royal Hunt Cup. Sindon came from the last crop sired by Hyperbole prior to his sale to the Swedish Government in 1954. The only other winner of note sired by Hyperbole in these islands was the Lincolnshire winner Monawin. Cotton Wool, by Donatello II out of a mare by Loaningdale, won once before being sold carrying Sindon for only 340gns. Sindon was expensive in comparison to Hard Ridden, having cost his trainer and joint-owner, Michael Dawson, all of 1150gns at Ballsbridge, where Hard Ridden was bought for less than a quarter of that amount!

Following the well-publicised breach between Mrs More O'Ferrall and her trainer, P. J. Prendergast, her horses had been transferred from Rossmore Lodge to the care of Michael Dawson at Rathbride Manor. Mrs More O'Ferrall – now calling herself Mrs Anne Bullitt-Biddle – subsequently purchased a half-share in Sindon, who ran in her colours. Fourth in the Beresford Stakes on his only appearance as a two-year-old, Sindon had finished a most promising second to Hard Ridden in the Irish Two Thousand Guineas. Had it not been for his subsequently disappointing run behind Tharp in the Gallinule Stakes, Sindon would certainly have started a much shorter price to become the first maiden to win the Irish Derby since Piccadilly thirteen years earlier. Starting joint-favourite with Royal Highway for the Irish St

Leger, Sindon did well to run that dour stayer to two lengths in soft ground over a distance beyond his best. Having won only one race – albeit the Irish Derby – Sindon could scarcely be said to have proved his class, particularly in view of the luckless record of Paddy's Point. By running him in the Champion Stakes at Newmarket, Mrs Biddle and Michael Dawson sought to silence Sindon's critics. As it turned out, their courageous gambit came close to outright success. Hitting the front a little too soon, Sindon was only narrowly beaten by Bella Paola, winner of both the English fillies' Classics that year and arguably the best of her age in Europe. Sindon was then sold to race in the United States, where he failed to add to his reputation. Retired to stud there and subsequently sent to Japan, Sindon failed to make a name for himself as a stallion, which, in view of his breeding, was not altogether surprising.

Anne Bullitt-Biddle is the daughter of a former United States Ambassador to Spain, where she began racing with success, prior to moving to Ireland, shortly before her marriage to Roderic More O'Ferrall. She had already become well-known in National Hunt circles by the Galway Plate and Hurdle triumphs of Amber Point and Knight Errant. Having parted from More O'Ferrall, Ireland's most glamorous owner established the Palmerstown Stud near Naas in 1956. Since then she has continued to breed and race on a lavish scale. Her 'purple patch' on the flat occurred in the early 'sixties when, with Tommy Shaw as her private trainer at Palmerstown, she won scores of good races, many with the progeny of the resident stallion, Milesian. Zenonbia, in the Irish One Thousand Guineas, remains her only Classic winner since Sindon, but such as China Clipper, Ionian, Le Prince, Mystery, Partholon, Satan and Scissors kept the 'Navy blue, white hoop on body, white cap' constantly to the fore. When women were eventually granted licences to train in Ireland, Mrs Brewster, as she had now become, following her marriage to a US Congressman, took out a licence and became the first woman to train a winner in Ireland. Since then she has continued to supervise the training of her own horses, though without the success that she formerly enjoyed.

In sending out Sindon to win the Irish Derby, Michael Dawson was carrying on the tradition of his famous father, who had ridden three winners of the race and trained a further four. Following the death of his elder brother, Joseph Dawson, in 1946, Michael took over the reins at Rathbride Manor and proceeded to turn out a steady if unspectacular stream of winners. The majority of his success was achieved in handicaps, for he seldom got anything better to train, nor was he a man to go looking for wealthy owners and expensive horses. Best-known of his earlier charges was his own Bold Baby, whose numerous victories included an Irish Cesarewitch and a Naas November Handicap. In 1954 he saddled Cloudless Days to win the Galway Hurdle. But a more memorable Galway meeting for Michael Dawson was the one at which he sacked his jockey immediately after a race. Though he owned a motor car, Dawson had never learned to drive and, as was usually the case, his jockey had driven him to the races, in this instance over a hundred miles from home. Having dismissed his 'chauffeur' Dawson obviously had a difficulty. However, not one to publicise his problems, he set about driving himself home, arriving in the early hours of the morning, having driven the entire distance in bottom gear! As his owners, mostly of an age with himself, retired from racing, Michael Dawson allowed his stable to dwindle to nothing and finally retired quietly in 1970. Having seen

Nijinsky, whom he regards as the greatest horse it has been his fortune to see, storm to victory in the Irish Derby, Michael Dawson said farewell to racing, immersed himself happily in his family and farm and has not set foot on a racecourse since.

Liam Ward, the rider of Sindon, was the most consistently successful Irish flat jockey throughout the 'fifties and 'sixties. Apprenticed initially to Roderic More O'Ferrall at Kildangan and subsequently to Martin Quirke at Mountjoy Lodge, he rode the first of his ten Irish Classic winners when Do Well gave Morny Wing his biggest training success in the Irish St Leger of 1951. The following year he won the Irish Two Thousand Guineas on D.C.M. for a very youthful Mickey Rogers, who remembers Liam Ward as his favourite Irish jockey, whom he 'admired both as a rider and a person'. Having been associated with the Prendergast stable, Ward retained his links with Mrs Biddle when she transferred her horses to Michael Dawson and in 1958 he scored the coveted Irish Derby–Oaks double when Amante was successful in the latter event. Leading jockey in Ireland in 1959 and 1961, Ward continued his association with the Biddle horses, whose participation in non-handicap races enabled him to overcome the handicap of a non-competitive weight. In 1962 a chance ride on the Irish-trained Sicilian Prince provided him with his greatest overseas success when the partnership combined to win the French St Leger, the first foreign-based victory in a French Classic for many years.

When the craze for Australian jockeys waned in Ireland Liam Ward entered into an agreement with Vincent O'Brien to ride his runners in Ireland and with the powerful Ballydoyle stable behind him Ward became almost invincible on the Curragh, his favourite track. Scene of innumerable victories, the Curragh also provided Liam Ward with his most spectacular failure, when beaten on Sir Ivor in the Irish Sweeps Derby. However, an Irish Oaks on Gaia and a St Leger on Reindeer the following season provided some consolation and when he rode Nijinsky to a scintillating victory in Ireland's greatest race the bitter memory was successfully erased. Quietly-spoken and reserved in his manner, Liam Ward was often mistakenly described as arrogant. The qualities which his critics misconstrued as conceit were an unshakeable confidence in his own ability allied to a burning ambition to excel at anything to which he put his mind. Anyone who has ever witnessed his handling of a golf club or a shotgun, both latter-day pursuits, will realise the results of this determination to excel. As polished as he was powerful in the saddle, Ward never attempted to 'modernise' his style, riding with a length of leather which made his handling of two-year-olds both an education and a pleasure to watch. The pity was that so many Irish apprentices should have ignored his example, striving vainly to emulate O'Brien's overseas jockey. On his retirement Liam Ward concentrated his energies on his Ashleigh Stud near Dublin, where he and his wife, formerly Jackie Hylton, have achieved notable success, particularly with the produce of that wonderful broodmare Zanzara.

The luckless Paddy's Point, until then the only Epsom Derby runner-up to have sought compensation on the Curragh and failed, won one small race before being transferred to the North of England. The following year his half-sister, named Paddy's Sister, was trained by Paddy Prendergast to win the Queen Mary Stakes, the Gimcrack Stakes and the Champagne Stakes, proving herself in the process the leading filly of her generation. Royal Highway, like so many of Straight Deal's progeny, continued to improve with age, winning the Blandford Stakes, the Irish St

Leger and the Champion Stakes, all at the Curragh. Retired to his owners' Eyrefield House Stud, Royal Highway became a recognised sire of tough, staying National Hunt horses. Nagami, third in all three English colts' Classics, gained belated compensation in the Gran Premio del Jockey Club in Milan, ridden by Lester Piggott*. Taken all round, the field for this Irish Derby were fairly representative of their mediocre generation.

Wednesday, 25th June, 1958	**£7345**	**12 Ran**	**1½m**

The Irish Derby. A sweepstakes of 5sovs each for yearlings entered on 20th June, 1956, or of 15sovs for those entered on 7th November, 1956, 20sovs extra for all if not struck out on 23rd October, 1957, and 25sovs additional for all if not struck out on 28th May, 1958, with 4000sovs added to be contributed by the Turf Club and the Racing Board. The winner will receive 75%, second 15%, and third 10% of the whole stakes after deduction of the bonuses of 100sovs to the owner (at entry) of the winner, 50sovs to the owner (at entry) of the second and 25sovs to the owner (at entry) of the third. For three years old entire colts and fillies. Colts, 9st; Fillies, 8st 11lb. One mile and a half.

(263 subs)

1	Mrs A. B. Biddle's	SINDON (L. Ward) Ch. colt Hyperbole – Cotton Wool by Donatello.	9. 0	M. Dawson
2	Mr F. W. Shane's	PADDY'S POINT (G. W. Robinson) B. colt Mieuxce – Birthday Wood.	9. 0	G. Robinson
3	Mrs W. Macauley's	ROYAL HIGHWAY (N. Brennan) B. colt Straight Deal – Queen's Highway.	9. 0	H. V. S. Murless
4	Mrs Arpad Plesch's	NAGAMI (J. Mercer) Ch. colt Nimbus – Jennifer.	9. 0	H. Wragg (GB)
5	Major J. Alexander's	ADVANCE GUARD (P. Powell, jr) B. colt Vic Day – Venturesome.	9.0	Owner
6	Major M. W. Beaumont's	MESEMBRYANTHEMUM (John Power) B. colt Migoli – Anaphalis.	9.0	J. Oxx
7	Mr R. W. Hall-Dare's	TERN (P. Matthews) B. colt Tenerani – Chough.	9.0	M. Hurley
8	Mr Terence J. S. Gray's	LAO TZU (W. Elliott) B. colt Arctic Star – Maighdean Mara.	9.0	M. Hurley
9	Mr A. A. Thorn's	IRISH PENNY (A. Brabazon) Br. colt Hindostan – Penny on the Jack.	9.0	D. St J. Gough
10	Mr Ralph Lowe's	KENTUCKY SUN (W. Swinburn) Gr. colt Numbus – Kennie II.	9.0	E. M. Quirke
11	Mr Joseph McGrath's	PRESTEL (J. Eddery) Ch. colt Preciptic – Stella's Sister.	9.0	S. McGrath
12	Mr G. A. Oldham's	LORENZO (E. Mercer) B. colt Tenerani – Haymaker.	9.0	H. Wragg (GB)

SP 6/4 Paddy's Point; 9/4 Nagami; 10/1 Lorenzo, Royal Highway; 100/8 SINDON; 100/7 Mesembryanthemum; 20/1 Lao Tzu; 25/1 Irish Penny, Advance Guard; 50/1 Bar. TOTE (2/6 unit) 27/6. Places 6/-, 4/-, 5/6.

Short head, 4 lengths. 2m 58.9s.

Winner trained by Mr Michael Dawson at Rathbride Manor, Curragh.

*Kept in training as a four-year-old, Nagami won the Coronation Cup at Epsom and was subsequently sold to Italy as a stallion.

1959

In keeping with what was now an established pattern, the Epsom Derby runner-up sought consolation in the Irish equivalent. In 1959 the horse in question was the Newmarket-trained Fidalgo, whose participation was sufficient to deter any other English or French challengers. An impressive winner of the Chester Vase, Fidalgo had only been caught close home by Parthia at Epsom. His ability to act on the prevailing hard ground, combined with the lack of talent among the home-trained brigade, made his task an apparent formality. Of the ten that opposed him, only El Toro and Anthony were given even a reasonable chance of success. The former, trained by Vincent O'Brien and ridden by his new Australian stable jockey, Garnet Bougoure, had won both the Madrid Free Handicap and the Irish Two Thousand Guineas, but had yet to prove his ability to stay the Derby distance. Anthony, trained by Mickey Rogers, had made all the running to win the Gallinule Plate, beating the subsequent Royal Ascot winners, Lucky Guy and Vivi Tarquin. However, the breeding purists, undeterred by Hard Ridden and Sindon the year before, refused to accept that any son of Merry Boy out of an Owenstown mare could conceivably win the Irish Derby. Fidalgo, looking magnificent in the sweltering sunshine, seemed a worthy odds-on favourite.

As he had done in his previous race, Anthony attempted to make every post a winning one, leading until joined briefly in the straight by Randwick. Having beaten off that challenge, the tiring leader had no answer to Bois Belleau, brought with a smooth run on the rails by Liam Ward. However, no sooner had Bois Belleau got the measure of Anthony than Joe Mercer shot Fidalgo through between them to win going away by an easy four lengths. Bois Belleau held off the renewed challenge of Anthony by half a length in their struggle for the minor placings. Of the others, Light Horseman finished a promising fourth, whereas El Toro, the second favourite, made no show at all. Despite the ease of Fidalgo's victory, the time for the race was 2.5 secs faster than Parthia's at Epsom.

By the McGrath stallion Arctic Star, Fidalgo was out of Miss France and thus a three-parts brother to Harry Wragg's previous Irish Derby winner, Talgo. Both Arctic Star and Krakatao, Talgo's sire, were sons of Nearco. Arctic Star had retired to stud in 1946 unraced owing to injury and with nothing other than his pedigree to recommend him to breeders. It was the exploits Solar Slipper and Peter Flower, both out of his half-sister Solar Flower that first brought Arctic Star to notice. In 1954 Arctic Wind provided him with his first Classic winner when successful in the Irish Two Thousand Guineas. The following year Roistar emerged as the leading two-year-old in Ireland and thereafter Arctic Star had a full book, only for an immensely promising stud career to be abruptly terminated by his early death in 1958. As so often happens, his best progeny appeared on the racecourse after his death. They included Fidalgo, Arctic Storm, Arctic Slave, Arctic Kanda and Ross Sea.

A well-made bay colt, if rather upright of his pasterns, Fidalgo, like Talgo, was bred by Brigadier C. M. Stewart and bought privately for 3000gns by Peter Wragg, the trainer's son, having failed to reach his reserve at Ballsbridge. Second at

1958 Sindon, *(L. Ward), undoubtedly a better horse than his solitary success in the Irish Derby might have made him appear. Source:* The Irish Horse.

1959. Fidalgo, *equally impressive as his three-parts brother, Talgo, had been three years earlier. Source:* The Irish Horse.

Newmarket in both his runs as a two-year-old, Fidalgo had shown promise on his reappearance and then scored a most impressive victory at Chester. The subsequent form of that race had seen him backed down to third favourite for the Epsom Derby. Hitting the front sooner than his trainer would have wished, Fidalgo failed to withstand Parthia's relentless run, which put one and a half lengths between them at the line. To have been caught and beaten so close to home in the Epsom Derby must have been bad enough, but by your father-in-law . . . By waiting until he did in the Irish Derby, Joe Mercer had obviously been determined to avoid a repetition. After his Curragh success Fidalgo started favourite in the Eclipse Stakes, finishing a somewhat lacklustre fifth behind St Crespin III. Later in the season he redeemed his reputation with a good second to Cantelo in the St Leger in which he finishd ahead of Parthia. A tendon injury after that race necessitated his retirement to stud. Exported to Japan in 1966, Fidalgo left behind him Twelfth Man, winner of the Ebor Handicap for the Wragg stable, as well as the dams of Full Dress II and Lucky Wednesday.

Just as Talgo and Fidalgo were closely related, so were their respective jockeys, for Fidalgo was ridden by Manny Mercer's younger brother Joe. Not to be outdone, Manny Mercer was in the saddle when Harry Wragg sent over Discorea to complete the Irish Derby–Oaks double as he had done three years earlier. Born in 1934, Joe Mercer served his apprenticeship with Major Sneyd, a hard taskmaster, who had been responsible for launching the Smith brothers, Eph and Doug, on the path to success. One of the best English jockeys riding over the past twenty years, Joe Mercer achieved his first Classic success when winning the Epsom Oaks on Lord Astor's Ambiguity as long ago as 1953. Since then he has won all the English Classics except the Epsom Derby, his most famous mount being Brigadier Gerard, conqueror of Mill Reef in the Two Thousand Guineas and beaten only once in three seasons. A long-standing and extremely successful association with Dick Hern and the West Ilsey stable was dissolved when Joe Mercer was replaced by a younger jockey at the owners' insistence. Far too good a jockey to be thus discarded, Joe Mercer was promptly retained by Henry Cecil to ride for his powerful Warren Place stable, for which he stands every chance of gaining that elusive Epsom Derby success. In the meantime Joe Mercer's skill and powerful, rythmic style place him second only to the peerless Piggott among the senior English jockeys of the present day.

Of those that finished behind Fidalgo on that sunny afternoon at the Curragh, Light Horseman revealed the greatest measure of improvement. Beaten a short head in the Warren Stakes at Goodwood, he won the Desmond Stakes at the Curragh before suffering another short head defeat by Barclay and an inspired Garnet Bougoure in the Irish St Leger. Kept in training as a four-year-old, Light Horseman upset the 4-to-1 ON favourite Primera when winning the Ormonde Stakes at Chester. He was subsequently placed in both the Vaux Gold Tankard and the John Porter Stakes. Anthony, as his breeding suggested, proved to be even better over hurdles, winning six such events before becoming a decent National Hunt sire. Randwick

Wednesday, 24th June, 1959   **£7212 10 0**   **11 Ran**   1½m

The Irish Derby. A sweepstakes of 5sovs each for yearlings entered on 19th June 1957, or of 15sovs for those entered on 6th November, 1957, 20sovs extra for all if not struck out on 22nd October, 1958, and 25sovs additional for all if not struck out on 27th May, 1959, with 4000sovs added to be contributed by the Turf Club and the Racing Board. The winner will receive 75%, second 15%, and third 10% of the whole stakes after deduction of the bonuses of 100sovs to the owner (at entry) of the winner, 50sovs to the owner (at entry) of the second and 25sovs to the owner (at entry) of the third. For three years old entire colts and fillies. Colts, 9st; Fillies, 8st 11lb. One mile and a half.

(251 subs)

1 Mr G. A. Oldham's	FIDALGO (J. Mercer)	9.0	H. Wragg (GB)	
	b. colt Arctic Star – Miss France by Jock.			
2 Mrs A. B. Biddle's	BOIS BELLEAU (L. Ward)	9.0	T. Shaw	
	B. colt Bois Roussel – War Loot. (FOALED IN FRANCE.)			
3 Lord Fingall's	ANTHONY (T. P. Burns)	9.0	J. M. Rogers	
	Ch. colt Merry Boy – Grey Anna.			
4 Lord Ennisdale's	LIGHT HORSEMAN	9.0	P. J. Prendergast	
	(W. Swinburn) B. colt Guersant – Lumine.			
5 Mr B. Kerr's	BEAU ROSSA (P. Canty)	9.0	E. M. Quirke	
	Ch. colt Beau Sabreur – Cara Rossa.			
6 Mr J. Ismay's	BABU (G. Cooney)	9.0	D. Rogers	
	B. colt My Baby – Nella.			
7 Mr P. W. McGrath's	SOLAR DUKE (O. O'Neill)	9.0	S. McGrath	
	B. colt Solar Slipper – Archduchess.			
8 Mr B. Kerr's	RANDWICK (J. Mullane)	9.0	K. R. Kerr	
	B. colt Tehran – Windway.			
9 Mr G. Verling's	BUMPER HARVEST (G. W.	9.0	Owner	
	Robinson) B. colt Artist's Son – The Reaper.			
10 Mr C. M. Kline's	EL TORO (G. Bougoure)	9.0	M. V. O'Brien	
	Ch. colt Cagire – Early Milkmaid.			
11 Mr Joseph McGrath's	CARRIGEEN DUFF (J. Eddery)	9.0	S. McGrath	
	Bl. colt Hill Gail – Beauty Royal.			

SP 1/2 FIDALGO; 4/1 El Toro; 10/1 Anthony; 20/1 Bois Belleau, Bumper Harvest, Randwick; 33/1 Bar. TOTE (2/6 unit) 4/-. Places 3/6, 6/6, 5/-.
4 lengths, ½ length. 2m 33.5s.
Winner trained by Mr H. Wragg at Abington Place, Newmarket.

won races in America over the next two seasons, while Beau Rossa went on to achieve his greatest victory in the Zetland Gold Cup at Redcar. Considering that the Epsom Derby was worth over five times more to the winner, this year's Irish equivalent could be said to have achieved a reasonable standard, though it still fell a long way short of the showpiece required to reflect Ireland's proclaimed prominence among the leading racing and breeding nations of the world.

1960

In what was a sensational year in Irish racing, most of the drama and excitement involved the Irish Derby. The year got off to an excellent start for Irish interests when Paddy Prendergast saddled Martial to win the English Two Thousand Guineas, providing Ron Hutchinson, his new Australian stable jockey, with a dream debut in European racing. For good measure the partnership combined to win the Irish equivalent with Kythnos. However, on Friday, May 13th, the racing world was shattered by two events. The first was the news from Paris that the Aly Khan had met his death in a motoring accident. Mourned by all in racing, who shared his love of horses and admired his fearless tilts at the Ring, Aly died as he lived – at speed. The second shock was contained in a terse announcement from the Turf Club: 'The Stewards of the Turf Club met . . . to hear Mr M. V. O'Brien's explanation of the presence of a drug and stimulant in the samples of saliva and sweat taken from Chamour, trained by him, after the colt had won the Ballysax Maiden Plate at the Curragh on April 20th.

'The Stewards of the Turf Club, having heard the evidence of . . . were satisfied that a drug or stimulant had been administered to Chamour for the purpose of affecting his speed and/or stamina in the race. The Stewards accordingly withdrew Mr O'Brien's licence to train under Rule 102(v) Rules of Racing and declared him a disqualified person under that rule and under Rule 178, from May 13th, 1960 until November 30th, 1961. They also disqualified Chamour for the Ballysax Maiden Plate . . .

'At the conclusion of the case, when Mr O'Brien had been informed of the decision of the Stewards, he was warned by them that none of the horses under his care could fulfil their engagements unless and until they had been transferred to another licenced trainer or trainers.

'Mr O'Brien was further informed that such transfers should be notified to the Registry Office in the normal way and that the Stewards, when satisfied that the transfers had actually taken place, would immediately issue instructions to the Keeper of the Match Book to allow such horse or horses to fulfil their engagements.' The Stewards who sat on the enquiry were Joe McGrath, Sir Cecil Stafford-King-Harman and Major Victor McCalmont. To their verdict a shocked Vincent O'Brien could only respond that: 'I did not drug this, or any other, horse, and I trust my staff. My personal gain from Chamour's victory was twenty pounds – ten per cent of the stake.'

While the racing world absorbed the impact of this bombshell and began to discuss the consequences of the dissolution of one of the most powerful stables in Europe, the Jockey Club extended the sentence to England and Chamour's part-owner, Walter Burmann, offered £5000 reward for information which led to the apprehension of the true culprit. Within a week of their pronouncement, amid rumours of legal action, the Stewards, who had not banned the 'doped' Chamour from running again, performed a volte face by announcing that the powerful Bally-doyle stable could remain intact under the supervision of Vincent O'Brien's younger brother, A. S. 'Phonsie' O'Brien, who already trained a small string nearby. On May 27th Chamour returned to the Curragh to win the Gallinule Stakes, a successful prelude to his principal objective, the Irish Derby.

Of the five Irish-trained colts that took part in the Epsom Derby, the most strongly-fancied was the Phonsie O'Brien-trained Die Hard. He could only finish fifth to St Paddy. However, of Paddy Prendergast's three runners Alcaeus had run an excellent race to finish second, half a length in front of his stable companion Kythnos. Consequently, the presence of Alcaeus in the field for the Irish Derby frightened off any worthwhile opposition, with the exception of Chamour. Alcaeus, unbackable at 3-to-1 ON, was accompanied by his pacemaker Woodforest, while Chamour and Prince Chamier represented the O'Brien stable. Like Chamour, Prince Chamier was from the first crop of Vincent O'Brien's controversial Irish Derby winner Chamier. Like his sire, Prince Chamier carried the colours of Mrs F. L. Vickerman. The remaining three runners, including the English-trained Inter-vener looked to have no chance.

Ridden by 'Spurs' Nolan, Woodforest immediately dashed into a clear lead, followed at an interval of ten lengths by Alcaeus, Chamour, Djebe Boy and Prince Chamier. Only when they had turned into the straight did Alcaeus, Intervener and Chamour range up to the longtime leader, as Royal Buck flattered briefly and faded. In the straight Alcaeus took it up, looking certain to justify his prohibitive price. However, Ron Hutchinson had simply played into the hands of a fellow-Australian, who was older and wiser than he. Waiting until inside the distance, Bougoure pounced with Chamour, winning a short, sharp tussle by a length. Five lengths further back Prince Chamier stayed on to give the Ballydoyle stable first and third in the race. Alcaeus, in finishing second both at Epsom and the Curragh, thus emulated the invidious achievement of Paddy's Point.

When St Brendan beat Port Blair in the Irish Derby nearly sixty years earlier his victory was greeted 'by scenes unparalleled on any Irish racecourse'. What happened on that memorable occasion was positively subdued by comparison with the welcome that greeted Chamour. The stands erupted, the crowd went wild and Chamour was led back to a prolonged storm of cheering, which reached its crescendo with a repeated roar of 'We want Vincent!' To the excited, exultant, well-nigh vengeful crowd Chamour's victory represented O'Brien's vindication. Why, in the name of sanity, would the greatest trainer in Europe dope a Derby winner to win a maiden plate? Walter Burmann voiced the sentiments of most people present when he told the Press: 'Chamour is a really good horse, who was trained by the greatest trainer in the world.' Meanwhile, Vincent O'Brien, fishing on the Blackwater at the time of Chamour's triumph, remained an exile in his own land, barred from his own home. Thereafter events moved fitfully to a conclusion. In the face of expert veterinary opinion that sweat and saliva samples were utterly unreliable, samples from brood mares, cart-horses and even police horses had given positive readings, the Stewards of the Turf Club discontinued the old procedure, appointed their own analyst and announced that in future the winner of every race would be tested on samples of both urine and saliva. In October O'Brien was quietly informed that he was at liberty to resume living at Ballydoyle and in December he was further informed that his sentence had been commuted by six months. Justice had still not been done, but Chamour, the unwitting agent of his trainer's catastrophe, had done more than any judge and jury to vindicate him by his utterly convincing success in the Irish Derby.

An attractive chestnut colt by Chamier out of Cracknel, Chamour had been bred at the Ballykisteen Stud, where his dam had died shortly after foaling him, leaving Chamour to be fostered by a mare who otherwise pulled a cart. Chamour was the last of eleven winners produced by Cracknel, the best of the others being Maddalo, winner of the 1959 Zetland Gold Cup. Sold as a foal for 500gns, Chamour had cost O'Brien 1100gns as a yearling. Owned in partnership by Walter Burmann and Jacqueline O'Brien, the trainer's wife, Chamour had run twice unplaced as a two-year-old. Following his disqualification at the Curragh he had finished fourth behind his stable companion Die Hard at Leopardstown, before winning the Gallinule Stakes. After his historic victory in the Irish Derby, run on very hard ground, Chamour became plagued by splints, which prevented his preparation for the Irish St Leger or the Washington DC International, in which he had been invited to represent Ireland. Retired into winter quarters to contest the Cup races as a four-year-old, Chamour hit the headlines yet again in February 1961. He had dropped dead in training. Five years later his sire, Chamier, was exported to Denmark, by which time Vincent O'Brien had become more firmly established than ever before as the undisputed leader of his profession. Never the most communicative of men, O'Brien had maintained a dignified silence throughout the whole, harrowing, heart-breaking ordeal. Nonetheless, he must, on occasion at least, have reflected that for Michael Vincent O'Brien, success in the Irish Derby was a perilous pleasure.

Walter Burmann, in whose colours Chamour raced, was at that time a London-based Lloyds underwriter, whose extensive racing and breeding interests were divided between Ireland and France, where Willie Head trained for him. In 1960 he headed the list of winning owners in Ireland, where the Blandford Stakes and Champion Stakes success of Hunch combined with those of Chamour to place their owner ahead of Joe McGrath in the table. Subsequently transferred to France, Hunch won several good races, including the Prix Gladiateur, the longest flat race in Europe. Walter Burmann's biggest success as an owner-breeder was also achieved in France, where in 1966 Willie Head sent out Bon Mot, ridden by his grandson Freddie Head, to win the Prix de l'Arc de Triomphe.

At the time of his success in the Irish Derby Chamour was officially trained by A. S. O'Brien, known to the racing world as 'Phonsie' and much more readily associated with National Hunt racing. An accomplished amateur rider, Phonsie had finished second in the Aintree Grand National on Royal Tan, before following in the footsteps of his older brother and taking up training. Pitchforked into prominence when called upon to do duty for his banished brother, Phonsie O'Brien emerged as leading Irish trainer in 1960. Having filled the breach in the hour of need and kept the Ballydoyle stable intact, Phonsie happily reverted to his first love, steeplechasing. As relaxed and outgoing as Vincent is tense and introspective, Phonsie O'Brien identifies much more readily with the cheerful camaraderie of the 'winter game'. In this respect he has the best of both worlds, being somewhat of a summer 'chasing specialist and for a number of years he deposed Paddy Sleator as the uncrowned King of Galway by sending out four consecutive winners of the historic Galway Plate, highlight of the mid-summer festival meeting. And memorable were the celebrations on each occasion! Having sold his South Lodge stables to Adrian Maxwell, Phonsie O'Brien moved to Ballynonty, where he trains for a select band of owners, who can both afford and appreciate the fruits of his skilful and patient approach.

Years of riding and wasting in hot climates had left their mark on the lined and leathery features of Garnet 'Garnie' Bougoure. However, Irish racegoers soon discovered just why this wizened, frail-looking little Australian – he was in fact only thirty-six – had achieved such a reputation in his native land and subsequently in the Far East. Like all Australian jockeys, Garnie Bougoure had learned to ride with a 'clock in his head'. Acclimatising quickly to the variations of Irish racecourses and the state of the ground, he finished a close second to Liam Ward in the jockeys' championship, having given an exhibition performance on Barclay to land the Irish St Leger. That epic victory on Chamour in the Irish Derby the following season provided consolation for a disappointing ride on the fancied Die Hard at Epsom. Once again he finished second in the jockeys' table, this time to Bobby Beasley. In 1962 he moved from Ballydoyle to the Curragh, succeeding his compatriot Ron Hutchinson as stable jockey to Paddy Prendergast and scored his first major success in England when winning the Timeform Gold Cup on Noblesse, the best animal he ever rode.

1963 was a golden year for Prendergast and Bougoure, who combined to win the Epsom Oaks with Noblesse, the Irish Sweeps Derby, King George VI and Queen Elizabeth Stakes and St Leger with Ragusa, the Eclipse Stakes with Khalkis and the Irish St Leger with Christmas Island. Continuing their all-conquering run the following year, trainer and jockey won the English One Thousand Guineas with Pourparler, the Eclipse Stakes with Ragusa and the Champagne Stakes and Timeform Gold Cup with Hardicanute. That was Garnie Bougoure's last full season in Ireland and by the time that Paddy Prendergast had sent out Meadow Court to win another Irish Sweeps Derby, Bougoure was about to depart these shores for sunnier climes, returning to Singapore, where he became a successful trainer. What he lacked in strength in the saddle, Garnie Bougoure compensated with skill and timing. Moreover, like Scobie Breasley, he rode with a length of leather which enabled him to get the best out of big, ungainly animals like Khalkis. Invariably photographed with his whip at the ready, he rarely resorted to hitting his horse, using the stick rather to keep the animal balanced and running straight. Such skilful restraint provided the perfect compliment to the training talents of Paddy Prendergast, unrivalled as a handler of two-year-olds, whose future prospects were enhanced in the sympathetic hands of Garnie Bougoure.

While the Chamour saga dragged on much more positive and heartening news was forthcoming in connection with the Irish Derby; not Chamour's Derby, but one scheduled to take place in two years' time. Its import was to have profound significance for the entire bloodstock industry in Ireland. At a joint Press conference, staged by the Turf Club, the Racing Board and the Hospitals' Trust Ltd, plans were announced for a new and vastly different Irish Derby, which, if successful, would become the richest race in Europe, vying with its Epsom, French and Kentucky counterparts. The concept was disconcertingly simple; the Hospitals' Trust Ltd, the company which administered the Irish Hospitals Sweepstakes, had obtained the consent of the Turf Club and the Racing Board to sponsor the Irish Derby to the tune of £30,000, in return for which the race would be called the Irish Sweeps Derby. Responsibility for the success of this mammoth promotion rested with the Irish Sweeps Derby Co-ordinating Committee, which included Mr Joseph McGrath and Captain Spencer Freeman. Thus was born Joe McGrath's brilliant brainchild, and around its successful growth and development revolved the future of Irish racing. The initial entry stage drew 500 and the second stage (in November) attracted a further 127, the total constituted a new world record; the first signs were healthy . . .

Wednesday, 22nd June, 1960 £7442 10 0 **7 Ran** 1½m

The Irish Derby. A sweepstake of 5sovs each for yearlings entered on 18th June, 1958, or of 15sovs for those entered on 5th November, 1958, 20sovs extra for all if not struck out on 21st October, 1959, and 25sovs additional for all if not struck out on 25th May, 1960, with 4000sovs added to be contributed by the Turf Club and Racing Board. The winner will receive 75%, second 15%, and third 10% of the whole stakes after deduction of bonuses of 100sovs to the owner (at entry) of the winner, 50sovs to the owner (at entry) of the second and 25sovs to the owner (at entry) of the third. For three years old entire colts and fillies. Colts, 9st; Fillies, 8st 11lb. One mile and a half.

(241 subs)

1	Mr F. W. Burmann's	CHAMOUR (G. Bougoure) Ch. colt Chamier – Cracknel by Manna.	9.0	A. S. O'Brien
2	Sir Richard Brooke's	ALCAEUS (Ron Hutchinson) Ch. colt Alycidon – Marteline.	9.0	P. J. Prendergast
3	Mrs F. L. Vickerman's	PRINCE CHAMIER (T. P. Burns) Ch. colt Chamier – Princesse Janique.	9.0	A. S. O'Brien
4	Mrs V. Vanden Bergh's	DJEBE BOY (L. Ward) Br. colt Djebe – Sea Princess.	9.0	C. Collins
5	Mr N. L. Cohen's	ROYAL BUCK (Herbert Holmes) B. colt Buckhound – Royal Charge.	9.0	K. Kerr
6	Mrs J. Forrestal's	WOODFOREST (M. Nolan) Gr. colt Djebe – Love in the Forest.	9.0	P. J. Prendergast
7	Mr Stanhope Joel's	INTERVENER (W. Snaith) B. colt Supreme Court – My Poppet.	9.0	H. L. Cottrill (UK)

SP 1/3 Alcaeus; 3/1 CHAMOUR; 18/1 Intervener; 25/1 Prince Chamier; 50/1 Djebe Boy; 66/1 Royal Buck; 150/1 Woodforest. TOTE (2/6 unit) 10/-. Places 3/-, 3/-.
1 length, 5 lengths. 2m 37.5s.
Winner trained by Mr A. S. O'Brien at Ballydoyle, Co. Tipperary.

1961

That the Irish Derby of 1961 should have seemed an anti-climax was inevitable. Worth a total of £10,670, of which the Turf Club and the Racing Board contributed £4000, it was the richest Irish Derby since the race had begun almost a hundred years earlier. However, such was the excitement and anticipation concerning the first running of the Irish Sweeps Derby – prize fund approximately £60,000 – that this, the last of the 'old' Irish Derbies, seemed like very small beer. Adding to the air of anti-climax on Derby Day itself were the signs of expansion and improvement at the Curragh; new car parks, more covered stand area, better facilities and an overall air of anticipation – none of which seemed relevant to the immediate proceedings. Nor did the standard of the largest field in the history of the race help to redeem the situation, for they were a moderate lot, representative of their generation. The best of them seemed to be Light Year, saddled by A. S. O'Brien to win the Irish Two Thousand Guineas and now in the hands of a recently-reinstated M. V. O'Brien. He started a short-priced favourite to beat seventeen rivals, including the Irish-trained Epsom failures, Time Greine, Neanderthal, Cipriani and Supreme Verdict. The two English challengers were Dual, another Epsom flop, and Your Highness, whose two recent successes hardly seemed good enough. The fact that Haven and Soysambu, the joint second favourites, were both still maidens, further underlined the mediocrity of the Classic crop. Light Year, backed from 3-to-1 to 2-to-1 to provide Vincent O'Brien with a triumphant return, was led to the start with the Stewards' permission.

The Paddy Prendergast-trained Baynard set off at a furious pace and was soon well clear of Indian Judge, Your Highness and Anner Banks. Still clear entering the straight, Baynard showed no signs of weakening and a growing murmur from the stands suggested a repetition of Psidium's shock success at Epsom three weeks earlier. It was only in the last quarter of a mile that Baynard began to falter and as he did so Herbert Holmes brought Your Highness through to take the lead. He in turn was challenged at the distance by Soysambu and Haven. Try as he might, the gigantic Soysambu could not wear down Your Highness, who stuck grimly to his task to win by half a length in a photo finish. Two and a half lengths further back came Haven, whose rider Lester Piggott reported that he had felt the colt falter at the entrance to the straight. It transpired that Haven had broken down in running, but for which he must have won. Nonetheless, Your Highness' victory was as well-deserved as it was unexpected and he returned to a warm reception, much of the applause being directed at his rider, the veteran 'Bert' Holmes.

A heavily-built chestnut colt, Your Highness provided a notable breeding double for the Joel family, for he was by Stanhope Joel's wartime St Leger winner Chamossaire out of Mrs Joel's prolific mare Lady Grand, who had foaled Your Highness at the Joels' Snailwell Stud near Newmarket. Bred by the Aga Khan, Lady Grand was by Solario. Having won one small race, she had been bought by Mrs Joel, for whom she bred nine winners in all, of whom no fewer than four won races in 1961. Unplaced in his three starts as a backward two-year-old, Your Highness had shown rapid improvement in recent weeks, beginning with a modest success in maiden company at Birmingham, he had won at Epsom and was now completing his hat-trick in a Classic.

The manner of Your Highness' victory at the Curragh indicated a bright future as a Cup horse and, in line with this thinking, the Irish St Leger seemed an obvious objective. Having finished a good fourth in the Vaux Gold Tankard at Redcar, Your Highness returned to the Curragh, where he started favourite for the final Irish Classic. Ridden by Paddy Powell in place of the recently-retired Herbert Holmes, Your Highness was found wanting in pace rather than stamina, being beaten by the maiden Vimadee, trained by Tommy Burns and ridden by his son T. P. Burns. In six runs as a four-year-old Your Highness came closest to success when running Dicta Drake to a neck in the Coronation Cup. The same year he was exported to Japan as a stallion. By no means an outstanding racehorse, Your Highness did not have to be anything special to win the last running of the 'old' Irish Derby.

For Mr and Mrs Stanhope Joel, on a visit from their residence in Bermuda, the summer of '61 was one of incredible and almost unbroken racecourse success. Only a week earlier Brud Fetherstonhaugh, their trainer in Ireland, had sent three of their horses to the Royal Ascot meeting; Prince Tor won the Windsor Castle Stakes, Silver Tor, his three-parts brother, won the King's Stand Stakes and Bun Penny won the Cork and Orrery Stakes! As if to emphasise their luck, the Joels had virtually decided that Your Highness should not run in the Irish Derby as they had not been able to arrange 'plane reservations to Ireland to see the colt run. Hearing of their plight, some of the jubilant Irish contingent at Ascot had prevailed upon their national airline with the consequent happy results. Students of fashion rather than form might have benefited from observing that Mrs Joel wore the same hat that she had worn the previous Friday at Ascot, when both Prince Tor and Silver Tor had been successful! Alas, even the magic hat could not bring off another notable double, for Flumeri, Your Highness' older half-brother, could only manage third place in the last race on the card.

Though Stanhope Joel's jet-hopping schedule contrasted vividly with his father's more leisurely progress – 'Solly' Joel had crossed the Channel in his steam yacht to witness the success of his colt Kopi in the 1929 Irish Derby – he had inherited his father's enthusiasm for racing in full measure. Born in 1903, educated at Eton and called to the Bar, Stanhope Joel had inherited his father's business and bloodstock interests on the latter's death in 1931. The best horse to carry his 'Green and pink stripes, pink cap' in those earlier years had been Chamossaire, winner of the St Leger at York in 1945. Chamossaire spent his entire stud career at the Joels' Snailwell Stud, where a life-sized statute was erected in his memory. Your Highness was the second of three Irish Derby winners sired by Chamossaire – the greatest of these was still to come. Towards the end of his life – he died in 1976 – Stanhope Joel had the pleasure of breeding and owning such high-class performers as Busted, Caliban and St Pauli Girl, while under National Hunt Rules he owned that spectacular and flamboyant 'chaser Frenchman's Cove, trained by his son-in-law Harry Thompson Jones. American-born Mrs Joel pursued a relatively independent policy with the horses that carried her pink and green checks, frequently employing trainers other than those favoured by her husband. Apart from Your Highness the best animal owned by Mrs Joel was her home-bred filly Lupe, winner of the

Cheshire Oaks, Epsom Oaks and Yorkshire Oaks in 1970 and the Coronation Cup a year later.

Your Highness was trained at Newmarket by Humphrey Lawson Cottrill. Son of the Lambourn trainer Harry Cottrill, Humphrey had assisted his father in the late 'twenties and 'thirties, during which time the stable provided Sir Abe Bailey with his only Classic winner in forty years of trying when Lovely Rosa won the Oaks at Epsom. Having spent a number of years in South Africa as a stipendiary steward, Humphrey Cottrill returned to England, becoming assistant to Willie Pratt and then to Marcus Marsh. In 1952 he accepted the post of private trainer to Lionel Holliday at LaGrange. In training for Jimmy White, the self-made millionaire and for Sir Abe Bailey, Cottrill's father had demonstrated his ability to train owners as well as horses and the fact that Humphrey remained for six years with Holliday, a cantankerous old Yorkshireman, showed that he had learned his lessons well. On becoming a public trainer at Newmarket, Humphrey Cottrill continued to saddle his share of winners, though nothing of the calibre of such Holliday horses as Narrator, Pirate King and Gratitude. In 1974, in a characteristically forthright protest against the absurd economics of his profession, Humphrey Cottrill handed in his licence and set out to make some real money as a bloodstock agent.

The warm reception accorded to Your Highness after the Irish Derby was directed almost entirely at his diminutive rider, the veteran lightweight Herbert Holmes, for it was generally felt that 'Bert' had been needlessly and unfairly 'jocked off' the Joel-Fetherstonhaugh winners at Ascot the previous week. The truth of the matter was that an agreement existed between Brud Fetherston' and Paddy Brudenell-Bruce, the Joels' son-in-law and racing manager, whereby English jockeys rode the Joel runners in England and Irish jockeys had the rides on runners in Ireland. Having kept his side of the bargain at Ascot, Brud had insisted that Holmes, his stable jockey, be given the mount on Your Highness, even though the ride had already been offered to Harry Carr, who, notwithstanding the Chamier-Premonition episode, found himself free to accept. Fetherston's loyalty to his jockey

1960. Chamour, *victory by the 'doped' colt provided triumphant popular vindication for his banished trainer, Vincent O'Brien, whose enforced exile found him fishing on the Blackwater at the time of Chamour's Classic success. Source:* The Irish Horse.

1961. Your Highness, *scraping home from Soysambu (far right) to win the last of the 'old style' Irish Derbies. Source:* The Irish Horse.

Wednesday, 21st June, 1961   **£7921 5 0**   **18 Ran**   **1½m**

The Irish Derby. A sweepstakes of 5sovs each for yearlings entered on 24th June, 1959, or of 15sovs for those entered on 4th November, 1959, 20sovs extra for all if not struck out on 26th October, 1960, and 25sovs additional for all if not struck out on 31st May, 1961, with 4000sovs added to be contributed by the Turf Club and the Racing Board. The winner will receive 75%, second 15%, and third 10% of the whole stakes after deduction of the bonuses of 100sovs to the owner (at entry) of the winner, 50sovs to the owner (at entry) of the second and 25sovs to the owner (at entry) of the third. For three years old entire colts a nd llies. Colts, 9st; Fillies, 8st 11lb. One mile and a half.

(237 subs)

1	Mrs Stanhope Joel's	YOUR HIGHNESS (Herbert Holmes) Ch. colt Chamossaire – Lady Grand by Solario.	9.0	H. L. Cottrill (GB)
2	Mr G. M. Bell's	SOYSAMBU (T. Gosling) Ch. colt Sicambre – Safari Moon. (FOALED IN FRANCE.)	9.0	P. J. Prendergast
3	Mr W. F. Pinnington's	HAVEN (L. Piggott) Ch. colt Borealis – Quick Arrow.	9.0	J. M. Rogers
4	Mr C. M. Kline's	NEANDERTHAL (G. W. Robinson) Ch. colt Nearula – Marteline.	9.0	M. V. O'Brien
5	Lord Ennisdale's	BAYNARD (J. G. Winter) Ch. colt King of the Tudors – Lumine.	9.0	P. J. Prendergast
6	Lady Honor Svejdar's	CIPRIANI (Ron Hutchinson) B. colt Never Say Die – Carezza.	9.0	P. J. Prendergast
7	Sir Harold Wernher's	DUAL (J. Lindley) B. colt Chanteur II – Duplicity.	9.0	J. M. Gosden (GB)
8	Mrs Thomas O'Brien's	ANNER BANKS (John F. Rafferty) B. colt Black Tarquin – Mill Vine.	9.0	Thomas O'Brien
9	Mr T. E. Hallinan's	LIGHT YEAR* (G. Bougoure) Ch. colt Chamier – Spring Light.	9.0	M. V. O'Brien
10	Mr Joseph McGrath's	TIME GREINE (W. Williamson) B. colt Arctic Time – Blaith na Greine.	9.0	S. McGrath
11	Mrs E. J. King's	WISE BOY (M. Kennedy) Br. colt Le Sage – Dusky Slipper.	9.0	Sir H. Nugent
12	Mr Joesph McGrath's	RULLAHGEELAGH (J. Wright) Br. colt Valerullah – Inchigeelagh.	9.0	S. McGrath
13	Lord Harrington's	ARCHIPELAGO (T. P. Burns) Ch. colt Acropolis – Pharwin.	9.0	C. Chute
14	Mr J. B. Turner's	GARLAND KNIGHT (John Power) Ch. colt Sadani – Garland.	9.0	A. D. Turner
15	Mrs A. B. Biddle's	LE PRINCE (L. Ward) Br. colt Prince Bio – Atlantida.	9.0	T. Shaw
16	Mr J. Audain's	SUPREME VERDICT (P. Powell, jr) Ch. colt Supreme Court – Valona II.	9.0	J. M. Rogers
17	Mrs A. B. Biddle's	COUNTER-ATTACK (L. Browne) Ch. colt Never Say Die – Kilcarn Victory.	9.0	T. Shaw
18	Mr B. Kerr's	INDIAN JUDGE (G. McGrath) B. colt Sayajirao – Northern Beauty.	9.0	K. R. Kerr

SP 2/1 Light Year; 11/2 Soysambu, Haven; 8/1 Time Greine; 9/1 Dual; 100/8 Cipriani, Anner Banks; 20/1 Neanderthal; 25/1 Rullahgeelagh, Supreme Verdict; 33/1 YOUR HIGHNESS; 50/1 Wise Boy; 66/1 Le Prince; 100/1 Bar. TOTE (2/6 unit) 80/6. Places 17/6, 6/6, 7/6.

½ length, 2¼ lengths. 2m 33.5s.

Winner trained by Mr H. L. Cottrill at Beverley House, Newmarket.

*Light Year led to the start by permission of Stewards.

on this occasion was no less than Bert Holmes deserved for many years' service to Brud and his father before him.

Born in England, where he served his apprenticeship with Fred Darling at Beckhampton and rode his first winner in 1928, Bert Holmes had tried his luck in East Africa before coming to Ireland to join the J. T. Rogers stable. So long had he been riding in Ireland that few people any longer regarded him as other than an Irishman. Having moved across the Curragh to ride the lightweights for Bob Fetherstonhaugh, Bert Holmes became stable jockey on Jack Moylan's retirement. Apart from his success on Your Highness, Bert Holmes scored his greatest personal triumph when riding Circus Lady to upset the odds on the crack French filly Coronation V in the 1949 Irish Oaks. Having broken his leg in five places in a fall the previous year and fought his way back to ride the winner of the Irish Derby, Bert Holmes wisely decided to hang up his boots while his luck was in. Not that the poor fellow's luck was destined to last, for a year later, having made all the preparations to begin training, likeable little Bert Holmes dropped dead.

The seventeen beaten runners in the Irish Derby did little afterwards to enhance the form. Neither Soysambu nor Haven ever saw a racecourse again. The talented but excitable Time Greine went to America, while Light Year and Rullahgeelagh retired to stud in Ireland. Le Prince proved consistent but luckless – an unfortunate characteristic of Mrs Biddle's horses – though he did win the Welsh Cesarewitch before retiring to his owner's stud, alongside the very successful Milesian. Garland Knight, a good, tough stayer, won the Naas November Handicap and the Edinburgh Gold Cup and later sired hardy types like himself. The best of the lot of them was Cipriani, who beat Vienna in the Coronation Stakes and finished second to Romulus in the Sussex Stakes before joining Your Highness in Japan.

1962

The inaugural running of the Irish Sweeps Derby constituted the greatest sports spectacular that had ever been staged in Ireland. Three years of planning, promotion and hard work had produced an international field to contest the richest race ever run in Europe. Besides being the best quality horse race ever to take place in Ireland, the Irish Sweeps Derby had caught the public imagination as one of the most glamourous social occasions of the year. A glorious summer's day drew a crowd estimated at between forty and seventy thousand people, including HE President de Valera, everybody who was anybody in political, social and business circles in Ireland, as well as Turf celebrities and dignitaries from all over the world. The vision of Joe McGrath, allied to the promotional genius of Spencer Freeman, had combined to elevate Irish racing to the international status that Irish-bred horses had gained many years before.

As if to celebrate this breakthrough in Irish racing, Irish-bred and Irish-trained horses were sweeping the board, not only at home, but also in England and France. It seemed entirely appropriate that the Epsom Derby should recently have fallen to an Irish-trained colt, Larkspur. Trained by Vincent O'Brien, Larkspur was about to become the first Epsom Derby winner since Orby to lay his laurels on the line at the Curragh. A record field of twenty-four included four runners from England and two from France. Despite Pat Glennon's decision to remain loyal to Sebring, fifth to his victorious stable companion in the all-fall-down Epsom Derby, in which the favourite, Hethersett, had been one of seven fallers, Larkspur remained a firm favourite to pull off the double. His most strongly supported rivals, aside from Sebring, were Arctic Storm, winner of the Irish Two Thousand Guineas in record time, Saint Denys, successful in the Gallinule Stakes, and the French pair, Arcor and Tambourine II. Roger Poincelet, having ridden Arcor into second place at Epsom, had declared that he would win at the Curragh. However, he had since been claimed by Pollet to ride Tambourine II, while Neville Sellwood had been obliged to ride Arcor, leaving the mount on his Epsom Derby winner to yet another Australian, Scobie Breasley. In order to give the huge crowd a better view of the proceedings, the parade ring had been temporarily transferred to in front of the grandstand, yet another of the imaginative innovations which created such a favourable impression with all present.

First to show from a walk-in start were Saint Denys and Gail Star, who set a rare gallop, ahead of London Gazette, Cyrus and Trade Wind. A mile from home Gail Star faded, leaving Saint Denys in the lead ahead of Atlantis, Trimatic, Cyrus and Tambourine II. Turning into the straight Saint Denys began to weaken and it was at this point that the race was won and lost. As Poincelet shot Tambourine II into a clear lead, Larkspur and Sebring lay fifth and sixth, with Arctic Storm, drawn on the wide outside, now pocketed on the rails in tenth position. Having stolen first run, Tambourine looked like coming home an easy winner, for neither Sebring nor Larkspur were making any impression in pursuit. Suddenly Arctic Storm, extricated at last by Williamson, came flying through his field with a blistering late run, which brought him level with Tambourine II in the final strides. Amid intense excitement the two colts flashed past the post together, inseparable to the naked eye. Some lengths further back Sebring outran Larkspur for third place, followed by Atlantis and Saint Denys. Amid scenes of feverish excitement the judge's verdict was announced: Tambourine II by a short head. Both the winner and the second returned to a rousing reception, leaving one to reflect what might have happened if the short head had gone the other way . . . With a typically Gallic gesture, the lad leading in Tambourine II whipped off the colt's blinkers in his enthusiasm to show the hero of the hour at his best. In the spirit of the occasion this infringement of the Rules was rightly overlooked.

When interviewed afterwards Poincelet said that he had gone on as early as he did because he thought the pace too slow – the time, 2mins 28.8secs, beat Talgo's record by over two seconds. When still clear at the two furlong marker he had felt certain of victory and it was only inside the final furlong, where he thought that the roar of the crowd had caused Tambourine II to check, that Arctic Storm's late challenge had worried him. Bill Williamson confirmed Poincelet's version by saying that Arctic Storm had merely run on at the one pace, indicating that his late flourish was in reality an illusion caused by the winner slowing, rather than by Arctic Storm quickening. Neither Breasley nor Glennon had any excuses to offer for the failure of the O'Brien-trained pair, though Glennon's quip 'Mission accomplished!' indicated his pleasure at having his faith in Sebring as the better of the two vindicated. Immediately after the race John D. Schapiro, the man responsible for the Washington International invitation race, confirmed that the connections of Arctic Storm had accepted an invitation to run the colt at Laurel Park. He added that an invitation would also be issued to Mrs Howell E. Jackson, the winning owner, who had been unable to be present. In her absence a delighted Etienne Pollet would not commit himself concerning future plans for Tambourine II, whom he described as a triumphant vindication of his belief in the La Mirambule bloodline. However, the most excited people of all at the Curragh that afternoon were a certain Mr and Mrs Albert Smith from Melbourne, Australia. A dairy farmer and bookmaker of Scots-Irish descent, Albert Smith had dreamed that a horse called Golden Fire would win the Chester Cup and had backed his hunch successfully. With his winnings he had bought the £50,000 winning ticket, in partnership with a Melbourne judge. For his Dutch-born wife this first visit to Ireland was an occasion to remember!

Bred at his owner's Bull Run Stud in Virginia, Tambourine II was a good-looking bay colt by the American champion sire Princequillo, made famous in America by his record-breaking son Round Table, and notorious in England as the sire of Prince Simon, touched off in both the Guineas and the Derby. La Mirambule, Tambourine II's dam, had an all-French pedigree going back six generations. The leading French two-year-old of 1951, La Mirambule had won the Prix Vermeille and finished second in the English One Thousand Guineas, the French Oaks and the Prix de l'Arc de Triomphe. La Mirambule's family had gone to France in 1898 through the export of the Irish-bred Kendal Beauty, whose third dam was Gramachree, own-sister to Birdcatcher and Faugh-a-Ballagh and the grandam of Selim. Thus, by curious coincidence, the winners of both the first Irish Derby and the first Irish Sweeps Derby, though separated by almost a century, sprang from the same world-renowed Irish taproot.

Unraced as a two-year-old, Tambourine II had previously won over ten furlongs at Longchamp in May and then finished fourth to Val de Loir, Pickfort and Exbury in the Prix du Jockey Club, beaten only a length and two necks. Even in a season of muddling Classic form, this was quite good enough to justify his trip to Ireland, as events proved. Not long after his return to France Tambourine II went lame and was taken out of training. Tambourine II was retired to stud in France on the understanding that breeders agreed to send him a mare for four years at the comparatively modest fee of £550. When Tambou, one of his first crop, realised £13,460 as a yearling at Deauville, this began to look like a remarkably good deal. However, his early promise was not fulfilled and he was not a successful sire.

Mrs Howell E. Jackson, the winning owner-breeder, had been unable to make the journey from Paris to see her colt's thrilling victory, celebrating instead with Pollet and Poincelet in Paris that night. American-born Mrs Jackson, whose husband owned the Bull Run Stud as well as having interests in several racetracks, had been deeply involved in racing and breeding all her life. Her colours, registered for the first time in 1825, were among the oldest in America. Though she had spent a lot of time hunting in England, Mrs Jackson regarded Paris as her adoptive home, so much so that during the War she had raised and financed an entire ambulance unit in the Infanterie Coloniale, for which she subsequently received the Legion d'Honneur. Prior to her success in the Irish Sweeps Derby, Mrs Jackson had won the English

One Thousand Guineas and Oaks with that exquisite filly Never Too Late II. That was in 1960, the same year that La Mirambule became the last mare ever covered by the celebrated Nasrullah. Subsequently named Nasram II, the produce of that mating provided Irishmen with another more painful memory of Mrs Jackson and her marvellous mare when he beat Santa Claus fair and square in the King George VI and Queen Elizabeth Stakes in 1964, the same year in which Baldric II credited Mrs Jackson with the English Two Thousand Guineas.

Tall, distinguished and umistakably French, Etienne Pollet had for many years been at the top of the training profession in France, where he had been champion trainer during the war years. As far back as 1952 he and Poncelet had combined to win their first English Classic with Thunderhead II in the Two Thousand Guineas. However, at the time of Tambourine II's success in the Irish Sweeps Derby Pollet's greatest charge had only just been foaled. That was Sea Bird II, brilliant winner of the Epsom Derby and the Prix de l'Arc de Triomphe and one of the truly great racehorses seen in Europe since the War. Vaguely Noble was yet another world-beater to pass through his immensely capable hands, while he always held that the brilliant but wayward Gyr could have proved himself greater than either of those champions.

In his autobiography, 'Souvenirs d'une cravache d'or', Yves Saint-Martin devoted a chapter to 'Les jockeys', in which he had this to say: 'Roger Poincelot restera le meilleur jockey que j'ai vu monter. Le plus grand.' He went on to cite the advice of his master and mentor, Francois Mathet: 'Regarde monter Poincelet . . . Observe-le bien: il n'y a pas de meilleur exemple.' That was written in 1968, by which time Roger Poincelet was in the twilight of a long and immensely successful career, during which his stylish blend of strength, coolness and dash had gained him acceptance in England as a top-class jockey; an accolade not bestowed on any Frenchman since George Stern almost half a century earlier.

Outstanding among a vintage crop of apprentices in pre-war France, where he served his time with Charles Barriere, Poincelet went jumping as soon as he had lost his claim, that being common practice in France at that time. Without altering either his flat race style or length of leather, he became recognised as a brilliant jump rider, notably through his association with the outstanding wartime hurdler, Wild Risk. When the war ended he had established himself as the leading jockey in France. However, in common with other jockeys the world over, he was determined to prove himself in England, the birthplace of horseracing.

In the years immediately after the war French horses seemed almost invincible in England, mostly ridden either by Charlie Elliott, an Englishman, or Rae Johnstone, an Australian, and it is no exaggeration to say that when French jockeys were employed the consequences, win or lose, were frequently disastrous. Moreover, English jockeys riding in France would return with hair-raising accounts of the lunatic behaviour of the native jockeys. Amid all the rancour and ridicule one name stood out – Roger Poincelet, whose victories in races such as the Coronation Cup, the Ascot Gold Cup, Goodwood Cup and Champion Stakes marked him out as a talented jockey in any country. By the time that Saint-Martin had burst upon the scene, compelling comparison with his very much older compatriot, the latter had gained the most spectacular and satisfying success of his career. That crowning moment came at Epsom in 1961, when Poincelet got the Derby mount on Harry

Wragg's non-staying no-hoper, Psidium. George Moore had been flown especially from Australia to ride Wragg's better-fancied runner, Sovrango. Settling Psidium at the rear of the field and riding as though his mind were a million miles away, Poincelet trailed the entire field as they swung down around Tattenham Corner. Pulling wide in the straight, he conjured such a burst of speed from his much-maligned mount that they passed their struggling opponents as though they were standing still and swept to a stupefying success. Later that year he returned to England and rose Right Royal V to humble St Paddy at Ascot. Two years later Roger Poincelet scored his last major success in England when he won the One Thousand Guineas on Hula Dancer. Having signed off with a typically stylish swansong on Prince Royal in the Prix de l'Arc de Triomphe the following year, Poincelet retired to take up training, making the most of what was entrusted to his care, before cancer claimed him at an all-too-early-age in 1977. When many more memorable Epsom Derby winners have been long forgotten, Psidium will be remembered, and with him the genius of rider Roger Poincelet.

1962. *The greatest sporting spectacular ever staged in Ireland. . . . The Irish Sweeps Derby provided a fitting finish, as* **Tambourine II** *(rails) repelled the late challenge of the locally-trained Arctic Storm, with the Epsom Derby winner, Larkspur back in fourth place. Source:* The Irish Horse.

While Tambourine II returned to France to complete his racing career, Arctic Storm took on the older horses in the King George VI and Queen Elizabeth Stakes at Ascot. By finishing third, beaten less than a length by the four-year-olds Match III and Aurelius, with Val de Loir, Tambourine II's conqueror in the Prix de Jockey Club, well behind him, Arctic Storm looked more than ever to have been a desperately unlucky loser of the Irish Sweeps Derby. Reappearing on the Curragh to contest the Irish St Leger, for which he seemed a certainty, Arctic Storm got a deplorable ride, finishing only sixth to the unconsidered Arctic Vale. Remaining loyal to his hapless jockey, who insisted that Arctic Storm simply did not stay, Oxx put Williamson up again in the Champion Stakes, in which Arctic Storm proved himself conclusively the best of his generation in these islands. He headed the English Free Handicap and was retired to John Oxx's Park Stud, dying before he got sufficient opportunity to prove whether he could transmit sufficient of his racecourse brilliance to outweigh his distinctly plebeian breeding. Larkspur, having finished behind Sebring yet again when both were unplaced in Hethersett's St Leger, was syndicated and retired to his owner's Ballygoran Stud. Of those that finished further down the field in the inaugural Irish Sweeps Derby, London Gazette, once offered as a prize in a golf club raffle, proved the best, winning the Churchill Stakes at Ascot and five other races. His very first runner, Quayside, turned out to be even better than his sire. Running Rock, Talgo Abbess and Ticonderoga went on to make their names over hurdles.

The participants, the Press and the public were unanimous in their verdict: the Irish Sweeps Derby, the most ambitious venture in the history of Irish racing, was an unqualified success.

Saturday, 30th June, 1962   **£50,027 10 0**   **24 Ran**   **1½m**

Irish Sweeps Derby. A sweepstakes of 10 sovs each for yearlings entered on 27th July, 1960, or of 30sovs for those entered on 2nd November, 1960; 40sovs extra for all if not struck out on 25th October, 1961; an additional 100sovs for all if not struck out on 20th June, 1961, with 30,000sovs added, to be contributed by the Irish Hospitals' Sweepstakes. The winner will receive 75%, second 15%, and third 10% of the whole stakes after deduction of bonuses of 500sovs to the breeder of the winner, 300sovs to the breeder of the second and 200sovs to the breeder of the third. For three years old entire colts and fillies. Colts, 9st; Fillies, 8st 11lb. One mile and a half.

Note—Subject to the usual conditions the Racing Board will pay special allowances as follows towards the transport costs of runners from abroad in this race:– Great Britain, £200 per horse; other European countries £250 per horse; other countries, £500 per horse.

In consultation with the appropriate Stud Book Authority the Stewards shall determine the identity of the breeder and their decision shall be final.

(627 subs)

1	Mrs Howell E. Jackson's	TAMBOURINE II (R. Poincelet) 9.0	E. Pollet (FR)
		B. colt Princequillo – Le Mirambule by Coaraze.	
2	Mrs E. M. Carroll's	ARCTIC STORM 9.0	J. Oxx
		(W. Williamson) Br. colt Arctic Star – Rabina.	
3	Mr Townsend B. Martin's	SEBRING (T. P. Glennon) 9.0	M. V. O'Brien
		B. colt Aureole – Queen of Speed.	
4	Mr Raymond R. Guest's	LARKSPUR (A. Breasley) 9.0	M. V. O'Brien
		Ch. colt Never Say Die – Skylarking.	
5	Mrs A. B. Biddle's	ATLANTIS (L. Ward) 9.0	T. Shaw
		B. colt Milesian – Atlantida.	
6	Princesse N. d'Imeretie Mrs Gray's	SAINT DENYS (P. Canty) 9.0	M. Hurley
		Ch. colt Dionisio – Fand.	
7	Mr J. O. Hambro's	CYRUS (W. Rickaby) 9.0	G. T. Brooke (GB)
		Br. colt Darius – Good Line.	
8	Mrs Stanhope Joel's	OUR GUILE (E. Smith) 9.0	H. L. Cottrill (GB)
		Ch. colt Court Martial – Lady Grand.	

9 Mr Fred Turner, jr's	SOLPETRE (G. McGrath)	9.0	K. R. Kerr
	B. colt Sunny Boy III – Blue Pet.(FOALED IN FRANCE.)		
10 Mr Clifford Nicholson's	TRADE WIND (H. J. Greenaway) Ch. colt Never Say Die – Following Breeze.	9.0	W. Elsey (GB)
11 Mr Thomas P. Power's	SNOWHOUND (M. Kennedy) Br. colt Buckhound – Obla.	9.0	C. L. Weld
12 M. Marcel Boussac's	ARCOR (N. Sellwood) B. colt Arbar – Corejada. (FOALED IN FRANCE.)	9.0	H. Nicolas (FR)
13 Mr Michael Kennedy's	RUNNING ROCK (John Power) Gr. colt Royal Challenge – Ouranna.	9.0	P. Norris
14 Major Victor McCalmont's	Le PIRATE (P. Boothman) B. colt Zarathustra – Marsh Mallow.	9.0	R. N. Fetherstonhaugh
15 Mrs Victor McCalmont's	LONDON GAZETTE (G. Starkey) Ch. colt Panaslipper – Court Circular.	9.0	H. Thompson Jones (GB)
16 Mr R. B. Beaumont's	MUMZOWA (T. P. Burns) Ch. colt Preciptic – Torc Anna.	9.0	K. Bell
17 Mrs A. B. Biddle's	MARCH WIND (G. W. Robinson) B. colt Hill Gail – War Loot.	9.0	T. Shaw
18 Comdr A. R. Bradshaw's	T. V. (P. Powell, jr) Ch. colt Darius – T.S.F.	9.0	H. V. S. Murless
19 Mr Joseph McGrath's	GAIL STAR (D. Page) Br. colt Hill Gail – Silken Star.	9.0	S. McGrath
20 Colonel J. Reid's	TICONDEROGA (P. Sullivan) B. colt Talgo – Marjorie Castle.	9.0	J. Oxx
21 Mr T. Scahill's	TALGO ABBESS (R. Moylan) B. colt Talgo – Mount Abbess.	9.0	Private
22 Mr Peter McCarthy's	SIR PAT (W. Berg) Ch. colt Acropolis – Jury Woman by Fair Trial.	9.0	C. Magnier
23 Mrs J. R. Mullion's	BORGHESE (G. Bougoure) B. colt Macherio – Eastern Glamour.	9.0	P. J. Prendergast
24 Mrs H. Taylor's	TRIMATIC (E. J. Cracknell) B. colt Talgo – Miss Maisie.	9.0	P. Norris

SP 9/4 Larkspur; 6/1 Sebring; 15/2 TAMBOURINE II, Arctic Storm; 10/1 Arcor; 100/7 Saint Denys; 25/1 Cyrus; 33/1 London Gazette, Our Guile, Le Pirate, Running Rock; 66/1 Atlantis, March Wind, T.V., Gail Star; 75/1 Trade Wind; 100/1 Bar. TOTE (2/6 unit) 22/-. Places6/6, 5/-, 5/6.

Short head, 5 lengths, 2½ lengths. 2m 28.8s.

Winner trained by M. E. Pollet at Chantilly, France.

1963

The second running of the Irish Sweeps Derby seemed destined to follow its predecessor to France, for the event was dominated by Mme Dupre's Relko, cantering winner of the French Two Thousand Guineas and the Epsom Derby. Though opposed again by Ragusa and Tarquogan, third and fourth in the Epsom race, Relko seemed invincible. In a situation of 12-to-1 bar one, Relko's most serious rival appeared to be his compatriot Cervinia, recently runner-up in the

French Oaks and a chance mount for Nicky Brennan, as her French trainer and jockey had been stranded in Paris by an airport strike. Of the two English challengers, Tiger, winner of his last two races, seemed to have better credentials than the Middleham-trained Paddy's Birthday, a half-brother to the luckless Paddy's Point. Vic Mo Chroi's win in the Gallinule Stakes gave him an outside chance, but the only real hope of keeping the great prize at home seemed to lie in Ragusa, who was quietly fancied to finish much closer to Relko than he had done at Epsom. Once again the runners paraded in front of the packed grandstand, the only untoward incident being the antics of Relko, who lashed out repeatedly in his attempts to unseat Saint-Martin.

As the runners circled at the start and the crowd settled down to watch the race for second place behind Relko, the lengthening delay indicated that something was seriously amiss. That something was the odds-on favourite, who had become progressively more and more lame on arrival at the start. As Saint-Martin spoke no English and Major Tyrell, the starter, spoke even less French, it had been necessary to put Saint-Martin in touch with Francois Mathet, the trainer, over the starter's field telephone. Having listened to his jockey's account of Relko's dramatic loss of action behind, Mathet had no alternative but to instruct him to seek permission to have the favourite withdrawn. As speculation mounted among the expectant crowd, the shattering news came over the loudspeakers: 'Number 16, Relko, is lame and has been withdrawn.' Just as a disgusted Saint-Martin was seen to hurl his helmet to the ground came the familiar announcement: 'They're Off!'

First to show was Christmas Island, who set a moderate pace ahead of Diritto, Vic Mo Chroi, Tarquogan and Partholon. Having increased his gallop after the first quarter of a mile, Christmas Island still led entering the straight, where he gave way to Vic Mo Chroi, with Partholon, Ragusa and Lock Hard in close pursuit. Stalking Vic Mo Chroi up the straight, Ragusa swept to the front at the distance, winning comfortably from Vic Mo Chroi, with the fast-finishing Tiger squeezing his way through on the rails to take third place. The Stewards promptly enquired into an incident concerning the placed horses near the finish, but decided not to alter the placings. It was generally admitted by those who took part that it had been a rather rough race, in which the principal sufferer appeared to have been L'Homme Arme, on whom Liam Ward felt he would otherwise have certainly been placed.

Having satisfied themselves about the race as it had been run, the Stewards then enquired into the cause of the delay at the start and found that in the circumstances it had been unavoidable. They then interviewed Mathet and Saint-Martin, whose accounts of Relko's misfortune were corroborated by Bob Griffin, the official vet, who stated that Relko appeared to be suffering from muscular trouble high up in his near hind quarter. In order to eliminate any suspicion of foul play the Stewards ordered a dope test on the stricken favourite. This proved negative. However, the Relko saga did not end there, for on July 11th the Jockey Club announced that certain routine dope tests taken at Epsom had proved positive and it duly transpired that one of the animals involved was Relko . . . At the end of August the Jockey Club revealed that: 'The Stewards were satisfied that a substance other than a normal nutrient was present in the horse.' It was not until October that Relko finally receved that All Clear, with the announcement that: 'They (the Stewards) found no evidence which would justify a disqualification of Relko under Rule 66(c).' The tests had revealed that, while urine samples had proved positive, the saliva samples had been negative. In the face of such inconclusive evidence the Stewards had little choice but to act as they did. Nevertheless, a cloud of suspicion lingered over Relko, which his performance at the Curragh had done nothing to dissipate.

A medium-sized bay colt by Ribot out of Fantan II, Ragusa provided a striking example of the increasingly international aspect of breeding and racing. He had been conceived in Italy, where the mighty Ribot then stood, and foaled in Ireland, where his American-based dam was visiting Red God. As Captain Guggenheim, his breeder, had decided that Fantan II should remain in Ireland to be mated with Red God again the following season, her under-sized colt was reared at Middleton Park Stud in Co. Westmeath, which belonged to Mrs Iris Boyd-Rochfort, whose brother-in-law, Cecil Boyd-Rochfort, trained for Captain Guggenheim in England. Unfortunately for Captain Guggenheim, his trainer had conceived an irrational dislike of Ribot and his progeny. Accordingly, on Boyd-Rochfort's advice, the 'Ribot rat' was put up for sale as a yearling, being bought by P. J. Prendergast for 3800gns, on behalf of Mr J. R. Mullion.

Given plenty of time to mature, as befitted such a late foal, Ragusa scored his first success in the Suir Stakes over seven furlongs in October 1962 and went into winter quarters, earmarked by his talented trainer as a potential Derby colt, for whom the Epsom Derby might simply come too soon. Having finished second at Chester, Ragusa had only just attained his third birthday when taking third place in the Epsom Derby. While neither Prendergast nor Bougoure was prepared to claim that Ragusa would definitely have reversed that form with Relko at the Curragh, the subsequent careers of the two colts suggested that there would have been very little between them. Next time out Ragusa swept to a majestic success in the King George VI and Queen Elizabeth Stakes at Ascot and was then aimed for the St Leger at Doncaster. Having given his supporters heart failure by the narrowness of his victory over Only For Life in the Great Voltigeur Stakes, owing to Bougoure's over-confidence, Ragusa came home alone in the St Leger, creating a new European stakes-winning record. Though rated 1lb below Relko in the English Three-year-old Free Handicap, Ragusa gained ten times as many votes as his rival in the Racing Journalists Three-year-old of the Year Award. Thanks almost entirely to Ragusa, Ribot became the first foreign-based sire to head the list in England since Flageolet in 1879.

Although he remained in training as a four-year-old – his sporting owner having declined an American offer of £600,000 – Ragusa was unluckily denied an opportunity to try conclusions with Relko. He reappeared in the Ardenode Stakes at Naas, sponsored by his owner, in April, beating two stable companions in a common canter and went on to collect the Royal Whip at the Curragh, in what should have been no more than a gallop in public. The ground was extremely heavy, Ragusa was quite unable to act in it, finishing a floundering third to Cassim and Wily Trout, mere handicappers, and was found to have strained muscles. Off the course until July, his campaign in ruins, Ragusa made a triumphant comeback in the Eclipse Stakes, slamming Baldric II, that year's winner of the English Two Thousand Guineas. On his only other run Ragusa finished down the field in the Prix de l'Arc de Triomphe and was then retired to his owner's Ardenode Stud, syndicated at £10,000 per share. His death at the early age of thirteen was regarded as a disaster

1963. Ragusa, *benefitting from the last-minute withdrawal of the red-hot favourite, Relko, the 'Ribot rat' storms home to climax an incredible year for his trainer, Paddy Prendergast. Source:* The Irish Horse.

That man again, **Paddy Prendergast,** *first-ever Irish-based trainer to head the list in Britain, with Jim and Meg Mullion, whose Ragusa he had trained to become the record-breaking stakes winner in Europe in that golden year, 1963. Source:* The Irish Horse.

Saturday, 29th June, 1963 **£48,732 10 0** **16 Ran** **1½m**

Irish Sweeps Derby. A sweepstakes of 10sovs each for yearlings entered on 26th July, 1961, or of 30sovs for those entered on 1st November, 1961; 40sovs for all if not struck out on 24th October, 1962; and an additional 50sovs for all if not struck out on 27th March, 1963; an additional 50sovs for all if not struck out on 15th May, 1963; and an additional 100sovs for all if not struck out on 12th June, 1963, with 30,000sovs added, to be contributed by the Irish Hospitals' Sweepstakes. The winner will receive 75%, second 15%, and third 10% of the whole stakes after deduction of bonuses of 500sovs and to the breeder of the winner, 300sovs to the breeder of the second and 200sovs to the breeder of the third. For three years old entire colts and fillies. Colts, 9st; Fillies, 8st 11lb. One mile and a half.

Note—Subject to the usual conditions the Racing Board will pay special allowances as follows towards the transport costs of runners from abroad in this race:– Great Britain, £200 per horse; other European countries, £250 per horse; other countries, £500 per horse.

In consultation with the appropriate Stud Book Authority the Stewards shall determine the identity of the breeder and their decision shall be final.

(545 subs)

1	Mr J. R. Mullion's	RAGUSA (G. Bougoure) B. colt Ribot – Fantan II by Ambiorix II.	9. 0	P. J. Prendergast
2	Comte Antoine de de Laubespin's	VIC MO CHROI (P. Boothman) Ch. colt Chamier – Vic Girl by Vic Day.	9. 0	M. Hurley
3	Mr Michael Sobell's	TIGER (A. Breasley) Br. colt Tamerlane – Desert Girl.	9. 0	Sir G. Richards (GB)
4	Mr Joseph McGrath's	TARQOGAN (W. Williamson) Br. colt Black Tarquin – Rosyogan.	9. 0	S. McGrath
5	Lord Ennisdale's	CHRISTMAS ISLAND (P. Matthews) Ch. colt Court Harwell – Tahiti.	9. 0	P. J. Prendergast
6	Mrs A. B. Biddle's	PARTHOLON (P. Powell, jr) B. colt Milesian – Paleo II.	9. 0	T. Shaw
7	Mr W. J. Kavanagh's	LOCK HARD (G. McGrath) B. colt Hard Tack – Dunlavin Star.	9. 0	M. Hurley
8	Mrs A. B. Biddle's	L'HOMME ARME (L. Ward) B. colt Milesian – Palestrina.	9. 0	T. Shaw

9 HH Aga Khan's	CERVINIA (N. Brennan)	8.10	A. Head (FR)
	B. filly Phil Drake – Noorani.		
10 Mrs John Thursby's	FINAL MOVE (W. H. Carr)	9. 0	J. M. Rogers
	B. colt Botticelli – Checkmate.		
11 Mrs John M. Olin's	PRADO (T. P. Burns)	9. 0	P. J. Prendergast
	B. colt Sicambre – Princess Charming.		
12 Mr F. W. Burmann's	PHILEMON (J. Roe)	9. 0	M. V. O'Brien
	B. colt Never Say Die – Winged Foot.		
13 Lt-Comdr G.	DIRITTO (W. Swinburn)	9. 0	H. V. S. Murless
Lennox-Cotton's	B. colt Straight Deal – Syracruse.		
14 Mr Joseph McGrath's	GALA CHIEF (D. Page)	9. 0	S. McGrath
	B. colt Rockefella – Solanum.		
15 Mr F. N. Shane's	PADDY'S BIRTHDAY (J. Sime)	9. 0	S. Hall (GB)
	B. colt Eudaemon – Birthday Wood.		
16 Mr F. W. Burmann's	CHAMERO (T. P. Glennon)	9. 0	M. V. O'Brien
	Ch. colt Chamier – Arctic Peace.		
W M. Francois Dupre's	RELKO* (Y. Saint-Martin)	9. 0	F. Mathet (FR)
	Br. colt Tanerko – Relance III.		

SP 8/11 Relko; 100/8 Cervinia; 100/7 RAGUSA; 100/6 Chamero; 18/1 Tiger; 20/1 Tarqogan; 22/1 Christmas Island, Paddy's Birthday; 25/1 L'Homme Arme, Final Move; 28/1 Vic Mo Chroi; 50/1 Lock Hard, Prado; 66/1 Partholon, Philemon; 100/1 Diritto; 250/1 Gala Chief. TOTE (2/6 unit) 24/-. Places 6/6, 10/-, 7/6. Refund on Relko.

2½ lengths, 2 lengths, 2½ lengths. 2m 45.6s.

Winner trained by Mr P. J. Prendergast at Rossmore Lodge, Curragh.

*Relko withdrawn, not under starter's orders, and therefore 10/- in the £ is deducted from winning bets.

The Stewards gave permission for the withdrawal of Relko which was due to the fact that this horse was found to be lame when he arrived at the start. At a subsequent enquiry the Stewards heard the evidence of Y. Saint-Martin, jockey, Mr Con O'Kelly, MRCVS, who examined the horse at the start, and Mr J. H. Tyrrell, starter, the Stewards were satisfied that the delay was unavoidable.

The Stewards also enquired into an incident concerning the placed horses near the finish of the race. Having viewed the Patrol Camera film of the race they decided that no action was necessary.

The Stewards of the Turf Club ordered samples to be taken from Relko after this race. The report from the Analyst was negative.

by Irish breeders, for he had sired a succession of good racehorses of the calibre of Ballymore, Caliban, Homeric and Duke of Ragusa. The disaster of his premature demise deepened to catastrophe when, less than a month later, his son Morston won the Epsom Derby. The following year another son, Ragtime, won the Ascot Gold Cup.

Owned by one of the best-known and liked couples in Irish racing, Ragusa was one of comparatively few runners to carry the distinguishing Robertson Tartan sash of Jim Mullion, the majority of their horses running in the name of his chic and charming wife, Meg. With extensive shipowning interests in Hong Kong and a home in the Bahamas, Scots-born Jim Mullion bought the Ardenode Stud in Ballymore Eustace, Co. Kildare, from Captain Spencer Freeman in 1956. Three years later the Mullions hit the headlines through the success of that brilliant filly Paddy's Sister, the beginning of their long and successful association with trainer Paddy Prendergast. Since then they have had the good fortune to see their colours carried by a whole succession of high-class horses – many of them home-bred – in Ireland, England and France. Apart from Ragusa they have owned and raced such as Floribunda, champion sprinter and successful sire, Gazpacho, winner of the Irish One Thousand Guineas, Prominer and Hardicanute, two immensely promising juveniles, whose careers were ruined by a virus which decimated the Prendergast stable, and Ballymore, a son of Ragusa and Paddy's Sister, whose racecourse debut resulted in a spectacular success in the Irish Two Thousand Guineas. Ballymore eventually replaced his sire at Ardenode, making an equally auspicious start with More So, winner of the Irish One Thousand Guineas in the popular Mullion livery.

Ragusa's victory in the Irish Sweeps Derby – however fortuitous – was just one more milestone in the all-conquering campaign of his trainer Paddy Prendergast, whose other English raiders, Noblesse in the Oaks, Khalkis in the Eclipse Stakes and Pourparler in the National Stakes and the Lowther Stakes, broke all training records in England and enabled him to become the first Irish-based trainer ever to head the list in England. In Ireland his runners carried off four of the five Classics, contributing to a stakes total more than three times greater than that of his nearest rival, John Oxx. Linacre, with whom he had won the Irish Two Thousand Guineas, rounded off a triumphant Sweeps Derby weekend by winning the Prix de la Porte Maillot at Longchamp the next day, also ridden by stable jockey Garnie Bougoure, who shared in most of the jewels in P.J.P.'s trainer's crown.

Recovered from his mysterious affliction, Relko made a triumphant reappearance in the Prix Royal Oak (French St Leger), in which he beat Sanctus, winner of the Prix du Jockey-Club and the Grand Prix de Paris. His victory inspired a remarkable public demonstration in tribute to Francois Mathet, otherwise a thoroughly unpopular figure among 'turfistes'. As had been the case in Ireland with Vincent O'Brien and Chamour, Relko's emphatic defeat of the best of his generation, was regarded as absolute vindication of his trainer, still under suspicion of doping his Epsom Derby winner. Though he could finish only sixth to Exbury in the Prix de l'Arc de Triomphe, Relko went through the following season undefeated in his three races, the Prix Ganay, the Coronation Cup and the Grand Prix de Paris. This three-parts brother to Match II and Reliance II was then syndicated by Mme Dupre and Lord Sefton, who had purchased a half-share in the horse, and located at the Lavington Stud in Sussex. Despite the successes of such as Breton, Freefoot and Relay Race, Relko proved a disastrous failure as a sire, a situation which his son Selko seems unlikely to redeem.

Vic Mo Chroi, one of the last good colts sired by Chamier, went on to win races in the USA, as did Lock Hard. Tiger, having scored an incredible last-to-first success in the Gordon Stakes at Goodwood, was retired to stud in Ireland and was later exported to Japan, leaving behind him that brilliant but ill-fated 'chaser Killiney. Christmas Island remained in America after his unsuccessful effort in the Washington DC International, in which he had become Ireland's representative by virtue of his successes in the Ulster Harp Derby and the Irish St Leger. Partholon won the Ebor Handicap and became a leading sire in Japan, while Diritto and L'Homme Arme both won races before retiring to stud in Ireland. Philemon proved himself an out-and-out stayer by victories in the Great Yorkshire Handicap and the Brown Jack Stakes and then caused consternation among breeding pundits when being credited with siring Whip It Quick, a very fast two-year-old and winner of the Coventry

Stakes. Apart from the winner and the equally celebrated non-runner, the 1963 Irish Sweeps Derby contained one other high-class colt in Tarquogan. Fourth in both the English and Irish Derbies, he went on to be placed in the King George VI and Queen Elizabeth Stakes, the Eclipse Stakes and the Lincolnshire and Cambridgeshire Handicaps. As a five-year-old he finally got the reward that his class and consistency deserved when successful in the Chesterfield Cup and the Cambridgeshire. Retired to the Brownstown Stud, Tarquogan proceeded to sire numerous winners as game, courageous and consistent as himself.

1964

Once again the Irish Sweeps Derby had attracted the winner of the Epsom Derby, bidding for the double only Orby had accomplished, all of fifty-seven years earlier. Not, indeed, that success at Epsom was any guarantee of further laurels at the Curragh, as Larkspur and Relko had demonstrated in dramatically different ways. Moreover, both had achieved victory at Epsom in much more convincing fashion than Santa Claus, whose narrow win over Indiana and Dilettante II might have owed everything or nothing to Breasley's exaggerated waiting tactics. However, on his form, both in the Irish Two Thousand Guineas and at Epsom, Santa Claus appeared to have nothing to fear from his eighteen rivals, whether trained in Ireland, England or France. In fact the biggest danger to Santa Claus appeared to be the inexperience of his rider Willie Burke, who was having only his sixth ride in public that season. However, Burke had ridden Santa Claus in his only three races prior to Epsom, all at the Curragh, and their spectacular successes in both the National Stakes and the Irish Guineas had provided ample proof of Burke's ability to do justice to his brilliant mount. Just as they had done twelve months earlier, the layers fielded 12-to-1 bar the Epsom Derby winner, best backed of his opponents being Dilettante II now ridden by Lester Piggott, and Neptunus, winner of the French Two Thousand Guineas.

Ominous, the Prendergast pacemaker, dashed into an early lead ahead of Master Barry, ridden by Joe McGrath's amateur grandson, Neptunus, Red Vagabonde and Crete, with Santa Claus settled on the wide outside, towards the rear of the field. Down the hill into the straight Biscayne, Neptunus and Crete went past the early leader, as Master Buck slipped and fell. Biscayne, having faltered momentarily, faded, giving way to Crete, who was headed in turn by Lionhearted. Having made up ground swiftly at the entrance to the straight, Santa Claus ranged effortlessly alongside the battling leaders, as an enormous roar from the stands greeted the first mention of his name. Sitting like a graven image, Willie Burke allowed Santa Claus to toy with his struggling rivals, before sending him rocketing away at the distance to win, hard-held, by four lengths. It took the aid of the camera to sort out the wall of horses who fought out an exciting, if remote, struggle for the minor placings in his wake. Lionhearted was shown to have held off Sunseeker and Crete by two short heads, while All Saved and Dilettante II were only a head and a neck further back. All Saved might have been closer with a clear run, while Piggott reported that Dilettante II had never been going well. However, the unbelievable ease of Santa Claus' victory was summed up by Harry Carr, the rider of Lionhearted, who reported that, from the time Santa Claus had joined the leaders: 'I knew then that my chance was gone. He was going incredibly well – and the rest of us were all under full pressure.' Willie Burke, who returned to a hero's welcome, confirmed that Santa Claus had never been out of a canter. As all Ireland toasted their champion, now worthy to rank with Arkle, the idol of steeplechasers, rapturous reporters wrote that this magnificent racing machine, an incredible combination of stamina and speed, would never again be beaten . .

A tall, rangy, brown colt, whose plain head and shambling slower gaits belied his splendour at speed, Santa Claus was by the aged Chamossaire out of Aunt Clara, by Arctic Prince. Moreover, his name neatly reflected his fairytale background. The story of Santa Claus began in 1938, when Clarence, an unraced product of the National Stud, gave birth to her first foal, a bad-legged filly by the unfashionable Scarlet Tiger. By the time that filly, later named Sister Clara, had been bought by Major E. C. Doyle for all of 20gns, Clarence had produced a very different filly, destined to become famous as Sun Chariot, winner of three Classics in the Royal colours and the outstanding filly of her era. Thus it was a vastly more valuable Sister Clara who passed through the sales ring in 1944, making 11,000gns to the bid of Dorothy Paget. Though Sister Clara bred a few winners, they were of little account and her filly by Arctic Prince fetched only 130gns as an unraced two-year-old. For that price she became the property of Dr Frank Smorfitt, who raced her three times before retiring her to his small stud in Warwickshire, where her arrival doubled the broodmare strength. Her first two foals sold quite well, but accomplished little, so when her gangling colt by Chamossaire fetched 800gns as a foal Dr Smorfitt was pleased enough. The buyer on that occasion, Bertie Reynolds, was less than ecstatic when a year's keep showed a profit of only 400gns. However, the only outright loser to date had been Dorothy Paget, true to her role as the somewhat unlikely-looking fairy godmother of British racing. After Santa Claus had confirmed his brilliance in the Irish Two Thousand Guineas, Dr Smorfitt received his reward when Tim Rogers, the trainer's brother, paid a hefty price for Aunt Clara, the dam of Santa Claus. And so, as it should be in the Santa Claus stories, everybody was happy.

Bought for 1200gns at Newmarket by Mickey Rogers, this long-legged, loose-limbed colt became the property of octogenarian John Ismay, a long-standing patron of the Rogers stable, who subsequently sold a half-share to Mrs Darby Rogers, the trainer's mother. Santa Claus made his debut in the Anglesey Stakes at the Curragh. Ridden by Willie Burke, his constant partner at home, he started completely unfancied, was slowly away and finished a flying fifth behind Dromoland. On his second and final appearance as a two-year-old, in the seven-furlong National Stakes on the same course, Santa Claus, in the words of one experienced reporter: 'put up one of the most electrifying displays ever seen at headquarters', when an astonishing burst of speed saw him slam the Royal Ascot winner Mesapotamia by an extending eight lengths. Suddenly a star had been born and Santa Claus immediately became winter favourite for the Epsom Derby, for which Bernard Sunley, an English owner, backed him to the tune of £6000 each way. Ladbrokes, to their eternal credit, laid him at 9¼-to-1 and his winning dividend of £69,375 established a world record for a single winning bet.

Santa Claus had only one race before Epsom, the Irish Two Thousand Guineas. Ridden as always by Willie Burke, who had not sat on a winner in the intervening five months, Santa Claus looked beaten three furlongs out, when fully ten lengths behind the leader, Young Christopher. Then, to a growing roar of 'Here he comes!', Santa Claus lengthened his stride, swept past an incredulous Jimmy Lindley on Young Christopher a furlong out and won going away. Long confident that only bad luck could prevent Santa Claus from winning both the Epsom and Irish Derbies, Mickey Rogers had set about securing the best possible jockey for the notoriously tricky Epsom course. On being advised by Noel Murless that Lester Piggott, his first choice, would almost certainly be required to ride a Warren Place runner, Rogers had tentatively booked Scobie Breasley, who now confirmed his availability.

1964. *The Curragh Comet,* **Santa Claus,** *streaks clear of his pursuers to become the first winner of the Epsom and Irish Derbies since Orby in 1907.* Source: The Irish Horse.

Now in his fiftieth year, Breasley had won everything except the Epsom Derby. As he walked out to mount the red-hot favourite, a colt that he had only sat on twice, Breasley must have felt that this, his greatest chance, was also his last. Rogers' orders were simplicity itself; he wanted Santa Claus ridden from well behind and he wanted him brought on the outside of his field. If the latter instruction were anathema to a confirmed rails rider like Breasley, the come-from-behind strategy was his speciality and in executing his orders Scobie Breasley proceeded to shave years off the lives of those who believed in Santa Claus. Delaying his challenge until the last possible moment, he produced Santa Claus two furlongs out and once again that blinding speed – the hallmark of true brilliance – saw Santa Claus the winner by a length from Indiana, ridden by the hapless Jimmy Lindley. The manner of his success sparked off a furious controversy over whether Breasley's brilliance had won the Derby, or whether, ridden with less panache, Santa Claus would have won by a greater margin. By his devastating performance in the Irish Sweeps Derby Santa Claus confounded his critics, confirming for once and for all that Breasley's tactics had affected only the winning margin and not the result itself.

Incredibly, Santa Claus was never to win another race. Sent over to Ascot for the King George VI and Queen Elizabeth Stakes, an apparent formality in the absence of Relko, Santa Claus failed to act on the hard, rough ground. That famous finishing flourish was not forthcoming and his struggling second to the all-the-way winner Nasram II made him look like just another, rather ordinary racehorse. On a line through Nasram II, Santa Claus would, in the words of a disbelieving John Lawrence, have needed spectacles to see where Relko had finished in front of him. This debacle, for which Rogers blamed himself, having risked the colt on such unsuitable ground, placed Santa Claus' connections in a quandary. Months earlier they had decided that he would achieve sufficient as a three-year-old to retire at the end of that season as undisputed all-aged European champion. As syndication plans were already far advanced to this end, a clearcut success in the Prix de l'Arc de Triomphe offered the only means to restore his tarnished reputation.

Relko's retirement after the Grand Prix de Paris robbed Santa Claus of the opportunity to test John Lawrence's contention. Nevertheless, the effect of that Ascot fiasco on his reputation was reflected in the fact that he started only third favourite behind Le Fabuleux and Ragusa. Ridden by Jimmy Lindley in Breasley's absence, Santa Claus overcame interference to beat everything except his contemporary Prince Royal II, champion of his generation in Italy. That he should have finished within a length of the winner, having been impeded in his run, was unfortunate. However, any horse that must be brought from behind is always at risk in the Arc, and Lindley was afterwards adamant that, ridden otherwise, Santa Claus would not have finished as close as he did. Thus Santa Claus, the first dual Derby winner since Orby, retired to stud as the highest stakes-winning three-year-old in the history of European racing, though no longer undisputed champion of his age. However, it is not what he won, nor indeed what he beat, rather is it the manner of his winning that will ensure that Santa Claus remains a vivid memory to those privileged to witness it, long after more recent racecourse heroes have been forgotten. And how many will argue with Mickey Rogers' quiet confident claim that Santa Claus was the greatest horse ever to race the Curragh?

For octogenarian English owner John Ismay, Santa Claus' success in the Epsom Derby held an additional savour. John Ismay was old enough to remember a vastly different Derby scene, all of fifty-one years earlier, when C. Bower Ismay's Craganour had finished first past the post, only to lose the Derby on the Stewards' initiative. Like his less fortunate relation, John Ismay had come into racing through steeplechasing, owning those good pre-war hurdlers Victor Norman and Bimco. Back in the last century the Ismay family had been large shareholders in the Belfast shipyard of Harland and Wolff, and these long-vanished Irish connections were revived in the last years of the Second World War, when John Ismay put some horses in training with Captain Darby Rogers. Among them was Spam, who became the last gelding to compete in an Irish Classic when successful in the Irish St Leger in 1945. At that time John Ismay concerned himself primarily with the management of the Swinley Paddocks Stud at Ascot and though he continued to pay steep prices for yearlings, he enjoyed little success until Santa Claus blazed like a comet across the twilight of his years, then spent in Monte Carlo, where this quiet and unassuming man died in 1972, having outlived his wonderful horse by two years.

Tall, lean, athletic, exuding nervous energy . . . the words used to describe Santa Claus could have applied equally to his talented trainer, J. M. Rogers. Son and grandson of trainers, whose names were inscribed in the annals of Irish racing, Mickey Rogers gained his initial experience at Crotanstown with his grandfather, the legendary J. T. Rogers, and it was there that he became convinced that it was total dedication, concentration and absorption in his horses that formed the basis of his grandfather's outstanding success. Equally aware that modern-day stable staff would not accept the demands of J. T. Rogers' fourteen-hour working day, irrespective of example, Mickey Rogers embarked on a policy of quality rather than quantity. From the time he began training at Stepaside, the Curragh, in 1950, until he retired twenty years later, his stable never exceeded eighteen. From this deliberately restricted string he produced two Epsom Derby winners, the winners of five Irish Classics and a succession of high-class horses, such as Stephanotis, Prince Poppa, Royal Sword, Candy Cane and Barrons Court.

Quite how this young man achieved to win two Epsom Derbies, with colts purchased at public auction for less than 1500gns the pair and prepared in a stable smaller than some point-to-point yards, remains as much a mystery as the man himself. He attributes his success to his total and utter dedication to what he regarded as his Classic contenders. This degree of concentration is reflected in his statement that the only times he went racing during 1964 were when Santa Claus was running. The other Stepaside runners were accompanied by his travelling head lad, Willie Burke. In the case of Santa Claus, Rogers was fortunate that this tall, rangy colt required very little work, for in a string of whatever size trial tackle to extend 'the best colt in the British Isles' would have been difficult to find. Thus, unlike with Hard Ridden, his 280gns Derby winner, Rogers did not need to seek the cooperation of his friend Vincent O'Brien. In any case, O'Brien had no Ballymoss in his yard in 1964.

Towards the end of that unforgettable year a rumour emerged that Mickey Rogers had advised John Ismay that Santa Claus could not remain in training for a further season, not because the colt would not stand the strain, but rather because his trainer could not! Though only partly correct, this story aptly reflects the tension to which Rogers felt himself subjected by the demands of striving constantly in the highest echelons of horse racing. Consequently, when Mickey Rogers relinquished his licence in 1970, still only forty-five years old, the news came as a disappointment, but not as a surprise to those who knew the intensity of his nervous, introspective nature. His retirement to the more leisured life of studfarming left many wondering whether his remarkable receipe for success would ever be repeated. It seems unlikely.

That Santa Claus should have been ridden in all his races in Ireland by a stable lad was quite in keeping with the other ingredients of his fairytale career . . . useless dam, small-time breeder, bargain yearling, octogenarian owner intense trainer with tiny stable, aged Australian rider at Epsom, and so on. Naasborn Willie Burke was twenty-nine when he became the first Irish jockey to win the Irish Sweeps Derby. On leaving school at fourteen he had joined the Rogers stable, where he had remained ever since. Although he had previously ridden the Rogers-trained Prince Poppa to win the valuable Phoenix Stakes, Willie Burke never thought of himself as a jockey, nor, indeed, did anybody else. Nonetheless, it was to the man that rode Santa Claus in all his work at home that much of the credit belonged for enabling the colt to realise his enormous potential. The ability to relax in the early stages of a race, retain his balance around Epsom's tricky contours and answer instantly his rider's call with that blinding burst of speed; all were due to the patient and skilful horsemanship of Willie Burke. To the everlasting credit of both trainer and rider, the faith and trust of one was repaid in full by the other in the Irish Sweeps Derby. Willie Buke's preoccupation after the greatest moment of his career was getting home 'to do his two' at evening stables. His disappearance from the limelight rivalled the suddenness of his arrival in the public eye. However, far from being commiserated, Willie Burke would rather be congratulated for following Pollonius' advice to Hamlet: '. . . and this above all, to thine own self be true.'

To complete this Santa Claus tale . . . his owner died not long afterwards, his trainer retired, his rider returned to doing his two and his Curragh victims vanished into obscurity, though Biscayne did win the Irish St Leger. As a supporting cast quit the stage, so, shortly afterwards, did the principal actor. Having sired Santa Tina, winner of the Irish Oaks, Reindeer (Irish St Leger) and Bonne Noel (Ebor Handicap) from only five crops, Santa Claus suddenly died in 1970. The Curragh Comet, a brief but brilliant blaze, was gone but not forgotten.

Saturday, 27th June, 1964   **£53,725**   **19 Ran**   **1½m**

Irish Sweeps Derby. A sweepstakes of 10sovs each for yearlings entered on 25th July, 1962, or of 30sovs for those entered on 7th November, 1962; 40sovs extra for all if not struck out on 23rd October, 1963; and an additional 50sovs for all if not struck out on 25th March, 1964; an additional 50sovs for all if not struck out on 13th May, 1964; and an additional 100sovs for all if not struck out on 10th June, 1964, with 30,000sovs added and a trophy value 300sovs to the owner of the winner both to be contributed by the Irish Hospitals' Sweepstakes. The winner will receive 75%, second 15%, and third 10% of the whole stakes after deduction of bonuses of 500sovs to the breeder of the winner, 300sovs to the breeder of the second and 200sovs to the breeder of the third. For three years old entire colts and fillies. Colts, 9st; Fillies, 8st 11lb. One mile and a half.

Note—Subject to the usual conditions the Racing Board will pay special allowances as follows towards the transport costs of runners from abroad in this race:– Great Britain, £200, per horse; other European countries, £250 per horse; other countries, £500 per horse.

In consultation with the appropriate Stud Book Authority the Stewards shall determine the identity of the breeder and their decision shall be final.

(590 subs)

1 Mr J. Ismay's	SANTA CLAUS (W. Burke) B. colt Chamossaire – Aunt Clara by Arctic Prince.	9. 0	J. M. Rogers
2 Sir Humphrey de Trafford's	LIONHEARTED (W. H. Carr) B. colt Never Say Die – Thunder.	9. 0	Boyd-Rochfort (GB)
3 Mr J. Cox Brady's	SUNSEEKER (W. Pyers) Ch. colt Aureole – Sun Deck.	9. 0	M. V. O'Brien
4 Lady Honor Suejdar's	CRETE (G. Bougoure) B. colt Mossborough – Carezza.	9. 0	P. J. Prendergast
5 Mr Joseph McGrath's	ALL SAVED (J. Roe) Ch. filly Never Say Die – Silken Glider.	8.11	S. McGrath
6 Mr Lawrence M. Gelb's	DILETTANTE II (L. Piggott) B. colt Sicambre – Barizonnette.	9. 0	P. J. Prendergast

0 Mme Jean Couturie's	NEPTUNUS (T. P. Glennon)	9. 0	E. Pollet (FR)
	B/Br. colt Neptune II – Bastia.		
0 Mrs J. P. Herdman's	CARRICKLEE (P. Powell, jr)	9. 0	C. L. Weld
	B. colt Premonition – Queen's Orders.		
0 Mr J. H. Kartz's	RED VAGABONDE (G. Pezeril) 9. 0		C. Bartholomew, Jr
	Ch. colt Red God – La Vagabonde		(FR)
0 Mr T. E. Kelly's	MASTER BARRY (Mr J. M.	9. 0	S. McGrath
	McGrath) Ch. colt Court Harwell – Slippery Fox.		
0 Mr Joseph McGrath's	FRENCH STAR (G. McGrath)	9. 0	S. McGrath
	Br. colt Vimy – Silken Star.		
0 Mrs J. Reid's	BISCAYNE (P. Sullivan)	9. 0	J. Oxx
	B. colt Talgo – Marjorie Castle.		
0 Mr E. E. Dale Shaffer's	HORSE POWER (T. P. Burns)	9. 0	M. Dawson
	B. colt Alcide – Tiona.		
0 Mr R. N. Webster's	OMINOUS (P. Matthews)	9. 0	P. J. Prendergast
	Ch. colt Ommeyad – Peribanoo.		
0 Mr Billy Fury's	ANSELMO (A. Robson)	9. 0	K. PIGGOTT (UK)
	B. colt Aureole – Aranda.		
0 Mrs L. McVey's	DEVASTATION (J. Sime)	9. 0	S. Hall (UK)
	B. colt Tamerlane – Daughter of Sylvia.		
0 Mrs M. V. O'Brien's	HOVERCRAFT (J. Purtell)	9.0	M. V. O'Brien
	B. colt Pardal – Wave Crest.		
0 Mrs M. E. Whitney Tippett's	KING PADDY (L. Ward)	9. 0	K. Prendergast
	B. colt Mister Gus – My Endeavour.		
PU. Comte Antoine de Laubespin's	MASTER BUCK* (R. F. Parnell) 9. 0		M. Hurley
	Br. colt Buckhound – Bezique.		

SP 4/7 SANTA CLAUS; 100/8 Neptunus, Dilettante; 100/7 Crete; 100/6 Lionhearted; 20/1 King Paddy; 25/1 All Saved; 33/1 Hovercraft; 40/1 Anselmo, Master Buck; 50/1 Devastation; 66/1 Sunseeker, Master Barry; 100/1 Bar. TOTE (2/6 unit) 3/6. Places 3/6, 8/6, 26/6.

4 lengths, short head, same. 2m 35.6s.

Winner trained by Mr J. M. Rogers at Stepaside, Curragh.

*The Stewards inquired into the fall of Master Buck coming into the straight and decided that the fall was an accident and attached no blame to anyone.

1965

Sea Bird II, brilliant winner of the Epsom Derby, had not been asked to emulate Santa Claus' Derby double, being held in reserve for the Grand Prix de Saint-Cloud. In the absence of the French champion the Irish Sweeps Derby was dominated by Meadow Court, a respectful two-length second to Sea Bird II at Epsom. Ridden again by Lester Piggott, Paddy Prendergast's charge was a short-priced favourite to confirm his Epsom superiority over the English-trained trio, Niksar, Convamore and Ballymarais. The best of his home-trained opponents appeared to be the O'Brien-trained pair, Donato and Baljour. Donato had won the Wills Gold Flake Stakes, while Baljour had won the Gallinule Stakes and was the choice of O'Brien's latest

Australian stable jockey, Jack Purtell. Beddard, successful in four of his last five races, including the two-mile Queen's Vase at Ascot, was fancied by his trainer Stuart Murless, though he seemed short of real pace for an event of this class. The rest lacked either proven or potential ability; both in some cases. Shortly before the race Meadow Court's Canadian owner, Max Bell, had sold shares in the colt to his good friends Frank McMahon and Bing Crosby, who were among the huge crowd that made Meadow Court a firm favourite.

From the customary walk-in start Indian Snow made the early running, ahead of Baljour and Ballymarais. At the top of the hill Baljour took it up, only to give way almost immediately to Ballymarais, who led the field into the final bend, with Piggott poised motionless behind him on the favourite, just waiting for the moment to strike. These two were now most closely pursued by Khalife, Convamore and Wedding Present. No sooner had Meadow Court hit the front in the straight than he was challenged by Convamore, these two racing together into the final furlong. Suddenly, what had looked like an epic duel in the making turned into a procession, as Meadow Court strode clear to win by a very easy two lengths. Wedding Present ran on well to deprive Ballymarais of third prize. The first four to finish were all bred in Ireland, while three of them, including the winner, had been bought at Ballsbridge. Of the rest, only Jealous, Khalife and Zend Avesta emerged with any credit, though the riders of Western Wind, Niksar and Kilcoran all returned with excuses for their mounts in what must have been a fairly rough race. The winner returned to a rousing reception, which Bing Crosby's impromptu rendering of 'When Irish Eyes are Smiling' turned into a memorable scene in the winner's enclosure.

Bred by Mrs Pansy Parker Poe, an American patron of the Prendergast stable, Meadow Court had been born and reared at the Kildangan Stud, where his dam, Meadow Music, was boarded. Though bred by an American, part-owned by a Canadian, trained by an Irishman and ridden by an Englishman, Meadow Court meant most of all to the breeders of Argentina. His grandam, Miss Grillo, won the Argentine Derby and Oaks in 1945, before becoming equally successful in North America. Among the winners she bred was Meadow Music, by champion racehorse Tom Fool. But of infinitely greater significance to Argentine breeders was the fact that Meadow Court's sire, Court Harwell, was now at stud in their country The first of many good horses to carry the Mullions' colours, Court Harwell had won the Oxfordshire Stakes and the Jockey Club Stakes, besides finishing second to Ballymoss in the St Leger. Retired to his owners' Ardenode Stud, Court Harwell had received such scant patronage that in 1961 Jim Mullion had accepted an offer of £40,000 from Senor Martinez de Hoz, who took Court Harwell back to his successful Haras Comalal near Mar del Plata. Thus it was that Court Harwell had crossed the Atlantic before any of his stock had ever set foot on a racecourse. Just what breeders in these islands had let slip away was highlighted by Court Harwell's becoming leading sire both in Britain and in Ireland in 1965. Unfortunately for his new owners, who had refused all manner of temptations designed to secure Court Harwell's repatriation, their champion broke a leg in January 1968 and had to be destroyed.

Meadow Court's next appearance was in the King George VI and Queen Elizabeth Stakes at Ascot, where he dominated his opponents both in the paddock and in the race, which he won with almost insulting ease from Soderini and

1965. Meadow Court *carries Lester Piggott to his first success in an Irish Classic, leaving many to wonder how far Prendergast's 'top class' colts would have won, had they not fallen prey to the dreaded virus. Source:* The Irish Horse.

1965. The presentation ceremony; *(left to right) Bing Crosby, Joe McGrath, Mrs Frank Mahon and Max Bell. It was the last Irish Sweeps Derby that its founder would live to see. Source:* The Irish Horse.

Oncidium, with four of the previous season's Classic winners toiling in his wake. Unbackable for his next race, the St Leger, Meadow Court proved totally unable to cope with the bog-like conditions and trailed in a mud-covered and leg-weary second to the mud-loving Provoke. In the final race of his European career Meadow Court showed signs of having trained off when a fading ninth to Sea Bird II in the Prix de l'Arc de Triomphe. Syndicated for £40,000, Meadow Court was retired to the Sandley Stud in Dorset, where serious fertility problems soon became evident. After four unsatisfactory seasons Max Bell bought in all the shares in Meadow Court and put him back in training in Canada. This proved equally unsuccessful and Meadow Court was again retired to stud. On Bell's death in 1972, Meadow Court became the property of his daughter and covered a very restricted number of mares with success. That he should have proved such an abject failure at stud was particularly unfortunate in view of the export and premature demise of his sire, Court Harwell.

For Paddy Prendergast, who had now won his second Irish Sweeps Derby and his fourth Irish Derby in all, 1965 was an extraordinary year of fluctuating fortunes. Leading trainer in England the previous season, Prendergast had gone into winter quarters with the best Classic prospects of any trainer in Europe – Prominer, Carlemont and Hardicanute, unbeaten in their English campaigns. Although Meadow Court had won on his back-end debut, he was not mentioned in the same breath as the stable stars. By the time the 1965 Classics came round Prendergast's stable had been ravaged by the virus, his crack colts sidelined indefinitely and his dreams dispersed on the breezes that forever blow across the Curragh of Kildare. Slowly the stable began to emerge from the shadows and by the end of the season the victories of Meadow Court, Carlemont, Young Emperor and Celtic Song had enabled Paddy Prendergast to retain his English trainers' championship for the third year in succession. At home the success of Meadow Court in the Irish Sweeps Derby enabled Prendergast to regain the Irish title that he had surrendered to Mickey Rogers the year before.

The only remarkable feature of Lester Piggott's victory in the Irish Sweeps Derby was that it should have been his first success in an Irish Classic. Since then he has more than made up for lost time by winning the race on a further three occasions, in addition to riding the winners of eight other Irish Classics. The main reason for his relatively late entry to the Irish Classic scene was his long-standing retainer from Noel Murless, which almost invariably required him to ride in England. Since his widely-criticised decision to ride as a freelance in 1966 Piggott has become a familiar feature of the major Irish meetings, latterly through his association with Vincent O'Brien's powerful stable. Though his participation is a sure crowd-puller at any Irish meeting, his presence, allied to his enormous public following, frequently makes nonsense of the betting market; not, indeed, that he can be held responsible for that phenomenon! Not always the darling of the Irish crowds, Piggott has been booed when beaten on a succession of falsely-priced favourites, censured by the Stewards for trying too hard as well as for not trying hard enough and frequently reviled by trainers for his alarmingly candid replies to the queries of breathless owners. Paddy Prendergast was once quoted in the Press to the effect that Piggott would never ride for him again, while even Vincent O'Brien has been moved to reflect that, in the best of all possible worlds, Lester Piggott would ride his horses in all their major races, but in none of their trials! Books have been written about poker-faced Piggott and there are doubtless more to follow. In this instance perhaps a rare Piggot quotation can be turned upon himself. When asked who, in his opinion, was the greatest trainer in the business, he replied with characteristic brevity: 'It's got to be O'Brien; look at his record'. Applied to jockeys, the same will stand for Lester Piggott for many, many years to come.

Meadow Court's merit as an Irish Sweeps Derby winner must be assessed on his running with Sea Bird II at Epsom and on his superlative performance in the King George VI and Queen Elizabeth Stakes, rather than on his success in the Irish race, although he won very easily that day. The truth emerged only after the Doncaster debacle, when Piggott disclosed that even on the good ground at the Curragh Meadow Court was not the horse that he had proved himself at Epsom and again at Ascot, where he got the top-of-the-ground conditions which were essential to enable him to show his best form. Moreover, the subsequent exploits of his Curragh victims

Saturday, 27th June, 1965	£55,900	21 Ran	1½m

Irish Sweeps Derby. A sweepstakes of 10sovs each for yearlings entered on 31st July, 1963, or of 30sovs for those entered on 6th November, 1963; 40sovs extra for all if not struck out on 21st October, 1964; and an additional 50sovs for all if not struck out on 31st March, 1965; an additional 50sovs for all if not struck out on 12th May, 1965; and an additional 100sovs for all if not struck out on 9th June, 1965, with 30,000sovs added and a trophy value 300sovs to the owner of the winner both to be contributed by the Irish Hospitals' Sweepstakes. The winner will receive 75%, second 15%, and third 10% of the whole stakes after deduction of bonuses of 500sovs to the breeder of the winner, 300sovs to the breeder of the second and 200sovs to the breeder of the third. For three years old entire colts and fillies. Colts, 9st; Fillies, 8st 11lb. One mile and a half. The Racing Board will contribute a sum equal to 5% of the whole stakes after deduction of the bonuses to the owner of the fourth horse if there are eight or more runners.

Note—Subject to the usual conditions the Racing Board will pay special allowances as follows towards the transport costs of runners from abroad in this race: Great Britain, £200 per horse; other European countries, £250 per horse; other countries, £500 per horse.

In consultation with the appropriate Stud Book Authority the Stewards shall determine the identity of the breeder and their decision shall be final.

(649 subs)

1 Mr G. M. Bell's	MEADOW COURT (L. Piggott) 9.0		P. J. Prendergast
	Ch. colt Court Harwell – Meadow Music by Tom Fool.		
2 Mr E. R. More O'Ferrall's	CONVAMORE (J. Lindley) 9.0		R. V. Smyth (GB)
	Br. colt Court Harwell – Absolution by Petition.		
3 Lord Donaughmore's	WEDDING PRESENT 9.0		J. Oxx
	(W. Williamson) Ch. colt Macherio – Muscosa.		
4 Mr W. T. Stoker's	BALLYMARAIS (B. Connorton) 9.0		W. H. Gray (GB)
	Ch. colt Ballymoss – Skylarking.		
5 Princess Elizabeth Oettingan-Spielberg's	JEALOUS (W. Rickaby) 9.0		J. Oxx
	Ch. colt Above Suspicion – Leidenschaft.		
6 Mr Terence J. S. Gray's	ZEND AVESTA (J. Massard) 9.0		M. Hurley
	Gr. colt Zarathustra – Overboard.		
7 Mrs Mary B. Hecht's	KHALIFE (P. Matthews) 9.0		P. J. Prendergast
	Ch. colt Montaval – Jill Scott.		
8 Mrs A. B. Biddle's	WESTERN WIND (L. Ward) 9.0		M. Dawson
	Ch. colt Milesian – Palestrina.		
9 Mr Wilfred Harvey's	NIKSAR (R. Poincelet) 9.0		W. Nightingall (GB)
	Ch. colt Le Haar – Niskampe.		
10 Mr S. McGrath's	SIERRA DE MIZAS (C. J. 9.0		Owner
	Mulhall) B. colt Hill Gail – Katty's Slipper.		
11 Mr C. Clore's	SCRAPANI (W. Pyers) 9.0		M. V. O'Brien
	B. colt Tenerani – Scrap.		
12 Mr Joseph McGrath's	BALLYCIPTIC (G. McGrath) 9.0		S. McGrath
	Ch. colt Preciptic – Bally Tickle		
13 Mr Michael Kennedy's	FLAMING RED (J. Roe) 9.0		P. Norris
	B. colt Red God – Rosheen.		
14 Mr R. B. Beaumont's	MABROUK (T. P. Burns) 9.0		K. Bell
	B. colt Babur – Ma Davies.		
15 Comte Antoine de Laubespin's	GA-GREINE (P. Powell, jr) 9.0		M. Hurley
	Ch. colt Preciptic – After the Show.		
16 Mr R. S. Reynolds, jr's	BEDDARD (P. Sullivan) 9.0		H. V. S. Murless
	B. colt Quorum – Miss Pepita.		
17 Countess de la Valdene's	DONATO (A. Breasley) 9.0		M. V. O'Brien
	B. colt Alycidon – Mamounia.		
18 Mr Joseph McGrath's	INDIAN SNOW (G. Bougoure) 9.0		S. McGrath
	Br. colt Arctic Time – Sliprullah.		
19 Mr J. McShain's	BALJOUR (J. Purtell) 9.0		M. V. O'Brien
	Ch. colt Ballymoss – Day Dreaming.		
20 Mrs D. Archer Houblon's	SOLWEZI (G. W. Robinson) 9.0		P. Mullins
	B. colt Zimone – Solfarana.		
21 Mr B. Kerr's	KILCORAN (M. Kennedy) 9.0		K. R. Kerr
	Br. colt Gilles de Retz – Chislet.		

SP 11/10 MEADOW COURT; 6/1 Donato; 10/1 Baljour, Beddard; 100/9 Niksar; 100/7 Western Wind; 20/1 Convamore; 25/1 Ballymarais; 28/1 Kilcoran; 33/1 Wedding Present, Zend Avesta; 40/1 Khalife, Jealous; 66/1 Flaming Red; 100/1 Mabrouk, Ga-Greine, Solwezi; 200/1 Bar. TOTE (2/6 unit) 7/-. Places 4/6, 12/-, 16/-.

2 lengths, ¾ length, 4 lengths. 2m 46.8s.

Winner trained by Mr Patrick J. Prendergast at Rossmore Lodge, Curragh.

paid him scant compliment. Convamore, Ballymarais and Donato all finished even further behind him in the Doncaster mud and were promptly banished to stud in Australia. Niksar never regained the form which had enabled him to beat Silly Season in the Two Thousand Guineas and, having finished third to that colt in the Champion Stakes, Niksar joined the Australian exodus. Ballyciptic, disqualified after winning the Queen Anne Stakes at Ascot, was placed in both the Eclipse and Champion Stakes, before being retired to his owner's Brownstown Stud, where he became reasonably successful. Taken all round, it was not a vintage Irish Sweeps Derby.

1966

An outbreak of the dreaded Swamp Fever on the Continent in the Spring of 1966 had prompted the Irish Department of Agriculture to impose a ban on the importation of horses from the Continent. One week later England followed suit, to the fury of the French, who regarded the feature races in these islands as being at their mercy. One effect of the enforced French withdrawal from the Irish Sweeps Derby was a marginal decline in the prize fund for the race, run on this occasion over the 'old course', though not started from the stalls, which had recently been introduced in Ireland. Despite the absence of French challengers, Ireland's premier prize still looked destined for export, for the three-horse English raiding party was headed by Charlottown, who had recently credited the ageless Australian, Scobie Breasley, with his second success in the Epsom Derby. Pretendre, a close second at Epsom, had since paid his conqueror a compliment by a smooth success at Royal Ascot. The much-vaunted Irish colts had performed dismally in the big races in England and neither Paveh nor Democrat, first and fourth in the Irish Two Thousand Guineas, looked likely to keep the great prize at home. If Charlottown, odds-on favourite to emulate Santa Claus' Derby double, was to be beaten, the one most likely to do it was Sodium. Well fancied for the Epsom Derby, Sodium had finished fourth, highly distressed. Frankie Durr had reported that his mount had choked at a critical point in the race. While a dope test had proved negative, Sodiium had run a temperature as well as developing a mouth ulcer. Now fully recovered, Sodium looked a picture of health and vigour and his irrepressible little rider confidently expected to avenge that Epsom defeat. Apart from his faith in Sodium's ability, Durr was well aware that Charlottown's tendency to hang to the left would most likely be increased by the effect of the faster ground on his notoriously thin-soled feet.

From a perfect start Not So Cold went on from Ascot, Reubens, Agogo and Busted, with Charlottown and Sodium being held up at the rear of the large field. Approaching the half way mark Busted tore into the lead, swinging into the straight ahead of Paveh. It was here, at the elbow, that the race was won and lost. Unwilling to risk interference, Breasley took Charlottown around his field, whereas Durr, taking a calculated chance, threaded his way through on the inside, meanwhile Paveh had taken the lead from the faltering Busted. Launching Sodium with a smooth run on the inside, Durr swept past Paveh at the distance, as the challenging Charlottown continued to hang towards the stand side. Though Breasley managed to straighten the favourite, he failed by a length to peg back Sodium. Paveh, having put up a brave show over a distance well beyond his best, held on to take third place, ahead of the Stuart Murless-trained pair, Baylanx and Agogo. Crozier, the third cross-Channel challenger, was never a factor, while the erstwhile 'talking horses', Democrat, Radbrook and Khalekan, never looked likely to live up to their home reputations. After the race Breasley was widely criticised for having left Charlottown with too much ground to make up in the straight. However, both he and Frankie Durr were adamant that Charlottown had, in fact, turned into the straight marginally in front of Sodium. Both jockeys contended that victory had gone to the better horse on the day, an opinion with which most rational observers were inclined to agree.

Bred by Major E. O'Kelly at the Kilcarn Stud, near Navan, Co. Meath, Sodium was a well-made bay colt from the first crop of the surprise Epsom Derby winner, Psidium, out of Gambade. Though useless on the racecourse, Gambade was a full-sister to the Epsom Oaks winner, Ambiguity, and Sodium was her fourth winning produce. Just as she was fully entitled to produce a Classic winner, so was the much-maligned Psidium, whose first two crops had not found favour in the sale rings. Even Sodium's success failed to overcome this strange aversion to his sire, and Psidium departed to the Argentine in 1970, leaving behind him such as Richmond Fair, Crocus and Trillium

In 1964 Radha Sigtia, a millionaire chemical manufacturer from Bombay, who had come to live in London, commissioned his trainer, George Todd to spend up to a total of 10,000gns on two or three likely-looking yearlings, no doubt encouraged by Todd's handling of his delicate colt River Chanter. Todd had trained River Chanter to win four times as a two-year-old, including the valuable Dewhurst Stakes, and although this one-time favourite for the Epsom Derby of 1962 had disappointed his connections on that occasion, he went on winning races for a further two seasons in Mr Sigtia's colours. True to his painstaking and conscientious nature, George Todd had found only one yearling that he considered suitable, and that was Sodium, bought at Newmarket for only 3500gns. Though he had failed to win as a two-year-old and had beaten very little when gaining a hard-won first success in the Brighton Derby Trial, Sodium had been strongly fancied by his connections at Epsom. His next race after the Irish Sweeps Derby was in the King George VI and Queen Elizabeth Stakes at Ascot, where he ran Aunt Edith, the best older filly in Europe, to half a length. He then met Charlottown for the third time in the Oxfordshire Stakes at Newbury and caused a major shock when trailing in thirteen lengths behind his old adversary. He was then found to have been sickening for a drastic bout of kidney trouble. Having got over that, he renewed rivalry with Charlottown for the fourth time in the St Leger at Doncaster. As at the Curragh, he was given very little chance of turning the tables on the favourite. In an enthralling race, Charlottown wore down David Jack a furlong out and looked to have won his race, when Sodium came with a tremendous run to get his head in front on the line.

In an effort to resolve which was the better of the puzzling pair, they were both kept in training as four-year-olds, at which stage the honours definitely belonged to Charlottown, who won the John Porter Stakes, beating Salvo, and the Coronation

Cup, in which Sodium could finish only sixth. The nearest that Sodium came to victory that year was when beaten half a length by Salvo in the Hardwicke Stakes at Ascot. Sodum retired to Daniel Wildenstein's Haras du Victot in Normandy, failed to sire anything of note and was sent to Japan in 1973, while Charlottown, having proved almost as disappointing at stud in England, was dispatched to Australia two years later. Though they were both good, game colts, one cannot help feeling that they were lucky not to have had to contend with their French contemporaries.

Veteran trainer George Todd did not accompany Mr Sigtia to Ireland to witness Sodium's victory, for, having returned alive to England after the First World War, he had vowed never to leave English soil again! Born into a Lincolnshire farming family in 1895, George Todd had learned his trade with Bert Lines and Tom Coulthwaite, before taking out his own licence in 1925. Having trained at Royston and then at West Ilsey, he took over historic Manton House at the end of the last war. In common with Alec Taylor, the man who had made Manton famous, George Todd was a masterly stableman and a martinet, both with staff and owners. Unlike his celebrated predecessor, Todd liked a tilt at the Ring and the successes of Dramatic in the Stewards' Cup and the Lincolnshire Handicap, followed by French Design in the Goodwood Stakes and the Cesarewitch left the layers in no doubt that George Todd could not only bring a horse back to his best, but that he knew only too well how to take advantage of such rejuvenations. Towards the end of his career George Todd began to get a better type of horse, and his performances with such as River Chanter, Roan Rocket, Oncidium and Sodium indicated that, had his talents received earlier recognition, as they deserved, he might have been known as more than simply a trainer of somewhat unglamorous stayers.

However, it is as such that he will be remembered, for no other trainer since the war could rival George Todd in his ability to teach horses to stay. Moreover, this strict disciplinarian was equally good at teaching his apprentices to ride over a distance and nothing gave him greater pleasure than to land an occasional 'touch' with patched-up old geldings, ridden by unknown claimers; Shira, John Hayward, and Caught Out, Glyn Foster, being just two that come to mind. Appropriately, George Todd trained the greatest old stayer to run in England since the war – Trelawny. By his Royal Ascot doubles in the Ascot Stakes and the Queen Alexandra Stakes in 1962 and 1963, this gallant old gelding captured the affection of the racing public to an extent unknown since the days of Brown Jack. On the second occasion Trelawny went on to win the Goodwood Cup, ridden as usual by Scobie Breasley and sporting the narrow sheepskin which was the hallmark of a Todd-trained runner. He returned to a reception rarely accorded to a Derby winner and the normally taciturn Todd was moved to remark that it wasn't a bad performance for a seven-year-old who had broken his cannon-bone three years previously and whose career had been prolonged on the flat only because he so clearly disliked the rough and tumble of hurdle racing! On his retirement in 1973 this highly-respected master of his profession retired to the Imperial Hotel in Torquay, a favourite haunt for many years, and died not long afterwards.

Sodium was not the first big-race success in the Sigtia colours for diminutive Frankie Durr, who had worn them to victory three years earlier in the Ayr Gold Cup on Egualita, trained by Sam Hall. Nor was Sodium the first Irish Classic winner for the Liverpudlian lightweight, who had won the Irish One Thousand Guineas in

1957 on Even Star, trained in Newmarket by Reg Day, his former master. After a slow start in his riding career, Frankie Durr gradually gained recognition as an exceptionally powerful lightweight, particularly effective in long-distance handicaps, where strength and stamina can be as vital in the jockey as in his mount. Three Chester Cups – one of them on Trelawny – two Ascot Stakes and two Ebor Handicaps, almost all for different trainers, indicated his ability to make the best of relatively limited opportunities. Those two Classic victories on Sodium represented the vital breakthrough in Durr's career, resulting in a retainer to ride for David Robinson's powerful private stables at Newmarket. With the Michael Jarvis and Paul Davey 'winner machines' behind him, Durr was constantly in the headlines, winning the Gimcrack Stakes three times in four years.

Despite being branded as a 'veteran' in the sporting Press, Frankie Durr seemed to improve with age, though he would be the first to observe that good horses make good jockeys. His brushes with the Stewards became less frequent and even his peculiar style, which he never altered, became positively fashionable as Willie Carson demonstrated its undoubted effectiveness. In 1973, almost thirty years after riding his first winner, Frankie Durr won the Two Thousand Guineas on the outsider Mon Fils and the St Leger on Peleid, despite the fact that he was devoting progressively more of his time and energy to his farm near Newmarket. Having sprung another Classic upset when Roland Gardens left Try My Best trailing in the 1978 Two Thousand Guineas, Frankie Durr retired at the end of the season to begin training in Newmarket, taking over the yard from which the late Peter Robinson had sent out Prince de Galles to successive victories in the Cambridgeshire, ridden by none other than Frankie Durr.

Of those that finished behind those constant rivals, Sodium and Charlottown, at the Curragh, one was destined to prove himself a far, far greater horse than either. However, taking them in order in which they finished . . . Paveh won the Sussex Stakes at Goodwood, confirming his excellence as a miler. Retired to stud in Ireland, he was unfortunately let go to Japan before his only three crops had had the chance to prove his undoubted ability to sire numerous winners. Agogo, owned by Mrs E. N. Graham – otherwise better known as Elizabeth Arden – went to race in the USA. Khalekan came closest to redeeming his earlier promise with a courageous second in the Irish St Leger, later becoming a successful stallion in Australia. Alciglide matured into a formidable stayer, whose victories included the Queen Alexandra Stakes and the Prix Gladiateur. He went to stud in Germany. Al-Alawi won the Irish Lincolnshire as a four-year-old. Crozier retired to stud in England as the winner of thirteen races, including the Jockey Club Stakes and the Doncaster Cup, but did not prove successful as a sire. White Gloves won the Desmond Stakes and the Irish St Leger, before finishing third in the Gran Premio del Jockey Club in Milan, while his stable companion, Beau Chapeau, transferred to Phonsie O'Brien's stable, proved himself a high-class hurdler, before emerging as a National Hunt sire of infinite promise.

The best horse in that Irish Derby field finished exactly in the middle of the twenty-three runners, having burned himself out in the earlier stages of the race. His name was Busted. Second to Agogo at Naas in May, Busted had scored his first success when holding off Pieces of Eight in the Gallinule Stakes. It was not until after the Irish Sweeps Derby that the value of that form became apparent, for Pieces of Eight proceded to win both the Eclipse Stakes and the Champion Stakes. Runner-up to White Glves in the Desmond Stakes, Busted disappointed in his remaining two races and was removed to England by his disgruntled owner. An unknown quantity on his arrival at Noel Murless' Newmarket stable, Busted showed signs of returning to his best form with a success in the Coronation Stakes at Sandown in April. On his next outing he slammed Great Nephew in the Eclipse Stakes, earning from Bill Rickaby the accolade of the best horse he had ever ridden. A scintillating success in the King George VI and Queen Elizabeth Stakes from an international field entitled him to be regarded as the best horse in Europe, a title which he confirmed with a facile finale in the Prix Henri Foy at Longchamp. Retired to the Snailwell Stud at Newmarket, Busted immediately established that his stud career was destined to match his racecourse distinction, by siring such as Weavers' Hall, Bustino, Crash Course, Blustery, Cheveley Princess and Sorbus.

Saturday, 2nd July, 1966	£52,157 10 0	23 Ran	1½m

Irish Sweeps Derby. A sweepstakes of 10sovs each for yearlings entered on 15th July, 1964, or of 30sovs for those entered on 4th November, 1964; 40sovs extra for all if not struck out on 20th October, 1965; and an additional 50sovs for all if not struck out on 30th March, 1966; an additional 50sovs for all if not struck out on 11th May, 1966; and an additional 100sovs for all if not struck out on 8th June, 1966, with 30,000sovs added and a trophy value 300sovs to the owner of the winner both to be contributed by the Irish Hospitals' Sweepstakes. The winner will receive 75%, second 15%, and third 10% of the whole stakes after deduction of bonuses of 500sovs to the owner (at entry) of the winner, 300sovs to the owner (at entry) of the second and 200sovs to the owner (at entry) of the third. For three years old entire colts and fillies. Colts, 9st; Fillies, 8st 11lb. One mile and a half.

The Racing Board will contribute a sum equal to 5% of the whole stakes after deduction of the bonuses to the owner of the fourth horse if there are eight or more runners.

Note—Subject to the usual conditions the Racing Board will pay special allowances as follows towards the transport costs of runners from abroad in this race:– Great Britain, £200 per horse; other European countries, £250 per horse; other countries, £500 per horse.

(561 subs)

1	Mr R. J. Sigtia's	SODIUM (F. Durr) B. colt Psidium – Gambade by Big Game.	9.0	G. E. Todd (GB)
2	Lady Zia Wernher's	CHARLOTTOWN (A. Breasley) B. colt Charlottesville – Meld.	9.0	G. Smyth (GB)
3	Mr P. A. B. Widener's	PAVEH (P. Powell, jr) B. colt Tropique – Persian Shoe.	9.0	T. D. Ainsworth
4	Mr W. G. Reynold's	BAYLANX (R. P. Elliott) B. colt Helioscope – Close Ranks. (FOALED IN USA).	9.0	H. V. S. Murless
5	Mrs E. N. Graham's	AGOGO (N. Brennan) Ch. colt Never Say Die – Speed Bird.	9.0	H. V. S. Murless
6	Mr E. R. More O'Ferrall's	KHALEKAN (D. Lake) Ch. colt Alycidon – Tenebel.	9.0	P. J. Prendergast
7	Mr S. McGrath's	ALCIGLIDE (G. McGrath) Gr. colt Alcide – Silken Glider.	9.0	Owner
8	Mrs H. V. S. Murless's	REUBENS (P. Sullivan) Ch. colt Panaslipper – Peribanoo.	9.0	H. V. S. Murless
9	S. A. S. Princesse N. d'Imeretie Mrs Gray's	Al-ALAWI (R. Sheather) B. colt Aureole – Andromeda Nebula.	9.0	M. Connolly
10	Mr P. McManus's	POLEMIC (J. Roe) B. colt Quorum – Polar Point.	9.0	J. Oxx

11 Mr A. D. G. Oldrey's	CROZIER (J. Mercer) B. colt Zarathustra – Vimere.	9.0	P. T. Walwyn (GB)
12 Mr Stanhope Joel's	BUSTED (P. Boothman) Ch. colt Crepello – Sans le Sou.	9.0	R. N. Fetherstonhaugh
13 Comte Antoine de Laubespin's	NOT SO COLD (W. Swinburn) B. colt Arctic Time – Rose Vale.	9.0	M. Hurley
14 Mr Richard Greene's	PETIT JEAN (G. W. Robinson) Ch. colt Petition – Hiera II.	9.0	M. Hurley
15 Lady Sassoon's	RADROOK (T. P. Burns) Ch. colt Ballymoss – Alare.	9.0	J. M. Rogers
16 Mr Miles Valentine's	BEAU CHAPEAU (J. Murtagh) Ch. colt High Hat – Beau Co Co.	9.0	M. V. O'Brien
17 Mrs Anne Ford's	AMBERICOS (L. Ward) Ch. colt Darius – Ambergris.	9.0	M. V. O'Brien
18 Mr A. S. Hewitt's	DEMOCRAT (M. Kennedy) B. colt Pinza – Fair Plea.	9.0	J. M. Rogers
19 Mr H. Dolan's	ASCOT (L. W. Johnson) Ch. colt High Hat – Light Action.	9.0	C. L. Weld
20 Mrs M. A. Moore's	WHITE GLOVES (John Power) Ch. colt High Hat – Gallamond.	9.0	M. V. O'Brien
21 Mr S. McGrath's	MILESVENA (P. McEntee) B. colt Milesian – Venarctic.	9.0	Owner
22 Mrs H. P. Gallagher's	RIPPING TIME (J. Larkin) B. colt Arctic Time – Mill Baby.	9.0	C. Grassick
23 Mr H. Dolan's	DRUMLANE (P. Vaughan) Br. colt Arctic Time – Rocint.	9.0	C. L. Weld

SP 8/11 Charlottown; 13/12 SODIUM; 100/8 Paveh, Democrat; 100/7 Crozier; 20/1 Khalekan; 22/1 Ambericos, Busted; 50/1 Radrook, Beau Chapeau; 100/1 Bar. TOTE (2/6 unit) 25/6. Places 5/6, 3/-, 4/6.

1 length, 2½ lengths. 2m 31.5s.

Winner trained by Mr George E. Todd at Manton House, nr. Marlborough, Wiltshire.

1967

As had become the accepted pattern, the Irish Sweeps Derby was dominated by Epsom form. In the English Derby Royal Palace had beaten Ribocco, Dart Board and Royal Sword, and in the absence of the winner Ribocco became a firm favourite to confirm that form with the other two. He was again ridden by Lester Piggott, whose decision to split with Noel Murless the previous season looked like costing him dear, for Murless had won both the English Guineas and the Epsom Derby with Royal Palace and Fleet, ridden by his new stable jockey, the Australian ace, George Moore. This all-conquering combination was now represented by Sucaryl, well backed ante-post, despite not having run that season. Dart Board, the mount of Scobie Breasley, had been held up in his work since Epsom by a bruised foot, giving way in the market to the Mickey Rogers-trained Royal Sword, now thought to be at his best and strongly fancied to improve on his Epsom placing. Atherstone Wood, awarded the Irish Two Thousand Guineas on the disqualification of Kingfisher, was not certain to get the extra half mile, while the other home-trained runners seemed lacking in class. The most spectacular move in the Ring concerned the sole French raider, Steady II, backed at all rates from 100-to-6 to half those odds. El Mighty, the subject of yet another of those 'I dreamed he won the Derby', who had done the bookes such a favour at Epsom, was kept at conservative odds of 100-to-1, on the off-chance that the clairvoyant had got his Derbies confused! The huge crowd, which included Mrs Jacqueline Kennedy, fidgeted restlessly on the packed stands as Rare Jewel was replated, thus delaying the start for several minutes.

Starting stalls were not yet in use for Classic races and from a level break Skamander led the other twenty-two runners, with Palmas, Sovereign Slipper, Dan Kano and Royal Sword most prominent of his pursuers. Approaching half way disaster struck when Royal Sword broke his foreleg and fell, hampering Rare Jewel and Dart Board. Dan Kano then hit the front, only to be headed by Sovereign Slipper, who gave way in turn to Signa Infesta at the entrance to the straight, where Dan Kano, Sucaryl and Ribocco began to emerge as the main contenders. Two furlongs out George Moore hit the front on Sucaryl, as Atherstone Wood delivered a short-lived challenge on his outside. Poised patiently on the leader's heels, Piggott waited until Atherstone Wood had dropped back, coolly switching Ribocco off the rails to come and beat Sucaryl by a clever three-parts of a length. Dart Board, whose chance had been ruined by Royal Sword's fatal fall, ran on to be third, ahead of Gay Garland, thus competing the rout of the home-trained hopefuls. Appreciative of the particular significance of Ribocco's victory for his rider, the crowd greeted Piggott with a chorus of 'Smile, Lester!' to which 'Old Poker-face' responded with unfeigned delight.

A medium-sized, well-made bay colt, Ribocco was bred by Mrs Julie Rogers at the Idle Hour Farm in Kentucky. By Ribot, then based in America, Ribocco was out of the Hyperion mare Libra, who had never raced beyond five furlongs prior to going to the United States in 1958. Bought for 35,000 dollars as a yearling at Keeneland by David McCall, Charles Englehard's racing manager in Europe, Ribocco had proved himself one of the best two-year-olds of 1966 in England, where he had won the Observer Gold Cup and been beaten only once, by Bold Lad in the Champagne Stakes. As a three-year-old he had been slow to find his form and had begun to show ominous signs of temperament, characteristics of Ribot's stock. Just as had been the case with Ragusa four years earlier, the Epsom Derby had come too soon for Ribocco, who only reached his peak at the Curragh.

Beaten by his seniors, Busted and Salvo, in the King George VI and Queen Elizabeth Stakes at Ascot on his next appearance, Ribocco then met Dart Board again at Goodwood. After the Irish Sweeps Derby Scobie Breasley had been adamant that only interference had robbed him of victory. Those – and they were in the majority – who had scoffed at Scobie and dismissed his claims as signs of senility, were dumbfounded when Dart Board left Ribocco floundering at Good-wood. As a consequence, they were more confused than ever when Piggott brought Ribocco from last to first in the straight at Doncaster to win the St Leger, in which Dart Board, pinnioned on the rails, could finish only fourth. The pair met for the last time in the Prix de l'Arc de Triomphe, where Salvo and Ribocco came weaving like snipe through beaten horses and just failed to overhaul Topyo. Dart Board finished well down the field. Ribocco made his final appearance in the Washington

DC International, in which he ran deplorably behind Fort Marcy and then retired to stud in America. Lack of immediate success resulted in his expulsion to the Land of the Rising Sun and those of his progeny that did race on this side of the Atlantic exhibited the same signs of temperament which had once threatened to wreck Ribocco's own racing career.

Ribocco was one of a whole host of good horses to carry the colours of Charles William Englehard, the American-born son of a German emigré, who was reputed to have laid the foundations of a vast family fortune by sieving the sweepings he was employed to clean off the floor of a factory where platinum was processed. Already a leading owner in America, where he owned Assegai, and in South Africa, where he owned the champion Hawaii, Charles Englehard made his initial impact on European racing with Romulus, the leading miler in Europe in 1962. Two years later Indiana gave him his first Classic success when winning the St Leger at Doncaster, the first occasion on which his owner had seen him run. That same year his Double Jump emerged as the leading two-year-old in England, so it was hardly surprising that Charles Englehard should have taken the opportunity, in the course of his speech at the traditional Gimcrack dinner, to extol the pleasures of racing in England!

Both Englehard and his European racing manager, David McCall, fervently believed that the stock of Ribot, currently finding little favour in America, were infinitely better suited to European racing. Their faith was rewarded in spectacular fashion by the triumphs of Ribocco, Ribero and Ribofilio, to name but three. The last-named had the dubious distinction of being beaten favourite in the three Triple Crown races in England in 1969. However, any disappointment that he may have caused his owner was swept away the very next year, when the majestic Nijinsky became the first Triple Crown winner in England since Bahram thirty-five years earlier. In the winner's enclosure after Nijinsky's St Leger, Charles Englehard declared – à la Mary Queen of Scots – that when he died the word 'Nijinsky' would be found inscribed upon his heart. Six months later he was dead, killed by the effects of gross overweight, which he had persistently ignored his doctors' advice to curb. Only fifty-four, he was a man that racing could ill-afford to lose and the recent success of Ile de Bourbon, the last animal associated with the short-lived Englehard racing empire, served as a poignant reminder of the void created by his premature demise.

Ribocco was trained in Steve Donoghue's former yard, at Blewbury in Berkshire, by the youthful Fulke Johnson Houghton, who might be regarded as the most successful exponent of Ribot's stock in Europe. Born in 1940, Johnson Houghton lost his trainer father, Gordon Johnson Houghton, as the result of a hunting accident when he was only twelve. Thereafter the stable was carried on by his mother, Fulke Walwyn's twin sister Helen, with the licence being held by a succession of assistants, one of whom, Charles Jerdein, was officially credited with the Two Thousand Guineas victory of outsider Gilles de Retz in 1956. Jerdein was followed by Peter Walwyn, Mrs Johnson Houghton's cousin, and by the time that he decided to go out on his own in 1961, young Fulke, who had spent time with Major Goldsmith in England and Jack Cunnington in France, was ready to take over as licence-holder. He got off to a flying start with Romulus, who provided insights into the peculiarities of Ribot's stock, which later proved invaluable in handling Ribocco, Ribero, Ribofilio, Ad Lib Ra and Rose Bowl. Other high-class winners to have emerged from Fulke Johnson Houghton's powerful yard include Habitat, champion miler and phenomenal sire, and Ile de Bourbon, winner of the King George VI and Queen Elizabeth Stakes in 1978.

Sucaryl, having put up such a fine performance in what was his seasonal reappearance at the Curragh, went on to win the David Robinson Stakes at Newbury and the News of the World Stakes at Goodwood. He later became a successful sire in New Zealand. Dart Board, an unlucky animal, went to Argentina. Dan Kano, not even quoted in the betting when proving best of the home-trained brigade in the Irish Sweeps Derby, confirmed his merit with successive victories in the Ulster Harp Derby, the Grand Prix de Vichy and the Irish St Leger, in which he made every yard of the running, ridden by Lester Piggott. Kept in training as a four-year-old, Dan Kano came closest to success when third in the Coronation Cup to Royal Palace. The best of the others proved to be Fortissimo, winner of the John Porter Stakes and unplaced only three times in seventeen races.

Saturday, 1st July, 1967   **£57,610**   **23 Ran**   **1½m**

Irish Sweeps Derby. A sweepstakes of 10sovs each for yearlings entered on 14th July, 1965, or of 30sovs each for those entered on 3rd November, 1965; 40sovs extra for all if not struck out on 19th October, 1966, an additional 50sovs for all if not struck out on 29th March, 1967, an additional 50sovs for all if not struck out on 10th May, 1967, and a further additional 100sovs for all if not struck out on 7th June, 1967, with 30,000sovs added and a Trophy value 300sovs to the owner of the winner, both to be contributed by the Irish Hospitals' Sweepstakes. The winner will receive 75%, second 15%, and third 10% of the whole stakes after deduction of bonuses of 500sovs to the owner (at entry) of the winner; 300sovs to the owner (at entry) of the second and 200sovs to the owner (at entry) of the third. For three years old entire colts and fillies. Colts, 9st; Fillies 8st 11lb. One mile and a half.

The Racing Board will contribute a sum equal to 5% of the whole stakes (after deduction of bonuses) to the winner of the fourth horses if there are eight or more runners.

Note—Subject to the usual conditions the Racing Board will pay special allowances as follows towards the transport costs of runners from abroad in this race– Great Britain, £200 per horse; other European countries, £250 per horse; other countries, £500 per horse.

1	Mr C. W. Engelhard's	RIBOCCO (L. Piggott) B. colt Ribot – Libra by Hyperion.	9.0	R. F. Johnson- Houghton (GB)
2	Lady Sassoon's	SUCARYL (G. Moore) Ch. colt St. Paddy – Sweet Angel	9.0	C. F. N. Murless (GB)
3	Mr Michael Sobell's	DART BOARD (A. Breasley) Ch. colt Darius – Shrubswood.	9.0	Sir G. Richards (GB)
4	Mr A. B. Askew's	GAY GARLAND (Ron Hutchinson) B. colt Shantung – Festoon.	9.0	H. Wragg (GB)
5	Mr S. Raccah's	DAN KANO (P. Powell, jr) Ch. colt Dicta Drake – Gillylees.	9.0	J. Lenehan
6	Mr Stephen O'Flaherty's	ATHERSTONE WOOD (R. F. Parnell) B. colt Buisson Ardent – Reine des Bois.	9.0	S. Quirke
7	Mr D. Drewery's	DANCING MOSS (G. Starkey) Ro/Ch. colt Ballymoss – Courbette.	9.0	R. N. Fetherstonhaugh
8	Mr A. Tsiatalous's	EL MIGHTY (G. Thiboeuf) Ch. colt Sheshoon – Delicious.	9.0	D. L. Hanley (GB)
9	Mr A. J. Richards's	TAPIS ROSE (R. McCarthy) B. colt Tissot – Rosace.	9.0	D. L. Hanley (GB)

10	Major Victor McCalmont's	FORTISSIMO (P. Boothman) Gr. colt Fortino II – Choir Practice.	9.0	R. N. Fetherstonhaugh
11	Mr S. McGrath's	SIGNA INFESTA (G. McGrath) Ch. colt Saint Crespin – Certosa.	9.0	Owner
12	Mr R. S. Reynolds's	CREPE CLOVER (P. Sullivan) Br. colt Crepello – Honey Flower.	9.0	H. V. S. Murless
13	M. le Baron G. de Waldner's	STEADY II (R. Poincelet) B. colt Fast Fox – Seed Pearl.	9.0	F. Palmer (FR)
14	Mr J. McNamee-Sullivan's	RUGGED MAN (T. P. Burns) B/Br. colt Hard Ridden – Night Operation.	9.0	A. Brabazon
15	Mrs Martin Andree's	SKAMANDER (J. Roe) Br. colt Arctic Storm – Sara Polly.	9.0	J. Oxx
16	Mr R. H. Preston's	SOVEREIGN SLIPPER (D. Lake) B. colt Fortino II – Solar Echo.	9.0	P. Murphy
17	Mr R. G. Angus's	KISS OF LIFE (L. Browne) B. colt Never Say Die – Poste Restante.	9.0	G. N. Robinson
18	Mr T. McCairn's	RARE JEWEL (P. Matthews) B. colt Princely Gift – Royal Pageant.	9.0	P. Prendergast, jr
0	Mrs T. E. Kelly's	HEAVE HO (L. Ward) B. colt Le Levanstell – Vallombrosa.	9.0	S. McGrath
0	Mr A. S. D. Scott's	MARK SCOTT (J. Murtagh) B. colt Milesian – Tonakhan.	9.0	P. Norris
0	Mr G. A. Newsome's	PALMAS (P. J. Willett) B. colt Pardal – Choosey.	9.0	E. Davey (GB)
0	Mr J. G. Barnett's	ZARACARN (L. Johnson) Br. colt Zarathustra – Kilcarn Goddess.	9.0	C. L. Weld
F.	General R. K. Mellon's	ROYAL SWORD (M. Kennedy) Br. colt Right Royal – The Blonde.	9.0	J. M. Rogers

SP 5/2 RIBOCCO; 11/2 Royal Sword; 8/1 Sucaryl, Steady II; 9/1 Dart Board; 100/9 Signa Infesta; 18/1 Fortissimo, Gay Garland; 22/1 Atherstone Wood; 28/1 Dancing Moss, Rugged Man; 40/1 Heave Ho, Sovereign Slipper; 66/1 Mark Scott; 100/1 Crepe Clover, Skamander, El Mighty; 150/1 Bar. TOTE (2/6 unit) 8/6. Places 5/6, 8/6, 7/-.
1 length, 3 lengths, 2m 32.4s.
Winner trained by Mr Fulke Johnson-Houghton at Blewbury, Berkshire.

1968

This was 'The Year of Sir Ivor', as the film then in the course of production was entitled. This American-bred colt, trained in Tipperary by Vincent O'Brien and ridden by Lester Piggott, had captured the imagination of the Irish racing public to an extent equalled only by Santa Claus, since the heady days of Ballymoss. Scintillating successes in the National Stakes at the Curragh and the Grand Criterium at Longchamp had established Sir Ivor as the best staying two-year-old in Europe. Having wintered in Italy, with others of O'Brien's star-studded string, Sir Ivor had won the Guineas Trial at Ascot, slaughtered his English counterpart, Petingo, in the Two Thousand Guineas at Newmarket and annihilated Connaught in the Epsom Derby with a burst of acceleration which left all who saw it gasping in sheer disbelief. Sir Ivor was, quite simply, invincible and the fact that he was being ridden in his bid to emulate Santa Claus by Liam Ward, O'Brien's first jockey in Ireland was not expected to make any difference. Ward knew the colt well and had quite rightly rejected Piggott's repeated entreaties to surrender the mount. Unbackable at 3-to-1 ON, Sir Ivor was followed in the market by the headstrong Giolla Mear, winner of the Gallinule Stakes, Val d'Aoste, third in the French Derby and Ribero, ridden by Lester Piggott. Unable to run in the Epsom Derby, Ribero had since been beaten twelve lengths by Connaught at Ascot. On a line through the latter he had no earthly chance of beating the favourite, even allowing for the abnormal degree of improvement that could be expected in an own-brother to Ribocco. As the huge crowd massed on the stands, the chief topic of conversation concerned what would be second. Even this fascinating topic began to pall in the time it took for Giolla Mear to reach the start, for T. P. Burns, mindful of what his fractious mount had done to his good friend Paddy Powell, was adamant that he be led all the way across the Curragh.

A further delay was caused by the reluctance of Home Farm to enter the stalls, in use for the first time. When at last they were away, Giolla Mear tore into the lead, accompanied by Stitch, who showed ahead of Ribero, with Sir Ivor settled nicely towards the rear of the small field. There was little change in the order until half a mile from home, where the race began to take on its final shape, as Ribero and Val d'Aoste shadowed Giolla Mear and Stitch into the straight, followed closely by an improving Sir Ivor. As they lined out for home Piggott drove Ribero into the lead, with Sir Ivor now on level terms. These two now had the race between them and as they approached the two-furlong pole the crowd waited expectantly for that now-familiar burst of speed, which would sweep Sir Ivor to success. To their utter dismay, no such fireworks were forthcoming and as Ward strove desperately to rally his faltering mount, Piggott pushed Ribero clear to win by two lengths, with Val d'Aoste a similar distance away in third place, ahead of Laudamus. In contrast to the previous year, Piggott and his winning partner returned to the winner's enclosure amid stony silence, as an incredulous crowd, still stunned by Sir Ivor's defeat, strove to discover the reason.

On the end of the grandstand at the Curragh there is a clock, and underneath that clock runs the legend: 'Time discloses all'. In that old adage lay the explanation to the inexplicable, for Ribero had covered the stiff Curragh course in fully 4.6secs faster time than that taken by Sir Ivor at Epsom. Before the Epsom Derby many had insisted that Sir Ivor could not possibly stay a mile and a half in a truly-run race. As the race had been run, and ridden as brilliantly as he was on that occasion, Sir Ivor had not done so. Only Piggott knew the true extent of Sir Ivor's stamina and, in employing the forcing tactics that he did on Ribero, he had put that unique knowledge to devastating use, riding Ribero not merely to be second, as any other jockey would have been entitled to do, but to beat the favourite, by blunting his speed. It was, in fact, cruel luck on Liam Ward, whose insistence upon his rights had brought about both his own downfall and that of Sir Ivor, a public idol, for it could be said – as, inevitably, it was – that Piggott would have won on Sir Ivor. He would, simply because no other jockey would have known or dared to take him on.

Bred, like Ribocco, by Mrs Julie Rogers at the Idle Hour Farm, Lexington, Kentucky, Ribero had cost 50,000 dollars as a yearling at Keeneland. Even slower to come to hand than his smaller brother, Ribero had not been rated among the top twenty in the English Two-year-old Free Handicap. Prior to his victory at the Curragh, which surprised even his trainer, he had finished a close third to Lucky Finish in the Dante Stakes at York and a distant second to Connaught at Ascot, though Piggott afterwards attributed at least the margin of that defeat to inexperience. On his next appearance, in the King George VI and Queen Elizabeth Stakes at Ascot, he emulated the feat of Ribocco in getting rid of Piggott before the start. Having gorged himself on rhododendrons prior to his recapture, he then ran all too freely to finish fourth to Royal Palace. Sent to France in an effort to get him resettled, Ribero trailed in behind Pardallo, having relaxed so effectively that, in the words of his trainer: 'He never came out of his coma.'

Perhaps fortunately for his supporters, Ribero was denied a run in the March Stakes at Goodwood, the race that Ribocco had disgraced himself in the previous year. Still following in his older brother's footsteps, Ribero turned up at a rain-lashed Doncaster to contest the St Leger, for which he started second favourite to his Ascot conqueror, Connaught. Slowly away, Ribero worked his way steadily through the field to tail Connaught into the straight. As the favourite tired and sprawled, Piggott swooped into the lead on Ribero, only to face a desperate late challenge from the Irish-trained Canterbury. Not daring to stir on his flagging mount, Piggott nursed him home with hands and heels, throwing everything into the final strides, which saw him home by a short head. It was a brilliant performance on Piggott's part to snatch victory from what had seemed certain defeat. Asked afterwards why he had not resorted to the whip, Piggott explained that Ribero had been giving his all. What he forbore to add was that the courageous colt was also suffering from an abcess on his jaw.

In his final race as a three-year-old Ribero was kicked at the start of the Prix de l'Arc de Triomphe and made no show behind the majestic Vaguely Noble. Unplaced in his first two outings as a four-year-old, Ribero was withdrawn without coming under starter's orders in the Coronation Cup and subsequently retired to the Sandringham Stud. Well patronised, Ribero got numerous winners from his early crops, though none of exceptional merit, with the inevitable result . . . in 1977 he joined his brother in Japan. By their victories at the Curragh Ribocco and Ribero became the first full-brothers to win successive runnings of Ireland's greatest race. Portmarnock (1895) and Carrigavalla (1901) were full-brothers, as, indeed, were Harinero (1933) and Primero (1934), but the latter had only managed to share the honours with Patriot King. Both excellent racehorses, Ribocco and Ribero reflected enormous credit on their young trainer for his ability to reconcile temperament with talent to such memorable effect.

Sir Ivor finished third to Royal Palace and Taj Dewan in the Eclipse Stakes, and it was this run, over ten furlongs, which made Vincent O'Brien begin to wonder whether staleness rather than lack of stamina might have been the cause of his downfall at the Curragh a week earlier. Rested until the autumn, Sir Ivor finished second to Prince Sao in the Prix Henri Delamarre and then beat everything except Vaguely Noble in the Prix de l'Arc de Triomphe. After four successive defeats, Sir Ivor showed his own courage and his trainer's skill when concluding his career with brilliant victories in the Champion Stakes at Newmarket and the Washington DC International at Laurel Park. Retired to stud in Ireland for two seasons as a gesture to European breeders by his owner Raymond Guest, Sir Ivor then returned to the land of his birth, missed more than ever when his daughter, Ivanjica, won the Prix de l'Arc de Triomphe in 1976.

Saturday, 29th June, 1968   **£55,340**   **14 Ran**   1½m

Irish Sweeps Derby. A sweepstakes of £10 each for yearlings entered on 13th July, 1966; or of £30 each for those entered on 2nd November, 1966; £40 extra for all if not struck out on 18th October, 1967, an additional £50 for all if not struck out on 27th March, 1968, an additional £50 for all if not struck out on 15th May, 1968 and a further additional £100 for all if not struck out on 12th June, 1968. With £30,000 added and a trophy value £300 to the owner of the winner both to be contributed by the Irish Hospitals' Sweepstakes. The winner to receive 75%, second 15% and third 10% of the whole stakes after deduction of bonuses of £500 to the owner (at entry) of the winner, £300 to the owner (at entry) of the second and £200 to the owner (at entry) of the third. For three years old entire colts and fillies. Colts, 9st; Fillies, 8st 11lb. One mile and a half.

The Racing Board will contribute a sum equal to 5% of the whole stakes (after deduction of bonuses) to the owner of the fourth horse if there are eight or more runners.

Note—Subject to the usual conditions the Racing Board will pay special allowances as follows towards the transport costs of runners from abroad in this race:– Great Britain, £200 per horse; other European countries, £250 per horse; other countries, £500 per horse.

(582 subs)

1	Mr. C. W. Engelhard's	RIBERO (L. Piggott) B. colt Ribot – Libra by Hyperion.	9.0	F. Johnson-Houghton (GB)
2	Mr R. R. Guest's	SIR IVOR (L. Ward) B. colt Sir Gaylord – Attica.	9.0	M. V. O'Brien
3	Baron de Rothschild's	VAL D'AOSTE (J. Deforge) B. colt Val de Loir – Nourouche.	9.0	M. Clement (FR)
4	Mr J. McGrath's	LAUDAMUS (G. McGrath) B. colt Lauso – Damarctic.	9.0	S. McGrath
5	Mrs C. B. Nathorst's	LUCKY FINISH (B. Taylor) B. colt Milesian – Campanette.	9.0	H. Leader (GB)
6	Mr J. R. Mullion's	NEW MEMBER (W. Williamson) Ch. colt Alcide – Maiden Speech.	9.0	P. J. Prendergast
7	Mrs M. V. Philippi's	ALARIC (J. Roe) B. colt Arabian – Anet II.	9.0	J. Oxx
8	Mr J. McGrath's	STITCH (P. Matthews) B. colt Lauso – Silken Princess.	9.0	S. McGrath
9	HE the President's	GIOLLA MEAR (T. P. Burns) B. colt Hard Ridden – Lacobella.	9.0	M. Hurley
10	Mr W. J. Simms's	PANCO (P. Boothman) Ch. colt Panaslipper – Counsel's Opinion.	9.0	R. Jarvis (GB)
11	Lord Harrington's	SARAGAN (M. Kennedy) Gr. colt Sicambre – Ash Plant	9.0	M. V. O'Brien
12	Mr R. S. Reynolds jr's	MEADSVILLE (C. Williams) Ch. colt Charlottesville – Honey Flower.	9.0	H. V. S. Murless
13	Mr J. Smyth's	SUNSET GLORY (A. C. McGarrity) B. colt Sayajirao – Sun Shower	9.0	K. Bell
14	Mr B. Kerr's	HOME FARM (R. F. Parnell) B. colt Bairam II – Pitcher Girl.	9.0	K. R. Kerr

SP 1/3 Sir Ivor; 10/1 Giolla Mear; 100/6 RIBERO, Val D'Aoste; 25/1 New Member; 28/1 Lucky Finish; 33/1 Meadsville; 50/1 Laudamus; 66/1 Alaric; 100/1 Stitch, Saragan, Home Farm; 200/1 Bar. TOTE (2/6 unit) 45/-. Places 5/-, 3/-, 5/-.

2 lengths, same, 5 lengths. 2m 33.9s.

Winner trained by Mr R. F. Johnson-Houghton at Blewbury, Berkshire, England.

Of the others in what will always be remembered as a two-horse race, Giolla Mear did best, winning the Irish St Leger. Retained by the Irish National Stud, he became a very successful National Hunt sire. New Member won ten races on the flat and four over hurdles, before retiring to stud in England. Stitch won the Ulster Harp Derby, while Saragan won the Munster equivalent and finished second in the Irish St Leger, before finding his way to Poland. Whether in victory or in defeat, 1968 will be recalled as 'The Year of Sir Ivor'.

1969

That four out of the first five past the post in the Epsom Derby should turn out for the Irish Sweeps Derby was a fair indication of the muddled Classic form that year. Moreover, Ribofilio, the last of those on that occasion, was again favourite, a reflection of the charisma of his connections, bidding for a hat-trick in the race. In the Epsom race Blakeney had got a trouble-free run along the rails to beat Shoemaker, Prince Regent, Moon Mountain and Ribofilio. Blakeney had been dismissed in many quarters as an extremely lucky winner, for the Comtesse de la Valdene's pair, Prince Regent and Moon Mountain, had both received singularly ill-judged rides from their French jockeys, never particularly happy around Epsom. These two were now ridden by a Welshman and a Scot, Geoff Lewis replacing Deforge on Prince Regent and Sandy Barclay taking over from Saint-Martin on Moon Mountain. Ribofilio, representing the team connected with Ribocco and Ribero, had started favourite for the Two Thousand Guineas at Newmarket, in which he had run so badly that Lester Piggott had actually pulled him up. However, he had been noted running on well at Epsom and, being by Ribot, was expected to have made abnormal improvement in the interim. Of the remainder, Beaugency, second in the French Derby, appeared to have the best chance, though there was some support for Onandaga, winner of the Gallinule Stakes and the choice of Liam Ward, in preference to Moon Mountain and Vincent O'Brien's three other runners in the race.

Ballantine, the O'Brien pacemaker, went into a clear lead from the start, followed by Moon Mountain, in the same colours, with Vivadari, Tanzara and Northern Mist most prominent of the others. Blakeney and Ribofilio had been settled towards the rear, while Prince Regent was last but one in the early stages. Ballantine continued to lead coming down the hill, where his stable companions, Onandaga and Reindeer, came to take it up, with Ribofilio and Prince Regent also taking closer order. Two furlongs out Piggott came with his run in Ribofilio, sweeping past Onandaga and Reindeer and looking certain to achieve that unique hat-trick. However, Geoff Lewis, under orders to ride Prince Regent for speed, had merely been biding his time. Making his challenge in the middle of the course, Prince Regent produced a remarkable burst of speed inside the distance, which saw him a length to the good at the post. Reindeer just held off the fast-finishing Blakeney for third place, while Onandaga finished fifth. The winner, a well-backed second favourite, returned to an enthusiastic reception, which became quite a family affair in the unsaddling area, for Prince Regent was owned by the Comtesse de la

Valdene, while the third horse, Reindeer, belonged to her brother, Raymond Guest, until recently US Ambassador to Ireland.

Bred in France by his owner, who kept her broodmares near Deauville, Prince Regent was a big, heavy-topped, almost black colt by Right Royal V out of Noduleuse, who had bred only one other moderate winner before killing herself by galloping into a tree a year or so earlier. Right Royal V, a high-class racehorse, whose victories included the Grand Criterium, the French Guineas and Derby and the King George VI and Queen Elizabeth Stakes in three seasons' racing, had already become established as a sire by the successes of such as Ruysdael (Italian Derby), Right Away (French Guineas), Salvo and Royal Sword. Twice successful as a two-year-old, Prince Regent had won the Prix Greffuhle and the Prix Lupin prior to his luckless essay at Epsom. Though he subsequently finished only fifth in the Prix de l'Arc de Triomphe, behind Levmoss and Park Top, Prince Regent was the first three-year-old past the post and could thus be regarded as the leading Classic colt in Europe in what was a mediocre vintage. Having won once as a four-year-old, at Evry, Prince Regent was retired to the Collinstown Stud in Co. Kildare, where he has sired numerous winners, of whom the best to date has been Red Regent.

The Comtesse de la Valdene, compensated for her near-misses at Epsom, emerged as the leading owner in Ireland that season, while her brother, Raymond Guest, occupied third place, just as he had at the Curragh. The American-born Comtesse, who later became Mrs Manning, had won the Eclipse and Champion Stakes three years earlier with Pieces of Eight, trained by Vincent O'Brien, while in France her Sea Hawk won the Grand Prix de Saint-Cloud for the Pollet stable. Having looked likely to prove the leading French colt of his year, Sea Hawk unfortunately broke down and was retired to stud in Ireland.

For Etienne Pollet, in what was to have been his last season as a trainer, Prince Regent also provided compensation for what he considered a singularly unfortunate performance at Epsom, where Prince Regent had finished like a train, when the race was over. Having saddled Tambourine II to win the inaugural running of the Irish Sweeps Derby seven years earlier, Pollet knew exactly what was required to win the race and considered Prince Regent a much more likely winner than his predecessor. In the meantime Pollet had trained two champions in Sea Bird II and Vaguely Noble, both winners of the Prix de l'Arc de Triomphe. Though still a comparatively young man, Pollet had made up his mind to retire at the end of the 1969 season. The emergence of the two-year-old, Gyr, had persuaded him to defer his retirement in order to supervise that colt's Classic career. Two factors frustrated the success of that plan, one was Gyr's temperament and the other was a rival called Nijinsky.

Geoff Lewis, who had given Prince Regent such a good ride, was just then on the threshold of the golden period of his riding career, three seasons during which he seemed to win every prestige race in the European Calendar. Already that year he had ridden Right Tack to become the first-ever winner of both the English and Irish Two Thousand Guineas. Born in Wales, he had gone to work as a pageboy in a London hotel, where his size had prompted Tim Molony, then reigning National Hunt champion jockey, to suggest a career in racing. Having become apprenticed to Ron Smyth at Epsom, Lewis rode his first winner on his local track in 1953 and has retained his happy association with Epsom ever since. Three times second in the apprentices' table, he rode his first big winner in 1959, when the Epsom-trained

354

Saturday, 28th June, 1969　　　　£53,390　　　　15 Ran　　　　1½m

Irish Sweeps Derby. A sweepstakes of £10 each for yearlings entered on 12th July, 1967; or of £30 each for those entered on 1st November, 1967. £40 extra for all if not struck out on 17th October, 1968, an additional £50 for all if not struck out on 26th March, 1969, an additional £50 for all if not struck out on 14th May, 1969 and a further additional £100 for all if not struck out on 11th June, 1969. With £30,000 added and a trophy value £300 to the owner of the winner both to be contributed by the Irish Hospitals' Sweepstakes. The winner to receive 75%, second 15% and third 10% of the whole stakes after deduction of bonuses of £500 to the owner (at entry) of the winner, £300 to the owner (at entry) of the second and £200 to the owner (at entry) of the third. For three years old entire colts and fillies. Colts, 9st; Fillies, 8st 11lb. One mile and a half.

The Racing Board will contribute a sum equal to 5% of the whole stakes (after deduction of bonuses) to the owner of the fourth horse if there are eight or more runners.

Note—Subject to the usual conditions the Racing Board will pay special allowances as follows towards the transport costs of runners from abroad in this race:– Great Britain, £200 per horse; other European countries, £250 per horse; other countries, £500 per horse.

(537 subs)

1	Comtesse de la Valdene's	PRINCE REGENT (G. Lewis) Br. colt Right Royal V – Noduleuse by Nosca.	9.0	E. Pollet (FR)
2	Mr C. W. Engelhard's	RIBOFILIO (L. Piggott) B. colt Ribot – Island Creek.	9.0	Johnson-Houghton
3	Mr Raymond R. Guest's	REINDEER (T. P. Burns) B/Br. colt Santa Claus – Reine des Bois.	9.0	M. V. O'Brien
4	Mr A. M. Budgett's	BLAKENEY (E. Johnson) B. colt Hethersett – Windmill Girl.	9.0	Owner
5	Mr J. W. Galbreath's	ONANDAGA (L. Ward) Ch. colt Ribot – Red Pippin.	9.0	M. V. O'Brien
6	Mr J. Cox Brady's	SELKO (J. Roe) Ch. colt Relko – Sijui.	9.0	M. V. O'Brien
7	Mr T. Geekie's	NORTHERN MIST (J. D. Coleman)　B. colt Arctic Storm – Polar Point.	9.0	J. Oxx
8	Mr J. R. Mullion's	AGUSTUS (W. Williamson) B. colt Ribot – Ela Marita.	9.0	P. J. Prendergast
9	Mme P. Wertheimer's	BEAUGENCY (F. Head) B. colt Val de Loir – Biobelle.	9.0	A. Head (FR)
10	Comtesse de la Valdene's	MOON MOUNTAIN (A. Barclay)　B. colt Mourne – Trip to the Moon.	9.0	M. V. O'Brien
11	Comtesse de la Valdene's	BALLANTINE (V. Rossiter) Ch. colt Ballymoss – Palmavista.	9.0	M. V. O'Brien
12	Mr S. McGrath's	SANTAMOSS (G. McGrath) Ch. colt Santa Claus – Feemoss.	9.0	Owner
13	Mr S. McGrath's	VIVADARI (M. Kennedy) B. colt Pindari – Ballyvive.	9.0	Owner
14	Mr B. Kerr's	BUNKERED (R. F. Parnell) B. colt Entanglement – Golf Ball.	9.0	K. R. Kerr
15	Comte Antoine de Laubespin's	TANZARA (F. Berry) Ch. colt Tanavar – Fujiyama.	9.0	M. Hurley

SP 2/1 Ribofilio; 7/2 PRINCE REGENT, Blakeney; 9/1 Beaugency; 100/8 Onandaga; 100/7 Moon Mountain, Reindeer; 33/1 Agustus, Northern Mist; 40/1 Santamoss; 66/1 Selko; 150/1 Vivadari; 200/1 Bar. TOTE (2/6 unit) 11/6. Places 5/6, 6/-, 6/-.
1 length, 5 lengths, short head. 2m 36.1s.
Winner trained by M. Etienne Pollet at Chantilly, France.

Faultless Speech won the Royal Hunt Cup. Two years later he won the same race on King's Troop for Kingsclere trainer, Peter Hastings-Bass, thus beginning an association with the Kingsclere stable, which was to provide him with his most famous mount – Mill Reef, on whom he won the Coventry, Gimcrack and Dewhurst Stakes in 1970.

The following year Geoff Lewis succeeded Sandy Barclay as first jockey to Noel Murless, scoring an unforgettable Epsom treble on Mill Reef in the Derby, Lupe in the Coronation Cup and Altesse Royale in the Oaks. On Mill Reef he went on to win the Eclipse Stakes, the King George VI and Queen Elizabeth Stakes and the Prix de l'Arc de Triomphe, while Altesse Royale gave him another Classic success in the Irish Oaks. Frequently compared to Gordon Richards, whose short-legged stature and upright, whip-swinging style he closely resembles, Geoff Lewis is a very good jockey, who seems equally likely to succeed in his new career as a trainer, based, naturally enough, at Epsom.

The wretched Ribofilio – ironically dubbed by his owner 'the last of the cheap Ribots' – disappointed yet again when favourite for the St Leger in which he finished second to Intermezzo. Another inglorious display in the Prix de l'Arc de Triomphe preceded his deportation to South Africa. Reindeer won the Irish St Leger, stood for two seasons in Ireland and then went to New Zealand, taking with him any chance of perpetuating a Santa Claus line in these islands. Blakeney's only other success was achieved in the Ormonde Stakes as a four-year-old, though his seconds to Precipice Wood in the Ascot Gold Cup and to Nijinsky in the King George VI and Queen Elizabeth Stakes provided ample evidence of his class courage and versatility. Nevertheless, this stigma of 'undeserving Derby winner' remained and his purchase by the English National Stud was widely criticised. By siring Juliette Marny, winner of the English and Irish Oaks, in his very first crop, Blakeney proved his purchase to have been inspired. Since then he has got such as Norfolk Air, Sexton Blake and Julio Mariner, while his half-brother, Morston, emulated his success in the Epsom Derby four years later.

1970

Just as 1968 had been the year of Sir Ivor, so 1970 was the year of Nijinsky, trained, like Sir Ivor, by Vincent O'Brien. Unbeaten in his eight races, including the English Two Thousand Guineas and Derby, Nijinsky came to the Curragh looking even more invincible than Sir Ivor; and so it proved. As had been the case in Sir Ivor's year, Liam Ward was first jockey to the O'Brien stable in Ireland. His presence on Nijinsky left Piggott free to ride Meadowville, winner of the Lingfield Derby Trial and fifth to Nijinsky at Epsom, where Approval, the other English challenger, had finished seventh, having previously won the Dante Stakes. Master Guy, the lone French challenger, represented the owner-trainer combination successful with Prince Regent the year before. A narrow winner of the Prix Jean Prat, Master Guy was known to be inferior to his stable companion Gyr. As the latter had been easily beaten by Nijinsky at Epsom, the odds-on favourite seemed to have little to fear from that quarter. The remaining nine home-trained hopefuls were quoted at prices ranging from 33-to-1 to 500-to-1, which seemed an accurate assessment of their chances on all known form.

The early running was made by Double Dick, who showed ahead of Illa Laudo and Dubrava, with Nijinsky and Master Guy settled at the rear of the field. The order remained unchanged until they reached the straight, where Double Dick weakened rapidly and Approval came under pressure. As Illa Laudo hit the front, ahead of Nor and Meadowville, Nijinsky cruised up into fourth place, with Master Guy also taking closer order. At the distance Nijinsky swept majestically into the lead, leaving the one-paced Meadowville to fight off the renewed challenges of Master Guy and Nor for the minor placings. Though few had cared to take the odds, Nijinsky returned to a hero's welcome, not a little of which was directed at Liam Ward, a relieved and happy man.

Bred in Canada by E. P. Taylor, Canada's 'Mr Racing', Nijinsky was an upstanding bay colt by Northern Dancer out of Flaming Page. Having won the Kentucky Derby (in record time) and the Preakness Stakes in 1964, Northern Dancer had bowed a tendon and been retired to Taylor's Windfields Stud in Canada. Having sired Viceregal, Canadian juvenile champion and Horse of the Year, in his first crop, Northern Dancer was transferred to Kentucky, where better opportunities enabled him to emerge as one of the foremost sires in the world, whose progeny to race in these islands include The Minstrel, Be My Guest, Lyphard and Try My Best. Flaming Page, the leading three-year-old filly in Canada in 1962, had previously produced the winning filly Fleur. Nijinsky, one of the first Taylor draft ever to be offered to the Canadian Thoroughbred Horse Society sales, cost Charles Englehard 84,000 dollars and the following year he paid a Canadian record of 140,000 dollars for Nijinsky's chestnut full-brother. Put in training with O'Brien and named Minsky, he won the Railway and Beresford Stakes in 1970.

Nijinsky won his first four races, all at the Curragh, including the Railway, Anglesey and Beresford Stakes, and concluded his first season with a cantering success in the Dewhurst Stakes. Top of the Two-year-old Free Handicap both in England and in Ireland, he became a firm winter favourite for the Two Thousand Guineas and the Derby. An easy victory over Deep Run and Prince Tenderfoot at the Curragh in April preceded his successes in the first two legs of the English Triple Crown. His presence in the King George VI and Queen Elizabeth Stakes frightened away his contemporaries. Opposed by Blakeney, winner of the Derby, Caliban, winner of the Coronation Cup, Karabas, winner of the Washington DC International, and Hogarth, the Italian champion, Nijinsky won in a style which saw him hailed as Horse of the Century.

Despite a setback in training, caused by an attack of American ringworm, Nijinsky travelled to Doncaster in search of the elusive Triple Crown. An apparently easy success over the luckless Meadowville meant that Nijinsky became only the fifteenth winner of the English Triple Crown, while crediting Charles Englehard with his fourth St Lever in seven years. Committed to retiring Nijinsky to stud in America as a four-year-old, to the disappointment of European breeders, Englehard and his advisers decided to go for the Prix de l'Arc de Triomphe, in a bid to establish Nijinsky as the greatest colt in European racing history, in his only two

The Irish Derby

Saturday, 27th June, 1970   £52,992½   **13 Ran**   1½m

Irish Sweeps Derby. A sweepstakes of 10sovs each for yearlings entered on 10th July, 1968, or of 30sovs each for those entered on 6th November, 1968; 40sovs extra for all if not struck out on 15th October, 1969, an additional 50sovs for all if not struck out on 25th March, 1970, an additional 50sovs for all if not struck out on 13th May, 1970, and a further additional 100sovs for all if not struck out on 10th June, 1970, with 30,000sovs added and a Trophy value 400sovs to the owner of the winner, both to be contributed by the Irish Hospitals' Sweepstakes. The winner will receive 75%, second 15%, and third 10% of the whole stakes after deduction of bonuses of 500sovs to the owner (at entry) of the winner; 300sovs to the owner (at entry) of the second and 200sovs to the owner (at entry) of the third. For three years old entire colts and fillies. Colts, 9st; Fillies, 8st 11lb. One mile and a half.

The Racing Board will contribute a sum equal to 5% of the whole stakes (after deduction of bonuses) to the owner of the fourth horse if there are eight or more runners.

Note—Subject to the usual conditions the Racing Board will pay special allowances as follows towards the transport costs of runners from abroad in this race:– Great Britain, £200 per horse; other European countries, £250 per horse; other countries, £500 per horse.

(571 subs)

1	Mr C. W. Engelhard's	NIJINSKY (L. Ward)	9.0	M. V. O'Brien
		B. colt Northern Dancer – Flaming Page by Bull Page.		
2	Mr David Robinson's	MEADOWVILLE (L. Piggott)	9.0	M. A. Jarvis (UK)
		Ch. colt Charlottesville – Meadow Pipit.		
3	Mrs A. Manning's	MASTER GUY (J. Taillard)	9.0	E. Pollet (FR)
		B. colt Relko – Musical.		
4	Mr R. W. Hall-Dare's	NOR (A. Simpson)	9.0	P. Mullins
		B. colt Tiger – Lucky Day.		
5	Mr P. W. McGrath's	ILLA LAUDO (G. McGrath)	9.0	S. McGrath
		B. colt Lauso – Four Two's.		
6	Mrs J. R. Mullion's	DUBRAVA (J. Miller)	9.0	P. J. Prendergast
		B. colt Ragusa – Maiden Speech.		
7	Sir H. de Trafford's	APPROVAL (G. Starkey)	9.0	H. Cecil (UK)
		Ch. colt Alcide – Success.		
8	Mr M. Gallagher's	NOBLE LIFE (M. Kennedy)	9.0	C. Grassick
		Br/Bl. colt Only For Life – Suburb.		
9	Mr Hugo Dolan's	RINGSEND (R. F. Parnell)	9.0	C. L. Weld
		B. colt Tamerlane – Scyllinda.		
19	Mr S. Raccah's	HONEST CROOK (T. P. Burns)	9.0	J. Lenehan
		B. colt Arctic Storm – Ma Tendresse.		
11	Mr J. McShain's	NIP AND TUCK (J. D. Coleman)	9.0	J. Oxx
		Br. colt Klairon – Bottalina.		
12	Mrs Rochford Hyde's	DOUBLE DICK (J. Roe)	9.0	M. Connolly
		B. colt Dual – Lucelle.		
13	Mrs W. J. Kavanagh's	OH BROTHER (L. W. Johnson)	9.0	M. Hurley
		B. colt Escart III – Dunlavin Star.		

SP 4/11 NIJINSKY; 10/1 Meadowville, Approval; 100/7 Master Guy; 33/1 Ringsend; 66/1 Nor, Illa Laudo; 100/1 Nip and Tuck; 200/1 Dubrava; 300/1 Honest Crook; 500/1 Bar. TOTE (2/6 unit) 3/6. Places 3/-, 4/-, 5/6.

3 lengths, same, ½ length. 2m 33.6s.

Winner trained by Mr M. Vincent O'Brien at Ballydoyle House, Cashel, Co. Tipperary.

seasons on the racecourse. Thus Vincent O'Brien faced the task of bringing Nijinsky to the post at Longchamp fit to run for his life, after a season which had begun six months earlier, encompassed the Triple Crown, a decisive defeat of the best older horses in Europe, a good deal of travelling and a setback in training. It was a brave gamble, but one that should perhaps not have been taken, for, in the event, it did not quite succeed. In a race where the presence of two pacemakers ensured a scorching gallop throughout Piggott rode Nijinsky from behind, always a risky strategy in the Arc, though, as the race was run, he had very little choice. Getting a miraculously clear run, Nijinsky came to challenge the leader, Sassafras, a furlong ut, got his head in front and then appeared to hang, allowing Sassafras to win by a head. Piggott was widely blamed for overdoing his waiting tactics and his recent record in the race lent strength to the view that it had become a bogey for him. In an all-judged attempt to make amends, Nijinsky was pulled out once more for the Champion Stakes at Newmarket. Visibly upset in the preliminaries, Nijinsky ran away below his best and was beaten by Lorenzaccio, a decent horse, but never likely to be hailed as the Horse of the Century. That was the end of Nijinsky's racecourse career, for he was promptly hustled off to stud in America, whence he sent back reminders of his brilliance in the form of African Dancer, Green Dancer, Caucasus, Lord of the Dance and Ile de Bourbon.

That Nijinsky's racecourse career should have ended, not in a blaze of glory, but in a cloud of defeat, was as unfair to a great horse as it was unjust. More versatile in his talents than either Santa Claus or Sir Ivor, though he never had to rival their brilliant speed, Nijinsky must rank with Windsor Slipper as the greatest winners of the Irish Derby. Whereas Windsor Slipper, who raced during the war, could not be asked enough to preserve his place among the immortals of European racing, Nijinsky was asked, quite simply, to do the impossible. On the other hand, had he not failed – and it was only by a head – what fields would be left for his successors to conquer?

Meadowville returned to the Curragh in search of Classic consolation in the absence of his nemesis, Nijinsky. Betrayed once again by his fatal lack of foot, he finished second in the Irish St Leger to the McGrath colt, Allangrange. Like many Glencairn runners, Allangrange had begun winning in modest company and continued to improve. In fact, so modest was his mid-season form that one well-known English National Hunt trainer had rejected him as a potential hurdle winner at Newton Abbot! Meadowville won the John Porter Stakes as a four-year-old and later went to stud in South Africa. Approval, never as good as the day he won the Observer Gold Cup, was exported to Australia. Noble Life and Nip and Tuck went on to success over hurdles, the former winning the Gloucestershire Hurdle at Cheltenham. Dubrava won the Ulster Harp Derby, while Nor's connections reaped the rewards of their adventurous policy when that colt finished third to Connaught and Karabas in the Eclipse Stakes.

1971

The absence of Mill Reef robbed the Irish Sweeps Derby of a star attraction, though it did make it infinitely more intriguing as a horse race. A fifteen-strong field included two colts from England and two from France and once again the form revolved around the Epsom Derby and those who finished behind Mill Reef. Linden Tree, Irish Ball and Lombardo, second, third and fourth at Epsom, met again, with each confidently supported to emerge victorious. Linden Tree, winner of the Observer Gold Cup and the Chester Vase, had been forced to make his own running at Epsom, where he had been caught and beaten by the brilliant Mill Reef. Having tried without success to purchase a pacemaker for this occasion, Linden Tree's connections now depended upon an outsider setting a good early gallop. A deserving favourite, Linden Tree had an infinitely better chance than his compatriot, Bayons Manor, recent winner of his maiden at Kempton. Irish Ball, third at Epsom, had failed to act coming down the hill, where, according to his French jockey, he had been 'battered repeatedly' off the rails. The gentle gradients of the galloping Curragh course were expected to suit both horse and rider much better. On the Prix Lupin form Irish Ball appeared to hold the other French raider, Music Man, owned by Mrs Howell E. Jackson, and by her inaugural Sweeps Derby winner Tambourine II. Lombardo, fourth at Epsom, now had the services of Lester Piggott and was strongly fancied by his trainer, Paddy Prendergast, to reverse that form. Prendergast also ran Guillemot, carrying his own colours and ridden by Liam Ward. Of the others, Parnell, unbeaten in six races that season, including the two-mile Queen's Vase, seemed to have better credentials than the O'Brien-trained Grenfall, winner of the Gallinule Stakes.

The favourite, Linden Tree, who was running in blinkers, was drawn No 1 on the wide outside. As such he was the last to be loaded into the stalls, under the watchful eye of Peter Walwyn's travelling head lad. As the doors were closed behind him, Linden Tree flicked his tail out over the doors, prompting one of the handlers to put it back. An instant later the stalls flew open for the start, Linden Tree took one full stride, whipped out to the left, dug in his toes and was out of the race – the most dramatic defector since Relko eight years earlier. In the absence of the favourite – left to canter around behind his field – the early running was made by Wacoso and Turbulent Eddy, with Music Man prominent and Irish Ball settled in sixth place. The order remained virtually unchanged until they turned to swing into the straight, where Swinburn made his move on Music Man, shadowed by Irish Ball and Guillemot. Slipping Irish Ball smoothly through on the rails, Gibert then switched him outside Music Man and bade his rivals farewell. Thereafter the race became a procession, though a patriotic roar from the packed stands signalled the emergence of Piggott and Lombardo in hot pursuit. However, nothing ever looked likely to trouble Irish Ball, who passed the post three lengths ahead of the exhausted Lombardo, who, in turn, held off the late flourish of his stable companion, Guillemot, by a short head. Lucky Drake, Nor's half-brother, emulated his relation by taking fourth place and a handsome £4000. Grenfall never showed with a chance, while Parnell had faded just when his stamina might have been expected to come into play.

Through an interpreter, Alfred Gibert declared that Irish Ball, much better suited by the stronger gallop than at Epsom, had enjoyed a trouble-free passage. Once in the straight he had felt confident of victory. Piggott reported that Lombardo had failed to stay, while Liam Ward, delighted with the resolution shown by a son of Sea Bird II, said that Guillemot never had any chance with the winner. But the jockey whose account everybody wanted to hear was Duncan Keith, the victim of ironic applause as he cantered forlornly back on the recalcitrant Linden Tree. As he reported to Peter Walwyn: 'There was nothing drawn outside us, or it might never have happened. He just ducked out to the open space and dug his heels in. I could do nothing about it . . . I'm sorry.' Sharing his sorrow were the thousands who had backed Linden Tree to solid favouritism, who were left to console themselves that the ease of Irish Ball's victory, in which he beat Lombardo further than at Epsom, suggested that it would have been a very close-run affair in any case. The rumour that Linden Tree's tail had got trapped in the rear doors of his stall was quickly exposed as a physical impossibility and, although connections scoffed at the suggestion, the fact that Linden Tree never saw a racecourse again indicated that his gruelling battle against Mill Reef at Epsom had ruined his zest for racing.

At the post-race Press conference, where Captain Spencer Freeman interviewed the connections of the winner in front of an audience of journalists – yet another Irish Sweeps innovation – the owner of Irish Ball, Emile Littler, the theatrical impresario, revealed that, while he had successfully launched the careers of such as Julie Andrews and Greer Garson, Irish Ball was the first four-legged star of his creation! He went on to say that, having bought Irish Ball as a yearling at Deauville, he and his trainer had given the colt plenty of time as a two-year-old. His win in the Prix Daru (in a record post-war time) had indicated 'that Classic fire' which made Mr Littler confident of Derby success. Disappointment in England had turned to delight in Ireland, a country which had fond memories for him, for it was in Ireland that he had successfully wooed his wife!

A plain-looking, rather leggy bay colt, Irish Ball was by Baldric II out of Irish Lass, bred at the Haras de la Gastine by M. Enrique Cruz-Valer and M. Eric Coupey, for whom he had realised 180,000Fr. Baldrick II, winner of the English Two Thousand Guineas and Champion Stakes, and second to Ragusa in the Eclipse Stakes in 1964, had covered his first mares in 1966 and from his second crop had now sired two Classic winners, for Favoletta had won the Irish One Thousand Guineas earlier in the year. Unfortunately, not even this auspicious start to his stud career was sufficient to protect Baldric II from the purchasing power of the yen, and he departed to Japan in 1973. Irish Lass, bred at the Baroda Stud, was, at 13,000gns, the third highest-priced yearling sold at public auction in 1963, largely on account of being a full-sister of Lynchris, winner of the Irish Oaks, the Yorkshire Oaks and the Irish St Leger. Twice a winner in France, where she had bred Irish Ball, Irish Lass and since been repatriated and was now immensely more valuable, not only through the exploits of Irish Ball, but because poor Lynchris was killed by lightning in her paddock in Kentucky.

Though he could finish only fifth to Mill Reef on his next appearance, in the King George VI and Queen Elizabeth Stakes at Ascot, Irish Ball's running with

Saturday, 26th June, 1971   **£62,120**   **15 Ran**   **1½m**

The Irish Sweeps Derby. £30,000 and a Trophy value £400 added to the stakes by Irish Hospitals' Sweepstakes. For three years old entire colts and fillies. One mile and a half.

Sweepstakes, £10 at entry on 9th July, or £30 at second entry on 5th November, 1969; £40 extra for acceptors on 14th October, 1970, £50 extra for acceptors on 24th March, 1971, £50 extra for acceptors on 12th May, 1971, £100 additional for final acceptors on 9th June, 1971. Second to receive 15%, third 10% of the whole stakes after deduction of bonuses to owners at entry as follows – winner £500, second £300, third £200. Weights: Colts 9st; Fillies 8st 11lb.

The Racing Board will contribute a sum equal to 5% of the whole stakes (after deduction of bonuses) to the owner of the fourth horse if there are eight or more runners.

Note—Subject to the usual conditions the Racing Board will pay special allowances as follows towards the transport costs of runners from abroad in this race:– Great Britain, £200 per horse; other European countries, £250 per horse; other countries, £500 per horse.

(613 subs)

1	M. Emile Littler's	IRISH BALL (FR) (A. Gibert)	9.0	P. Lallei (FR)
		B. colt Baldric II – Irish Lass by Sayajirao.		
3	Mrs J. R. Mullion's	LOMBARDO (L. Piggott)	9.0	P. J. Prendergast
		B. colt Ragusa – Midnight Chimes.		
3	Mr P. J. Prendergast's	GUILLEMOT (USA) (L. Ward)	9.0	Owner
		B. colt Sea Bird II – Belle Jeep.		
4	Mr R. W. Hall-Dare's	LUCKY DRAKE (Thomas Murphy) Ch. colt Dicta Drake – Lucky Day.	9.0	P. Mullins
5	Mrs Howell E. Jackson's	MUSIC MAN (USA) (W. Swinburn) B. colt Tambourine II – Way We Go.	9.0	H. Nicolas (FR)
6	Mr E. A. Holt's	ST. IVES (R. F. Parnell)	9.0	S. Quirke
		Ch. colt St Paddy – Night Court.		
7	Mrs J. W. Hanes's	TANTOUL (USA) (T. P. Burns)	9.0	M. V. O'Brien
		Ch. colt Tatan – Lebkuchen.		
8	Mr J. W. Galbreath's	GRENFALL (USA) (J. Roe)	9.0	M. V. O'Brien
		Ch. colt Graustark – Primonetta.		
9	Mr R. More O'Ferrall's	PARNELL (A. Simpson) Ch. colt St Paddy – Nella.	9.0	S. Quirke
10	Mr J. R. Brown's	TURBULENT EDDY (S. G. Spinks) B. colt Whistling Wind – Natty.	9.0	C. L. Weld
11	Mr T. W. Nicholson's	MERRY SLIPPER (T. Carberry)	9.0	P. Mullins
		Ch. colt Red Slipper – Merry Tola.		
12	Sir Gervais Tennyson D'Eyncourt's	BAYONS MANOR (P. Cook) Ch. colt Saint Crespin III – Lovely Lady II.	9.0	A. M. Budgett (GB)
13	Mr A. D. Brennan's	WACOSO (L. W. Johnson) Ch. colt Soderini – Waco II.	9.0	K. Prendergast
14	Mr S. McGrath's	ALL TAN (G. McGrath) Br. colt Tarqogan – All Saved.	9.0	Owner
15	Mrs D. McCalmont's	LINDEN TREE (FR) (D. Keith) Ch. colt Crepello – Verbena.	9.0	P. T. Walwyn (GB)

SP 7/4 Linden Tree; 7/2 IRISH BALL; 13/2 Lombardo; 7/1 Parnell, Grenfall; 16/1 Guillemot, Music Man; 22/1 Tantoul; 100/1 Bar. TOTE (20p unit) 96p. Places 48p, 46p, 82p.
3 lengths, short head. 2m 36.6s.
Winner trained by M P. H. Lalei at Chantilly, France.

Guillemot in that race suggested that Mill Reef was simply improving with every race. They met again in the Prix de l'Arc de Triomphe, where Mill Reef set the seal on his greatness, while Irish Ball finished well down the field. In his final race Irish Ball finished six lengths off Run the Gauntlet in the Washington DC International and was then retired to stud in England, whence he followed his sire to Japan, before any of his stock had even seen a racecourse.

Irish Ball provided Emile Littler – later knighted for his services to the theatre – with his greatest racecourse success. In previous years he had had horses in training with Walter Nightingall at Epsom, many of them named after his stage productions. By this time his racing and breeding activities were concentrated in France, under the care of Chantilly trainer, Philippe Lallie, at Chantilly. A former amateur rider, Lallie trained a string of seventy horses for his distinguished clientele, besides being extensively involved in bloodstock breeding. He had previously been responsible for such good performers as Fric, winner of the Coronation Cup in 1957, Miss Dan and Girl Friend.

Twenty-six-year-old Alfred Gibert, who had made a winning debut in Ireland, had come in for a lot of criticism for his handling of Irish Ball at Epsom, a course which has proved the downfall of so many of his countrymen. After that race he had been dismissed, both unfairly and inaccurately as a 'jump jockey', though he had never in fact ridden over obstacles. His smooth performance at the Curragh showed the qualities which were to make him champion jockey in France some years later.

Parnell recovered his earlier form to win the Irish St Leger, in which Lucky Drake finished third, and went on to prove himself a high-class, consistent and courageous racehorse. Twice successful in the Prix Jean Prat, he won the Jockey Club Cup at Newmarket and gave the great Brigadier Gerard a memorable race in the King George VI and Queen Elizabeth Stakes at Ascot. Having spent one season at stud in Ireland and another in France, Parnell was exported to Brazil in 1976. The other runners in the Irish Sweeps Derby of 1971 did little by their subsequent performances to enhance the value of that form. Linden Tree went to stud in France, All Tan in England and Guillemot in Colombia.

1972

For the eighth time since its inception the Irish Sweeps Derby had attracted the Epsom Derby winner and almost inevitable favourite, Roberto. Though Roberto had credited Vincent O'Brien with his fourth victory in Britain's greatest race, and Lester Piggott with his sixth, his success had not been by any means generally popular, specifically because the owner, John Galbreath, had stood down the recently-injured Bill Williamson at the eleventh hour, giving the mount to Piggott instead. Left without a mount in the Epsom Derby, a race he had never won, the Australian ace had won on his only two rides later that day, each time returning to a tremendous public ovation. On this occasion neither Williamson nor Piggott had the mount on Roberto, which went to the reigning Irish champion, Johnny Roe, retained by O'Brien in Ireland. Deprived of the Sweeps Derby ride on Roberto, as he had been on Sir Ivor and Nijinsky, Piggott had opted for Paddy Prendergast's charge, Ballymore. In spite of his particularly dreadful joints, which had kept him off the course as a two-year-old, Ballymore had made a spectacular winning debut in the Irish Two Thousand Guineas. In that race he finished a long way in front of High Top, Roberto's conqueror in the English Two Thousand Guineas, being acclaimed by Paddy Prendergast as the best that he had ever trained. Though Ballymore's only subsequent race had been a fiasco, Piggott was quietly confident that he would enable him to carry off the Derby treble previously accomplished only by Rae Johnstone in 1948. The sole French challenger was Lyphard, second favourite at Epsom, where he had all but careered off the course. Ridden once again by Freddy Head, Lyphard now sported blinkers and was expected to appreciate the sweeping Curragh bends more than the tricky Epsom track. Of the others, Scottish Rifle had finished in front of Steel Pulse and Manitoulin at Epsom, where Steel Pulse had received a very rough passage. Ridden by Bill Williamson, Steel Pulse was a popular choice to provide his rider with compensation for that Epsom disappointment. Perhaps more to the point, he was rated a clear winner by the Sporting Life's form expert, Dick Whitford. Despite his desperately hard race against Rheingold at Epsom, Roberto looked a picture of health in the parade, happily oblivious of the predictions of another Sporting Life pundit, biodynamics expert Patrick Evens, whose calculations indicated that 'Roberto will have an off day'.

After Scottish Rifle had caused a mild panic in the parade by unseating Ron Hutchinson, Extension then refused to enter the stalls. Eventually dragged in by his jockey, Christy Roche, Extension came out the other side like a bat out of hell, true to his role as pacemaker for Ballymore. Soon in a clear lead, Extension made the running for six furlongs, with Star Lark, Scottish Rifle, Ballymore and Steel Pulse most prominent amongst his pursuers. At the half way stage Extension faltered, giving way to Star Lark, who turned into the straight ahead of Scottish Rifle, Steel Pulse and Ballymore. Already Roberto had begun to show that only believers in biodynamics were likely to benefit from his performance. Sweeping past Star Lark, Scottish Rifle and Steel Pulse drew clear of the rest of the field, locked in an unremitting struggle, in which Steel Pulse gradually inched ahead of his tenacious opponent to pass the post a length to the good. All at sea under pressure, Ballymore pursued an erratic course up the straight to take third place six lengths further back, just ahead of the outsider Star Lark. Both Lyphard and Manitoulin came with belated runs, which never looked likely to succeed. Even the soft ground in the early stages could not explain Roberto's dismal performance, which saw him beat only two others, the pacemaking Extension and the injured Bog Road. Putting financial considerations aside, the sporting crowd gave Bill Williamson a rousing reception as he returned to the winner's enclosure. A double on Pidget in the supporting race, the Pretty Polly Stakes, made this a day to remember for the normally sad-faced Australian.

A well-made dark brown colt by Diatome, Steel Pulse was bred in England by Mr Eric Covell at the Southdown Stud and had been bought as a yearling for 4000gns by his jubilant owner, Mr Ravi Tikkoo, who revealed at the traditional post-race interview session that, in sixteen years of ownership, Steel Pulse was the first animal that he had bought entirely on his own judgement. By the French champion racehorse and sire Sicambre, Diatome was a top-class performer, whose misfortune it had been to be foaled in the same year as Sea Bird II and Reliance. As it was, his six successes included the Prix Ganay and the Washington DC International. Steel Pulse came from Diatome's second crop, and he sired such as Margouillat, Jakomima and Claudio Nicolai, before joining the endless exodus of stallions to Japan. Rachel, the dam of Steel Pulse, was a leading three-year-old in England in 1961, winning the Nassau Stakes at Goodwood. Her maternal grandsire was Phideas, winner of the Irish Derby in 1937. Trained by Sam Armstrong until the spring of his second season, Steel Pulse had won four times as a two-year-old, including twice in France, where he also finished a close and somewhat unlucky second to Hard to Beat in the Grand Criterium. Hard to Beat went on to win the French Derby and when he in turn was comfortably beaten by Rheingold in the Grand Prix de Saint-Cloud the Classic picture became more than ever confused. Nor did the subsequent performances of Steel Pulse do anything to clarify the situation, for he never ran up to his Curragh form again. Having finished a respectable fourth to Brigadier Gerard in the King George VI and Queen Elizabeth Stakes, he then started favourite for the St Leger, only to trail in last behind Boucher. Unplaced in both the Prix de l'Arc de Triomphe and the Champion Stakes, Steel Pulse showed a flash of his best form when third behind Droll Role and Parnell in the Washington DC International. After two unsuccessful runs as a four-year-old Steel Pulse was sold to go to Australia as a stallion.

The inspiration which had prompted him to buy Steel Pulse on his own judgement was characteristic of the flair and judgement which had made Kashmiri Ravi Tikkoo the owner of the largest fleet of tankers in the world. At the time of his Curragh victory, which marked his first visit to Ireland, Ravi Tikkoo was awaiting delivery of two super-tankers, costing almost £20,000,000. Having become one of the most lavish and successful owners in these islands, Tikkoo transferred his racing interests to France in 1975, in protest against the Value Added Tax levied on bloodstock in Britain. Having campaigned both there and in the United States, Tikkoo relented sufficiently to resume racing, though on a much reduced scale in England in 1978.

The success of Steel Pulse in the Irish Sweeps Derby provided consolation not only for Bill Williamson but also for his trainer A. E. 'Scobie' Breasley, thrice placed in the race as a jockey, notably on Charlottown. It was one of the few major races to elude him in a lengthy and distinguished riding career, which saw him recognised as the most successful, if not actually the greatest Australian to ride in these islands since the last World War. Born in Wogga Wogga – beloved by the British sporting Press – Scobie, so called after an Australian trainer of that name, was apprenticed to T. B. Quinlan in 1928 and rode his first big winner the following year, aged only fifteen. Having won the valuable Caulfield Cup for four years in a row, Scobie accepted an offer to go to England to ride for J. V. Rank in 1949, won the Two Thousand Guineas on Ki Ming in 1951, and returned to Australia. Two years later he set out for England again, for what he announced as his last season in the saddle . . . Fully fourteen years later, having survived four dreadful falls, won the Epsom Derby twice, and headed the jockeys' list on four occasions, 'the ageless Australian' finally retired to begin training at Epsom. One of his most successful partnerships had been with Sir Gordon Richards, whose own inimitable riding style had contrasted so vividly with Breasley's ice-cool, come-from-behind, hands and heels technique. During their lengthy association as trainer and jockey Richards never gave Breasley any instructions, reasoning that a good jockey needs no orders and a bad jockey is unable to execute them anyway!

Throughout the early sixties the dying weeks of the English Flat season were frequently enlivened by the battles for the jockeys' championship between this quiet-spoken, popular veteran and the comparatively youthful Lester Piggott. By then firmly established as one of the great jockeys of all time, Piggott found himself repeatedly locked in combat with a man who had been married on the same day that he, Lester, had been born! After forty years in the saddle Scobie Breasley retired at the end of 1968 to begin training. Steel Pulse provided him his greatest training success in these islands, as a prelude to his departure to France with the Tikkoo horses. Having moved yet again to America, at Tikkoo's behest, Scobie Breasley returned to England in 1978, set up at Epsom as a public trainer, and rapidly resumed his old winning ways.

Though Scobie Breasley seemed to have been in the forefront of English racing for so long that many believed him to be at least as old as Charlie Chaplin, he looked positively youthful compared to Steel Pulse's rider, fellow-Australian Bill Williamson, aptly dubbed 'Weary Willie'. Actually eight years Breasley's junior, Bill Williamson had come to Europe in 1960 to ride for Seamus McGrath. The pair met for the first time at Sandown, where they promptly kicked off on a winning note in the Coronation Stakes with Lucky Guy. This auspicious start was the prelude to three immensely successful seasons for the McGrath stable, during which their beautifully-bred horses realised their true potential in the hands of this quiet, relaxed, world-class rider, who was rated second only to George Moore in his native country. One of their most memorable triumphs was achieved with Le Levanstell, who upset the peerless Piggott-Petite Etoile partnership at Ascot, Williamson's lucky course. Thereafter Williamson moved to England to ride for Harry Wragg, winning the One Thousand Guineas and the Timeform Gold Cup twice, as well as the Prix de l'Arc de Triomphe on Vaguely Noble. In 1969 Williamson and Seamus McGrath renewed their allegiance through the medium of a son of Le Levanstell. This was Levmoss, on whom Williamson achieved an unique treble in the Ascot Gold Cup, the French Gold Cup and the Prix de l'Arc de Triomphe, a feat which led Williamson to rate Levmoss the greatest horse he ever rode. His success in the Irish Sweeps Derby on Steel Pulse completed a nap hand in the Irish Classics, besides erasing the memory of that narrow defeat on Arctic Storm in the inaugural Irish Sweeps Derby ten years earlier. The following season Bill Williamson, the supreme big-race rider, gave up his long battle with the scales, becoming Ravi Tikkoo's racing manager, before returning to Australia three years later to act as Assistant Starter in his native Melbourne, where he died in 1978 after a prolonged illness.

By curious coincidence, both Steel Pulse and Scottish Rifle, the dominant forces in that Irish Sweeps Derby, both belonged to shipping magnates. However, there the similarity ended, for Mr Struthers' unfashionably-bred colt continued to improve, winning the Eclipse Stakes the following season, and being placed in both the King George VI and Queen Elizabeth Stakes and the Benson and Hedges Gold Cup, before retiring to stud in England. Ballymore, unable to race again as a three-year-old, reappeared the next year to beat both Roberto and Weavers' Hall. With Exdirectory and More So amongst his first crop, Ballymore seems certain to prove a worthy successor to his sire, Ragusa, at the Mullions' Ardenode Stud. Lyphard had already emerged as the leading first-season stallion in France before his hurried and regrettable removal to America in 1977.

Saturday, 1st July, 1972   **£58,905**   **14 Ran**   **1½m**

The Irish Sweeps Derby (Group 1). £30,000 and a trophy value £500 added to the stakes by Irish Hospitals' Sweepstakes. For three years old entire colts and fillies. One mile and a half.

Sweepstakes, £10 at entry on 8th July, 1970, or £30 at second entry on 4th November, 1970; £40 extra for acceptors on 13th October, 1971, £50 extra for accepts on 22nd March, 1972, £50 extra for acceptors on 10th May, 1972, £100 additional for final acceptors on 7th June, 1972. Second to receive 15%, third 10% of the whole stakes after deduction of bonuses to owners at entry as follows – winner £500, second £300, third £200. Colts, 9st; Fillies, 8st 11lb.

The Racing Board will contribute a sum equal to 5% of the whole stakes (after deduction of bonuses) to the owner of the fourth horse if there are eight or more runners.

Note—Subject to the usual conditions the Racing Board will pay special allowances as follows towards the transport costs of runners from abroad in this race:– Great Britain, £200 per horse; other European countries, £250 per horse; other countries, £500 per horse.

(569 subs)

1	Mr Ravi N. Tikkoo's	STEEL PULSE (W. Williamson) 9.0 Br. colt Diatome – Rachel by Tudor Minstrel.	A. E. Breasley (UK)
2	Mr A. J. Struthers's	SCOTTISH RIFLE (Ron 9.0 Hutchinson) Br. colt Sunny Way – Radiopye.	J. L. Dunlop (UK)
3	Mrs J. R. Mullion's	BALLYMORE (L. Piggott) 9.0 B. colt Ragusa – Paddy's Sister.	P. J. Prendergast
4	Comte Antoine de Laubespin's	STAR LARK (Thomas Murphy) 9.0 B. colt Le Levanstall – Fuiseog.	M. Hurley
5	Mme P. Wertheimer's	LYPHARD (F. Head) 9.0 B. colt Northern Dancer – Goofed.	Alec Head (FR)
6	Mrs J. W. Galbreath's	MANITOULIN (M. Kennedy) 9.0 B. colt Tom Rolfe – Oak Cluster.	M. V. O'Brien
7	Mr M. McStay's	BOLD BID (T. Carberry) 9.0 Br. colt Bold Lad (IRE) – Meld's Relation.	M. Connolly
8	Mrs P. W. McGrath's	PARDNER (R. F. Parnell) 9.0 B. colt Pardao – Messene.	S. McGrath
9	Mr J. R. Brown's	KING CHARLES (J. V. Smith) 9.0 B. colt Le Levanstall – King's Victress.	D. K. Weld
10	Mr N. Bunker Hunt's	FALAISE (B. Marsh) 9.0 Br. colt Pretendre – Festiva.	T. Curtin
11	Mr E. P. Taylor's	BUCKSTOPPER (H. Cope) 9.0 Ch. colt Buckpasser – Northern Queen.	M. V. O'Brien
12	Mr J. W. Galbreath's	ROBERTO (J. Roe) 9.0 B. colt Hail to Reason – Bramalea.	M. V. O'Brien
13	Mrs J. R. Mullion's	EXTENSION (C. Roche) 9.0 B. colt Continuation – Sliprullah.	P. J. Prendergast
14	Mr S. McGrath's	BOG ROAD (G. McGrath) 9.0 B. colt Busted – Royal Danseuse.	Owner

SP 15/8 Roberto; 3/1 Ballymore; 7/2 Lyphard; 10/1 STEEL PULSE, Bog Road; 16/1 Scottish Rifle; 33/1 Buckstopper, Manitoulin; 66/1 Pardner; 100/1 Bar. TOTE (20p unit) £2.84. Places 62p, 60p, 48p.

1 length, 6 lengths, 1 length. 2m 39.8s.
Winner trained by Mr A. E. Breasley at Epsom, England.

It was perhaps inevitable in such a topsy-turvy Classic year that Roberto, having trailed in nearly last at the Curragh, should reappear to do what no other horse ever managed to do – defeat Brigadier Gerard. They met in the ten-furlong Benson and Hedges Gold Cup at York. Piggott opted to ride Rheingold, so O'Brien offered the ride on Roberto to Williamson, Ironically, he was already engaged to ride at Ostend, where he landed a double. Once again John Galbreath intervened, importing the American ace, Braulio Baeza. The mighty Brigadier Gerard, unbeaten in three seasons, was attempting to equal Ribot's unbeaten sequence and was regarded as a certainty. Setting off in front, with Baeza crouched almost invisible on his neck, Roberto proceded to run Brigadier Gerard into the ground, winning utterly convincingly in record time. An incredulous Jean Hislop, at a loss to account for the humilation of her hitherto invincible champion, could only suggest that Roberto had been stung by a bee! The truth of the matter was that Roberto, given the top of the ground and allowed to make his own running, was a very, very good racehorse, as he demonstrated by his ridiculously easy success in the Coronation Cup the following season, prior to his return to America to take up stud duty.

1973

In yet another year of clouded Classic form the millions of words written before the Epsom Derby had not contained more than a passing reference to the ultimate winner, Morston, a half-brother to Blakeney, by the recently-deceased Irish Sweeps Derby winner Ragusa. At Epsom Morston had narrowly, but convincingly, beaten Cavo Doro, thus thwarting Lester Piggott's bid to become the first man ever both to breed and ride the winner of that race. Morston had never been an intended runner at the Curragh and Cavo Doro had subsequently been withdrawn with an injured shoulder. This left Freefoot, Ksar, Ragapan and Natsun, third, fourth, fifth and eleventh respectively behind Morston, as representatives of the Epsom form. The blinkered Freefoot was still a maiden, Ksar seemed fatally lacking in finishing speed, and Natsun had finished a long way behind them at Epsom. This left Ragapan. This Irish record-priced yearling half-brother to the Irish One Thousand Guineas win ners, Front Row and Black Satin, was by Ragusa and thus likely to show continued improvement. Moreover, his jockey Bill Williamson was adamant that only interference had prevented him finishing a lot closer than he had at Epsom. Accordingly, he was made favourite in an undistinguished field for the Curragh spectacular, until displaced by an avalanche of money for Hail the Pirates, O'Brien's substitute for Cavo Doro, and the mount of Lester Piggott. The winner of four of his five races, including the Player-Wills and Gallinule Stakes, Hail the Pirates and Piggott caught the public's imagination in the absence of any outstanding runner. The McGrath-trained pair, Weavers' Hall and Park Lawn had both failed to live up to their juvenile promise and seemed to have little chance to credit their trainer with success in the race that he and his family mostly dearly wished to win. However, Weavers'

Hall had beaten Hail the Pirates as a two-year-old and Park Lawn, a half-brother to Park Top, had won the Railway Stakes. In any event, the McGraths had always adopted the policy that 'If you're not in, you can't win', both in their racing ventures and in promoting the Irish Hospitals Sweepstakes, with conspicuous success in both instances.

Blinkered for the first time in an effort to sharpen him up, Park Lawn reacted all too well to the stimulus, bolting out of the stalls and careering into a clear lead, with Buster Parnell, for once, powerless to apply restraint. Assisted by the gale force wind which howled across the Curragh, Park Lawn increased his lead to twenty and then thirty lengths. By the time his pursuers had caught him at the half way mark most of them were already off the bridle, two notable exceptions being Buoy and Weavers' Hall, who swept past the tiring Park Lawn as they turned into the buffeting headwind in the straight. Aware of Buoy's tendency to hang left-handed, George McGrath pushed Weavers' Hall into the lead earlier than intended and proceded to make the best of his way home, with Buoy and Hail the Pirates in unavailing pursuit. The only possible threat to Weavers' Hall now appeared in the form of Ragapan, under pressure from a long way out and racing with his head held high. With a furlong to run it became obvious that Weavers' Hall would not be caught and he galloped past the post amidst tumultuous applause, more fitted to a red-hot favourite than to the longest-priced winner since Zarathustra. As Weavers' Hall was led back to the winner's circle the cheering erupted again with renewed vigour, reflecting popular satisfaction at a thoroughly appropriate success in the race he had inspired for the 'Green, red seams and cap' first registered by the late Joe McGrath.

Bred by the McGrath Trust Company, Weavers' Hall was owned and trained by Seamus McGrath at Glencairn. Seamus, who had sent out Panaslipper to win the 'old' Irish Derby for his father almost twenty years earlier, revealed at the wind-swept post-race Press conference that the Irish Sweeps Derby had always been the main objective for Weavers' Hall and that his main fear had been the firm state of the going, despite extensive watering during the preceding week. Sharing in Seamus McGrath's success were his brothers Paddy, Chairman of the Racing Board, and Joe, responsible for the family's bloodstock breeding interests and, as such, the man directly concerned with the mating which had produced this, the most satisfying of the numerous McGrath triumphs in high-class races throughout Europe. Weavers' Hall descended from one of the most prolific and successful Brownstown families. His grandam, Damians, was useless on the racecourse, but bred Sixpence, the fastest two-year-old of her generation, Continuation, winner of the Royal Hunt Cup, and, finally, Marians. Successful as a two-year-old, Marians was rated initially with Pall Mall and produced All In All, winner of the Irish Lincolnshire. It was the desire to increase the stamina of the line, which, though successful all over the world, had never produced a winner at distances in excess of a mile, which had prompted Joe McGrath to mate Marians with Busted, the leading racehorse in Europe as a four-year-old. The result brilliantly justified his choice, for Weavers' Hall provided the McGraths with a resounding triumph in the race which remains a monument to the memory of one of the outstanding figures of Irish racing.

George McGrath, the winning rider, was no relation to the owner, trainer and breeder, the similarity in surnames being quite coincidental, as well as reminiscent of the Connollys, Tom the trainer and John the jockey, a century earlier. Champion apprentice when attached to Kevin Kerr's Summerseat stable, George McGrath became stable jockey at Glencairn in 1965 and won the first of his two Irish jockeys' championships that year. In 1970 he rode his only previous Irish Classic winner, and headed the list for the second time. Having fulfilled his greatest ambition by winning the Irish Sweeps Derby on Weavers' Hall, George McGrath became attached to Richard Annesley's Curragh stable when the McGraths reduced their number of horses in training. With the closure of the Annesley stable a year later George McGrath found good rides less plentiful. However, his forceful, bustling style is still seen to good effect when opportunities allow, and nowhere with greater effect than at Leopardstown, where he has few peers.

Following his convincing success in the Irish Sweeps Derby the prospects seemed unlimited for Weavers' Hall, particularly with the enforced retirement of Morston. Sadly, Weavers' Hall only made one more racecourse appearance, when fourth to that brilliant filly Dahlia in the King George VI and Queen Elizabeth Stakes at Ascot, where he finished in front of such as Parnell, Hard To Beat, Scottish Rifle and Roberto. Subsequent training problems forced his retirement to stud at Brownstown, where he now stands. Ragapan, second in the Irish Sweeps Derby, never quite lived up to expectations. Unplaced both in the St Leger and the Prix de l'Arc de Triomphe, he was retired to stud in Co. Cork, Buoy, who did best of the English quintet at the Curragh, finished second to Peleid in the St Leger and won the Coronation Cup, the Yorkshire Cup and the Princess of Wales Stakes as a four-year-old, prior to his departure to New Zealand. Hail the Pirates won another semi-Classic, the Desmond Stakes, the Chesterfield Cup under 10st, and the PTS Laurels as a five-year-old before his departure to the United States. Freefoot finally won a race when he scrambled home in the John Porter Stakes at Newbury as a four-year-old. His ultimate destiny proved to be Poland. Ksar won at Deauville and San Siro and finished second to Scottish Rifle in the Eclipse Stakes, while Laurentian Hills won the Moet et Chandon 'Amateurs' Derby' at Epsom.

Best of a moderate lot proved to be Star Appeal, only seventh behind Weavers' Hall. Having finished a poor third in the Irish St Leger, Star Appeal was then successful at Baden Baden, where he was purchased for £10,000 by Mr Zeitelhack to remain in training in Germany in the care of Theo Grieper. Undistinguished as a four-year-old, Star Appeal came good with a vengeance the following season, during which he was successful in England, France, Germany and Italy. This blinkered but courageous product of Italian and German parentage caused mild surprise when winning the Gran Premio di Milano, downright dismay when successful in the Eclipse Stakes, and utter consternation when weaving his way like a snipe through the field to slam the best in Europe in the Prix de l'Arc de Triomphe. Reluctantly recognised as the best racehorse in this part of the world, he was retired to stand at the English National Stud. Whatever his claims to international fame, Star Appeal will forever remain the greatest horse ever to run at imperilled Dundalk, should they race there till Doomsday!

Saturday, 30th June, 1973   **£62,495**   **15 Ran**   **1½m**

Irish Sweeps Derby (Group 1). £30,000 and a trophy value £500 added to the stakes by Irish Hospitals' Sweepstakes. For three years old entire colts and fillies. One mile and a half.

Sweepstakes £25 to enter, 23rd February, 1972; £60 extra for acceptors on 11th October, 1972; £50 extra for acceptors on 21st March, 1973; £60 additional for acceptors on 6th June, 1973; £100 extra if declared to run. Second to receive 15%, and the third 10% of the whole stakes after deduction of bonuses to breeders as follows – Winner £500; Second £300; Third £200. Weights – Colts 9st; Fillies 8st 11lb.

The Racing Board will contribute a sum equal to 5% of the whole stakes (after deduction of the bonuses) to the owner of the fourth horse if there are eight or more runners.

Note—Subject to the usual conditions the Racing Board will pay special allowances as follows towards the transport costs of runners from abroad in this race:– Great Britain, £200 per horse; other European countries, £250 per horse; other countries, £500 per horse.

1	Mr Seamus McGrath's	WEAVERS' HALL (G. McGrath) 9.0	Owner
		B. colt Busted – Marians by Macherio.	
2	Mr F. O'Sullivan's	RAGAPAN (W. Williamson) 9.0	K. Prendergast
		B. colt Ragusa – Panaview.	
3	Mr R. D.	BUOY (J. Mercer) 9.0	W. R. Hern (GB)
	Hollingsworth's	Ch. colt Aureole – Ripeak.	
4	Mr Daniel M.	HAIL THE PIRATES 9.0	M. V. O'Brien
	Galbreath's	(L. Piggott) B. colt Hail to Reason – Bravura.	
5	Lady Rotherwick's	KSAR (W. Carson) 9.0	B. van Cutsem (GB)
		Ch. colt Kalydon – Castle Mona.	
6	Mr N. Cohen's	NATSUN (F. Head) 9.0	B. Hills (GB)
		B. colt Soleil – Venante.	
7	Mrs Mehl-Muelhens's	STAR APPEAL (H. Cope) 9.0	J. Oxx
		B. colt Appiani – Sterna.	
8	Mr R. Eastwood's	NORTH WALL (P. Sullivan) 9.0	M. A. O'Toole
		B. colt King's Troop – Romp.	
9	Mrs J. F. C. Bryce's	LAURENTIAN HILLS 9.0	R. W. Armstrong
		(G. Starkey) Br. colt Hill Rise – Rave Notice. (GB)	
10	Lady Iveagh's	DECIMO (C. Roche) 9.0	P. J. Prendergast
		B. colt Stupendous – Padante.	
11	Mr R. B. Moller's	FREEFOOT (J. Lindley) 9.0	H. Wragg (GB)
		B. colt Relko – Close-Up.	
12	Mr N. B. Hunt's	TALL NOBLE (Thomas Murphy) 9.0	T. G. Curtin
		B. colt Vaguely Noble – Lola Montes.	
13	Mr M. Gallagher's	ALCHOPAL (J. Roe) 9.0	C. Grassick
		B. colt Paveh – Smith Original.	
14	Mr J. B. Moss's	TEKOAH (G. Curran) 9.0	K. Prendergast
		B/Br. colt Great White Way – Tatelka.	
15	Mr Joseph McGrath's	PARK LAWN (R. F. Parnell) 9.0	S. McGrath
		Ch. colt Lauso – Nellie Park.	

SP 11/4 Hail the Pirates; 7/2 Ragapan; 4/1 Buoy; 5/1 Ksar; 13/2 Freefoot; 16/1 Natsun, Laurentian Hills; 33/1 WEAVERS' HALL; 40/1 Decimo; 80/1 North Wall; 200/1 Bar. TOTE (20p unit) £4.38. Places 88p, 52p, 56p.
2 lengths, 1½ lengths, 2 lengths. 2m 32s.
Winner trained by Mr Seamus McGrath at Sandyford, Co. Dublin.

1974

Yet another record prize fund for the Irish Sweeps Derby – over £100,000 – had attracted a very strong overseas challenge, which dominated the betting market. The favourite, Imperial Prince, a half-brother to the triple Classic winner Altesse Royale, had finished second in the Epsom Derby to the rank outsider Show Knight and was confidently supported to provide Colonel Hue-Williams, Noel Murless and Geoff Lewis with handsome compensation at the Curragh. A late foal, and consequently unraced as a two-year-old, Imperial Prince had made a winning debut in the Wood Ditton Stakes, in which Red Canute, another of the English-trained quartet, had finished third. Second to Jupiter Pluvius at Chester, with Sir Penfro well in arrears, Imperial Prince having only the third race of his life when staying on strongly to finish second at Epsom, with Mistigri in sixth place. Next in demand were the French pair, Caracolero and Mississipian, first and fourth in the Prix du Jockey-Club. Caracolero, Lester Piggott's ultimate choice in a season marred by dramatic jockey switching, was the first French Derby winner ever to challenge for the Irish equivalent. Gorfou, the third French participant, though a winner over the distance at Longchamp, did not seem up to this standard. The home-trained contingent was headed by Sir Penfro and Furry Glen. The latter had beaten Pitcairn in a desperate finish for the Irish Two Thousand Guineas and had subsequently been short-headed by Sir Penfro in the Gallinule Stakes. For many among the glamourous, sun-baked throng the biggest danger to Imperial Prince was English Prince, owned by Mrs Hue-Williams and trained especially for this race by Peter Walwyn. Only the previous week English Prince had broken the course record when winning the King Edward VII Stakes over a mile and a half at Royal Ascot. Spurned by Lester Piggott, English Prince was ridden by the French champion Yves Saint-Martin in place of stable jockey Pat Eddery, under suspension for his part in a remarkable Queen Anne Stakes at Ascot, where the Stewards had disqualified the first three past the post. The start was scarcely delayed by a bomb scare in the packed grandstand, swiftly and efficiently dealt with by racecourse manager Paddy Connolly's well-drilled staff. The general reluctance to evacuate the stand confirmed to the many overseas visitors present that it takes more than a threat of being blown to bits to deter Irish racegoers from witnessing the fate of their fancy!

From a level break Pythia settled down in his role as pacemaker for Mississipian, showing ahead of Appleby Fair, English Prince and the stable companions Furry Glen and Love Tale. The order remained unchanged until the field began to swing downhill towards the straight, when Appleby Fair took over, shadowed by English Prince, with Imperial Prince, Mississipian, Mistigri and Sir Penfro all still in close contention. What looked to be anybody's race then developed into a procession, for fully five furlongs out Saint-Martin went on with English Prince, who swept majestically up the long straight to hold off the unavailing challenge of Imperial Prince. Behind these two Mississipian ran on under pressure to take third place, veering right across the course in the process interfering with the chances of Sir Penfro. The Stewards promptly announced an inquiry and reversed the placings of third and fourth, a verdict with which not even the most biased supporters of Mississipian could disagree. Furry Glen found the going too fast and the journey too far, while Caracolero never at any stage looked likely to repay the compliment of being Piggott's chosen mount.

By their unique one-two Colonel Hue-Williams and his wife netted £90,993, in addition to the 10 per cent breeders' premium under the recently-instituted Irish Stallion Incentive Scheme. At the Press conference conducted by the suave and smiling Spencer Freeman, Russian-born Vera Hue-Williams related in husky tones how she and her husband had talked endlessly about the possibility of either of their colts winning the Irish Derby, emphasising that they had discussed their prospects as partners rather than rivals! Their obvious delight was enhanced by the fact that both colts had been bred at their Rathasker Stud at nearby Naas. Mrs Hue-Williams was no stranger to success in big races, for over twenty years earlier, as Mrs T. Lilley, she had won the Festival of Britain Stakes (forerunner to the King George VI and Queen Elizabeth Stakes) with Supreme Court. On the death of her second husband, Tom Lilly, of Lilley & Skinner fame, in 1959, she had carried on their breeding operations at the Woolton House Stud near Newbury and the Rathasker Stud at Naas, where the Irish Two Thousand Guineas winner Kythnos was bred. Two years later, having married industrialist and stockbroker Roger Hue-Williams, she had achieved her first Classic success when Aurelius won the St Leger. Her husband, who adopted the late Tom Lilley's colours, had also achieved Classic success both in England and in Ireland through Altesse Royale, who added the Irish Oaks to her triumphs in both English fillies' Classics.

The victory of his son English Prince over Imperial Prince, a son of Sir Ivor, provided Petingo with a measure of consolation as it were for his defeat by the brilliant Sir Ivor in the Two Thousand Guineas six years earlier. Unbeaten until then, Petingo had won the Gimcrack and Middle Park Stakes and went on to win the St James' Palace Stakes at Ascot and the Sussex Stakes at Goodwood. Retired to the Simmonstown Stud, as one of Tim Rogers' galaxy of high-class stallions, Petingo had got off to a flying start by siring Satingo, the leading two-year-old in France, in his first crop. Satingo was followed by such as Pitskelly, Miss Petard and Pitcairn, and the tragedy of Petingo's premature demise in 1976 was emphasised by the dual Oaks success of his daughter Fair Salinia two years later. English Miss: a winner at two and three years, had bred seven foals, best of whom had been Mirella, Rascolnik and Relate, prior to producing English Prince.

Success in the Irish Sweeps Derby was a matter of third time lucky for trainer Peter Walwyn, atoning for the earlier disappointment of Crozier and the disaster of Linden Tree, the reluctant favourite three years previously. Peter Tyndall Walwyn had learned his trade under Geoffrey Brooke at Newmarket before succeeding Charles Jerdein as the licence-holder for his cousin Helen Johnson Houghton. In 1961 he had struck out on his own at Windsor House, Lambourn, achieving recognition through the consistent successes of that gallant old gelding Be Hopeful. He subsequently moved into Seven Barrows, where he saw his pursuit of perfection rewarded by the Classics exploits of Mable, Linden Tree, Shoemaker, Humble Duty and Polygamy, successful in the Epsom Oaks a few weeks earlier, making a vital contribution to Peter Walwyn's first English training championship, narrowly exceeding Dick Hern's record stakes total achieved two years before.

Peter Walwyn refused to be drawn concerning future plans for English Prince and his eager interrogators had to content themselves instead with information on the colt's career to date. Training problems had made it impossible to get him onto a racecourse as a two-year-old and a promising debut at Newbury in April had prefaced an impressive success in the White Rose Stakes at Ascot, which had brought him into the reckoning as an Epsom Derby contender. However, one gallop on the old Derby Trial Ground, with its left-handed, downhill turn similar to Tattenham Corner, had caused such difficulties for English Prince that Walwyn had promptly advised his owner to forget about Epsom and aim for the Curragh instead, with the consequent happy outcome. Having won four of his five races, English Prince was rested with the St Leger in view. In the meantime Walwyn's stable was virtually shut down for a while by a virus and when English Prince reappeared in a three-horse race for the Great Voltigeur Stakes there were fears that he might not be at his best. Starting odds-on, he failed to cope with Bustino, injured himself in running and was subsequently retired to Ballylinch Stud, Co. Kilkenny at a fee of £2000. In his only season to race English Prince had won four times and been second in his other two races with winnings of £91,284. As it transpired, he would have been put to the pin of his collar to beat Bustino, who went on to a convincing success in the St Leger and the following season gave Grundy the hardest race of his life in the King George VI and Queen Elizabeth Stakes.

For French champion Yves Saint-Martin it was also a case of third time lucky at the Curragh. In 1963 he had paid his first visit to Ireland, seemingly certain to add yet another Derby to his growing tally, only to be left to hurl his helmet to the ground as Relko's mysterious lameness and enforced withdrawal left the way clear for Ragusa. Eight years later Saint-Martin's Curragh jinx had struck again as he brought Vincennes to challenge Altesse Royal in the Irish Oaks. With the race in the balance, Vincennes had jumped a shadow across her path, losing her momentum, and with it the race. However, in the intervening years since the Relko fiasco Francois Mathet's brilliant protege had won a further two English Classics on Altesse Royale and Nonoalco, the Washington DC International on Match and numerous French Classics in a career which saw him recognised as the only world-class French jockey since Roger Poincelet. In the process of winning the coveted cravache d'or – the French jockeys' championship – seven years in succession he had broken Frank O'Neill's record of 161 winners in one season which had stood since 1911. Though this dapper little Frenchman has always vigourously denied any antagonism towards his greatest rival, Lester Piggott, he was once suspended for a month for bringing down Piggott's mount in a race, while his jubilation knew no bounds when he conjured that incredible rally out of Sassafras to foil Nijinsky and Piggott in the Prix de l'Arc de Triomphe, a race that he was shortly to win again on his most famous mount, the fabulous filly Allez France.

Like his Curragh conqueror, Imperial Prince was destined never to win another race, though he did manage to turn the tables on Snow Knight when they finished second and third to Dahlia in the Benson & Hedges Gold Cup at York. Fourth to Bustino in the St Leger, Imperial Prince failed in his two races as a four-year-old and was promptly sold as a stallion to Australia. Sir Penfro won the Desmond Stakes and won on his final appearance in England the following season, prior to his departure to Japan. Mississipian, the leader of his generation in France as a two-year-old, won the Prix Neil Longchamp, finished down the field behind Allez France in the Prix de

Saturday, 29th June, 1974   **£74,945**   **13 Ran**   **1½m**

Irish Sweeps Derby (Group 1). £30,000 and a trophy value £500 added to the stakes by Irish Hospitals' Sweepstakes. For three years old entire colts and fillies. One mile and a half.

Sweepstakes, £25 to enter, 28th February, 1973; £60 extra for acceptors on 10th October, 1973; £50 extra for acceptors on 20th March, 1974; £60 additional for acceptors on 5th June, 1974; £100 extra if declared to run. Second to receive 15% and the third 10% of the whole stakes after deduction of bonuses to breeders as follows – Winner £500; Second £300; Third £200. Weights – Colts, 9st; Fillies, 8st 11lb.

The Racing Board will contribute a sum equal to 5% of the whole stakes (after deductions of bonuses) to the owner of the fourth horse if there are eight or more runners.

The Management Committee of the I.S.I.S. will pay to the breeder of each horse which is placed and which is qualified under that scheme an amount equal to 10% of the prize money payable to that horse.

Note—Subject to the usual conditions the Racing Board will pay special allowances as follows towards the transport costs of runners from abroad in this race:– Great Britain, £200 per horse; other European countries, £250 per horse; other countries, £500 per horse.

(744 subs)

1	Mrs V. Hue-Williams's	ENGLISH PRINCE (Y. Saint Martin) B. colt Petingo – English Miss by Bois Roussel.	9.0	P. T. Walwyn (GB)
2	Mr F. R. Hue-Williams's	IMPERIAL PRINCE (G. Lewis) B. colt Sir Ivor – Bleu Azur.	9.0	C. F. N. Murless (GB)
3	Mr J. R. Philipps's	SIR PENFRO (Thomas Murphy) Br. colt Sir Ivor – Running Blue.	9.0	M. V. O'Brien
4	Mr N. B. Hunt's	MISSISSIPIAN (USA)* (F. Head) B. colt Vaguely Noble – Gazala.	9.0	M. Zilber (FR)
5	Mr David Robinson's	RED CANUTE (B. Raymond) B. colt Hardicanute – Rosy Gleam.	9.0	M. A. Jarvis (GB)
6	Mr Alan Clore's	GORFOU (USA) (J. C. Desaint) Ch. colt Sea Bird – Sanelta.	9.0	G. Delloye (FR)
7	Mr P. W. McGrath's	FURRY GLEN (G. McGrath) B. colt Wolver Hollow – Cleftess.	9.0	S. McGrath
8	Mme Maria Felix Berger's	CARACOLERO (USA) (L. Piggott) Ch. colt Graustark – Betty Loraine.	9.0	F. Boutin (FR)
9	Mr J. J. Astor's	APPLEBY FAIR (J. Mercer) B. colt Charlottown – Vardo.	9.0	W. R. Hern (GB)
10	Mr E. R. More O'Ferrall's	MISTIGRI (C. Roche) B. colt Misti – Nyanga.	9.0	P. J. Prendergast
11	Mr S. McGrath's	FLOWER ROBE (R. F. Parnell) B. colt Ribero – Blaithne.	9.0	Owner
12	Mr N. B. Hunt's	PYTHIA (USA) (T. P. Burns) Ch. colt Vaguely Noble – Make Sail.	9.0	T. G. Curtin
13	Mr S. McGrath's	LOVE TALE (J. Roe) Br. colt Levmoss – Tuna Gail.	9.0	Owner

SP 11/5 Imperial Prince; 7/2 Caracolero; 5/1 Mississipian; 8/1 ENGLISH PRINCE; 12/1 Sir Penfro; 15/1 Furry Glen; 16/1 Appleby Fair, Mistigri; 33/1 Red Canute; 50/1 Gorfou; 100/1 Love Tale; 300/1 Bar. TOTE (20p unit) £1.48. Places 60p, 34p, 42p.

1½ lengths. 2m 33.4s.

Winner trained by Mr Peter T. Walwyn at Seven Barrows, Lambourn.

---

*Mississipian finished third, a length behind Imperial Prince, with Sir Penfro 3 lengths behind fourth. After a Steward's Enquiry the placings of Mississipian and Sir Penfro were reversed.

l'Arc de Triomphe, and retired to stud in America. Mistigri, responding to blinkers, won the Irish St Leger, before embarking on a singularly luckless career in high-class stayers' races. The others did little to enhance the standing of what was, nonetheless, a good Irish Sweeps Derby.

1975

This was the year of a flashy little chestnut called Grundy, and after his scintillating successes in the Irish Two Thousand Guineas and the Epsom Derby he became an odds-on favourite to achieve the Classic treble previously accomplished only by Santa Claus. The long, hot summer was all in his favour, for Grundy was at his best on the prevailing firm ground, which had caused the withdrawl of the fancied Irish colts, Sea Break and Nuthatch, both of whom had failed to act on similar terrain at Epsom. By his sparkling success over Nobiliary and Hunza Dancer in the Epsom Derby Grundy had dispelled any doubts concerning his stamina and only two factors prevented him starting at prohibitive odds for the Curragh Classic. The first was the high failure rate among Epsom Derby winners attempting the double previously achieved only by Orby, Santa Claus and Nijinsky. The other was the fantastic form in recent weeks of Vincent O'Brien and Lester Piggott OBE. O'Brien had taken eight horses to Ascot and won with seven of them, while Piggott, who had shared in four of those triumphs, had won nine races at the meeting. These champions in their respective spheres now combined to oppose Grundy with King Pellinore. A half-brother to Thatch and Lisadell, this $230,000 yearling had won his only two races that season, beating the Convivial Stakes winner Phoenix Hall by six lengths in the Gallinule Stakes. If Grundy were to be overthrown, this was the alliance most likely to cause his downfall. Maitland, the sole French challenger, had won his three previous races, all at Saint-Cloud. However, on a line through Parako, Val de l'Orne and Patch, he hardly seemed good enough, notwithstanding the services of Yves Saint-Martin. Sea Anchor had recently won the King Edward VII Stakes at Royal Ascot, the stepping stone to success employed by English Prince a year earlier, while Anne's Pretender, fourth at Epsom, was still fancied by his ever-optimistic trainer to reverse that form. Looking his best in the brilliant sunshine, as chestnuts always do, Grundy began to appear increasingly invincible.

Bent on exploiting the only possible flaw in Grundy's armour – his stamina – Saint-Martin shot Maitland out of the stalls ahead of Hobnob, Giggery, Anne's Pretender and the free-running King Pellinore, as Eddery calmly settled Grundy among the backmarkers. Having cut his own throat, Maitland gave way over half a mile from home to Anne's Pretender, on whom Tony Murray tried, as he had at Epsom, to get first run on his opponents. As Piggott slipped King Pellinore through a wall of horses in pursuit, Grundy was momentarily obscured from view. A split second later his flaxen mane and tail appeared on the outside. Once clear Grundy became a blond blur as he sped past his seemingly stationary rivals. The race was over there and then, for only King Pellinore managed to make any impression on

Grundy's lead as the winner galloped past the post with Eddery patting him on the neck. Beaten two lengths in the end, King Pellinore finished a long way in front of Anne's Pretender, who soldiered on to keep Sea Anchor out of third place. The others had long since ceased to count, other than as courtiers to the king of the day, Grundy.

Rescued from a swarm of well-wishers, Peter Walwyn recovered his composure in the sanctuary of a minibus to speak of Grundy as '. . . an extraordinary horse. I've never known another like him. He's so tough you can't keep him down.' At the ritual Press conference Walwyn quipped: 'I find coming to Ireland is good for the health'. Asked his views on Pat Eddery's riding, he answered: 'He's improving.' In response to an absolute gem from the hapless Noel Reid: 'Did last year's win by English Prince prove of any value to you?', the efferverscent Walwyn replied: 'The ten per cent certainly helped'. No less ecstatic at the success of his champion and the enthusiasm with which it was popularly acclaimed was wealthy Milanese industrialist Dr Carlo Vittadini, who had already witnessed Grundy's triumph in the Irish Two Thousand Guineas and had since seen his Orange Bay win the Italian Derby. Entering into the spirit of the occasion, Dr Vittadini caused momentary scandal among racing scribes by declaring that becoming a grandfather recently had given him greater pleasure than all his Classic successes!

For Pat Eddery, on his way to his second consecutive English jockeys' championship, success in the Irish Derby was particularly poignant; triumph in front of his countrymen compensating as it did for his missing the ride on English Prince twelve months earlier. Moreover, Grundy had enabled him to go one better than his father, Jimmy Eddery, who, twenty years previously, had gone so close on Panaslipper at Epsom prior to gaining consolation at the Curragh. One of a squad of children, Pat Eddery had been put up on racehorses in McGraths' at the age of ten by his father, who never doubted Pat's potential, declaring that he had 'the God-given gift of hands'. Sent over to 'Frenchie' Nicholson at Cheltenham to be both taught and tamed, Pat Eddery followed in the footsteps of Nicholson's earlier protege, Paul Cook, by becoming champion apprentice in 1971. When weight problems finally forced Duncan Keith to retire, Eddery landed the plum job of first jockey at Seven Barrows, rewarding Walwyn's initial faith and subsequent unswerving loyalty with the most consistently accomplished performance of any jockey now riding in England. Champion jockey in Britain – the first-ever Irishman to achieve that distinction under Jockey Club Rules – for four years in a row, Pat Eddery has developed into a delightfully stylish little rider, whose earlier impetuosity has matured into an uncanny sense of positioning and finesse unrivalled in Britain since Breasley's retirement.

A flashy but compact chestnut, distinguished by a bizarre white blaze, Grundy was bred by Edward and Tim Holland-Martin at their Overbury Stud in Gloucestershire, leading breeders in Britain in 1975. By Great Nephew, runner-up in both the Two Thousand Guineas and the Eclipse Stakes, Grundy was out of the Worden mare Word From Lundy. Having cost 11,000gns as a yearling, Grundy went through his first season undefeated in four races, including the Champagne Stakes and the Dewhurst Stakes, and was rated the top English two-year-old of his generation.

A severe kick in the face in March delayed Grundy's three-year-old preparation and successive defeats in the Greenham Stakes, by Mark Anthony, and in the Two

Thousand Guineas, by Bolkonski, led many to declare that Dr Vittadini and Peter Walwyn were doomed to a repetition of the disappointment they had suffered with Habat, a brilliant two-year-old that had failed to train on. Sent over to the Curragh to contest the Irish Two Thousand Guineas, Grundy won very easily from Monsanto and Mark Anthony. On the strength of this performance he returned to favour for the Epsom Derby, second in the betting to the impressive Prix Lupin winner, Green Dancer. Previewing that race, Tony Morris, the Sporting Life's breeding expert, wrote: 'Only at the highest level in racing can a study of breeding ever be a guide to winner-finding.' Of Grundy he had this to say: 'The only pattern race winner yet sired by his disappointing sire, he is out of a slow mare who was at her indifferent best around two miles. This does not look like the breeding of a Derby winner, but he has already won a classic, so he must not be underestimated.' Handsome is as handsome does, and Grundy's Derby double decisively vindicated the English National Stud's purchase of a three-parts share in him for £750,000 after Epsom.

Regrettably, the conditions of the National Stud deal stipulated that Grundy should retire at the end of his three-year-old career and that his permitted maximum of four more races after Epsom be confined to these islands. That effectively ruled out a tilt at the Prix de l'Arc de Triomphe and an opportunity to try conclusions with Allez France, a champion in her own country, whose prowess had repeatedly been endorsed by the exploits of Dahlia, always her bridesmaid at home, but virtually invincible abroad. Thus Grundy took on his seniors for the first time in the King George VI and Queen Elizabeth Stakes at Ascot. Though Allez France declined the challenge, France was represented by Dahlia, successful in the last two runnings of the race, Card King, On My Way and Ashmore. Star Appeal, whose recent surprise win in the Eclipse Stakes had been the first German victory in Britain since 1850, was also in the field, which included the Classic winners Dibidale and Busted, who had gone on to win the Coronation Cup in record time. The presence of not one but two pacemakers for Bustino evoked memories of the epic Ascot Gold Cup duel between Alycidon and Black Tarquin twenty-five years earlier . . .

The fateful day started well for Carlos Vittadini and Peter Walwyn, who won the first race on the card with Hard Day, ridden by Vittadini's accomplished daughter Franca. The stage was set for what many would describe quite simply as the greatest race they had ever seen. When Bustino stormed past his two exhausted pacemakers and blazed up the short Ascot straight he was fully four lengths ahead of Grundy, whose reputation now hung precariously in the balance. Answering unflinchingly to Eddey's every demand, Grundy closed with Bustino, both colts hurtling towards the line as straight as gunbarrels. Only inside the last hundred yards did Grundy's sheer class overcome Bustino's dogged courage and he passed the past half a length to the good after a titanic battle, which neither of these supremely courageous colts deserved to lose. Finishing five lengths further back in third place, Dahlia provided irrefutable evidence of Grundy's achievement, for, in finishing third, Dahlia beat the previous record for the race by more than a second.

Apparently fully recovered from his heroic performance at Ascot, Grundy reappeared in the Benson & Hedges Gold Cup at York a little over three weeks later. Opposed again by his Ascot victims, Star Appeal, Card King and Dahlia, successful in this race a year earlier, Grundy seemed to have an easy task. In the short time since its inception the Benson & Hedges Gold Cup had proved a

Saturday, 28th June, 1975   **£64,063**   **13 Ran**   **1½m**

Irish Sweeps Derby (Group 1). £30,000 and a trophy value £500 added to the stakes by Irish Hospitals' Sweepstakes. For three years old entire colts and fillies. One mile and a half.

Sweepstakes £25 to enter, 27th February, 1974; £60 extra for acceptors on 9th October, 1974; £50 extra for acceptors on 19th March, 1975; £60 additional for acceptors on 4th June, 1975; £100 extra if declared to run. Second to receive 20% and the third 10% of the whole stakes after deduction of bonuses to breeders as follows: Winner £500, Second £300, Third £200. Weights – Colts 9st; Fillies 8st 11lb.

The Racing Board will contribute a sum equal to 5% of the whole stakes (after deduction of bonuses) to the owner of the fourth horse if there are eight or more runners.

The Management Committee of the I.S.I.S. will pay to the breeder of each horse which is placed and which is qualified under that scheme an amount equal to 10% of the prize money payable to that horse.

Note—Subject to the usual conditions the Racing Board will pay special allowances as follows towards the transport costs of runners from abroad in this race:– Great Britain £200 per horse; other European countries £250 per horse; other countries £500 per horse.

1 Dr Carlo Vittadini's	GRUNDY (P. Eddery)	9.0	P. T. Walwyn (GB)
	Ch. colt Great Nephew – Word From Lundy by Worden.		
2 Mr John A. Mulcahy's	KING PELLINORE (USA)	9.0	M. V. O'Brien
	(L. Piggott) B. colt Round Table – Thong.		
3 Sir Charles Clore's	ANNE'S PRETENDER (USA)	9.0	H. R. Price (GB)
	(A. Murray) Ch. colt Pretense – Anne La Douce.		
4 Mr R. D. Hollingsworth's	SEA ANCHOR (J. Mercer) Ch. colt Alcide – Anchor.	9.0	W. R. Hern (GB)
5 Mr W. Zeitelhack's	IRISH STAR (W. Swinburn) Br. colt Relko – Chanter.	9.0	J. Oxx
6 M Daniel Wildenstein's	MAITLAND (FR) (Y. Saint- Martin) Br. colt Stupendous – Maintenon.	9.0	A. Penna (FR)
7 Mr R. B. Moller's	HOBNOB (FR) (E. Eldin) Ch. colt Gyr – Forever.	9.0	H. Wragg (GB)
8 Mr S. McGrath's	DERBY COURT (G. McGrath) B. colt Continuation – Court Time.	9.0	Owner
9 Mrs M. E. Farrell's	DOWDALL (K. F. Coogan) Ch. colt Dike – Pavella.	9.0	D. K. Weld
10 Mr C. Crowley's	MASQUED DANCER (USA) (R. F. Parnell) B. colt Nijinsky – Bonnie Google.	9.0	D. K. Weld
11 Mr Ravi N. Tikkoo's	PHOENIX HALL (USA) (F. Durr) B. colt Nearctic – Copra Girl.	9.0	D. K. Weld
12 Mrs J. J. Prendergast's	GIGGERY (USA) (Thomas Murphy) B. colt Captain's Gig – In A Moment.	9.0	S. McGrath
13 Mr S. McGrath's	NEVER SO GAY (M. Kennedy) Ch. colt Never Say Die – Gliding Gay.	9.0	Owner

SP 9/10 GRUNDY; 7/2 King Pellinore; 6/1 Maitland; 10/1 Sea Anchor; 20/1 Anne's Pretender; 66/1 Derby Court, Hobnob, Irish Star; 80/1 Never So Gay; 100/1 Masqued Dancer, Phoenix Hall; 200/1 Bar. TOTE (20p unit) 44p. Places 28p, 34p, 56p.

2 lengths, 6 lengths. 2m 31.1s.

Winner trained by Mr P. T. Walwyn at Lambourn, Berkshire.

graveyard for favourites. 1975 was to be no exception. Jumping her out in front, Piggott proceeded to dominate the race on Dahlia and fully two furlongs out it became painfully clear that Grundy was not going to catch that remarkable mare. Only fourth in the end to Dahlia, Card King and Star Appeal, Grundy confirmed that his hard race at Ascot had left its mark, for Dahlia's success represented a turnaround of fifteen lengths. It also enabled her to overtake her famous adversary, Allez France, as the leading stakes winner in Europe.

Characteristically accepting full responsibility for Grundy's defeat, Peter Walwyn could only say that he would never have run his champion, had he not believed him to have recovered completely after that Ascot epic. While a disappointed Dr Vittadini mooted the Champion Stakes as a likely target to enable Grundy to retire on a winning note, Walwyn and Eddery promptly combined to win the next two races, the Yorkshire Oaks with May Hill and the Lowther Stakes with Pasty – both owned by Walwyn's longest-standing patron, Mr G. Williams – en route to heading the trainers' and jockeys' lists respectively. Walwyn's winning total of £382,527 was very nearly double the record which he had set the previous year. On October 1st it was announced that Grundy, while perfectly sound and healthy, had lost his earlier sparkle and was thus being retired forthwith to the National Stud. So ended the sadly abbreviated racecourse career of this supremely courageous little chestnut, whose flying flaxen mane and tail had flowed to success in three Classics, and whose name would forever come to mind whenever racing enthusiasts foregathered, glass in hand, to relive what had already become immortalised as 'the Race of the Century'.

King Pellinore, second to Grundy at the Curragh, beat the Champion Stakes winner Hurry Harriet by a short head in the Blandford Stakes and then started favourite for the St Leger. King Pellinore won a good race, but it was for second place, in the wake of a brilliant Bruni, whose electrifying acceleration in the straight made his rivals appear rooted to the ground. Among these were Hobnob, who finished fourth, and the disappointing Sea Anchor. However, the latter made ample amends as a four-year-old, winning the Goodwood Stakes, the Henry II Stakes at Sandown and the Doncaster Cup, besides finishing third in the Ascot Gold Cup. Anne's Pretender went on racing for a further two seasons, including among his six victories a defeat of Green Dancer in France, where he eventually retired to stud. Returning to race in the land of his birth, King Pellinore earned the title 'Grass Horse of 1976' in California.

1976

Empery's decisive rout of the English Classic colts at Epsom resulted in the first Irish Derby for almost twenty years without an English-trained challenger. However, the French were by no means as convinced of Empery's invincibility and he was accompanied to the Curragh by five compatriots, including his pacemaker, Oilfield. The latter had recently acted in that role for Youth, who had provided Texan oil tycoon, Nelson Bunker Hunt, with a Derby double when winning the Prix du Jockey-Club. Malacate, third on that occasion, had won his previous three races and travelled to the Curragh in an attempt to maintain trainer Francois Boutin's spectacular run of success in recent major races, notably with Sagaro and Trepan, both Royal Ascot winners. Far North, a three-parts brother to Nijinsky, had so far failed to recover the form which had made him one of the leading juveniles in France, while No Turning, blinkered for the first time, had finished only seventh to Empery at Epsom and looked unlikely to reverse that running. In the face of this Gallic invasion the Irish defence looked pitifully weak. Only Hawkberry, a promisng fourth at Epsom, Northern Treasure, shock winner of the Irish Two Thousand Guineas, and the hitherto disappointing Niebo appeared to hold any chance of preventing an all-French finish. In the absence of a likely home-trained winner, the sporting Press made great play of Navarre, the first runner in the race to be trained by woman, Mrs Brewster, who had become the first woman to saddle a winner in Ireland when licences had been granted to women ten years earlier. They also highlighted the participation of a 'jockette', Joanna Morgan. Riding Riot Helmet for her master, Seamus McGrath, this very capable Welsh-born apprentice was to become the first of her sex to ride in a Classic race anywhere in Europe – as far as anybody knew. A smaller, though more suntanned crowd than in recent years reflected the mass exodus to the seaside during this, the finest summer in living memory. Those that did pay homage to the highlight of the Irish racing year, attired in anything from nightdresses to bowler hats, happily backed Empery and Lester Piggott from even money to odds-on. Though the favourite sweated up in the sweltering sunshine more than he had at Epsom, he was a model of composure in contrast to his compatriot Far North, whom Bill Pyers was forced to lead all the way down to a much-delayed start.

When they at last got away Oilfield set a cracking pace ahead of Empery, King Mousse and Malacate, on whom Paquet was obviously intent on tracking the favourite. The order remained unchanged to the final bend, where Alain Lequeux obligingly pulled Oilfield off the rails to let Empery through, followed instantly by Malacate, while Northern Treasure and No Turning made up ground on the outside. Already Piggott's posterior had dropped from perpendicular to horizontal, indicating his unease on the leader, who was under increasing pressure with Malacate breathing down his neck. Stalking his prey into the final quarter of a mile, Paquet then nudged Malacate into full flight. As Piggott reported: 'He came past us as though we were standing still.' So indeed it appeared from the stands, as Malacate strode clear to win by two and a half lengths to win with his ears pricked. Staying on surprisingly well, Northern Treasure held off Hawkberry for third place. Hawkberry's running with Empery suggested that Malacate would have won the Epsom Derby, had he been in the field. It also made Youth appear the outstanding colt in a year of total domination by the French.

The winning owner, Maria-Felix Berger, resplendent in a peach-coloured trouser suit, showed much more restraint when welcoming her winner than she usually did on such occasions in France, where pictures of her kissing Lester Piggott in the winner's enclosure aroused reactions ranging from unashamed envy to downright disbelief! In view of her lack of English, rivalled by her trainer, it was all the more regrettable that Spencer Freeman's traditional interview for the benefit of the Press had been discontinued. In the circumstances the scribes were forced to reiterate the few well-known facts of Maria-Felix Berger's acting career, which had apparently elevated her to Brigitte Bardot status in her native Mexico. Since moving to France a few years previously, she had become interested in racing and had been fabulously lucky, winning the Two Thousand Guineas with Nonoalco and the Prix de Jockey-Club with Caracolero, for whose failure in the Irish Derby Malacate had now made handsome amends. Francois Boutin, a much more likely-looking film star than his owner, and his protege Philippe Paquet declared through the jubilant jockey that they had always been confident with success, as well they might, for on numerous lines of form Malacate had been fully entitled to beat Empery. However, they owed their good fortune, at least in part, to a most improbable guardian angel, Stewards' Secretary, Jim Marsh. On the previous evening this much-maligned official had gone down to the stables to inspect the passports of the foreign runners. As he was doing this, Malacate, who was being walked around at the time, suddenly reared up, knocked over his handler and got loose. Only Jim Marsh's prompt action in seizing the flying lead rein prevented Malacate careering off across the wide open wastes of the Curragh.

Born into a farming family in Dieppe, the tall and urbane Francois Boutin looked much more like a typical French film star than the popular image of a racehorse trainer. Having got his first taste of racing through training trotters on country tracks, he had done his 'service militaire' in Tunisia, before renewing his association with horses on stud farms in Normandy, where he met Etienne Pollet. A year as assistant to 'le maitre' was followed by a year as private trainer to Marcel Boussac. In 1966 Francois Boutin set up on his own, with three horses, and won two races. One of the talents that he had most admired in Pollet was his gift of selecting yearlings. Boutin proved himself a good learner, for in that make-or-break first year on his own he selected a white-faced yearling filly by Val de Loir. Two years later, when the white face of La Lagune swept up the straight to success in the Epsom Oaks, Boutin's career was made. La Lagune was followed by Nonoalco, Caracolero, Ribecourt and Sagaro, and by 1974 Boutin controlled a string of 125 in his rented stables in Lamorlaye. At the recent Royal Ascot meeting Boutin had sent out Trepan to a shock success in the Prince of Wales' Stakes, which he won in record time. Just a few days after the Irish Derby it was announced that the routine dope test on Trepan had proved positive. Attributing this to the belated administration of a diuretic, a defiant Francois Boutin assured the Press that Trepan would confirm his merit in the Eclipse Stakes. He was right. Trepan slaughtered the Guineas winner, Wollow, to win the Eclipse in record time. Boutin and Paquet continued on their all-conquering progress when winning the Irish Oaks with Lagunette, a full-sister to La Lagune. Then came the news that rocked the racing world: Trepan's dope test after the Eclipse had also proved positive. The outcome of a lengthy Jockey Club hearing was that Boutin was fined £1250 and the official statement contained a strange implication to the effect that, had the races involved been of less consequence, Boutin's trainer's licence would have been withdrawn. In the light of Francois Mathet's allegations that the majority of trainers in France were regularly administering 'les traitements', Boutin's was an unenviable position, worsened when Trepan finished a dismal last in the Benson & Hedges Gold Cup at York. Boutin's furious allegation that that was the one occasion on which his horse surely had been doped was made to look less than convincing by the official post-race test, which proved negative. Fortunately for him, Boutin was by now much too well established in his profession to suffer unduly and he continues to turn out a succession of high-class winners.

Having joined the Boutin stable in 1966 as a fourteen-year-old apprentice, through the offices of the local labour exchange, Philippe Pacquet got his big break in 1973 when a homesick Sandy Barclay resigned his position as stable jockey and Tony Murray declined the job. Though regularly displaced by Lester Piggott on Boutin's overseas raiders, Paquet, by his consistency on the Paris tracks, eventually convinced his extremely professional employer that he was worth his chance abroad. By his performances on Malacate and Lagunette at the Curragh and on the controversial Trepan at Ascot and Sandown, Paquet not only rewarded Boutin's trust, but also revealed the ability which would make him champion jockey in his native land in 1977. Though possibly lacking the occasional brilliance of Saint-Martin, whose style he closely resembles, Philippe Paquet probably rides fewer bad races than his celebrated rival, indicated by the fact that he has already gained that grudging English accolade 'a good jockey', seldom conferred on his countrymen – and never lightly!

Bred by Don and Thomas Sturgill at their Beaconsfield Farm in Kentucky, Malacate had been purchased for $40,000 as a yearling by bloodstock agent George Blackwell, who had previously bought both Nonoalco and Caracolero as yearlings on Madame Berger's behalf. By the Santa Anita and Kentucky Derby winner, Lucky Debonair, and the seventh winner out of the prolific My Babu mare, Eyeshadow, Malacate repesented a good, honest American family, which had not produced a Classic winner for generations, stretching back to the Oaks winner of 1841, Ghuznee, from whom had descended Fair Maid of Kent, dam of both Kentish Fire, winner of the Irish Derby, and of the Grand National heroine Frigate. A winner as a two-year-old, Malacate had won three races in succession prior to meeting defeat at the hands of Youth in the Prix du Jockey-Club. Fifth to his compatriot Pawneese in the King George VI and Queen Elizabeth Stakes, Malacate returned to Ireland to contest the inaugural running of the ten-furlong Joe McGrath Memorial Stakes at Leopardstown. Starting odds-on favourite and ridden by Lester Piggott in place of the currently suspended Paquet, Malacate easily confirmed his superiority over Mart Lane, Niebo and Northern Treasure. In the Champion Stakes Malacate headed the group on the stands' side to finish fourth to Vitiges. However, the fact that Northern Treasure, racing with the winner, took third place, suggested that Malacate's draw had placed him at an impossible disadvantage.

After the Irish Sweeps Derby Tim Rogers had acquired a substantial share in Malacate, who now retired to his Airlie Stud near Dublin. In buying Malacate as a stallion Tim Rogers had secured a tail-male descendant of Swynford, in itself a marvellous sire line. However, in this instance he took a calculated risk, for Malacate descended from Swynford through his son St Germans, second to Sansovino, another son of Swynford, in the Epsom Derby of 1924. St Germans went to stud in the USA, where he sired Twenty Grand. Unfortunately, St Germans subsequently proved to be almost completely sterile, a fault which he transmitted to the majority of his male offspring, already few enough in number. Consequently, it was not so much surprising as disappointing that Malacate should have proved to suffer from hereditary infertility. Put back in training with Francois Boutin, Malacate won the Prix Foy at Longchamp the following season, finished unplaced in the Benson & Hedges Gold Cup, the Prix de l'Arc de Triomphe and the Champion Stakes, and was retired once more to Airlie, later being sold to Japan for a reputed £750,000. In view of his obvious shortcomings, Malacate stands out as one of the few Classic winners whose departure to the Land of the Rising Sun caused little regret.

Beaten fair and square by Malacate at the Curragh, Empery was promptly retired and went to stud in the USA. The marvellously tough and consistent Northern Treasure went on to win the Blandford Stakes, finished fourth to Malacate at Leopardstown, reversed the placings in the Champion Stakes and was sold to go to stud in New South Wales, never having been out of the first four in his seventeen races, a remarkable tribute to his trainer Kevin Prendergast, whose horses invariably hold their form throughout their hard-working careers. Hawkberry went to be trained in France and finished third in the Ascot Gold Cup two years later, while Decent Fellow vindicated Eddie Harty's judgement by emerging as the leading juvenile hurdler of his generation in England and subsequently winning the John Porter Stakes at Newbury, before being sent back to his native land by Toby Balding to carry off the Sweeps Hurdle. If it was not a particularly memorable Irish Sweeps Derby, it did serve once again to underline the fact that it takes an exceptional Epsom Derby winner to defend those laurels successfully on the Curragh of Kildare.

Saturday, 26th June, 1976	£66,016	17 Ran	1½m

Irish Sweeps Derby (Group 1). £30,000 and a trophy value £500 added to the stakes by Irish Hospitals' Sweepstakes. For three years old entire colts and fillies. One mile and a half.

Sweepstakes, £25 to enter, 26th February, 1975 or £1000 each if entered on 10th December, 1975. £60 extra for acceptors on 12th November, 1975, £50 extra for acceptors on 10th March, 1976, £60 additional for acceptors on 2nd June, 1976, £100 extra if declared to run. Second to receive 20% and the third 10% of the whole stakes after deduction of bonuses to breeders as follows – Winners £500, Second £300, Third £200. Weights – Colts 9st; Fillies 8st 11lb.

The Racing Board will contribute a sum equal to 5% of the whole stakes (after deduction of the bonuses) to the owner of the fourth horse if there are eight or more runners.

The Management Committee of the I.S.I.S. will pay to the breeder of each horse which is placed and which is qualified under that scheme an amount equal to 10% of the prize money payable to that horse.

Note—Subject to the usual conditions the Racing Board will pay special allowances as follows towards the transport costs of runners from abroad in this race:– Great Britain £200 per horse; other European countries £250 per horse; other countries £500 per horse.

1	Mme Maria-Felix Berger's	MALACATE (USA) (P. Paquet)	9.0	F. Boutin (FR)
		B. colt Lucky Debonair – Eyeshadow by My Babu.		
2	Mr N. B. Hunt's	EMPERY (USA) (L. Piggott)	9.0	M. Zilber (FR)
		B. colt Vaguely Noble – Pamplona.		
3	Mr A. D. Brennan's	NORTHERN TREASURE	9.0	K. Prendergast
		(G. Curran) Ch. colt Northfields – Place d'Etoile.		
4	Mr Lawrence M. Gelb's	HAWKBERRY (C. Roche)	9.0	P. J. Prendergast
		B. colt Sea Hawk – Khalberry.		
5	Mr Robin Scully's	FAR NORTH (CAN) (W. Pyers)	9.0	J. Fellows (FR)
		B. colt Northern Dancer – Fleur.		

6 Mr Kevin O'Donnell's BRANDON HILL (R. F. Parnell) 9.0   P. Mullins
B. colt Wolver Hollow – Debatable.
7 Mrs Walter Haefner's NIEBO (USA) (Thomas Murphy) 9.0   M. V. O'Brien
Ch. colt Arts and Letters – Firey Angel.
8 Mrs D. B. Brewster's NAVARRE (T. Carberry) 9.0   Owner
B. colt Le Prince – Missa.
9 Mrs E. McMahon's FINSBURY (R. Carroll) 9.0   C. Collins
B. colt Levmoss – Miss Millicent.
10 Mr N. B. Hunt's OILFIELD (USA) (A. Legueax) 9.0   M. Zilber (FR)
B/Br. colt Hail to Reason – Ole Liz.
11 Mrs J. R. Mullion's NO TURNING (USA) 9.0   F. Palmer (FR)
(A. Murray) B. colt Never Bend – Secret Story.
12 Mr Patrick O'Leary's DECENT FELLOW 9.0   Owner
(W. Swinburn) B. colt Rarity – Takette.
13 Mr S. McGrath's MART LANE (G. McGrath) 9.0   Owner
B. colt Le Levanstell – Marians.
14 Mrs P. W. McGrath's RIOT HELMET (Miss J. Morgan) 9.0   S. McGrath
B. colt Levmoss – Hunting Cap.
15 Mrs G. Robinson's TALARIAS (D. Hogan) 9.0   G. W. ROBINSON
B/Gr. colt Silver Shark – Starlighter.
16 Mr S. McGrath's KING MOUSSE (M. Kennedy) 9.0   Owner
B. colt Kauai King – Feemoss.
17 Mr John Ringling North's IMPERIAL FLEET (FR) 9.0   G. W. Robinson
(J. Roe) B. colt King Emperor – Anchor Song.

SP 4/5 Empery; 5/1 MALACATE; 9/1 Far North; 10/1 Hawkberry; 16/1 Niebo, Northern Treasure; 20/1 Mart Lane; 33/1 No Turning; 40/1 Decent Fellow; 100/1 Brandon Hill, Oilfield; 200/1 Bar. TOTE (20p unit) £1.20. Places 40p, 28p, 44p.
2½ lengths, ¾ length. 2m 31.2s.
Winner trained by M F. Boutin at Chantilly, France.

1977

In a year in which the ups and downs of racing were never more vividly illustrated than by the fluctuating fortunes of the O'Brien stable, that quietly-spoken master of his craft had eventually decided to let The Minstrel, his fifth winner of the Epsom Derby, defend his title at the Curragh. Whether you liked him or not – and many still did not – this flashy little chestnut, with the curious head carriage and the cotton wool in his ears, had won the hard way at Epsom, where his sheer courage and Piggott's artistry had combined to wear down the gallant Hot Grove in a gruelling contest. After two hard losing races in both the English and Irish Guineas, The Minstrel had only run in the Epsom race on Piggott's insistence that he would win. Even after that punishing race Piggott remained adamant that the colt, who appeared to thrive on this treatment, was capable of winning at the Curragh, and once again Piggott's persuasive powers prevailed.

Of the fourteen that opposed the short-priced favourite, Monseigneur, Lucky Sovereign and Milverton had finished behind him at Epsom. Only Monseigneur, who had failed to act down the hill, could be expected to finish any closer to The

Minstrel than the eight lengths that had separated them on that occasion. Monseigneur was accompanied from France by the unbeaten Ercolano, whose three victories might amount to anything or nothing. Best of the five English-trained challengers was thought to be Classic Example, recent winner of the King Edward VII Stakes at Royal Ascot, beating Ad Lib Ra and Remezzo. Out of a full-sister to Altesse Royale, Classic Example was attempting to repeat the path to victory which the Hue-Williamses and their trainer Peter Walwyn had taken with English Prince three years previously. While there seemed no reason why Ad Lib Ra should reverse that Ascot form with Classic Example, the former was, after all, a half-brother to Ribocco and Ribero . . . With the obvious exception of The Minstrel, the Irish defenders looked outclassed in this company, though Orchestra would have had an infinitely better chance with some give in the ground. With his ears once again stuffed with cotton wool during the preliminaries, The Minstrel looked more cool, calm and collected than many of his supporters, who had contributed to an Irish Totalisator record of £176,249. This figure suggested a combined turnover, between bookmakers and the Tote, of over £750,000 for the meeting.

The start took place without incident and when the field settled down King Ashoka made the early running ahead of Aristocracy, Star's Salute and Ad Lib Ra. The latter took it up approaching the half way mark, chased by Orchestra and Ercolano, with The Minstrel still travelling smoothly towards the rear of the field. With half a mile to run Orchestra hit the front and as he did so a roar from the stands signalled the emergence of The Minstrel in ever-closer pursuit, shadowed by Lucky Sovereign, with Classic Example seeking and finding an opening on the rails. Two furlongs from home The Minstrel hit the front, with Piggott poised to give him as easy a race as possible and eyeing Classic Example's challenge on his right. Suddenly The Minstrel began to veer left-handed towards the stands, right across the path of Lucky Sovereign, whom Frankie Durr switched to make his run between the other two. Still confident with success, Piggott almost reluctantly pulled his whip through into his less favoured left hand, straightened The Minstrel out, and went on to beat Lucky Sovereign by a length and a half, with Classic Example a neck further back in third place, some way ahead of Orchestra.

Scarcely had Piggott pulled up his fourth winner of the Irish Sweeps Derby than the Stewards announced an inquiry, and as the bemused crowd rushed to watch the re-run of the race on television Frankie Durr lodged an objection to the winner for crossing inside the final furlong. As the Stewards deliberated the evidence of the two jockeys and scrutinised the camera patrol film, an anxious Vincent O'Brien silenced one gloomy but garrulous reporter by inviting *his* opinion of the outcome! After what must for him have been an agonising wait, reminiscent of the Chamier drama almost a quarter of a century earlier, O'Brien masked his relief and delight as the enclosure erupted to the announcement: 'No change in the placings.' Once again the absence of a properly organised Press conference became evident as journalists bombarded O'Brien with questions concerning The Minstrel's future. Mindful of The Minstrel's arduous season, O'Brien intimated that he would contest the King George VI and Queen Elizabeth Stakes, all being well. Winning owner, Robert Sangster, was quoted as saying that, provided European breeders were prepared to support him, The Minstrel would retire to stud in Ireland. Otherwise the power of the dollar would prevail. It was left to Mrs O'Brien to reveal that The Minstrel's threatened problems of temperament, now happily overcome, were trivial by comparison to those that her husband had encountered with Nijinsky. In the euphoria of success none chose to dispute her assertion that only Vincent could have got a race out of Nijinsky, let alone four Classics.

A small, compact, white-splashed chestnut, The Minstrel was by Northern Dancer out of Fleur and thus a three-parts brother to Nijinsky, whose dam, Flaming Page, had produced Fleur. The temperament to which Mrs O'Brien referred had come out to an almost unmanageable degree in Fleur's first produce, Far North, whose tantrums had delayed the start of the Irish Sweeps Derby only the year before. Bred in Canada by Eddie Taylor, the breeder of Nijinsky, The Minstrel had fetched $200,000 at Keeneland as a yearling. On his racecourse debut at the Curragh The Minstrel had broken the six-furlong course record for two-year-olds. The first leg of a treble for Lester Piggott on the day he won the Joe McGrath Memorial Stakes on Malacate, The Minstrel had concluded his first season by a clearcut success in the Dewhurst Stakes, being rated 8lbs below J. O. Tobin in the English Free Handicap.

On the same day that Red Rum galloped to everlasting glory in his third Grand National The Minstrel made his seasonal debut in the Two Thousand Guineas Trial Stakes at Ascot. Despite his evident dislike of the heavy going, he won with sufficient authority to become a red hot favourite for the Two Thousand Guineas. Always struggling, The Minstrel looked like another flash in the pan when only third to the Kevin Prendergast-trained Nebbiolo. The following day Sangster, O'Brien and Piggott suffered another and more bitter blow when the brilliant but wayward Cloonlara flopped in the One Thousand Guineas. Worse was to follow at the Irish Guineas meeting, at which the O'Brien-Piggott fortunes reached their nadir. Though O'Brien won the Irish One Thousand Guineas with the unraced outsider Lady Capulet and the Royal Whip with the 33-to-1 chance Alleged, the longest-priced double of his entire career brought little solace to anguished Piggott fans. He rode in eleven of the twelve races, partnered eight favourites, two of them odds-on, and failed to ride a single winner. One of those setbacks was provided by The Minstrel, short headed by Pampapaul in a desperate finish for the Irish Two Thousand Guineas. At the end of a disastrous meeting, during which he had been booed by the crowd, cautioned by the Stewards and dubbed Svengali by the Press, an ashen-faced Piggott assured an equally despondent O'Brien: 'If you run The Minstrel in the Derby, I'll ride him and he'll win.' Having fulfilled that prophesy, Piggott had now brought The Minstrel home first in the Irish Sweeps Derby: he was the hero of the hour. No one knows better than Lester Piggott that, in the eyes of the public, a jockey is just as good as his last winner. If he needed any reminding he got it in the very next race. His stirrup broke as he left the stalls on Glencoe Lights in a six-furlong race. Fighting desperately to maintain his balance and control his mount, Piggott managed to pull up at the finish before toppling to the ground in pain and exhaustion. Advised on medical grounds to rest for the remainder of the day, the puckish Piggott caused uproar in the weighroom when he admonished the startled doctor: 'Don't be . . . silly. I've got to go out there and earn my £14 riding fee in the next race!' By strange coincidence, he had had an even closer escape after winning the Epsom Derby when unseated and dragged by Durtal. On that occasion a broken stirrup saved his life. To complete the coincidences: O'Brien and Piggott had narrowly failed to follow up their Epsom triumph when Artaius was just beaten in the Prix du Jockey-Club: The day after their success at the Curragh they had again to be content with second place in a major French race when Valinsky was beaten in the Grand Prix de Paris.

Always favourite for the King George VI and Queen Elizabeth Stakes. The Minstrel faced a formidable field at Ascot, which included no fewer than six Classic winners of older generations. They were Orange Bay (Italian Derby), Bruni (St Leger), Crow (St Leger), Exceller (French St Leger), Rheffissimo (Spanish St Leger) and Trainer's Seat (Norwegian Triple Crown). Crystal Palace, the only three-year-old to oppose The Minstrel, had beaten Artaius in the Prix du Jockey-Club. In the meantime Artaius had provided O'Brien and Piggott with a record-breaking win in the Eclipse Stakes. The Minstrel, who had never looked better, terrified his supporters by dwelling in the stalls. Unperturbed, Piggott settled him calmly towards the rear of his field and was still only sixth turning into the straight, where Pat Eddery kicked for home on the blinkered Orange Bay. Showing that priceless ability to accelerate, which is the hallmark of true class, The Minstrel magically shrank the gap, heading Orange Bay at the furlong pole. But Orange Bay was far from done with and under Eddery's inspired urging he fought back to join battle in a manner reminiscent of Bustino and Grundy. After a titanic struggle the younger horse prevailed by a short head, with Exceller and Crystal Palace well beaten in third and fourth places. Having achieved the treble previously accomplished only by Nijinsky and Grundy, The Minstrel had become the greatest stakes winner ever trained in these islands, fully deserving the accolades from O'Brien and Piggott, who rated him among the best they had ever trained or ridden. Robert Sangster, ecstatic about his courageous little colt, revealed that he and his partners had recently turned down an American offer of $10,000,000 for the Minstrel.

In August The Minstrel was announced as a definite acceptor for the Washington DC International, where he would meet the American Triple Crown winner, Seattle Slew, as well as Forego, three times 'Racehorse of the Year' in the States. Within days came further news that Sangster and his partners had sold a half-share in The Minstrel to his breeder Eddie Taylor, who owned the Windfields Stud Farm in Maryland. At his valuation of $9,000,000 The Minstrel became the most expensive thoroughbred ever sold. Prospects of his remaining in Europe began to seem remote . . . By the end of August Vincent O'Brien had exceeded Peter Walwyn's two-year-old record for stakes won in Britain. When Be My Guest won the Waterford Crystal Mile at Goodwood O'Brien's British winnings for the season reached £399,270, contributed by 12 winners of 17 races. Walwyn had won 121 races with 69 different horses. On September 6th Robert Sangster announced that Alleged, rather than The Minstrel, would represent him in the Prix de l'Arc de Triomphe. Two days later came the startling news that The Minstrel had already been flown to Taylor's Windfields Farm and would never race again. His hasty departure had been caused by fear that America would follow Australia's lead in banning importation of horses from Britain and Ireland, owing to the rampant Equine Metritis, which had ravaged stud farms in these islands throughout 1977. The very next day the Americans announced their embargo.

A remarkable racehorse, The Minstrel was owned by equally remarkable people:

Saturday, 25th June, 1977   **£72,797.50**   **15 Ran**   1½m

Irish Sweeps Derby (Group 1). £30,000 and a trophy value £500 added to the stakes by Irish Hospitals' Sweepstakes. For three years old entire colts and fillies. One mile and a half.

Sweepstakes, £25 to enter, 25th February, 1976 or £1000 each if entered on 8th December, 1976, £60 extra for acceptors on 10th November, 1976, £50 extra for acceptors on 16th March, 1977. £100 additional for acceptors on 1st June, 1977, £100 extra if declared to run. Second to receive 20% and the third 10% of the whole stakes after deduction of bonuses to breeders as follows – Winner £500, Second £300, Third £200. Weights – Colts 9st; Fillies 8st 11lb.

The Racing Board will contribute a sum equal to 5% of the whole stakes (after deduction of the bonuses) to the owner of the fourth horse if there are eight or more runners.

The Management Committee of the I.S.I.S. will pay to the breeder of the winner and which is qualified under that scheme an amount equal to 10% of the prize money payable to that horse.

Note—Subject to the usual conditions the Racing Board will pay special allowances as follows towards the transport costs of runners from abroad in this race:– Great Britain £200 per horse; other European countries £250 per horse.

1	Mr R. E. Sangster's	THE MINSTREL (CAN)	9.0	M. V. O'Brien
		(L. Piggott)		
		Ch. colt Northern Dancer – Fleur by Victoria Park.		
2	Mr R. B. Moller's	LUCKY SOVEREIGN (USA)	9.0	H. Wragg (GB)
		(F. Durr) B. colt Nijinsky – Sovereign.		
3	Mr F. R. Hue-Williams's	CLASSIC EXAMPLE (P. Eddery)	9.0	P. T. Walwyn (GB)
		Ch. colt Run The Gauntlet – Royal Saint.		
4	Lord Donoughmore's	ORCHESTRA (R. Carroll)	9.0	J. Oxx
		Ch. colt Tudor Music – Golden Moss.		
5	Mr Arthur Seeligson's	MONSEIGNEUR (USA)	9.0	F. Boutin (FR)
		(P. Paquet) Ch. colt Graustark – Brown Berry.		
6	M. Jacques Wertheimer's	ERCOLANO (USA) (F. Head)	9.0	A. Head (FR)
		B. colt Sir Ivor – Green Valley.		
7	Mr Tjo Eng Tan's	MILVERTON (C. Roche)	9.0	C. Collins
		Br. colt Royal Palace – Melodina.		
8	Mr Charles J. Haughey's	ARISTOCRACY (J. Roe)	9.0	R. J. McCormick
		B. colt Lord Gayle – Roxboro.		
9	Mr D. A. N. Allen's	LIMONE (G. Starkey)	9.0	G. Harwood (GB)
		B. colt Relko – Palmavista.		
10	Captain M. D. Lemos's	REMEZZO (G. Dettori)	9.0	C. Brittain (GB)
		Ch. colt Ribero – Camina Bay.		
11	Mrs Mehl-Muelhens's	STAR'S SALUTE (G. Curran)	9.0	K. Prendergast
		B. colt Sallust – Sterna.		
12	Mrs Julian G. Rogers's	AD LIB RA (USA) (A. Murray)	9.0	R. F. Johnson-Houghton (GB)
		B. colt Droll Role – Libra.		
13	Mrs Walter Haefner's	PADROUG (USA) (Thomas Murphy) B. colt Sir Ivor – Running Blue.	9.0	M. V. O'Brien
14	Mr Patrick S. Gallagher's	LATH (USA) (D. Hogan)	9.0	C. Grassick
		B. colt Nijinsky – Moll Flanders.		
15	Mr W. Zeitelhack's	KING ASHOKA (T. Carmody)	9.0	J. Oxx
		Br. colt Relko – Softly Glowing.		

SP 11/10 THE MINSTREL; 4/1 Monseigneur; 10/1 Ercolano; 12/1 Orchestra; 14/1 Classic Example; 20/1 Ad Lib Ra; 22/1 Lucky Sovereign; 25/1 Limone; 40/1 Milverton; 50/1 Padroug; 66/1 Remezzo, Star's Salute; 100/1 Aristocracy; 200/1 King Ashoka, Lath. TOTE (20p unit) 50p. Places 30p, 96p, 62p.

1½ lengths, neck. 2m 31.9s.

Winner trained by Mr M. V. O'Brien at Ballydoyle House, Cashel, Co. Tipperary.

Stewards' Enquiry and an objection to the winner by the second, for taking his ground in the final furlong. The Stewards' overruled the objection and made no alteration to the judges placings.

Robert Sangster, Simon Fraser, Vincent O'Brien and his son-in-law, John Magnier. O'Brien's legendary career has already been chronicled – however inadequately John Magnier has overall responsibility for the Coolmore–Castlehyde stud complex, with its worldwide ramifications. His record speaks for itself in the increasingly sophisticated sphere of bloodstock breeding. Simon Fraser has sought successfully to avoid the limelight in his role as a 'sleeping partner' in this extraordinary amalgam of wealth and talent. That leaves the 'front man', figurehead and financier-extraordinary – Robert Sangster. Millionaire managing director of Vernons' Pools, youthful member of the Jockey Club Sangster conducts his international business, bloodstock and racing operations from his tax exile headquarters in the Isle of Man. After a short, but by no means unsuccessful, spell in conventional racehorse ownership, Sangster decided that his hobby was too costly and withdrew. That was not the end, rather the beginning . . .

His return to the ranks of ownership was on an investment basis, in which return on capital employed was to be a more important consideration than the vainglory of the winner's enclosure. The initial investment was reputed to be in the region of £3,000,000, the foundation of his 'internationalist' policy, which has led to his involvement in racing and breeding on three continents. In a lengthy and lucid interview with 'Pacemaker' after The Minstrel had fulfilled his ambition to own a world-class racehorse and potential stallion, Robert Sangster outlined his 'modus operandum'. Briefly, it consists of buying the very best yearlings, whose all-important stallion potential can be maximised by their racecourse success, syndicating them for stud purposes and retaining a substantial interest in their subsequent careers. The Minstrel provided a perfect illustration of this policy at its most successful: purchase price $200,000; stakes $600,000 approx; syndication $9,000,000. During 1977 Sangster bought the top-priced yearling at all four of the major American sales. But long before they would see a racecourse another had emerged to fill the void left by The Minstrel. This was Alleged, dual winner of the Prix de l'Arc de Triomphe. In that same golden year for the Sangster 'empire' it seemed that he and his partners might have produced one greater still – Try My Best . . .

1978

The smallest field since the Irish Sweeps Derby had first been run sixteen years earlier promised to provide one of the most informative renewals of the race. The favourite was Shirley Heights, whose last-stride victory in the Epsom Derby had posed more questions than it had provided answers. By diving through a gap on the rails to head Hawaiian Sound at Epsom, Shirley Heights had sparked off furious controversy as to whether he owed his victory to the opportunism of his jockey, Greville Starkey, to the incompetence of American ace, Willie Shoemaker, whose waiting-in-front tactics on Hawaiian Sound had so nearly won the day, or, as Starkey claimed, he would have won much more easily but for getting into trouble coming down the hill into the straight. Hawaiian Sound opposed him again at the Curragh, but was not expected to appreciate this more severe test of stamina. Moreover, there were those who contended that Willie Shoemaker, for all his 7500 winners on left-handed American tracks, would be totally bemused by the right-handed Curragh course. Exdirectory and Inkerman, two costly Irish flops at Epsom, were both fancied to leave that form far behind. Inkerman, favourite at Epsom, had swallowed his tongue and now had it tied down to prevent a reoccurrence. Exdirectory had lost his place completely coming down the hill and never got back into the race. If everything that his trainer, Paddy Prendergast, claimed on his behalf was true, he would not only gain revenge over Shirley Heights, he would beat him out of sight! Of the others, Remainder Man, second in the Two Thousand Guineas and third in the Derby, had recently run well below that form at Ascot and looked more in need of a rest than a race, while El Badr, recent winner of a maiden race at Chantilly, might be anything or nothing.

The start was delayed by the antics of Remainder Man, who got thoroughly upset when resaddled in the parade ring and took little interest in proceedings subsequently. When at last they did get away Hawaiian Sound immediately pulled his way to the front ahead of Encyclopaedia, Rathdowney, Valley Forge and Strong Gale. Shoemaker then managed to settle his headstrong partner sufficiently to allow Encyclopaedia, carrying the same colours, to take up the running, but only on sufferance, for, rounding the final turn, Hawaiian Sound went on again, followed now by Inkerman on the rails and Shirley Heights coming wide with Exdirectory. As these four swept up the straight in line abreast, Shirley Heights, as he had several times before, began to hang further and further to his left, bringing the hapless Exdirectory out towards the stands. As these two fought their own duel, Hawaiian Sound, having beaten off the challenge of Inkerman, was now left to race alone on the rails. Inside the final furlong Exdirectory appeared to head Shirley Heights for a few strides. But Starkey then straightened Shirley Heights out and conjured a last desperate rally out of him, which saw him home, neck outstretched and nostrils flared, by a head from Exdirectory. Almost unnoticed in the general excitement, Hawaiian Sound had galloped on with lonely courage to finish a very close third on the far side of the course, only a neck behind Exdirectory, with Inkerman a length further back in fourth place.

Those who anticipated a Stewards' Inquiry were disappointed, though nothing like as upset as Paddy Prendergast, who castigated the wretched Christy Roche for his stupidity in making his challenge on the outside of a horse that any half-wit knew invariably hung to his left. Adding fuel to the heated post mortems were the backers of Hawaiian Sound, who insisted that, ridden in a more restrained fashion, he must have won. Then came word of Lester Piggott's downright disgust at Inkerman's failure to see out his race. However, even his most partisan opponents took time off to accord Shirley Heights the ovation that his indomitable display so richly deserved.

Bred in Yorkshire by Lord Halifax and his son Lord Irwin, Shirley Heights came from the second crop of the brilliant Mill Reef, winner of fourteen of his sixteen races, including the Epsom Derby, Eclipse Stakes, King George VI Stakes and the Prix de l'Arc de Triomphe. By siring Acamas, recent winner of the Prix du Jockey-Club, in the same crop, Mill Reef had achieved the unique feat of siring the winners of the English, Irish and French Derbies in the same year. Hardiemma, the dam of Shirley Heights, was by Hardicanute, winter favourite for the Epsom Derby of 1965 before succumbing to the virus which had devastated Paddy Prendergast's stable that year. Hardicanute had retired to the Mullions' Ardenode Stud, where he had covered Hardiemma's dam. As the Mullions owned Exdirectory they may well have reflected that that was one service fee they would happily have foregone! With every ray of sunshine a little rain must fall, and Lord Halifax and Lord Irwin, having bred Shirley Heights, had sold Hardiemma, in foal to Mill Reef, for 15,000gns, the cost of getting her in foal. The benificiaries on this occasion were the owners of the Ballyrogan Stud in Co. Wickow, for whom Shirley Heights' yearling full-sister was to fetch a world record price of 250,000gns when offered at Goffs Premier Yearling Sales.

Winning trainer John Dunlop had watched the race from the far side of the course and was thus uncertain as to whether Shirley Heights had won or even been better than fourth. As he said afterwards: 'I just can't take any more finishes like this!' As all who follow flat racing in these islands know only too well, John Leeper Dunlop is far too much of a professional in his approach to the uncertain science of racehorse training to allow such situations to do other than whet his appetite for more. Having learned the rudiments of his profession in a National Hunt stable, John Dunlop joined Gordon Smyth, at that time private trainer to the Duke and Duchess of Norfolk at Arundel Castle. When Smyth left to become a public trainer John Dunlop took over and helped the Duke of Norfolk to realise one of his life's ambitions when Ragstone won the Ascot Gold Cup for the Arundel stable. Although he had won the Irish One Thousand Guineas with Black Satin in 1970, John Dunlop had not won a colts' Classic in Ireland, having come very close with both Pitcairn and Scottish Rifle, second to Steel Pulse in the Irish Sweeps Derby six years earlier. His most recent winner in Ireland prior to Shirley Heights had been North Stoke, whose success in the Joe McGrath Memorial Stakes had brought his sequence to six, leading many people to believe that this bargain-basement yearling would have won that year's Derby had he been entered. Since becoming a trainer in his own right John Dunlop had formed a very happy partnership with Ron Hutchinson and it was particularly hard luck on this very likeable Australian that he should have decided to retire at the end of the 1977 season, having ridden Shirley Heights in two of his three juvenile successes.

On the day that Ron Hutchinson had crossed to Ireland to ride North Stoke at Leopardstown John Dunlop had sent out two other good winners at Ascot. One was Trusted in the Queen Elizabeth II Stakes and the other Shirley Heights, ridden by Greville Starkey to beat Bolak and Hawaiian Sound in the Royal Lodge Stakes. That performance had served to earn Shirley Heights a 25-to-1 quote for the Derby and had also decided Greville Starkey on his Derby mount, all things being equal. Beaten a long way by Whitstead on his seasonal reappearance at Lingfield, Shirley Heights had then proceeded to give weight and a beating to Ile de Bourbon at Newmarket and, in the Dante Stakes, his final race before Epsom, he had defeated Julio Mariner, Sexton Blake and Remainder Man. In view of the fact that he had now beaten every Classic colt of his generation in England and Ireland, some of them on several occasions, it was a pity that injury should have necessitated Shirley Heights' premature retirement to stud. Just what a pity became increasingly evident as Ile de Bourbon won the King George VI and Queen Elizabeth Stakes and then Julio Mariner redeemed his promise in the St Leger. Had Shirley Heights been able to confirm his superiority over two colts that he had already beaten decisively, he would demand comparison with Nijinsky, Grundy and The Minstrel. As it is, Shirley Heights, still only the sixth horse ever to win both the English and Irish Derbies, commenced his career as a stallion at the Sandringham Stud in Norfolk in 1979.

Hawaiian Sound, who simply did not know how to run a bad race, finished third to Ile de Bourbon in the King George VI and Queen Elizabeth Stakes, won the Benson & Hedges Gold Cup at York and completed his hard-working season by finishing second to Swiss Maid in the Champion Stakes. In contrast, Exdirectory, having promised so much at the Curragh, disappointed dreadfully in both the King George VI and Queen Elizabeth Stakes and in the Prix de l'Arc de Triomphe. Inkerman regained his earlier winning form in the Joe McGrath Memorial Stakes, before going to America, where he remained. Encyclopaedia won the Ulster Harp Derby, Strong Gale won in Munich and Valley Forge won the Blandford Stakes. The combined efforts of his Irish Sweeps Derby victims merely confirmed that Shirley Heights was the best colt of his generation.

Just as other years remain forever associated with the triumphs of particular horses, so 1978 became the year of a jockey – Greville Starkey. Born in Lichfield in 1939, Greville Starkey served his apprenticeship with Harry Thompson Jones at Newmarket, rode his first winner in 1955 and became leading apprentice in 1958. The following year he began an association with John Oxley's Hurworth House stable, which was to last until 1969 and provided him with his first English Classic winner when Homeward Bound won the Oaks in 1964. Four years later he won the Lincolnshire Handicap on Lady Halifax's Frankincense, landing the gamble which enabled Starkey's friend and hunting companion, Barry Hills, to set up on his own as a trainer. However, much as Hills liked and admired his friend, he, like too many others in racing, had come to think of Greville Starkey as a horseman rather than a jockey – the worst thing that can happen to a flat race jockey. When Henry Cecil signed him up as stable jockey in 1970 it looked as though Greville Starkey might at last have got the opportunity to prove that he could not only 'make' horses, but could ride them winners as well. Unfortunately, though the alliance did provide him with his first Irish Classic winner – Cloonagh in the Irish One Thousand Guineas in 1973 – Starkey could not tolerate being stood down in favour of Lester Piggott on the big occasion. He then began to ride for Guy Harwood, who was gradually making his name as a flat race trainer and in 1975 Starkey startled those who had written him off as a middle-division, journeyman jockey when winning the Eclipse Stakes on the German-trained outsider, Star Appeal. Surprise turned to astonishment when this unlikely combination carried off the Prix de l'Arc de Triomphe.

However, none of what had gone before prepared the racing world for Greville Starkey's triumphal progress through 1978, when he appeared to win every worthwhile race in the Calendar. His last-stride success on Shirley Heights in the Epsom Derby was followed by an even closer win on Fair Salinia in the Oaks. On to the Royal Ascot meeting, where he carried off the Ascot Gold Cup on Shangamuzo and the Norfolk Stakes on Schweppshire Lad. Shirley Heights and Fair Salinia then proceeded to give the 'jockey of the year', as Starkey had already become known, an incredible second Classic double on the Curragh. Schweppshire Lad provided a double of a different type when carrying Starkey to success in the National Stakes at Sandown. Fair Salinia in the Yorkshire Oaks, Vaigly Great in the Ayr Gold Cup and, finally, Swiss Maid in the Champion Stakes set the seal on an unforgettable year for silent, solemn-faced Greville Starkey.

Saturday, 1st July, 1978   **£72,172.50**   **11 Ran**   1½m

Irish Sweeps Derby (Group 1). £30,000 and a trophy value £500 added to the stakes by Irish Hospitals' Sweepstakes. For three years old entire colts and fillies. One mile and a half.

Sweepstakes, £25 to enter, 23rd February, 1977 or £1000 each if entered on 7th December, 1977, £60 extra for acceptors on 9th November, 1977, £50 extra for acceptors on 15th March, 1978, £1000 additional for acceptors on 7th June, 1978, £100 extra if declared to run. Second to receive 20% and the third 10% of the whole stakes after deduction of bonuses to breeders as follows – Winner £500, Second £300, Third £200. Weights – Colts 9st; Fillies 8st 11lb.

The Racing Board will contribute a sum equal to 5% of the whole stakes (after deduction of bonuses) to the owner of the fourth horse if there are eight or more runners.

The Management of the I.S.I.S. will pay to the breeder of the winner and which is qualified under that scheme an amount equal to 10% of the prize money payable to that horse.

Note— Subject to the usual conditions the Racing Board will pay special allowances as follows towards the transport costs of runners from abroad in this race:– Great Britain £200 per horse; other European countries £250 per horse; other countries £500 per horse.

1	Lord Halifax's	SHIRLEY HEIGHTS	9.0	J. L. Dunlop (GB)

1 Lord Halifax's   SHIRLEY HEIGHTS   9.0   J. L. Dunlop (GB)
                      (G. Starkey)   B. colt Mill Reef – Hardiemma by Hardicanute.
2 Mrs J. R. Mullion's EXDIRECTORY (C. Roche)   9.0   P. J. Prendergast
                      Ch. colt Ballymore – Regal Bell by Princely Gift.
3 Mr R. E. Sangster's HAWAIIAN SOUND   9.0   B. W. Hills (GB)
                      (W. Shoemaker)
                      B. colt Hawaii – Sound of Success by Successor.
4 Mr Simon Fraser's   INKERMAN (L. Piggott)   9.0   M. V. O'Brien
                      B. colt Vaguely Noble – Crimea by Princequillo.
5 Mrs Mehl-Muelhens's STRONG GALE (R. Carroll) 9.0   J. Oxx
                      Br. colt Lord Gayle – Sterntau by Tamerlane.
6 Mr R. E. Sangster's ENCYCLOPAEDIA (T. Murphy) 9.0   M. V. O'Brien
                      B. colt Reviewer – Arkadina by Ribot.
7 Mrs D. J. Jardine's REMAINDER MAN (T. Ives) 9.0   R. Hollinshead (GB)
                      Ch. colt Connaught – Honerone by Sammy Davis.
8 Mr P. J. Prendergast's RATHDOWNEY (J. Roe)   9.0   Owner
                      Ch. colt Ballymore – Roanoke by Charlottesville.
9 Mr Bertram R.   VALLEY FORGE (W. Swinburn) 9.0   D. K. Weld
  Firestone's   B. colt Petingo – Border Bounty by Bounteous.
10 Mr Mahmoud Fustok's EL BADR (Y. Saint-Martin) 9.0   M. Zilber (FR)
                      B. colt Weavers' Hall – Indian Maid by Astec.
11 Mr J. Hanson's   MAJESTIC MAHARAJ   9.0   Owner (GB)
                      (J. Bleasdale)
                      Br. colt Taj Dewan – Canaan by Santa Claus.

SP 5/4 SHIRLEY HEIGHTS; 3/1 Inkerman; 6/1 Hawaiian Sound; 8/1 Exdirectory; 9/1 Strong Gale; 16/1 El Badr; 18/1 Remainder Man; 40/1 Majestic Maharaj; 50/1 Valley Forge; 100/1 Encyclopaedia, Rathdowney. TOTE (20p unit) 64p. Places 30p, 48p, 50p. Head, neck, 1 length. 2m 32.3s. Winner trained by Mr John L. Dunlop at Arundel, West Sussex.

1979

The concluding chapter of this saga of the Irish Derby to date opens on a note of consciously Irish irony with the admission that the interminable strike in the postal service eventually obliged the sponsors to abandon their annual sweepstake on the Irish Sweeps Derby! However, emerging a glorious green after the longest winter in living memory, the Curragh provided the perfect setting for the richest Irish Derby ever run, this auspicious occasion being marked in appropriate style by the opening of a new champagne bar overlooking the parade ring.

For the fifth year in succession the race had attracted the Epsom Derby winner. His name was Troy and by his scintillating burst of acceleration in the Bicentennial Epsom Derby he had won by the longest winning margin since Manna in 1925. Of those that had followed Troy home at Epsom, only two cared to renew rivalry with Sir Michael Sobell's magnificent colt. They were Dickens Hill and Laska Floko. The former had won the Ballymoss Stakes prior to crediting his ebullient trainer Mick O'Toole with his first Classic success in the Irish Two Thousand Guineas. Hitting the front two furlongs out at Epsom Dickens Hill had looked the likely winner until demolished by Troy. Even his invariably optimistic trainer seemed doubtful that Dickens Hill could do more than reduce the deficit, even though he was to be ridden for speed on this occasion. Laksa Floko, an exasperating maiden of undoubted ability, had run deplorably at Epsom, where he had finished last, and even the presence of Lester Piggott on his back failed to arouse any appreciable support. Of the two French challengers the unbeaten Fabulous Dancer seemed more likely to cause an upset than Scipio. In any case a line through Northern Baby, third at Epsom, suggested that the French Classic colts were a moderate lot. The nine-strong field was dominated during the preliminaries by Troy, whose principal rival in the paddock was undoubtedly Princess Caroline of Monaco, cynosure of all eyes as she accompanied the infinitely more alluring Madame Binet, part-owner of Dickens Hill.

Deprived of even a worthwhile forecast betting opportunity, the large and colourful crowd assembled on sunlit, windblown stands to witness a repetition of the Epsom result. As retiring Senior Starter Hubie Tyrrell despatched his last Irish Derby field Brian Proctor shot Rivadon into a clear lead in an effort to ensure a strong gallop for Troy and thus to blunt Dickens Hill's speed. Setting a headlong gallop ahead of his nearest pursuers, The Bart, Scorpio and Fabulous Dancer, Rivadon had the entire field off the bridle by the time he surrendered his lead to The Bart at the top of the hill turning for home. So far the plot had unfolded with boring predictability. However, as Christy Roche hurtled towards the straight on The Bart, a swelling murmur from the stands signalled that the favourite might be in trouble. Such gleeful surmise was, alas, shortlived. Once in the straight Carson pulled Troy outside The Bart and the two French colts, put down his head and began to scrub, slap and drive in his inimitable style. As at Epsom the effect was instantaneous. Devouring the ground with ever-lengthening strides Troy surged away to win un-challenged. Saved for a late run, Dickens Hill finished a clear second, reducing the deficit to only three lengths, while Bohemian Grove came with an even more delayed run to snatch third place, a short head in front of Scorpio. Willie Shoemaker's performance on this rank outsider was even more commendable in view of the fact that he had injured his foot so badly leaving the stalls that he was unable to carry his saddle back to scale. Though still limping badly the pint-sized American went on to ride the next two winners, thus completing a treble.

While most of those present at the Curragh had seen Troy's Epsom triumph on television, not many had appreciated that blistering burst of speed and relentless acceleration that had suddenly left his rivals floundering in his wake. Having seen it now in the flesh, it was a somewhat subdued, almost awestruck crowd which applauded the return to the unsaddling area of only the sixth dual Derby winner since Orby seventy-two years earlier.

A strongly-made dark bay colt, whose three white socks emphasised his exceptionally long pasterns, Troy was bred at Ballymacoll Stud, Dunboyne, by his joint owners, Sir Michael Sobell and his son-in-law, Sir Arnold Weinstock, who had purchased the 300-acre property, along with all her bloodstock, from the executors of that remarkable character Dorothy Paget following her death in 1960. From the last full crop of the much-lamented Petingo, Troy was also the last produce of his dam, the Hornbeam mare La Milo. Successful four times as a three-year-old in the Sobell colours when trained by Sir Gordon Richards, La Milo bred seven foals, all of whom proved successful on the racecourse. The best of these, other than Troy, being Admetus, winner of the Washington DC International, the Grand Prix d'Evry, the Prince of Wales's Stakes and the Prix Maurice de Neuil. Due to visit Reform in the hopes of producing another Admetus, La Milo carried Troy for so long and in such obvious pain from rapidly worsening arthritis, that it was decided to have her put down as soon as her weak and gangling colt had been weaned. As Petingo had died from a haemorrhage at Simmonstown Stud in February 1976, only a month before the birth of his most famous son, Troy was truly an orphan. However, the line remains secure at Ballymacoll through Silk Rein, the only filly that La Milo ever bred. After an upbringing which Peter Reynolds, the courteous and extremely competent manager at Ballymacoll, recalls as unexceptional, Troy joined Dick Hern at West Ilsley. Twice successful as a two-year-old, Troy was narrowly defeated by Ela-Mana-Mou in the Royal Lodge Stakes. In Reynolds' understandably biased estimation this big and backward colt had done sufficient in his first season to justify winter-long dreams of Epsom glory. Impressive victories at Sandown and Goodwood convinced stable jockey Willie Carson to opt for Troy rather than the Royal colt, Milford, in the Bicentennial Epsom Derby; an act of faith which was triumphantly vindicated.

Octogenarian Jockey Club member Sir Michael Sobell had made his fortune in the electrical industry – subsequently receiving a knighthood – before becoming deeply involved in racing. Fired by the success of London Cry in the Cambridgeshire in 1958, he purchased the late Dorothy Paget's bloodstock interests, lock, stock and barrel – approximately 120 thoroughbreds. Maintaining the association with Sir Gordon Richards and Scobie Breasley, Michael Sobell raced with consistent, if unspectacular success up to the time of Sir Gordon's retirement in 1970. During that period the combination had twice been third in the Irish Derby, with Tiger in 1963 and Dart Board in 1967. The Sobell horses then moved to West Ilsley, where Major Dick Hern trained for the Astor family and their friends, among them HM the Queen. That long-sought first Classic success for the 'Pale blue, yellow and white check cap' was achieved when Gaily triumphed in the Irish One Thousand Guineas in 1974, while others of the calibre of Reform, Sallust and Sun Prince continued to enhance the record of Ballymacoll breeding. In 1976 the West Ilsley stable hit the headlines in less happy circumstances when the news broke immediately after Lady Beaverbrook's Relkino, ridden by long-standing stable jockey Joe Mercer, had finished second in the Epsom Derby that Mercer was being replaced as stable jockey at the end of the season by Willie Carson. Amidst a welter of rumour, counter-rumour, evasion and denial it finally emerged that Sobell and his hard-headed son-in-law, as owners of the stable, called the tune and neither the Queen, Lady Beaverbrook, the Astors nor, least of all, Dick Hern had any say in the matter. Far too good a jockey to be thus discarded, Mercer was quickly secured by the powerful Henry Cecil stable and continues to ride with success appropriate to his supremely stylish talent. That unfortunate episode apart, the Sobell colours have always had a popular following with the racing public, who appreciate Troy's owners as staunch, if unsentimental supporters of the Turf.

The man caught in the middle of the Mercer–Carson affair was one William Richard Hern, a mild-mannered former major in the Irish Horse, whose career had subsequently taken him through Porlock Vale Equestrian Academy, Michael Pope's Blewbury stable and a successful spell as private trainer to the hot-tempered Lionel Holliday, for whom he saddled Hethersett to win the St Leger in 1962, partially atoning for that colt's ill fortune in being brought down when favourite for Lark-spur's Epsom Derby. Leading trainer that year, Dick Hern moved into West Ilsley on the retirement of Jack Colling in 1965 and commenced a lasting association with the Astor family, which got off to a flying start when Provoke won the St Leger and Craighouse annexed the Irish equivalent that same season. Since then the Hern stable has seldom been long out of the Classic limelight, achieving notable successes with such as Brigadier Gerard, Bustino and the Royal fillies Highclere and Dunfermline. Unlike the majority of his fellow trainers, Dick Hern is fortunate in being free to concentrate his consummate care and skill on the horses in his charge without having to train the owners as well and in an age of spiralling costs and staggering capital outlay necessary to practise his exasperating art he is doubtless thankful for that.

Willie Carson, who succeeded Joe Mercer at West Ilsley, is the most forceful, effective and uniquely unstylish jockey riding in England today. Born in Stirling, Scotland, he started his apprenticeship with Gerald Armstrong, concluded it at brother Sam Armstrong's famous 'academy' and emerged as first jockey to Lord Derby. Having ended Lester Piggott's eight-year reign as champion jockey in 1972, he held the title for a further year, relinquished it to Pat Eddery and regained it from his Irish-born rival in 1978. To date he has won each of the English Classics with the exception of the One Thousand Guineas, while Dibidale's victory in the Irish Oaks provided compensation for being robbed of certain success in the Epsom equivalent by a slipping saddle. Cocky, cheerful, past master of the lightening riposte, Willie Carson radiates an inexhaustible fund of nervous energy which has seen him time and again induce performances from sluggish or wayward horses, which no one, least of all the animals themselves, would have believed them of being capable.

When Troy demolished his opponents at Epsom it was widely contended that he had beaten a bad bunch. Within weeks this theory was exploded. Lyphard's Wish ran the older Crimson Beau to a length at Royal Ascot, while at the same meeting Ela-Mana-Mou confirmed Epsom form with Hardgreen, Lake City and Man Of Vision. Then Milford reappeared successfully at Newmarket. But most convincing testimony to Troy's merit was provided by Dickens Hill, whose clearcut victory over Crimson Beau and Epsom third, Northern Baby, in the Eclipse Stakes only a week after the Irish Derby prompted his rider Tony Murray to declare that there could seldom, if ever, have been better than Troy. The dual Derby winner duly reappeared to confirm his greatness in that established all-age Classic, the King George VI and Queen Elizabeth Stakes, where he encountered older horses for the first

Saturday, 30th June, 1979	**£96,910**	**9 Ran**	**1½m**

Irish Sweeps Derby (Group 1). £50,000 added to the stakes (of which £30,000 and a trophy value is contributed by Irish Hospitals' Sweepstakes). For three years old entire colts and fillies. One mile and a half.

Sweepstakes, £25 to enter, 22nd February, 1978 or £1000 each if entered on 6th December, 1978. £60 extra for acceptors on 8th November, 1978. £50 extra for acceptors on 14th March, 1979, £100 extra if declared to run. Second to receive 20% and the third 10% of the whole stakes after deduction of bonuses to breeders as follows – Winner £500, Second £300, Third £200. Weights – Colts 9st; Fillies 8st 11lb.

The Racing Board will contribute a sum equal to 5% of the whole stakes (after deduction of the bonuses) to the owner of fourth horse if there are eight or more runners.

Note—Subject to the usual conditions the Racing Board will pay a special allowance of £500 towards the transport costs of runners from abroad which finish out of the first four.

1 Sir Michael Sobell's   TROY (W. Carson)   9.0   W. R. Hern (GB)
B. colt Petingo – La Milo by Hornbeam.

2 Mme J. P. Binet's   DICKENS HILL (A. Murray)   9.0   M. A. O'Toole
Ch. colt Mount Hagen – London Life by Panaslipper.

3 Mr William   BOHEMIAN GROVE   9.0   A. J. Maxwell
  McDonald's   (W. Shoemaker)
B. colt Personality – Frimanaha by Crafty Admiral.

4 Mr G. A. Oldham's   SCORPIO (P. Paquet)   9.0   F. Boutin (FR)
B. colt Sir Gaylord – Zambara by Mossborough.

5 Mr Franklin N.   THE BART (C. Roche)   9.0   T. G. Curtin
  Groves's   B. colt Le Fabuleux – Liscia by Saint Crespin III

6 Captain M. D. Lemos's LASKA FLOKO (L. Piggott)   9.0   C. Brittain (GB)
B. colt Thatch – Prima by Alcide.

7 Mme Alec Head's   FABULOUS DANCER (F. Head) 9.0   Miss C. Head (FR)
B. colt Northern Dancer – Last of the Line By The Axe II.

8 Exors the late F. H.   BALLYBOGGAN PRINCE   9.0   John M. Oxx
  Langan's   (R. Carroll)
B. colt Brigardier Gerard – Pale Jasmine by Continuation.

9 Lady Beaverbrook's   RIVADON (B. Proctor)   9.0   W. R. Hern (GB)
B. colt Riva Ridge – Sarah Bernhardt by Buckpasser.

SP 4/9 TROY; 9/2 Dickens Hill; 7/1 Fabulous Dancer; 12/1 Scorpio; 40/1 Laska Floko; 50/1 The Bart; 66/1 Bohemian Grove; 100/1 Ballyboggan Prince; 300/1 Rivadon. TOTE (20p unit) 32p. Places 24p, 32p, 60p.
4 lengths, 2½ lengths, short head. 2m 30.6s.
Winner trained by Mr W. R. Hern at Newbury, Berkshire.

time. In the enforced absence of the previous year's winner, Ile de Bourbon, Troy started at long odds-on to confirm Epsom form with Ela-Mana-Mou and to beat the four-year-olds, Swiss Maid and Gay Mecene. Though less spectacular than at Epsom or the Curragh, Troy once again surged clear in the closing stages to beat Gay Mecene and Ela-Mana-Mou, laying claim to be regarded as the outstanding race-horse in Europe, where his racecourse earnings constituted a new record. Within days of that Ascot triumph came the announcement that Troy had been syndicated at a valuation of £7 million and that he would retire to stud in England at the end of his three-year-old career.

RECORD OF OWNERS IN THE IRISH CLASSICS 1866–1979

	Fst Wnr	2000	1000	Derby	Oaks	St Leger	Total
HH Aga Khan (1878–1957)	1925	–	2	5	5	1	13
Major Dermot McCalmont (1887–1968)	1927	1½	2	2	2	1	8½
Mr William Barnett (18 –1946)	1929	1	1	1½	–	4	7½
Mr Joseph McGrath (1895–1966)	1942	1	2	2	1	1	7
Mr Daniel Sullivan (18 –1940)	1915	1	2	1	2	1	7
Colonel Giles Loder (1885–1966)	1918	1	1	2½	–	2	6½
Sir Victor Sassoon (1882–1961)	1935	3	–	2	–	1	6
Prince Aly Khan (1911–1960)	1947	–	2	–	1	2	5
Mr Robert E. Sangster	1977	1	2	1	1	–	5
Mr Charles J. Blake (18 –1917)	1883	–	–	3	1	–	4
Sir Thomas Dixon (1868–1950)	1915	2	–	–	2	–	4
Sir Percy Loraine (1880–1961)	1934	2	1	–	1	–	4
Mrs J. R. Mullion	1963	1	3	–	–	–	4
Mr Y. J. J. Kirkpatrick	1944	1½	1	–	–	1	3½
Mr James Cockin (18 –1876)	1866	–	–	3	–	–	3
Mr Richard Croker (1841–1922)	1905	–	–	1	2	–	3
Mr Charles W. Engelhard (1917–1971)	1967	–	–	3	–	–	3
Sir Harold S. Gray (1867–1951)	1931	1	1	1	–	–	3
Mr John Ismay (1885–1972)	1945	1	–	1	–	1	3
Mr Charles L. Mackean (18 –1943)	1921	1	1	–	1	–	3
Mr John McShain	1957	–	–	1	1	1	3
Mr James McVey, jr	1943	–	1	1	1	–	3
Mr Frederick S. Myerscough (1881–1954)	1941	1	1	1	–	–	3
Mr Gerald A. Oldham	1956	1	–	2	–	–	3

TRAINING RECORDS IN THE IRISH CLASSICS 1866–1979

	Stables	Fst Wnr	2000	1000	Derby	Oaks	St Leger	Total
M. Vincent O'Brien	Cashel, Ireland	1953	2	3	4	4	6	19*
Colonel Arthur J. Blake	Maryborough, Ireland	1925	5	6	2	2	2	17
Patrick J. Prendergast	Curragh, Ireland	1950	3	5	4	1	3	16*
James Dunne	Curragh, Ireland	1883	–	–	4	5	3	12
Hubert M. Hartigan	Curragh, Ireland	1941	1	6	–	3	2	12
John T. Rogers	Curragh, Ireland	1931	3	2	2	1	3	11
S. C. Jeffrey	Maryborough, Ireland	1895	2	1	3	3	1	10
Harry Wragg	Newmarket, England	1951	1	2	3	3	–	9*
Robert Fetherstonhaugh	Curragh, Ireland	1933	½	2	2	2	2	8½
John Oxx	Curragh, Ireland	1943	1	–	–	4	3	8
Captain Darby Rogers	Curragh, Ireland	1940	2	2	1	1	2	8
Richard C. Dawson	Whatcombe, England	1925	–	–	2½	2	3	7½
Philip Behan	Curragh, Ireland	1906	2	–	1	3	1	7
Henry S. Persse	Stockbridge, England	1913	1	2	2	2	–	7
Captain Sir Cecil Boyd-Rochfort	Newmarket, England	1924	–	–	–	4	2	6
Michael Dawson	Curragh, Ireland	1902	–	–	4	2	–	6
Seamus McGrath	Sandyford, Ireland	1955	1	1	2	1	1	6*
James J. Parkinson	Curragh, Ireland	1901	–	1	2	4	–	6
Peter P. Gilpin	Newmarket, England	1918	1	–	2½	–	2	5½
J. A. Frank Butters	Newmarket, England	1932	–	–	4	1	–	5
Michael C. Collins	Curragh, Ireland	1942	2	1	1	–	1	5
Alec Head	Chantilly, France	1956	–	3	–	1	1	5*
Roderic More O'Ferrall	Kildangan, Ireland	1930	2	1	–	1	1	5
J. Michael Rogers	Curragh, Ireland	1952	4	–	1	–	–	5

*currently holding licence to train.

RIDING RECORDS IN THE IRISH CLASSICS 1866–1979

	Nat	Fst Wnr	2000	1000	Derby	Oaks	St Leger	Total
Mornington Wing	England	1920	2		6	1	7	23
Thomas Burns	Scotland	1916	5	5	1	4	6	21
Joseph Canty	Ireland	1924	3	5	3½	1	2	14½
Lester Piggott	England	1965	2	2	4	3	3	14*
Stephen Donoghue	England	1908	2		5	2	2	11
Liam Ward	Ireland	1951	1	1	2	3	3	10
E. Martin Quirke	Ireland	1919	5	1	1	2		9
Michael Beary	Ireland	1919			2	4	2	8
Charles Smirke	England	1940	2	1	2	3		8
W. (Bill) Williamson	Australia	1960	1	1	1	3	2	8
W. Rae Johnstone	Australia	1948	2	1	2	1	1	7
John Moylan	Ireland	1926	½	1	2	1	2	6½
Thomas P. Burns	Ireland	1957	2	1	1		2	6
Edward Gardner	England	1931	1	2		1	2	6
Garnet Bougoure	Australia	1959	1		2		2	5
John Doyle	Ireland	1896			2	3		5
Herbert Holmes	England	1949		2	1	2		5
George Archibald	USA	1922	1		1½		2	4½
Cecil Ray	England	1933			1½	1	2	4½
Algernon Anthony	England	1899			2	2		4
John Connolly	Ireland	1879			4			4
James Dines	Ireland	1922	1			1	2	4
Ron Hutchinson	Australia	1960	1	3				4
Emanual Mercer	England	1956	1		1	2		4
Christopher Roche	Ireland	1972	1	2			1	4*

*currently riding.

RECORD OF SIRES IN THE IRISH CLASSICS 1866–1979

			2000	1000	Derby	Oaks	St léger	Total
GALLINULE	1884	Isonomy – Moorhen by Hermit	–	–	6	1	–	7
SPION KOP	1917	Spearmint – Hammerkop by Gallinule	1	2	1	–	2	6
BLANDFORD	1919	Swynford – Blanche by White Eagle	–	1	1½	–	3	5½
ACHTOI	1912	Santoi – Achray by Martini Henry	2	1	1	1	–	5
SPEARMINT	1903	Carbine – Maid of the Mint by Minting	1	–	2	–	2	5
ARGOSY	1914	Bachelor's Double – Fragrant by Spearmint	2	–	1	–	1	4
CAPTIVATION	1902	Cyllene – Charm by St Simon	–	–	–	1	3	4
CHAMOSSAIRE	1942	Precipitation – Snowberry by Cameronian	1	–	3	–	–	4
DASTUR	1929	Solario – Friar's Daughter by Friar Marcus	1	1	1	1	–	4
NEARCO	1935	Pharos – Nogara by Havresac	–	–	1	3	–	4
RIBOT	1952	Tenerani – Romanella by El Greco	–	–	3	1	–	4
ROI HERODE	1904	Le Samaritain – Roxelane by War Dance	1	–	1	2	–	4
SAYAJIRAO	1944	Nearco – Rosy Legend by Dark Legend	–	2	–	1	1	4
STARDUST	1937	Hyperion – Sister Stella by Friar Marcus	1	1	1	1	–	4
TREDENNIS	1898	Kendal – St Marguerite by Hermit	1	–	2	–	1	4
UNCAS	1865	Stockwell – Nightingale by Mountain Deer	–	–	4	–	–	4

IRISH OAKS

Year	Winner & Rider	Owner	SP	Trainer	Ran	Sire
1 mile						
1895	SAPLING (J. Wynne)	Mr C. Hannan	8/1	James Dunne	10	Marmiton
1896	KOSMOS (John Doyle)	Mr W. J. Goulding	4/9f	W. P. Cullen	3	Atheling
1897	DABCHICK (Alf. Aylin)	Capt. F. Fetherstonhaugh	1/1f	S. C. Jeffrey	7	Gallinule
1898	SABINE QUEEN (T. Doyle)	Mr F. F. MacCabe	1/2f	T. Doyle	5	Hackler
1899	IRISH IVY (T. Almack)	Capt. Peel	1/2f	W. Behan	5	Marmiton
1900	MAY RACE (A. Anthony)	Capt. Eustace Loder	2/1	D. McNally	6	Melanion
1901	ROYAL MANTLE (J. Thompson)	Mr P. J. Brophy	1/1f	J. J. Parkinson	5	Henry VIII
1902	MARIEVALE (D. Condon)	Mr W. Dunne	7/2	M. Dawson	5	Buckingham
1903	MARY LESTER (W. Higgs)	Mr C. J. Blake	4/1	S. C. Jeffrey	5	Lesterlin
1904	COPESTONE FILLY (W. Higgs)	Mr J. Lonsdale	4/1	James Dunne	5	Laveno
1905	BLAKESTOWN (J. Thompson)	Mr R. Croker	1/5f	J. J. Parkinson	3	Lesterlin
1906	JULIET (A. Anthony)	Mrs Sadleir-Jackson	5/2	Philip Behan	6	Troubadour
1907	REINA (F. Hunter)	Sir E. C. Cochrane	1/1	James Dunne	2	Count Schomberg
1908	QUEEN OF PEACE (S. Donoghue)	Mr R. Croker	2/1	J. Allen	5	General Peace
1909	FREDITH (John Doyle)	Mr Joseph Cooper	1/1f	M. Reidy	7	Hackler
1910	BLAIR ROYAL (S. Donoghue)	Mr E. Tanner	10/1	Capt. Dewhurst (GB)	5	Blairfinde
1911	TULLYNACREE (M. Colbert)	Mr J. Hutton	6/1	M. Dawson	6	Fowling-piece
1912	SHINING WAY (J. Thompson)	Mr J. C. Galstaun	4/7f	J. J. Parkinson	6	Oppressor
1913	ATHGREANY (T. Bennett)	Mr P. Murphy	4/1	J. J. Parkinson	7	His Majesty or Galloping Simon
1914	MAY EDGAR (John Doyle)	Mr P. Cullinan	5/2jf	James Dunne	6	Sir Edgar
1 mile, 4 furlongs						
1915	LATHARNA (W. Barrett)	Sir T. Dixon	8/1	J. Hunter	9	Kosmos Bey
1916	CAPTIVE PRINCESS (T. Burns)	Mr W. A. Wallis	5/1	James Dunne	6	Captivation
1917	GOLDEN MAID (T. Burns)	Mr P. Nelke	5/1	C. Pickering (GB)	8	Goldon Rod
1918	JUDEA (B. Carslake)	Capt. C. Moore	2/1	C. Pickering (GB)	4	Roi Herode
1919	SNOW MAIDEN (M. Breary)	Mr J. J. Maher	5/2jf	P. Behan	6	The Tetrarch
1920	PLACE ROYALE (M. Beary)	Cap. C. Moore	9/4	S. C. Jeffrey	6	Royal Realm
1921	THE KIWI (M. Beary)	Sir W. J. Goulding	2/1f	P. Behan	7	Kosmos Bey
1922	MISS HAZELWOOD (J. Dines)	Capt. B. Daly	25/1	F. Grundy	10	Royal Canopy
1923	BECKA (F. Bullock)	Mr W. M. G. Singer	4/1	Alec Taylor (GB)	10	Sir Eager
1924	AMETHYSTINE (J. Childs)	Lady Nunburnholme	3/1	Boyd-Rochfort (GB)	8	Hainault
1925	IXIA (F. Bullock)	Mr W. M. G. Singer	4/1	Alec Taylor (GB)	6	Rossendale

Year	Winner & Rider	SP	Owner	Trainer	Ran	Sire
1926	RESPLENDENT (T. Burns)	1/1f	Mr D. Sullivan	H. S. Persse (GB)	7	By George
1927	CINQ A SEPT (J. Childs)	6/1	Mr Marshall Field	Boyd-Rochfort (GB)	7	Roi Herode
1928	HAINTONETTE (F. Winter)	2/1jf	Mr J. A. Hirst	R. W. Colling (GB)	7	Hainault
1929	SOLOPTIC (E. M. Quirke)	1/10f	Mr C. L. Mackean	Col. A. J. Blake	4	Soldennis
1930	THERESINA (M. Beary)	4/5f	HH Aga Khan	R. C. Dawson (GB)	8	Diophon
1931	NITSICHIN (C. Richards)	5/1	Mr D. S. Kennedy	P. Thrale (GB)	8	Achtoi
1932	SANTARIA (E. M. Quirke)	5/1	Mr E. J. Hope	J. Ruttle	9	Santorb
1933	SALAR (C. Ray)	3/1jf	Mr R. C. Dawson	Owner (GB)	14	Salmon Trout
1934	FOXCROFT (J. Childs)	1/3f	Mr Marshall Field	Boyd-Rochfort (GB)	5	Foxlaw
1935	SMOKELESS (E. Gardner)	5/1	Mr R. J. Duggan	J. T. Rogers	8	Prince Galahad
1936	SILVERSOL (W. Nevett)	10/11f	Mr M. Peacock	Owner (GB)	6	Solario
1937	SOL SPERANZA (M. Wing)	8/1	Mr D. Sullivan	Col. A. J. Blake	7	Ballyferis
1938	CONVERSATION PIECE (P. Gomez)	3/1	Lady Furness	H. S. Persse (GB)	8	Orpen
1939	SUPERBE (P. Beasley)	5/4f	Duchess of Marlborough	Boyd-Rochfort (GB)	8	Bosworth
1940	QUEEN OF SHIRAZ (C. Smirke)	5/2	HH Aga Khan	F. Butters (GB)	11	Bahram
1941	UVIRA (T. Burns)	1/6f	Sir T. Dixon	H. G. Wellesley	5	Umidwar
1942	MAJIDEH (Joseph Canty)	1/6f	HH Aga Khan	H. M. Hartigan	8	Mahmoud
1943	SUNTOP (Joseph Canty)	4/5f	HH Aga Khan	H. Ussher	12	Dastur
1944	AVOCA (J. Moylan)	7/1	Major D. McCalmont	R. Fetherston'	9	Mr Jinks
1945	ADMIRABLE (A. Barrett)	25/1	Sir P. Loraine	R. More O'Ferrall	14	Nearco
1946	LINARIA (C. Smirke)	10/11f	Mr A. P. Reynolds	R. J. McCormick	10	Turkhan
1947	DESERT DRIVE (M. Molony)	2/1f	Mr G. Y. Kinnaird	Capt. D. Rogers	14	Admiral's Walk
1948	MASAKA (A. Brabazon)	1/1f	HH Aga Khan	H. M. Hartigan	10	Nearco
1949	CIRCUS LADY (Herbert Holmes)	3/1	Major D. McCalmont	R. Fetherston'	12	Fun Fair
1950	COREJADA (W. R. Johnstone)	4/7f	M Marcel Boussac	Semblet (FR)	16	Pharis
1951	DJEBELLICA (C. Smirke)	4/1	Comte de Chambure	C. Clout (FR)	13	Djebel
1952	FIVE SPOTS (J. Mullane)	11/2	Mr A. L. Hawkins	P. J. Prendergast	13	Blue Train
1953	NOORY (C. Smirke)	2/1	HH Aga Khan	R. Carver (FR)	11	Nearco
1954	PANTOMIME QUEEN (G. Cooney)	100/7	Miss Eileen McLean	H. M. Hartigan	15	Stardust
1955	AGAR'S PLOUGH (Herbert Holmes)	10/1	Major Victor McCalmont	R. F. Fetherston'	12	Combat
1956	GARDEN STATE (E. Mercer)	13/2	Mr H. Wragg	Owner (GB)	8	Krakatao
1957	SILKEN GLIDER (Jas. Eddery)	11/4	Mr Joseph McGrath	S. McGrath	15	Airborne
1958	AMANTE (L. Ward)	11/4	Prince Aly Khan	A. Head (FR)	11	Tehran
1959	DISCOREA (E. Mercer)	100/7	Mrs Arpad Plesch	H. Wragg (GB)	9	Dante
1960	LYNCHRIS (W. Williamson)	11/4f	Mrs E. M. Fawcett	J. Oxx	17	Sayajirao

1961	AMBERGRIS (J. Lindley)	6/4f	Mr R. More O'Ferrall	H. Wragg (GB)	10	Sicambre
1962	FRENCH CREAM (W. Rickaby)	100/9	Mr R. F. Dennis	G. T. Brooke (GB)	12	Faubourg

Irish Guinness Oaks

1963	HIBERNIA (W. Williamson)	6/4f	Dr M. Andree	J. Oxx	15	Masetto
1964	ANCASTA (J. Purtell)	3/1	Mr F. W. Burmann	M. V. O'Brien	9	Ballymoss
1965	AURABELLA (L. Ward)	22/1	Lt-Col. J. Silcock	M. V. O'Brien	10	Aureole
1966	MERRY MATE (W. Williamson)	100/9	Mr J. McShain	J. Oxx	10	Ballymoss
1967	PAMPALINA (J. Roe)	100/8	Mr Hans Paul	J. Oxx	14	Bairam
1968	CELINA (A. Barclay)	4/1	Mrs J. R. Hindley	C. F. N. Murless (GB)	12	Crepello
1969	GAIA (L. Ward)	9/1	Mrs J. W. Hanes	M. V. O'Brien	7	Charlottesville
1970	SANTA TINA (L. Piggott)	5/2f	Mrs S. O'Flaherty	C. Milbank (FR)	14	Santa Claus
1971	ALTESSE ROYALE (G. Lewis)	1/2f	Col. F. R. Hue-Williams	C. F. N. Murless (GB)	13	Saint Crespin
1972	REGAL EXCEPTION (M. Phillipperon)	4/1	Mr Robin F. Scully	J. B. Fellows (FR)	12	Ribot
1973	DAHLIA (W. Pyers)	8/1	Mr N. B. Hunt	M. Zilber (FR)	12	Vaguely Noble
1974	DIBIDALE (W. Carson)	7/4f	Mr N. J. F. Robinson	B. W. Hills (GB)	8	Aggressor
1975	JULIET MARNEY (L. Piggott)	5/2f	Mr J. I. Morrison	A. J. Tree (GB)	14	Blakeney
1976	LAGUNETTE (P. Paquet)	3/1	Mr Souren Vanian	F. Boutin (FR)	18	Val de Loir
1977	OLWYN (J. Lynch)	11/1	Mr S. Hanson	R. Boss (GB)	8	Relko
1978	FAIR SALINIA (G. Starkey)	3/1f	Mr R. E. Sangster	M. Stoute (GB)	12	Petingo
1979	GODETIA (L. Piggott)	6/4f		M. V. O'Brien	13	Sir Ivor

IRISH ONE THOUSAND GUINEAS

Year	Winner & Rider	SP	Owner	Trainer	Ran	Sire
1922	LADY VIOLETTE (M. Wing)	100/30	Mr A. Le Roch	S. C. Jeffrey	11	Rossendale
1923	GLENSHESK (M. Wing)	5/1	Capt. Dixon	F. Grundy	6	Junior
1924	VOLTOI (James Doyle)	4/5f	Mr J. J. M'Auley	T. Coombs	6	Achtoi
1925	FLYING DINAH (R. Cullen)	100/8	Capt. G. F. Dunne	Col. A. J. Blake	11	White Eagle
1926	RESPLENDENT (J. Moylan)	2/1f	Mr D. Sullivan	H. S. Persse (GB)	12	By George
1927	WEST INDIES (T. Burns)	2/1f	Lady Mahon	F. Grundy	9	Jackdaw
1528	MOUCHERON (John Doyle)	8/1	Capt. R. B. Brassey	H. M. Hartigan	13	Herodote
1929	SOLOPTIC (E. M. Quirke)	9/4	Mr C. L. Mackean	Col. A. J. Blake	9	Soldennis
1930	STAR OF EGYPT (T. Burns)	7/1	Mr G. A. Allen	R. More O'Ferrall	9	Allenby
1931	SPIRAL (M. Wing)	4/6f	Mr J. J. Maher	Col. A. J. Blake	7	Spion Kop
1932	PETONI (John Doyle)	8/1	Mr D. J. Cogan	W. Magee	12	Zanoni
1933	SPY-ANN (T. Burns)	5/1jf	Mr T. K. Laidlaw	R. Fetherston'	17	Spion Kop
1934	KYLOE (T. Burns)	1/3f	Sir P. Loraine	John Murphy	6	Blandford
1935	SMOKELESS (E. Gardner)	4/5f	Mr R. J. Duggan	J. T. Rogers	9	Prince Gallahad
1936	HARVEST STAR (E. Gardner)	100/8	Mr W. Barnett	J. T. Rogers	6	Trigo
1937	SOL SPERANZA (M. Wing)	4/7f	Mr D. Sullivan	Col. A. J. Blake	7	Ballyferis
1938	LAPEL (B. Carslake)	8/11f	Major D. McCalmont	Lambton (GB)	12	Apelle
1939	SERPENT STAR (Joseph Canty)	100/8	Sir Harold Gray	James Canty	7	Sea Serpent
1940	GAINSWORTH (M. Wing)	4/1	Mr E. A. Robinson	Col. A. J. Blake	12	Bosworth
1941	MILADY ROSE (G. Wells)	1/2f	Mr F. S. Myerscough	Col. A. J. Blake	9	Knight of the Garter
1942	MAJIDEH (Joseph Canty)	4/6f	HH Aga Khan	H. M. Hartigan	13	Mahmoud
1943	SUNTOP (J. Tyrrell)	7/2	Mr G. J. Ellis	H. Ussher	12	Dastur
1944	ANNETTA (Joseph Canty)	5/2	Mr P. E. Burell	H. M. Hartigan	10	Fairway
1945	PANASTRID (M. Wing)	7/2jf	Mr Joseph McGrath	M. C. Collins	16	Panorama
1946	ELLA RETFORD (Joseph Canty)	100/8	Mr J. McLean	H. M. Hartigan	13	Turkhan
1947	SEA SYMPHONY (M. Wing)	11/2	Lt-Col. Giles Loder	H. M. Hartigan	20	Fairhaven
1948	MORNING WINGS (Joseph Canty)	5/1	Mr Y. J. Kirkpatrick	E. McGrath	16	The Phoenix
1949	SUNLIT RIDE (Herbert Holmes)	6/1jf	Capt. G. A. Clark	R. Fetherston'	18	Solenoid
1950	PRINCESS TRUDY (M. Molony)	1/1f	Mr R. McIlhagga	P. J. Prendergast	18	His Highness
1951	QUEEN OF SHEBA (Hbt. Holmes)	3/1	Major D. McCalmont	H. S. Persse (GB)	16	Persian Gulf
1952	NASHUA (C. Smirke)	7/2	HH Aga Khan	H. M. Hartigan	14	Nasrullah
1953	NORTHERN GLEAM (T. Burns)	5/2	Lady Bury	Capt. D. Rogers	15	Borealis
1954	PANTOMIME QUEEN (W. Nevett)	6/1	Miss Eileen McLean	H. M. Hartigan	16	Stardust

Year	Horse (Jockey)	Odds	Owner	No.	Sire	Trainer
1955	DARK ISSUE (P. Canty)	6/1	Sir W. Churchill	16	Sayajirao	Capt. D. Rogers
1956	PEDEROBA (W. R. Johnstone)	4/1	M Pierre Wertheimer	16	Djebe	A. Head (FR)
1957	EVEN STAR (F. Durr)	6/1	Mr Rex A. L. Cohen	15	Abernant	R. Day (GB)
1958	BUTIABA (J. Massard)	2/1	Prince Aly Kyan	15	Prince Chevalier	A. Head (FR)
1959	FIORENTINA (G. Moore)	1/1f	Prince Aly Khan	19	Tulyar	A. Head (FR)
1960	ZENOBIA (L. Ward)	100/8	Mrs A. B. Biddle	15	Sayajirao	T. Shaw
1961	LADY SENATOR (T. Gosling)	6/4f	Mr G. H. Freeman	12	The Phoenix	P. Ashworth (GB)
1962	SHANDON BELLE (T. P. Burns)	20/1	Mr S. B. I. Abbott	16	Hook Money	R. N. Fetherston'
1963	GAZPACHO (F. Palmer)	9/1	Mrs J. R. Mullion	18	Hard Sauce	P. J. Prendergast
1964	ROYAL DANSEUSE (J. Roe)	7/4	Mr Joseph McGrath	13	Prince Chevalier	S. McGrath
1965	ARDENT DANCER (W. Rickaby)	5/1	Mrs P. McAllister	13	Buisson Ardent	T. Gosling (GB)
1966	VALORIS (John Power)	9/1	Mr C. Clore	15	Tiziano	M. V. O'Brien
1967	LACQUER (Ron Hutchinson)	4/1	Mr R. B. Moller	15	Shantung	H. Wragg (GB)
1968	FRONT ROW (E. Eldin)	7/1	Mrs F. G. Allen	13	Epaulette	R. Jarvis (GB)
1969	WENDUYNE (W. Williamson)	2/1	Mrs J. R. Mullion	13	Moutiers	P. J. Prendergast
1970	BLACK SATIN (Ron Hutchinson)	3/1	Mr W. L. Reynolds	13	Linacre	J. Dunlop (GB)
1971	FAVOLETTA (L. Piggott)	5/2	Mr R. B. Moller	17	Baldric	H. Wragg (GB)
1972	PIDGET (W. Swinburn)	20/1	Mr Norman Butler	16	Fortino	K. Prendergast
1973	CLOONAGH (G. Starkey)	7/1	Mr A. Boyd-Rochfort	12	High Hat	H. Cecil (GB)
1974	GAILY (Ron Hutchinson)	11/5	Sir Michael Sobell	17	Sir Gaylord	Maj. W. R. Hern (GB)
1975	MIRALLA (R. F. Parnell)	14/1	Lady Lister-Kaye	11	Allangrange	H. Nugent
1976	SARAH SIDDONS (C. Roche)	9/2	Mrs J. R. Mullion	14	Le Levanstell	P. J. Prendergast
1977	LADY CAPULET (Thomas Murphy)	16/1	Mr R. E. Sangster	14	Sir Ivor	M. V. O'Brien
1978	MORE SO (C. Roche)	2/1jf	Mr L. Gelb	17	Ballymore	P. J. Prendergast
1979	GODETIA (L. Piggott)	4/6f	Mr R. E. Sangster	12	Sir Ivor	M. V. O'Brien

IRISH TWO THOUSAND GUINEAS

Year	Winner & Rider	SP	Owner	Trainer	Ran	Sire
1921	SOLDENNIS (T. Burns)	4/1	Mr C. L. Mackean	S. C. Jeffrey	10	Tredennis
1922	SPIKE ISLAND (G. Archibald)	11/10f	Major Giles Loder	P. P. Gilpin (GB)	11	Spearmint
1923	SOLDUMENO (T. Burns)	4/1	Mr D. Sullivan	S. C. Jeffrey	9	Diadumenos
1924	GRAND JOY (S. Ingham)	10/1	Lord Glanely	C. Marsh (GB)	8	Grand Parade
1925	ST DONAGH (J. Dines)	7/1	Mr A. B. Coyle	E. Fordred	8	Roi Herode
1926	EMBARGO (S. Donoghue)	1/1f	Maharajah of Rajpipla	Bartholomew (GB)	10	Argosy
1927	FOURTH HAND (H. H. Beasley)	4/7f	Major D. McCalmont	H. S. Persse (GB)	9	Tetratema
1928	BAYTOWN (F. Fox)	3/1jf	Sir C. Hyde	N. C. Scobie (GB)	8	Achtoi
1929	SALISBURY (E. M. Quirke)	3/1	Mrs C. L. Mackean	Col. A. J. Blake	7	The Boss
1930	GLANNARG (E. M. Quirke)	4/1	Mr P. Fitzgerald	Col. A. J. Blake	10	Argosy
1931	DOUBLE ARCH (E. Gardner)	25/1	Mr J. T. Rogers	Owner	10	Arch-Gift
1932	LINDLEY (M. Wing)	2/1	Capt. G. F. Dunne	Col. A. J. Blake	12	Spion Kop
1933	CANTEENER (C. Richards)	20/1	Mr D. S. Kennedy	P. Thrale (GB)	12	Son & Heir
1934	CARIFF (Joseph Canty)	4/5f	Sir T. Dixon	P. Behan	10	Achtoi
1935	MUSEUM (E. M. Quirke)	100/1	Sir V. Sassoon	J. T. Rogers	11	Phalaris or Legatee
1936	HOCUS POCUS (Joseph Canty)	7/4f	Mr H. S. Gray	P. Behan	9	Mascot
1937	PHIDEAS (S. Donoghue)	4/6f	Sir V. Sassoon	J. T. Rogers	9	Pharos
1938	NEARCHUS (E. M. Quirke)	10/1	Mr P. Loraine	R. More O'Ferrall	12	Lemnarchus
1939	CORNFIELD (T. Burns)	7/4f	Mr W. Barnett	F. Armstrong (GB)	16	Trigo
1940	TEASEL (G. Wells)	10/1	Col. A. J. Blake	Owner	6	Pharian
1941	KHOSRO (E. M. Quirke)	4/1	Sir P. Loraine	R. More O'Ferrall	14	Sir Cosmo
1942	WINDSOR SLIPPER (M. Wing)	1/5f	Mr Joseph McGrath	M. C. Collins	12	Windsor Lad
1943	THE PHOENIX (Joseph Canty)	2/1jf	Mr F. S. Myerscough	Owner	12	Chateau Bouscaut
1944	GOOD MORNING (Jas. Eddery)	100/6	Mr Y. J. Kirkpatrick	H. G. Wellesley		Sir Cosmo
1944	SLIDE ON (J. Moylan)	9/4f	Major D. McCalmont	R. Fetherston'	14	Bobsleigh
1945	STALINO (Jas. Eddery)	6/4f	Mr John J. Blake	Col. A. J. Blake	20	Stardust
1946	CLARO (Joseph Canty)	100/8	HH Aga Khan	H. M. Hartigan	14	Colombo
1947	GRAND WEATHER (T. Burns)	3/1	Mr Y. J. Kirkpatrick	E. McGrath	8	Dastur
1948	BEAU SABREUR (T. Burns)	7/1	Mr A. B. Macnaughton	C. Brabazon	12	His Highness
1949	SOLONAWAY (M. Hartnett)	100/6	Mr R. A. Duggan	M. C. Collins	12	Solferino
1950	MIGHTY OCEAN (A. Brabazon)	10/1	Mr A. W. Gordon	Capt. D. Rogers	10	Coup de Lyon
1951	SIGNAL BOX (M. Molony)	5/4f	Mr F. W. Dennis	Capt. D. Rogers	16	Signal Light
1952	D.C.M. (L. Ward)	7/4	Mrs J. Thursby	J. M. Rogers	11	Distingue

Year	Horse (Jockey)	Odds	Owner	Trainer		Sire
1953	SEA CHARGER (W. R. Johnstone)	6/1	Mr Martin F. Molony	K. R. Kerr	13	Royal Charger
1954	ARCTIC WIND (J. Mullane)	25/1	Mr J. H. Thursby	J. M. Rogers	14	Arctic Star
1955	HUGH LUPUS (W. R. Johnstone)	13/8	Lady Ursula Vernon	J. Lenehan	20	Djebel
1956	LUCERO (E. Mercer)	5/1	Mr G. A. Oldham	H. Wragg (GB)	13	Solonaway
1957	JACK KETCH (C. Smirke)	7/4f	Mrs M. P. Annesley	E. M. Quirke	13	Abadan
1958	HARD RIDDEN (C. Smirke)	9/2	Sir V. Sassoon	J. M. Rogers	13	Hard Sauce
1959	EL TORO (T. P. Burns)	100/9	Mr C. M. Kline	M. V. O'Brien	15	Cagire
1960	KYTHNOS (Ron Hutchinson)	5/4f	Mr E. R. More-O'Ferrall	P. J. Prendergast	14	Nearula
1961	LIGHT YEAR (G. Bougoure)	6/1	Mr T. F. Hallinan	A. S. O'Brien	21	Chamier
1962	ARCTIC STORM (W. Williamson)	20/1	Mrs E. M. Carroll	J. Oxx	17	Arctic Star
1963	LINACRE (P. Matthews)	40/1	Lord Ennisdale	P. J. Prendergast	14	Rockefella
1964	SANTA CLAUS (W. Burke)	1/1f	Mr J. Ismay	J. M. Rogers	16	Chamossaire
1965	GREEN BANNER (N. Brennan)	100/7	Mr B. Kerr	K. R. Kerr	21	Palestine
1966	PAVEH (T. P. Burns)	9/1	Mr P. A. B. Widener	T. D. Ainsworth	15	Tropique
1967	ATHERSTONE WOOD (R. F. Parnell)	100/7	Mrs S. O'Flaherty	S. Quirke	19	Buisson Ardent
1968	MISTIGO (R. F. Parnell)	10/1	Mr F. Feeney	S. Quirke	15	Miralgo
1969	RIGHT TACK (G. Lewis)	1/1f	Mr J. R. Brown	Sutcliffe, jr (GB)	15	Hard Tack
1970	DECIES (L. Piggott)	8/13f	Mr N. B. Hunt	B. Van Cutsem (GB)	13	Pardal
1971	KING'S COMPANY (F. Head)	9/2	Mr B. Firestone	G. W. Robinson	14	Kings Troop
1972	BALLYMORE (C. Roche)	33/1	Mrs J. R. Mullion	P. J. Prendergast	14	Ragusa
1973	SHARP EDGE (J. Mercer)	5/2	Mr J. J. Astor	Maj. W. R. Hern (GB)	16	Silver Shark
1974	FURRY GLEN (G. McGrath)	10/1	Mr P. W. McGrath	S. McGrath	10	Wolver Hollow
1975	GRUNDY (P. Eddery)	10/11f	Dr C. Vittadini	P. T. Walwyn (GB)	12	Gt. Nephew
1976	NORTHERN TREASURE (G. Curran)	33/1	Mr A. D. Brennan	K. Prendergast	17	Northfields
1977	PAMPAPAUL (G. Dettori)	16/1	Mr Hans Paul	H. V. S. Murless	21	Yellow God
1978	JAAZEIRO (L. Piggott)	11/4f	Mr R. Sangster	M. V. O'Brien	12	Sham
1979	DICKENS HILL (A. Murray)	5/2	Mme J. P. Binet	M. A. O'Toole	9	Mount Hagen

IRISH ST LEGER

Year	Winner & Rider	SP	Owner	Trainer	Ran	Sire
1915	LA POLOMA (F. Hunter)	6/1	Mr D. Sullivan	James Dunne	6	Prospector
1916	CAPTIVE PRINCESS (T. Burns)	2/1f	Mr. W. A. Wallis	James Dunne	8	Captivation
1917	DOUBLE SCOTCH (T. Burns)	7/4	Mr W. A. Murphy	James Dunne	5	Seaforth
1918	DIONYSOS (S. Donoghue)	2/1f	Lord D'Abernon	G. Lambton (GB)	7	Llangibby
1919	CHEAP POPULARITY (T. Burns)	3/1	Mr A. Lowry	H. Powney	5	Tredennis
1920	KIRK ALLOWAY (M. Wing)	3/1	Mr T. K. Laidlaw	J. Hunter	3	Tracery
1921	KIRCUBBIN (M. Beary)	1/1f	Major D. Dixon	P. Behan	5	Captivation
1922	ROYAL LANCER (F. Lane)	4/6f	Lord Lonsdale	A. Sadler, jr (GB)	8	Spearmint
1923	O'DEMPSEY (M. Wing)	2/1	Mr H. Baillie	S. C. Jeffrey	5	Flying Orb
1924	ZODIAC (G. Archibald)	2/1	Major Giles Loder	P. P. Gilpin (GB)	8	Sunstar
1925	SPELTHORNE (G. Archibald)	1/2f	Col. Giles Loder	P. P. Gilpin (GB)	6	Spearmint
1926	SUNNY VIEW (J. Dines)	2/5f	Sir A. Bailey	R. Day (GB)	2	Sir Berkeley
1927	BALLYVOY (P. Beasley)	5/1	Mr H. Pulitzer	S. Darling (GB)	4	Captivation
1928	LAW SUIT (J. Dines)	2/1	Sir A. Bailey	R. Day (GB)	4	Son-in-Law
1929	TRIGO (M. Beary)	1/7f	Mr W. Barnett	R. C. Dawson (GB)	5	Blandford
1930	SOL DE TERRE (M. Wing)	1/1f	Mrs C. L. Mackean	Col. A. J. Blake	4	Soldennis
1931	BEAUDELAIRE (T. Burns)	4/6f	Count J. McCormack	R. More O'Ferrall	3	Argosy
1932	HILL SONG (E. Gardner)	4/5f	Major E. C. Shirley	J. T. Rogers	4	Spion Kop
1933	HARINERO (C. Ray)	1/4f	Mr W. Barnett	R. C. Dawson (GB)	6	Blandford
1934	PRIMERO (C. Ray)	4/7f	Mr W. Barnett	R. C. Dawson (GB)	8	Blandford
1935	MUSEUM (S. Donoghue)	1/2f	Sir V. Sassoon	J. T. Rogers	5	Phalaris or Legatee
1936	BATTLE SONG (E. Gardner)	10/11f	Major E. C. Shirley	J. T. Rogers	4	Spion Kop
1937	OWENSTOWN (J. Taylor)	5/2	Sir T. Dixon	M. Peacock (GB)	5	Apron
1938	OCHILTREE (M. Wing)	2/5f	Lord Talbot de Malahide	Col. A. J. Blake	7	Tolgus
1939	SKOITER (J. Moylan)	20/1	Mr J. V. Rank	R. Fetherston'	6	Singapore
1940	HARVEST FEAST (T. Burns)	100/8	Mr W. Barnett	Capt. D. Rogers	5	Trigo
1941	ETOILE DE LYONS (Joseph Canty)	2/1	Mr H. M. Hartigan	Owner	6	Coup de Lyon
1942	WINDSOR SLIPPER (M. Wing)	8/100f	Mr Joseph McGrath	M. C. Collins	8	Windsor Lad
1943	SOLFERINO (John Power)	8/1	Mr J. McVey, jr	J. Oxx	4	Fairway
1944	WATER STREET (Joseph Canty)	6/4jf	Mr M. S. Carroll	C. A. Rogers	7	Early School
1945	SPAM (M. Wing)	6/4jf	Mr J. Ismay	Capt. D. Rogers	9	Coup de Lyon
1946	CASSOCK (J. Moylan)	4/1	Major D. McCalmont	R. Fetherston'	9	Casanova
1947	ESPRIT DE FRANCE (M. Wing)	4/9f	Prince Aly Khan	H. M. Hartigan	5	Epigram

Year	Horse (Jockey)	Odds	Owner	Trainer		Sire
1948	BEAU SABREUR (T. Burns)	9/2	Mr A. B. Macnaughton	C. Brabazon	8	His Highness
1949	BROWN ROVER (W. H. Carr)	3/1	Mr William Woodward	Boyd-Rochfort (GB)	13	Fighting Fox
1950	MORNING MADAM (P. Canty)	20/1	Mr Y. J. Kirkpatrick	P. Connolly	12	Limekiln
1951	DO WELL (L. Ward)	10/11f	Mr J. Lunn	M. A. Wing	10	Rosewell
1952	JUDICATE (W. H. Carr)	6/4	Lady Zia Wernher	Boyd-Rochfort (GB)	7	Hyperion
1953	SEA CHARGER (W. R. Johnstone)	5/2	Mr Martin F. Molony	K. R. Kerr	10	Royal Charger
1954	ZARATHUSTRA (P. Powell, jr)	7/4	Mr Terence J. S. Gray	M. Hurley	5	Persian Gulf
1955	DIAMOND SLIPPER (D. Page)	100/8	Mrs E. J. King	H. Nugent	9	His Slipper
1956	MAGNETIC NORTH (W. Elliott)	8/1	Mr W. A. Phillips	D. F. G. Hastings (GB)	8	Borealis
1957	OMMEYAD (J. Massard)	5/4f	Prince Aly Khan	A. Head (FR)	11	Hyperion
1958	ROYAL HIGHWAY (N. Brennan)	7/4	Mrs W. Macauley	H. V. S. Murless	6	Straight Deal
1959	BARCLAY (G. Bougoure)	1/2f	Mr J. McShain	M. V. O'Brien	7	Guersant
1960	LYNCHRIS (W. Williamson)	4/6f	Mrs E. M. Fawcett	J. Oxx	8	Sayajirao
1961	VIMADEE (T. P. Burns)	100/9f	Mrs T. McCairns	T. Burns	10	Vimy
1962	ARCTIC VALE (P. Matthews)	40/1	Mrs E. Goring	P. J. Prendergast	9	Arctic Time
1963	CHRISTMAS ISLAND (G. Bougoure)	6/1	Exors. of Lord Ennisdale	P. J. Prendergast	10	Court Harwell
1964	BISCAYNE (W. Williamson)	4/1	Mrs J. Reid	J. Oxx	8	Talgo
1965	CRAIGHOUSE (J. Mercer)	6/1	Lord Astor	Maj. W. R. Hern (GB)	14	Mossborough
1966	WHITE GLOVES (L. Ward)	4/1	Mrs M. A. Moore	M. V. O'Brien	14	High Hat
1967	DAN KANO (L. Piggott)	1/1f	Mrs S. Raccah	J. Lenehan	8	Dicta Drake
1968	GIOLLA MEAR (F. Berry)	8/1	HE the President	M. Hurley	10	Hard Ridden
1969	REINDEER (L. Ward)	5/2	Mr Ramond R. Guest	M. V. O'Brien	9	Santa Claus
1970	ALLANGRANGE (G. McGrath)	9/1	Mr J. McGrath	S. McGrath	8	Le Levanstell
1971	PARNELL (A. Simpson)	11/5	Mr R. More O'Ferrall	S. Quirke	8	St Paddy
1972	PIDGET (T. P. Burns)	13/2	Mr Norman Butler	K. Prendergast	7	Fortino II
1973	CONOR PASS (P. Jarman)	5/1	Mrs R. Moore	K. Prendergast	7	Tiepolo II
1974	MISTIGRI (C. Roche)	9/1	Mr E. R. More O'Ferrall	P. J. Prendergast	7	Misti IV
1975	CAUCASUS (L. Piggott)	3/1	Mrs C. W. Engelhard	M. V. O'Brien	13	Nijinsky
1976	MENEVAL (L. Piggott)	4/5f	Mrs G. F. Getty	M. V. O'Brien	11	Le Fabuleux
1977	TRANSWORLD (Thomas Murphy)	13/2	Mr Simon Fraser	M. V. O'Brien	9	Prince John
1978	M-LOLSHAN (B. Taylor)	2/1f	Mr E. Alkhalifa	Capt. H. R. Price (GB)	8	Levmoss
1979	NINISKI (W. Carson)	11/10f	Lady Beaverbrook	Maj. W. R. Hern (GB)	10	Nijinsky

INDEX TO RUNNERS IN THE IRISH DERBY 1866–1979

Estrapade (1903)
Etoile de Lyons (1941)
Evora (1873)
Exdirectory (1978)
Extension (1972)
Eyrefield (1880)

Fabulous Dancer (1979)
Fainne Geal (1913)
Fair Ashton (1948)
Fair Contract (1951)
Fairest Flower (1890)
Fair Ray (1948)
Fairwargor (1939)
Fairy Isle (1896)
Falaise (1972)
Fanessa (1892)
Faria (1913)
Far North (1976)
Faustin (1881)
Faux Pas (1951)
Favoloo (1895)
Fermoyle (1902)
Ferns (1903)
Fethard (1887)
Fidalgo (1959)
Field Day (1897)
Final Move (1963)
Finesse (1869)
Finsbury (1976)
Fire Eater (1866)
First Flier (1917)
First Flower (1893)
Fitzorb (1915)
Flaming Red (1965)
Flash Arin (1949)
Flax Park (1905)
Flaxman (1937)
Flirt, The (1880)
Flower Robe (1974)
Flying Comet (1911)
Fomelhault (1910)
Fortissimo (1967)
Fort Osway (1942)
Foxlaw (1925)
Fraise du Bois (1951)
Franz Hals (1933)
Freefoot (1973)
Freighter (1930)
Frenchhaven (1897)
French Star (1964)
Fulminator (1898)
Furore (1916)
Furry Glen (1974)

Gael Rhu (1912)

Ga-Greine (1965)
Gail Star (1962)
Gala Chief (1963)
Galgreina (1905)
Gallinaria (1900)
Gallini (1931)
Galway Prince (1922)
Garinish Island (1909)
Garland Knight (1961)
Gaultier (1906)
Gauntlet (1894)
Gawsworth (1889)
Gay Garland (1967)
Gazetter (1894)
Georgetown (1907)
Geraldina (1917)
Geraint (1926)
Giggery (1975)
Gilbert the Filbert (1916)
Giolla Mear (1968)
Gipsy George (1934)
Glandine (1880)
Glanmerin (1919)
Gleg (1907)
Glen Albyn (1926)
Glenamoy (1904)
Glenbower (1896)
Glengariff (1896)
Gold Amulet (1932)
Golden Bay (1900)
Golden Crest (1955)
Golden Glen (1933)
Golden Lancer (1936)
Golden Plover (1867)
Golden Rose (1881)
Golden Sovereign (1938)
Golden Tiger (1940)
Goldminer (1890)
Good-time (1900)
Gorfou (1974)
Grand Ecart (1932)
Grand Inquisitor (1942)
Grand Terrace (1929)
Grand Weather (1947)
Grecian Bend (1884)
Greek Bachelor (1923)
Greek Star (1944)
Greenfield (1881)
Green o' My Eye (1899)
Green Witch (1900)
Grenfall (1971)
Grey Bachelor (1930)
Grey-Green (1904)
Grundy (1975)
Guestmaster (1893)
Guillemot (1971)

Gulsalberk (1896)
Gyneth colt (1902)

Hail the Pirates (1973)
Haine (1924)
Handcuff (1881)
Happy Medium (1902)
Hare Warren (1905)
Harinero (1933)
Hartstown (1894)
Haven (1961)
Hawaiian Sound (1978)
Hawk, The (1900)
Hawkberry (1976)
Head the Trick (1897)
Heavo Ho (1967)
Hebron (1894)
He Goes (1920)
Helen Mar (1880)
Henry George (1887)
Hidalgo (1954)
Highlandmore (1922)
Hill Song (1932)
Hindostan (1949)
Hindu Festival (1957)
Hobnob (1975)
Hocus Pocus (1936)
Holly (1887)
Hollywood (1874)
Home Farm (1968)
Honest Crook (1970)
Honor's Choice (1938)
Hooton (1873)
Horse Power (1964)
Hospodar (1888)
Hovercraft (1964)
Howitzer (1869)
Hugh Lupus (1955)
Hyperina (1944)
Hyrcania (1945)

Idolator (1898)
Illa Laudo (1970)
Illyrian (1924)
Illyric (1952)
Immorata (1878)
Impeccable (1947)
Imperial Fleet (1976)
Imperial Prince (1974)
Impressario (1900)
Indian Judge (1961)
Indian Snow (1965)
Ingomar (1875)
Inishowen (1869)
Inkerman (1978)
Innishowen (1875)

Mediator (1891)
Melliflor (1882)
Melody (1869)
Melra (1923)
Merrion (1901)
Merry May (1882)
Merry Slipper (1971)
Mesembryanthemum (1958)
Mespilus (1883)
Michaelis Liber (1920)
Mighty High (1952)
Mighty Ocean (1950)
Milesian (1956)
Milesvena (1966)
Miller (1942)
Millman (1899)
Milverton (1977)
Minnie (1882)
Minstrel, The (1978)
Miser (1879)
Mississipian (1974)
Miss Kate (1880)
Miss Pitt (1888)
Miss Snap (1894)
Mistigri (1974)
Mistress, The (1899)
Molino (1934)
Momentum (1946)
Mondragon (1939)
Monmouth (1899)
Monseigner (1977)
Montserrat (1900)
Moon Mountain (1969)
Mumzowa (1962)
Museum (1935)
Music Man (1971)
Mute, The (1896)
Myosotis (1933)

Nagami (1958)
Narraghmore (1891)
Nathoo (1948)
Natsun (1973)
Navarre (1918)
Navarre (1976)
Neanderthal (1961)
Nemo (1910)
Neptunus (1964)
Nettleweed (1937)
Never So Gay (1975)
New Member (1968)
Niebo (1976)
Nightmare (1886)
Nijinsky (1970)
Niksar (1965)
Nip and Tuck (1970)

Noble Duchess (1882)
Noble Howard (1898)
Noble Life (1970)
No Comment (1956)
Nollikens (1893)
Nor (1970)
Northern Mist (1969)
Northern Treasure (1976)
North Wall (1973)
Not So Cold (1966)
No Turning (1976)
Notus (1877)
Nova Herculis (1949)
N.P.B. (1929)

Ocean Echo (1951)
O'Curry (1928)
O'Dorney (1922)
Oh Brother (1970)
Oilfield (1976)
Old Brown Bess (1900)
Old Napoleon (1951)
Ominous (1964)
Onandaga (1969)
Oppidan (1948)
Oppressor (1899)
Orby (1907)
Orchestra (1977)
Orpine (1923)
Our Guile (1962)

Pacifier (1944)
Paddy's Birthday (1963)
Paddy's Point (1958)
Padroug (1977)
Palmas (1967)
Panaslipper (1955)
Panco (1968)
Panther, The (1919)
Pardal (1950)
Pardner (1972)
Parisian (1935)
Park Lawn (1973)
Parnell (1971)
Partholon (1963)
Patriot King (1934)
Paul's Cross (1955)
Paveh (1966)
Peat Smoke (1947)
Pendragon (1917)
Pericles (1887)
Pet Fox (1887)
Petit Jean (1966)
Pheonician, The (1909)
Phideas (1937)
Philammon (1877)

Philemon (1963)
Philistine, The (1887)
Phoenix, The (1943)
Phoenix Hall (1975)
Physician (1928)
Piccadilly (1945)
Pink Larkspur (1949)
Pioneer (1880)
Pitched Battle (1930)
Pleasure Seeker (1872)
Polar Prince (1957)
Polemic (1966)
Port Blair (1902)
Portmarnock (1895)
Prado (1963)
Premonition (1953)
President Steyn (1901)
Prestel (1958)
Primero (1934)
Priory, The (1905)
Prince Chamier (1960)
Prince Herod (1920)
Prince Lionel (1917)
Prince of Fairfield (1902)
Prince Regent (1969)
Pythia (1974)
Python (1946)

Queen May (1889)
Queen of the Bath (1877)
Queen's Eyot (1942)

Rachel (1922)
Radbrook (1966)
Raeburn (1936)
Ragapan (1973)
Ragusa (1963)
Randwick (1959)
Rao Raja (1941)
Rare Jewel (1967)
Rath, The (1885)
Rathdowney (1978)
Rathmore (1934)
Rattleaway (1871)
Rebel Chief (1872)
Redbay (1945)
Red Branch Knight (1915)
Red Canute (1974)
Red Clover (1929)
Red Heart's Pride (1904)
Red Rhetoric (1920)
Red Shaft (1938)
Redskin (1877)
Red Vagabonde (1964)
Red Wine (1867)
Refuge (1879)

Sucaryl (1967)
Summer Solstice (1939)
Sunny Slipper (1953)
Sunrise (1890)
Sunseeker (1964)
Sunset Glory (1968)
Supreme Verdict (1961)
Suspender (1947)
Sweet Lester (1908)
Sweetness (1886)
Sweet Thought (1876)
Swindon Light (1933)
Sylph (1883)

Talarias (1976)
Tale of Two Cities (1954)
Talgo (1956)
Talgo Abbess (1962)
Tall Noble (1973)
Tambourine (1962)
Tantoul (1971)
Tanzara (1969)
Tapis Rose (1967)
Tara (1955)
Tara Hill (1923)
Tarqogan (1963)
Tauranga (1910)
Teasel (1940)
Tekoah (1973)
Tenacity (1926)
Tern (1958)
Terror (1878)
Theatre Royal (1901)
Theodemir (1886)
Theodolite (1888)
Theodosius (1917)
Theologian (1884)
Theorist (1882)
Thirteen of Diamonds
  (1952)
Thunderbolt (1942)
Tice (1885)
Tickler (1912)
Ticonderoga (1962)
Tiger (1963)
Timberland (1953)
Time Greine (1961)
Tiverton (1941)
Tolago (1940)

Tolman (1937)
Tom King (1866)
Too Good (1899)
Tower, The (1908)
Town's Wall (1954)
Toy Label (1923)
Trade Wind (1962)
Tragedy (1889)
Transatlantic (1949)
Trapper (1932)
Treetops Hotel (1953)
Tremola (1921)
Tribal Song (1949)
Trickstress (1872)
Trimatic (1962)
Troy (1979)
Truehaven (1902)
Tullynacree (1911)
Turbulent Eddy (1971)
Turco (1875)
Turkhan (1940)
Turkish Prince (1950)
T.V. (1962)
Twenty-third (1908)
Tyrconnel (1877)

Ulster Man (1915)
Umpire (1876)

Val d'Aoste (1968)
Valedictory (1938)
Valentine Slipper (1957)
Valerie (1882)
Valiant (1922)
Valley Forge (1978)
Vaquero (1956)
Vaudemont (1956)
Velocity (1905)
Venice (1878)
Veno (1906)
Vic Mo Chroi (1963)
Victor Hugo (1943)
Victory Roll (1953)
Vivadari (1969)

Wacoso (1971)
Waddler (1905)
Wales (1897)

War Cloud (1892)
Warminster (1925)
War Wolf (1902)
Waterkoscie (1926)
Water Street (1944)
Wavetop (1928)
Waygood (1923)
Weavers' Hall (1973)
Wedding Present (1965)
We Don't Know (1953)
Western Wind (1965)
Westview (1921)
What Next (1901)
Whistling Duck (1921)
White Gloves (1966)
White Hackle (1897)
White Orb (1926)
Wild Bouquet (1908)
Wild Corn (1930)
Wild Johnnie (1948)
Wild Attorney (1920)
Windsor Slipper (1942)
Windsor Whisper (1948)
Windy Torrent (1952)
Winkfield's Fortune (1903)
Wise Boy (1961)
Without Benefit (1935)
Wolfdog (1910)
Wondrous (1928)
Wonersh (1939)
Woodforest (1960)
Woodland Star (1947)
Wordsworth (1892)
Worsted (1893)
Writ (1930)

Yakoob Khan (1882)
Young Abercorn (1905)
Your Highness (1961)

Zaracarn (1967)
Zarathustra (1954)
Zefus (1916)
Zelne (1896)
Zend Avesta (1965)
Zionist (1925)
Zodiac (1924)
Z.Z. (1918)

Total number of Runners in Irish Derby 1866 to 1979 = 1110

Horses with 'The' in the name are without the definite article. *eg*. The Sleeping Beauty listed under S. Although nowadays (within the past 10 years) this practice has been discontinued, in the interest of clarity, we feel that we must stick by the old tradition because 'The Sleeping Beauty', for example, is freely referred to as simply 'Sleeping Beauty.'

General Index